POLITICAL
LEADERS
OF THE
CONTEMPORARY
MIDDLE EAST
AND
NORTH AFRICA

POLITICAL LEADERS OF THE CONTEMPORARY MIDDLE EAST AND NORTH AFRICA

A Biographical Dictionary

EDITED BY
BERNARD REICH

Greenwood Press

NEW YORK · WESTPORT, CONNECTICUT · LONDON

Library of Congress Cataloging-in-Publication Data

Political leaders of the contemporary Middle East and North Africa : a
  biographical dictionary / edited by Bernard Reich.
      p.   cm.
    Bibliography: p.
    Includes index.
    ISBN 0–313–26213–6 (lib. bdg. : alk. paper)
      1. Statesmen—Middle East—Biography—Dictionaries.   2. Statesmen—
    Africa, North—Biography—Dictionaries.   I. Reich, Bernard.
    DS61.5.P65   1990
    920′.056—dc20   89–7498

British Library Cataloguing in Publication Data is available.

Library of Congress Catalog Card Number: 89–7498
ISBN: 0–313–26213–6

First published in 1990

Greenwood Press, Inc.
88 Post Road West, Westport, Connecticut   06881

Printed in the United States of America

The paper used in this book complies with the
Permanent Paper Standard issued by the National
Information Standards Organization (Z39.48–1984).

10 9 8 7 6 5 4 3 2 1

To Suzie

CONTENTS

PREFACE

The purpose of this volume is to provide political-biographical profiles of a select group of leaders who have made significant contributions to the political evolution and development of the Middle East and North Africa since World War II.

A work of this sort requires a large number of choices. The period is post–World War II—a time span that often includes the attainment of modern independence, the inauguration of contemporary political life, and the formative years of many of the states. Some figures from earlier periods are, of course, significant, and while they are not individually profiled, they are referred to in various entries and can be located through the use of the index. The geographical area of coverage goes beyond the narrow definition generally employed in works dealing with the Middle East and includes Algeria, Bahrain, Egypt, Iran, Iraq, Israel, Jordan, Kuwait, Lebanon, Libya, Morocco, Oman, Qatar, Saudi Arabia, South Yemen, Sudan, Syria, Tunisia, Turkey, the United Arab Emirates, and Yemen.

More than seventy Middle Eastern and North African political leaders who have been instrumental in the evolution of political life in their own states or other political systems in the Middle East, North Africa, and beyond have been included. The choice of personalities was difficult, and several techniques were used to construct the final list. A form of reputational analysis was employed in which the major works on the region were surveyed to determine which figures were considered to be significant for the development of the region since World War II. Also, specialists on the region, many of them authors of the profiles that follow, were queried about the appropriateness and relative weight of the figures to be included, and were asked to identify potential subjects. They reacted to an initial list and made the suggestions that contributed to the compilation of the ultimate roster of subjects, although not all would agree with its final content.

The roles of personalities and leaders in political life have varied over time and in different states and regions, and while they have been the subject of much discussion, there have been relatively few systematic examinations of this phenomenon. This volume provides a large empirical base that will facilitate further investigation and analysis of that question. The profiles include the basic information contained in a who's who but the number of entries was limited to permit detailed analyses and assessments of the careers and achievements of the various figures rather than simply providing biographical data.

Each profile includes essential facts (such as birth dates and career patterns) but focuses on a discussion of the individual and his contribution to the political past and present as well as the probable future of his country, of the Middle East and North Africa, and of the international arena. Each individual was selected not simply because he attained an office or position of consequence but because he is a contemporary leader of note with a substantial and lasting effect on politics in the Middle East and North Africa. Each essay explores the personal and political evolution of the individual including his initial appearance on the political scene (how he was drawn into politics), his efforts to develop political programs and goals, and the methods he pursued to achieve his political and related goals. The profiles vary in their length but they all seek to identify the salient biographical details of the personality's life and to evaluate and assess the political career and contribution. The essays do vary in detail as some authors faced problems caused by the uneven coverage of the personalities in the literature and the resultant lack of materials, data, and even official information.

A brief bibliography of works by (where appropriate) and about the subject follows each entry. The bibliography provides sources for further research and information, and generally is limited to works in English that will be useful to the reader. A brief general bibliography on political elites in the Middle East and North Africa will allow the reader to draw comparisons between leaders and to approach them from a more general framework.

The Arabic, Turkish, Persian, and Hebrew languages all pose problems of transliteration and of spelling in English. This volume uses the transliteration generally utilized in works on the region and in the media—that is, the most common and widely or generally accepted usage—although some variations occur even with this rule. Thus, the reader will find Nasser rather than Nasir as the preferred rendition in this volume. Diacritical marks have been omitted. With Arab names the last name is used as the family name and the entry is in alphabetical order accordingly (that is, Nuri Said is located under Said). Kings and princes (amirs and sheikhs) are listed by their first names (that is, King Farouk under Farouk). The Arabic "al" or "Al" is disregarded in the alphabetical listing.

Foreign words and terms have been defined in parenthetical phrases in the text where employed. A list of subjects by country follows the biographical sketches. To facilitate the use of the volume and to provide a context for the reader, a detailed chronology of important events in the region has been constructed in which important dates in the lives and careers of each of the profiled figures are included.

The index facilitates cross-references between entries and provides access to information about people not individually profiled. In studying a particular personality, the reader will find it useful to utilize the index as well as to peruse the profiles of other figures from that country.

The preparation of this large and complex work required the assistance and cooperation of many people. Most important were the contributors of the profiles, but a number of others were instrumental in ensuring an end product of high quality. Ahmed Mohamed El-Bashari, Mohammed Alluhaymaq, Noah Dropkin and Joe Helman helped in the proofreading and indexing of the book. Wendy Kolker and Ann McQueary facilitated the process of dealing with the authors and administering the project. Mildred Vasan, Politics and Law Editor at Greenwood Press, is a unique and positive asset in any scholarly publication and played the role of godmother for this effort while Lynn Sedlak Flint was most helpful in the production of this book. Nevertheless, the book would have been impossible without the constant help and support of my wife, to whom this book is dedicated.

POLITICAL
LEADERS
OF THE
CONTEMPORARY
MIDDLE EAST
AND
NORTH AFRICA

A

FERHAT ABBAS (1899–1985) is the first president of the Provisional Government of the Algerian Republic and the first president of the National Assembly of independent Algeria. Ironically, this French-educated moderate, whose name for a time was almost synonymous in Western minds with Algerian nationalism and violent revolution, had spent the twenty-five years prior to 1956 seeking negotiated, nonviolent ways to end his people's social, economic, and political subjugation.

Ferhat Abbas was born on October 24, 1899, near Taher in Algeria's eastern department of Constantine. Ferhat's grandfather had been driven from the family lands during the French repression of the Kabylie revolt. His father, Said Ben Ahmed, was obliged to hire out on a *colon* (settler) farm, but then rose into increasingly responsible positions, attracted the attention of regional government, and eventually won appointment to a series of native administrative posts. Ultimately, Said Ben Ahmed was made commander of the Legion of Honor.

As the son of a moderately affluent Muslim family, Ferhat could look forward to the advantages of the French education to which such families increasingly directed their sons. He attended elementary school in the small coastal city of Djidjelli, and went on to secondary school at Constantine. Most of his three years of compulsory military service were spent at Bône in the army medical corps, from which he was discharged with the rank of sergeant in 1923.

After his military service, Abbas studied pharmacy for eight years at Algiers. In 1926 he was elected president of the Association of Muslim Students, a position he held for several years. From his early years he displayed a passionate interest in the political and cultural issues absorbing the young *évolués* of the 1920s. Beginning in 1922, Abbas contributed occasional articles on such issues to publications sympathetic to native viewpoints. On the occasion of the 1930 centennial of the French conquest of Algiers, he published the best of his articles in a volume entitled *De la colonie vers la province: Le jeune Algérien*. Among the many themes with which Abbas deals in the volume, four are especially worthy of note.

The first is a call for recision of the *code de l'indigénat*, which subjected Algerian Muslims to an arbitrary juridical regime totally foreign to French legal tradition. The second urged compulsory free primary education as a means to help Algerian peasants and the subproletariat lift themselves out of their abject social and economic position.

A third less frequently cited group of articles defended the Islamic heritage and its fraternal and inclusive social vision against the ill-informed and racially intolerant attacks of settler publicists, comparing the Islamic worldview favorably to the polarizing ideologies of nationalism and Marxism. Finally, Abbas expressed in many ways the deep resentment of educated Muslims about the systematic discrimination that colonialism visited even on their class. One of his most poignant articles ends with the ringing challenge to France to "Help us reconquer our dignity or take back your schools!" (1981:144).

Upon completing his university studies, Abbas opened a pharmacy in the *sous-préfecture* of Sétif that before long became a favorite gathering spot for reform-minded politicians. The constituency he cultivated in Sétif launched him on a political career that saw him elected successively to the General Council of the Constantinois (1933), the Municipal Council of Sétif (1935), and the Délégations Financières at Algiers (1936). He also joined the Fédération des Elus Musulmans, which during the mid–1930s was the principal organization through which native officeholders sought to coax a reluctant colonial establishment into admitting natives to the benefits of the French liberal tradition. In 1933, Ferhat Abbas founded his weekly newspaper, *L'Entente*, which until the outbreak of World War II was the most prominent publication pressing for reform within the framework of French Algeria.

In their struggle against the colonial system, middle-class French-educated liberals like Abbas sometimes collaborated with, but more often competed with, movements whose assessment of the Algerian problem differed markedly from their own. The first of these was the Etoile Nord-Africaine headed by the charismatic and often demagogic Messali Hadj, whose thinking blended aspects of Marxist social analysis, communist-style organization, and militant nationalism. The Etoile in 1937 became the Parti du Peuple Algérien (PPA) and after World War II the Mouvement pour le Triomphe des Libertés Démocratiques (MTLD). The other competing organization was the Association of Algerian Ulama (religious leaders), headed during the 1930s by Shaykh Abd al Hamid Ben Badis. These Islamic reformers believed the path to Algerian emancipation lay through the renewal and rejuvenation of Islamic belief, practice, and education.

The contrast between the analyses of Abbas and Ben Badis is nowhere better illustrated than in a 1936 newspaper exchange. In a February 23 *Entente* article, Abbas wrote that after questioning history, the living and the dead, and visiting the cemeteries, he had concluded that the Algerian fatherland did not exist and that therefore one should link the future of the country definitively to that of France. He cautioned, however, that without political and economic emancipation of the native people, there could be no durable French Algeria.

From the beginning, Algerians who disagreed with Abbas's program of change within the system dwelt on the first part of the analysis to the exclusion of his portentous conclusion. Ben Badis responded in the ulama's organ, *Ech-Chihab*, that the Algerian nation indeed existed, and that that nation "is not France, cannot be France, and does not wish to be France" (quoted in Charles-André Julien, *L'Afrique du Nord en marche* [Paris: Julliard, 1972], p. 104).

With the advent of the Popular Front in France in May 1936, the moderate reformers were swept up in a wave of enthusiastic optimism. In June, an Algerian Muslim Congress in which Abbas played a major role adopted a "Charter of Demands of the Algerian Muslim people" which demanded abolition of the Code de l'Indigénat; separation of church and state; the right of Algerians to preserve their Islamic civil status while becoming French citizens; the adoption of Arabic as a second official language; the fusion of French and Arabic education and its universalization; universal suffrage; proportional representation in the French parliament; and complete integration of Algeria politically and administratively into France.

By December the Popular Front had responded by introducing into Parliament three modest reform proposals, the most celebrated of which was the Blum-Violette Bill, which would have extended French citizenship to between twenty and thirty thousand Muslims of the more privileged classes. Messali Hadj and his followers bluntly rejected the bill as an attempt to divide native society by coopting its most privileged elements. The reformist ulama gave the bill modest support, probably because they believed that any measure empowering more Muslims was a step in the right direction. The most enthusiastic supporters were Abbas, the Fédération des Elus Musulmans, and others of the French-educated elite who would, it has been frequently—if somewhat unfairly—observed, have been the principal beneficiaries of the bill. Thanks to the power of the colon delegation in the National Assembly, Blum-Violette languished in committee and never made it to the floor of the Chamber of Deputies.

The refusal of France to promulgate even such a limited reform was a bitter disappointment to assimilationist liberals. As a result of this disappointment, Abbas would eventually cease promoting assimilation and start demanding autonomy, but he would spend the rest of his life attempting to justify to his nationalist compatriots why in the 1930s he had been such an ardent advocate of merging Algeria into France.

In the preface to the 1981 edition of *De la Colonie vers la Province*, Abbas explained that the new generation did not understand the times or the range of reasonable options they presented. He and his contemporaries were few and they had very little power. In spite of this they dared to speak out when most were silent, and in speaking they initiated the process of mass awareness and mobilization that led ultimately to freedom. Abbas admitted that by temperament he was essentially a pacifist; knowing the bloody history of earlier repression in Algeria, he, in fact, preferred honorable compromise to violent upheaval. He continued to believe even in 1981 that if he and his colleagues had been able to induce the French to institute liberal and scientific education across Algeria and to extend political participation, Algerians would have had tools enough for improving their personal, economic, and political condition. Independence would have come gradually, naturally, and amicably, and a million lives would have been spared.

Convinced that mass mobilization would be one way to extract concessions from the colonial authorities, in 1938 Ferhat Abbas founded his first political party, the Union Populaire Algérienne. However, when World War II broke out, he suspended political activity in the interest of national unity, volunteered at the age of forty for the army, and served in the Medical Corps at Troyes until the fall of France.

Profoundly shaken by the defeat of France and the collapse of the Third Republic, Abbas returned to his pharmacy at Sétif and to his functions as city councilman. In April 1941 he composed a "Report to Marshal Pétain" whose analytical section displays a peculiar blend of quasi-Marxism, racist colonial theory, 1848 liberalism, and elitism. According to the report, France had modernized Algeria in a material sense, but by basing that modernization upon a "landed feudalism" dominated by European propertied and ruling elements, France had neglected the modernization of the people. The report stated that "on a European land with European elites live six million Orientals" in the most extreme poverty and degradation. It so happened that "a handful of men of French education [were] trying to transform the lives and habits of a decadent society," but found themselves blocked at every turn by a racist colonial mentality. "One must choose," Abbas contended, "to go forward to enlarge the circle of modern life, or resign oneself one day to seeing the medieval Orient submerge the entire achievement and destroy it" (Lacouture, 1961: 280–281). Abbas goes on to elaborate an extraordinarily comprehensive program of agrarian reform coupled with a rural political restructuring based on communes designed to serve as channels of material, moral, and educational transformation.

Having experienced rejection of his assimilationist vision by the French as well as by many Muslims, Abbas's thinking was already beginning to move in the direction of a federative solution by the time of the November 1942 Allied landing in Algeria. The contrast between the respectful interest of the Americans who were coauthors of the Atlantic Charter and the weakened condition of the rejectionist French was the catalyst that decisively transformed Abbas into a partisan of a separate Algerian entity in association with France.

A caucus of native politicians authorized Ferhat Abbas to draft the *Manifesto of the Algerian People*, which was delivered in February 1943 to French and U.S. officials. After rehearsing the repeated failures of the Algerian people to win emancipation within the framework of the French legal and political systems, the manifesto concludes that an Algerian identity, nationality, and citizenship offer the only logical avenue to native development and emancipation. The manifesto poses a list of six demands, the most important of which is the granting of a separate constitution to Algeria that would guarantee (1) the absolute equality of all inhabitants regardless of race or religion; (2) freedom of speech, press, assembly, and religion; (3) agrarian reform; and (4) free compulsory education for children of both sexes. A spring 1943 *addendum* elaborated on the nature of the federative relationship with France.

When the governor general announced that France could entertain no talk of a separate status for Algeria, Ferhat Abbas and his colleagues decided to boycott the September 1943 session of the Délégations Financières. For this act of resistance, Abbas was jailed for the first time. Released in December 1943, he refused to adjust his goals but for a period adopted less confrontational tactics.

Though the French refused to consider an Algerian constitution, they soon unilaterally extended a number of concessions to the Muslims, including a vast expansion of the electorate, abolition of the hated Indigénat, and French citizenship for several tens of thousands of évolués. What Abbas would have welcomed in 1936, however, was not even marginally acceptable in 1944. His response to these concessions was to return once again to the idea of mass mobilization, this time by founding an organization called Amis du Manifeste et de la Liberté (AML).

Having previously won the support of the Association of Algerian Ulama and of Messali Hadj, Abbas saw the AML grow rapidly to a membership of hundreds of thousands. The bulk of this membership consisted of militant younger men loyal to Messali Hadj, however. Ferhat Abbas and his moderate colleagues watched in dismay as their own organization escaped increasingly from their control.

On May 8, 1945, as France and her allies celebrated victory over Germany, Muslim demonstrations in Sétif and Guelma degenerated into riots and then into a massacre. In three days' time, some one hundred Europeans and between ten and forty-five thousand Muslims were killed. Since some implicated Muslims were found to be members of the AML, the organization was summarily banned. Ferhat Abbas, who said he knew nothing of the bloody events until two weeks later, was in Algiers to pay his respects on the occasion of France's victory when he was arrested in the governor general's waiting room.

Upon his release under a general amnesty in March 1946, Abbas founded a new party, the Union Démocratique du Manifeste Algérien (UDMA). Having learned from his AML experience, Abbas did not even consider making the new party a common front for patriotic elements. While the UDMA was to be extremely influential in Algerian politics down to the Revolution, it was clearly the party of the middle-class Constantinois and to a lesser extent of middle-class intellectuals in other regions.

Partly because the more popular Messali Hadj was still in prison, the UDMA won the bulk of the seats in the second French Constituent Assembly. By August 1946, Ferhat Abbas was sitting in the French National Assembly. Algerians had waited 116 years for admission to that forum, but, ironically, the bill that Abbas and his colleagues presented on their behalf was the draft constitution of an independent Algerian republic loosely associated with France. The draft's reception was hostile and the debate acrimonious. Abbas preferred not to stand for Parliament again.

After much parliamentary wrangling, a compromise Statute of Algeria enacted in 1947 created for the first time a separate Algerian Assembly, half of whose members were to be Muslims. In spite of many misgivings, both the MTLD and the UDMA decided to give the new system a trial. During the next few years, however, the colon establishment regularly sabotaged the statute by crudely rigging elections in such a way as to exclude most credible Algerian candidates. The underlying premise of Abbas and other moderates—that political action could lead to an improvement of Algerian prospects—was yanked away. As late as summer 1954, Abbas was still pleading with French authorities to respect and enforce France's own laws, but by that time the logic of the colonial dialectic was pushing forth, behind the scenes, a new leadership committed to revolutionary action.

While he expressed fear that revolt might be brewing, it is clear that Abbas, like the great majority of his compatriots, was caught off guard by the scattered violence that erupted on November 1, 1954. What grew into the Algerian War of Independence began as the work of a handful of revolutionaries whose early achievements were so unimpressive that Abbas labelled the first ten months of insurrection a "*drôle de rébellion*" (phony rebellion). As an influential member of the Algerian Assembly, Abbas worked for reconciliation, helping to secure the release of numerous political prisoners and making three trips to Paris in vain search of a negotiated settlement.

At the same time, FLN (National Liberation Front) recruiters were actively working to broaden their base of support. According to Abbas, Abdane Ramdane and Amar Oumrane contacted him in May 1955, at which time he quietly began to collect funds and medical supplies for the movement. By late August, grossly disproportionate French reprisals for guerrilla killing of European civilians accelerated a process of communal polarization that pushed Abbas ever closer to open embrace of the revolution. In September 1955 he joined other elected officials in sponsoring a "Declaration of the Sixty-One" recognizing "the Algerian national idea" and demanding that Algeria be treated as France's associate. Finally, on April 26, 1956, at a press conference in Cairo's Hotel Sémiramis, Abbas announced his adhesion to the FLN.

It is worth noting that Ferhat Abbas delivered his pronouncement in French because, like many Algerians of his generation, he had never mastered literary Arabic. He always seemed as ill at ease in Cairo as he was with the Pan-Arabist ideology fashionable at the time. By choice he spent most of the exile years in the less alien environments of Switzerland, Tunisia, or Morocco. It is apparently during these exile years, as well, that Abbas formulated the conviction that Algeria's past as well as its future could only be realistically approached as part of an Arabo-Berber Greater Maghrib. He felt affinity for Tunisia and Morocco that he never displayed for the Arab East.

In August 1956, the Soummam Congress met to reorganize the now dramatically expanded leadership of the FLN. The Congress created a representative authority in the form of a Conseil National de la Révolutoin Algérienne (CNRA), on which Abbas was awarded a seat. In the next year he also became a member of the principal executive organ, the Comité de Coordination et d'Exécution. When in 1958 the provisional government of the Algerian Republic (GPRA) was created, Abbas was its first president.

As one of the best known Algerian political figures of the era, Abbas's presence helped to strengthen both the internal base and the international credibility of the FLN. He occupied himself variously with information, finance, supply, and mediating amongst factions. The preponderance of power continued to reside in members of the original revolutionary group, however, and in 1961, as negotiations with France intensified, Abbas and other moderates were removed from the GPRA. The presidency was transferred to Benyoussef Benkhedda of the former MTLD. Explanations for Abbas's expulsion vary. It was alleged that French General Charles de Gaulle questioned Abbas's credibility within the FLN and preferred a negotiating partner with greater authority. Abbas himself believed that de Gaulle was still smarting from an alleged slight dating back to 1943. Others believe that Abbas was simply a victim of the scramble for position that gripped the FLN as it became apparent that Algerians would soon in fact hold power.

In 1962, as independence dawned, the authority of Benkhedda's GPRA was challenged by a ''Tlemcen Group'' headed by Ahmed Ben Bella* of the FLN's new Political Bureau and Houari Boumediene* of the General Staff. Still bitter at his exclusion from the GPRA and wanting to play a role in the shaping of independent Algeria, Abbas allied himself with the Tlemcen Group.

Ben Bella accepted the support of Abbas and other ideologically distant elements in order to strengthen his hand against the GPRA, but once Ben Bella attained power, Abbas became one of the many victims of his drive to consolidate it. As president of the National Constituent Assembly elected in September 1962, Abbas believed it was the duty of this broadly representative body to formulate through careful study and open debate a constitution truly reflective of Algerian personality and opinion. He also believed that until the constitution was adopted, legislative authority as well as ultimate supervision of the government should reside in the Assembly. Such views brought him into direct conflict with Ben Bella, whose institutional model was based on the single party and a far more centralized view of political authority.

When Ben Bella submitted for Assembly adoption a constitution drafted by his own Political Bureau and approved by a hand-picked selection of FLN members, Abbas resigned as president of the Assembly. Three days later, on August 16, 1963, Ben Bella announced his expulsion from the party. Thirteen months after Algerian independence, the active political career of the pharmacist from Sétif had ended.

Abbas spent the bulk of the twenty-two years remaining to him at his modest villa in Algiers or in Sétif. He was also arrested for the third and fourth times in his life. Ben Bella arrested him during a summer 1964 crisis, holding him in a villa in southern Oranie until June 1965. Boumediene placed him under house arrest for fifteen months in 1976 after Abbas signed an ''Appeal to the Algerian People'' condemning the break with Morocco over the Western Sahara, which he ascribed to the fact that in place of truly representative institutions, the leaders had substituted unbridled personal power.

During the retirement years, Abbas published in France *Autopsie d'une Guerre*, his history of the War of Independence, and *L'Indépendance confisquée*. In the latter work he deplored the usurpation of power by Ben Bella and Boumediene who, in his view, prevented the Algerian people from creating authentic and truly legitimate national institutions. Looking to Moscow rather than to the humane tradition of Islam and the liberal tradition of France, the leaders burdened Algeria with Stalinist communism, a so-called democratic centralism, and the cult of personality. The emancipation for which two generations of Algerian patriots and martyrs had fought had been confiscated by men bent on personal power.

In 1961, Jean LaCouture observed that Ferhat Abbas had spent his entire adult life searching for his country—first in France, then alongside France, and then outside France. When this liberal heir of two of civilization's greatest traditions died on December 24, 1985, he was still searching for that country.

BIBLIOGRAPHY

Works by Abbas:

Guerre et Révolution d'Algérie. La Nuit coloniale. Paris: Julliard, 1962.
Autopsie d'une Guerre. Paris: Garnier, 1980.
De la Colonie vers la Province. Le jeune Algérien. Paris: Garnier, 1981.
L'Indépendance confisquée. Paris: Flammarion, 1984.

Other Works:

Gordon, David. *The Passing of French Algeria*. London: Oxford University Press, 1966.
Lacouture, Jean. *Cinq hommes et la France*. Paris: Editions du Seuil, 1961.
Naroun, Amar. *Ferhat Abbas*. Paris: Denoel, 1961.
Quandt, William B. *Revolution and Political Leadership: Algeria, 1954–1968*. Cambridge, Mass.: M.I.T. Press, 1969.

JOHN RUEDY

ABDALLAH AL-SALIM AL-SABAH (1895–1965) is remembered by Kuwaitis as one of the most effective rulers in their nation's history. Abdallah ruled Kuwait for fifteen years, from 1950 through 1965. Those years saw Kuwait move from a poor British protectorate to an independent, wealthy state. Abdallah was the architect who oversaw this transition with remarkable skill. During a period of rapid change in a region experiencing tremendous domestic instability,

Abdallah, with few examples to draw on, mapped a course for Kuwait that brought it prosperity and political continuity. The stability and internal cohesion that Kuwait knows today is in no small measure the consequence of choices made by Abdallah during this critical period.

Abdallah was born in Kuwait in 1895. He was the first of several sons of Sheikh Salim Mubarak, who ruled Kuwait from 1917 to 1921, and the grandson of Mubarak the Great, who ruled Kuwait from 1896 through 1915. Abdallah grew up in the political shadow of his very powerful grandfather. Mubarak had become amir through a violent coup—unusual in Kuwaiti history—in which he assassinated his own half-brothers. After consolidating his position at home, Mubarak then radically reoriented Kuwait's position in the international arena by maneuvering Kuwait away from its Ottoman alliance and placing it under British protection. Abdallah thus came of age in a political world dominated by one strong leader; his own rule, when it came, would mirror that of his grandfather in its power and purpose, while carefully avoiding Mubarak's more authoritarian tendencies. Abdallah was to take the best from his predecessors. From Mubarak he learned the importance of strong leadership during a sustained period of transition and crisis. When Mubarak died in 1915, he was succeeded by his son Jabir, who ruled less than two years. On his death in 1917, Jabir was succeeded by his brother, Abdallah's father, Sheikh Salim, who ruled until 1921.

Abdallah began his own political career under the tutelage of his father, Sheikh Salim, who ruled Kuwait from 1917 to 1921. Under Jabir, Salim had held the position of tribal liaison, an important role given that tribal relations were key to defining relations with Kuwait's Saudi neighbor. Abdallah assisted his father in tribal affairs, thus acquiring both domestic- and foreign-policy experience. During World War I, Abdallah also worked with British officials in blockading trade to Syria and Arabia.

During this period, Salim positioned his son carefully, with an eye to his eventual succession. In the long run Salim's efforts were successful, but in the short run they were not. Salim's rule was crowded with crises, key among them border raids from the Saudis. Salim's policy of opposition to Abd al-Aziz ibn Saud,* who would soon rule Arabia, was neither popular nor successful, and when Salim died, many key members of the Sabah family—brothers, uncles, and cousins of the ruler who were historically consulted on matters of succession—wanted a clean break with his policies. Other family members supported Abdallah, who assumed temporary rule on his father's death; still others backed Abdallah's cousin Ahmad al-Jabir, who was older and who enjoyed the support of the Saudis and the British. In the end, the family came to a decision that would have longstanding consequences for Kuwait. They decided on a new succession pattern, an alternation between the Jabir and Salim lines (each a son of Mubarak), a pattern that continues today. Ahmad, not Abdallah, took power, ruling from 1921 to 1950.

Abdallah never fully reconciled himself to this displacement. No sooner had Ahmad taken power then Abdallah began to assist him in every way he could.

It was not long before he was issuing orders directly in the ruler's name, threatening to reduce Ahmad to a mere figurehead. Abdallah finally overstepped his mark when he tried to introduce fixed stipends for the ruling family, giving himself a salary far higher than the others and equal to that of the amir. The result was a stormy scene, and Abdallah was forced to retreat temporarily.

In the 1930s, Abdallah made another bid for power. During this decade, the first oil concession was signed and the first oil revenues began arriving in Kuwait. These revenues, and the promise of more, sharpened cleavages within Kuwaiti society at large and within the ruling family. In 1938 these differences came out in the open as dissident merchants joined forces with dissident members of the ruling family under the leadership of Abdallah Salim and his brothers Fahd and Sabah. The merchants' opposition culminated in an assembly over which Abdallah presided during its six-month lifespan. In the end, Sheikh Ahmad resorted to force to put down the uprising. Abdallah, unable or unwilling to continue his opposition, backed down, and the uprising ended. Nonetheless, the political events of the 1930s left their mark on Abdallah. They played a role in his decision, years later as amir, to introduce an elected National Assembly to Kuwait. They also forged an enduring relationship between the trading community and Abdallah's branch of the ruling family. That legacy survives Abdallah; it is popularly believed that Abdallah's relatives, and in particular his son, crown prince Saad Abdallah (who played an important role in reconvening the Assembly in 1981) are more committed to the Assembly. After 1986, when the Assembly was suspended by Sheikh Jabir of the rival branch, this belief offered hope to the Assembly's supporters.

With the defeat of the Assembly in the 1930s, Abdallah sought another institutional mechanism to develop his power. He found it in the finance department, which he established and ran from 1937 to 1950. The department was in part a way for Ahmad to placate and contain Abdallah. Their personal relationship never became cordial, but this division of labor allowed a cold peace to emerge. A finance department was also becoming a practical necessity given the new oil revenues. Both the Assembly and the British had called for institutions to maintain financial control of those revenues. Abdallah spent the decade following the uprising in developing this department. During World War II, he expanded the post to include handling rationed food supplies.

In 1950 Ahmad had a fatal heart attack. As Abdallah Salim was out of the country, the British, who had always preferred Ahmad over Salim and his son Abdallah, and who perhaps feared a genuine succession crisis, brought in a squadron of armored cars and boats, and discussed flying-in troops. However, Britain underestimated the family's discipline. On the news of his cousin's death, Abdallah returned to Kuwait and assumed rule. This time, after a month's debate, the family confirmed Abdallah. Abdallah's accession caused no radical break with the past. He had been ready to assume the post for decades.

Abdallah immediately set about putting in place a development program. Ahmad had limped by with ad hoc policies, particularly in his last years of increasing ill health, but the magnitude of oil revenues after World War II, when exports finally got underway, demanded a more coherent policy. Abdallah's planning was not wholly successful and, especially in the first years, vast amounts of money were wasted on poorly designed, poorly executed, and inappropriate projects. However, although Abdallah made many mistakes, his planning and organization insured far more successes. His first task fell in the area of foreign policy. In his last years Ahmad had tried, without success, to renegotiate the oil agreement with the two foreign concessionaires, British Petroleum and Gulf Oil. Now, the success of other states (notably Saudi Arabia) in negotiating more profitable arrangements, combined with Kuwait's growing importance following the rise of Mohammed Mossadegh* in Iran and the decline of oil export there, gave Abdallah more leverage. After a year in power he was able to negotiate a new oil agreement.

The new agreement produced revenues on an unprecedented scale. Abdallah's next task was to oversee the distribution of those revenues. Ahmad had used the early trickle of revenues to placate ruling family dissidents. In Ahmad's last years his touch had weakened, and in the power vacuum that began to emerge, a few family members (Abdallah among them) had begun to develop their own bureaucratic fiefdoms. In the early 1950s, this nascent battle for control of the new state institutions broke into the open. Three personalities led the fight: Abdallah's brother, Fahd al-Salim; Abdallah's uncle, Abdallah Mubarak; and Abdallah's nephew, Jabir al-Ahmad* (later *amir* or ruler). Their struggle focused on the formal demand that Abdallah name a crown prince. This he refused to do. Instead, Abdallah first set about exercising control over these bureaucratic barons. Through a decade of administrative reforms and new family alliances, Abdallah finally succeeded in instituting his central control over these contenders. Fahd died defeated toward the end of the decade; Abdallah Mubarak left for an angry exile, and Jabir, the survivor, eventually became amir. The ousters of Fahd and Abdallah were more than the elimination of family rivals; they were the first step toward instituting a modicum of rational administration. Their ouster announced that Abdallah would place a limit on corruption at the highest levels. To mollify the rest of the ruling family and contain their ambitions, Abdallah insisted that British contractors, who were taking advantage of growing local investment, take local partners, a lucrative arrangement for Kuwaitis. Many such partners were from the Sabah family.

Abdallah also rallied the support of the merchants to his side. Through carefully protecting their economic interests and guaranteeing them freedom from government intervention, he purchased their withdrawal from public politics, an arrangement that has largely held since and would have been far harder to negotiate had Abdallah not already enjoyed significant confidence from the merchant community, stemming from his support of the uprising of 1938.

Abdallah also turned to the national population, using the new revenues to develop a popular support base. First, he improved the standard of living by investing heavily in infrastructure; communications and transportation. In this he relied heavily on the advice of a handful of British advisers. When it turned out that much of their advice was self-serving and bad, he had the sense to cut his losses and completely reorganize his development plans in the mid–1950s. After focusing on infrastructure, he introduced a massive, broad-based program of social services, providing Kuwaitis with free health, education, and welfare benefits, as well as guaranteed employment. He built hospitals and opened schools. In all this, he assured himself not only of another pillar of support to use against dissident family members, but also outflanked Arab nationalists who sought a popular support base. The 1950s were the era of Gamal Abdul Nasser,* and his potential support in Kuwait was large, especially given that Abdallah needed initially to rely heavily on expatriate, mainly Egyptian, teachers to provide the education he had promised Kuwaitis. However, Abdallah's social programs eliminated many of the popular grievances on which Nasserists liked to feed. Just to be sure, Abdallah also kept good lines of communication open with Nasser himself, striking an accommodation in which Nasser left Abdallah for the most part alone and Abdallah continued to hire Egyptians, providing Nasser with badly needed hard currency.

In his personal life, Abdallah had, over the years, a number of wives, illustrating, perhaps unintentionally, his political constituency. From the ruling family, he married his cousin Mariam al-Sabah, a sister of Amir Ahmad (likewise, one of Abdallah's sisters, Bibi, married Sheikh Ahmad). From the merchants, he married Hasa al-Ghanim, a member of one of Kuwait's largest trading families. From the popular sector, he married a slave who eventually became the mother of Kuwait's current heir apparent, Sheikh Saad.

By the end of the 1950s, Abdallah had made remarkable progress. Not only had he asserted control over his family rivals, but he had gone beyond that goal and used his new centralized power to develop a variety of state services that benefited the population at large. In a decade, Abdallah had laid in place a basic infrastructure, established a system of social programs, and built a bureaucracy capable of extending basic services.

In the 1950s, Abdallah was able to focus on domestic issues. This was in keeping with his interests and background. Abdallah had traveled little in the West (with the notable exception of a 1953 visit to England for the coronation of Queen Elizabeth), although he was decorated by the British, the French and the Pope. He had traveled extensively in the region: in the Arab world and India. In the 1950s, his foreign-policy projects were primary regional—for example, early on he introduced a significant foreign-aid program.

In the 1960s, circumstances forced Abdallah to focus on foreign policy. In 1961, Britain granted Kuwait independence. Within days Iraq had placed a claim on Kuwait, threatening to annex the new state. At Abdallah's request, British and Arab League forces landed to prevent the Iraqis from exercising their claim. Abdallah's stand brought him much popularity at home. His success stemmed from his ability to maneuver outside powers into defending Kuwait's independence and transforming a position of extreme vulnerability into one of strength.

At home, Abdallah used the opportunity of an outside threat to strengthen his domestic coalition. First he asserted control over the ruling family. In 1962, he finally named an heir apparent, his brother Sabah, then deputy prime minister and foreign minister. This move marked the end of his long struggle with the supporters of Fahd al-Salim and Abdallah Mubarak. When Abdallah died in 1965, Sabah succeeded him without incident.

Second, Abdallah extended a measure of participation to groups outside the ruling family, notably through the inauguration of the National Assembly. The Iraqi threat and the need for a national front at home were the immediate catalyst, but Abdallah's positive experience with the brief interwar Assembly doubtless played a role. Abdallah's ouster of Fahd al-Salim and Abdallah Mubarak, two family members who opposed expanding participation, helped pave the way. In 1963, Kuwait held its first elections and produced a body with vocal opposition that proved strong enough in 1965 to prompt a cabinet removal. In a period of Arab nationalism, when dissent in much of the Arab world was increasingly stifled by regimes wary of opposition, Abdallah's decision was a brave one. Even when the Assembly proved contentious, Abdallah was more likely to respond with techniques drawn from the democratic repertoire—gerrymandering and selective suffrage expansion—than with outright repression (although this sometimes occurred). His successors, Sabah and Jabir, would not hesitate to suspend the Assembly when it proved too vocal.

Abdallah died November 24, 1965, at the age of 70, from a heart attack during the opening session of the new National Assembly. His death was widely mourned in Kuwait. He was succeeded by the crown prince he had named, his brother Sabah. His final legacy was the continuity of succession.

Abdallah's achievements are impressive. His rule oversaw Kuwait's transition from a British dependency to an independent state. At home, Abdallah actively oversaw Kuwait's transition from poverty to wealth. He laid the groundwork in the 1950s for the economic development of the next thirty years. He designed the new state institutions, financial and participatory, that would ease that transition. In particular, Abdallah had the political imagination to smooth this transition by adding a degree of participation, drawing on a Kuwaiti tradition that is popularly valued. Economically as well as politically, Kuwait was one of the first oil states to face these transitions. When Abdallah made what were generally solid decisions, he had few examples to draw on—indeed, Kuwait became the example for the others. The smoothness of the transition owes much to his leadership. His critics, however, argue that the sudden oil revenues gave Abdallah far more political space than most rulers enjoy. The revenues masked mistakes and gave Abdallah, as they would any leader, the appearance of great capability.

In part, Abdallah's personal style predisposed him to focus on economic and political development. Abdallah was a respected leader in his own time. Physically imposing, tall and heavyset, he commanded attention. He had a reputation for hard work; observers noted he began his day at the palace at 6:30 A.M. In his private life, Abdallah was relatively frugal and restrained. Although journalists called him the richest man in the world (which he was not), he abjured the lavish lifestyle that characterized not only his predecessors, Ahmad and Mubarak, but also neighboring leaders. His private villa was, by regal standards, small. True, he took a substantial royal salary, but, given the opportunities at hand, his personal spending was constrained. His private interests ran more to reading and religion than revelry. Contemporary observers remark on his interest in and knowledge of history, poetry, religion, and politics. These were skills dearly acquired; when Abdallah was a child, Kuwait still lacked a formal school system. He was educated by tutors. From this, perhaps, he came to value what he himself had so dearly acquired. In particular, Abdallah clearly invested something of himself in his enthusiastic expansion of public education in Kuwait, a step taken at some political risk.

For all his virtues, Abdallah could not have achieved what he did without a concentrated purpose. He spent literally decades trying to achieve power. Perhaps it was the years of waiting, during Ahmad's rule, that gave him the time to develop his skills. The waiting and the focus on one goal also gave him the political ruthlessness he occasionally needed. Abdallah's combination of ruthless realism and political vision served Kuwait well during this critical period.

BIBLIOGRAPHY

Abu-Hakima, Ahmad Mustafa. *The Modern History of Kuwait*. London: Luzac & Co., 1983.
Burke's Royal Families of the World. Vol. 2. *The Middle East and North Africa*. London: Burke's Peerage, 1980.
Crystal, Jill. *Oil and the State in the Gulf: Rulers and Merchants in Kuwait and Qatar*. Cambridge: Cambridge University Press, forthcoming.
Daniels, John. *Kuwait Journey*. Luton; England: White Crescent Press, 1971.
Dickson, H.R.P. *Kuwait and Her Neighbors*. London: George Allen & Unwin, 1956.
Freeth, Zahra, and Victor Winstone. *Kuwait: Prospect and Reality*. London: George Allen & Unwin, 1972.
Ismael, Jacqueline. *Kuwait: Social Change in Historical Perspective*. Syracuse: Syracuse University Press, 1982.
Rush, Alan. *Al-Sabah: History and Genealogy of Kuwait's Ruling Family: 1752–1987*. London: Ithaca Press, 1987.
al-Sabah, Y.S.F. *The Oil Economy of Kuwait*. London: Kegan Paul, 1980

JILL CRYSTAL

ABD AL-AZIZ IBN SAUD (1881–1953) was the son of Abd al-Rahman, the defeated ruler of the second Saudi state of the Saud family, the ruling family in Nejd, Central Arabia. In early 1902 he emerged from exile in Kuwait and established the present Kingdom of Saudi Arabia, which he ruled until 1953. He became king of the Hejaz in 1926 and of Nejd in 1927. These regions and others were incorporated into the Kingdom of Saudi Arabia in 1932. Ibn Saud established a relatively stable, dynastic rule in his kingdom, and became a major Arab leader and a figure acquainted with leaders such as Franklin Roosevelt and Winston Churchill.

There were three main components that shaped ibn Saud's personality and conduct of public affairs through his tenure as leader of Saudi Arabia (1902–1953). First was his ancestral legacy to reestablish an empire committed to spreading the ideas of the Wahhabi creed. This legacy was anchored in the Wahhabi ideology, manifested in the successes of the first and second Saudi states in the eighteenth and nineteenth centuries, which were abruptly terminated in the late nineteenth century when the Saudi realm fell into internal war and ultimate collapse.

The aim of Wahhabism has been the purification of Islam from popular innovations and distortions which, over centuries, have melded with the Islamic scholastic and monotheistic core. Muhammad Ibn al-Wahhab, the clergyman who founded this denomination in the eighteenth century, drew both on the pedant Hanbali school of law prevalent in central Arabia and on the scholarship of a fourteenth-century scholar, Ahmad Ibn Taymiyya. Ibn Abd al-Wahhab's interpretation of these works focused on the centrality of God's oneness as the heart of Islamic theology and on the rejection of any anthropomorphism, which was regarded as a major sin. In Abd al-Wahhab's perception, his revivalist denomination should dominate Muslim life and the Muslim state in order to destroy any group that was lax about God's oneness or abhorrent of the practices that follow therefrom.

After some futile attempts, Abd al-Wahhab struck an alliance with the ruler of the Saudi chieftaincy of Nejd, Muhammad ibn Saud, in 1744. Like the original Muslim state led by the prophet Muhammad, the Saudi state emerged as a vehicle to spread the purifying creed of Wahhabi Islam. In a series of conquests carried out in the late eighteenth century, the Saudi-Wahhabi state captured most of northern Arabia and, in the early nineteenth century, even the Holy Places in the Hejaz. Due to the difficulties the Saudis caused to surrounding populations and to the Ottoman government, the official authority of the Arab World, the latter engaged the governor of Egypt, Muhammad Ali, to fight the challenging Wahhabis. After several years of fighting the Egyptians conquered and destroyed the Wahhabi force and turned their capital, Dariyya, into ruins in 1818.

The second Saudi-Wahhabi state, which emerged in 1821 following the Egyptian withdrawal from Nejd, was bound to principles similar to those that guided the first Saudi state, but its achievements were less impressive. Moreover, internal fighting among factions of the Saudi family spread starting in the 1860s, which precipitated the demise of their state. The Rashidi dynasty of Jabal Shammar gradually took over the realm until its final collapse in 1891.

Ibn Saud was a youth of ten when he and his family went in exile from Nejd to Kuwait in 1891, after the downfall of the second Saudi state. Ibn Saud grew up there as part of the entourage of Kuwait's ruler Mubarak, who came to power in 1897. He acquired traditional education in chivalry, riding, and fighting, and even led occasional raids against the Rashidis. He was also a keen observer of the political wheeling and dealing that Mubarak, tribal leaders, and foreign representatives carried on in the Royal palace. Ibn Saud first married at fifteen but his wife died; after a short time he remarried at eighteen, which led to the birth of his first son, Turki. As a son of the last reigning Saudi ruler, Abd al-Rahman, and as grandson of Feisal ibn Turki, ibn Saud carried a very specific mission to establish a state that would follow the example of the earlier states and would conquer and expand. The state would be governed according to the pious Wahhabi doctrine and would be bound to purify the Islamic practice as far as possible. Ibn Saud commenced this mission in January 1902. With only forty men, he conquered Riyad, the capital of the second Saudi state. However, his policies during the next years reveal that there was also a second component that shaped his personality and political perception. Ibn Saud displayed a degree of pragmatism and insight into regional strategic conditions uncommon among his ancestors and contemporaries. He probably acquired these skills during his exile in Kuwait, which constituted a formative period in his development. Under the leadership of Mubarak, Kuwait was a local center for the great powers' diplomacy and for international trade between India and the Ottoman Empire or Europe. Ibn Saud could thereby learn that the Arabian Peninsula, notably the Gulf Littoral, had become a focus for competition between the great powers, a situation that generated new political conditions: the emergence of Britain as a new, lasting superpower in the Gulf and the ensuing of a rivalry among local rulers over British favors. Ibn Saud apparently drew two main conclusions from these new conditions: that the Nejdi state should embark on long-term cooperation with great powers, mainly Britain, to secure its future; and that he should consolidate his state internally, in order to persevere in regional disputes.

Despite his inclination to develop strategies for the future, ibn Saud was well-grounded in the realities of his time as evident in a third component that shaped his outlook and behavior. This was his tribal heritage. Ibn Saud was a student of tribal values, mainly of tribal leadership, warfare, and mediation, both during his early youth in Nejd and later in Kuwait. The entity he established after the occupation of Riyadh in 1902 indeed emulated the type of tribal chieftaincies that prevailed in the region. It was based on a loose alliance of several nomadic tribes and townspeople of Nejd and Qasim, tied together only by ad hoc and personal bonds, which easily broke and collapsed. Ibn Saud spent his early years of leadership in a slow piecing-together of the Mutayr tribal groups and the townspeople of Qasim, both of whom were often lured by the main enemies of the Saudis, the Rashidis, and their Ottoman supporters.

Ibn Saud thus combined traditional qualities of leadership, which focused on tactical maneuvering among tribal segments, with more ambitious and innovative qualities, bound on a long-term alliance with Britain and on building a stable and institutionalized state. Driven by his ancestral legacy to reestablish the Wahhabi empire, ibn Saud embarked on both traditional and innovative means in order to realize this ambition.

During the first decade of his reign, ibn Saud had to fight exhausting struggles for the very existence of the Nejdi state. The struggle with the Rashidis spread over several years and peaked in 1906 with the killing of the incumbent Rashidi ruler. At the same time, ibn Saud had to thwart attempts by the Mutayr to align with his rivals, and gained some regional relief in this respect only in 1909. He was also forced to tackle other members in the Saudi family, who during these years contended for the throne. Under this burden, ibn Saud did not embark on substantial changes in state formation, but mainly sought to align with the British and thereby forge a long-term axis of cooperation that would counter the Ottoman alliance with the Rashidis. The British authorities in London prevailed over their counterparts in India and decided against the weakening of the Ottoman Empire, whose rule in the Middle East they still regarded as the best means to secure British interests en route to India.

Gulf-based British officers, such as Percy Cox, the British Resident in the Gulf, sensed ibn Saud's potential, but Cox's recommendation of 1906 to have Britain recognize an independent and friendly Saudi rule was to no avail. Ibn Saud succeeded in attracting growing British attention only after his forces had taken the Gulf region of al-Hasa in 1913 from the Ottomans and obtained direct access to a region that was vital for British interests.

Seeking to dominate this region, which constituted an outlet to the maritime route to India, the British then reached an agreement with the Ottomans to that effect and attempted to develop a rapprochement with the Saudi ruler, too. In an attempt to both increase his stake with the British and yet exploit his new influential position with the Ottomans who did not want to relinquish the Gulf, ibn Saud also entered new negotiations with the latter. At that stage, Saud clearly maneuvered between the two powers in order accomplish the best gain. On May 15, 1914, he signed an agreement with the Ottomans that recognized their sovereignty in the region but in practice left him as the governor of Nejd and al-Hasa, thereby recognizing his rule there.

As World War I commenced, the British authorities divorced themselves from the interests that had hitherto bound their policies to the Ottoman well-being. Ibn Saud too, decided to throw in his lot with the British, the superpower he deemed would dominate in the future. Following several months of negotiations between ibn Saud and the British agent in Kuwait and then with Cox, a treaty was concluded between the parties on December 26, 1915. Ibn Saud gained important advantages. The treaty assured British aid to ibn Saud against foreign aggression and granted the Saudi state practical independence from any great power. Ibn Saud had to commit himself to refrain from encroaching into the British-protected principalities in the Gulf and from ceding territories to a foreign government without British consent. Otherwise, however, the treaty signified the recognition of an international independent status for the Saudi state, a much-cherished ambition of ibn Saud. Moreover, the treaty did not commit ibn Saud to engage in any specific military actions on the British side, which allowed the Saudi ruler relative calm to develop his state.

In spite of this achievement, the positions of Nejd and of ibn Saud personally were rather insignificant during the early stages of World War I. Supported by the Arab Bureau, the Cairo-based British office for intelligence and liaison with the Arabs, it was mainly Sherif Abdullah ibn Hussein* of the Hashemite family of Jordan, the keeper of the Holy Places in the Hejaz, whom the British designated as leader of the Arab Movement and head of the Anti-Ottoman Arab Revolt. The considerable amount of money Hussein received, the tribal forces he was thereby able to attract, and the military successes the Hashemites encountered against the Ottomans overshadowed ibn Saud's position. It took him several months to draw the attention of other British authorities (notably those of Eastern Arabia, answerable to the India Office) to his fear of Hashemite expansion. With the encouragement of such officials, notably Cox and his secretary, H. B. St. John Philby, ibn Saud acquired some real dividends from his cooperation with Britain. Starting in early 1917 he received a modest monthly subsidy and was given a role in the regional anti-Ottoman efforts, to harass the Rashidi forces. Following a visit from Philby to ibn Saud in November 1917, the Saudi campaign against ibn Rashid was enhanced, making it possible for the Nejd chieftaincy to expand its territories.

During 1916 and 1917, ibn Saud commenced a campaign of state building in Nejd to transform the traditional nature of the chieftaincy into an organized state. He embarked on this campaign in response to changes that British and Ottoman intervention had introduced in Arabia, which shook the old system of chieftaincies and forced them to transform. The assistance the British Arab Bureau gave Sharif Hussein was echoed by other British authorities and by the Ottomans, who cultivated, to a considerably smaller extent, their own local protégés. The blocking of ports and the shifting of trade routes, which were part of war efforts, and the use Hussein made of British gold to enlist tribes, enhanced rivalries among rulers and caused tribes to change loyalties among chieftaincies. Ibn Saud's grasp of great-power politics led him to understand that only large, strong, and organized states would survive the war and the postwar era in Arabia. He therefore started altering the structures and practices of the Saudi chieftaincy in several respects. Ibn Saud embarked on conquests, and subsequently gained the image of a builder of empires "by his sword."

In fact, he was careful not to challenge the British by fighting any of their other protégés, and avoided exposing his forces to difficult battles. For years he limited his actions to a sporadic attack on ibn Rashid's forces in September 1918 (an initiative mainly instigated by Philby) and to diplomatic assistance to the people of Khurma (located between Nejd and the Hejaz, northeast of Mecca), who had revolted against Hussein and asked for Saudi help. Ibn Saud finally dispatched a force to assist them in May 1918, but was not involved in the subsequent massacre the Khurma people inflicted on Hussein's forces in Turaba, on May 25, 1919.

Only in the fall of 1920, after ibn Saud had discovered a plot against him by Hussein, with the participation of the Sheikh of Kuwait and other rulers of the region, he embarked on a systematic campaign of conquest. Ibn Saud was then organizing his forces, both nomads and townspeople in regional commands, and engaged them in several arenas. His forces established settlement at Jarriyya al-Ulya near the city of Kuwait, and defeated a Kuwaiti contingent. Being careful not to destroy a British-protected chieftaincy, ibn Saud did not pursue fighting on this front. He rather turned against one of Nejd's archenemies, the Rashidi chieftaincy. After winning some of the local Shammar tribe groups over to his side, ibn Saud laid siege to the Rashidi capital, Hail. This chieftaincy finally collapsed and fell into Saudi hands in November 1921. Exploiting a call for help from the Idrisi ruler of Asir against a rebel chieftain in Abha, ibn Saud dispatched a force led by his son Faisal bin Abd al-Aziz Saud* to Asir. Abha and the northern parts of Asir had already been captured in 1920, but following recurrent rebellions against Saudi control there, it was consolidated only during 1923. On January 7, 1925, ibn Saud concluded a treaty with the Idrisi ruler that gave the Saudi state complete control of the whole of Asir.

Saudi conquests were crowned with the occupation of the Hejaz, which signified the return of the Wahhabi to control the Holy Places. The Saudi conquest did materialize only after relations with the British had further improved; notably after London ceased subsidizing local rulers and after Hussein had wrecked his relations with Britain, which lost patience with the Hejazi ruler. An attempt for a comprehensive settlement between ibn Saud and the Hashimites which took place in Kuwait between fall 1923 and spring 1924 also failed. The Saudi campaign attests to ibn Saud's grasp of international affairs: He took full notice of the Muslim and European interests in the Hejaz, and accompanied his moves with propaganda publications and letters to foreign consuls. After his forces inflicted a massacre on the population of Taif in July 1924, he laid siege on Mecca and Jidda to ease the impact of the attack on the resident foreign legation. By early 1926, the Hejazi town surrendered, and the last Hashimite ruler, Ali, went into exile. Ibn Saud's attention to foreign powers then paid off, as a Muslim conference convened in Mecca after the Saudi occupation, and which had originally preferred an international rule in the Holy Places, finally endorsed Saudi rule there.

The formation of a large territorial base for the Saudi state was only one means of state building on which ibn Saud embarked. After 1917 he seriously attempted to consolidate his chieftaincy internally. During the next decades he exercised some of the traditional tribal devices: He, his brothers, and other members of his family married tens of wives for short periods to integrate their families with bonds of loyalty and produce princes. He also kept paying subsidies to tribal rulers. He further tried a new method: He started sedenterizing nomads in special settlements, where they were supposed to assume a quiet life of agriculture and religious studies. They were also supposed to function as a standing army for ibn Saud. This campaign was supposed to stifle the turbulence of the major nomadic tribes, install ideological zeal among them, and render them ready to fight for the state.

It became evident that the *Ikhwan* (Brethren) movement that thus emerged had mixed blessings. The Ikhwan indeed functioned as an important component in Saudi conquests and as a pioneer spreading Wahhabi ideas, thereby helping to integrate tribes around the Wahhabi ideology. However, after the late 1910s, the Ikhwan developed problems. They were overzealous in their fighting and proselytizing, and unseasoned by previous government experience. Different groups in society complained about the Ikhwan's enforcement methods. They even tried to dictate revivalist methods to ibn Saud. The Ikhwan were also relentless in raiding into neighboring states, exceeding ibn Saud's orders; particularly in the 1920s, when he had to accommodate to British-initiated frontier lines with Iraq and Transjordan. Most of all, the Ikhwan maintained tribal habits and disliked subordination to a central authority in administrative and economic spheres.

Ibn Saud's dissatisfaction with the Ikhwan's conduct enabled him to initiate a set of new devices, which attested to the emergence of an organized state. They were manifested in centralization and in administrative and economic reforms. Ibn Saud started to develop two Gulf regions, Jubail and Qatif, and to levy customs on the trade in these places. This was to replace Saudi trade in Kuwait, which had not adequately benefited the Saudi state. He also increased direct taxes on the local population. After the occupation of the Hejaz, ibn Saud established government offices, improved communication through a telegraph system, and brought in some initial vehicle transportation.

In a parallel manner, he sought improved relations with surrounding states and with Britain; the new Jedda treaty of May 20, 1927, signed with Britain, finally granted the Saudi state complete, unimpeded independence. Apparently, ibn Saud had developed a perception of a centralized, peaceful kingdom geared at economic development. The Ikhwan then emerged as his main opponents: They resisted centralization and association with "infidel" foreigners, and raided, against ibn Saud's will, into Iraq. They were advocates of the traditional chieftaincy. Initially the two camps sought to persuade each other rather than fight out their differences.

The Saudi religious sages, who were called on to adjudicate the dispute in a series of conferences during 1927–1928, did not come up with a clear decision concerning the legitimacy of the parties' demands. Consequently, ibn Saud fought the main Ikhwan malcontents during 1929; it remains unclear who started the actual fight, but as the fighting subsided, in January 1930, ibn Saud had defeated his rivals and gained a major victory.

In the next twenty-three years, ibn Saud strived to entrench, institutionalize, and develop the centralized polity he had introduced. The effect of the war with the Ikhwan, his former allies, and the accumulating effects of continuous stomach and eye problems, made ibn Saud withdraw from the direct management of state affairs. He remained the major force behind strategic decision making and the architect of both Saudi foreign policy and economic development. However, he was not involved with daily affairs, which were left to the new administrators.

As such, ibn Saud's influence was marked in several spheres. In the early 1930s, the Saudi regime faced two tribal rebellions, in the northern Hejaz and in Asir. They were provoked by the worldwide economic depression and by the increased taxation the Saudis imposed; but there was also a plot designed by a group of Hejazi exiles and assisted by Hashemites from Jordan and Iraq and by the Imam Yahya* of Yemen that stimulated the rebels. The rebellions were easily crushed in the Hejaz in May 1932 and in Asir in November of that year. However, the skirmishes in Asir developed into a full-scale war with Yemen in February or March of 1934. Ibn Saud personally, and his forces as a whole, proved resilient and decisive. Three Saudi columns rushed into the eastern, central, and western-coastal regions of Asir, destroyed the forces that confronted them, and penetrated Yemen. The most impressive Saudi conquest was that of the significant Red Sea port, Hodieda. However, with British and Italian intervention, Saudi forces retreated to their territory. In May 1934, a treaty of friendship was signed between Saudi Arabia and Yemen in Taif. It concluded the immediate dispute between the two parties and left Asir in Saudi hands.

Ibn Saud then grew to value stable relations with surrounding states as a crucial determinant for internal stability and development in Saudi Arabia. This development coincided with a British policy to demarcate frontier lines among Britain's different client states in Arabia and stabilize their interrelations. Ibn Saud concluded a treaty of friendship with Iraq in 1931 and again in 1936, and with Transjordan in 1933, which terminated Hashemite plotting in the Northern Hejaz. Following extensive discussions between Saudi and British officials in the mid–1930s, the southern and southeastern Saudi frontier was principally outlined to include the Rubal-Khali desert in Saudi hands. Through these agreements, ibn Saud was able to reassert Saudi Arabia's regional status and to create surrounding conditions conducive for internal development.

The convoluted relationship that ibn Saud had hitherto had with Britain enabled him to diversify his foreign policy in the next years. The achievements of his pro-British policy, notably the demarcation of frontiers and improved relations with neighbors, notwithstanding, ibn Saud saw definite shortcomings along these lines. Britain did not settle the Palestinian problem in the ultimate Arab favor as the Saudi leader had wished. London also refused to conclude a military alliance with Saudi Arabia and to sell arms to Riyadh. Ibn Saud's sense of international relations presumably guided him in searching for collaboration with other ascending powers active in the region. He negotiated with Germany for the sale of light weapons, which he stopped when German soldiers invaded Poland in September 1939, prompting Britain to declare war on Germany. Ibn Saud maintained a policy of benevolence toward the Allies during World War II, but did not engage in any active operations.

During the war, ibn Saud also witnessed the ascending role of the United States. He realized the superior financial American position in comparison with the limited British resources, and particularly benefited from the direct and indirect support afforded by the American oil companies. The political and superior military might of the United States became apparent toward the end of the war. Ibn Saud's meeting with President Franklin D. Roosevelt aboard a ship in the Red Sea in February 1945 crowned the new relationship: Both men were impressed with each other and pledged future cooperation. Although Roosevelt died two months later and the future U.S. policy on Palestine was not favored by Riyadh, U.S. Middle Eastern policy thereon became tied with Saudi security and economic development. The meeting ibn Saud had with Winston Churchill in Fayum, Egypt, three days after he had seen Roosevelt, was considerably cooler and proved fruitless. It symbolized Britain's declining position in Saudi foreign policy.

Following the Saudi victory over the Ikhwan, the centralizing Saudi regime had still to be institutionalized and exercised. Ibn Saud's style of internal building was twofold: On one hand, he generated centralization by reinforcing the authority of the new government offices, and he encouraged policies of mineral research and imposition of high taxation. A new elite of local and foreign businessmen ran public affairs. Regional integration was manifested in the unification of the different parts of the realm into the Saudi Arabia Kingdom, declared on September 16, 1932.

The most impressive project of development on which ibn Saud embarked was the exploitation of oil. He took full advantage of the interest of American companies to search for mineral resources in the region and to pay in advance for each concession. According to the treaty of May 1933 with Standard Oil of California, the Saudi government got "dead rent" even before oil was struck in al-Hasa in 1938. In May 1939, the concession in Dahran, al-Hasa, was enlarged, but the outbreak of the war paralyzed the production of oil.

Thanks to the Saudi potential of exporting oil, ibn Saud received financial aid from both the British government and, mostly, the U.S. government (although the latter refrained from doing so in the open and acted through the oil companies), which amounted to $6 million, and was aimed at securing his goodwill during the war. After the war, the American companies, which in the meantime organized themselves as the Arabian American Oil Company (ARAMCO), started building the Trans-Arabian Pipeline, delivering oil through Syria to the Mediterranean, which was finally completed in September 1950. The oil companies also developed the standard of living for their workers in al-Hasa. They offered them education, medical service, and improved conditions for housing facilities and for purchasing homes.

On the other hand, tribal practices and loyalties still dominated public life underneath the new institutions and were continuously used by ibn Saud. Paramount decision-making was limited to a group of princes (notably the king's sons Fahd bin Abd al-Aziz Al Saud,* who became heir apparent in 1932, and Faisal) and several top officials, and was conducted in informal procedures. Provincial governors were selected among members of the Royal Family. Subsidies to tribal chiefs and intermarriage with their members still constituted the government's most effective means of integration. The Royal Family became the largest melting pot in the realm. Ibn Saud's own thirty-six living sons, whose mothers came from different quarters, set the example.

Consequently, segments in the Saudi state usually maintained their tribal-regional identity and cooperated with their counterparts and with the government in alliances or coalitions that did not destroy their primordial structure. While this dual state of affairs attests to the modest and limited changes that evolved in the Saudi entity, it also indicates that the old and traditional balanced the innovative and the new. Saudi society therefore developed gradually, and in a balanced manner. Hence, ibn Saud's slow mode of change in state building had marked assets.

From the mid–1930s and until ibn Saud's death on November 8, 1953, no serious upheavals were reported in Saudi society. His sons as well as offshoots of other factions of the Royal Family (notably the Jilawi faction, which emerged in the al-Hasa region near the Gulf) were actually serving as the main ministers of the realm, the main regional governors, and heads of important public and ministerial agencies. The Royal Family thereby became an actual elite in the realm, in both numerical and functional respects. During ibn Saud's lifetime, several of his sons already occupied major positions. Saud was heir apparent since 1932 and the governor of Nejd. Faisal governed the Hejaz and was foreign minister. Saud was a tribal diplomat: Faisal was an organizer and experienced in dealing with foreign countries. The younger sons were less in line; Tallal was known as a zealous agitator for social reform; Mishari brought disgrace on ibn Saud when, while drunk, he murdered a British diplomat in 1951. The affair was concluded through the payment of blood money. However, most of the sons served well in their positions. Hence, when ibn Saud died both Saud and Faisal swept aside any disagreements they had harbored toward each other and allowed a smooth succession to ibn Saud's era.

In the 1950s, new challenges emerged for the Saudi Kingdom. In the light of the impact of the cold war on the Middle East, and of the changes initiated by ARAMCO in al-Hasa, some Saudi princes and officials demanded changes in the Saudi process of decision making. Consequently, in addition to a Ministry of Defense and Aviation established in 1944, a Ministry of Interior was established in 1951. In 1953, Ministries of Education, Agriculture, and Communications were added. Laws of income tax and an organized budget introduced in 1950 were followed in May 1952 by the establishment of the Saudi Arabian Monetary Agency to function as a state bank. These changes were only a partial remedy to the deep economic crisis the Saudi Kingdom was then undergoing. Only King Faisal's reforms in the mid–1960s changed this situation. Ibn Saud's skills were insufficient when it came to the transformation of Saudi Arabia into a modernized state, but he was definitely a ruler who led a mere tribal grouping to become an organized monarchy that spread over a large territory.

BIBLIOGRAPHY

Almana, Mohammad. *Arabia Unified: A Portrait of Ibn Saud.* London: Hutchinson Benhom, 1980.

Aramco. *Directory of the Royal Family, Officials of the Government, Diplomats and Other Prominent Persons*. 2d ed. Dhahran, Saudi Arabia: Aramco, 1957.

Bligh, Alexander. *From Prince to King*. New York: New York University Press, 1984.

Habib, John S. *Ibn Saud's Warriors of Islam*. Leiden, The Netherlands: Brill, 1978.

Helms, Christine Moss. *The Cohesion of Saudi Arabia: Evolution of Political Identity*. London: Croom Helm, 1981.

Holden, David, and Richard Johns. *The House of Saud*. London: Sidgwick and Johnson, 1981.

Howarth, David. *The Desert King: Ibn Saud and His Arabia*. New York: McGraw Hill, 1964.

Philby, H. B. St. John. *Arabian Jubilee*. London: Hale, 1952.

————.*Saudi Arabia*. Beirut: Librarie du Libon, 1968.

al-Rashid, Ibrahim (ed.). *Documents on the History of Saudi Arabia*. 3 vols. Salisbury N.C.: Documentary Publications, 1976.

Rihani, Ameen. *Ibn Saoud, His Land and People*. London: Constable, 1928.

————. *Makers of Modern Arabia*. Boston: Mifflin, 1928.

Troeller, Gary. *The Birth of Saudi Arabia, Britain and the Rise of the House of Saud*. London: Cass, 1976.

Williams, Kenneth. *Ibn Saud, the Puritan King of Arabia*. London: Cape, 1933.

JOSEPH KOSTINER

ABDULLAH IBN HUSSEIN (1882–1951) (amir of Transjordan, king of Jordan) is a controversial figure in the history of the modern Middle East. Owing to his leadership of the Arab Revolt during World War I, he claimed a position in the pantheon of Arab nationalist leaders. However, his subsequent dependence on Britain in ruling Transjordan caused many to consider him a British puppet. This judgment appeared to be confirmed when he accepted the British plan for the partition of Palestine in 1937 and when he added the West Bank portion of Palestine to his kingdom after the 1948 Arab-Israeli war amid a flurry of ill-kept secret meetings with Israeli emissaries.

Abdullah was born in Mecca in the Ottoman province of the Hejaz. He was the second son of Hussein ibn Ali and Abdiyya bint Abdullah, first cousins who traced their descent from the Prophet's great-grandfather Hashim (hence Hashemite) through the Prophet's grandson, Hasan (hence the title *Sharif*). At the time of his birth, Abdullah's great-uncle was the sharif of Mecca, a religious and political office recognized by the Ottomans. Abdullah's mother died when he was four, at or soon after the birth of his brother Faisal (1886–1933; king of Iraq, 1921–1933).

Owing to factional rivalry in Mecca in 1891, Hussein was summoned to Istanbul by Sultan Abdulhamid. In Istanbul, Abdullah and his brothers, Ali (1879–1935; king of the Hejaz 1924–26), and Faisal, were educated by tutors at home. Their social and political circle included other sharifian exiles and the Turkish elite. Hussein's second wife, Adilé Hanum, was a granddaughter of a former grand vizier. She bore one son, Zeid, and three daughters.

In 1902 Abdullah married his paternal cousin, Misbah. She bore two children, a daughter, Haya, and Abdullah's son and heir, Talal (King of Jordan, 1951–

1952). Later Abdullah married two more women, both of whom had been part of his household. The first, a Turk, bore a son, Nayyif, and two daughters, Maqbula and Munira. The second, a Sudani named Nahida, was ostracized by Amman society and was never officially recognized as his consort.

Abdullah's public political life began in 1908 when his father was named Sharif of Mecca by Sultan Abdulhamid following the Young Turk revolution. The family returned to Mecca at that time, and Abdullah became his father's chief go-between with Istanbul, where he attended the Ottoman Parliament as deputy for Mecca from 1910 to 1914. During this period, Sharif Hussein and the Ottoman government were locked in a battle over the limits of his jurisdiction. Hussein was intent on protecting the traditional autonomy of the Hejaz while Istanbul was making an effort to centralize and regularize its authority. Passing through Egypt on his way to Istanbul early in 1914, Abdullah met Lord Kitchener, then British high commissioner of Egypt, and solicited Britain's support for Hejazi autonomy. Although he was unsuccessful, British officials in Egypt remembered him and his request when World War I broke out several months later.

Through Abdullah, Britain sought Sharif Hussein's support in the war. The ensuing correspondence with Hussein, conducted by Sir Henry McMahon (British high commissioner of Egypt, 1914–1916), led in 1916 to the Arab Revolt. According to T. E. Lawrence, Abdullah was the "spur" in encouraging his father to rebel against Ottoman control. However, exactly what was promised in the correspondence in terms of an independent Arab kingdom is still a matter of historical debate (the correspondence is reprinted in Antonius, 1938). It is also a matter of continued historical controversy whether the Hashemites led the revolt motivated by Arab nationalism with the aim of making a complete break with the Ottoman Empire or whether their ambitions were dynastic and did not necessarily envision the destruction of the empire.

The Arab Revolt was declared in June 1916. For most of the revolt, Abdullah camped in the vicinity of Medina in order to harass its line of supply with Turkish strongholds further north. Meanwhile, his younger brother Faisal moved northward into geographic Syria, eventually reaching Damascus simultaneously with Allied troops in July 1918. Faisal's sphere of action in the north brought him into immediate contact with European allies and Arab nationalists of the Fertile Crescent, and during this time he supplanted Abdullah as Britain's chief interlocutor with the Hashemites and built a reputation among the growing group of Arab nationalists.

Abdullah's interests during the war seem to have centered on expanding familial dominance further into the Arabian peninsula. From Medina he diverted tribal forces into Nejd against Abd al-Aziz ibn Saud* who was expanding his domain from Riyadh. Skirmishes east of Taif in the vicinity of Khurma oasis and the village of Turaba increased in the spring of 1918 when tribes there refused to pay taxes to Mecca. After Medina capitulated in February 1919, Abdullah moved southward with his troops to enforce Hashemite authority.

Instead, he was disastrously defeated at Turaba by forces loyal to ibn Saud. Many of his comrades were killed, and Abdullah himself narrowly escaped in his nightclothes. In the contest between Mecca and Nejd for Arabian dominance, ibn Saud eventually triumphed. Mecca fell in 1924, and ibn Saud remained a lifelong enemy of Abdullah, who returned to Arabia only once (and never to Mecca), in 1948, in an effort to garner support for his role in Palestine. The two states did not develop close relations until after the death of both leaders.

After his defeat by ibn Saud's forces in 1919, Abdullah returned in disgrace to Mecca. The wartime alliance he had championed with Britain had soured; the Hejaz, though now an independent kingdom, was of dubious viability outside of a larger framework, and Britain and France were carving up the territory of geographical Syria and Iraq in ways that the Hashemites and their Arab nationalist supporters felt were at odds with British promises in the Hussein-McMahon correspondence. Briefly, his ambitions turned on Iraq, but in the end Britain created an Iraqi throne for Faisal after he had been ousted from Damascus by the French. Thereafter, the relations between the two brothers grew increasingly rancorous, fueled by jealousy and resentment on Abdullah's side.

French troops had occupied Damascus in July 1920, destroying the administration Faisal had been organizing since 1918. The nationalist coterie that had gathered around him scattered, some moving south to the village of Amman in Transjordan. Transjordan was a part of geographic Syria and had been administered from Damascus under the Ottomans and subsequently by Faisal. However, it was not occupied by the French in 1920 since it was in the British sphere of influence according to the wartime Sykes-Picot agreement, which had divided the Fertile Crescent between France and Britain. Close to Damascus, sparsely populated, on the Hejaz railway, without an established government, and not occupied by British troops, Amman was an ideal place for Faisal's nationalist followers to regroup. From there they wrote to Hussein in Mecca asking him to send another son to be their standard-bearer in the struggle to return to Damascus. Abdullah arrived in Amman in March 1921 on the eve of the Britain's Cairo conference, which was to decide on the form of British Mandate administrations in the Middle East.

Owing to the absence of a clear and agreed-on British policy toward Transjordan, and to Britain's fear that Abdullah, if not given some position, would cause trouble, Colonial Secretary Winston Churchill settled Transjordan's future with Abdullah on the spot. Abdullah agreed to keep Transjordan quiet for the next six months with the aid of a British subsidy. According to the minutes of the conference, Churchill encouraged Abdullah by suggesting that if he prevented anti-French activities, he would improve his chances of a reconciliation with the French, and might end by becoming King of Syria under French patronage. Churchill also said that if Abdullah did his part, Britain would help him to achieve this end. Abdullah construed Churchill's remarks as a promise to which he attempted to hold Britain in later years. However, in the face of adamant Syrian and French opposition, Britain was unwilling and unable to deliver the

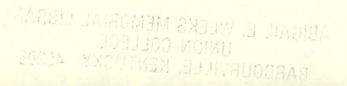

Syrian throne. Whether Churchill was guilty of deliberate deception is another point of controversy.

Abdullah's six-month agreement turned into a lifetime's undertaking. Begun on the strength of a handshake, his position in Transjordan was formalized in stages, and was always dependent on his good behavior. In April 1923, Britain issued a carefully worded statement that had been framed in discussions between Abdullah and the Colonial Office the previous November. Called simply an "assurance," its text is as follows: "Subject to approval of the League of Nations, [Britain] will recognize the existence of an independent Government in Transjordan, under the rule of His Highness the Amir Abdullah ibn Husain, provided such government is constitutional and places [Britain] in a position to fulfil their international obligations in respect of the territory by means of an agreement to be concluded between the two Governments" (quoted in Uriel Dann, *Studies in the History of Transjordan, 1920–1949: The Making of a State* (Boulder & London: Westview, 1984, pp. 70–71). By 1928 the conditions outlined in this assurance had been fulfilled: A constitution and an Anglo-Transjordanian agreement had been written that guaranteed Britain's interests. In these documents, Transjordan was formally fixed in a position of dependence in external as well as internal affairs.

The structure of colonial supervision rested on a British subsidy that made up for Transjordan's lack of a sufficient tax base and resources to support the dual Anglo-Arab governmental structure. At the top of the structure was a British Resident who, with the help of several British advisers, oversaw all internal and external government functions. For example, British diplomats negotiated the borders of Transjordan and its treaty relations with surrounding states, British financial and judicial advisers supervised the budget and lawmaking, and British army and police officers created and commanded the local armed force, the Arab Legion. On the Arab and subordinate side, Abdullah was at the head of a structure that included a council of ministers and, after 1928, an elected legislative council that could comment on but could not initiate legislation. Transjordan was divided into two juridical areas defined by geography and personal allegiance: a settled area, which was subject to constitutional law derived from Ottoman, British, and Islamic sources, and a tribal area, which was subject to "tribal" law derived from customary usage. After 1930, the final arbiter and executor of tribal law was the British officer John Bagot Glubb Pasha, who created and led the desert patrol and later became the commander of the Arab Legion.

British control of Transjordan based on a few key officers and administrators was easily maintained throughout the Mandate Period owing to the demographic and economic structure of the country. There were no cities (which in the interwar period were the bases of the Arab nationalist movement), the population was sparse (some 235,000 in 1920) and scattered, and the population lacked the merchant, professional, and bureaucratic classes, which provided the Arab nationalist leadership of the period. Economically, the administration of Transjordan was dependent on a British subsidy, and Britain enjoyed a monopoly of armed force with Royal Air Force bases and the British-led Arab Legion. The only concerted revolt against Abdullah's British-backed power, the Adwan revolt of 1923, grew out of local tribal politics upset by Abdullah's tax policies and was put down in one morning owing to Britain's superior equipment.

Although Transjordan's population nearly doubled during the Mandate Years, and the population of Amman grew from at most 5,000 in 1921 to 20,000 in 1938, no new structures of possible political mobilization took root. The army remained firmly under British control, education facilities were limited, industrial establishments were few and tiny, and the formal institutions of national government lacked independence from their two taskmasters, Abdullah and the British. Party politics were nonexistent in all but name; manifestations of popular sentiment occurred mainly in conjunction with issues in the larger Arab arena, especially those having to do with Palestine.

These structural realities severely restricted Abdullah's political options. Unlike the other mandated states, Transjordan did not have a nationalist movement to speak of. Although Abdullah used the rhetoric of Arab nationalism, he was unable to distance himself from Britain within Transjordan, and was unsuccessful in identifying his interests with those of the Arab nationalist movement at large. While Transjordanians generally credit him with saving their country from the Jewish settlement to which Palestine under a British mandate was subject, other Arabs feel that his subsequent dependence on Britain made him a British puppet.

After independence in 1946, little immediately changed in the Anglo-Transjordanian relationship. British officers and administrators remained important in internal affairs and Britain continued to support the Arab Legion. Sir Alec Kirkbride (British Resident, 1939–1946, and British minister in Amman, 1946–1951), felt that despite his change of title, his role and sphere of activity changed little with independence. The same might be said of Abdullah, who took the title of king in 1946.

Of course, Abdullah was not the only ruler of the period to accept a throne from British hands. Indeed, most of the political elite of the interwar period, including the nationalist elite, were only able to exercise power in national politics owing to some degree of compromise with Britain or France. Notably, Abdullah's brother Faisal became King of Iraq owing to Britain's support. However, Faisal and other nationalist leaders were able to deal with Europe from a certain position of strength, created by their ability to mobilize popular support in order to make things difficult for Britain or France. The concessions they gained during the Mandate Years were won in a complex process of manifesting political strength through strikes and demonstrations on the one hand, and negotiating with the mandatory power on the other.

Abdullah also gained certain concessions from Britain as the years passed, but what he gained was given in recognition of his cooperation. He opposed the conventional benchmarks of increasing independence, such as elections and constitutions, which he saw as further limiting his personal power, which had already been drastically curtailed by Britain. Hence, a constitution was written and elections held in 1928 owing to Britain's insistence and despite his objections. Popular discontent focused on the limited nature of Britain's idea of a constitutional government for Transjordan; Abdullah did not want a constitutional government at all. The concessions Abdullah won from Britain were more often personal than public, and did not necessarily serve to enhance his prestige. He was kept on a very tight budget by Britain throughout the Mandate and any particular cooperation above and beyond the dictates of the Mandate was often rewarded by an augmentation of his income in some shape or form.

It would be wrong to conclude, however, that Abdullah was happy in Britain's rather close embrace. In order to escape it, and lacking the resources that could help create the latitude that Feisal, for example, had won in Iraq, Abdullah aimed at territorial expansion. His most constant ambition was a throne in Syria, but he also at times looked to add Palestine, Iraq, or the Hejaz to his domain. However, it was not until Britain proposed the partition of Palestine between Jews and Arabs in 1937 that any sort of expansion became at all feasible. Attached to the 1937 partition plan was the notion that Abdullah would rule what was left of Arab Palestine. His acceptance of partition, which was opposed by the Palestinians and by other Arab leaders, and was eventually dropped by the British, earned him the opprobrium of the Arab world and exacerbated the enmity between himself and the Palestinian leadership of Hajj Amin al-Husseini. In view of the subsequent loss of Palestinian territory in 1948 and 1967, some have credited Abdullah with uncanny foresight. However, the majority view among his contemporaries was that he was acting in his own interests and in a way that, at the time, was detrimental to Arab efforts to save Palestine.

In 1947, the idea of the partition of Palestine was revived by the United Nations. Passed as UN Resolution 181 on November 29, 1947, the new partition was more generous toward the Jewish state than the 1937 plan, but unlike the prior plan it also created an independent Palestinian Arab state. However, no overseer was provided to see that the two states emerged peacefully and as drawn. Britain abstained from the UN vote and withdrew from Palestine rather than enforcing a policy it viewed as harmful to its position in the Middle East. Fighting between Zionist and Arab forces began the moment the partition resolution was passed, and escalated when Britain formally withdrew from Palestine on May 14, 1948. On May 15, the Arab states, including Transjordan, sent regular forces in.

At that time, the Arab Legion was armed by Britain, commanded by British officers, and supported by a British subsidy. In keeping with this dependence, the legion entered Palestine with Britain's knowledge and subject to the proviso that it not enter the UN-designated Jewish portion of Palestine. A secret agreement to this effect had been reached in London in February 1948.

At the same time, Abdullah carried on other secret negotiations with Zionist representatives in order to divide Palestine between them and avoid war between Zionist forces and the Arab Legion. Thus Abdullah met Golda Meir* on November 17, 1947, and they agreed that partition suited both their needs. The hope of a peaceful partition, however, evaporated with the fighting that erupted in Palestine after the Partition Resolution was passed, and in particular with the advance of Zionist forces into Arab-designated territory and into the international zone of Jerusalem in April and early May 1948. Arab losses were such that a United Arab Command was hastily assembled, nominally under Abdullah's leadership, and troops from the surrounding states were sent into Palestine on May 15. A last-minute meeting between Abdullah and Golda Meir was not sufficient to avert a clash between Israeli and Tansjordanian forces.

In the 1948 war, the Arab Legion occupied East Jerusalem and the West Bank; these were later added to Transjordan, which was renamed Jordan. All the fighting between the legion and Israeli forces occurred in Arab-designated territory or in the international enclave of Jerusalem, and thus Abdullah appears to have lived up to his undertaking with Britain. What sort of understanding he may have had with Israel, if any, is less clear. In any event, Israeli success on the battlefield carried Israeli troops beyond the partition borders on all sides.

Talks between Israeli representatives and Abdullah resumed as soon as fighting between the Arab Legion and Israeli forces stopped. These talks, coupled with the legion's lack of arms and ammunition, allowed Israel to engage Egypt unilaterally in October and December 1948, all but eliminating that country from the Palestinian arena. The point of ongoing talks with the Israelis was to secure Abdullah's hold on the West Bank from further Israeli aggression and from Arab rivals. Jordan formally annexed the West Bank in 1950, with tacit Israeli approval, though not before more Palestinian territory had been lost by Abdullah at the negotiating table.

Although some details of Abdullah's meetings with Zionist representatives have only recently been published, and some may never see the light of day, it has been generally known in the Arab world since 1947 that Abdullah carried on secret negotiations with Zionist, and later Israeli, representatives. These negotiations were instrumental in shaping the outcome of the struggle for Palestine. Arab judgment of him has consequently been harsh, while the West generally views him with approbation.

These sorts of judgments are made in light of what has happened to Palestine and among Palestinians since 1948. However, another way to look at Abdullah is to look at what has happened to Jordan since 1948, and here, what Abdullah achieved by his occupation of the West Bank was a restructuring of Jordan's position in the region and the diversification of its sources of support. Because Jordan took on the task of satisfying the immediate social and economic needs of the greatest concentration of Palestinians, it came to serve the interests of the United States, Britain, Israel, and the Arab states. Both the United States and Britain thought an independent Palestinian state would cause them problems in the region; Israel was able to shift onto Jordan's shoulders the task of pacifying and controlling the greatest concentration of Palestinians on its borders; and the Arab states gradually came to understand that Jordan saved them either from having to champion the Palestinian cause directly or from having to absolutely admit their inability to do so. Hence Abdullah and his successors were finally able to expand their sources of political and financial support beyond Britain.

The inclusion of Palestinians in Jordan also transformed the social and economic structure of the country internally. The Palestinians came with some capital, doubling Jordan's money supply virtually overnight; they attracted more capital as refugees, workers, and entrepreneurs, and they were better educated and had stronger contacts with the Arab world and with Europe than had the relatively isolated Transjordanians.

Abdullah, however, had gotten what he wanted, but had also gotten more than he bargained for. The patriarchal world that he had created in Transjordan began to pass away with the addition of some 800,000 Palestinian subjects. He now presided over a far more complex polity of clashing interests and better-articulated class and political identities. In this new world, few of his Palestinian subjects had any historical ties to the Hashemite monarchy.

Abdullah was assassinated by a Palestinian in Jerusalem in July 1951 for what was viewed by many as his collusion in the partition of Palestine. It is not clear that at the time of his death he understood exactly what he had achieved, that he had created a regional role for Jordan that would provide for the continuity of his state. Abdullah viewed the addition of the West Bank to Jordan as only the first step in the creation of a larger Hashemite state, and his political ambitions at the end of his life, as in 1921, were focused on Damascus. However, although he failed to achieve the goal dearest to his heart, he nonetheless passed on to his heirs a solid legacy in the form of a community of interests that guaranteed not only the survival of Jordan but of the Hashemite dynasty itself. His grandson Hussein ibn Talal* (b. 1935, king of Jordan, 1952) is the longest reigning monarch in the region, and the dynasty has outlasted the regimes of Abdullah's Arab nationalist rivals and detractors.

BIBLIOGRAPHY

Works by King Abdullah:

Mudhakkirati. Amman, Jordan: n.p., 1945. Abridged and translated by Philip Graves and G. Khuri as *Memoirs of King Abdullah of Transjordan*. London: Jonathan Cape, 1950.
al-Takmilah. Amman, Jordan: n.p., 1951. Published in English as *My Memoirs Completed*. London: Longman, 1978.

Other Works:

Antonius, George. *The Arab Awakening*. London: Hamish Hamilton, 1938.
Dawn, C. E. *From Ottomanism to Arabism*. Urbana, Ill.: University of Illinois Press, 1973.
Glubb, John Bagot. *The Story of the Arab Legion*. London: Hodder and Stoughton, 1948.
Kirkbride, Alec. *A Crackle of Thorns*. London: John Murray, 1956.
Louis, William Roger. *The British Empire in the Middle East 1945–1951*. Oxford: Clarendon Press, 1984.

Mousa, Suleiman. *Ta sis al-Imara al-Urduniyya* (The Foundation of the Jordanian Amirate). Amman: Al-Matba a al-Urduniyya, 1971.
Shlaim, Avi. *Collusion across the Jordan*. New York: Columbia University Press, 1988.
Wilson, Mary C. *King Abdullah, Britain and the Making of Jordan*. Cambridge: Cambridge University Press, 1987.

MARY C. WILSON

MICHEL AFLAQ (1910–1989) was a Syrian leader whose life span matches almost exactly the growth, success, and decline of the Arab nationalist cause, to which he devoted his intellect and energies. He was born in Damascus in 1910, in a period when political figures in Syria were beginning to comprehend what the Turkish nationalism of the Committee of the Union and Progress, in control of the Ottoman Empire after 1908, could mean for non-Turkish elements in that state. The program of the "Young Turks" acted as a strong stimulant to the nascent ideas of Arab nationalism in Syria and neighboring districts of the eastern Arab world. Aflaq and his associate, Salah al-Din Bitar,* together articulated a philosophy of pan-Arab nationalism and founded a party to propagate it. Their greatest success came with the formation of the United Arab Republic in 1958, an event widely considered at the time to be but the first step toward pan-Arab unity. Their influence and the pull of pan-Arabism have declined since then, but the post–World War II history of Iraq, Jordan, Lebanon, Egypt, and Libya, as well as of their native Syria, would have been vastly different without their influence.

The decade of 1918 until 1928, when Aflaq left for Paris to attend the Sorbonne, was a period of extraordinary activity that left its mark in the future political life of Aflaq and Bitar. Four centuries of Ottoman rule ended in 1918. The attempt of nationalists to establish an Arab state with its capital in Damascus ended in 1920 when French troops easily routed the forces available to the state. Ottoman Syria—the area from the Taurus Mountains to Sinai and from the Mediterranean Sea to the desert—was divided into a British Mandate for Palestine and Transjordan and a French Mandate for Syria and Lebanon. The French attached districts that had historically adhered to Damascus to the Sanjak of Mount Lebanon, to form, along with the coastal cities, the twentieth-century Republic of Lebanon. From 1925 to 1927, a bloody uprising against the French, which had begun in the Jabal Druze, raged in and around Damascus. The Syrian Constituent Assembly of 1928 drafted a constitution asserting that Syria, including Palestine, Lebanon, and Transjordan, was an indivisible political entity.

During the decade of the 1930s, when Aflaq and Bitar were students in Paris and then secondary-school teachers in Damascus, a critical development in the content of Arab nationalism occurred. For the nationalist leaders of World War I and after, the Arab nation was confined to Iraq, former Ottoman Syria, and the Arabian Peninsula; it did not include North Africa. In efforts to define and explain what the essence of Arab nationalism consisted of, and especially to distinguish it from Islam, thinkers such as Abd al-Rahman Bazzaz, Sati al-Husri, and Edmond Rabbath argued that language—Arabic as native tongue—defined who was an Arab and therefore what were the boundaries of the Arab nation. The concept of pan-Arabism appealed to Aflaq's generation, which had witnessed the carving up of the eastern Arab world to suit the requirements of European chanceries.

Aflaq taught secondary school for ten years, but he and Bitar resigned their posts in 1942 to devote their full time to political activity. The British–Free French seizure of Syria and Lebanon from Vichy French control in 1941 opened up a greater possibility for political activity in Damascus during the remainder of the war period. The two friends, joined by Bitar's cousin, Midhat Bitar, and the young son of a land-owning family from Dayr al-Zur, Jalal al-Sayyid, were the nucleus of a political movement that grew to wield enormous influence in the Arab world. The Arab Resurrection Party (al-Hizb al-Baath al-Arabi), as it termed itself from 1945 on, took the ideas of Husri, Bazzaz, and others, enlarged on them, added concepts of its own, and gave organizational strength to the entire vision. The Baath Party, formally established with a constitution and executive body in 1947, was the first and by far the most important and influential political organization devoted to pan-Arabism. Founded in Damascus, and with a preponderance of Syrians in its early membership, it was intended from its inception to be for all Arabs. Its goal was the political unification of the entire Arab world. Aflaq's slogan, "One Arab nation with an immortal mission," appeared for the first time in 1945. It has remained the Baath slogan ever since.

The professor, as he was known to Baath party associates, achieved his success through his ability to persuade and inspire his followers. He was at his best in this regard when guiding and directing men younger than he; that is, through a teacher-student relationship. Although there were some of his and Bitar's contemporaries among the early adherents to the party, the majority of Baath recruits were students whom he attracted in the classroom or who came to the virtually continuous seminar in politics that he conducted at his home or in coffee shops in the capital. Slight of build, caring little for appearance, Aflaq was intense in his devotion to political affairs and to the articulation and propagandization of his ideology. Only once in his life did he hold public office, as minister of education in Syria for three months in 1949.

Aflaq was the son of a moderately prosperous grain merchant whose economic status fluctuated with the vagaries of that trade. The family was Greek Orthodox in religion, and his father was active in politics, opposing the policies of the French Mandate authorities. The Aflaqs lived in the Maydan Quarter, a district outside the old walled city stretching along the road from Damascus south toward the grain-growing regions of the Hauran. Politically, the district was a center of anti-French nationalist activity in the Mandate Period. After completing secondary school, Michel studied history at the Sorbonne in Paris from 1928 through 1932, in addition reading widely in literature and philosophy. Fluent in French, Aflaq chose, as a nationalist, to write exclusively in Arabic.

After resigning from the teaching profession in 1942, Aflaq's life was exclusively bound up with his Baath Party. It was a life dominated by political
discussions, seminars for student prospects and members, writing, speaking, and
occasionally participating in demonstrations. When the party started its own
publication, the newspaper *al-Baath*, in July 1946, Aflaq was the political editor.
At the formal founding conference in April 1947, Aflaq was chosen *amid* (dean
or headmaster) of the party, a title later converted to secretary-general.

Aflaq stepped aside as secretary-general at the Eighth National Baath Congress
in April 1965, to be replaced by his contemporary, the Jordanian Munif Razzaz.
Both moves by Aflaq were in reaction to attacks from within the party on him
and on his deficiencies as a leader. At the end of 1965, supported by Bitar and
others in the old guard, he made an attempt to impose National Command
authority on the Syrian regional party structure, succeeding briefly and super-
ficially. On February 23, 1966, the military elements associated with the ousted
Regional Command seized control of both party and government. Aflaq went
into exile a few weeks later, never to return to his native city.

The Baath Party split over this event. Since 1966, there have been two Arab
Socialist Resurrection Parties, one in Iraq and one in Syria, and each with a
(nominal) pan-Arab National Command and a regional party structure. Aflaq
accepted the post of secretary-general in the Baghdad-based Baath Party in 1968.
He visited Iraq for stays of a week to several months, finally taking up permanent
residence there in the 1980s. He retained the post of secretary-general, although
it was largely a formality, until his death June 23, 1989, following heart surgery.
Real power lies with Assistant Secretary-General Saddam Hussein,* who is also
secretary of the Iraq Regional Command, president of the Republic, and commander of the armed forces.

In the lively political atmosphere of Syria's early years of independence, Aflaq
and his Baathists played an active part. The last French troops left on April 17,
1946, which is celebrated as independence day. Aflaq offered himself as a
candidate in the July 1947 parliamentary elections, failing to win as he had failed
in 1943, and would again fail in 1949. Upon losing in 1949 he resigned from
the office of minister of education to which he had been appointed three months
earlier. Keeping the party going and growing in the complex political drama of
Syria's early independence years had become a full-time task for him. Beginning
in 1949, the Syrian military began its history of involvement in political life.
Before parliamentary life was restored in 1954, the party newspaper had been
suppressed several times, Aflaq and Bitar had been jailed twice, and Aflaq had
been exiled for a year. While living in Beirut, the two Baathist leaders arranged
the unification of their party with the personal political organization of Akram
Hourani, the Arab Socialist Party. Hourani brought to the merger a substantial
following among the peasants of his native Hamah region, where he fought for
land reform. He also brought considerable practical political skills, which helped
the merged party over the next few years.

In February 1954, the third of Syria's postwar dictators was ousted by army units whose leaders turned the governance of the country back to civilians through the freest elections that Syrians have enjoyed, before or since. The newly merged party, named the Arab Socialist Resurrection Party, won sixteen seats in the Parliament, and at least as many leftists could be numbered among the independent candidates who also won. In a few years this leftist wave, which combined programs of domestic social reform with pan-Arab nationalism and opposition to Western influence in the region, took the direction of Syrian politics out of the hands of the men who had led the struggle for independence. Its success was due in good part to the work of Aflaq and his Baathists in propagating their triple message of Arab unity, independence, and social reform.

Syrians were not alone in their surge toward pan-Arab nationalism. The 1950s witnessed the growth of nationalist sentiment throughout the eastern Arab world. Heading the list of countries bursting with nationalist sentiment was Egypt, where a group of majors and colonels overthrew the monarchy in 1952 and got Britain in 1954 to agree to abandon its Suez Canal military bases. In Iraq, Jordan, Libya, and even in less politically advanced states, young officers were eager to emulate the Egyptian example. They were supported by steadily growing numbers of citizens being turned out by the equally growing educational system, where teachers routinely indoctrinated their charges with nationalist sentiment. Aflaq and Bitar had had their teaching counterparts in Husri and Darwish Miqdadi in Iraq, and they were followed by thousands of lesser-known enthusiasts for the nationalist cause. They and their students chafed under the rule of men who were on the whole well-to-do, conservative, inclined to cooperation with Western powers, and who, as a group, had been in power for twenty or thirty years.

The swing to the left in Syria and the rise of the charismatic Gamal Abdul Nasser* to the presidency of Egypt combined to lead Aflaq and Bitar to their greatest success—uniting two Arab states, Syria and Egypt, into one United Arab Republic (UAR) in February 1958. When Iraqi officers destroyed the Hashemite monarchy in Baghdad a few months later, it seemed as if Arab nationalism was about to take another great leap forward. However, it did not happen. The Iraqi Free Officers Movement and the new government were taken over by Abdul Karim Qassem,* a man whose political horizons were limited to Iraq and who quickly crushed the pan-Arabists in the Free Officers Movement. In retrospect, it is clear that Qassem's policy stopped the pan-Arab movement in its tracks, although this was not apparent at the time. For Aflaq and Bitar, the failure of the Iraqis to join the UAR was a blow that turned an earlier serious mistake into a disastrous one.

The Baath Party and other nationalists had created the atmosphere in Syria which made the establishment of the UAR possible. Indeed, they had forced it upon the older generation of Syrian political leaders, who knew in their hearts that they would live to regret it. When the terms of the union were being arranged in early 1958, Nasser insisted that all political parties in Syria be dissolved as a condition of Egypt's participation in the UAR. They were to be replaced by an all-embracing National Union. Aflaq, together with Bitar and Hourani, agreed to Nasser's stipulation. Aflaq believed that Nasser lacked a political philosophy, that such a philosophy was necessary, and that the Baath would provide it.

It did not work out that way. Nasser was an authoritarian who governed Syria through loyal subordinates. Baathists held nominally important positions but had very little power. When the National Union was brought to Syria in 1959, the dissolved Baath Party was in such disarray that only a few hundred of the 9,445 elected members of the union's local committees were from the party. For a variety of reasons—drought leading to poor economic conditions and Egyptian heavy-handedness being the chief ones—the UAR experiment quickly lost its initial popularity in Syria. Syrian troops took over the country in September 1961, and Syria seceded from the UAR. The political figures who had taken credit for bringing the UAR into existence were badly hurt by its failure.

Aflaq and his two top associates in addition suffered much damage among the party membership. Aflaq, although not a dynamic leader, was a man of great tenacity of will and stubborn adherence to his own views. However, he had grown accustomed over the years to making decisions in the name of the Baath, which was "his" brainchild (or his and Bitar's), even though the party organization provided a means for obtaining the views of the membership. He was convinced that dissolution would serve his movement's long-term goals. He, Bitar, and Hourani took the decision to dissolve the party organization in Syria without consulting non-Syrian members of the party's (pan-Arab) National Command or even the Regional Command, which was the highest party body for Syria. Many party members were outraged, a large number simply dropped out of political activity, and others turned against the founders.

The formation of the UAR in 1958 was the high point of Aflaq's career. It was a concrete step toward the all-inclusive Arab unity in which he passionately believed. Even its failures did not dampen his ardor. When Baathist officers seized power in Damascus in March 1963, he joined with Iraqi Baathists, who themselves had seized power the previous month, and went to Cairo to try to persuade Nasser to make another attempt at unity. After several weeks of wrangling discussions, a tripartite unity formula was worked out, but it never went into effect. The Baathist officers who held the real power in Syria wanted no part of another union with Nasser.

The three years of 1963 through 1966 were a time of frustration and ultimate defeat for Aflaq. The Baath Party in Syria was split between an old guard— Aflaq, Bitar, and a small number of contemporaries and devoted followers, with some allies in the military—and a second, more numerous, generation of military and civilian party members. The latter group had been brought into the party by Aflaq's disciples and had had little direct contact with him. They were rural rather than urban in background, and were among the strongest objectors to the party's dissolution in 1958. Aflaq could count on the support of most of the non-Syrian members of the pan-Arab National Command, which totalled thirteen in those years, but the Syrian Regional Command was controlled by the new generation. Aflaq continued his usual activities of speaking, writing, and discussing. This had always been more important to him than organization, and he did not comprehend the limitations on the influence he could wield in the Syrian arena.

In trying to draw up a balance sheet on Aflaq's political career, it would be gravely distorting to focus on the two regimes, in Syria and in Iraq, that bear the Baath name today. Both have grown a long way from Aflaq's romantic notion that forging a united, eventually pan-Arab state would solve most of the Arab world's problems. Each has developed an authoritarian system of rule, with heavy reliance on security forces to stay in power. Neither is avidly pan-Arab in its external policy, in part because pan-Arabism is in broad decline throughout the region. However, neither would call itself Baathist, nor have the political structure it has today, were it not for Michel Aflaq's success in inspiring a generation of Arab youth with his vision of Arab nationalism.

The essence of Aflaq's ideology is summed up in the second of the two principal Baath slogans: *Wihdah, Hurriyah, Ishtirakiyah* (Unity, Freedom, Socialism). Of the three concepts, unity was the most important to him. In Aflaq's view, the second and third were subsumed in the concept of pan-Arab Unity. Freedom meant freedom of Arab territory—mandates, colonies, and protectorates—from foreign rule; there was no way that Arab polities could unite unless and until they had thrown off external control. Through the first two decades of his party's existence, the Arabs did just that either directly (for example, termination of the mandate over Syria), or indirectly, by ousting rulers who were beholden to external powers, as happened in Egypt in 1952 and Iraq in 1958. That the Arab states, from Morocco to the Gulf and from the Taurus Mountains to the Arabian Sea, contained sizable non-Arab populations—Berbers, southern Sudanese, and Kurds—was a matter that he glossed over. His party insisted, however, on the need to recover several pieces of "lost" Arab land: the Sanjak of Alexandretta taken by Turkey in 1939, the district of Khuzistan in southwest Iran, and occupied Palestine, that is, Israel.

Although Aflaq and Bitar had been exposed to communism during their student days in Paris and maintained contacts for a time with Syrian communists, they soon found that there were two issues on which their ideology was in fundamental disagreement. Communists, with their goal of world revolution, were squarely opposed to Arab nationalism. Second, the class struggle had no place in Aflaq and Bitar's ideology. They and most of the first generation of Baathist leaders were middle-class in origin and outlook. They were elitist, in the sense of believing that they knew best how to lead the masses to a better life. Socialism in Aflaq and Bitar's view was a matter of social justice. The party constitution of 1947, written under Aflaq's direction, called for a just redistribution of wealth and opposed the exploitation of some citizens by others, but it endorsed the right to private property and inheritance. A second generation of Baathists contained many who had a much more rigorous concept of socialism, and differences on this issue contributed to the struggle of the 1960s that split the Baath Party into two separate organizations. For Aflaq, however, the socialist–social justice issue was always secondary to the cause, the achievement of Arab unity.

Michel Aflaq had the capacity to instill ideas and enthusiasm in the young men who gathered around him. His timing in founding the Baath Party was nearly perfect. Others wrote and spoke about Arabism and unity, but he and a few close associates established an organization to do something about it. That organization got the jump on the competition, as it were, to the degree that, until the powerful personality of Nasser adopted Arab nationalism in the mid–1950s, the Baathists were the only organized pan-Arabists.

As the leader of an organization, Aflaq must be judged wanting in certain practical skills. Like many a person who founds his own business or other organization and sees it grow, he never understood that a party with branches throughout Syria and in other countries required vastly different management techniques than did a movement of a few dozen intellectuals, nor did he deal adequately with the inevitable differences over policy and organization that arose in the growing party. He and Bitar brought great political strength to the movement when they joined the Baath to Akram Hourani's personal political following. The strains that grew out of this merger were enormous; many early colleagues quit. Aflaq totally misjudged Nasser in 1958, and, according to Munif al-Razzaz, his short-term successor as secretary general, he never understood that he had very little support in the Syrian party apparatus from 1963 through 1966. The man who was an inspiration to a generation of nationalist youth in the 1940s and 1950s was not a man who could lead the following generation in the political arena.

BIBLIOGRAPHY

Works by Aflaq:

Marakat al Masir al Wahid (The Campaign for a Single Destiny). Beirut: Dar al-Ilm li al-Malayin, 1958.
Fi Sabil al-Baath (Toward Resurrection). Rev. and enlarged ed. Beirut: Dar al-Taliah, 1963.
Nidal al-Ba'th (The Baath's Struggle). Beirut: Dar al-Taliah, 1963–1965. Vols. 1–4 contain items by subject.
Nuata al-Bidayah: Ahadith bad al-Khamis min Huzayran (The Starting Point: Discussion after June 5th). Beirut: Muassassah al-Arabiyah li al-Dirasat wa al-Nashr, 1970.
Choice of Texts from the Ba'th Party Founder's Thought. Florence: n.p., 1977.

Other Works:

Abu Jaber, Kamel S. *The Arab Ba'th Socialist Party*. Syracuse, N.Y.: Syracuse University Press, 1966.
Devlin, John F. *The Ba'th Party: A History from Its Origins to 1966*. Stanford, Calif.: Hoover Institution Press, 1976.
Hourani, Albert H. *Arabic Thought in the Liberal Age, 1798–1939*. London: Oxford University Press, 1962, Ch. 11.
Al-Jundi, Sami. *Al-Ba'th*. Beirut: Dar al-Nahar li al-Nashr, 1969.

Kaylani, Nabil A. "The Rise of the Syrian Baath 1940–1958: Political Success, Party Failure." *International Journal of Middle East Studies* 3, no. 1 (January 1972): 3–23.

Khadduri, Majid. *Arab Contemporaries: The Role of Personalities in Politics*. Baltimore: Johns Hopkins Press, 1973, Ch. 12.

Khalidi, Tarif. "A Critical Study of the Political Ideas of Michel Aflaq." *Middle East Forum* 42, no. 2 (1966): 55–67.

Rabinovich, Itmar. *Syria under the Ba'th 1963–1966: The Army-Party Symbiosis*. Jerusalem: Israel Universities Press, 1972.

Salem-Babikian, Norma. "Michel Aflaq: A Biographic Outline." *Arab Studies Quarterly* 2, no. 2 (1980): 162–179.

Al-Sayyid, Jalal. *Hizb al-Ba'th al-'Arabi* (The Arab Baath Party). Beirut: Dar al-Nahar li al-Nashr, 1973.

Seale, Patrick. *The Struggle for Syria: A Study of Post-War Arab Politics, 1945–1958*. London: Oxford University Press, 1964, 2d ed., New Haven: Yale University Press, 1987.

JOHN F. DEVLIN

SALIM RUBAY ALI (1934–1978) was one of the founders of the People's Democratic Republic of Yemen (PDRY or South Yemen). A radical populist (even a "Maoist"), yet ultimately a pragmatist, he was South Yemen's most charismatic leader, its president, and a member of its ruling triumvirate (with Abd al-Fattah Ismail* and Ali Nasser Mohammed*) throughout its formative years.

Rubay Ali came from a peasant background in Zinjibar (near Aden) and had been a farmer, teacher, bookkeeper, and justice of the peace by the late 1950s. He was also an adherent of the Arab Nationalist Movement and joined its South Arabian offshoot, the National Liberation Front (NLF), when it was formed. The NLF was distinguished in South Arabia by its insistence that only armed struggle could rid the territory of its imperialist foes; furthermore, violent struggle was seen as a positive strategy, purifying society while heightening solidarity and morale among the strugglers. This focus on violent struggle drew on the theories of Mao Zedong and Franz Fanon; it was also pragmatically based on the propensity of tribal society to seek redress of its grievances through violence. Thus, for its less sophisticated adherents, the NLF offered a simplified goal: throwing out the local rulers, and with them the British who supported them.

The armed struggle in Aden's hinterland began on October 14, 1963, with what appeared at first to be a tribal uprising with the usual motives (albeit with backing from Egypt) in the Radfan Mountains on the border with Yemen. Although not successful in its immediate goal, the rebellion was much better organized and led than previous tribal uprisings, and inspired the anti-British struggle in the rest of South Arabia. One of its leaders, (although not the overall commander) was Salim Rubay Ali.

Little has been revealed of Salim Rubay Ali's activities before South Yemen's independence in December 1967. However, he achieved enough distinction to be considered one of the "secondary leadership," the in-country struggle leaders; in 1965 and 1966 he was prominent in their successful fight to prevent political leaders of the NLF based in North Yemen from compromising the commitment to armed struggle in a merger with opposition groups owing allegiance to Gamal Abdul Nasser.* Apparently, it was this experience and the subsequent loss of Egyptian support which led the broad NLF leadership to adopt (or openly to profess) various strains of Marxism.

Rubay Ali tended to some form of Maoist populism, set incongruously (as was the case with most South Yemeni political figures) in a society in which tribalism remained dominant. He was given a junior position in the relatively moderate first South Yemeni government. After joining in the call for greater radicalization of the NLF at its Fourth Congress in 1968, he was included in a purge of leftists by the more moderate faction. However, unrest within the country and tension on its borders forced the government to call on the leftists for assistance. Rubay Ali led them in defense of the regime. A year later, under the leadership of Abd al-Fattah Ismail and Salim Rubay Ali, the leftists seized power. Ismail took the more important position of secretary-general of the party, and Rubay Ali became president.

The next nine years saw an uneasy cooperation between the two men (and the factions they led and personified) in some policy areas, overlaid by conflict rooted in personality, in differences over goals, methods, and the desired pace of change; and ultimately in the struggle for power. Initially, they were united in their hostility towards the conservative governments on the Arabian Peninsula, especially Saudi Arabia; and they were united in their active support for other revolutionary movements, in particular the Popular Front for the Liberation of Oman (PFLO), which began as a low-intensity conflict in Dhofar in 1968. They were also united in aligning the PDRY with the socialist countries, although Rubay Ali (while by no means hostile to the Soviet Union) looked to the People's Republic of China for aid and inspiration until China turned away from radical leftism. By mid-decade, however, this overall unity on foreign policy orientation had been fractured, largely because of Rubay Ali's willingness to follow a more pragmatic line in response to a changing regional environment.

The differences between the two men on the domestic front arose more quickly, although both were committed to radical social transformation. Both supported the nationalization of foreign-owned firms in November 1969, and later the collectivization or transformation into cooperatives of the handicrafts and retail trades. In agriculture, both supported widespread transformation, with policies first of redistributing the arable land and then of partial collectivization. However, Rubay Ali put his stamp on the changes in 1972 (and earned widespread popularity as the "father of the agricultural revolution") by encouraging peasants and fishermen to seize their means of livelihood in popular uprisings and settle their scores with old and new landlords.

The local anarchy and "voluntarism" that were the result of this policy were integral parts of his Maoist approach to revolutionary social and political organization, and were probably inspired by his trip to Beijing in August 1970. Not coincidentally, Ismail favored a system dominated by a highly centralized and bureaucratized party, a type of organization that began to appear after the Fifth Congress of the National Front in March 1972. Rubay Ali responded in July (while Ismail was touring Eastern Europe) with urban uprisings (the ''Seven Glorious Days''), during which his followers staged demonstrations in favor of spontaneous participation of the masses in decision making (including, reportedly, a demand for lower salaries for themselves, which was accommodated by a 30 percent cut.) He also persisted in the rapid expansion of the Chinese-armed and -trained militia to balance the regular military.

Whatever the disputes among the leadership, the first five years of independence wrought startling changes in South Yemen, although these did not go as deeply into society as they appeared to. The land had been redistributed, and collective and state farms and various types of cooperatives had been established; land reclamation projects were in the works. A family law had been promulgated which significantly advanced the equality of women. The number of schools and students had approximately doubled, and adult literacy programs were underway. A start had been made at expanding health facilities. Tribal conflicts were under control, although often only by the time-tested methods of bribery or threat from the center. Tribalism was under attack, and it was expected that the spread of National Front cadres and the growth in the number of militia members with rudimentary indoctrination would lead to the development of supra-tribal loyalties. Many economic endeavors had been subjected to the plan. Income redistribution was highly effective.

However, all this was taking place in an economy that had virtually collapsed. With negative or very slow economic growth, one-third of the work force fled. Agricultural production fell below preindependence levels, and well over half the country's food requirements had to be imported. The PDRY's realignment with the socialist countries and its hostile stance toward its neighbors had led to a virtual cutoff of aid from the West, and there was little chance of a successful appeal for a share of the Arab oil riches that began to appear after 1971. The Soviet Union and China had given vital (but relatively small) amounts of economic aid, which had kept the country afloat and started useful technical and infrastructure projects, but which was insufficient to promote rapid economic growth. To compound the problem, the PDRY's aggressive stance and its ideological position had been reciprocated with hostility from North Yemen and Saudi Arabia, where exile groups kept pressure on the South Yemeni border areas. This situation required a substantial defense effort, and closer ties to the Soviet Union (which was willing to supply relatively large amounts of military aid after 1969) than Rubay Ali may have been comfortable with.

Whether this was his reason, the South Yemeni president did begin to moderate his foreign policy stance by the end of 1972. Brief conflicts on the border with Saudi Arabia and (more extensively) with North Yemen brought victory, and the PDRY and YAR (Yemen Arab Republic) signed an agreement committing them to negotiations on Yemeni unification. The October War in 1973 gave some momentum to his more moderate policy. The conservative oil states' tougher line meant that the PDRY did not have to move so far to join the Arab mainstream; at the same time, their burgeoning oil revenues enhanced the likelihood that moderation could generate the levels of economic aid needed for South Yemen's moribund economy. Consequently, throughout 1974 and 1975, Rubay Ali made overtures to Egypt, Saudi Arabia and the other Gulf Arab states, West Germany, and even the United States. He was helped by the accession of a new North Yemeni leader, Ibrahim al-Hamdi, who was interested in distancing his country from Saudi Arabia; by the defeat of the (Aden-supported) PFLO in Dhofar in 1975; and by disastrous floods in the same year in the PDRY, which caused even more economic hardship.

Rubay Ali's policies appeared to have paid off in March 1976 when Saudi Arabia and the PDRY established diplomatic relations; this was reported to have been preceded by a Saudi payment of $40 million and accompanied by the promise of a $300-million annual subsidy. (By contrast, the PDRY drew $6.6 million in 1976 from its Soviet aid package, and total Soviet aid committed by 1977 was estimated to be $97 million.) South Yemen continued its move to the center, attending a conference promoted by Saudi Arabia and Egypt on Red Sea security (which was judged to have anti-Soviet and anti-Ethiopian overtones), and moving toward accommodation with Oman; in August 1977, Salim Rubay Ali visited Saudi Arabia.

However, this moderation in foreign policy was not reflected in internal policy beyond a slight relaxation in the state's grip on economic conditions, including invitations to several Western oil companies to take up exploration contracts. The convocation of a Unification Congress in October 1975, which moved the PDRY much closer to a highly bureaucratized vanguard party that would tightly control the government, demonstrated the strength of Ismail. After a well-publicized spy trial, a law was forced on Rubay Ali that forbade South Yemenis from speaking with foreigners, especially Arabs (with whom he was seeking to expand contacts), except on official business. Furthermore, there was no reduction in the Soviets' role or presence in the PDRY; advisers from the Soviet Union and its allies continued to function in the government ministries, in the party, in the higher education system, and in the military and security services. The USSR continued to be the sole source of weapons.

Nevertheless, there were events external to the PDRY that prevented Salim Rubay Ali from succeeding in reorienting the country's foreign policy and ultimately from remaining in power. The promise of Saudi aid was not fulfilled; although the initial payment was substantial, it was not repeated, as Riyadh awaited proof that Aden's change of direction was more than tactical. This reluctance in turn strengthened opposition in Aden to the change. Rubay Ali attempted to maintain the momentum of his policies by inviting the United States to send a representative to Aden in early 1978 for discussions that might lead to renewal of relations. However, the assassination of YAR President al-Hamdi, widely believed to have been engineered by the Saudis, angered and weakened Rubay Ali (who was thought to believe that progress toward Yemeni unity under himself and al-Hamdi could dilute the domestic pressure from Ismail). After that, the balance of power in the regime began to shift decisively in Ismail's favor, as the Ministry of Defense was taken out of the hands of Prime Minister Ali Nasser Mohammed (a relative moderate) and given to a member of the Ismail faction.

Events in the Horn of Africa made it impossible for the South Yemeni President to recover. In November 1977, Moscow intervened decisively in the Horn of Africa with a massive lift of materiel and Cuban troops to Ethiopia, much of it through Aden. Saudi Arabia, infuriated and alarmed by the sudden shift in the regional correlation of forces and by its inability to respond effectively, immediately cut off all aid to South Yemen. Rubay Ali's foreign policy was in tatters.

Armed clashes were reported on the Saudi border. Salim Rubay Ali, his options almost entirely foreclosed, nevertheless struggled on. He continued to press for a visit by an American mission, initiated another high-level contact with Riyadh, and attempted to restore relations with the YAR's new president, Ahmad al-Ghashmi. However, by the spring of 1978, Ismail clearly had the upper hand. The ruling group had become more radical under the impact of events in the Horn and on the Arab-Israeli front, and in this they were receiving encouragement from Moscow. Soviet prestige grew markedly as a result of the USSR's successful intervention in the Horn, with little or no response from the United States. Soviet arms had flooded into Aden, a fact much appreciated by the military as tensions with Saudi Arabia rose.

Adding momentum to the president's decline were a succession of poor harvests and the revelation of bizarre economic policies and administrative practices. Ever suspicious of bureaucracy, and the centralized party bureaucracy in particular, Rubay Ali had relied on family and tribal supporters to cut through red tape and bottlenecks, using his substantial presidential budget (augmented, it was reported after his death, by a significant portion of the Saudi aid). It was not that he used this money for personal gain; he was not charged with corruption, but rather with appointing incompetents. As a result, millions of dollars were wasted in impossible development projects and foolish commercial deals. For the bureaucrats who had taken over the party, this situation was not only frustrating, it was anathema to their goal of scientific planning.

Salim Rubay Ali's career and life came to an end after the bizarre events of June 24 through 26 1978. On June 24, a suitcase bomb carried by a South Yemeni emissary killed the North Yemen president. It has never been credibly explained, let alone proven, whether the bomb was sent by Rubay Ali or by Abd al-Fattah Ismail's faction, nor is it clear who started the fighting in South Yemen the next day. However, by the time it was over, Rubay Ali's military and tribal allies had been defeated, and he himself had been summarily tried and executed.

Salim Rubay Ali failed, ultimately, because of the growing tensions in the Arabian Peninsula–Horn of Africa region, which made it prudent for Aden to reject pragmatism in favor of strengthening its relationship with its superpower patron, and because of the unremitting poverty and cleavages within the society and polity of the PDRY. His preference for a quasi-traditional, personalized rule offended the new elites advocating a "modern" state, highly centralized and controlled by a tightly knit bureaucratic party. The apparently quixotic and (more importantly) unsuccessful nature of his foreign and domestic policies left him in the end vulnerable to attack from other factions within the regime.

The author wishes to acknowledge the assistance of the Advisory Research Committee, Queen's University, in the preparation of this entry.

BIBLIOGRAPHY

Bell, J. Bowyer. *South Arabia: Violence and Revolt*. London: The Institute for the Study of Conflict, Conflict Studies no. 40, November 1973.
Bidwell, Robin. *The Two Yemens*. Boulder: Westview Press, 1983.
Halliday, Fred. *Arabia without Sultans*. London: Penguin, 1974.
————. "Yemen's Unfinished Revolution: Socialism in the South." *MERIP Reports* (October 1979).
Kostiner, Joseph. *The Struggle for South Yemen*. New York: St. Martin's Press, 1984.
Novik, Nimrod. "On the Shores of Bab al-Mandab: Soviet Diplomacy and Regional Dominances." *Crossroads* (Winter 1979): 61–101.
Page, Stephen. *The Soviet Union and the Yemens: Influence in Asymmetrical Relationships*. New York: Praeger, 1985.
Stookey, Robert W. *South Yemen: A Marxist Republic in Arabia*. Boulder: Westview, 1982.
Stork, J. "Socialist Revolution in Arabia." *MERIP Reports* (March 1973).
The World Bank. *People's Democratic Republic of Yemen: A Review of Economic and Social Development*. Washington, D.C.: The World Bank, 1979.

STEPHEN PAGE

YASSER ARAFAT (1929–   ) became chairman of the Palestine Liberation Organization (PLO) in 1969, after working many years as an organizer in the Palestinian nationalist movement. His years as PLO chairman were marked by his attempts to win the PLO's inclusion in the Arab-Israeli peace process. From 1974 on, Arafat nudged the PLO toward the political moderation that was the price of entry into the peace process; but he was still careful not to strain the Palestinian national consensus on vital issues, such as recognition of Israel, beyond the breaking point. Under Arafat, the PLO suffered grave military setbacks in Jordan in 1970 and in Lebanon in 1982. However, in late 1987, the PLO gained new relevance, and when Palestinians in the West Bank and Gaza launched a prolonged uprising against Israel's occupation of their regions, they proclaimed the PLO as their only representative. In late 1988, with the uprising still raging, Arafat finally met the conditions the United States had set for holding talks with the PLO. There was thus a strong possibility that the years that followed would see the fulfillment of his goal of the PLO's inclusion in the mainstream of Arab-Israeli diplomacy.

The future PLO chairman was born in December 1929 to a minor branch of one of the leading Arab families of Jerusalem, the Husseinis. Yasser Arafat himself was probably born in Cairo, Egypt, but his boyhood was spent in Jerusalem and Gaza. During his youth, he witnessed the Palestinian Arab revolt of 1936–1939 and the Arab-Jewish fighting that accompanied the creation of Israel in 1948. He reportedly spent some time in virtual apprenticeship to his older cousin Abdel-Qader al-Husseini, who in the mid–1940s was the military leader of the ragtag Palestinian fighting forces, until he died in action in 1948.

After the Palestinians were defeated in 1948, Arafat went to study engineering at Cairo University. He was strongly affected by his experiences during and after the 1948 war, when he witnessed the scattering of over a million of his compatriots from their homes in the areas now held by Israel, and the destruction of the Palestinian national leadership at the hands of Israel and its Arab neighbors. In 1952, he was one of the prime organizers of a new, highly political Palestinian Students' Union in Cairo: Two key colleagues from that group, Salah Khalaf and Khalil Wazir, would later join him in founding the Palestinian guerrilla group Fatah. The twin political themes that marked their work in the Students' Union, as in the decades that followed, were that the Palestinians could rely on no one but themselves to regain their rights, and that Palestinian national unity was more important than any of the ideologies sweeping the Arab world at that time.

During the 1956 Egyptian-Israeli war, Arafat joined an engineering corps in Port Said as a reserve officer with the Egyptian army. The following year he left for Kuwait, where many Palestinian exiles found they were able to make a decent living. He and a number of other Palestinian nationalists living there then started patching back together the torn fabric of Palestinian political life as a prelude to fighting for the "Return" to their native homes which was then the dream of all the Palestinian exiles. In the late 1950s and early 1960s, a number of nascent Palestinian nationalist networks came together to form Fatah, an organization whose name is a reverse acronym for *Harakat al-Tahrir al-Watani al-Filastini* (Palestinian National Liberation Movement). In the first leadership of Fatah, on a more or less coequal basis, were Arafat, Khalaf, Wazir, Khaled al-Hassan, and six or eight other activists. Because they were engaged in a cat-and-mouse game with hostile Arab intelligence services, the Fatah leaders built up a series of overlapping networks, each responsible to one of the leading "barons": This organizational pattern remained in place in Fatah through the late 1980s.

From the beginning, there was some tension inside the leadership between those who argued for steady, long-term organizational work and those, like Arafat, who wanted to adopt an action program more quickly. In May 1964, the Arab states set up their own shell Palestinian organization, which was the Palestine Liberation Organization (PLO). Most Fatah leaders saw this as a threat to their group's continued growth, so they tried to regain the political initiative by going ahead with the activists' program. On January 1, 1965, they launched Fatah's first sabotage operation against Israel. This operation was not successful, but its date is still remembered as the birthdate of Fatah's "armed struggle" against Israel.

The June 1967 Arab-Israeli war resulted in a stunning victory for the Israel Defense Forces (IDF). It also, by weakening the political standing of the Arab government leaders, gave Fatah an unexpected new opportunity to organize in the Palestinian diaspora. In the atmosphere of general public humiliation that pervaded the post–1967 Arab world, the ability of Fatah's operatives to launch any attacks against Israel, however slight, received wide support from Palestinian and non-Palestinian Arabs alike.

Arafat's first proposal after June 1967 was to try to counter Israeli might from within the IDF's new defense perimeter. In the weeks following the cease-fire, he and some colleagues crossed into the Israeli-occupied West Bank to stir up a popular revolt against the occupation. They were unsuccessful for a number of reasons; and toward the end of 1967, Arafat retreated to Jordan. By then, the Israelis had killed two hundred suspected members of his resistance movement, imprisoned another thousand, demolished the houses of scores of suspected sympathizers, and deported scores more.

Fatah turned its energies to organizing among the large Palestinian refugee populations of Jordan and Lebanon, whence they sought to mount cross-border raids against Israel. The rulers of these countries were at first little able to curb the guerrillas' activities. At the political level, meanwhile, the Arab regimes considered it wisest to reach an accommodation with the Palestinian groups. Under an agreement brokered in 1968–1969 by Egypt's President Gamal Abdul Nasser,* Fatah took over the PLO in coordination with a number of other guerrilla groups. At a February 1969 meeting of the PLO's supreme governing body, the Palestine National Council (PNC), Fatah installed its candidate as PLO chairman: he was Yasser Arafat, who had emerged during the previous few months as Fatah's own "first among equals."

Fatah's specific weight within the PLO (in political terms, and as reflected in budgetary allocations) stabilized at about two-thirds of the PLO's total weight; but the other guerrilla groups that had entered the PLO along with Fatah in 1968 retained their own organizational identity within the PLO umbrella. These groups included some that were recognized as authentically Palestinian, like George Habash's* Popular Front for the Liberation of Palestine (PFLP); they also included some with indisputable ties to Arab regimes, like the Syrian-controlled Saiqa. Their presence, along with the Palestinian activists' lack of a territorial base, ensured the continued intervention of the Arab regimes in PLO decision making through the late 1980s.

In Jordan, the Palestinian guerrillas posed a threat to King Hussein ibn Talal's* regime both by their influence within his own political system (in which the Palestinians outnumbered the purely Jordanian population), and by the instability they caused along his border with Israel. By September 1970, Hussein was ready to regain the political initiative he had lost three years earlier. After members of the PLO-affiliated PFLP forced three hijacked Western aircraft to land at a guerrilla-controlled airstrip in Jordan, Hussein sent his army into action against the PLO. Arafat appealed for support from the other Arab regimes, but they did nothing effective to help; and after a series of battles, Hussein was able to regain total control of his country. Arafat and those of his guerrillas who survived the Jordanian onslaught then joined their compatriots who were building up a Palestinian armed presence in Lebanon.

In October 1973, the Egyptian and Syrian rulers launched a limited military offensive against Israel. Arafat's forces played only a small part in that war effort, but when the post-war diplomacy got underway, the question of PLO participation in the peace talks became an important issue at the Arab and international levels. Several of Arafat's political mentors, including the leaders of Algeria and the Soviet Union, urged him to seek a place at the talks on the basis that the PLO sought to create an independent Palestinian state alongside Israel, after the latter's withdrawal. Urging him in this direction, too, were numerous messages coming to him from Palestinian residents of the occupied territories.

Adopting such a stance meant changing Fatah's traditional doctrine, which held that armed struggle should be the Palestinians' major mode of operation, and that their goals should be the return of all Palestinian exiles to their homes and farms inside the 1948 State of Israel and the replacement of the entire Jewish state with a vaguely defined "secular democratic state." In spring 1974, the Fatah leaders agreed to a change in doctrine; and that summer they won official PLO backing for the goal of creating a "Palestinian national authority" in any Palestinian area from which Israel should withdraw. (The PNC still spelled out, however, that this ministate would be only a first step, pending the creation of the Palestine-wide "secular democratic state." Furthermore, the new formula was inserted only into the PLO's program, leaving its original charter unchanged.)

Despite some continuing internal opposition to the new program, Arafat tried to push the diplomatic option forward. At an Arab summit in Rabat in October 1974, he won the support of all major Arab states except Iraq for the PLO's new program. The following month, the PLO leader took his campaign to the United Nations General Assembly in New York, where he referred to the fact that he now carried "both a gun and an olive branch." This speech to the General Assembly on November 14 did nothing to open up the diplomatic process; but it did elicit a vast show of support from the Palestinians of the occupied territories, who mounted a wave of pro-PLO demonstrations that continued for a number of weeks. When the Israelis sponsored municipal elections on the West Bank eighteen months later, pro-PLO activists won nearly all the contested mayoral seats.

The PLO's 1974 doctrinal switch was designed to allow the organization to enter the post–1973 round of diplomacy, but it came too late. By summer 1974, both Egypt and Syria had committed themselves to a military disengagement with Israel that left little room for discussion of Palestinian issues. Then, in 1975, the PLO's burgeoning base in Lebanon came under attack from the Maronite Christian militias there. The PLO, supported by its allies from the Lebanese leftist and Muslim militias, struck back, but in June 1976 Syria moved troops in to save the Maronites. At first, the PLO leaders decided to resist the Syrian advance, but by September 1976, they decided instead to disengage from the Lebanese imbroglio. They soon succeeded in this aim. However, the continuation of intra-Lebanese rivalries prevented the restoration of any effective government in Beirut; and the PLO's political-military infrastructure continued to grow, especially in the southern region bordering Israel.

After Jimmy Carter became U.S. president in 1977, Arafat tried to capitalize on his interest in the Middle East, and through the summer of 1977 the two sides engaged in indirect contacts to try to work out precisely how the Palestinians might be represented at a reconvened peace conference. That fall, however, Egypt's President Anwar al-Sadat* jettisoned the last pretense of an all-Arab approach and started suing for peace with Israel on his own. As Sadat's intentions became clear, the PLO joined the militant anti-Sadat coalition which was called the Steadfastness and Confrontation Front. The following year, Sadat signed the Camp David Accords, which set the terms for the Egyptian-Israeli peace accord that was concluded the following year and obliged the parties to continue discussions on an "autonomy" plan for residents of the West Bank and Gaza. This second Camp David Accord proved unacceptable both to the PLO leadership and most residents of the occupied territories, who feared the planned autonomy would merely mask Israel's continuing control over their lives, lands, and resources.

In 1981, Israeli Prime Minister Menachem Begin's* appointment of Ariel Sharon as Defense Minister brought new threats to the Palestinians both within and outside the occupied territories. Inside the territories, the Israelis now tried to counter PLO influence by building up alternative organizations called Village Leagues. Outside the territories, Sharon meanwhile planned a blow against the PLO buildup in Lebanon.

This blow came in June 1982, in a massive military campaign that took the IDF to the outskirts of Beirut, and that after eleven weeks forced the PLO to evacuate its troops from the city. However, the PLO's evacuation was something other than the rout Sharon had planned. Arafat had commanded the PLO forces in person during the deadly siege of Beirut, and he negotiated an agreement that enabled his troops to leave the city with heads held high and carrying sidearms, while he received what he thought were cast-iron guarantees for the security of Palestinian civilians left behind. (This proved not to be the case the following month, when Israeli-backed local militias engaged in an orgy of killing against Palestinian families in Beirut.) The PLO forces left Beirut, moreover, with the political part of the PLO infrastructure still intact, while Sharon found his forces bogged down in a Lebanese campaign from which there was no clear exit.

In the years after 1982, Arafat's career was dominated by two major inter-related themes. The first was his continued bid for inclusion in Arab-Israeli peace deliberations, and the second was the increasing attention he and his colleagues, especially Khalil Wazir, devoted to building up Fatah's clandestine networks inside the occupied territories.

In September 1982, U.S. President Ronald Reagan unveiled a peace plan that called for the Palestinians' inclusion in a Jordanian team negotiating peace with Israel. Arafat and most of his colleagues understood that this meant that the PLO should upgrade its relations with Jordan, but Syria's President Hafez al-Assad,* whose interests had been left out of the Reagan peace plan altogether, was strongly opposed to this development. In the summer of 1983, Assad fomented an anti-Arafat schism inside the PLO, which included some second-tier members of Fatah's own leadership along with some PLO activists who were not in Fatah.

In fall 1984, Arafat and his loyalist colleagues decided to make a more de-termined effort to join the peace process that Jordan was trying to pursue with Israel, even though this meant risking a more lasting split in their movement. In November 1984, Arafat convened a PNC session in the Jordanian capital, from which all the Syrian-backed groups pointedly stayed away, as did the PFLP and the Democratic Front. However, the PLO leader's willingness to risk splitting his movement as a price for entering the peace process brought him no quick return. In February 1985, Hussein joined Arafat in endorsing a joint stand toward negotiations. However, from the end of the year on, the Jordanian monarch moved rapidly away from the PLO and into an alliance with Syria. Throughout 1986, Arafat was thus left at odds with both Syria and Jordan, while the U.S.-backed peace process was also at a standstill.

The Soviets, the Algerians, and the Libyans all helped to bail out the PLO chairman at this point. They brokered a process of reconciliation that brought all but the most abjectly pro-Syrian of the Palestinian groups back into the PLO fold at the eighteenth PNC session, which was held in Algiers in April 1987.

Also urging the Palestinian exile groups to reunite were numerous commu-nications from the Palestinian population under occupation, which had become considerably more militant in the years following 1982. The PLO's dispersal from Lebanon had led the "resident" Palestinians to understand they would now have to take a larger part in their own liberation; the PLO leaders had also come to understand that their resident compatriots would have to play a larger role in the movement in the future. Inside Fatah, Khalil Wazir was in charge of organ-izing inside the territories: During the mid–1980s, he succeeded in building his organization there into a many-layered conglomeration of overlapping clandestine networks. The other groups with significant networks in the territories included the PFLP, the Democratic Front, the Palestinian Communist Party, and some Islamic organizations. The one bloc that notably did not enjoy much support there was the pro-Syrian bloc.

In December 1987, the ferment in the territories exploded into an all-out *intifada* (uprising) against the Israeli occupation. During the first year after December 1987, the militancy of the resident Palestinians, the sophistication of their clandestine organizations, and the discipline with which they kept their protests short of the use of armed violence, left the IDF unable to beat back their intifada. Even the Israelis' April 1988 assassination of Wazir did not dampen the spirits of the resident Palestinians, who continued to signal clearly that the Israelis could no longer maintain a cost-free occupation of their areas. While they showed themselves willing to discuss minor police matters with the Israelis, at the overall political level the residents still unanimously insisted that the PLO was their only representative.

The intifada immensely boosted the internal legitimacy and the international standing of PLO Chairman Arafat. Throughout 1988, it also boosted his long-held political agenda. In the early months of the year, U.S. Secretary of State George Shultz felt obliged to restart the stalled contacts concerning the status of the occupied territories; and in July, King Hussein abandoned his claim to represent the Palestinians. This latter step faced Arafat with the challenge of gaining the PLO's entrance to any peace process on its own account. Nationalist activists inside the occupied areas, including Abdel-Qader al-Husseini's newly-prominent son Faisal al-Husseini, were meanwhile urging him to make the unequivocal commitments to UN Security Council Resolution 242, and to a renunciation of terrorism, that were the U.S. preconditions for starting any direct talks with the PLO. In December, Arafat finally made a statement in Geneva that Shultz considered fulfilled the American conditions. American diplomats immediately commenced political contacts with the PLO.

Yasser Arafat's political career had been nearly coterminous with the existence of the State of Israel. Clearly, he was much more than the terror-gang leader he was portrayed as in some Western media. Over the four decades following 1948, he and his colleagues had succeeded in redefining a durable form of Palestinian nationalism. They had built a durable set of organizations to embody this ideal, and steered these organizations through the multiple minefields of inter-Arab, Arab-Israeli, and international politics.

Arafat remained unmarried, devoting long workdays and extensive travel to the Palestinian cause. While the Husseini organization in which he had served his political apprenticeship had had quite a strong Islamic tinge, he became much more of a secularist in his maturity: He welcomed into Fatah many Christian Palestinian activists, while he himself remained a generally observant Muslim. Quick in his wits, Arafat was a master of political tactics, maintaining the balance between the historic barons of the Fatah leadership even when, as over the question of Lebanon in 1976, there were sizable differences between them.

In the early 1960s, the stockily built Arafat with his characteristic checkered headdress and two-day growth of beard, was identified as an "activist" within Fatah, but he was more cautious in the years between 1968 and 1987. In those years, he appeared generally unwilling to risk his domestic political capital by experimenting with radically new approaches to the nationalist cause. Meanwhile, in successive internationally brokered cease-fire agreements in Lebanon between 1978 and 1982, he proved himself a man of his word; he also proved that his apparatus was capable of enforcing these agreements from the Palestinian side.

In 1987, the outbreak and continuation of the intifada gave Arafat new self-confidence, and he adopted a clear prenegotiating stance. This was a risky move. If it should not bring tangible results within an acceptable time period, Arafat's domestic opposition could be expected to mount. Waiting to challenge his leadership of the reconstituted Palestinian nation were irredentists of the ideological right and left and a resurgent Islamic fundamentalist movement. However, whether or not Arafat and his secular, scaled-down version of Palestinian nationalism will survive, the achievement of having rebuilt the Palestinian nation from its post–1948 despair will remain.

BIBLIOGRAPHY

Abou Iyad (Khalaf, Salah) with Eric Rouleau. *My home, My Land*. New York: Times Books, 1981.
Cobban, Helena. *The Palestinian Liberation Organization: People, Power and Politics*. New York and Cambridge, U.K.: Cambridge University Press, 1984.
Cooley, John. *Green March, Black September*. London: Frank Cass, 1973.
Dimbleby, Jonathan, and Don McCullin. *The Palestinians*. London: Quartet Books, 1980.
Kelman, Herbert C. "Talk with Arafat." *Foreign Policy* (Washington, D.C.), no. 49 (Winter 1982–1983): 119–139.
Khalidi, Rashid. *Under Siege; PLO Decisionmaking during the 1982 War*. New York: Columbia University Press, 1986.
Sahliyeh, Emile. *The PLO after the Lebanon War*. Boulder, Colo.: Westview Press, 1986.
Sayigh, Rosemary. *Palestinians: From Peasants to Revolutionaries*. London: Zed Press, 1979.

HELENA COBBAN

HAFEZ AL-ASSAD (1930–   ), ruler of modern Syria, is one of the most powerful, intriguing, and controversial leaders of the contemporary Middle East. His is indeed an exceptional life story, of a boy from a poor peasant family named *Wahsh* (wild beast) who changed his family name to *Assad* (lion) and made an unprecedented rise to the supreme position as Syria's president. More significantly, although a member of the esoteric, heterodox, and rural Alawite minority sect, which represents only 12 percent of the total population, Assad rules over a predominantly Sunni (Orthodox) Muslim country (although in the eyes of many Sunni Muslims it is a military-sectarian dictatorship). Assad has managed to stay in power since 1970—longer than any previous regime in Syria's modern history.

In a country that for decades has been a breeding ground for military coups and countercoups, Assad established an unchallenged, highly centralized regime, and at the same time was able to transform Syria from a notoriously weak and vulnerable country into a strong, stable, and assertive state. Moreover, Assad has turned his country from an object of encroachment on the part of neighboring countries into a regional power, challenging or affecting a number of countries and other forces in the region and beyond. Starting as coleader of the 1973 war against Israel, Assad now aims to single-handedly challenge Israel's military superiority in the Middle East by working systematically to achieve a "strategic balance" with the Jewish state. Simultaneously, Assad has endeavored to create a political-military alliance of "Greater Syria," with Lebanon, Jordan, and the Palestinian people under his leadership.

In addition, Assad continued to muster both political backing and financial assistance from Saudi Arabia (thereby demonstrating the weakness of Arab criticism of Syria's alliance with Iran) in its Gulf war with Arab-backed Iraq. To be sure, Assad's support of Ruhollah Khomeini's* Islamic fundamentalist regime is essentially designed to help him gain the upper hand in his intense rivalry with Iraq's Saddam Hussein* over the leadership of the Baath and eventually for hegemony over the Fertile Crescent region.

Finally, although Assad's domestic and regional achievements were realized with substantial Soviet military, political, and economic support, he has by no means become a client of the USSR. Furthermore, Assad has sometimes dealt directly with the United States without apparently coordinating his moves with the USSR. Even as he labelled the United States as Syria's arch enemy, Assad has never closed the door to independent bilateral relations with Washington, D.C.

Assad's external and domestic policies have faced grave problems and suffered serious setbacks. On balance, though, his achievements, especially in regional affairs, seem to be quite remarkable, all the more so when one considers that most, if not all, of those achievements have been accomplished single-handedly by Assad himself. Naturally, Assad is assisted by scores of advisers, ministers, and army officers, but he makes all the important decisions and runs the country as a one-man show. He is as close to a one-person regime as is possible.

Assad was born on October 6, 1930, to a poor peasant family in Qardaha, an Alawite mountain village which is southeast of Latakia, a predominantly Sunni-Muslim town and a Mediterranean port. This social milieu as well as contemporary political developments may signify the ambivalent or contradictory circumstances that may have had a strong impact on Assad as a boy. Initially he belonged to the minority Alawite sect, which for generations had been looked down on with great contempt by many Sunni Muslims for being religiously heretic, politically separatist, and socially inferior. Such harsh conditions presumably created not only an inferiority complex but also a deep urge to fare better than the Sunnis.

The political developments coupled with the ideological trends in Syria during his youth provided Assad, like other Alawite boys, suitable opportunities to board together with young Sunni Muslim children. Indeed, the ineffective struggle of the old Syrian-Arab nationalist parties against the French Mandate and their conservative socioeconomic policies, coupled with the growing grievances and aspirations of many deprived young Syrians, all contributed during the 1930s and 1940s to the emergence of new radical parties in Syria which stood for socioeconomic change and a new nonsectarian society. One of these parties was the Baath. Assad, who at the age of fourteen moved to the nearby town of Latakia for his secondary schooling, soon immersed himself in this new, radical political environment. Receiving Arab nationalist education and developing a keen interest in Arab history and geography, the ambitious, stealthy, proud, and stubborn Assad became involved in anti-French political activities and thus emerged as a high-school student leader. Joining the newly formed Baath Party in 1947, Assad organized the party's students' cell in his secondary school at Latakia. Like many non-Sunni youngsters, Assad was attracted by the secularist, nationalist, and socialist notions of this party, and sought to be an equal member in a new nonsectarian Syrian-Arab national community. However, a few years later Assad decided to embark on a military career which he felt was a more promising avenue for political involvement and social mobilization.

Indeed, unlike the Baath Party, which was still numerically small and politically marginal, the Syrian army has since 1949 become deeply involved and greatly influential in postindependence national politics. Following the traditional enlistment of young Alawites (as well as other minorities) in the armed forces, Assad joined the Syrian army in 1952, registering in the Military Academy of Homs. Possibly impressed by the fact that two Alawite officers had successively commanded the Syrian Air Force in 1950 and 1952, Assad went to the Air Force Academy in Aleppo. His flying talent won him the best-aviator trophy on graduation as a combat pilot in 1955. Holding the rank of lieutenant, Assad continued advanced training in Egypt together with a young Egyptian pilot, Hosni Mubarak.* Promoted in 1957 to squadron commander, Assad subsequently went to the USSR for a course in flying Mig–17s.

However, Assad was not content with a professional military career. He regarded it as an avenue for political ascent. He thus joined the Baath military faction in the army, which in 1957–1958 acquired a predominant position. At that juncture, however, fresh political upheavals threatened his military-political career. The union between Syria and Egypt in 1958, initiated by the Baath Party, paradoxically dealt a severe blow to the party, its leaders, and its activists. While the party was dissolved and its leaders were given junior government positions, its military partisans were either dismissed or transferred (exiled) to Egypt. Among the latter was Captain Assad.

He did not despair. Hardworking, discreet, skillful, and highly ambitious, Assad, still a junior officer, became, along with senior Alawite and Druze officers, one of the leaders of the Baathist Military Committee, which was established in Egypt in the late 1950s with the aim of seizing Syria. However, when Syria seceded from the United Arab Republic (UAR) in September 1961, Assad like other Baathist officers, was eased out from the army by the new rightist regime in Damascus and was given a minor clerical position at the Transportation Ministry.

Assad again did not give up. He continued his activities in the clandestine Baath Military Committee, playing a significant role in the March 1963 Baathist military coup. Promoted to the rank of major and subsequently to lieutenant colonel, Assad was put in charge of the Syrian Air Force by the end of 1963. By the end of 1964, he was appointed commander of the Syrian Air Force with the rank of major general. He then turned the Air Force into his power base by lavishing special privileges on its officers, appointing his confidants to senior and sensitive positions, and establishing an efficient intelligence network. Thus, under the command of Muhammad Khuli, the Air Force Intelligence network became independent of Syria's other intelligence organizations and was given assignments beyond the Air Force arena. Apparently, Assad prepared himself at that time to take an active role in the power struggles that lay ahead. During that period, from 1963 to 1970, Assad demonstrated a unique combination of traits—ambition and single-mindedness, patience and caution, coolness and manipulativeness—in order to reach the supreme position in the country. During the first stage of the power struggle, Assad remained the junior partner in the leading Alawite Triumvirate of the Military Committee, together with generals Muhammad Umran and Salah Jadid. However, when a struggle for power erupted between General Umran, the leader of the Military Committee, and General Amin al-Hafiz, the newly emerging strongman of the Baath regime, Assad and Jadid sided with the Sunni leader Amin Al-Hafiz against their Alawite comrade Muhammad Umran. To be sure, Assad's choice was based on a cool evaluation of the power balance between Umran and Al-Hafiz. However, because of similar calculations, and drawing upon his powerful Alawite military faction, Assad later joined forces with Jadid against the Sunni-backed government of Al-Hafiz in the military coup of February 1966.

Now also assuming the portfolio of defense minister, and becoming number 2 in the neo-Baath regime, Assad systematically prepared the ground for ousting Jadid and climbing to the top. Indeed, turning the army into his power base, Assad employed brutal force and political manipulation as well as ideological and strategic argumentation in order to undermine Jadid's position and gain supremacy.

Paradoxically, the defeat of the Syrian army by Israel in 1967 and its 1970 fiasco in Jordan, were both skillfully utilized by Assad, the defense minister, to discredit Jadid and extend his own control over the armed forces and the Baath party. In addition, in two successive military coups in February 1969 and November 1970, Assad evicted and arrested Jadid and his senior followers in the government, and assumed an unchallenged control of Syria.

Once in power, Assad was not content with sustaining his control only by means of military force and coercive measures. While greatly expanding his control over the army and establishing a wide network of security organizations,

Assad systematically sought to build a large support base among the Syrian population, Sunnis and non-Sunnis alike.

Indeed, from the outset of his rule, Assad greatly endeavored to avoid an image of his regime as being based on Alawite military support. He rather sought to project his government as constitutional and democratic, and himself as a national popular leader deriving his authority from the people. It is conceivable that Assad was indeed motivated not only by his strong lust for power but also by a genuine sense of nationalist mission. He has thus believed that his leadership served the national interests of the Syrian people as well as the Arab cause at large.

In any event, to gain legitimacy in the eyes of his people, Assad needed first to appear as the legal leader and representative of the ruling Baath Party. Thus, arresting or discharging the incumbent party leaders and delegates late in 1970, Assad established a new Baath Regional Command composed of his own supporters. They promptly elected him the new party's secretary-general, and early in 1971 appointed a new People's Assembly (parliament) which immediately nominated him as the sole candidate for Syria's presidency. In March 1971, Assad was subsequently endorsed as president by a referendum with 99.2 percent of the vote. In 1978 he was reelected as president with 99.6 percent of the vote and in 1985 with 99.9 percent of the referendum ballot.

While continuing to use the Baath party, its ideology, and its expanding apparatus as instruments of his rule and policies, Assad established for the first time in Syria's modern history a powerful centralized presidential system with absolute authority. Indeed, in addition to becoming ex officio the supreme leader of the army and armed forces, Assad has assumed almost unlimited powers in legislature, administration, and policy, both domestic and foreign.

Undoubtedly it was a remarkably bold move on Assad's part to rule Syria from the position of president, for Syrian constitutions had repeatedly stated that the president should be a Sunni Muslim, and Assad was an Alawite. To be sure, since his ascendancy, Assad had tried to present himself in public as a devout Muslim while hailing the role of Islam in national life. Reportedly in the early 1970s he was verified by the Sunni Mufti of Damascus as an authentic Muslim, participated in public prayers and religious ceremonies in various mosques, and made the minor Hajj (an *umra*, or pilgrimage to Mecca at an irregular time). While using in his speeches Islamic terms such as *jihad* (holy war) and *shahada* (martyrdom)—both terms referred to fighting Israel), Assad made various gestures toward the Orthodox Muslim population. For example, he encouraged the construction of new mosques, raised the salaries of many religious functionaries, and appointed a Sunni religious leader as minister of religious endowments. Along similar lines, in an attempt to project his regime as predominantly Sunni Muslim, Assad appointed Sunni Muslims who were personally loyal to him to senior positions in the government, the army, and the party. For instance, all prime ministers of defense and foreign ministers as well as most cabinet ministers in Assad's governments have been Sunni Muslims. Among them, the most veteran have been Mustafa Tlas and Abd al-Halim Khaddam, defense and foreign ministers respectively, as well as vice presidents since 1984. Other Sunnis in prominent positions include Hikmat Shihabi, the army's chief of staff, and Zuhayr Masharqa, vice president since 1984 and deputy secretary-general of the Baath party.

However, in addition to this Sunni Muslim facade, Assad has also sought to portray his regime as a popular democratic system. Thus, the Syrian People's Assembly, or parliament, consisted of several nationalist and socialist parties; and together with the leading Baath Party, they formed a "National Progressive Front" in both the parliament and the cabinet. About half the members of the parliament have been representatives of peasants and workers, and a number of popular organizations of peasants and workers, women, students, and the like were established in the country allegedly to participate in the decision-making process.

Still, while relying heavily on these social groups—notably peasants, workers, and youth (and obviously the army and the Alawite community)—as a support base for his regime, Assad has also attempted to win the allegiance, or at least to neutralize the opposition, of other large sections of the Syrian population. He has sought to implement this by acting as a leader-reformer, a state-builder as well as a nation-builder; namely, by developing and modernizing the country's socioeconomic infrastructure, while supplying the population with political stability and economic opportunities as well as ideological consensus. The latter objective—ideological consensus or national unity—could also be cultivated, according to Assad, by a dynamic regional policy, while stepping up the national struggle against Zionism and imperialism. To be sure, Assad has sought to carry out these policies—domestic and external alike—primarily in order to strengthen the legitimacy of his regime. However, interwoven with these motives or calculations may have been Assad's deep sense of mission to his country and nation as well as possibly his sincere care for the well-being of his people, notably the underprivileged sections. Labelling his domestic reform policies as a corrective movement, Assad made great efforts and achieved substantial results, particularly during the first six or seven years of his rule, in the various economic and social fields. For example, the completion in 1974 of the Euphrates Dam, one of the biggest dams in the world, with its huge water reservoir, Lake Assad, greatly increased the irrigation of arable lands, provided electric power to many regions of the country, and fostered industrial as well as technical development in Syria. Parallel to his efforts to advance agriculture and develop modern industry, the conditions of many peasants and workers were noticeably improved in matters of financial income and social security as well as health and educational services. The urban middle classes—merchants, artisans, shopkeepers, and the like— which had been hurt by Jadid regime's policies were now given new economic opportunities by Assad.

However, Assad's domestic policy encountered serious difficulties and setbacks, and produced new problems and ill feelings particularly among the Sunni

Muslim urban classes; the orthodox sections among these classes also continued to oppose Assad's regime for being a military sectarian dictatorship. As it happened, the continued Muslim opposition to his regime as well as the shortcomings of his socioeconomic policies served to further enforce Assad's initial tendency to give prime attention to Syria's regional affairs—namely intra-Arab and anti-Israeli policies. This tendency did not stem only from Assad's expectations to score quick and spectacular gains in his foreign policies at a time when the crucial socioeconomic problems of Syria required long-term and painstaking efforts without the promise of immediate positive results. Furthermore, in addition to his strong ambition to turn Syria into a regional power and himself become a pan-Arab leader, Assad may have calculated that working for Arab unity and stepping up the struggle against Israel were likely to strengthen his legitimacy and leadership among the various sections of the Syrian population.

Assad's very first foreign policy actions after he came to power were to join the newly established federation of Arab Republics along with Egypt, Libya, and Sudan (pending), and to sign a military pact with Egypt. Simultaneously, Assad gave high priority to quickly building a strong military force and preparing it for a confrontation vis-à-vis Israel—both for defensive and offensive purposes and to enable him to politically negotiate the return of the Golan Heights from a position of military strength. Allocating up to 70 percent of the annual budget to the military buildup and receiving large quantities of modern arms from the USSR, Assad was ready to join Anwar al-Sadat* in the October 1973 Yom Kippur War against Israel.

Even though the Syrian army was badly defeated in the war, while Sadat signed unilateral agreements with Israel, Assad emerged from the war as a national hero in Syria as well as in other parts of the Arab world. This was due not only to his bold decision to go to war against Israel and subsequently carry out single-handedly a war of attrition against the IDF in the spring of 1974. Assad's skills as a cool, proud, tough, and shrewd negotiator in the postwar period enabled him to gain not only the town of Kuneitra but also the respect and admiration of many Arabs in Syria and elsewhere. Many of his followers now regarded Assad as the new pan-Arab leader, and a worthy successor of Gamal Abdul Nasser.*

To be sure, since his ascendancy in November 1970, which symbolically occurred a few weeks after Nasser's death, Assad has alluded in various ways to the fact that he regards himself as Nasser's successor. He constructed his presidential system according to Nasser's mold and hailed Nasser for his pan-Arab leadership, while displaying Nasser's photos alongside his own posters in public places.

Nonetheless, a greater hero and a supreme model for Assad has been Salah ad-Din (Saladin) al-Ayyubi, the legendary Muslim Kurdish leader who in the twelfth century succeeded in unifying the Muslim East, defeating the Crusades in 1187 at Hittin (near Tiberias) and subsequently conquering Jerusalem. Assad has demonstrated his admiration of Saladin and his heritage by having in his office a large painting depicting Saladin's tomb in Damascus and issuing a currency bill with Saladin's figure. In his speeches and conversations, Assad frequently hails Saladin's successes and his victory over the crusades while equating Israel with the crusader state.

While promoting his personality cult as a historical leader along the models of Nasser and Saladin, Assad has indeed regarded his supreme twofold goal to be Arab unity and an uncompromising struggle against Israel. The latter goal, with its military, political, economic, and cultural ramifications, does not only stem from Assad's need for legitimacy as an Alawite ruler of Syria who wishes to present himself as a genuine Arab and Muslim leader. Moreover, Assad has apparently been convinced that Israel presents a severe threat to the integrity of the Arab nation from the Nile to the Euphrates, and that it is, therefore, his historic mission to defend Arabdom from this alleged neo-Nazi invasion. He regards the confrontation with Israel as a zero-sum struggle, and as a good strategist who understands power politics, he has sought to counterbalance Israeli military might with an all-Arab political-military alliance. However, since Egypt, under Sadat's leadership, defected from this alliance following the 1973 war, Assad endeavored during the middle and late 1970s to establish an alternative all-Arab alliance with Iraq, Jordan, Lebanon, and the PLO (Palestine Liberation Organization). However, facing grave difficulties to reach an understanding with Baathist Iraq (Assad himself was not too keen to play a secondary role in an Iraqi-Syrian union), Assad resorted to implement his (and his country's) historic goal, namely, to create under his leadership a Greater Syria union or alliance with Jordan, Lebanon, and the PLO. As it happened, during the second half of the 1970s Assad managed to significantly advance political, military, and economic cooperation with Jordan; to extend his control over large parts of Lebanon while intervening in the Lebanese civil war; and, for a while, also to sustain his strategic alliance with the PLO.

To be sure, parallel to his regional accomplishments, Assad also scored significant gains in his relations with the superpowers. In 1974 he embarrassed the USSR by negotiating with the United States regarding the military disengagement on the Golan Heights, and in 1976 he ignored Soviet pressure and requests to refrain from invading Lebanon and subsequently to refrain from attacking the PLO and the Lebanese radical forces. Simultaneously, Assad renewed and markedly improved his relations with the United States, and made both presidents Richard Nixon and Jimmy Carter his great admirers.

However, neither Assad's international and regional achievements nor his domestic gains lasted long, and soon showed signs of collapse, partly owing to his miscalculations and partly because of changing circumstances. The major source of his initial successes—his regional politics—turned out to be the main causes of his severe setbacks.

Primarily, Assad's direct intervention in Lebanon proved to be a grave miscalculation; indeed, within a year or two it turned from an important asset to a grave liability, both regionally and domestically. Thus Assad's maneuvers among the two main rival factions, playing one against the other, served to alienate both. The PLO, experiencing Assad's blows in 1976, distanced itself from him and consolidated its autonomous infrastructure in southern Lebanon, paradoxically with Israel's indirect assistance (Israel firmly objected to the deployment of Syrian troops south of the Sidon-Jazzin "red line").

The Christian Maronites, fearing Syrian domination, in 1978 started a guerrilla warfare against Syrian troops in Beirut and northern Lebanon. Here again Israel's moral support and material aid contributed to foster the Maronites' autonomy and their resistance to Assad's de facto occupation of Lebanon. Furthermore, while Syria was drenched in the Lebanese quagmire, the newly formed Likud government in Israel (founded in 1977) not only developed political and military relations with the Maronite "Lebanese Forces," but took a further important step, which contributed to undermining Assad's regional position: Israel welcomed Sadat's initiative of November 1977 and signed the Camp David Accords with Egypt and the United States in 1978, to be followed by the Egypt-Israel Peace Treaty in 1979.

To be sure, apart from a deep psychological shock, Assad's regional strategic posture also suffered serious blows as Egypt, the major Arab country, departed from the all-Arab confrontation against Israel, in effect exposing Syria to a growing Israeli threat. Indeed, apart from a short-lived rapprochement with the PLO, Assad became increasingly isolated in the region. His brief unity talks with the Iraqi leaders collapsed in mid–1979; and with Iraq's 1980 involvement in the war with Iran, this second major Arab state also virtually departed from the conflict against Israel.

Simultaneously, in 1979, under the impact of the Egypt-Israeli Peace Treaty, and in view of Syria's regional predicament, King Hussein ibn of Talal* of Jordan pulled away from his association with Assad in favor of a closer relationship with Iraq. Finally, Assad's regional strategic position was further damaged as the Carter administration in the United States was geared to abandon its new Syrian-oriented policy in favor of the Egyptian-Israeli peace process. In this critical situation, with his political skills exhausted, Assad still demonstrated his stamina, obstinacy, and single-mindedness.

In 1980, with the first of a friendship and cooperation agreement with the USSR, Assad continued to develop his new doctrine of Strategic Balance, which he had initiated the previous year. Aiming primarily at confronting Israel single-handedly, this doctrine not only engendered fresh intra-Arab policies, it was also directed toward reconsolidating Assad's domestic front, which, similar to his regional posture, had suffered severe setbacks since 1977.

By 1977, it became clear that Assad's state-building and nation-building reforms, despite certain achievements, had largely failed to reach their goals. Here again, the causes for these failures were partly related to Assad's miscalculations or mistakes, and partly to factors that he was unable to control or change within a short period of time. Thus, the chronic socioeconomic difficulties of Syria mostly persisted, while new ones were created. The major problems were mismanagement, inefficiency, and corruption in the government bureaucracy as well as in the public and private economic sectors; illiteracy and low-level education, particularly in the rural areas, and an increasing brain drain of professionals; and a growing trade deficit and inflation, high cost of living, and shortages in consumer goods and the like. As it happened, Syria's involvement in Lebanon since 1976 with the resulting financial burden contributed not only to worsening the economic problems, it also fostered the spread of corruption and black-marketeering to high levels. The emerging new class of entrepreneurs and brokers now became involved with senior army officers (among them Rifat, Assad's brother) in smuggling contraband goods from Lebanon, thus affecting government revenues and spreading bribery among senior government officials.

Still more detrimental and threatening was the resurgence and expansion of the Islamic opposition to Assad's regime. Indeed, Assad's initial support of the Christian Maronites and his military action against the Muslim radicals in Lebanon provoked for the first time a new and unprecedented phase of Muslim resistance to Assad. It took the form of well-organized and effective urban guerrilla warfare against government, military, and Baathist officials and institutions. During the late 1970s and early 1980s, this Islamic *jihad* (holy war) became almost an open rebellion as many Alawite soldiers and officers as well as senior officials were killed, and government and military centers were bombed by the Muslim *mujahidun* (freedom fighters).

Facing a serious menace to his regime and perhaps even to his life, for the first time Assad lost his coolness and self-confidence, and reacted with fury and desperation; reportedly, his health also started to deteriorate during this period. Under his personal orders a ferocious campaign of repression and counterterror was launched against the Muslim Brothers. Thousands of them were arrested and inhumanely tortured, many of them were killed or "disappeared"; and in February 1982, the rebellious city of Hama was bombed by Assad's troops, killing up to thirty-thousand people, including women and children.

At that juncture, Assad finally realized that his previous great efforts to bring about a national unity in Syria—namely to gain legitimacy in the eyes of the Sunni Muslim urban population—had totally failed. He was confronted now not only with the resistance of the Muslim Brothers and their many thousands of Orthodox followers. Large sections of the urban intelligentsia—professionals and intellectuals, as well as former Baath members—also regarded his regime as an illegitimate Alawite sectarian military system.

Consequently, Assad has been geared to increasingly rely on and further cultivate his close constituencies as a support base and a new political community. These have consisted of a large section of peasants and workers, salaried middle-class and public employees, and Sunnis and non-Sunnis alike. Mostly organized in the Baath Party, mass syndicates, and trade unions, these sections, like most Alawites and many Christians, have greatly benefited from Assad's policies, and thus are dependent on him or are ideologically identified with his regime.

Another large section of the population that has a strong allegiance to Assad are many of the young Syrians, who for a generation or so have been educated or indoctrinated in the notions of the Baath Party as formulated by Assad. These sections of the population not only render legitimacy to Assad's regime, but from time to time they have been mobilized by Assad to actively support his policies and curb his domestic enemies. Nonetheless, the hard core of Assad's support base has remained the Alawite community, combined with the combat units of the Syrian army as well as with the wide network of security and intelligence organizations.

Indeed, members of the Alawite community as well as non-Alawites loyal to Assad virtually control the huge security, intelligence, and military apparatuses of Assad's regime. They man or command about a dozen security and intelligence networks as well as most armored divisions, commandos, and other combat units of the Syrian army. Having direct supervision and control over the commanders of these forces and units, Assad has employed them not only in order to protect his life, his regime, and country against the growing number of domestic and regional enemies, he has skillfully and brutally used both his armed forces and intelligence-security networks in order to back and carry out his domestic and regional policies. Thus, in addition to directing a state-run repression system against the Muslim Brothers in Syria, Assad has turned some of his intelligence networks into special apparatuses for terrorism against targets in the Middle East and in Europe. For example, Assad used terrorism and intimidation (in addition to other means) to extend his control over Lebanon: in 1977, his agents assassinated Kamal Jumblatt* the Druze leftist leader, and in 1982 the killed Bashir Gemayel, the newly elected Maronite president, both of whom had struggled against Assad's attempts to dominate Lebanon. By similar tactics, Assad managed to bring about the abolition of the 1983 Lebanon-Israel agreement, and through guerrilla warfare carried out by proxy in 1985 Assad indirectly caused the withdrawal of the Israel Defense Forces (IDF) from southern Lebanon. Terrorism against Palestinian and Jordanian targets contributed in the mid–1980s to thwart the rapprochement between King Hussein and the PLO, as well as to slowing down Jordanian-Israeli political cooperation in the West Bank.

To be sure, Israel has remained the major target of Assad's terrorist and guerrilla operations, not only in Lebanon but also in Europe. The attempt to bomb an El-Al airliner in London in April 1986 and the attack on an El-Al jet in Madrid in June 1986 are two examples of his policy. These actions were apparently part of an attrition campaign that Assad has been directing against Israel aimed at damaging its economy, morale, and social fabric, as well as weakening its military capacity. However, this campaign of attrition has merely been an auxiliary tactic in Assad's major strategy of strategic balance with Israel.

This doctrine of strategic balance or military parity was developed by Assad in the late 1970s, when Syria was largely isolated in the region and exposed to a potential Israeli threat. Assad was then determined to build a powerful military force (in addition to a sound economy and a cohesive national community) in order to single-handedly confront Israel, while exercising his influence over the neighboring Arab countries. The 1982 war with Israel in Lebanon only enhanced Assad's efforts to greatly increase and improve his army. Indeed, with the massive help of the Soviet Union, Assad succeeded during recent years in building a huge and modernized army equipped with modern tanks, airplanes, and long-range ground-to-ground missiles capable of launching chemical warheads into most Israeli centers.

Thus, although he is still far from achieving military superiority over, or a strategic balance with, Israel, Assad may nevertheless have reached a military parity with the Jewish state in quantitative terms. This military capacity, a major achievement for Assad, enables him to deter Israel from attacking Syria as well as to cause heavy losses to Israel in case of war. While possibly rendering him an option to regain the Golan, or part of it, by a surprise attack, Assad's enormous military power also enables him to sustain some of his major political gains in the region and at home.

However, Assad was not content with his military buildup, and continued to also employ his unique skills as a first-rate strategist and master manipulator in order to advance his prime regional policies, namely to mobilize all-Arab support for his assumed role as leader of the Arab struggle against Israel, while further isolating Egypt and counterbalancing the growing power of Iraq, Syria's major Arab rivals in the region.

The Islamic revolution that erupted in Iran in February 1979 was seen by Assad as an opportunity to further implement his policies. The new Khomeini regime promptly abolished Iran's pro-Western link with Egypt, potentially threatened Iraq, and turned Israel from a latent ally into a declared enemy of Iran. Assad thus established this unusual alliance with revolutionary Iran, whose political and social principles (except those concerning Israel and the United States) were dramatically opposed to the Baathist doctrines of his regime as well as of the Iraqi government.

Furthermore, Assad consistently extended military and diplomatic assistance to Iran in its long and bloody war with Iraq—aiming at achieving the following major goals: securing Shiite legitimacy and support for his Alawite rule in Syria and his policies in Lebanon; using the Iranian potential threat in manipulating Arab Gulf states to continue their financial and diplomatic support for Syria; weakening, and possibly toppling, his main political and personal opponent, Saddam Hussein; himself becoming the broker between Teheran and a would-be pro-Syrian regime in Baghdad; and subsequently employing Iraq and Iran for "strategic depth" and as allies in Syria's confrontation with Israel, thus emerging as leader of the all-Arab struggle against Israel.

To be sure, Assad repeatedly stated (and possibly also deeply believed) that the war between Iraq and Iran never should have occurred since it was waged against a potential ally of the Arabs (Iran), and caused the diversion of the Arabs' attention, resources, and efforts from their real arch enemy, Israel. In other words, according to Assad, most Arab countries have been wrongly led to support Iraq in an unnecessary war against Iran, rather than support Syria in its vital national-historical struggle against Israel.

However, except for securing Arab financial support and verbal commitments, and obtaining large quantities of free and discounted Iranian oil, Assad failed to achieve the main goals of his Gulf strategy. Moreover, this strategy served to further worsen Syria's regional position. Thus, Assad failed to further isolate Egypt because of her peace with Israel, to weaken or topple the Iraqi leadership because of their war against Iran, and to himself emerge as a leader of an all-Arab coalition vis-à-vis Israel. The growing Iranian threat to Iraq, which Assad indirectly fuelled, contributed to bringing Egypt back to the Arab fold and made many Arabs acquiesce with Egypt's peace treaty with Israel; it also served to develop a new alliance between Egypt and Iraq, the two major Arab states, while further isolating Syria in the Arab world; and finally, it helped to consolidate the Iraqi regime and create among its leaders intense feelings of hatred and revenge toward Assad.

Indeed, although it is difficult to predict the future of Iraqi-Syrian relations in the wake of the Iraqi-Iranian cease-fire and negotiations, it is highly likely that, under suitable circumstances, Saddam Hussein of Iraq will endeavor to "square accounts" with Hafez al-Assad. However, despite his grave miscalculations regarding the Gulf War, Assad would not be an easy prey to Iraq, since he is in full control domestically with a powerful military force under his personal command. He is enjoying noticeable intra-Arab legitimacy and respect owing to his courageous attempt to challenge Israel's military superiority in the region by his doctrine of strategic balance.

In conclusion, through his unique talents and traits—notably, consistency, shrewdness, manipulation, and brutality—Assad, once a low-ranking Alawite officer, rose to supreme power in Syria within a mere six years, and has managed to hold it for almost two decades. He has been able to render Syria unprecedented stability, but has failed to gain a national consensus. He succeeded in turning Syria into a regional power, but could not win a wide pan-Arab support to his regional policies. Assad has shaped a new Syria, militarily strong and politically active, but her economy is severely damaged and large parts of her society have been greatly suppressed.

BIBLIOGRAPHY

L. Bitterlin. *Hafez El-Assad, Le Parcours d'un Combattant*. Paris: 1986.
Alasdair Drysdale. "The Assad Regime and Its Troubles." *MERIP Report* no. 12 (1982).
Malcolm H. Kerr. "Hafiz Assad and the Changing Patterns of Syrian Politics." *International Journal* 28 (1975): 689–706.
Moshe Ma'oz. "Profile: Hafiz al-Assad of Syria." *Orbis* 31 (Summer 1987): 207–217.
————.*Asad: The Sphinx of Damascus: A Political Biography*. London and New York: Weidenfeld and Nicholson, 1988.

Moshe Ma'oz and Avner Yaniv (eds.). *Syria under Assad: Domestic Constraints and Regional Risks*. London and New York: St. Martin's 1986.

Patrick Seale. *Asad of Syria: The Struggle for the Middle East*. London: Tauris, 1988.

Nikolaos Van-Dam. *The Struggle for Power in Syria: Sectarianism, Regionalism, and Tribalism in Politics, 1961–1978*. London: Croom Helm, 1979.

MOSHE MA'OZ

B

SABRI KHALIL AL-BANNA (1937–) (nom de guerre Abu Nidal) remains the most elusive and shadowy figure in contemporary Palestinian politics. In contrast to the traditionally high public profile adopted by Palestinian activists from Ahmad Shukeiry to Yasser Arafat,* Abu Nidal has purposely cultivated a secretive image—consonant with his terrorist activities and his status as an extreme Palestinian rejectionist operating for more than a decade and a half on the fringes of Palestinian politics. Indeed, what is more striking about Abu Nidal are his staying power and his extremism—characteristics that have made him extremely useful to a number of Arab regimes over the years and a popular symbol for radicalized Palestinians. Equally important, the Abu Nidal phenomenon reflects both the violence and the fractiousness that characterize Palestinian national politics.

The uncertainty about Abu Nidal's early years reinforces the elusive image that would characterize his early career. We cannot even be certain of the date of his birth. Abu Nidal himself claims to have been born in 1937, although other accounts put his date of birth somewhat later. What we do know of his past suggests quite unremarkable middle-class origins. Born in Jaffa, to a wealthy Palestinian family, he apparently attended French and Islamic schools before the outbreak of the 1948 Arab-Israeli war.

With the outbreak of formal hostilities in 1948, the al-Banna family found its way to Nablus, although Abu Nidal himself claimed in a 1985 interview that he and his family first spent months in a refugee camp in Gaza. Abu Nidal claims to have spent time in Egypt where he studied engineering and was later employed by the American Arabian Oil Company (ARAMCO) to work in Saudi Arabia. He asserts that he was arrested by the Saudis, tortured, and later expelled from the country. There is no independent confirmation of this story, and it may well be that it was embellished to give a more exciting and revolutionary character to what may well have been an ordinary middle-class background.

By the early 1960s, Abu Nidal—like so many of his well-educated middle-class contemporaries—had been swept up in the swirling currents of an emerging

Palestinian nationalism. There were a range of different Palestinian nationalist orientations during these early years, but the organizational focus and inspiration for many young Palestinians was the Fatah organization, which by 1968 had laid its claim as the most important Palestinian constituent group within the newly created Palestine Liberation Organization (PLO).

Most likely al-Banna came into contact with Fatah in Jordan, then the PLO's primary base of operations against Israel. It was during these early years, in the wake of the devastating Arab defeat by Israel 1967 that the PLO began to establish itself—in the eyes of Palestinians—as the only Arab group willing and able to confront Israel. The Palestinians' credible performance against a larger Israeli force at Karameh in Jordan in 1968 reinforced this image and created the impression that a "new Arab man," embodied by the Palestinian *fedayeen* (commandos), had emerged to regain Arab honor.

Al-Banna appears to have been very much taken with the military aspects of the organization, and rose quickly, adopting his nom de guerre—*Abu Nidal* (Father of the Struggle)—and maintaining a close association with Fatah's intelligence and security organizations. This association drew him inside the more violent aspects of the Palestinian national movement and into contact with men such as Fatah's chief financial officer in Jordan, Ahmad Abd al-Ghafur, whose splinter group would later merge into Fatah's own terrorist arm, Black September. Here Abu Nidal was presumably exposed to the clandestine and shadowy world of Palestinian terrorism and its Arab state and international connections.

From this vantage point as well, al-Banna observed the growing tension between the Palestinian fedayeen and Jordan's King Hussein ibn Talal* who by 1969 was increasingly worried about the Palestinians' increasing independence within Jordan and Israel's retaliation for cross-border attacks. When the Jordanian-Palestinian confrontation came in September 1970 and Hussein pushed the PLO out of Jordan, Abu Nidal developed a hatred for the Hashemites that would follow him throughout his career. Although there is no evidence to support it, al-Banna's connection with Fatah intelligence may have brought him into contact with Black September during the early 1970s. This organization—responsible for major terrorist attacks against Jordanian, Israeli, and American targets—would have provided an ideal training ground for al-Banna's own terrorist operations a decade later.

By the early 1970s, al-Banna, although formally affiliated with Fatah, was beginning to strike out on his own. In 1971 he had taken up a position as head of the PLO's Higher Committee in Baghdad, where he quickly established a relationship with the Iraqi government and renewed his interest in Baathi ideology. Here Abu Nidal would begin the first of his three intimate associations with Arab regimes, which would support his operations over the course of a decade and a half.

There was nothing sentimental or mysterious about these relationships: They were rooted firmly in mutual self-interest. For the Iraqis—like Abu Nidal's future Syrian and Libyan patrons—Abu Nidal's organization would provide a useful vehicle to strike out at their opponents within the Palestinian community and in the Arab world. For Abu Nidal, the support and sanctuary provided by a rejectionist Arab regime offered him a powerful patron to maintain his own ideological extremism and provide him with sanctuary and support against his own adversaries. Although Salah Khalaf, a key Fatah official, would later claim that Abu Nidal did not represent an individual but a state, it would be inaccurate to see al-Banna as a simple Arab tool; rather, Abu Nidal saw and sought out these associations as vital to accomplishing his own objectives, and was willing to sacrifice some of his independence. Indeed, it is doubtful if he would have been able to survive without them. Moreover, Abu Nidal would play the inter-Arab game very successfully, never burning his bridges in one Arab capital without first securing a base of support in another.

The early 1970s would also witness Abu Nidal's formal break with the established Fatah and PLO leadership and a vendetta against Yasser Arafat* that constituted perhaps the most important influence on Abu Nidal's later activities. The original cause of the estrangement has never been clear; Abu Nidal claims that it originated as early as September 1970. Like many of the fissures within the Palestinian movement, tensions may have occurred as a result of personality conflicts or policy differences—perhaps both. In the early 1970s, the PLO remained a highly decentralized organization with numerous orientations and approaches within each constituent group. These fissures were even more apparent after Hussein's crackdown in 1970–1971, when the Palestinian movement entered a more diffuse underground phase as it struggled to regroup, redefine itself, and find a new base of operations.

It is likely that Abu Nidal, already in contact with one of Fatah's more militant factions, gravitated into an even more rejectionist orbit during his tenure in Baghdad. He may simply have been looking for a way to distinguish himself among the proliferation of Palestinian factions. In any event, capitalizing on his host's antipathy toward a PLO then allied with both Syria and Egypt, Abu Nidal appears to have gone into business on his own, forming his own group, and in September 1973 carrying out another attack on the Saudi embassy in Paris.

Relations between Fatah and Abu Nidal, who was soon to create his own group—''Fatah—The Revolutionary Council''—as a formal alternative to Arafat's Fatah, went rapidly downhill. Al-Banna was alarmed by Fatah's willingness to articulate a political strategy in the years following the 1973 October War and to distance itself formally from its previous terrorist operations. When Fatah officials discovered a plan to assassinate its top leadership (a plot in which Abu Nidal appears to have been implicated) there was no reason to sustain even the image of factional unity that had been so important to the Palestinian movement. For his involvement (which al-Banna continues to deny to this day), he was tried and sentenced to death in absentia. The break with Fatah now seemed irreparable.

Starting in the mid–1970s, al-Banna and his organization entered into a fairly predictable and consistent pattern, associating with Arab regimes that offered him sanctuary and supported his operations. From each of the capitals from which he would operate, Abu Nidal would try to accomplish four interrelated goals: building his own organization as the true heir to Fatah; pursuing terrorist activities as a self-sustaining rationale; creating a network of relations with a range of transnational terrorist groups to carry out these operations; and carrying on a war against Arafat's Fatah and any diplomatic efforts to resolve the Palestinian issue.

To a remarkable degree, these objectives also served the interests of each of his Arab state patrons. When his goals began to diverge, as they did in 1980 with Iraq and in 1986 with Syria, Abu Nidal was forced to find another sanctuary. Indeed, state patronage and the need for his services are critical elements in Abu Nidal's staying power. Similarly, Abu Nidal's association with his Arab patrons reflected the current level of tension between the PLO establishment and these regimes. During the period of greatest tension between Iraq and the PLO, Abu Nidal found a home in Baghdad; when Syria and Fatah were at odds, he operated out of Damascus. Given Libya's mercurical relations with the mainstream PLO and its commitment to a revolutionary brand of terrorism, Abu Nidal developed close ties with the Libyans, perhaps as early as the 1970s.

The years in which Abu Nidal operated out of Baghdad—roughly between 1973 and 1980—were spent creating a formal organization and conducting a variety of terrorist attacks, principally against Middle Eastern targets in the region. His choice of targets reflected in part the preferences of his patron. Consequently, much of Abu Nidal's effort was directed against Syria. In the wake of Syria's entry into Lebanon in June 1976 and its later confrontation with a variety of Palestinian groups, Abu Nidal went into action against Damascus. A number of operations were launched against Syria, including attacks on the Semiramis Hotel in Damascus, Syrian embassies in Rome and Islamabad, and the attempted assassination of the Syrian foreign minister in December 1976 and again in October 1977, all under the name of "Black June."

Typically, however, Abu Nidal also found a way to carry out his own objectives as well. Paradoxically, Israel was not his primary target during these years. Rather, this period would not only establish his credentials as an implacable foe of conservative Arab regimes, but also demonstrate his intense hatred for Palestinians interested even in the principle of formulating a political strategy to participate in Arab-Israeli negotiations. His anti-Fatah crusade was particularly virulent, and coincided with his Iraqi host's bitter disputes with Arafat for much of 1977 and 1978. Although the Camp David Accords would mitigate some of Baghdad's hostility as it tried to forge a united Iraqi-Syria-PLO front against Egypt, the flurry of diplomatic activity during this period also increased suspicion that Fatah was looking for a way into the negotiating process. Between January and June 1978, Abu Nidal's group claimed responsibility for the murder of three PLO representatives, one of whom, Said Hamammi, was known for his moderate views on Israel. For the rest of 1978 and much of 1979, not much was heard from Abu Nidal—a fact attributed to a heart attack he apparently suffered in early 1979.

By 1980, it appears that Abu Nidal, while not fully severing his ties with Baghdad, was in the process of shifting his base of operations to Damascus. The switch was extraordinary in many respects, not the least of which was Abu Nidal's previous attacks against Syrian targets, including the two assassination attempts against the Syrian foreign minister. However, the decision to move from Iraq was understandable given the shifting circumstances in the region. The Iraqis—increasingly preoccupied with the war with Iran and eager to solicit Western assistance—felt increasingly encumbered by Abu Nidal's presence and charges that it was supporting terrorism. The 1978 Baghdad summit had to some degree mended fences with the PLO and moderated the need for an active anti-Syrian strategy. Equally important, Syria sought a proven terrorist option for dealing with its opponents inside and outside the region. To Abu Nidal, Damascus offered access to Lebanon and a pool of Palestinian recruits, and a host whose relations with his number one enemy—Yasser Arafat—were increasingly strained.

Abu Nidal's sojourn in Syria between 1981 and 1985 coincided with a number of developments that would increase his utility to Syria and allow him to carry out his own agenda. Most important was the increasing rift and ultimate break-down in relations between Syrian president Hafez al-Assad* and Yasser Arafat. Syrian-PLO relations had always been complicated, set as they were against the backdrop of Syria's efforts to control the organization and Palestinian determi-nation to retain their independence. However, in the wake of the June 1982 Lebanon war, Arafat's public accusations that Syria had failed to support the Palestinians there, and Assad's opposition to close coordination between Jordan and the PLO, these ties deteriorated rapidly. Assad's support for the Fatah mutiny in the Bekaa valley and his decision to boot Arafat out of Damascus along with his efforts to drive Arafat's fighters from Lebanon pushed matters to a head.

What gave Abu Nidal centrality during this period was a flurry of inter-Arab and diplomatic activity in the peace process. The centerpiece of this activity was the evolving relationship between King Hussein of Jordan and Arafat. Assad saw a PLO focused on Amman, cooperating closely with Egypt, and jockeying for a role in the peace process, as a threat to his interests; Abu Nidal saw these developments as the latest and most insidious evidence of Arafat's betrayal of the Palestinian cause. This coincidence of interests would cement the Syrian–Abu Nidal connection until circumstances changed again.

King Hussein's decision to host the seventeenth session of the Palestine Na-tional Council in Amman in 1984 and to conclude an agreement with Arafat in February 1985 sparked a flurry of attacks by Abu Nidal against Jordanians and Palestinians. The attacks, ranging from the 1984 assassination of an exiled West Bank mayor recently appointed to the PLO's Executive Committee and a rocket attack against the Jordanian embassy in Rome in April 1985 to the murder of a Jordanian publisher in Athens in September 1985 were designed to send messages to both Hussein and Arafat. Abu Nidal saw an ideal opportunity to disrupt any Palestinian political coordination with Hussein, a logical first step into Palestinian accommodation with Israel. Syria saw an opportunity to use the Abu Nidal organization to demonstrate to Jordan that it was opposed to any unilateral moves on the Arab-Israeli peace process and that there were costs for close coordination with Arafat.

However, Abu Nidal's Syrian connection, like the Iraqi relationship, was not based on any permanent or unchangeable set of conditions. When circumstances began to change, as they did once again toward the end of 1985, Abu Nidal and the Syrians began to reexamine the utility of the connection. With the momentum of a Jordanian-PLO alignment sagging and the peace process at an impasse, Abu Nidal's importance as an anti-Jordanian surrogate diminished. Indeed, by 1986, after the Syrians had been implicated in an effort to blow up an Israeli airliner in London, Assad was increasingly sensitive to charges of Syrian support for terrorism. It is likely that Abu Nidal realized—as he had before—that it was necessary to develop another base of support.

By 1985, it appeared that Abu Nidal was already actively promoting his connection with Libya. This was not a new relationship. The early antecedents of Fatah's own terrorist organization, Black September, had had a Libyan connection, and it is likely that Abu Nidal maintained ties as well. Moreover, the move to Libya made sense. Libya's Muammar Qaddafi* was an avowed supporter of the more extreme Palestinian groups, and a bitter enemy of Israel, while his ties with the mainstream PLO had often been strained. Equally important, Qaddafi was not adverse to supporting terrorist operations in Europe—a theater in which Abu Nidal had expanded his operations after 1984. Indeed, in 1985 alone, two thirds of Abu Nidal's operations took place in Western Europe.

The Libyan connection may well prove to be Abu Nidal's most durable. Qaddafi's persistent pursuit of revolutionary goals and his hostility to Israel and Arab regimes interested in accommodation provide an environment well suited for Abu Nidal's own irredentist ambitions. Unlike Iraq and Syria, which appear to have been embarrassed by their associations with Abu Nidal, Libya has been surprisingly open about its Abu Nidal connection. Indeed, in September 1985, both the Libyan prime minister and Qaddafi himself met publicly with al-Banna.

While Abu Nidal's ties to various Arab states have shifted over the years, his ideology and political objectives have remained strikingly the same. As self-declared heir to Fatah's policies, Abu Nidal seeks to achieve the liberation of Palestine through armed struggle. However, unlike Fatah, which developed a relatively complex doctrine of armed struggle and political action with a view toward achieving a set of defined objectives that at times required some adjustment in approach, Abu Nidal pursues an open-ended, eschatological agenda that presumes to involve an eternal war against Zionism, Arab reaction, and Palestinian betrayal. Indeed, political ideology is subordinated to operations; armed struggle becomes not only the sole means to the end, but the end itself. Terrorism, not international recognition, Arab support, or even Palestinian grass-roots organization, is the primary vehicle for gaining legitimacy.

What is striking about Abu Nidal's ideology, however, is the way in which his theoretical objectives have been translated into practice. While in theory Zionism is the primary target, in practice the majority of Abu Nidal's sixty-some attacks over the past eight years have been directed at Palestinian and Arab targets. It is likely that this pattern reflected the simple fact that it was easier to strike out at Arabs than Israelis, as well as indicating the preferences of some of his Arab state patrons. However, it also reflected the intensity of Abu Nidal's hostility to those states and individuals whom he believed had betrayed the Palestinian cause. This was particularly true of his hatred of those in Arafat's Fatah organization who were willing to accept not only the need for a political strategy but the importance of an accommodation with Israel. Perhaps the most dramatic example of this was Abu Nidal's assassination of both Said Hammami and Isam Sartawi—both of whom played important roles in forging contracts with Israeli peace activists.

BIBLIOGRAPHY

Amos, John W. *Palestinian Resistance: Organization of a Nationalist Movement*. New York: Pergamon Press, 1980.

Melman, Yossi. *The Master Terrorist: True Story of Abu Nidal*. New York: Adama Books, 1986.

Miller, Aaron David. "The Man Who Loves to Kill Americans." *The Washington Post*, March 28, 1986.

AARON DAVID MILLER

MENACHEM BEGIN (1913–) has been one of the most significant leaders of Israel since its establishment. As prime minister (1977–1983) he personally conducted the country's foreign policy, leading first to the Camp David Accords in 1978 and then to the Egypt-Israel Peace Treaty in 1979. Other significant actions included Begin's support for a vigorous settlement of Jews on the West Bank, the annexation of the Golan Heights, the destruction of the Iraqi nuclear reactor near Baghdad, and finally the 1982 invasion of Lebanon. Begin's influence over the Israeli political system was not merely through his actions as Israel's prime minister, but also through his ability to articulate a general approach to Israel's problems, a right-wing philosophy that still prevails in many quarters.

Menachem Begin was born on August 16, 1913, in the city of Brest-Litovsk (now Brest in the Soviet Union). His father, Zeev Dov Begin, was an orthodox Jew as well as an ardent Zionist, who took an active role in the life of the city's large Jewish community. His mother, Hassia Korsovsky, came from a rabbinical family. Begin's education was diversified: he attended a Jewish elementary school and then a Polish secondary school, where he was sometimes a target of anti-Semitic attacks. At nine, Begin had already joined Hashomer Hatzair, the left-oriented Zionist youth organization, but at sixteen he left and became a member of the more fervently nationalist organization, Betar. His rise within Betar's ranks was meteoric: in 1938 Begin was appointed to head the organization in Poland, in effect commanding seventy thousand members.

When World War II erupted in September 1939, Begin, now a graduate of Warsaw University's School of Law, escaped to Vilna. There he was quickly arrested by the Soviet secret police; he was sentenced to eight years hard labor in Siberia for Zionist activity. However, following Hitler's assault on the Soviet Union, Begin was released by the Soviets in order to join the Polish army being formed in the USSR. In 1942 he arrived in Palestine as a soldier in General Anders's (Polish) army.

Begin was discharged from the army in December 1943. He immediately became commander of the radical underground organization in Palestine, the IZL or *Irgun Zvai Leumi* (National Military Organization, also known by its Hebrew acronym as *Etzel*, or simply the *Irgun*). The IZL disagreed with the policy of the *Yishuv* (Palestine's Jewish community), a policy that opposed a military challenge to the British authorities in Palestine as long as the war with Nazi Germany had not ended. On February 1, 1944, the Etzel under its new commander, Menachem Begin, proclaimed a revolt against Britain, trying to force it out of Palestine in order to establish a Jewish state on the western and eastern banks of the Jordan River.

Its maximalist ideological goals and the violent military tactics made Begin's IZL highly controversial in the eyes of the majority of the Yishuv. Although Begin tried to prevent violent clashes between his organization and other par-amilitary bodies within the Jewish community—activity that brought him universal acclaim within the Yishuv—the IZL's activity against the British (for example, the bombing of Jerusalem's King David Hotel on July 22, 1946) and the Arabs (for example, the assault on the Arab village of Deir-Yassin on April 9, 1948) was generally considered much less restrained. Some observers saw this activity as terrorism.

Ideologically, Begin represented the most radical nationalist position within the Yishuv. When the United Nations General Assembly decided on November 29, 1947, to partition Palestine into a Jewish and an Arab state, Begin and the IZL announced their opposition to the plan despite its endorsement by the political institutions of the Yishuv, led by David Ben-Gurion,* and the vast majority of the Jews in Palestine.

The IZL continued to hold to its position once the State of Israel came into being on May 14, 1948. The strained relations between the new state's institutions and the underground finally led to the bloody incident surrounding the ship *Altalena*. About a month after the establishment of Israel, in the midst of the UN-sponsored first Arab-Israeli cease-fire, the IZL tried to bring to Israel large amounts of weapons and ammunition, as well as nine hundred new recruits from Europe. Ben-Gurion, who suspected that the Etzel intended to rebel against his young government, ordered the army to shell the ship and sink it, which occurred on June 20, 1948. This dramatic incident brought the IZL chapter in Begin's life to an end.

Begin established the Herut (Freedom) Party in order to contest the parliamentary election of 1949. IZL veterans quickly became the dominant force within the party, with more moderate elements assuming peripheral positions. Herut's ideology emphasized territorial expansion and boldly called for the inclusion of Transjordan (later Jordan) in Israel. On all issues of foreign and defense policy, Herut was considered extremely hawkish, often finding itself outside Israel's national consensus. In 1952, Begin led the vigorous, and occasionally violent, party protest against the government's intention of negotiating a reparation agreement with West Germany. In 1956 he supported not only the military operation against Egypt (the Suez or Sinai campaign) but demanded that the war be expanded to include Jordan.

Nevertheless, with the departure of Ben-Gurion from the government in 1963, Herut's status as a legitimate political force started to rise in the eyes of the Israeli electorate. This process accelerated when Herut, under Begin, signed an agreement with the Liberals on April 1965 to form a new political bloc, *Gahal*. The leader of Gahal was Menachem Begin, and his acceptance by the Liberals signalled a new attitude of the middle class toward the hawkish, ex-IZL commander. The legitimation of Herut acquired further momentum when Begin joined, as a minister without portfolio, the national unity government formed a few days prior to the Six Day war.

Within the government, first under Levi Eshkol* and then under Golda Meir,* Begin sought to prevent negotiations with the Arab states that would lead to Israel's withdrawal from the West Bank and the Gaza Strip. When in 1970 the government accepted the U.S. initiative for peace talks with the Arabs, Begin took Gahal out of the government. In opposition, Begin became one of the most influential spokespeople in favor of the idea of greater Israel, first as leader of Gahal and then as leader of Likud.

Surprising almost all observers, Begin's Likud won the May 17, 1977, elections in Israel, ending a thirty-year period of Labor dominance of Israel's political scene. As prime minister, Begin not only applied Israeli law to the Golan Heights, but acted vigorously in order to guarantee the continuation of Israel's control over the West Bank and the Gaza Strip. Nevertheless, in September 1978, Begin signed the Camp David Accords with President Jimmy Carter of the United States and President Anwar al-Sadat* of Egypt, agreeing to return the Sinai Peninsula to Egyptian control and work toward a permanent solution for the West Bank and Gaza. The accords led to a full-fledged peace between Egypt and Israel, but proved less successful in producing a long-term solution for the Palestinian question.

In July 1981, Begin won another election. His victory reflected the fact that some of his most controversial decisions—notably the preelection decision to destroy the Iraqi nuclear reactor—were generally supported by the majority of Israeli voters, despite an almost universal condemnation abroad. The government ushered in by Begin following his 1981 victory reflected the growing hawkishness of the Israeli electorate: It included General Ariel Sharon as defense minister and Yitzhak Shamir* as foreign minister. Begin's second government initiated the unexpected annexation of the Golan Heights in December 1981, and, although it went through with the commitment to return the Sinai to Egypt, it authorized the invasion of Lebanon in early June 1982.

The Lebanon war was Begin's last major political act. The campaign met with general criticism abroad but also with significant protest at home. Begin found himself, for the first time since he had become prime minister, held responsible for a major political blunder.

Begin resigned as premier in September 1983, surprising even his closest advisers. He announced his decision to leave political life, generating tremendous speculation as to the reason. Some observers suggested that Begin was in the midst of serious depression, maintaining that Begin was a manic-depressive. Others suggested that in resigning, Begin was acting like a gentleman in accepting his responsibility for the Lebanese debacle and the failure to achieve his major political goal, the annexation of the West Bank and Gaza to Israel. Since his retirement, Menachem Begin has been living, secluded and politically uninvolved, in his Jerusalem apartment.

Throughout his political life, Menachem Begin represented the right wing of the Zionist movement and public opinion in Israel. During his period of political activity, stretching over more than fifty years, Begin remained loyal to an ideological framework developed in the era preceding the establishment of Israel by Vladimir (Zeev) Jabotinsky, one of Zionism's most important leaders. Jabotinsky's major political objective was the establishment of a Jewish state on both sides of the Jordan River. A fierce nationalist who did not believe in the possibility of Jewish-Arab accommodation, Jabotinsky advised his people to build a strong army and conquer the land through the force of arms. A gifted writer and a brilliant orator, Jabotinsky offered an alternative to Labor's myth of personal and national redemption through the establishment of a model society. Jabotinsky's myth was that of national grandeur: emphasis on military power, conquest, and territorial expansion. He dreamed poetically about the reemergence of *Malchut Israel*, the greater Kingdom of Israel.

Begin himself admitted that when he heard Jabotinsky's gospel, as a sixteen-year-old in Brest-Litovsk, he converted overnight and fully adopted it. However, Begin not only absorbed Jabotinsky's message but also changed it. In general, Begin radicalized and emotionalized the message. During the third Betar Congress in Warsaw in 1938, Begin, in an unprecedented challenge to Jabotinsky, called on the delegates to adopt military Zionism as their platform. Begin's trust of the world was considerably less than that of Jabotinsky, who was a devout Anglophile despite his disagreements with Britain's Palestine policy. Begin's emphasis on self-reliance was even stronger than Jabotinsky's. Even on the territorial issue, Begin's language carried an important nuance: For him, Greater Israel was not merely a political necessity but also a land belonging to the Jews by historical and even religious right. Begin unquestionably had a much more intimate link to Judaism as a religion than Jabotinsky, who was a secularist.

While Jabotinsky's ideology is generally known as Revisionism—his Revisionist movement tried to revise the political program of the Zionist majority, Begin's ideological legacy could be termed Neo-Revisionism. Although it rests, intellectually, on notions introduced by Jabotinsky, its emotional depth and fierce radical tone is Begin's. In some important ways, such as its fundamental mistrust of the world, Neo-Revisionism is not only different but even incompatible with the Revisionist tradition.

Begin's ideology was deeply influenced, as one would expect, by the life experience of Begin himself and that of his generation. It is fundamentally pessimistic, views the world as essentially anti-Semitic, and calls on the Jews to be entirely independent. Undoubtedly, the Holocaust is the center of gravity of Begin's ideology, a dominating, almost meta-historical event. Among the Neo-Revisionists, there is a tendency to see Israel's Arab problem as merely an extension of the fundamental problem of Jewish existence, the problem of anti-Semitism.

Despite its inherent pessimism, Begin's Neo-Revisionism is not entirely negative in content, it is a belief system with a powerful compensatory, positive element as well. Thus, Neo-Revisionism believes in total national power, it dreams about grandeur, it claims international recognition, and it desires full control over the nation's affairs. In brief, Neo-Revisionism, in whose development Begin contributed more than any other individual, should be looked on as a belief system composed on two different but connected images. The negative image focuses on powerlessness and victimization, conditions that reached culmination in the Holocaust, which the Neo-Revisionists view as an integral part of the Jewish condition in an almost metaphysical, ahistorical way. The positive image of the Neo-Revisionists is dominated by an effort to compensate for the negative image: Powerlessness is now translated into unlimited national power, victimization is transformed into victory over enemies, and total insecurity is converted into total security. Thus, in Begin's thought a Holocaust-fixated attitude was, almost organically, transformed into the pursuit of Greater Israel.

As a historical figure, Begin's importance was in the fact that through his policies, the West Bank (Judea and Samaria) and the Gaza Strip became, for most Israelis, part of what might be called their "cognitive map": Begin's policies of annexation, through settlement, land seizure, and other means, not only pushed Israel toward the crucial point of no return (where withdrawal from the West Bank would be simply impractical) but also significantly changed the perception of many Israelis as to the final disposition of the territories. Begin's commitment to the eventual annexation of Judea, Samaria, and Gaza could be regarded as the cornerstone of his foreign policy.

In general, Begin's territorial policy was loyal to Revisionism's traditional conception. In fact, the ideology served as the main basis for the policy, if not the only basis. Although Begin had doubts as to Israel's short-term ability to bring about a complete, open, de jure annexation of the territories, he took vigorous and consistent action to prevent the withdrawal of Israel from the areas. While he applied Israeli law to the Golan in December 1981, the agreement he reached with Egypt and the United States regarding the West Bank and Gaza guaranteed, at the very least, an Israeli veto over any permanent solution not to Israel's liking.

Regarding the Sinai Peninsula, Begin demonstrated from the very first days of his administration a substantially more flexible position. In the peace treaty with Egypt, signed March 26, 1979, Israel committed itself to return the entire Sinai. This seemingly inconsistent position could be explained ideologically and politically. In terms of ideology, the Zionist right (Jabotinsky and his supporters) had never formulated a territorial claim on the Sinai, while its commitment to the idea of *shlemut hamoledet* (the integrity of the motherland) in terms of Judea, Samaria, and Gaza was never in question. Opposition to any partition of *Eretz Israel* (Land of Israel) had always been the core belief of the Revisionists: In this sense, Begin's inflexible approach toward the West Bank and his flexible approach toward the Sinai were highly consistent, ideologically speaking.

Politically, Begin's agreement to return the Sinai meant the neutralization of Egypt as an anti-Israel, confrontational state. It therefore also meant the complete loss of a significant military option for the Arabs, a loss of ability to use military means to directly challenge Israel's continued domination of the West Bank. The Camp David Accords ought to be understood, therefore, not only as a diplomatic breakthrough leading to the first peace agreement between Israel and an Arab state. They must also be perceived as an understanding giving Begin the breathing space necessary to promote his policies on the West Bank. As for the East Bank, the Hashemite Kingdom of Jordan, an area over which Jabotinsky split with the rest of the Zionist leadership in 1922, Begin seemed to have arrived at the conclusion that, ideology aside, its acquisition was beyond Israel's capabilities.

In general, Begin's foreign policy could be seen as forming a comprehensible, logical whole only within the fundamentalist ideological context within which it operated. The policy was, on the whole, quite consistent with the prime minister's ideological commitments.

Begin's foreign policy could be divided into two distinct periods, which were unified by the persistent push toward an eventual annexation of the West Bank, but which were also significantly different in terms of operational style and personnel. The first period, 1977–1979, was characterized by relative moderation in terms of the pursuit of the prime minister's goals: Begin worked toward a long-term understanding with Egypt (through the Camp David process) so as to neutralize it as an active confrontation state and guarantee a free Israeli hand in determining the future of the occupied territories. This period saw the achievement of a number of great successes. Begin's foreign and defense policies were carried out during the initial period by ex-generals Moshe Dayan* and Chaim Weizmann,* but both of them resigned because of fundamental disagreements with Begin over policy issues. The second period, 1979–1983, was that of relative radicalism, at least as perceived by the international community. The Begin government—with Sharon as Defense Minister and Shamir as Foreign Minister—intensified the measures designed to control and eventually annex the West Bank. Furthermore, the Golan Heights and East Jerusalem were formally incorporated into Israel, and Lebanon was invaded.

During Begin's six-year tenure as Israel's prime minister, the reality and practice of maintaining control over the occupied territories also changed. In effect, Begin's foreign policy was implemented in two different yet complementary circles: the outer, diplomatic circle, where Begin successfully resisted any regional (mainly Egyptian) or international (mainly American) pressure for reaching an agreement on a West Bank, self-governing authority; and the inner, practical circle, where Begin tried and generally succeeded in neutralizing the opposition on the West Bank and in Israel itself to his annexationist policies.

Within the practical circle, Begin's government supported a few significant actions: (1) a vigorous settlement effort, which increased the number of Jews in the occupied territories from 3,200 to 28,400 and the number of Jewish settlements from 24 to 106 between 1977 and 1983; (2) the initiation of a new phase in the West Bank settlement activity, whereby Jewish settlements were established in central Samaria and at the Western Samaria foothills, close to and even inside major Arab population centers, with extensive political, organizational, and financial assistance of the government; (3) a concentrated effort to increase the Israeli control over land in the occupied territories, including a revision in the rationale for land acquisition (from military purpose under Labor to national rights under Likud, and finally to the massive seizure of property as "state land"); by 1983, when Begin resigned, more than 400,000 *dunams* (or quarter-acres) had already been taken, with a claim to millions of additional dunams publicly made; and (4) the establishment of a civilian administration for the occupied areas, an administration theoretically separated from the military authorities on November 8, 1981, as a signal for the transition from a temporary to a permanent system of Israeli domination.

In the international area, Begin's most important actions were the Camp David negotiations (successfully concluded on September 17, 1978); the peace treaty with Egypt leading to Israel's withdrawal from the Sinai, signed in April 1982; the destruction of the Iraqi nuclear reaction near Baghdad on June 7, 1981; the annexation of the Golan Heights on December 14, 1981; and, finally, the invasion of Lebanon on June 6, 1982. Of these actions, the first two were generally popular worldwide and also accepted by the great majority of Israelis. The other three were almost universally opposed throughout the world and vigorously challenged even in Israel itself.

Of all his policies, the invasion of Lebanon was and remains Begin's most controversial action. The goal of the operation was identified by Begin's supporters as the guaranteeing of the security of Israel's northern Galilee; Begin's detractors argued that the objectives were actually the destruction of Palestinian power in Lebanon, the establishment of new order in this country, and the imposition of Begin's will (particularly his autonomy plan) on the West Bank through the elimination of all independent Palestinian power bases.

From Begin's perspective, the Lebanon war was an unmitigated disaster. The power of the PLO as a political organization was not broken; the population on the West Bank not only remained loyal to Yasser Arafat* but intensified its commitment to the PLO; the Maronites failed in imposing their political will on Lebanon; Israeli morale, image, and consensus suffered as a direct result of the campaign, and so forth. It is no surprise that many observers linked the departure of Begin from political life to the Lebanon war.

On the whole, Menachem Begin was in many ways an effective leader of the Israeli right during the first thirty-five years of Israel's existence. A charismatic leader and capable orator, he maintained the zest of the nationalists in their long years in opposition. As prime minister he carried out vigorous policy designed to prevent eventual Israeli withdrawal from the occupied territories and guarantee their retention by Israel. Although he was unable to bring about the annexation of the West Bank and Gaza by Israel, he contributed significantly toward the attainment of that goal.

BIBLIOGRAPHY

Works by Begin:

The Revolt. Revised ed. New York: Nass, 1977.
White Nights: The Story of a Prisoner in Russia. New York: Harper & Row, 1979.

Other Works:

Freedman, Robert O. (ed.). *Israel in the Begin Era*. New York: Praeger, 1982.
Gavron, Daniel. *Israel after Begin*. New York: Houghton Mifflin, 1984.
Heydemann, Steven (ed.). *The Begin Era: Issues in Contemporary Israel*. Boulder: Westview, 1984.
Hirshler, Gertrude, and Lester S. Eckman. *From Fighter to Statesman: Menachem Begin*. New York: Shengold, 1979.
Hurwitz, Harry. *Menachem Begin*. Johannesburg: Jewish Herald, 1977.
Peleg, Ilan. *Begin's Foreign Policy, 1977–1983: Israel's Move to the Right*. Westport, Conn.: Greenwood, 1987.
Peleg, Ilan, and Ofira Seliktar (ed.). *The Emergence of a Binational Israel: The Second Republic in the Making*. Boulder: Westview, 1989.
Perlmutter, Amos. *The Life and Times of Menachem Begin*. Garden City, N.Y.: Doubleday, 1987.
Silver, Eric. *Begin: The Haunted Prophet*. New York: Random House, 1984.
Temko, Ned. *To Win or Die: A Personal Portrait of Menachem Begin*. New York: William Morrow, 1987.

ILAN PELEG

ZINE EL ABIDINE BEN ALI (1936–) became Tunisia's second president when he deposed the elderly and ailing Habib Bourguiba* on November 7, 1987. Prior to becoming president Ben Ali served in several positions where he was responsible for national security matters, including Director of Military Security, Secretary of State for National Security, and Minister of National Security. He entered political life through the Destourian Socialist Party where he rose to the position of Secretary General. Ben Ali's coming to power was more a "coup de constitution" that a "coup d'état." He had been named prime minister of Tunisia only five weeks earlier, and thus was the constitutionally ordained successor to Bourguiba. After receiving a report of seven medical doctors that confirmed Bourguiba's declining capacities, Ben Ali invoked Article 57 of the Tunisian constitution, which stated that the prime minister should immediately assume the presidency in the event of the president's "death, resignation or permanent inability." Ben Ali was a military man who came to power as a civilian, without brutality or violence. He treated Bourguiba with the respect owed to one of the Third World's greatest nation-builders.

Zine el Abidine Ben Ali was born in 1936 in Hammam Sousse, in the Sahel. After studying electrical engineering in Tunis, he graduated from the French military academy at Saint Cyr and attended the French artillery school at Chalons sur Marne. Initially pursuing a career as an artillery officer, Ben Ali continued his training at the U.S. Army's School of Field and Anti-Aircraft Artillery at Ft. Bliss, Texas. He soon transferred to intelligence, however, and completed the intelligence and military security course at Ft. Holabird, Maryland.

Returning to Tunisia in 1958, Ben Ali—then an officer in the Tunisian High Command staff—was appointed director of military security, a post he held for sixteen years. In 1974, Ben Ali began the first of what were to be two periods of "exile" after he reportedly criticized Bourguiba's decision to form a union with Muammar Qaddafi's* Libya. Several weeks later Bourguiba sent Ben Ali to the Tunisian embassy in Rabat to serve as military attaché.

Bourguiba revoked the agreement with Qaddafi only two months after signing it, and in 1977 Ben Ali was recalled to Tunis and appointed director general of national security. Within three years, however, he was again sent into exile, this time as Tunisian ambassador to Poland. Some sources claim this second exile was the result of a Libyan-backed raid on the southern Tunisian town of Gafsa by Tunisian rebels. Bourguiba, the argument runs, blamed Ben Ali for failing to foresee the Libyan incursion. Other sources claim then Prime Minister Mzali was behind Ben Ali's transfer. Still others believe that Ben Ali was simply the victim of the disfavor of Wassila Bourguiba, Habib Bourguiba's wife.

In January 1984, Tunisia was wracked by bread riots, and Ben Ali was brought back to Tunis to resume his position as head of national security. Nine months later, in October 1984, he was named secretary of state for national security; in October 1985, he became minister of national security; and in April 1986, he was appointed minister of the interior.

Although as a teenager Ben Ali was active in the Destourian youth movement (and served a brief jail sentence as a result), his first significant entry into the political ranks of the Destourian Socialist Party (PSD) came at the party's twelfth congress in June 1986, when he was appointed under secretary-general. On

October 2, 1987, Bourguiba appointed Ben Ali prime minister and secretary-general of the PSD.

Ben Ali's rapid rise after the 1984 bread riots attests to the importance that security issues (both internal and external) had come to play in Tunisian society. Previously, Bourguiba had gone to great lengths to keep military men far from politics. As minister of the interior, Ben Ali was responsible for monitoring the activities of the MTI (Islamic Tendency Movement) and other opposition groups. It was later revealed that during this period he cultivated contacts with Islamic leaders and Tunisian human-rights activists. Their favorable response to his accession to power would seem to confirm this.

When Ben Ali deposed Bourguiba and became president of Tunisia on November 7, 1987, he enjoyed the image of a technocrat with no long-standing ties to the PSD. He thus avoided association with the PSD's failures, its history of corruption, and the growing impression that it had become a stagnant institution. His practice of maintaining ties with the opposition while serving as Minister of the Interior, as well as the skillful way in which he brought about Bourguiba's removal, evidenced considerable political savvy.

The immediate catalyst for Ben Ali's action was his disagreement with Bourguiba over the outcome of the trial of a dozen Islamic activists. The activists had received a relatively lenient sentence, and Bourguiba demanded that Ben Ali call for their immediate retrial and insure that the new sentences were harsh. Ben Ali refused, fearing that a retrial, in addition to being of questionable legality, would spark violent disturbances. Faced with reports that the angered Bourguiba was about to replace him as prime minister, Ben Ali commissioned the medical report that justified his invocation of Article 57.

However, there were underlying reasons motivating Ben Ali. Tunisia had been obsessed with the question of succession at least since the late 1960s; as Bourguiba grew older and more feeble, the issue of succession loomed even larger. Moreover, the last decade of Bourguiba's rule was marked by a number of serious crises that threatened the national consensus he had forged in his early years of rule. As Bourguiba's physical and mental health began to fail, so did his vaunted ability to coopt the opposition, out-maneuver his foes, and inspire his people. By the end of his rule, Bourguiba was increasingly prone to using repressive measures to counter the country's mounting polarization. The result was a trend toward violence—by those with grievances, who had no other means of expression, as well as by government security forces, who feared a total breakdown in order.

Tunisia's once impressive economic growth began to deteriorate in the early 1980s as the result of a series of unsuccessful economic policies. By 1986, its economic problems had become acute: Foreign reserves were dwindling, the trade balance was chronically in deficit, oil income and tourism revenues were falling, and a series of bad harvests plagued Tunisian agriculture. Disparities in wealth, both among classes and among regions of the country, were creating growing discontent.

These economic problems were coupled with Bourguiba's authoritarianism and suppression of political expression. As a result, opposition forces began to resort to protest and violence: In January 1978, the General Union of Tunisian Workers (UGTT) staged a general nationwide strike, which quickly evolved into rioting by the urban poor; over one hundred people were killed before the army succeeded in suppressing the demonstrations. In January 1984, southern Tunisia was wracked by bread riots, as poor villagers protested the reduction of government food subsidies. Once again, the military was called in to restore order, but not before the protests had spread to Tunis.

One of the greatest beneficiaries of the economic hardship and the lack of outlets for political expression was the Islamic Tendency Movement (MTI). Founded officially in 1981 by Rachid Ghannouchi, and inspired by the Islamic Revolution in Iran, the MTI became a strong voice for social and economic justice. Adopting a nonrevolutionary program, the MTI developed a strong following among Tunisian youth, particularly in the universities. Nevertheless, it suffered the same fate as other opposition groups in Tunisia: Bourguiba had Ghannouchi and the rest of the MTI leadership arrested, forcing the group to go underground. This played into the hands of the more radical segments of the MTI, who were already more prone to espouse violence.

Ghannouchi was released from prison in 1984; but in 1987, Bourguiba launched a new campaign against the MTI, accusing it of favoring an overthrow of the government and the establishment of an Iranian-style Islamic regime. It was on these charges that Ghannouchi and eleven other MTI leaders were sentenced in the fall of 1987. It was Bourguiba's demand for harsher sentences that prompted Ben Ali to depose him.

The 1980s also witnessed a growing sense of external threat, deriving principally from Tunisia's neighbor, Muammar Qaddafi's Libya. In January 1980, Libya openly backed the raid on Gafsa by Tunisian rebels. In 1985, the two countries severed diplomatic relations after Libya expelled thousands of Tunisian guest workers. The Tunisians' sense of security was also undermined when Israel launched an air attack against PLO headquarters in a Tunis suburb in 1985.

Tunisians needed to confront their problems and debate solutions; it was clear that this would not be possible so long as Bourguiba remained at the helm. Until the 1980s Bourguiba had, for the most part, succeeded in suppressing opposition voices—both within and outside of the ruling party—through cooptation or imprisonment. These included former allies, such as Ahmed Mestiri, who became leader of the outlawed opposition party, the Democratic Socialist Movement (MDS), as well as the leaders of the UGTT and the MTI. However, as Tunisia's problems mounted, opposition forces became increasingly bold.

Moreover, throughout this decade of discontent and growing problems, Bourguiba evidenced increasing feebleness. His almost whimsical hirings and firings of prime ministers and other officials, and a succession of palace intrigues (many initiated by his wife, Wassila, who was ultimately "fired" herself via divorce), spoke of a growing leadership vacuum. Ben Ali's underlying motivation in deposing the "combattant supreme" was to fill this vacuum.

In a 1972 interview, Bourguiba said, "It will not be easy to replace a man like me" (*Le Monde*, November 8, 1987). This was all the more true given the tremendous number of political, economic, and social challenges that Bourguiba left his successor. Foremost among these, in the words of Ben Ali, was the need for "national reconciliation" (Tunis Radio Domestic Service, August 2, 1988). Thirty years after independence, Tunisia found itself torn by growing dissent spearheaded by the UGTT and the Islamists, a stagnating ruling party (which had actually lost ground to independent candidates in the 1981 and 1986 elections), continuing economic difficulties, and looming demographic pressures.

Ben Ali acted quickly. In his first address to the nation he announced pending changes in the constitution, including abolition of the presidency for life and automatic succession, "in which the people are not involved." Instead, presidents would be limited to three five-year terms and replaced only through popular election. He vowed to bolster democracy by opening the political system to parties other than the PSD and by declaring that "there is no room for repression and injustice" (*Le Monde*, November 8, 1987). In a gesture to Tunisia's Islamic heritage (and to the MTI), Ben Ali closed his address with a verse from the Koran.

Over the next several months, Ben Ali granted clemency to over four thousand political prisoners, abolished the state security court (whose constitutionality was questionable), launched a reconciliation process with the UGTT, and announced a new campaign against government corruption. In an effort to break with the past, he changed the name of the PSD to the Democratic Constitutional Rally (RCD); the cabinet he formed in April 1988 and reshuffled in July of that year included members without strong links to the PSD. Among them were younger technocrats, some of whom had links with the opposition. The new minister of public health, for example, had formerly been the head of the Tunisian Human Rights League, a group that had been highly critical of Bourguiba. At a special Congress of the RCD, held in July 1988, Ben Ali claimed that a multi-party system, free speech, and fair elections would lead ultimately to separation of party and state. In November 1988, on the first anniversary of his ascension to power, he announced early presidential and legislative elections for April 1989, and recognized two new opposition parties.

In foreign affairs, Ben Ali's early pronouncements pledged greater emphasis on Tunisia's relations with the Arab and Islamic worlds and his commitment to the elusive goal of Maghrib unity. He was one of the moving forces behind the establishment of the Arab Maghrib Union in early 1989. Ben Ali pursued a rapprochement with Qaddafi, and voiced strong support for the Palestinian movement and for the continued presence of both the PLO and the Arab League headquarters in Tunis. He also reaffirmed Tunisia's traditionally close ties to the United States and Western Europe.

Ben Ali's "constitutional coup" was welcomed almost unanimously among Tunisians. Opposition forces in particular were encouraged by his conciliatory words and actions, such as the releasing of political detainees. Even the MTI, which during Bourguiba's last years in power had suffered severe repression, was cautiously optimistic.

Indeed, reconciliation with Tunisia's Islamic forces was one of Ben Ali's principal early goals. It was not difficult for Ben Ali to initiate the reconciliation process, since his predecessor had been so stridently secular. Ben Ali could thus assuage the Islamists by symbolic measures alone, such as declaring publicly that "Islam is the most prominent factor that unites Tunisia," by ordering the state radio to broadcast the daily call to prayer, and by making a religious pilgrimmage to Saudi Arabia. Ben Ali also took tangible steps such as establishing a new university for religious education.

At the same time, Ben Ali declared that Islam must not be "a cause of rifts, conflicts, fanaticism, or extremism" (Foreign Broadcast Information Service, August 28, 1988). The new Political Parties Law, which the Tunisian Parliament promulgated in the summer of 1988, forbade any party from claiming to be the sole representative of Islam or from using Islam in its name. The MTI would thus have to change its name and behave as any other party if it wished to participate in a multiparty system.

Ben Ali's early reforms reflected both his commitment to a more pluralistic and open system and his conception of Tunisian security. During his rise through the ranks of the international security system, Ben Ali had become convinced that Tunisia's future security and stability depended on a new national consensus among the various groups that Bourguiba had alienated, a sharing of political power and increased outlets for political expression, and a greater emphasis on Tunisia's Islamic and Arab roots. It was this conviction as much as anything else that prompted his initial reforms; the fact that these reforms were so popularly received indicated the degree to which virtually the entire Tunisia political spectrum desired change.

Ben Ali introduced to Tunisians a new style of leadership in sharp contrast to that of Bourguiba. Determined to keep his finger on the country's pulse, he periodically paid unannounced visits to poor and working-class neighborhoods during his first year in office, and initiated personal contact with exiled opposition activists. Ben Ali involved a greater number of Tunisians in the decision-making process. He established a National Security Council to advise him on foreign policy and defense issues, and several presidential commissions to investigate such issues as press reform.

Any new leader as widely welcomed as Ben Ali can indulge in a honeymoon period in which reforms are relatively easy to carry out and favorably received. However, honeymoons ultimately come to an end; the new leader must then address the country's more serious, devisive, and long-term problems. For Ben Ali, these problems are mostly structural economic ones: chronic balance of payments deficits; a shortage of foreign exchange; un- and underemployment; a system of inefficient government subsidies and price controls; and a dependence on international financial support. They are compounded by demographic problems: a birth rate that, while declining, is still producing more people than there are jobs; continued rural-urban migration; and a growing class of disaffected university educated youth seeking meaningful employment.

None of these problems will be easy to solve, yet Ben Ali's long-term success will depend on his ability and willingness to confront them. The initial steps he took to open the political system, if fully carried out, will help insure that these issues will be debated.

BIBLIOGRAPHY

de la Gueriviere, Jean. "M. Ben Ali: Un homme d'ordre ouvert au dialogue." *Le Monde*, Sunday, November 8, 1987, p. 3.
"Un entretien avec le president tunisien Ben Ali." *Le Monde*, September 10, 1988, pp. 1–2.
Gharbi, Samir, and François Soudan. "Bourguiba C'est Fini: Ca Succession C'est Reglé." *Jeune Afrique*, November 18, 1987, pp. 26–57.
Moore, Clement Henry. "Tunisia and Bourguibisme: Twenty Years of Crisis." *Third World Quarterly* (January 1988); 176–190.
———. "La Tunisie après vingt ans de crise de succession." *Maghreb-Machrek* (Summer 1988); pp. 5–15.
Ouertani, Mustapha. "Kurzbiographien: Zine el-Abidine Ben Ali." *Orient* (September 1987); 297–302.
Perkins, Kenneth J. *Tunisia: Crossroads of the Islamic and European Worlds*. Boulder, Colo.: Westview Press, 1986.
Vandewalle, Dirk. "From the New State to the New Era: Toward a Second Republic in Tunisia." *Middle East Journal* (Autumn 1988); pp. 602–620.
Ware, L. B. *Tunisia in the Post-Bourguiba Era*. Montgomery, Ala.: Air University Press, 1986.
———. "Ben Ali's Constitutional Coup in Tunisia." *Middle East Journal* (Autumn 1988); pp. 587–601.

WILLIAM MARK HABEEB

AHMED BEN BELLA (1918–), one of the nine "historic chiefs" who launched the Algerian revolution, went on in 1962 to become the first president of the Peoples Democratic Republic of Algeria until ousted in a coup in 1965. He was born on December 25, 1918, to a peasant family of seven children at Maghnia, a small town near the Moroccan frontier. While the family's ownership of a rocky, thirty-hectare farm placed it in a distinctly better position than that of the bulk of Algerian peasantry, its material situation was nevertheless modest.

Ben Bella retained largely positive memories of his childhood at Maghnia and of the French-staffed elementary school he attended there. A promising pupil, his father sent him on to *lycée* (high school) in the district capital of Tlemcen, where he lodged with family friends. It was at Tlemcen that Ben Bella first became conscious of the wide gulf separating Europeans from native Algerians and where he encountered for the first time the multitude of discriminatory attitudes and practices designed to assure the subordination of the native population to the *colons* (settlers). Being of athletic physique and inclination, he worked out much of his frustration and hostility playing soccer, a sport in which he gradually became something of a star. At the age of fifteen, however, he failed his *brevet* (diploma) examination, dropped out of school, and returned to Maghnia where he helped his father on the farm, worked for a time as an insurance company secretary, and played a great deal more soccer.

Drafted into the army in 1937, Ben Bella attended noncommissioned officers school and rose to the rank of sergeant. The camaraderie of barracks life, the exposure to a system that recognized and rewarded performance, and the acceptance accorded him by metropolitan Frenchmen in spite of his race and religion, all made a deep impression on the young Algerian. Awarded the *Croix de Guerre* in 1940, he was demobilized after the fall of France and returned to Maghnia. Because his father and two surviving brothers had recently died, he spent the next years attending to the family farm, a backbreaking physical experience that deepened his appreciation for the lot of Algerian peasantry. Returning to the colors in 1943, he served with valor in some of the most savage fighting of the Italian campaign, received four citations, and was eventually decorated with the *Médaille militaire* by General Charles de Gaulle himself. As the war drew to a close, Ben Bella's superiors urged him to consider a military career, offering as inducement the opportunity to attend officer candidate school. At this point, however, the May 1945 massacre at Sétif convinced him that in spite of the personal satisfactions of such a course, the philosophical and moral impediments to a life of service to France were too great.

Returning to Maghnia, Ben Bella won a seat on the Municipal Council as a candidate of the *Mouvement pour le Triomphe des Libertés Démocratiques* (MTLD). The quasi-Marxist MTLD, with its earliest roots among the Algerian proletariat of France, was the most popular and most militantly nationalist of the parties then competing for native Algerian loyalties. As a municipal councilman, Ben Bella incurred the antipathy of his European colleagues by refusing to allow them to monopolize the town's administrative offices and by attracting large numbers of local Muslims into the suspect MTLD. According to Ben Bella, the Europeans retaliated by providing a total stranger with manufactured documentation and inciting him to claim and occupy Ben Bella's ancestral farm. Legal recourse under the circumstances being fruitless, Ben Bella physically evicted the occupants and subsequently shot and wounded one of them. At the age of twenty-eight, Ben Bella's foray into the politics of late colonial Algeria had ended.

In 1947, Ben Bella fled to Algiers, assumed a false identity, and joined the *Organisation Spéciale* (OS), a clandestine appendage of the MTLD, which was planning for direct action against the colonial regime. As a result of increasingly blatant French manipulation of the electoral process and colon determination to block even the most minimal reforms, Ben Bella was convinced that the only road to liberation lay through revolutionary action. He felt increasing contempt for the politicians of the MTLD, who continued to squabble among themselves for access to the few benefits an inherently unjust system accorded to those who would play the game.

Ben Bella soon came to head the OS, helped to organize its most celebrated accomplishment, the February 1950 attack on the Oran Post Office, and was subsequently arrested and condemned to eight years' imprisonment. With aid from militants outside, he and OS companion Ahmed Mahsas escaped from the Blida prison in spring 1952. After going underground in Algiers and Paris, Ben Bella arrived virtually penniless in Cairo in 1953, where he and former OS members Mohammed Khider and Hocine Ait Ahmed began to plead Algeria's cause with the increasingly Pan-Arabist regime of Gamal Abdul Nasser.*

Dialogue with the Egyptians was slowed by ideological, tactical, and even linguistic differences. When Ben Bella first spoke to the Arab League about his cause, he had to do so in French. Eventually, however, the Egyptians agreed to help subsidize a revolution once the Algerians should launch it. The timing of the insurrection on November 1, 1954, was determined by internal members of the *Comité révolutionaire d'unité et d'action* (CRUA), who communicated the order to their three external colleagues of the Cairo delegation. During the next two years, Ben Bella traveled extensively between Cairo, Italy, Libya, and ultimately Tunisia and Morocco, performing a variety of diplomatic functions and arranging arms shipments to the *maquisards* (guerrillas).

It is unclear whether Ben Bella could not or would not attend the clandestine Congress of the FLN (National Liberation Front) held in the Soummam Valley in August 1956. At any rate, many interior leaders blamed him for shortages of guns and money, and expressed misgivings about behind-the-scenes negotiations he was known to be conducting with the French. As it broadened the FLN leadership to include most major political tendencies in Algeria, the Congress emphatically affirmed the primacy of the internal over the external leadership, and the principle of collegial decision making, for which purpose it created a broad-based Conseil National de la Révolution Algérienne (CNRA). Looking back at these decisions from the 1960s, Ben Bella expressed great pride in his achievements as a gunrunner and deplored the admission into the FLN's inner circles of the political class that had preferred self-serving political games with the French to armed struggle. Once admitted to the revolutionary leadership, these individuals, in his view, created a bureaucratic apparatus that diverged increasingly from the realities of the independence struggle, sowed confusion and contradiction, and were responsible for catastrophic mistakes like the Battle of Algiers and the abandonment of the interior *wilayas* (military districts), which turned them into autarchic fiefdoms.

By the fall of 1956, repeated contracts with representatives of Premier Guy Mollet's Socialist Party had resulted in a tentative agreement on a negotiated settlement, which Ben Bella and other "externals" determined should be discussed with the governments of Morocco and Tunisia before final approval. On October 22, a DC–3 carrying Ben Bella, Ait Ahmed, Mohammed Khider, Mohammed Boudiaf, and Moustapha Lacheraf from Rabat to Tunis was forced down at Algiers. The flight was presumably diverted on orders of Governor General Robert Lacoste in order to sabotage any negotiated settlement. A politically vulnerable Premier Mollet acquiesced, and Ben Bella was incarcerated for the next five and a half years.

The most physically difficult years for the prisoners were those spent at La Santé in Paris, but beginning in March 1959, they occupied a series of more comfortable accommodations, ending with the commodious Château d'Aulnoy. While in prison, Ben Bella read innumerable issues of *Les Temps Modernes* and *France Football*, more than seven hundred books—mainly on Arab history and socialist thought—and devoted much time to improving his literary Arabic.

In the meantime, direction of the Algerian struggle and the subsequent peace negotiations devolved on others, some of whom had expressed dissatisfaction with Ben Bella's style and contributions even before his imprisonment, and who were not totally despondent at having the impulsive and strong-willed peasant's son out of the way. Throughout the prison years, however, Ben Bella and his prison-mates remained formal members of the CNRA and were accorded honorary membership on its executive committee as well as portfolios within the Provisional Government (GPRA). While Ben Bella was able to communicate intermittently with the FLN leadership, the major responsibility for the decisions of this difficult period lay with the heterogenous, often fractious, active membership of these bodies. As the years went by, the fissures dividing constituent elements of the FLN became increasingly apparent. Moderate reformist politicians of the Ferhat Abbas* tradition competed with radicals of the MTLD tradition. Former OS and other revolutionary activists resented both. Politicians and the military mistrusted each other, while the military itself was divided among the externally based National Liberation Army (ALN) and various of the mostly independent wilaya commands of the interior.

Aided by the fact that he and his fellow prisoners had remained largely untainted by the infighting, errors, and compromises of the later war years, Ben Bella, upon his release from Aulnoy in March 1962, set about trying to restore his weakened leadership position. At the Tripoli Congress of the CNRA, which was convened just before the referendum on Algerian independence, Ben Bella won adoption of a political program sharply critical of the stewardship of the GPRA and looking in general terms toward a centralized socialist model of Algerian development. He also sought approval of a list of nominations to a party Political Bureau which was to supplant the GPRA as the supreme authority in the country. That list, dominated by himself and the four other recently released prisoners, included none of the prominent men who over the past six years had borne the burden of the struggle. The Congress refused to ratify the nominations and broke up in disarray.

Ben Bella and Mohammed Khider then allied with Houari Boumediene,* chief of the General Staff of the ALN, who had his own grievance against the GPRA; with the leaders of the frontier wilayas geographically close to the ALN, and with the key reformist politicians who were angry at having been pushed out of the GPRA the preceding year by former MTLD politicians. As independence dawned, Ben Bella's coalition installed itself at Tlemcen in direct challenge to the GPRA and its supporters, who were headquartered at Tizi Ouzou and Algiers. After two months of negotiations, military maneuvers, and civil conflict, the Ben Bella coalition prevailed. A National Constituent Assembly elected from a single list prepared by the Political Bureau chose Ben Bella as president of the Algerian Republic, an office he formally assumed on September 28, 1962.

Ben Bella could have chosen to use institutions such as the National Assembly, labor and other national organizations, and the various party organs as vehicles for attempting to integrate the diverse elements into the nascent political system. Instead, he chose to concentrate increasingly more power into his own hands, gradually excluding from positive political participation the enormous majority of men whose efforts had made Algerian independence possible.

Some observers have ascribed this taste for personal power to personality traits already evident in Ben Bella's school days. From a variety of his own pronouncements it is also clear that Ben Bella's earliest experiences in politics gave him an almost visceral contempt for politicians, political debate, and the processes of accommodation. His oft-expressed concern for the condition of the Algerian peasantry was no doubt genuine, although his propensity to identify his own political and economic vision with theirs bore a mark of naiveté if not arrogance.

Standing athwart the road to consolidation of power were forces both inside and outside Ben Bella's government. Outside the government stood potentially dangerous dissident forces in the Kabylie, Constantinois, and the south; national organizations such as the student and labor movements; and the National Constituent Assembly, which contained, along with many hand-picked Ben-Bellists, major representation of the disparate factions of which the Tlemcen group had been composed. The composition of the government itself also tended to represent the make-up of the coalition on which Ben Bella's rise had depended, including especially Houari Boumediene, minister of defense, and Mohammed Khider, secretary general of the FLN, the key engineers of his rise to power.

During early 1963, Ben Bella, aided by Khider, succeeded in subordinating the Algerian Labor Federation (UGTA) to the party. Next they won control of the financially powerful Fédération de France du Front de Libération nationale. Khider, in the meantime, was significantly strengthening his hold over the party apparatus, whose primary function, he asserted with increasing force, was to serve as a monitor of government activity. Tensions between him and the head of that government mounted rapidly, until in April 1963, Ben Bella was able to force his resignation as secretary general and to assume the leadership of the party himself. As far as Ben Bella was concerned, checks, balances, and diversity of opinion were luxuries Algeria could ill afford and that "the people" would not tolerate.

The power play against Khider triggered a wave of defections of early revolutionaries, culminating in the arrest of former prison companion Mohammed
Boudiaf and the July 9, 1963, announcement by Hocine Ait Ahmed that he and
other militants would mount an open fight against the government.

In the meantime, the National Constituent Assembly, presided over by the
prestigious Ferhat Abbas, had engaged regularly in debates featuring some very
explicit criticism of the government. The majority of the Assembly seem to have
believed that it was their function not only to monitor government but also to
elaborate and approve a constitution defining the key power relationships within
government and among government, the party, and other organizations. Against
these Assembly conceptions, Ben Bella repeatedly opposed his notion of the
supremacy of the party. Since at this time the party hardly existed as a functioning
entity, when Ben Bella invoked the party's name, he was actually referring to
the Political Bureau, which consisted of five men in fall of 1962 and only three
by the time of Khider's departure.

The showdown materialized in August 1963, when the president submitted
for Assembly approval a constitution drafted by the Political Bureau and rubber-
stamped by a largely handpicked assemblage of party faithful convened in an
Algiers cinema. When Abbas resigned his position rather than submit, Ben Bella
expelled him from the party. That expulsion was a prelude to exclusion from
the parliament of the most active members of the opposition, and this initiated
a drastic further narrowing of political participation. Ben Bella's next government, selected in September, was far less representative than his first.

A major contradiction resulted from Ben Bella's centralization of authority:
Many excluded leaders joined or threatened to join the still simmering resistance
centered on the dissident wilayas. The threat of armed resistance, which became
actual in fall 1963 and again during the summer of 1964, in turn increased Ben
Bella's dependence on his minister of defense and the regular army.

Internationally, Ben Bella's regime became noteworthy for its vigourous support of African and other Third World liberation issues, and also for the attempt
to endow Algeria with a decentralized, Trotskyite model of socialism (*autogestion*). This putatively democratic socialism is most clearly illustrated by the
March Decrees of 1963 which sequestered an enormous amount of vacant French
property, mandated the establishment of worker management assemblies on farms
and in factories, and established the principle of worker profit sharing. While
autogestion was to some extent a recognition of the existing situation, the particular form of these institutions was the creation of a group of largely foreign,
Trotskyite advisers. While Ben Bella always believed autogestion to be his finest
achievement, the irony is that his predilection for centralization of authority
would from the beginning deny most self-managed units the resources and freedom of action they required to be other than state appendages.

Beneath the surface of the first Congress of the FLN, convened in April 1964,
lurked the ill-concealed tension between Houari Boumediene and Ahmed Ben
Bella. That tension expressed itself in two major ways. The first was in ideo-

logical debate over the uncompromisingly Marxist tone and foreign origin of the proposals submitted to the Congress by the Political Bureau. The defense minister, with approval of the *ulama* (religious leaders) present, argued for greater emphasis upon Arabo-Islamic precedents. The second area of conflict lay in Ben Bella's proposal for the creation of popular militias, with which he presumably intended to undermine the military monopoly of force. The army was resolutely opposed to militias, but in the end permitted a compromise according to which these would fall under army control in the event of war.

During the ensuing year, tension between the president and Boumediene expressed itself in conflict and rumors of conflict between Ben Bella and military members of the cabinet. It also expressed itself in attempts by Ben Bella to negotiate with and rehabilitate military dissidents in the interior wilayas as a counterweight to Boumediene's forces.

While, by June 1965, Ben Bella enjoyed enormous prestige on the international scene, he had maneuvered himself domestically into a situation of precarious isolation. Early in the morning of June 19, as Boumediene's army moved swiftly to take over the country, a unit under the personal command of Chief of Staff Tahar Zbiri descended on the president's residence and arrested him while he was still in bed. Although Ben Bella was thought to be immensely popular among the masses, his deposition elicited almost no popular reaction; as for Algeria's political elite, they were almost unanimous in applauding his overthrow. Houari Boumediene and the Council of the Revolution accused him of mismanaging the economy, turning capricious personal power into a system of government, discrediting the real militants of the revolution, and imposing on the people a foreign-inspired brand of socialism inconsistent with their Islamic heritage.

Looking back on the coup in 1981, Ben Bella, for his part, believed that his overthrow was inevitable because he had moved too far too rapidly; if Boumediene had not been there, another man would have played his part. Asked by journalists if he had any regrets about the conduct of his presidency, Ben Bella responded that "the principal one was in not having gone far enough, for example by not taking advantage of the autogestion program to arm the people." He admitted that he had in fact succumbed to the temptation of Bonapartism, but said that his greatest error had lain in enthroning the single party which in Algeria and many other countries had proven to be the "single evil" (1982:59).

Ben Bella spent the entire Boumediene era under detention. For the first six years he was held in total isolation under surveillance of television cameras. Ben Bella claims that in order to maintain his sanity he had long conversations with himself in the mirror and read aloud by the hour from the Qur'an. In 1971 his mother arranged his marriage to the leftist journalist Zohra Sellami, who thereafter shared the Moorish style residence in Douéra where he was confined and provided him with some indirect contact with the outer world. In July 1979, Chadli Bendjedid* released Ben Bella to house detention in the out-of-the-way town of Msila, and finally, on the occasion of the twenty-sixth anniversary of the Algerian Revolution, freed him. To the consternation of security forces, Ben Bella began traveling the country, renewing old contacts and making new ones; after a brief stay in Algiers, where he was offered and declined a "golden retirement," he left the country and went into opposition.

Those who had known the old Ben Bella were astounded at his repudiation of the one-party system he had so self-confidently imposed on Algeria. They were equally astounded by the fervor with which this hero of the Soviet Union and holder of the Lenin Medal came out expounding social and economic paradigms he called Islamic. In an interesting blend of Islamic thought on the cultural side and dependency school analysis on the economic side, Ben Bella espoused a Pan-Islamic future in which the social solidarity of Islam would be reinforced by an economic base grounded in agricultural self-sufficiency and light industry—a combination that would free Muslim peoples from dependency on the core economies. The instrument for achieving these economic goals would be a multitude of autogestion units that would inescapably lead at the political level to a kind of "*auto-gouvernement.*" By trying to achieve economic self-sufficiency through heavy industrial development financed with hydrocarbon exports, Algerian leaders, in Ben Bella's view, had destroyed the country's agriculture, ended up with neither agriculture nor viable manufacturing, and produced a demoralized population increasingly out of touch with the great spiritual and ethical resources that are its heritage.

After going into exile, Ben Bella settled in Paris, but when the French police started monitoring his activities too closely, he moved his residence to Switzerland in 1983. In May 1982, he launched the French-language monthly *El Badil* (The Alternative), which attracted a considerable readership among the European émigré population. In May 1984 he founded the Mouvement pour la démocratie en Algérie (Movement for Democracy in Algeria) to popularize his views. In December of the next year, he joined the secular Hocine Ait Ahmed in London in calling for a unified opposition based on a "return to the founding ideals of the Algerian Revolution," respect for human rights, political pluralism, recognition of the Berber language as official on the same basis as Arabic, the separation of powers, and the election of a constituent assembly (*Jeune Afrique*, January 8, 1986, p. 42).

Ben Bella was a dedicated and energetic leader who felt deeply the pain and the shame to which the colonial system subjected the ordinary Algerian citizen. It is possible, however, that the inadequacy of his formal education left Ben Bella without the firm intellectual grounding necessary to evaluate the range of ideological formulations swirling about him and still less their relationship to the objective needs of his people. In place of a solid intellectual and ideological underpinning, he substituted a disarming confidence in his own abilities and analyses that hampered his ability to cooperate effectively with other elements of the political elite and that in the long run invited his own overthrow.

BIBLIOGRAPHY

Works by Ben Bella:

Ben Bella revient. Paris: Jean Picollec, 1982.
Min Zulamat al Sijn min Nur al Islam. Jerusalem: Wakalat Abu Arafah, 1982.

Other Works:

Gordon, David C. *The Passing of French Algeria*. London: Oxford University Press, 1966.
Humbaraci, Arslan. *Algeria: A Revolution That Failed*. New York: Praeger, 1966.
Merle, Robert. *Ahmed Ben Bella*. Paris: Gallimard, 1965.
Ottaway, David, and Marina Ottaway. *Algeria. The Politics of a Socialist Revolution*. Berkeley, Calif., and Los Angeles: University of California Press, 1970.
Quandt, William B. *Revolution and Political Leadership: Algeria, 1954–1968*. Cambridge, Mass.: M.I.T., 1969.

JOHN RUEDY

CHADLI BENDJEDID (1925–), Algeria's third president, has ruled since February 1979, when he was chosen by the Council of the Revolution to succeed Houari Boumediene,* who had succumbed to a rare blood disease in late 1978. Bendjedid, like Boumediene, was a respected career military officer, but was not well known beyond military circles at the time when he was selected for his country's highest office. For nearly a decade, his presidency was characterized by an improvement in Algeria's economic performance, stability and gradual political liberalization within the country, some reorientation of the country's foreign policy toward the immediate North African region, and continued emphasis on pragmatic, responsible problem solving, both at home and abroad. Riots in October 1988, however, were the worst in Algeria's modern history, and may result in radical changes in the presidency and other national political institutions.

Chadli Bendjedid was bórn on April 14, 1929, in the *Wilaya* (district) of Annaba to a farming family of modest means. As a youth, he became involved in independence activities, and in 1954, he joined the Armée Nationale Populaire (ANP), the professional army operating from the frontiers of Tunisia and Morocco.

Bendjedid rose quickly in the military, and was named head of a military region in his first year. In 1958, he was promoted to deputy commander of a larger unit, and in 1960 he was named commander of a battalion near the Tunisian border. The following two years, the last in the war against the French, he was chief of operations in Ghardimaou, Tunisia. During these years, one of his colleagues was Houari Boumediene, who played a part in his promotions. Bendjedid was not identified as part of a particular clan or clique around a senior personality, but was a respected if low-key officer, with the rank of major.

On the eve of independence, Algeria's two main fighting forces, the guerrillas and the professional army, turned on each other, and the country was effectively in a state of civil war. Bendjedid was arrested by the guerrillas and imprisoned. When the professional army, which was under Boumediene's command and linked politically with the FLN (National Liberation Front—the country's single political party) and Ahmed Ben Bella* (soon to become Algeria's first president), prevailed both over the guerrillas and the GPRA (the Provisional Government that negotiated the cease-fire and peace terms with France), Bendjedid's career was back on track. His solid reputation and association with Boumediene, President Ben Bella's choice as the country's first defense minister, led to steady advancement. In late 1962, he was named military commander of Constantine. In June 1964, he was transferred to command the Oran military district, where his popularity with both the civilian and military communities was noted. He remained in this position, with no national visibility, throughout the Boumediene presidency, which ended with the president's sudden death from a grave illness in December 1978. In a study of Algeria's socialist revolution, Bendjedid was described as "a minor political figure and a loyal officer of the ANP" (Ottaway and Ottaway, *Algeria: The Politics of a Socialist Revolution*, p. 302).

Boumediene had placed high priority on collegial leadership, and the Council of the Revolution, comprised of key military officers and some senior civilians, was the formal body for collective decision making. As commander of one of the country's five military districts, Bendjedid was a member of the Council. Thus he was party to the secret deliberations on the succession process that took place in late 1978 when the president's grave condition was discovered. Although the Algerian constitution provided for a vice president, Boumediene had never filled the position, and the task of designating a candidate to stand for elections to succeed the president was left to the political dynamics of the Council.

Western depictions of the leadership struggle emphasize ideological cleavages between the two known contenders, Mohamed Salah Yahiaoui, a military man and FLN Central Committee member, and Abdelaziz Bouteflicka, the country's activist foreign minister since 1963. The secret struggle was portrayed in the foreign media as a choice between the radical, Arab-oriented Yahiaoui, and the more Western-oriented Bouteflicka. Algerian sources, usually wary of ideological explanations explanations for political developments, stress instead a clash of personalities that deadlocked the Council over who should be named to succeed Boumediene.

It was in the context of protracted uncertainty that Bendjedid, who did not seek the job, emerged as a compromise candidate. His career had been beyond reproach; the only negative issue raised in public was reports of his family and associates becoming enriched during his long tenure as commander in Oran. Bendjedid was formally nominated as the sole presidential candidate by the Fourth Party Congress in January 1979, and elections were held in February. In an interview soon after his election, Bendjedid committed himself to continuing the revolution and demonstrating loyalty to the National Charter and to the late president.

Complementing his early economic initiatives were several political liberalization measures: he released some prominent political prisoners, allowed exiled dissidents to return, cancelled the onerous exit-visa policy for all citizens, lowered taxes, and reduced restrictions on private property ownership. Of particular note was Bendjedid's decision to name a prime minister, the first since independence; he chose Colonel Muhammed Ben Ahmed Abdelghani. This post was later made obligatory by constitutional amendments adopted by the National Assembly in mid–1979.

However, despite the change in tone, Bendjedid remained firmly in control of the instruments of power. In 1980, he instituted a streamlining of the FLN, which strengthened his control over it. He used the party as an advisory body, and retained the right to select members of the FLN political bureau.

Bendjedid did not hesitate to use force when dissident groups, including students and Berber and Islamic activists, took to the streets in the early 1980s. An anticorruption campaign, begun in the context of cleaning up the capital for the 1979 commemorations of the revolution, also served to intimidate any potential opposition; and numerous arrests of former officials on charges of financial mismanagement occurred in his first year in office. His approach to political liberalization was a gradual one.

In his first term, Bendjedid did not launch major initiatives in foreign policy, and generally favored a more pragmatic and low-key approach to diplomacy than his predecessors. He sought improved ties with Western countries, including the United States, and his government's rigorous and successful efforts to free U.S. hostages held in Iran contributed to that warming trend. Without forsaking the Third World commitments of his predecessors, Bendjedid sought to emphasize relations with Algeria's immediate neighbors; he also worked to improve relations with Morocco, although not at the expense of support for the Polisario, the guerrilla movement disputing Morocco's claim to the western Sahara.

The diversification of relations with major powers was manifest in new sources of military aid and equipment. This, according to some, has not been universally popular within the Algerian military, some of whom are explicitly Soviet-oriented. Under Bendjedid, Algeria's arms suppliers have been expanded to include a number of NATO (North Atlantic Treaty Organization) countries.

Bendjedid was reconfirmed as the party's choice for president at the fifth FLN conference, which was held in December 1983. This conference had as its slogan "Work and Rigor to Guarantee the Future," a sober acknowledgment that the consumerist expectations of the president's first term could not be achieved quickly. This was followed by national elections in January 1984, granting the president another five-year term. He began with a cabinet reshuffle, and appointed a new prime minister, Abdel-Hamid Brahimi. The president's second term was characterized by some scaled-back or modified economic goals, continued cautious evolution of political openness, further diversification of the country's trade and military partners, and foreign-policy emphasis on the immediate Maghreb region.

Economic issues posed important challenges to Bendjedid's second presidential term. The risky high-pricing strategy for liquid natural gas, on which much of Algeria's ambitious development plan depended, began to unravel. Major customers, including the United States, France, and Spain, began to balk at high prices set by Algeria, and several important deals fell through. In 1985, the serious downturn in the petroleum market, which affected oil and gas prices, took its toll on Algerian spending. Foreign exchange earnings fell from $13 billion in 1985 to $8 billion in 1986. This affected Algeria's debt and its previously favorable foreign creditworthiness. Bendjedid, who had pushed consumerist policies, was compelled to implement strict austerity measures. This led to sporadic public protests and violent opposition by those with economic grievances, a form of opposition apparently not linked to continued discontent by Berber, Islamic, and purely political groupings.

In 1985, the government launched an initiative to debate revisions of the National Charter, one of the centerpieces of Boumediene's presidency, which had been approved by referendum in 1975. The revisions, which can be seen as completing the process of de-Boumedienization, included toning down the doctrinaire socialism of the earlier document, advocating greater privatization of the economy, and promoting more conservative family values and the role of Islam in state ideology. The referendum was endorsed by a lopsided vote (98.4 percent in favor) in January 1986.

The foreign policy of the second term continued on a course of increasing pragmatism, more emphasis on regional relations, and further development of relations with Western countries, including the United States. Bendjedid's reputation for sober problem solving in a region fraught with explosive crises led to frequent use of Algeria as a crisis mediator or a venue for resolving terrorist incidents. On numerous occasions since the dramatic release of American hostages in Algeria in January 1981 the airport at Algiers has been the scene of negotiations to defuse potentially violent incidents between Middle Eastern guerrillas and their captives. In addition, Bendjedid dispatched his envoys to mediate in the Iran-Iraq war, and his role as facilitator of intra-Palestinian reconciliation deepened in the mid–1980s. Under Bendjedid, Algeria improved its standing as a formerly radical country that maintained its credibility both with conservative Western governments and Third World revolutionaries.

However, in many ways, Bendjedid's diplomacy in the second term demonstrated a preference for activism closer to home. During his second term, Algeria settled border disputes with Mali, Niger, and Mauritania. Most importantly, Bendjedid showed a desire to find a practical solution to the Western Sahara conflict, which began after the Spanish withdrawal in 1974, despite hardline pressure in the party and the military to offer no concessions to Morocco. Prospects for settling the Sahara conflict (allowing for effective Moroccan control over the territory, with some form of Saharan political autonomy) brightened in 1988, based on a sustained rapprochement underway between Rabat and Algiers, and increased momentum toward implementation of a UN plan involving a cease-fire and referendum to determine the future political status of the territory.

This latest improvement in the western Maghreb complemented efforts by President Bendjedid throughout his second term to expand intra-Maghrebi cooperation. Algeria mended its own fences with Colonel Muammar Qaddafi* (even leading to talk of an Algerian-Libyan union in early 1988), actively supported rapprochement between Tunisia and Libya, and tried to broker Libyan participation in an expanded version of the 1983 friendship pact linking Algeria with Tunisia and Mauritania. The push for Maghreb cooperation, including some calls for economic integration, a Maghreb parliament, and other European Community–like institutions, came strongly from Algeria, and its success will depend in large measure on the extent that Algerian-Moroccan rapprochement succeeds.

The mid–1980s were a time of notable improvement in U.S.-Algerian relations. In 1983, then U.S. Vice President George Bush visited Algeria, praised President Bendjedid, and indicated U.S. understanding of Algeria's nonaligned foreign policy. In June 1985, Bendjedid paid a state visit to Washington, D.C. which was heralded by many observers as the high point in relations with the United States since Algerian independence. One measure of the new state of relations was the U.S. decision that Algeria was eligible to purchase arms under the Foreign Military Sales program, which can be considered a ''seal of approval'' for customers of U.S. products. Cooperation in combatting terrorism, expanding trade and investment, and increasing cultural and educational exchanges are other signs of a maturing bilateral relationship.

As his second term came to an end in late 1988, Bendjedid faced the most serious domestic crisis of the entire independence period. On October 6, riots broke out across the country, and were subdued only after the army intervened, leading to what the Algerian government estimated as 159 dead and hundreds wounded. Among the causes of the riots were the cumulated toll of Algeria's economic decline and scaling-back of consumer-oriented policies, shrinking educational opportunities, and, more immediately, drought-caused food shortages, a tough presidential address in September on austerity, and a government decision to cancel foreign currency allocations for travel abroad. The rioters caused millions of dollars of damage in urban areas, and seemed to direct their rage against the symbols of government and party privilege, not against Bendjedid personally.

The president outlined his responses to the upheaval in a dramatic speech on October 10. He made a number of changes in key government positions. A series of political reforms were announced, including measures to strengthen the national assembly, to allow independents (not only FLN members) to run for Parliament, and to make the prime minister and his cabinet accountable to the will of the Parliament rather than the president. The reforms were approved in a national referendum on November 3. These reforms and other measures removing the party from any direct role in governing were endorsed at the Sixth FLN Congress in late November. At that Congress, Bendjedid was nominated for a third presidential term, and is generally viewed as having weathered the crisis with his leadership mandate intact.

The continued challenges of domestic economic pressures and raised expectations for political liberalization thus erupted as sources of instability for Algeria after a decade of President Bendjedid's rule. What had widely been considered his skill at managing a degree of internal restiveness without resorting to unduly harsh measures, and at achieving a new level of political equilibrium for Algeria, was called into question. Although expected to serve a third term, Bendjedid's generally successful presidency has been marred, at least temporarily, by his government's inability to adequately address the mounting economic and political challenges of governing Algeria.

BIBLIOGRAPHY

Work by Bendjedid:

Discours du President Chadli Bendjedid. Alger: Ministère de l'Information, annual volumes.

Other Works:

Entelis, John. *Algeria: the Revolution Institutionalized.* Boulder, Colo.: Westview Press, 1986.
Zartman, William. *L'Elite algerienne sous la presidence de Chadli Bendjedid.* Paris: Monde Arabe—Maghreb/Machrek, October-November-December 1984.
———. *Algeria: Implications of the Oil Price Collapse.* Washington, D.C.: Center for Strategic and International Studies, January 20, 1987.

ELLEN LAIPSON

DAVID BEN-GURION (1886–1973). At age thirty or even forty, it could scarcely have been predicted that David Ben-Gurion would become one of the towering figures of the twentieth century. His painstaking, careful, prudential style of operation and his personal characteristics yielded few clues to the profound impact he would have on Zionism, the Jewish community of Palestine, and the founding of the State of Israel. He was clearly a late bloomer as a national leader. After fifteen years heading the Histadrut, the labor federation he founded in 1920, he defeated the forces of Chaim Weizmann* and was elected chairman of the Jewish Agency Executive, serving from 1935 to 1948. Recognized as the founder of the new state of Israel, he served as prime minister from 1948 to 1963, except for two years from 1953 to 1955 when he retired to Sde Boker in the Negev to seek respite from the rigors of his long political career and to dramatize the significance of pioneering and reclaiming the desert. He remained in politics through the political party he created in 1965 (Rafi) until he resigned from the Knesset (Israel's parliament) in 1970. He died at age eighty-seven on December 1, 1973.

David Gruen was born in Plonsk, Poland, then under Czarist Russian control, on October 16, 1886. Plonsk was about thirty-five miles from Warsaw, a town of about ten thousand inhabitants, including forty-five hundred Jews living in a segregated *shtetl*, a small village ghetto to which Jews were typically confined in Eastern Europe. His father was a legal adviser (an unlicensed lawyer) in the shtetl and a person of some means. Under the influence of his father and grand-father, David became a committed Zionist in childhood. He often accompanied his father to the synagogue although he remained a secularist throughout his lifetime. He learned Hebrew from his grandfather and attended a modernized Hebrew-language school. He was eleven years old when Theodore Herzl con-vened the first Zionist Congress in Basel in 1897. His father was a cofounder of the Love of Zion Society in Plonsk in 1890. This movement was created by Russian Jews after the pogroms of 1882 and became the precursor of political Zionism established by Herzl in the 1890s. The publication of Herzl's *The Jewish State* in 1896 created excited talk in his father's synagogue, and at age ten, David probably heard about a messiah named Herzl.

At age thirteen, David continued his studies at a government school. In 1900, at fourteen, he became secretary of Ezra, a society teaching Hebrew to boys to encourage immigration to Palestine. Imbued with the tenets of Marxism and Zionism, he served as editor of a socialist Zionist newspaper. Arrested twice by Polish authorities for his Zionist political activity, he joined a group of two thousand to go to Palestine where he planned to become a Zionist labor organizer. Traveling via horse and buggy, train, and small cargo ship, in September 1906 he docked in Jaffa. He was immediately elected to the central committee of the Poalei Zion (Workers of Zion) and began organizing workers into unions. For four years, mainly in the Lower Galilee in Sejera, a forerunner of the *kibbutz* (cooperative agricultural settlement), he endured hunger, malaria, and Arab hostility while working the land, serving as watchman, organizing agricultural workers, and opposing Jewish farmers and landlords who employed Arabs.

In 1910, with Itzhak Ben-Zvi (the second President of Israel) and Rachel Yanait (later Mrs. Ben-Zvi), he joined the editorial staff of a new Poalei Zion paper, *Ahdut* (Unity) in Jerusalem and begun publishing articles under the name Ben-Gurion. In 1911 he and Ben-Zvi were elected delegates to the eleventh Zionist Congress. He also joined a group of young socialist Zionists to study at Turkish universities with the hope of establishing ties with some of the ruling circles in order to advance the goal of the Jewish Homeland in Palestine. At first he lived in Saloniki, but he moved in 1912 to the University of Constan-tinople, where he earned a law degree with highest honors. In Constantinople he suffered chronic starvation, as he depended on meager funds from his father in Plonsk. In 1914, he and Ben-Zvi returned to Palestine, and he resumed his work as a union organizer.

With the outbreak of World War I, Turkey was allied with the Central Powers. Because he spoke on behalf of the Allies, in 1915 the Ottoman authorities exiled Ben-Gurion. After a brief period in Egypt, he made his way to New York to advocate Jewish settlement in Palestine and establish the Hechalutz, and orga-nization of "pioneers" recruited to encourage Jewish settlement in Palestine.

He met a Brooklyn nurse, Paula Munweis, whom he married in 1917 at the Municipal Building in Manhattan. He welcomed the Balfour Declaration in November 1917, but he never deviated from his conviction that the Jewish Homeland could be achieved only by Jewish labor and capital. In May 1918 he enlisted in a Jewish Battalion of the British Royal Fusiliers and sailed to Egypt to join the expeditionary force. Paula and their first child, Geula, who was born in New York City, joined him in Palestine in 1919.

Ben-Gurion was a short, squat figure. In middle age, his heavy bushy eyebrows and white tufts of hair gave him a singular appearance. He had a quick jerky manner of moving, and his speech was staccato-like. He made no small talk and had almost no sense of humor. He seldom established close personal relations and had few intimate friends in his life. His favorite characters in history were usually zealots and dedicated persons.

Ben-Gurion was energetic, determined, and tough-minded. His biographers and associates remember him as fierce, aggressive, and tireless. He was also a gifted orator, yet at times his speeches were tediously long and boring. In his later years he was often impervious to opposition. He was a formidable hater of some major Zionist leaders, including Moshe Sneh, Moshe Sharett, and Nahum Goldmann. He frequently engaged in acrimonious argument even with his closest friends and political allies. On numerous occasions he resigned or threatened to resign from high office in order to have his way.

Ben-Gurion's intellectual capacity was superb. He was a voracious reader, concentrating on philosophy and, later, science. He loved languages and spoke Hebrew, Russian, Yiddish, French, German, English, and some Italian. He also read Greek, Spanish, and some Arabic.

In his early years in Palestine, Ben-Gurion's career had little coherence and provided him meager satisfaction. After World War I, however, he succeeded in merging into the Histadrut (the federation of labor) the unions of starving pioneers that he had previously organized. He had begun in 1906 as a firey young Zionist with a vision of a Jewish state organized along Marxist lines. By 1920, he had moved away from Marxism to embrace moderate socialism. Still later he demonstrated a capacity to move even further to embrace ideas of a mixed economy without weakening his goals of social justice, parliamentary democracy, and the rule of law.

From 1921 to 1935, Ben-Gurion was the general secretary of the Histadrut, whose activities encompassed many of the essential tasks of a sovereign state. As he conceived it, the Histadrut's objectives were to create the infrastructure of the future Jewish state, promote the economic development of the Jewish community of Palestine, and stimulate unlimited immigration of Jews to Palestine so that they would eventually become the majority population. At the same time, he was building an effective personal base of political power in Zionist politics.

Opponents within the Histadrut challenged Ben-Gurion's centralized leadership and especially his willingness to reach compromises with groups outside the Histadrut. Immediately after World War I, Ben-Gurion also founded the

United Labor Party. Eventually, this party became Mapai, the Socialist Zionist political party, and still later it evolved into the Labor Party.

In the 1920s and 1930s, Chaim Weizmann, the head of the World Zionist Organization and chief diplomatic negotiator of the Zionist movement, was in charge of overall Zionist affairs while Ben-Gurion headed Zionist activities in Palestine. This arrangement provided little visibility for Ben-Gurion, who deplored Weizmann's reliance on Britain and the Mandatory government as the best vehicle to a Jewish state.

In Palestine, Ben-Gurion's major rival for leadership was Vladimir Jabotinsky, who characterized the British action of taking Transjordan out of Palestine as a betrayal of the Balfour Declaration. He opposed Weizmann's relationship with the British, split with the Socialist Zionists, and vowed fervent opposition to the Mandatory government. He rejected Ben-Gurion's position of concentrating on creating the foundations for Jewish society and an infrastructure for a mixed economy. He organized Betar, a uniformed, militant Revisionist youth movement, and he preached war against the Mandatory government and the British. Convinced that Revisionist Zionists under Jabotinsky were endangering the drive toward eventual statehood by driving the British to retaliate, Ben-Gurion struggled to undermine and discredit Revisionism. When the British exiled Jabotinsky from Palestine in 1928, leadership passed to radicals in the Revisionist movement. Further radicalization of Betar and the Revisionist movement in the late 1930s led Etzel and Lehi—underground Revisionist groups—to begin a program of terror aimed at the British. When Menachem Begin* became leader of Revisionism in 1944 and increased terrorist acts against the British, Ben-Gurion intensified his efforts to destroy Revisionism and its leader.

The Arab Revolt of 1936 through 1939 led to the report of the Peel Commission in 1937, which proposed that Palestine be partitioned. The Zionist movement split sharply over the plan. Many groups in the Labor party, the kibbutz movement, and the Histadrut were ambivalent and uncertain. Weizmann's moderate forces in the West and in Palestine joined with Ben-Gurion's moderate left wing in Palestine to support partition as the most practical and expeditious means for securing Jewish sovereignty as early as possible. Britain renounced the plan in 1938. As the internal debate intensified, for the first time the Jewish community in Palestine had to confront critical issues of creating a Jewish majority, fixing territorial boundaries, dealing with the Arab countries, establishing relations with the great powers, and strengthening the Haganah, the defense arm of the Jewish community.

In the debate over partition and the character of the Jewish state, Ben-Gurion gambled his political future and won. During World War II in Palestine and in America he was eloquent and practical in outlining the case for early statehood, and he understood more clearly than others the historical circumstances underlying the case for statehood: the erosion of the Mandate; the painful unfolding of the tragedy of European Jewry under Hitler; the desperate need for open immigration to rescue the surviving remnants of the Jewish population; and the growth of Arab nationalism, which generated urgent requirements for more effective Jewish military forces.

In 1942 the battle over partition shifted to the American Zionist Conference at the Biltmore Hotel in New York. Ben-Gurion, with the support of Rabbi Abba Hillel Silver, an influential Zionist leader, defeated Weizmann and secured passage of resolutions demanding open mass immigration to Palestine immediately, transfer of authority over immigration and development in Palestine to the Jewish Agency, and establishment of a Jewish Commonwealth.

In Palestine, 1943 and 1944 were years of conflict within the Labor party. A faction split off in 1942 and established a new party, Ahdut Haavoda (United Labor) in 1944. Hashomer Hatzair (Young Guard), which called for a binational state, formed a party which became Mapam in 1948. Within the mainstream Mapai party, Ben-Gurion struggled to curtail Weizmann's authority and shift the struggle to Palestine and to the United States, which, he believed, was destined to become the dominant Western power after the war. Party leaders attacked Ben-Gurion's "cult of personality" and placed restrictions on his leadership.

At the Twenty-First Zionist Congress in December 1946, the restraints on Ben-Gurion were lifted. With a majority of 80 percent and an alliance with Rabbi Silver, Ben-Gurion forced the Congress to leave Weizmann's traditional post of president of the World Zionist Organization in London vacant. Ben-Gurion was reelected chairman of the Jewish Agency Executive.

When the War of Independence began in December 1947, following the UN resolution of November 29, 1947, favoring partition, Ben-Gurion devoted himself to the military struggle. He organized the fund-raising drive for the purchase of arms, the recruitment of military specialists, and the preparation of military plans. He directly influenced the character and shape of the Israeli Army, including the principle of civilian control.

From 1948 to 1953, as Israel's first prime minister, Ben-Gurion stressed the need to build a strong government to deal with urgent problems of national defense, mass immigration, economic development, and education. He boldly confronted crucial tasks of reducing the power of the prestate bodies, such as Palmach (the strike force of the Jewish defenses), the Jewish Agency, the Histadrut, and the Labor Party, which together had constituted the state in the making in the period 1920–1948.

He was most successful in consolidating into the new Israel Defense Forces the separate military organizations that the various political movements had developed. Under Ben-Gurion, the Israel Army would be nonpolitical. It would be a popular army based on universal military service and annual reserve duty. Members of the standing army would retire in the early forties to pursue civilian careers. Israel would prevent the development of an officer corps exercising excessive influence in society. The army would be educated in Jewish and Zionist history. Officers would lead men in battle, and their relations would be based on consent. The army would be a primary force for social integration and nation building.

It is probably impossible to overstate the burdens imposed by mass immigration. From 1948 to 1953, seven hundred thousand Jews came to Israel from Iraq, Yemen, Morocco, Libya, Egypt, Tunisia, Lebanon, and many other countries, more than doubling the Jewish population of 1948. Ben-Gurion gave strong leadership to the ingathering of the Jews from all over the world. In 1950 he persuaded the Knesset to enact the Law of Return, which gave every Jew in the world the right to immigrate to Israel and to claim citizenship immediately. Ben-Gurion orchestrated a superhuman effort to settle and absorb immigrants by organizing a national austerity regime. The new immigrants were settled in the principal cities, abandoned towns and villages, and temporary transit camps of tents and corrugated huts. In this on-going process, the Israeli Defense Forces became a major center of education and integration of young soldiers, with Hebrew as the language of instruction. Food and clothing were rationed, people were put to work building roads, villages, and kibbutzim (plural of kibbutz).

Ben-Gurion never stopped demanding that American Jews move en masse to Israel because Israel needed more Jews. He was convinced that people, not territory, constituted the most critical factor in national security. The refusal of the great majority of American Jews to emigrate to Israel was his greatest disappointment.

In November 1948, the Provisional Government established the electoral system of Israel, featuring a single national constituency and direct election by secret ballot. Candidates were nominated by political parties and voters cast ballots for party lists rather than candidates. The Constituent Assembly, later the Knesset, consisted of 120 delegates elected by proportional representation. As early as 1950, Ben-Gurion deplored the instability of the coalition government that the electoral system inevitably produced. The first cabinet crisis occurred in October 1950 when the United Religious Front defeated Ben-Gurion's proposal to add a new ministry headed by a non-Knesset member. The government fell; Ben-Gurion formed a new government whose principles were identical with those of its predecessor; and eleven of the thirteen ministers in the new government were carried over from the previous one. It too was brought down after only a few weeks, when the Religious Front demanded automatic assignment of Yemenite children to orthodox religious schools.

In April 1951, the Knesset enacted the Elections Law, which affirmed the familiar elections formula, made everyone eighteen years of age and older and registered as a resident of Israel eligible to vote, and fixed the Knesset term of four years. In an effort to reduce the number of parties, the law provided that a party list must receive at least 1 percent of the total number of valid votes in order to participate in the distribution of seats.

Following the election of 1951, it took Ben-Gurion seven weeks of hard coalition bargaining to form a new government. This third Ben-Gurion government closely resembled its predecessor, and the religious parties won concessions, including the exemption of orthodox women from military service, a ban on non-Kosher food imports, and state support of religious schools. In December 1952, another crisis was created when the Agudat Israel party withdrew from the cabinet on the issue of national service by orthodox women. The new government formed by Ben-Gurion at the end of 1952 remained in office with minor changes until June 1955. Ben-Gurion deplored the instability and brutal coalition bargaining that characterized Israeli governments from the beginning of statehood. Despite his stout advocacy, he never succeeded in winning majority support from electoral reform.

Ben-Gurion was determined to raise the educational, social, and economic levels of the immigrants to a standard of equality with veteran settlers. The Compulsory Education Law of September 12, 1949, established the principle of universal, free, compulsory education for children aged five to thirteen and required youths between fourteen and seventeen to complete elementary school or continue schooling until seventeen. The act left in place the prestate grouping of schools into four networks or "trends" organized by political parties.

Ben-Gurion undertook to introduce a unified educational system free from partisan indoctrination. After lengthy debates and innumerable amendments, the State Education Law was passed in 1953; it abolished the trend system and established a unified educational system from kindergarten through eight grades of elementary school. To keep the governing coalition in office, Ben-Gurion had reached a compromise with the ultraorthodox Agudat Israel Party, which permitted the party to maintain its own religious schools without government subsidy or to incorporate 75 percent of the standard curricula and receive in return a two-thirds public subsidy. Despite this major concession, the Education Act established a major separation between political parties and the education of children. When it went into operation in October 1953, immigration had already tripled the number of school children.

Ben-Gurion also led the drive to secure reparations from the West German government for the evil wrought upon the Jewish people. In September 1951, Chancellor Konrad Adenauer of West Germany for the first time acknowledged the need for reparations and his readiness to negotiate with Israel and world Jewry. Confronting the bitter, violent opposition led by Menachem Begin, Ben-Gurion stressed Israel's desperate need to finance the transfer and settlement of survivors of Nazi terror. He forced Begin to call off his demonstrations. The Reparations Agreement with West Germany, backed by the Knesset, was signed in 1952.

In December 1953, Ben-Gurion resigned as prime minister because of extreme fatigue brought on by the excessive demands of coalition politics, especially those of the religious parties, which commanded at most 15 percent of the national vote. He moved to Sde Boker, an obscure kibbutz deep in the Negev, the southern desert of Israel. He saw the Negev as the natural focus of pioneering idealism. He wanted others to follow him into the desert to create new communities, farms, and industries without displacing Arabs or aggravating the Arab-Israeli conflict.

He became a persistent promoter of the desalination of sea water and solar energy as keys to the transformation of the Negev.

In 1955, when Pinchas Lavon was forced by the disclosure of an Israeli military intelligence failure in Cairo to resign as minister of defense, Ben-Gurion left Sde Boker to head the Defense Ministry in the government headed by Moshe Sharett. After the election of 1955, Ben-Gurion undertook to form a new government. After eleven weeks of battling over the allocation of ministerial portfolios the resulting new government was similar to the one he had initially proposed.

Ben-Gurion was never able to formulate plans for sustained economic growth. The government was not sufficiently unified to enable it to consider, adopt, and execute comprehensive economic plans. The Histadrut, building on its prestate position, remained the senior partner in economic matters. Under Ben-Gurion's leadership, the husbanding of scarce water resources was accorded high priority, along with the exploitation of the resources of minerals, clays, and sands of the Dead Sea area. Despite the obstacles to rational development of the economy, many improvements were made, fueled by an inflow of capital from abroad in the form of investments, gifts, loans, German Reparations payments, and the beginning of American aid.

From the summer of 1952 to 1970, the dominant personality of the Arab world was Gamal Abdul Nasser.* Aspiring to be the champion of Pan-Arabism, he maintained a guerrilla campaign against Israel. With weapons from Czechoslovakia and Soviet support, he blockaded the Gulf of Aqaba and captured the Strait of Tiran. Ben-Gurion countered by winning support from France, which had begun to ship Mystère–4 fighters to Israel in 1954. When Nassar failed to obtain aid from the United States, Great Britain, or the Soviet Union to finance the construction of the High Aswan Dam on the Nile, he nationalized the Suez Canal on July 26, 1956. Anglo-French military preparations were stepped up when Nasser rejected international control of the waterway on September 9. For months Nasser had been intensifying Egyptian-trained *fedayeen* (Arab commando) raids from bases in Gaza, Jordan, and Syria, and he publicly announced his intent to liquidate Israel. Ben-Gurion had already replaced dovish Foreign Minister Moshe Sharett with Golda Meir,* and the groundwork was laid for an Anglo-French-Israeli assault on Egyptian forces. On October 29, 1956, with its virtual survival at risk, Israel began the Sinai campaign by having a squadron of Israeli transport planes cross the Negev frontier and a paratroop battalion land near Mitla Pass in Sinai. With French air support and an Allied bombardment of the Egyptian air force, the hundred-hour campaign advanced Israel's security significantly. It enhanced Israeli morale; it virtually ended fedayee raids from Gaza; it held open the Gulf of Aqaba for eleven crucial years; and it brought security to outlying border settlements. Ben-Gurion and Golda Meir then stubbornly resisted the powerful efforts of the United States and Britain to impose a settlement that would undermine Israel's security.

Coming at the end of its first decade of independent statehood and eight years under Ben-Gurion's leadership, the Sinai Campaign enabled Israel to enter into a period of rapid economic growth with increasing international stature. For the next ten years (1957 to 1967), its frontiers were reasonably secure and its prospects for national survival were dramatically improved.

Military success strengthened Ben-Gurion's coalition. After the election of 1959, Ben-Gurion countered growing agitation directed against the party's aging veterans by bringing into the government younger figures—Abba Eban, Moshe Dayan,* and Shimon Peres.* However, the eruption of the Lavon affair in 1960 (an intelligence failure which had begun during the tenure of Pinhas Lavon, Minister of Defense) brought disarray to Mapai and Ben-Gurion's political strength eroded. He resigned for the last time from the post of prime minister in June 1963.

Nonetheless, Ben-Gurion's final three years in office included notable achievements. On May 23, 1960, he electrified the nation by announcing that Adolf Eichmann, the chief administrator of the Nazi destruction of European Jewry, had been captured and imprisoned in Israel. Eichmann's subsequent trial had a profound impact on Israeli youth by dramatizing the horrors of the Holocaust and the imperative need of Jews for a homeland of their own. The trial also fostered improved relations between Israel and West Germany, which provided additional German payments for special projects in Israel.

Israel had little success in developing more fruitful relations with the European Economic Community. Limited quantities of Israeli industrial exports were granted a tariff reduction of 20 percent. However, Israel's relations with France prospered. France continued until 1967 to be Israel's main source of military equipment, and joint projects were developed in aircraft, rockets, and nuclear energy.

Following the Sinai Campaign, with Golda Meir in charge, Israel expanded its efforts to place Israeli advisers, scientists, and technicians abroad, concentrating on projects in which Israeli expertise excelled. Israel quickly became an international center for the Third World. Beginning with Ghana in 1956, major Israeli-led projects were organized in many African countries. From 1958 to 1970, about thirty-five hundred Israeli experts served in African countries and several thousand African students studied in Israel.

While Ben-Gurion had a remarkable capacity to deal with tactical details, he was preeminent in understanding the historical forces that were influencing nation building in Israel. He typically combined lofty vision, acute perception of historical trends, and practical means to achieve objectives. He frequently asserted that four factors would be decisive in determining Israel's future: the absorption of immigrants from all parts of the Diaspora; developing the country, including the south and the Negev, into a self-supporting economy that gave promise of economic independence and a decent standard of living; general and vocational education at primary and secondary levels, and higher institutions of learning that would transform Israel into an important center of science and learning; and molding a society without conflicting classes and founded on liberty, equality, love of humanity, justice, and peace.

Ben-Gurion was the primary formulator of the grand strategy that maintained Israel's security for at least twenty years. He assumed that the Arab-Israeli conflict would be deep and prolonged, that Israelis would always be inferior in numbers to the Arabs, and that the international system could not insure Israel's survival. Accordingly, immigration was essential to insure the Jewish character of the state; Israel's borders should minimize the number of non-Jews; Palestine refugees must not be permitted to return to their homes in Israel; and Israel must emphasize the development of its human resources in order to substitute quality for quantity. Because external guarantees were unreliable and ineffective, self-reliance must be stressed. Measures to overcome military weakness were adopted, such as the wide dispersal of the population. Both force and diplomacy, he argued, must be employed to achieve the goals of foreign policy and security, including external alliances. To promote security, he sought arrangements with countries on the periphery of Arab regimes: Ethiopia, Turkey, and Iran (under Shah Mohammad Reza Pahlavi*).

Israel, Ben-Gurion believed, must never confront a united Arab coalition. One means to avoid this was to develop relations with minority groups within Arab countries, whose attention would thereby be diverted from conflict with Israel. His military doctrine stressed preemptive and rapid offensive warfare and measures to combat terrorism.

Until 1967, Ben-Gurion's grand strategy was successful. It engaged wide public support and correctly assessed Israel's relative strengths and weaknesses. After the 1967 war and military occupation of the West Bank and Gaza, this strategy began to deteriorate. More emphasis was placed on Israel's strategic depth ("secure and defensible borders"), which Ben-Gurion had regarded as only one factor in a complex grand strategy.

Shortly before he died in 1973, Ben-Gurion admonished Israelis not to forget that two peoples claim Israel and that the Arabs outbreed the Jews. Therefore, a Jewish state must always maintain within her borders an undisputed Jewish majority. Peace, he asserted, would be achieved only if Israel returned in principle to the pre–1967 borders. Militarily defensible borders were important, he said, but by themselves they could not guarantee Israel's future. True security had to be founded on mutual respect among neighbors.

Perhaps Ben-Gurion's dominant feature was his single-minded pursuit of statehood and the strengthening of the state. In this life's work, he combined lofty visions with practical solutions. He called repeatedly for mass immigration and territorial concentration of Jews in Palestine in order to build a Jewish majority. He had an overwhelming dream of a land peopled by a prosperous and educated society of workers. He envisioned a national unity and a social integration in the Jewish state cemented by democracy, and independent judiciary, and the rule of law. He would rely on self-help, military strength, and reclamation of the wilderness by Jewish labor. His great skill was his ability to mobilize diverse forces to achieve practical results. His sense of timing was acutely perceptive, for example, in his insistence on declaring statehood on the eve of the termination of the Mandate.

As a visionary pragmatist, Ben-Gurion was able to concentrate powerfully on what was achievable. His acceptance of compromise to reach the attainable was geared to his perceptive analysis of historical circumstances, such as the decline of British power in the 1930s, the growing importance of the United States at the end of World War I, the acceptability of German reparation payments in 1951–1952, the impact of the destruction of Central and Eastern European Jewry on Jewish statehood, and the divisiveness of the Arab world as being Israel's secret weapon.

The period of Ben-Gurion's leadership was unprecedented in Jewish history. It was the time of the two world wars, the greatest of holocausts, and the greatest of rebirths, the creation of the State of Israel. In this context, Ben-Gurion grew prodigiously. With help from many quarters, he became the founder of the state. He changed course and shifted tactics and policy to fit events as he interpreted them with astounding acumen and tough-mindedness. His capacity for decision making produced spectacular achievements of nation building that may be without parallel in modern history.

BIBLIOGRAPHY

Works by Ben-Gurion:

Anachnu U'Sheineinu (We and Our Neighbors). Tel Aviv: Davar Publishing Co., 1929.
MiMa'amad l'Am (From Class to People). Tel Aviv: Davar Publishing Co., 1933.
Jewish Labor. London: Hechalutz, 1935.
The Peel Report and the Jewish State. Jerusalem: 1938.
B'Hilachem Yisrael (When Israel Fought). Tel Aviv: Mapai, 1949.
Ketavim Rishonim (Early Writings). Tel Aviv: 1952.
Rebirth of Destiny of Israel. New York: Philosophical Library, 1954.
B'Maarachah (In the Struggle). 5 vols. Tel Aviv: Am Oved, 1957.
Ma'arechet Sinai. Tel Aviv: Am Oved, 1959.
Israel: Years of Challenge. New York: Holt, Rinehart & Winston, 1963.
D'varim HeHavayatam (Things As They Happened). Tel Aviv: Am Hasefer, 1965.
The Jews in Their Land. Garden City: Doubleday, 1966.
Michtavim el Paula ve'ed haYeladim (Letters to Paula and the Children). Tel Aviv: Am Oved, 1968.
Recollections. Ed. Thomas H. Bernstein. Tel Aviv: Bitan, 1970.
Israel: A Personal History. New York: Funk and Wagnalls, 1971.
Letters to Paula. London: Vallentine Mitchell, 1971.
Zichronot (Memoirs). 5 vols. Tel Aviv: Am Oved, 1971–1972.
Igrot (Letters). 3 vols. Tel Aviv: Am Oved and Tel Aviv University, 1971–1974.
My Talks With Arab Leaders. Jerusalem: Keter, 1972.
Biblical Reflections. New York: Jonathan.

Other Works

Bar Zohar, Michael. *Ben-Gurion, A Biography.* Trans. Peretz Kidron. New York: Delacorte Press, 1978.

Cohen, Michael. *Palestine: Retreat from the Mandate, 1936–1945*. London: Paul Elek, 1978.
———. *Palestine and the Great Powers, 1945–1948*. Princeton, N.J.: Princeton University Press, 1982.
Sha'atiel, Eli. "David Ben-Gurion and Partition, 1937." *The Jerusalem Quarterly* (Winter 1979); pp. 38–59.
Teveth, Shabtai. *Ben-Gurion: The Burning Ground 1886–1948*. Boston: Houghton Mifflin Company, 1987.

MARVER H. BERNSTEIN

SALAH AL-DIN BITAR (1912–1980). Together with his fellow-Damascene, Michel Aflaq* Salah al-Din Bitar (Baytar) of Syria will be remembered as cofounder and leader of the Baath Party. Bitar was born in 1912 in Damascus, the son of a Sunni Muslim grain merchant from the Maydan quarter; the Bitars were one of the commercial-religious families that dominated social, political, economic, and religious life in the city. Well-to-do, they were notables, although not among the most important, and were very active in nationalist politics during the mandate period. An older cousin, Midhat Bitar, was active as the leader of a nationalist youth organization, the Steel Shirts, in the mid–1930s. By the mid–1940s, Bitar was living in the Salihiyah Quarter, northwest of the old city. Salah Bitar developed a lifelong personal and political friendship with Aflaq when both were students at the Sorbonne in Paris. Bitar received his licentiate in political science in 1934 and returned to teach secondary school in his native city.

The two friends, together with Midhat Bitar and Jalal al-Sayyid, joined in the early 1940s to form the nucleus of the Baath (resurrection) movement. The two shared a common view of the problems of Syria and the Arab world, and founded the Baath as an instrument dedicated to providing solutions to those problems. Their inclinations and abilities differed, with Bitar proving the more active in the give-and-take of the political arena than the introspective Aflaq. Salah Bitar was a member of the four-man executive committee, chosen at the founding congress in 1947, that headed the party for seven years. He then became one of three Syrians on the seven-member National Command of the party selected at the party congress in 1954 after the Baath merged with the Arab Socialist Party of Akram Hourani. His status in this command lapsed when the Baath Party in Syria dissolved itself as a condition set by Gamal Abdul Nasser* before he would agree to unite Egypt and Syria in the United Arab Republic (UAR) in 1958. Through most of this period, Bitar was the editor of *al-Baath*, the party paper.

Throughout his career in the Baath Party, Bitar was consistently prominent as a Baathist holding public office, or aspiring to hold office. He ran for a seat in the parliamentary elections of 1943 and 1947, but failed to win in either case. He was successful in a third attempt, securing a seat from Damascus in a close runoff in the uncontrolled elections of 1954 which brought sixteen Baathists into the Parliament. After the breakup of the UAR, new elections were held in

December 1961. Although these elections were formally conducted on a nonparty basis, the voters knew the political affiliation of the candidates. Egyptian rule over Syria, which was in effect what the UAR had turned out to be, had an adverse carryover effect on the Baath. Some former Baathists, who had local support independent of the party, won seats; others, who relied on their Baath credentials, were voted down, Bitar among them.

Bitar's indifferent showing at the polls—one narrow victory in four tries—indicates more about the Baath Party's political base than about Bitar's own abilities. Although he and Aflaq thought of the party as an organization for all Arabs, it was in essence a party of an educated elite, recruited in the schools, which felt it knew best how to lead the masses. Moreover, despite the fact that Bitar and Aflaq were Damascus-born and -bred, and that the former came from the traditional elite, they were never very successful in attracting members in the capital city. Most of their early adherents were students from the provinces who in turn recruited additional members from the provinces when they returned to Idlib, Latakia, or Dayr al-Zur. The party founders did not plan that their organization should grow in this fashion, but such growth came to have profound effects on them when a new generation of party activists challenged their judgment and authority in the 1960s.

Throughout independent Syria's history, however, the holding of executive office and the interaction of civilians with a highly politicized Syrian officer corps were of substantially more importance than electoral politics. Bitar played a prominent role in the executive side of Syrian affairs in the decade of 1956 to 1966. By mid–1956, strongly influenced by developments elsewhere in the Arab world, especially Egypt, the Syrian political balance tilted away from the conservative, nationalist complexion that had characterized civilian cabinets during the previous dozen years. In mid-June, Sabri al-Asali formed a nine-man cabinet containing two Baathists and two members of Khalid al-Azm's independent, but left-leaning, bloc. Salah Bitar was foreign minister, a post he held through one cabinet change later in 1956 until the resignation of the Syrian government when the UAR came into existence in February 1958.

In the UAR cabinets, which were in very large part staffed by Egyptians, Syrian Baathists held only a modest number of posts. Bitar was union minister of state throughout 1958 and union minister of culture and guidance in 1959 until he and other Baathists resigned from their posts, pursuant to a decision of the Baath Party pan-Arab National Command, at the very end of the year. That signalled the end of Baathist participation in the unity government in which Bitar and Aflaq had put such high hopes.

When the Syrian armed forces effected the withdrawal of Syria from the UAR in September 1961, Bitar joined a group of Syrian political figures who signed a statement approving the action. Under pressure from his colleagues in the party, he later repudiated his signature. By applauding the breakup of the UAR, however, Bitar added to his political enemies in Syria a bloc of Baathists who still believed in unity despite the problems of the UAR experiment. He and Aflaq had already incurred the opposition of many party militants for dissolving the party in Syria in 1958 without consulting the membership or even the elected Syrian Regional Command. Although Aflaq appointed his friend and colleague to a provisional Syrian party command in 1962, once the party was reconstituted in Syria, Bitar's opponents denied him election to either the regional or national command of the party he had founded.

His political career in Syria was far from finished, however. On March 8, 1963, Syrian military officers seized control of a country that had staggered from crisis to crisis over the previous eighteen months. Baathist officers dominated the group, and they selected Bitar to head the new cabinet. He remained prime minister until November, when he was replaced by General Amin al-Hafiz. He returned to the prime ministership in May 1964, and was also a member of a five-man Presidential Council during the same period. Despite being persona non grata to many party members, Bitar had several factors working in his favor. His experience in government was one; none of the second generation of Baathists had had much opportunity in their earlier careers to attain public office. With his urban, notable family, Bitar could serve as a link to an important element of Damascene society that was opposed to land reform and other nationalization measures that the Baathists of the 1960s were instituting in Syria. While traditional families bridled at their loss of influence, from time to time they at least had one of their own with whom to talk and who could pour a little oil on the troubled waters.

Bitar's final stint in public office lasted for just two months. When the old guard of the Baath Party made its last-ditch attempt to curb the power of the regionalists of the second generation by dismissing the Regional Command in late December 1965, they turned to Bitar to head the government. He was the only senior statesman that the old guard had on their side. The twenty-man cabinet installed on January 1, 1966, was swept out of office and into jail by a military coup on February 23, 1966. Bitar was jailed, but escaped and made his way to Lebanon in August of that year with the aid of a group of civilian and military Baathists who were organizing a coup to reverse the defeat of the previous February. He remained in Beirut, a traditional place of exile for Syrian politicians, until civil war and the arrival of Syrian troops in the mid–1970s caused him to flee. When several dozen adherents of Aflaq and the old guard line met in that city in 1968 for a national congress to reconstitute the organization, he refused to attend. Prior to the meeting he issued a statement stating that he had resigned from the Baath and calling for a comprehensive Arab movement to replace it. In his view, the Baath Party had failed to achieve its purposes and goals.

After living briefly in Cairo, Bitar paid a last visit to Damascus and then moved to Paris where he published a newspaper as a forum in Arab unity. The paper's name is significant, *al-Ihya al-Arabi* (Arab Revitalization), a term that he and Aflaq had used for their movement before they settled on the term "Baath." Bitar was also associated in some degree with externally-based movements opposed to the regime of Hafez al-Assad* in Syria. He was assassinated by an unidentified person on July 21, 1980. Suspicion has been directed at the Assad regime. In any event, the act was a waste of resources as well as the waste of a life. During his years of exile, Salah Bitar wielded little influence over opinion or political forces in or out of Syria.

Bitar was a transitional or bridging figure in twentieth-century Syrian politics. Sprung from a traditional, urban, and notable Sunni family, his political philosophy moved beyond Syria to embrace the entire Arab world. Like Aflaq he was no socialist; for him, too, socialism really meant social justice—decent wages, housing, and modest private ownership. In calling for this he went beyond the normal parameters of the stratum of society into which he was born. Grain merchants in early twentieth-century Syria as a class had little social conscience. In other respects, however, Bitar was a conventional Syrian politician. He devoted full time to politics, in or out of office, living on family support as was customary in the pre-UAR period. He could and did work with politicians of other parties when the situation demanded it.

Neither he nor Aflaq ever seems to have understood that the party they created was evolving into an organization with goals and concepts that they had neither thought of nor approved. They understood little about the background and aspirations of the second generation of Baathists, whose provincial origins drove them to effect revolutionary change in the governmental, social, and economic systems of Syria. Bitar was not a revolutionary; he was a nationalist who would modify and improve as he thought useful rather than uproot and overthrow.

BIBLIOGRAPHY

Works by Bitar:

Al-Siyasah al-Arabiyah bayn al-Mabda wa al-Tatbiq (Arab Policy in Principle and Practice). Beirut: Dar al-Taliah, 1960.
Nidal al-Ba'th (The Baath's Struggle). Beirut: Dar al-Taliah, 1963–1965. Vols. 1–4 contain items by subject.
"The Rise and Decline of the Baath." *Middle East International* (June 1971); 12–15 and (July 1971); 13–16.
"The Implications of the October War for the Arab World." *Journal of Palestine Studies* 3, no. 2 (1974); 34–45.

Other Works:

Abu Jaber, Kamel S. *The Arab Ba'th Socialist Party*. Syracuse, N.Y.: Syracuse University Press, 1966.
Devlin, John F. *The Ba'th Party: A History from Its Origins to 1966*. Stanford, Calif.: Hoover Institution Press, 1976.
Hourani, Albert H. *Arabic Thought in the Liberal Age 1798–1939*. London, New York and Toronto: Oxford University Press, 1962, ch. 11.
Al-Jundi, Sami. *Al-Ba'th*. Beirut; Dar al-Nahar li al-Nashr, 1969.

Kaylani, Nabil A. "The Rise of the Syrian Ba'th 1940–1958: Political Success, Party
    Failure." *International Journal of Middle East Studies* 3, no. 1 (January 1972);
    3–23.
Rabinovich, Itmar. *Syria under the Ba'th 1963–1966: The Army-Party Symbiosis.* Je-
    rusalem: Israel Universities Press, 1972.
Al-Sayyid, Jalal. *Hizb al-Ba'th al-'Arabi* (The Arab Baath Party). Beirut; Dar al-Nahar
    li al-Nashr, 1973.
Seale, Patrick. *The Struggle for Syria: A Study of Post-War Arab Politics, 1945–1958.*
    London: Oxford University Press, 1964; 2d ed., Yale University Press, 1987.
                                                                    JOHN F. DEVLIN

HOUARI BOUMEDIENE (1927–1978). Three years after independence had
been painfully won from France, Algeria's first defense minister, Houari Boumediene, wrested power from his colleague and revolutionary companion Ahmed
Ben Bella.* The Boumediene era lasted thirteen years, and was a critical period
for setting Algeria's political and economic course.

Houari Boumediene was an enigmatic figure. His coup against Ben Bella,
motivated largely by concerns about excessive powers concentrated in the presidency, in fact led to more centralized power than had prevailed under Ben Bella.
Boumediene was a man of strong, sometimes contradictory convictions. His
views on Islam, socialism, and the role of the military were not shared by all
the revolutionary leadership; once in power, he did not succeed in changing
official dogma fully to his presumed preferences. Despite his considerable skills
at consolidating power and keeping adversaries at bay, he was shy and a poor
public speaker. He did not thrive on the mass rallies and public demonstrations
that characterized Algeria's state-building stage. In his thirteen years in power,
he made a greater mark on independent Algeria than either his predecessor or
his successor, Chadli Bendjedid.* His legacy is surely a mixed one; he made
Algeria a symbol of fierce Third World pride, but was also responsible for many
of the economic and political policies that have been challenged in Algeria's
third decade of independence.

There is uncertainty about the early life of Boumediene, who was born Mohamed Ben Brahim Boukharouba in Clauzel, near Guelma in eastern Algeria.
His birthdate is in dispute; many sources cite 1927, although others suggest he
was born five years later. His father was a small landholder who sent his son to
French and Koranic schools. At the age of fourteen, Boumediene began his
studies at the Kettania Medersa, a conservative Muslim school near Constantine.
When called to the French army in 1952, he chose instead to flee, and began
working for the FLN (National Liberation Front) in Cairo. At the same time,
he continued Islamic studies at Al-Azhar. He would later prove to be one of the
only members of the ruling elite to have received serious training in Islamic
studies.

When the war with the French broke out in 1954, Bourmediene began commando training and soon joined the *maquisard* (insurgents organized in rural
clandestine activities), although his wartime career was essentially with the

external army, not the guerrillas incountry. It was in the mid–1950s that the young Boukharouba chose Houari Boumediene as his nom de guerre; it has saintly associations from the western city of Tlemcen. Unlike many of his compatriots, Boumediene never resumed the use of his given name, and would later tell interviewers that he could not remember where he was born.

Boumediene rose quickly in the ranks of the fifth military district, and was known for his effective recruitment of young people, even those of high-school age, to gather intelligence along the Moroccan frontier. He established a reputation as a reserved, courteous, and competent officer. By the fall of 1958, he was promoted to the head of the General Staff West, in command of three military districts. In less than two years, Boumediene was head of the General Staff headquartered in Tunisia, where he implemented a low-cost, low-key strategy that would serve to deceive the French Army Command into overestimating the French successes.

Boumediene's rapid rise in the ranks has been attributed to his considerable organizational skills and to his friendship with Abdelhafid Boussouff, one of the three most powerful members of the Provisional Government of the Algerian Republic (GPRA), which was formed in September 1958. With his focus on day-to-day military affairs, Boumediene was generally shielded from the fierce competition and infighting between the GPRA and the FLN (also known as the rivalry between the Alger Group versus the Tlemcen or Oujda Group) that soon dominated the political development of preindependence Algeria. In that struggle, the GPRA was generally viewed as willing to make compromises with France to expedite the transition to independence, while the FLN criticized any concessions to France and favored establishing an independent Algeria as a revolutionary, socialist state.

Boumediene emerged from political obscurity in 1961, when he defied the order of the provisional president of the GPRA, Ben Youccef Ben Khedda, to disband his general staff and subsume military authority to the provisional government. This proved to be a strategic turning point for Boumediene, who thus aligned himself with Ahmed Ben Bella, the charismatic revolutionary. This partnership proved key to both men's futures. Linked more by their common views of the struggle at that particular phase than by friendship or lasting compatibility, it appears that Ben Bella sought the alliance with the taciturn military officer and was intrigued with Boumediene. Ben Bella's emergence as the victor of these early internecine struggles is often attributed as much to the clout of Boumediene's support as it is to Ben Bella's own considerable political skills.

The Evian Accords, signed in March 1962, established the procedures for the transition to independence. Boumediene, who did not formally oppose Evian, had reservations about some unresolved issues and about the GPRA's political will to implement the accords in the ways that fully favored Algeria. From March until July 1, when the national referendum on independence was approved, Boumediene worked actively within Ben Bella's camp, maneuvering to consolidate Ben Bella's ascendancy over the GPRA and the forces within Algeria.

During the summer, Algeria was effectively in a state of civil war. The external military forces of Boumediene, renamed the *Armée Nationale Populaire* (ANP or People's National Army) occupied Constantine and Annaba, and forced the GPRA to yield certain functions to the FLN. The capital district (Wilaya IV) was most resistant to FLN domination, and forces there remained loyal to the GPRA after Boumediene's troops had established control in the rest of the country.

Boumediene was the last of the inner circle to enter Alger once the FLN triumph over the GPRA was achieved in September 1962. Boumediene was also the last to arrive at the meeting that was called to determine the new role of the military; he resisted calls to return the troops to the barracks and to place the army under civilian control. He favored instead a more original mandate for the army as a popular institution fully integrated into nation building, but that concept of the Algerian military was not adopted by his colleagues, who favored a more conventional role for the military in a civilian-controlled government.

Boumediene did not fully participate in the wild euphoria and near-anarchy that swept Alger and Ben Bella's entourage (in notable contrast to the somber discipline that prevailed in the areas under Boumediene's control). Instead, according to sympathetic French biographers, Boumediene was preoccupied by the challenges facing Algeria, and felt estranged from the demagoguery of the politicians.

It was no surprise that Boumediene was selected as the first minister of defense of the new government. He quickly applied himself to structuring and organizing the ministry, and worked to establish good relations between the central government and the regional military commands.

By late 1963, the time of the formation of the second government, Boumediene was the only one of Ben Bella's original clan to have survived the turbulent first year and to remain in the cabinet. Ben Bella named him vice president of the Revolutionary Council, and delegated power to Boumediene when he traveled abroad. Nonetheless, the differences between the two men were becoming clear: Boumediene gradually tired of Ben Bella's leadership, his policy improvisations and impetuous foreign commitments. He was reported to find *autogestion*—Ben Bella's radical agrarian reform, in which peasants took over the land they had worked during the colonial period—anarchic and imprecise. Ben Bella's constitutional referendum, setting up a presidential system in which the president was also commander in chief of the armed forces, further estranged Boumediene from his colleague, and Boumediene became the focus and catalyst for anti–Ben Bella sentiment within the ruling elite.

By 1964, signs that relations between Ben Bella and Boumediene had soured were evident. Despite stiff opposition, Ben Bella pushed for his National Charter, which affirmed the controversial autogestion as national policy and defined the relations among the state, party, and army; this exercise convinced Boumediene of the president's increasingly dictatorial tendencies.

Ultimately, military issues were the most divisive force in their relationship. Ben Bella, aware that the military had become an independent force, tried to assert his control over it, declaring that the ANP "only exists within the framework of the FLN" (Quandt 1969:219). As he became increasingly dependent on Boumediene and his powerful institution, he tried to undermine Boumediene's authority. Ben Bella used ideology to try to weaken Boumediene by emphasizing Boumediene's more traditional Islamic orientation in contrast to the scientific socialism of the revolutionary cadres. Ben Bella's deteriorating relationship with Boumediene manifested itself in the president's efforts to create a people's militia to serve as a counterweight to the national army. Boumediene was furious at this move, but a showdown was avoided with a compromise: The militia would be created but would be trained by the ANP. This face-saving solution bought some time for Ben Bella.

As Ben Bella prepared to host a large Afro-Asian conference, Boumediene conspired to depose the president with other Cabinet officers and key officials in the party and the military. The takeover on June 19, 1965, was bloodless. Ben Bella was informed by friends that he had been removed from office.

Boumediene announced the suspension of the constitution and the creation of the Council of the Revolution as the supreme political body in Algeria to be composed of twenty-six members, mostly from the military. He defended his action as necessary to rescue the revolution. This was a corrective coup, and was not a rejection of socialism or the fundamental directions chosen at independence. Boumediene promised gradual change, not an abrupt repudiation of the past. He was rejecting only what he saw as Ben Bella's distortions of the revolution, his flamboyant style, neglect of domestic development for the sake of foreign adventures, and encouragement of a cult of personality.

Boumediene's first government, established in July 1965, was dominated by military officers but also included technocrats and some of the party hard-liners. Boumediene appeared to favor strengthening the party, and to insist on collegial decision making. He created the Council of the Revolution, consisting of 26 members, and made speeches and statements giving the impression that it was the Council, and not Boumediene personally, that headed the government. Nonetheless, Boumediene's formal responsibilities included head of party, commander in chief of the armed forces, minister of defense, and president.

Boumediene's first priority was to consolidate his hold on power. Loyalty from the military was not an issue; much of the officer corps was relieved that Boumediene had acted against Ben Bella, and the ANP was in many ways the most effective national organization of the postindependence period. Rather, Boumediene, who had openly disdained professional politicians, had to prove his bona fides with the party leadership and with the government's bureaucratic cadres. This process of consolidation preoccupied the president's first few years in office, and no dramatic new policy initiatives were launched.

Boumediene faced early resistance from students, the union, and leftist forces in the party, who were concerned that his technocratic approach to governing would dilute or modify the socialism of Ben Bella. In these first years, there were two known attempts to oust Boumediene: one by a small group of disgruntled army officers in December 1967, and a second in April 1968, when the president was mildly injured by a guerrilla attack.

Boumediene became more active in setting his own policy agenda after 1968, focusing first on making government more effective in its tasks. He reorganized public finances, set up a state banking system, and created new public corporations. His most ambitious undertaking was the nationalization of the oil industry, with the takeover of all French-owned assets in February 1971. This was the first comprehensive nationalization of a Middle Eastern oil industry since Iranian Prime Minister Mohammad Mossadegh* made a similar move in 1953. The Algerian action presaged the creation of OPEC—the Organization of Petroleum Exporting Countries—in 1973.

The period after 1971 was characterized by more radical internal economic policy-making. Rapid industrialization, to move the country quickly into modernization, was emphasized, and became a centerpiece of Boumediene's presidency. Its benefits to the country as a whole were not realized quickly; the extended period of capital investment in industry did little to generate badly needed employment, and giant state corporations (of which the most notable was Sonatrech, the hydrocarbon company) became politically and economically costly. Ultimately, though, Boumediene's hopes for industrial development were thwarted by overly ambitious goals and inefficient management and design.

Boumediene also addressed agrarian reform. He had long been critical of the autogestion (self-management) policy of Ben Bella, which he felt provided no benefits to the real peasants while allowing those who had worked the French colons' (settlers') land to become landholders. Boumediene wanted more direction and management of the agrarian sector, a goal that was possibly at odds with autogestion. His new agrarian revolution was launched in three phases: first, the redistribution of foreign- and state-owned lands; second, redistribution of private estates; and third, transformation of the lives of nomads. These policies met considerable political resistance from conservatives, although they were supported by radical students who had previously been critical of the president. Boumediene succeeded in creating a new cooperative sector of agricultural production and marketing, but in general, agrarian reform was not considered a hallmark of his presidency, and chronic problems in food production, which struggled to keep pace with rapid population growth, plagued Boumediene's Algeria.

A decade after his accession to power, Boumediene launched an ambitious agenda in domestic politics, focusing on two major initiatives: to revitalize the FLN and to foster national consensus through approval of a national charter. His efforts to restore the FLN to its earlier, revolutionary dynamism by recruiting new socialist blood into its ranks was widely viewed as a failure. The central role the FLN had played before independence—as a symbol of liberation and a rallying point for national identity—could not be recaptured, particularly since the professional army and the bureaucracy had replaced the party as channels of policy formulation and debate. The party had been reduced to a messenger role, and Boumediene's goal of achieving popular mobilization behind policies that had been generated by a technocratic elite remained unrealized.

In June 1975, Boumediene announced new national elections for an assembly and for the presidency, to be preceded by a national referendum on a new charter or constitution. This bold initiative was generally considered a sign of Boumediene's political strength and his desire to demonstrate the extent of his command of national politics. Nonetheless, opposition from former leadership figures came quickly: Ferhat Abbas* and Ben Youssef Ben Khedda, among others, criticized Boumediene's totalitarianism in a manifesto published in early 1976, an action for which they were arrested.

The charter is a document of nearly two hundred pages, outlining in elaborate theories the country's underlying socialist and progressive orientation. It also pays homage to the FLN and its role in national life, and acknowledges the special Islamic and Third World dimensions of Algerian identity. The government encouraged active public debate over the charter, which was approved in June 1976. By year's end, Boumediene's new mandate as president was endorsed by 99 percent of votes cast. In February 1977, the last formal phase of the president's political agenda was completed, with the election of a new national assembly of 261 members chosen from a list of candidates prepared by the FLN. Other measures to strengthen and expand the role of the party were continued until the president's death in 1978.

Prominent in Boumediene's legacy is his activist and global foreign policy. Despite the fact that he was critical, even mocking, of Ben Bella's peripatetic involvement in far-flung liberation struggles, Boumediene continued to promote an energetic and ideological Algerian presence on the world scene, and made an important contribution to Algerian leadership of the nonaligned movement, the Arab League, and the Organization of African Unity.

At first, Boumediene did not alter the sensitive relationship with France, permitting continued French cultural and economic influence through a series of bilateral agreements. Early sources of friction stemmed from the 1971 nationalization of the petroleum industry and from French concerns about a growing Soviet influence, particularly in the military sphere. Eventually, Boumediene moved to begin a national healing process with France, and in 1975 he welcomed Valéry Giscard d'Estaing to Algiers, the first visit by a French president since the end of the war. During that visit, Boumediene departed from his practice of not speaking French in public, and told his French counterpart that a page had been turned and that Algeria was able to engage in a dialogue without bitterness or reservations. Boumediene could rightfully claim to have effected an evolutionary change in Algeria's approach to dealing with France, from acting as a former colonial dependent to serving as a respected trading partner.

Soviet-Algerian ties expanded under Boumediene, although he sought to avoid a dependent client relationship. From his tenure as Ben Bella's defense minister, Boumediene had looked to Moscow as a vital source for the modernization of the armed forces, and the Soviets provided large amounts of aid, equipment, and training. The heavy concentration of Soviet support led to Western concerns about an emerging client relationship, with strategic implications; and Algeria's strong support for Third World liberation movements, many Soviet-backed, was viewed as another dimension of Boumediene's pro-Soviet orientation. Algeria, for its part, insisted that its commitment to nonalignment prevented excessive reliance on any outside powers, and pointed to its refusal to let the Soviet Union use a naval base at Mers el-Kabir and other formerly French military facilities as firm evidence. Boumediene also considered support for revolutionary movements as a natural extension of Algeria's own revolutionary experience, not linked to its relations with the great powers.

In 1973, Algeria assumed the mantle of leadership of the nonaligned movement, and hosted the Non-Aligned Movement (NAM) conference in Algiers. This was a high point of Boumediene's foreign policy, enabling him to offer leadership to other developing countries; he urged them to avoid superpower domination, to work to end a biopolar world system, and to seek rapid development.

Leadership of the NAM provided Boumediene with a forum to rally international support for the Arab cause in the Arab-Israeli conflict. He was able to persuade many NAM countries to sever relations with Israel after the 1973 October Arab-Israeli War, and played a key role in improving the PLO's standing in the United Nations, culminating in Yasser Arafat's* address to the General Assembly in 1974.

In his immediate region, Boumediene's policies toward Morocco and the conflict in the western Sahara have had less clear results for Algeria's international standing. Although Algeria supported the initial efforts to disengage Spain from its former possession, and to allow Morocco and Mauritania to administer the territory until self-determination could be exercised, Algeria in 1975 became the principal backer of the Polisario movement, seeking independence of the disputed territory. This position seemed to marry Algeria's ideological principles with its interests in preventing Moroccan territorial expansion (Moroccan claims to the western Sahara could be extended to parts of the Algerian Sahara) and in protecting potential economic and strategic interests in the territory. Boumediene's deepening attachment to the Sahara cause appeared to isolate him in the Arab world, and the sharp deterioration of Algerian-Moroccan relations was the predominant national security problem at the end of his presidency.

BIBLIOGRAPHY

Balta, Paul, and Claudine Rulleau (eds.). *La Strategie de Boumediene*. Paris: Sinbad, 1978.
Braestrup, Peter, and David Ottaway. "In Algeria, It's Not 'Yah Yah Boumediene!' but Wait and See." *New York Times Magazine*, February 13, 1966.
Francos, Ania, and J. P. Sereni. *Un Algerien Nomme Boumediene*. Paris: Stock, 1976.
Mameri Khalfa. *Orientations Politique de L'Algerie: Analyse des discours du President Boumediene*. Alger: Société Nationale d'Edition et de Diffusion, 1973.

Ottaway, David, and Marina Ottaway. *Algeria, the Politics of a Socialist Revolution.*
     Berkeley: University of California Press, 1970.
Quandt, William. *Revolution and Political Leadership: Algeria 1954–1968.* Cambridge:
     MIT Press, 1969.

ELLEN LAIPSON

HABIB BOURGUIBA (1903–). On November 7, 1987, Habib Bourguiba, president-for-life of Tunisia and one of the last remaining Third World post-colonial political leaders was deposed, thus concluding a career that spanned eight decades of decisive change for Arab North Africa and the Middle East. That Bourguiba made a significant contribution to the evolution of the modern Tunisian personality, worked tirelessly for North African socioeconomic integration, and brought his unique philosophical perspective to bear on regional issues of global importance were facts recognized during his lifetime; and yet this recognition did not prevent a coup from being mounted against him, a coup that referred for its authority to the very constitution Bourguiba himself had struggled so arduously to manipulate in the service of his personal power.

To say as much, however, is not necessarily to class him with the petty dictators of which modern Africa and the Middle East can boast in such large numbers. Bourguiba was a dictator of the most benevolent kind. He was also an autocrat of liberal persuasions; he believed in the primacy of the state of law. However, his personal view of the world inclined him regrettably toward a political and philosophical pessimism that defeated his democratic instincts, for he understood history as an act of will and saw himself as the motor that imparted to time its élan vital; consequently, he was unable to imagine that history had meaning outside his capacity to valorize it and to personify the synthesis between events and the world in which he played so prominent a role. This megalomania, complicated in his declining years by the intensification of a manic-depressive psychosis, drove him deep into a solitude from which he was increasingly more reluctant to emerge.

However, like many geniuses afflicted with this malady, he was able to harness sickness to the material construction of his worldview. The peaks and troughs of his moods caused him only rarely to lose his center of gravity. Bourguiba demonstrated, even in ill health, his intuitive gift for pragmatic, tactical politics, a preference for nonviolence, and an aversion to political dogma. The result was the palpable creation of a state whose institutions revolved around his person. He erected a monolithic party structure and endowed it with a political character that reflected his own dynamism. In that both state and party conformed to his fluid conception of political culture, the state assumed a protean character. Anchored in Bourguiba's denial of the material basis for class struggle, the state would change with apparent ease during the thirty years of his reign from a monarch to a centralized presidency, from single-party politics to socialism, and finally from socialism to a liberal, laissez-faire pseudo-democracy.

Habib Bourguiba was born in 1903 to a petty bourgeois family in the Sahelian town of Monastir. His childhood was marked from an early age by the social values of his milieu that stressed the cohesiveness of Sahelian sedentary society, a frugal political economy, and a respect for individual achievement while, at the same time, it bred an oppressiveness of family relationships that could impose a rigid law of precedence in the distribution of scant resources. As a child, Bourguiba felt strongly the oppression of being the rival and ward of his older brothers. By the same token, revolt against the powerful males of the family engendered an overvaluation of his mother's role in his life and the desire for a spiritual son. In terms of Bourguiba's later politics, this psychosocial nexus was manifested in a personal tension between autonomous democracy and constraining autocracy, between the worship of reason and the cold efficiency of authority; in his savage intolerance of competition for pride of place from political rivals; and, finally, in the ambiguity of his reverence for, and distrust of, women. One thing clearly emerges from his childhood years: The lack of a unified family of his own would lead Bourguiba to unify the Tunisian people politically as a "family" under his spiritual fatherhood and to condemn as tribalism any sign of refractoriness.

Bourguiba spent his school days at Tunis's famous Sadiki school, and graduated from the Lycée Carnot, from which he received his baccalaureat in 1924. A chronic lack of funds made those years difficult but rewarding for the young scholar. However, despite the uncertainty of his position, he absorbed all that the Franco-Arabic curriculum of Sadiki could provide, and it was there that his lifelong admiration of French political culture was initially nurtured. Upon completion of his studies, he departed for Paris to study law and political science, but not before having lived through, and participated in, the first turbulent stirring of Tunisian nationalism. In 1926 he returned to Tunis. He opened a law office and turned immediately to political journalism sustained by the warm and devoted attention of his French wife, Mathilde, whom he had married in Paris, by whom he had his only child, and whom he was to divorce later for ostensibly political reasons.

At Sadiki, Bourguiba had read Sheikh Abdelaziz Thaalbi's *La Tunisie Martyre*. Profoundly impressed by this early independence manifesto, Bourguiba was encouraged to participate in demonstrations against the Protectorate and to join Thaalbi's *Destour* (Constitutionalist) Party in 1927. Bourguiba's writings covered a wide range of nationalist themes, perhaps none so fundamental to the Tunisian sense of authenticity as that of the status of women in society, a subject on which he gave his first public address in 1928 when he defended the wearing of the veil. That speech established Bourguiba's instinctive genius for the manipulation of symbols that would galvanize the Tunisian masses and touch them to the core. In 1932 he founded *l'Action Tunisienne*, the newspaper that would thereafter become the official organ for most intimate political and philosophic thoughts.

The interwar years saw everywhere in the Arab world a great nationalist effervescence with which the Destour was patently out of step, and so it was inevitable that Bourguiba would break with Thaalbi. It was not that Bourguiba disagreed with Thaalbi's assumption that France should cede to Tunisia its independence, only that the Destour's demands contributed to the restriction of its sphere of political action. Bourguiba's reaction to the Protectorate's politics was to confront the French with their tarnished ideals and combat the tendencies of Residents-General and *colons* (settlers) to centralize authority in their hands. He clearly realized that self-government must precede independence, and to this end continuing dialogue with France served a useful purpose. With small, pragmatic steps he exploited the Protectorate's weakness. The Destour was incapable of such finesse. Immured in the pride of their traditional caste system, the "old turbans" were hopelessly outdated politicians. In 1933, the Destour was outlawed; in 1934 Bourguiba led a rump congress in the Sahelian town of Ksar Hilal to a final schism with the parent body. Out of this conflict the Neo-Destour came into being as a reflection of the energy of a new class of Tunisian "Young Turks."

Bourguiba paid dearly for his political activism. He spent eight months under house arrest between September 1934 and April 1935. Released on the eve of the coming to power of Léon Blum's Popular Front in France, Bourguiba expected liberal reforms from the Protectorate. In this he was deceived. The Neo-Destour Party Congress voted in 1936 to pass into the opposition and, following the general strikes of 1938, Bourguiba was once more incarcerated. During the next five years, he was shunted from one prison to another in Tunisia, Vichy France, and Italy. The war years in prison never clouded his vision. He understood that Tunisia's destiny lay with a resurgent France, and he never once yielded to the temptation to bring the Neo-Destour Party into alignment with the Axis powers. When he was liberated in 1943, he returned to Tunisia enveloped in an aura of impeccable legitimacy, charged with charisma, and ready to continue the struggle. In the meanwhile, his party had held together in clandestinity aided by the increasingly powerful Tunisian trade union movement with which the Neo-Destour Party had established common political goals. While this commonality of interests allowed the Neo-Destour to survive under suppression, the resulting autonómy that the union enjoyed proved in later years to be a formidable impediment to national unity when the union challenged the party for domination of the postindependence polity.

However, Bourguiba had little time to consider this issue; he had already become an object of the official scrutiny of a Protectorate that was determined to proscribe his efforts. In 1945, Bourguiba fled Tunisia for Cairo to forestall arrest. He remained in Egypt for four years, toured the Mashriq, and endeavored to internationalize the Tunisian problem before the Arab League. The Arabs disappointed Bourguiba. Petty territorial squabbles, dynastic quarrels, and the Palestinian question preoccupied them, affording Bourguiba little hope that they would give more than lip service to his cause. His sojourn in the Arab East made him painfully aware of the Arabs' political provincialism. He quickly grasped that mythic, romantic pan-Arabism bore the seeds of perennial dissension, and that the pan-Arab world's militaristic intransigence toward Zionism would, in the final analysis, make the case for Israel's underdog status. Bourguiba demonstrated his prescience by insisting that the Arabs attack the international dimension of the Palestinian issue within the framework of Bourguibist tactics. History would exonerate him; but he made few Arab friends for his trouble.

By 1949 he was back in Tunis to pursue the politics of independence by stages. Once more, in 1952, the Neo-Destour was interdicted, its political bureau disbanded, and Bourguiba interned for the third time. The French had refused to take him seriously, his attempt to bring Tunisian grievances before the United Nations failed to produce results after a consultative assembly rejected the Protectorate's counterproposals for reform, and Farhat Hached, the secretary-general of the union and his confederate, was assassinated by colon extremists. Moreover, with the accession of Gamal Abdul Nasser* to power in Egypt, a current of pan-Arabism was beginning to sweep through the Neo-Destour Party, championed by the party's secretary-general, Salah Ben Youssef, who demanded complete and total independence. From prison, Bourguiba persevered. In March 1954, the party and the union rejected another series of French political reforms. Ben Salah's partisans (fellaghas) attacked the Protectorate from the south. Bourguiba was, however, not deterred from seeking accommodation with France. On June 1, 1955, he made a triumphant return to Tunis from exile; on June 3, a Franco-Tunisian accord was signed. Immediately the government of Mendès-France proclaimed Tunisian autonomy, the fellaghas laid down their arms, and the Neo-Destour Party entered the administration. In September, Ben Youssef, returning from Libya, took up a position against autonomy. For his defiance of Bourguiba he was excluded from the party. Incapable of clemency, Bourguiba had him assassinated in 1961.

Thus, after seventy-five years of French colonialism, Tunisia joined the community of independent nations on March 3, 1956. Bourguiba's first official act as president of the National Assembly was to promulgate a Code of Personal Status, abolish polygamy, suppress Islamic divorce, and enfranchise women. A year later the National Assembly did away with the monarchy, deposed the *bey* (the sovereign), proclaimed the republic, and unanimously designated Habib Bourguiba president of the republic. The first part of his illustrious career was over; a second and more controversial part was about to begin.

The history of postindependence Tunisia dovetails neatly with the three challenges to his power that Bourguiba was obliged to face at ten-year intervals during his reign. The first threat from Ben Youssef challenged the consolidation of state authority in Bourguiba's hands, and Bourguiba dealt with it savagely; the second threat came in 1969 from his minister of economics, Ahmed Ben Salah, when Ben Salah used the economic institutions Bourguiba had erected as a base for his own power; and the third threat came in the wake of the 1978 general strikes with the resurgence of union autonomy under its chief, Habib Achour.

Ben Youssef's downfall inaugurated a decade of significant successes. It could be fairly said that during that time Bourguiba achieved his right—as Charles de Gaulle was to say in his memoirs—to a greatness bigger than his small country. Against all ideological currents and entangling superpower alliances, Bourguiba maintained Tunisian sovereignty and neutrality. In the absence of natural resources, he put faith in the strengthening of Tunisia's human potential by allocating a large part of the state's budget to bilingual education. He stood firm for female emancipation and respect for civic rights and obligations, and gave Tunisians a clear and unambiguous notion of authentic modern culture.

Unfortunately, Bourguiba accomplished this at the expense of creating an elite tied to him by bonds of personal fidelity, and when, as in the case of Ahmed Ben Salah, one of his minions tried to institutionalize the implications of his concepts, Bourguiba took this as a gesture of lèse-majesté. Ben Salah's fall from grace in 1969 brought to a climax a five-year effort to cooperativize agriculture and bring ancillary industries in the public sector under governmental control. More importantly, the Ben Salah affair gave the lie to the political liberalization that an educated elite had been brought up to expect.

In the same year, Bourguiba's health began to fail. Personalistic politicking among the president's handpicked men intensified as he slowly withdrew from a supervisory role in national affairs, and many, such as Minister of Defense Ahmad Mestiri, who in 1971 demanded a reform of the party to free the nation from ossified socioeconomic structures, suffered permanent exclusion.

The early 1970s were a time of social and trade-union agitation. The population was increasing in disproportion to the state's ability to meet its aspirations; yet, curiously, this was also a time of relative prosperity (a prosperity, however, that benefited only the privileged few). A generation began to appear that had not been socialized to Bourguibist values and for whom Bourguiba was the example of a moribund political figure.

The sicker Bourguiba became, the more he acted out of character. Observers began to suspect that his mental faculties were degenerating when, in 1974, he agreed to merge Tunisia with Libya. Such an act was contrary to his convictions concerning the nature of Maghrib unity, his distrust of pan-Arabism, and his dislike of Muammar Qaddafi.* To some, this bizarre volte-face was indicative of Bourguiba's "Jugurtha" complex, a psychological disposition referring to the Berber patriot who, like Bourguiba, was simultaneously imaginative and indifferent, active and solitary, and never able to realize the contradictions of his own decisions.

Bourguiba survived this mistake which, unhappily, made worse the fierce competition to succeed him among the elites to whom he had relegated the practical business of running the government. On one hand, he divided and conquered them, using his occasional flashes of lucidity to disarm their coups; and, on the other hand, he constitutionally manipulated the succession issue to confound their machinations. In 1974 the National Assembly proclaimed him president-for-life. With his consecration as sole guarantor of the state of law, a "monarchy" was restored and the immobilism of the political process assured.

Against the background of deepening crisis, the trade union called for a general strike in early 1978. Ostensibly the strike was over the widening gap between wages and inflation. In point of fact, however, the strike represented a reaction to the curtailment of union political activities, the creation of parallel institutions in its place, and Bourguiba's desire to destroy the influence of the union's indomitable secretary-general, Habib Achour. Achour had been an important political militant and one of the few remaining elites to have participated in Bourguiba's independence movement. By imprisoning Achour, Bourguiba defeated the last old-guard Destourian around whom legitimate power might have coalesced. Victory was achieved at the expense of the Tunisian people, as a chasm between state and society began to open that threatened to become unbridgeable.

The general strike set the stage for the final decade of Habib Bourguiba's political career. Qaddafi capitalized on the internal chaos to mount a coup against the government in 1980 which, if it did not succeed in bringing Bourguiba down, still forced Tunisia to purchase defensive armaments it could little afford and thus exacerbated an already staggering debt service ratio of payments to GNP. A downturn in the tourism and petroleum markets, a failure to absorb the growing number of Tunisian youth into the economy, and paradoxically, the high per-capita income level, which was a product of the liberal seventies and the reason for disqualifying Tunisia for international development loans, combined to further weaken the strained socioeconomic fabric of the nation. In late 1983, Bourguiba consented to a program of forced savings whereby the price of government-subsidized basic foodstuffs would be raised. Bread riots broke out everywhere on the first of the new year. The army was called out to quell the disturbances and for the first time its politicization became a distinct possibility. Not long after, Bourguiba suffered a heart attack and disappeared from public view.

As a consequence, the struggle for succession intensified, taking the form of innumerable cabals and endless Florentine intrigues. Corruption was rife; the government seemed to have decamped, leaving in its wake unresolved problems of great magnitude. From the silence of the presidential palace, Bourguiba responded with a constant shuffling of his cabinet. The country was adrift without leadership or direction.

Aware of this and ready to take action was an indigenous Islamist movement, spawned by the resentment of moral decay and inspired by the example of militant Islamic revival in the Mashriq and Iran. The Islamists claimed to offer a political and economic alternative to national degeneration within the context of the political pluralism long promised but never carried out by Bourguiba. The president, who never waivered in his belief that Islam represented the force of cultural obscurantism (he was reported to have said to Muhammad Masmoudi, the architect of the Libyan union, that if God existed He was happy with Bourguiba, but that if He did not then Bourguiba was happy enough with himself), set about to crush the new competitors.

The conflict with the Islamists was Bourguiba's swan song. It evolved during a time of increasing ambiguity regarding the country's orientation toward both the West and the Arabs. PLO (Palestine Liberation Organization) headquarters in Tunis had been attacked in October 1985 by Israeli fighters, and the United States, with a surprising disregard of Tunisian sensibilities, applauded the event. Bourguiba had put much faith in the American ability to stabilize the Middle East and to bring the Arabs around to his way of thinking. Again he felt betrayed by his friends and deeply resented the Islamist suggestion that he had been duped by the West into serving the cause of imperialism and its systematic depredation of Muslim society. Bourguiba ordered the leaders of the Islamist movement to be imprisoned on a trumped-up charge of collaborating with Iran in the overthrow of the Tunisian state. When, in 1987, the Tunisian courts dealt a lighter sentence to the Islamists than Bourguiba thought warranted, he burst into an Olympian rage and demanded that they be retried and executed. There was no recourse but to oust the president. On November 7, 1987, Prime Minister Zine el Abidine Ben Ali* invoked Article 57 of the constitution, which provided for the removal of the chief executive in the event of mental incapacitation, and thus brought to an ignominious end the reign of Habib Bourguiba.

With the deposition of Bourguiba, the Arab world lost one of its great statesmen and a voice for moderation and political conciliationism. Tunisia itself lost the guiding spirit of its evolution toward modern nationhood. As Bourguiba's virtues were many, so were his vices. Because he wanted to be the personal guarantor of state legitimacy, he refused to institutionalize power in any political organism. Although his sickness prevented him from overseeing all aspects of government, he cashiered those who tried to do it in his place. Because he could trust no one but himself, he opened the way for intrigues against him and created the conditions of his debasement. Bourguiba believed unhesitatingly in his intuitive genius, and so he built state structures on the shifting sands of caprice and whimsy. Because he sacralized Tunisian nationalism and made it the religion of the state and the arbiter of the state's authenticity, he was unable to gauge the profundity of the Islamist reaction. Bourguiba attempted to be all things to all men; not only a political leader but a secular *imam* (prayer leader) who struggled to detach religion from its roots in the clientelism he despised and at the feet of which he laid the blame for the lack of real Arab democracy. His legitimacy rested on the uncanny way he assumed all Tunisian characteristics as his own and aligned Tunisia's Arabo-Islamic history with the unfolding of his career. He dictated to Tunisians to be sure. But he did so in a manner acceptable to their douceur de vivre; that is, to the dictatorship of an anxiety for the morrow.

In sum, Bourguiba was the total man of action, a leader deeply committed to the principles of a method without a plan for which no theory of state was ever devised. It was for that very reason that the social ideal to which he devoted so much skill and energy was ultimately unrealizable. The irony of Bourguiba's life was that he nourished the aspirations of a political class to realize the ideal of which he was incapable. Such is his greatest contribution and, in no small part, his departure from the scene was the sine qua non condition for the continuity of the state and the survival of his legacy.

BIBLIOGRAPHY

Brown, L. Carl (ed.). *State and Society in Independent North Africa*. Washington, D.C.: The Middle East Institute, 1966.
Camau, Michel. *Pouvoirs et Institutions au Maghreb*. Tunis: Cérès Productions, 1978.
Cohen, Bernard. *Bourguiba, Le Pouvoir d'un Seul*. Paris: Flammarion, 1986.
Micaud, Charles A. (ed.). *Tunisia: The Politics of Modernization*. New York: Praeger, 1964.
Moore, Clement Henry. *Tunisia since Independence*. Berkeley: University of California Press, 1965.
————. *Politics in North Africa*. Boston: Little, Brown and Company, 1970.
Périllier, Louis. *La Conquête de l'Indépendence Tunisienne*. Paris: Editions Robert Lafont, 1979.
Perkins, Kenneth J. *Tunisia: Crossroads of the Islamic and European Worlds*. Boulder, Colo.: Westview Press, 1986.
Salem, Norma. *Habib Bourguiba, Islam, and the Creation of Tunisia*. London: Croom Helm, 1984.

L. B. WARE

C

CAMILLE CHAMOUN (1900–1987) devoted his life to Lebanese politics. After winning election to the Chamber of Deputies at a young age, Chamoun rose through the ranks of Lebanese politics and played a key role in the national and international politics of his country. His political, legal, and business experience contributed to his election as president in 1952, a position he retained until 1958. Chamoun was a popular leader who pursued policies of greater economic and political freedom for Lebanon.

In the mountains southeast of Beirut lay the mixed Druze-Maronite district called the Shuf, seat of the palace of the former *amirs* (rulers) of Mt. Lebanon at Beit al-Din. Just across the valley from Beit al-Din is the Maronite market town of Dayr al-Qamr, site of a massacre of Maronite Christians by the Druze during the intercommunal hostilities of 1860. Despite the legacy of 1860, or possibly because of it, the Maronite inhabitants of the Shuf have tended to have a different view of Lebanon than their more isolated coreligionaires to the north. Whereas the Maronites of northern Lebanon have tended to view their country as a Christian homeland, those in the mixed districts of the Metn and the Shuf have grasped the multisectarian character of the modern Lebanese state. It is not surprising, therefore, that, as Lebanon gained its independence from France in 1943 and the need arose to establish an effective political system on the basis of cooperative sectarian relations, Lebanon's first two Maronite presidents, Bishara al-Khouri and Camille Chamoun, came from this region.

The town of Dayr al-Qamr was the birthplace of Camille Chamoun, although the ancestral home of the Chamoun clan was, and remains, Ayn al-Zhalta, higher up in the Shuf district. Both men based their political influence within Lebanon's Maronite community on the support of their coreligionaires in the mixed districts, and Chamoun also benefited from the patronage of Khouri, who helped raise him from relative obscurity to prominence in Lebanese politics.

Chamoun was born on April 3, 1900, the son of Nimr Chamoun and Antoinette Adib Nehme. His father was a relatively humble inspector of finances in the Ottoman provincial government of Mt. Lebanon, and continued in this function during the early years of the French Mandate. Educated at a small Catholic school in Dayr al-Qamr, the Petite Ecole des Soeurs de Saint-Joseph, and the College Français du Sacre-Coeur, a secondary school in Beirut, Chamoun was the product of a wholly French education, as were most members of the Maronite elite of his generation. In 1916, the family was exiled to Anatolia for three years during World War I for alleged anti-Turk activities on the part of Nimr Chamoun. In 1920, following the return of the family from exile, he entered the Faculty of Law of the Université de Saint-Joseph in Beirut, and in 1923 he obtained his license to practice law.

Chamoun's ambitious character was served by the changing times in which he lived. The French Mandate gave new scope for upward mobility to new classes of men who were interested in the pursuit of business, banking, journalism, or law. Chamoun interested himself in all these pursuits, and while establishing himself as a successful lawyer, businessman, and property owner during the 1920s, he also began making important social and political contacts through association with *Le Reveil* newspaper, for whom he wrote articles and served as a contributing editor. In 1926, the French Mandatory authority nudged Lebanon closer toward national independence by approving a constitution that defined the country as a republic and provided for an elected Chamber of Deputies.

The year 1929 proved to be a watershed in Chamoun's life. In that year his father died, he married, and he stood for his first election as a delegate from Dayr al-Qamr in the second stage of the election that would choose the country's Chamber of Deputies. In his memoirs, Chamoun gave credit to the good name of his late father in helping him to win this first electoral campaign as well as subsequent ones. He was never to be outside of Lebanese politics again. His choice that year of a wife, Zelpha Tabet, daughter of Nicolas Tabet of Dayr al-Qamr and Tabet's English wife, Maud Clayden, also proved to be significant. The English connection drew the Chamouns into British social circles in Beirut, led Chamoun to learn English well, and ultimately placed him in a position to play key intermediary roles during and after World War II with the British and American governments, which facilitated Lebanese independence and an enhanced international role for Lebanon in the postwar period. His central role in these affairs provided him, in turn, with national and international stature that contributed to his election as president of Lebanon in 1952.

Increasingly well known because of his various legal, business, journalistic and political activities, Chamoun successfully stood for election to the Chamber of Deputies itself in 1934. Now a member of Parliament, he associated himself with the Constitutional Bloc, led by Sheikh Bechara al-Khouri, which demanded full restoration of the 1926 Constitution that the French High Commissioner had abrogated in 1932. During the 1932 presidential elections, bitter rivalry between Khouri and National Bloc leader Emile Edde, from the Jbayl district in northern Lebanon, had led to the suspension of the constitution. To those who supported Khouri, including Chamoun, the politics of Edde, who favored a close relation with France and a perpetuation of the French Mandate, were hinderances to Lebanese independence.

Although Khouri's Constitutional Bloc remained in opposition until World War II, Chamoun was reelected deputy from the Shuf in 1937, and for the first time received appointment as a minister (finance). With the coming of World War II, the fortunes of the Constitutional Bloc began to improve, and Chamoun played a vital role in managing the events that finally led to the full establishment of Lebanese independence and the victory of the Constitutional Bloc in the general elections of 1943. Following the fall of France in June 1940 and the establishment of a Vichy-controlled administration in Lebanon, British and Free French forces began an invasion of Syria and Lebanon from Palestine in June 1941, announcing the full independence of both countries as they did so. Soon after the Allied occupation of Lebanon, it became clear that although Britain supported Lebanese independence, Free French attitudes were more recalcitrant. In these circumstances, the National Bloc supporters of Emile Edde sided with the French, while Khouri's Constitutional Bloc (particularly in the person of Camille Chamoun, who soon gained the label "agent of British intelligence") kept close touch with the British embassy and occupation forces in an effort to ensure continuing British support for Lebanese independence.

New elections in 1943 finally brought an overwhelming victory to the Constitutional Bloc, bringing into power a new parliament that quickly elected Bechara al-Khouri as the first president of independent Lebanon. Chamoun, now a powerful figure in the new government, became minister of the interior. However, within a year, because of his presumed influence with Great Britain, he was dispatched by Khouri as minister plenipotentiary to the Court of St. James. Enroute to London, he represented Lebanon in the September 1944 Alexandria (Egypt) Conference that laid the foundations for the League of Arab States. His primary mission, however, was to represent Lebanese interests in London and Washington against French efforts, led by General Charles DeGaulle, to retain a permanent foothold in Lebanon and to assure Lebanese participation and membership in the new United Nations. In all these missions he proved successful, with the result that when he finally returned to Lebanon in 1947 to resume his post as minister of the interior, he believed, as did many Lebanese, that he was next in line to succeed Khouri as president.

Parliamentary elections in 1947, however, returned an even larger majority of Khouri partisans to office, amid charges of corruption, purchase of votes, and intimidation by agents of the president. As the new Parliament moved in May 1948 to amend the constitution to enable Khouri to serve a second six-year term (by a forty-eight to seven vote) and subsequently to elect him, Chamoun resigned from the government and joined the opposition to Khouri. Numerous events in the late 1940s conspired to weaken the Khouri government and strengthen opposition to it.

New parliamentary elections in 1951 reflected the erosion of popular support for Khouri and encouraged opponents of the regime to unite against him. Under the leadership of Chamoun, a National Socialist Front came into being which included such disparate groups as the new Progressive Socialist Party of Druze leader Kamal Jumblatt,* also from the Shuf; the old National Bloc, now led by the sons of Emile Edde (Pierre and Raymond); the Phalangist Party of Pierre Gemayel;* the Parti Populaire Syrien (PPS), a member of which assassinated Prime Minister Riyad al-Sulh, an important Sunni Muslim ally of Khouri, in the summer of 1951; the Muslim Najjada Party; and numerous independent deputies. Although a temporary political alliance whose only common interest was opposition to President Khouri, the front gradually mobilized strong popular support so that it became possible in September 1952 during a cabinet crisis for the leadership of the front to call for a general strike and demand the resignation of President Khouri, fully two years prior to the legal expiration of his second term. So widespread had opposition become that Khouri elected to resign rather than force a bloody confrontation. To replace him, the Parliament elected Camille Chamoun as president of Lebanon on September 23, 1952.

As president of Lebanon between 1952 and 1958, Chamoun reached the pinnacle of his political career. A handsome, distinguished, and popular figure who unquestionably was Lebanon's most cosmopolitan head of state, Chamoun was also by now a wealthy, self-made man of modest origins who symbolized the aspirations of an emerging middle class in Lebanon's sectarian communities, which constituted the principal base of his popular support. Respected by neighboring Arab regimes for the helpful role he had played at the United Nations on behalf of Arab independence movements and the Palestine cause, he also was known and well thought of in the West, where he projected the image of a progressive, modern Arab statesman. In short, although he had come to power primarily because of opposition to Khouri, Chamoun was a popular choice to replace him.

Despite these credits, however, Chamoun's presidency also foundered. His first problem stemmed from the very means by which he had come to power. By participating in the movement to oust Khouri, Chamoun alienated many of his former colleagues of the Constitutional Bloc; as he extended himself to win back their support and to include them in his new administration, however, he quickly lost the support of many with whom he had allied against Khouri. This was especially true of Kamal Jumblatt, whom Chamoun systematically ignored and by whom he was regularly excoriated during the six years of his presidential term.

Never able to get a firm hand on Lebanon's traditional political establishment, Chamoun relied instead on popular support and reform efforts to strengthen the office of the president and his own control of the office. Among other things, he pushed through a reform of the electoral system, significantly expanding the number of electoral districts. This reform tended to weaken the political domination of Lebanon's traditional landowning aristocracy and urban notables, and provided more opportunity to new political aspirants to independently seek electoral office. In addition, Chamoun got the Parliament to grant women the right to vote, and he introduced several reforms that enhanced the independence of the judiciary.

The chief feature of Chamoun's presidency, however, was the atmosphere of economic and political freedom it secured for all Lebanese. Restrictions on free economic exchange were lifted, and a bank secrecy law was passed. As a result, capital began flowing into the country and Lebanon began to emerge as the leading banking center of the Middle East; the country entered a period of capitalist expansion and prosperity that continued virtually unabated until the civil war of 1975. Moreover, Chamoun encouraged total freedom of the press and political expression, even when it was used by his opponents to attack him. During the time he governed Lebanon, no newspaper or political party feared censorship, suppression, or arrest, in contrast to neighboring Arab regimes where political and economic restraints and controls were increasingly the order of the day.

Although Chamoun's policies made him popular in many sectors of Lebanese society, his supporters tended to be men without large political followings, while the traditional political leaders who did have large political followings viewed Chamoun with suspicion, fearing that his ultimate aim was to undercut the bases of their support. Although the sources of their dissatisfaction were primarily domestic, it was ultimately over issues relating to foreign policy that opposition to Chamoun was mobilized.

A feature of Chamoun's period of rule was the flowering of U.S.-Soviet Cold War rivalry in the Middle East. Under strong pressure, both internationally and domestically, to join the Western-sponsored Middle East alliances system known as the Baghdad Pact, he came under equally strong regional and domestic pressure, especially from Egypt and neighboring Syria, to oppose it. Caught in a dilemma, Chamoun avoided joining the pact, but he also refused to condemn it.

Issues came to a head in the 1956 Suez crisis when Chamoun came under strong pressure primarily from Lebanon's traditional Muslim politicians who, already upset with Chamoun's cavalier treatment of them, demanded that Lebanon break diplomatic relations with Great Britain and France. This Chamoun resolutely refused to do. The failure of the invading forces to secure their aims, however, transformed Gamal Abdul Nasser* into the leading political figure in the Arab world, placed Chamoun on the defensive politically, and energized pro-Nasser and anti-Chamoun forces in Lebanon.

In these circumstances, Lebanon conducted new parliamentary elections in the spring of 1957. Opponents of Chamoun allied together in a new National Front to mobilize support for anti-Chamoun candidates in the election. Perceiving his domestic political opposition increasingly in terms of the larger East-West conflict, in early 1957 Chamoun accepted the Eisenhower Doctrine, which promised military intervention in support of friendly regimes threatened by Soviet-inspired foreign aggression or domestic subversion. In so doing, he virtually transformed Lebanon's domestic political contest into a mirror of the larger East-

West conflict. In return, however, Lebanon received a twenty-million-dollar assistance package, at least some of which Chamoun used, or so his opponents charged, to influence the outcome of the election.

Despite the powerful opposition, pro-Chamoun candidates secured a majority in the Lebanese Chamber in the 1957 elections, while many powerful anti-Chamoun political figures—including Saeb Salam and Abdullah Yafi of Beirut, and Kamal Jumblatt and Ahmad al-Assad of al-Taybeh—were defeated. The outcome of the election placed Chamoun in a position to obtain a constitutional amendment that would enable him to serve a second term as president, a move his opponents were certain he would attempt.

Cut out of the established political process by the results of the 1957 election, some elements of Chamoun's opposition turned to violence and terrorism to demonstrate there were parts of the country the president did not control. The crisis escalated when, following the February 22, 1958, announcement of the political union of Egypt and Syria to form a United Arab Republic (UAR), massive Muslim demonstrations clamored militantly and sometimes violently in favor of Lebanese incorporation in the new UAR. In the midst of these circumstances, the mysterious assassination of a prominent Maronite journalist who happened to be an opponent of Chamoun sparked charges that Chamoun had been responsible. Chamoun's opponents called for a general strike, demanding his immediate resignation.

Interpreting the demand for his resignation as a demand for the dissolution of Lebanon as an independent state, and totally ignoring the domestic sources of his opposition, Chamoun refused. Almost immediately the general strike turned violent and became an insurrection. Strongly believing that Nasser's Egypt was behind what was happening in Lebanon, Chamoun submitted a protest to the United Nations. Efforts by the UN to investigate had proved inconclusive when on July 14, 1958, an apparently pro-Egyptian military coup d'état took place in Iraq, overthrowing the pro-Western monarchy that was a vital link in the Western-sponsored Baghdad Pact. Fearing a coup d'état against himself as well, Chamoun invoked the Eisenhower Doctrine and called on the United States to intervene militarily to support him. U.S. forces responded quickly, landing 15,000 troops during the next few days.

The U.S. intervention in Lebanon may have had some effect in helping to preserve Lebanese independence, but it did nothing to help Chamoun perpetuate himself in office. U.S. envoys who conducted negotiations among the conflicting parties soon realized that a smooth transition of power was necessary for the crisis in Lebanon to be resolved. They also learned that Lebanese Armed Forces Commander, General Fuad Chehab,* who had remained neutral in the conflict and had refused to deploy the army against Chamoun's opponents despite direct orders to do so, was the most acceptable Maronite candidate to replace Chamoun. Accordingly, Chehab was elected as the new president of Lebanon on July 31; Chamoun was enabled to serve out the remainder of his term until September 22; and Chehab was inaugurated to replace Chamoun on September 23, 1958.

Despite the disastrous end of his presidency, Chamoun quickly reemerged as the central Maronite political leader around whom opposition to the new president formed. Among Maronites, General Chehab proved a very unpopular president, and Chamoun, now at age fifty-eight and with a long active political career ahead of him, took the lead in opposing his policies. At the same time, Chamoun retained the strong political ties with important Maronite and non-Maronite politicians and business leaders that he had forged during his presidency. All these he sought to group in his new National Liberal Party that he established in 1959, after his departure from the presidency. Reelected to Parliament in 1960 and again in 1968 and 1972, the last being Lebanon's final electoral campaign before the outbreak of the civil war in 1975, Chamoun continued to play a central political role in Lebanon until his death by natural causes in August 1987.

Despite such a strong bloc of support, Chamoun never again was able to obtain reelection to the presidency. However, after a period of relative political weakness, he was able to reemerge as a central political kingmaker and -breaker in the Lebanese political system. Leading the drive to remove Chehabist political figures from office, he finally achieved success in 1970 with the election of Suleiman Franjieh as president. This was in a very real sense a personal victory for Chamoun, who was perceived as the principal behind-the-scenes power broker in Franjieh's government. Under Franjieh, Chamoun held several key ministerial positions (foreign affairs, defense, and interior), but more importantly he controlled important political appointments, including that of army commander in chief, which was held by General Iskander Ghanem, a Chamoun loyalist, during the first years of Franjieh's presidency.

By this time, the polarization of Lebanese politics that would finally deteriorate into civil war in 1975 had begun, and Chamoun had emerged as Lebanon's most vocal defender of the traditional political status quo against the challenge of those who sought to change it, centered in the Lebanese National Movement (LNM) headed by Kamal Jumblatt.

Although Chamoun preferred the Lebanese government and army to be the agents for enforcing the Cairo Agreement of 1969, which limited Palestine Liberation Organization (PLO) activities and movements in Lebanon, he also acted to form his own militia to defend Maronite interests and his own when political deadlock kept the army from intervening against the PLO. Never as large or as effectively organized as the militia raised by Pierre Gemayel's Phalange Party, Chamoun's Numur (Tigers) militia, commanded by his son Dany, nevertheless contributed to the defense of Maronite areas and the traditional political system against its enemies. In addition, the militia enabled Chamoun to remain a powerful political figure in Lebanon's increasingly violent political dialogue during the civil war. Still seeking to be perceived as the country's preeminent champion of the traditional Lebanese ethos, despite his relative lack of strength compared to the Phalangists, Chamoun rhetorically appeared more recalcitrant and unbending than Pierre Gemayel himself, supposedly the champion of Maronite preeminence in the Lebanese political system.

In keeping with the preeminent role he continued to seek to play, in early 1976, following the breakup of the Lebanese armed forces, Chamoun was the first Maronite politician to make contact with Israel, a step that helped to balance the competing forces in Lebanon as the tide of battle seemed to be turning against the Maronite militias. Reliance on Israeli support had the impact, however, not only of deepening the polarization of Lebanese politics, but also of dividing Maronite opinion between those, like Phalangist leader Pierre Gemayel and his son Amin, who feared the consequences of further internationalization of the Lebanese conflict, and others, including Gemayel's second son, Bashir, who considered the acceptance of Israeli support necessary. In this manner, an Israeli-supported component within the Phalangist militia, known as the Lebanese Forces, which was commanded by Bashir Gemayel but godfathered by Chamoun, came into being. In time the Lebanese Forces, with Israeli assistance, became the dominant Maronite militia and put an end even to Chamoun's Numur militia in July 1980. As a principal sponsor and patron of the new movement, however, Chamoun retained an important voice as president of the Lebanese Front, the political bureau of the Lebanese Forces militia.

The assassination of Bashir Gemayel in September 1982 resulted in a temporary eclipse of the ascendency of the Lebanese Forces. The more traditionally oriented Amin Gemayel was elected president and relied heavily on U.S. and West European support to the Lebanese government to help restore central authority in the country. Following the withdrawal of Western peacekeeping forces in February 1984, however, and as President Gemayel sought to reestablish the strongest possible "Government of National Unity" composed of the country's most dominant political figures, Chamoun once again was included as minister of finance and housing. Now an ancient figure in his mid-eighties, Chamoun no longer wielded immense influence and watched almost helplessly as the Lebanese economy deteriorated rapidly under his administration.

What was significant at this late stage of his life was not that he wielded power effectively—no one did so in the Lebanon of the mid–1980s—but that he remained a symbolically powerful individual. Until his death in 1987, Chamoun remained a powerful symbol of a vision of Lebanon that he had once served and championed in the prime of his life. It was basically a liberal vision of Lebanon as an independent state, Western-oriented but nevertheless on reasonably good terms with the majority of its Middle Eastern neighbors; of a country characterized by a high degree of political, economic, and social liberty; and of a multisectarian nation in which a special place of honor and respect was conserved for the Maronite community, but where there was also a place for other minorities of any kind of background. In defense of this liberal vision, he had demonstrated an almost unquenchable thirst for power and influence and a willingness to rely on the most extremist measures to keep his vision alive. Perceived almost as a messianic figure by those who supported him, he was equally reviled by his opponents as the principal symbol of all that was wrong with Lebanon.

Lawyer, journalist, businessman, financier, politician, patron of the arts, and even something of a scholar, Chamoun in many ways synthesized in his person the aspirations of many Lebanese of the twentieth century. A brilliant political tactician who understood every aspect of Lebanon's complex parochial and even tribal political system, he nevertheless lacked a strong strategic sense of what was required of Lebanon in order to adapt to the changing nature of Lebanese and Middle Eastern society in the latter half of the twentieth century. In this failing, he also symbolized many of his countrymen. Thus he was as much a part of the problem as well as a beloved leader who sought to survive in the increasingly hostile political environment of late-twentieth-century Lebanon.

BIBLIOGRAPHY

Works by Chamoun:

Crise au Moyen Orient (Crisis in the Middle East). Paris: Gallimard, 1963.
Crise au Liban (Crisis in Lebanon). Beirut, 1977. Also published in Arabic as *Azmat fi Lubnan*. Beirut: al-Fikr al-Hurr Press, 1977.
Memoire et Souvenirs. Du 17 Juillet 1977 au 24 Decembre 1978 (Memoir and Recollections from 17 July 1977 to 24 December 1978). Beirut: Imprimerie catholique, 1979.
A Soixante ans d'Inntervalles (To Sixty Years of Intervals). Beirut: Centre Libanais de Documentation et de Recherches (CEDR), 1980.

Other Works:

Cobban, Helena. *The Making of Modern Lebanon*. London: Hutchinson, 1985.
Gordon, David C. *The Republic of Lebanon: Nation in Jeopardy*. Boulder, Colo.: Westview Press, 1983.
Hudson, Michael C. *The Precarious Republic: Political Modernization in Lebanon*. New York: Random House, 1968.
al-Khoury, Bechara. *Haqa'iq lubnaniyah*. Beirut: Awraq lubnaniyah, 1961.
Rabinovich, Itamar. *The War for Lebanon 1970–1985*. Ithaca, N.Y.: Cornell University Press, 1985.
Salibi, Kamal S. *The Modern History of Lebanon*. London: Widenfeld and Nicholson, 1965.
———. *Crossroads to Civil War*. London: Ithaca Press, 1976.
Ziadeh, N. A. *Syria and Lebanon*. Beirut: Librarie du Liban, 1968.

MAX L. GROSS

FUAD CHEHAB (1903–1973) rose through the ranks of Lebanon's military, during a career which spanned nearly three decades, to become commander-in-chief of the Lebanese Army. He is often recognized as the founder of the Lebanese Army, which grew five-fold in size under his leadership. Chehab also served as minister of defense under President Camille Chamoun. Chehab was chosen president in July of 1958. He used the military as a base for popular support, and many of his advisors were trusted army colleagues. His tenure as president saw an increase in the role of the military in politics that mirrored events in other states in the region.

During the long centuries of Ottoman rule (1516–1918), Mt. Lebanon was governed (until 1841) by two different lines of hereditary princes (*amirs*) whose authority as local ruler was acknowledged and supported by the Turks in return for recognition of Ottoman suzerainty and payment of tribute. The first of these princely lines, the Maan, was supplanted by that of the Chehabs in 1697. Both families were apparently Druze, but over the centuries some members of the Chehab family converted to Maronite Christianity while others remained Sunni Muslims. Chehabs of all three sectarian communities may be found in modern Lebanon; yet all regularly retain the title amir as a sign of their aristocratic lineage and traditional social standing.

Amir Fuad Chehab (1903–1973), who served as independent Lebanon's third elected president (1958–1964), was a descendent of the Maronite branch of the family and was distantly related to Amir Bashir III Chehab, the last ruling amir of the Chehab dynasty (ruled 1840–1841). Born in Ghazir in the district of Kisrawan of central Mt. Lebanon, Fuad Chehab was the son of Amir Abdullah Chehab, a prominent aristocratic landowner of Kisrawan district, and his wife Badia Hobeiche. As a young boy, he attended local Maronite schools and then completed secondary school at the Collège des Frères Marists in Juniyah.

In 1921, at the age of nineteen, he decided to pursue a military career in the armed forces of the newly established French Mandate for Syria and Lebanon, and was admitted to the Military Academy in Damascus, which the French had taken over from the Turks. Two years later, he graduated as a sublieutenant in the Troupes Speciales du Levant, a Syrian legion created by the Mandatory authority to augment regular French forces in Syria and Lebanon. Over the next several years, he also attended infantry school and later army staff school in France. During these years he married a French woman, Rose Noiret, the daughter of a French officer serving in Syria during the 1920s. Promoted to captain in 1930, he received his first command experience as commandant of the garrison at Rashaya between 1931 and 1937. This assignment was followed by a year at the French War College in Paris during 1938.

Closely attached to France by education, military training, and marriage, Chehab welcomed the liberation of Lebanon from Vichy control by British and Free French forces in June 1941. Subsequently, he took charge of the effort to recruit, organize, and train detachments of the Troupes Speciales du Levant for service in support of the Allies in North Africa, Italy, and France. Promoted to lieutenant colonel in 1944, he briefly commanded the Lebanese light cavalry before being named general and commander of the new Lebanese Army to which Lebanese members of the Troupes Speciales du Levant rallied in August 1945.

Amir Fuad Chehab remained Lebanon's sole armed forces commander in chief until his election as president of Lebanon in 1958. In a sense, therefore, he was the founder of the Lebanese Army, although the history of the institution can be traced back through the French Mandate to Ottoman times. Starting as an army that numbered about thirty-five hundred men in 1948, it gradually expanded under Chehab's husbandship to about fifteen thousand by the end of his presidency in 1964. Provided with only a small amount of leftover French equipment from the Mandate period, Chehab nevertheless took personal interest in the development of the institution and its personnel and sought to develop a gradually expanding, well-educated, disciplined, and professional organization.

Under Chehab's command, the army participated in the Arab-Israeli war of 1948–1949. It conducted limited but reasonably well-coordinated cross-border operations that were clearly designed to demonstrate Lebanese solidarity with its fellow Arab states, but only in a secondary and supportive role. The army's success in countering an attempted coup d'état by the Parti Populaire Syrien (PPS) in July 1949 also illustrated its importance as a defender of Lebanon's fragile constitutional regime. Although Chehab probably opposed the execution of PPS leader Antun Saade for his role in the coup attempt, another PPS coup attempt against Chehab as president in December 1961 demonstrated continuing PPS bitterness over the role he had played in 1949.

Chehab and his army emerged as a highly significant political factor in Lebanon during the 1952 crisis, when President Bishara al-Khouri was forced to resign due to mounting political opposition. Although suspicious of Camille Chamoun,* a protégé of Khouri, who nevertheless now was a leader of the opposition against the president and who hoped to succeed him, Chehab informed Khouri that, although he was prepared to use the army to enforce the law, he would not take sides in political conflict. By abjuring political involvement, however, Chehab in fact took sides with the opposition. Lacking army support, Khouri resigned on September 18, appointing Chehab acting chief of state until a new president could be elected. Accordingly, Chehab governed Lebanon for a week prior to the formal election of Camille Chamoun as President on September 23, 1952.

Despite considerable popularity throughout the country, President Chamoun soon ran into difficulty because of divided political opinion about how Lebanon should align itself in the Cold War. Lebanese Muslims generally supported President Gamal Abdul Nasser* of Egypt, who strongly opposed the Western-sponsored Baghdad Pact, while Christian opinion represented by President Chamoun generally feared Nasser's radical Arab nationalism and tended to look to the West for guarantees of Lebanese Independence. A political crisis was reached in November 1956, when most Muslim politicians withdrew support from Chamoun to protest his unwillingness to break diplomatic relations with Great Britain and France, following their invasion of Egypt. To assure law and order, Chamoun declared martial law and appointed a new government which included General Chehab as minister of defense as well as armed forced commander, effectively making Chehab military governor of the country. Now demonstrating a firm willingness to use the army to maintain law and order, Chehab provided time for the crisis to pass and again demonstrated the centrality of the army and his own leadership of it in promoting political stability.

The polarization of Lebanese politics continued, however, and became more acute after Chamoun's acceptance of the Eisenhower Doctrine in March 1957. New parliamentary elections that gave the president commanding control of the Lebanese Parliament followed, making it technically possible for the Parliament to amend the constitution and enable Chamoun to serve a second term as president. Escalating violence in different parts of the country became a full insurrection against the president in the spring of 1958, following the union of Egypt and Syria as the United Arab Republic (UAR), a development that was hailed enthusiastically by Chamoun's political opposition. Despite direct orders to use the army against the opposition, Chehab, as he had in 1952, refused on the grounds that the crisis was political rather than Constitutional.

Unlike Khouri in 1952, however, Chamoun refused to resign. Believing the insurrection against him to have been inspired and supported by Egypt, he interpreted the apparently pro-Egyptian July 14, 1958, revolution in Iraq (a key member of the Baghdad Pact) as a prologue to a coup d'état against himself. Accordingly, he invoked the Eisenhower Doctrine and requested U.S. military intervention to save himself and the independence of Lebanon. U.S. forces, already in place off the coast of Lebanon, responded immediately and began landing troops on July 15.

Uninformed of President Chamoun's request, General Chehab deployed the Lebanese Army to resist the entry of U.S. forces into Beirut. Quick negotiations defused a potential clash and produced an agreement that enabled U.S. and Lebanese forces to work together under the overall authority of General Chehab. Meanwhile, U.S. Under Secretary of State Robert Murphy began meeting with various Lebanese personalities in an effort to untangle the conflicting threads of the Lebanese crisis. He soon realized that a smooth transition of power was necessary for the crisis to be resolved and that General Chehab, because of his neutral position in the conflict and his refusal to deploy the army, was the most acceptable Maronite personality to replace Chamoun as president. Accordingly, Chehab was elected president on July 31, but was not inaugurated until September 23, after Chamoun had completed his full term of office.

As president of Lebanon from 1958 to 1964, Amir Fuad Chehab represented a different sort of presidential leadership than the country had previously known. Aloof, aristocratic, disdainful of the traditional politicians, yet clearly a shrewd political pragmatist himself, his election in a sense represented more than another change in political leadership. In the context of Lebanon's traditional social order, it also represented a restoration of princely rule to which, at a time of crisis, the country now turned for salvation. His self-image, it is often asserted, was much like that of French General Charles de Gaulle, who also became president of France at a time of similar crisis in 1958 and whom some have argued served as an influential role model for the Francophile Chehab. President Nasser of Egypt, another Arab military officer become head of state, also seems to have influenced Chehab's way of thinking.

Lacking a strong political constituency of his own, Chehab turned for support to the one institution where he did have a popular base—the army. Trusted army colleagues were appointed to key sensitive posts, such as the directorships of the General Security Adminstration, the Internal Security Forces, and the National Police. Otherwise, Chehab tended to appoint educated professionals rather than protégés of powerful politicians to key administrative positions in the government, as he sought to govern Lebanon as an administrator rather than as a politician. Meanwhile, distrustful of the traditional politicians, Chehab kept a close watch on all political activity in the country by effective use of the army's Deuxième Bureau (military intelligence branch), an institution he had carefully built up over the years and which had helped him steer skillfully through the crises of 1952 and 1958. In this respect, his presidency represented a period of military control of politics in Lebanon, a phenomenon increasingly common in neighboring Arab countries. Although this aspect of his rule finally served as the focal point for growing opposition to Chehabist methods after him, it served Chehab effectively while he remained president of Lebanon.

Despite the fundamental autocracy of his presidency, however, Amir Fuad Chehab also realized the necessity of cultivating political alliances with powerful forces in each of Lebanon's sectarian communities. He built these alliances by drawing into collaboration with him the highly disciplined, ultranationalist Phalange Party of Pierre Gemayel* among the Maronites and the more radical Progressive Socialist Party (PSP) of Kamal Jumblatt* among the Druze. After experimenting briefly with various Sunni Muslim figures, he finally settled on Rashid Karami* of Tripoli, who served as prime minister during most of his presidency. In return for their collaboration, Chehab used his control of the Deuxième Bureau and the Security Forces to aid them politically in the parliamentary elections of 1960. In these elections, the hold of former President Chamoun, established in the 1957 elections, was broken, and the political strength of each of Chehab's allies was strengthened.

Soon after the 1960 elections, Chehab announced his decision to resign as president, stating that the political aims for which he had agreed to accept the office had been achieved. This unheard-of action in Lebanese politics actually served to consolidate his political authority in Lebanon. Demonstrations of support in various parts of the country finally allowed him to be prevailed on to serve out the remainder of his six-year term.

As he sought to control Lebanon politically, President Chehab also worked, as he had in the army, to develop a more effective and modern government. Before him, the Lebanese administrative system, as well as the services it provided, had been basically patrimonial in character, reflecting the interplay of the traditional politicians but no plan for the overall development of the country. Chehab believed that Lebanon's problems stemmed not from inherent sectarian differences in the society but from unequal treatment by the government, both in hiring practices and in the delivery of government services. Consequently, he embarked on an ambitious program to expand the size and scope of the government, to ensure equal hiring practices on the basis of quotas for Christians and Muslims, and to provide essential services—roads, electricity, schools, medical clinics, and hospitals—to all parts of the country that had been neglected by the government before him.

Improvement of agricultural production, welfare for the elderly and the handicapped, social security insurance for workers, a Central Bank to issue currency and manage the economy, and the establishment of a professional civil service were other important elements of his reform program. In no way did Chehab's reforms seek to undermine Lebanon's dynamic capitalist economic structure, which continued to flourish under his guidance, but they did seek to redistribute some of the surplus capital generated by that system into programs beneficial to the less prosperous citizens, with the overall aim of contributing to the stability of the country. As a result, although Chehab remained an aloof political figure without a high degree of charismatic appeal, he developoed a strong body of popular support, particularly in the army and the government, as well as among the more disadvantaged people in Lebanese society. His program soon came to be called *al-nahj al-shihabi* (the Chehabi Way), and those who supported it were called "nahjists" or "Chehabists"; it was a way of thinking about how to govern Lebanon that survived long after Chehab had left the scene of Lebanese politics.

At the same time, however, Chehabist polities stirred up a considerable opposition that grouped together a large portion of Lebanon's Maronite Christian population, an increasing number of traditional political figures, as well as much of the country's wealthy business and financial community. Maronite resentment occurred because Chehab's policies tended to benefit Muslim sectors of Lebanese society (which had been more neglected by previous administrations) more than they did Christian sectors, leading to charges that the president was pandering to Muslims at the expense of his Christian coreligionaires. Efforts to establish more effective government control over the country, moreover, were rightly seen by traditional politicians as tending to undermine their authority, a process they naturally resisted. Finally, the new taxes the government levied and the old taxes it more efficiently began to collect to pay for expanded government services upset the country's established business, banking and commercial classes who previously had had no habit of paying taxes at all.

As was the case with President Chamoun, domestic opposition to President Chehab ultimately expressed itself by opposition to his foreign policies. Ever mindful of the powerful Muslim opposition that had been rallied against President Chamoun because of his reliance on U.S. support and fears of Egyptian influence in Lebanon, President Chehab made strict neutrality in the East-West conflict and close coordination with Egypt the cornerstones of his foreign policy and the principal guarantee of Lebanese independence. As with his domestic policies, Chehab's deference to President Nasser of Egypt increased his popularity with Lebanon's Muslims, but decreased it among the Maronites who increasingly rallied around former President Chamoun.

President Chehab's deference to Egypt's Nasser was clearly demonstrated in September 1961 when, following the breakup of the United Arab Republic, he delayed extending recognition to the new Syrian regime. This frank manifestation of caution, and even fear, on the part of the Lebanese president to do anything that might be construed as anti-Egyptian sharpened anti-Chehabist opinion in Lebanon and gave rise in December to an attempted coup d'état against him by the PPS with the support of some affiliated army officers. Unsuccessful, the coup attempt led to the arrest of nearly six thousand people, while all opponents of the president, including ex-President Chamoun, a known friend of the PPS, came under suspicion. As a result, Chehab was led to place even greater reliance on the army to safeguard his regime, giving rise to increased criticism by his opponents of the antidemocratic and authoritarian nature of his government.

Despite growing criticism, however, Chehab also possessed a strong body of support both among the public and in the Parliament. As his Chehabists followers moved in 1964, in ways reminiscent of 1957, to elect a parliament strong enough to amend the constitution so as to enable Chehab to serve a second term, a powerful anti-Chehabist coalition emerged to resist the effort. Although the Chehabists gained strength in the election, their opponents retained enough strength to oppose any effort to perpetuate Chehab's presidency. Chehab subsequently declined to stand for reelection, thus making possible independent Lebanon's first peaceful transition of presidential power.

Despite Chehab's departure from the presidency in 1964, his influence and legacy continued to dominate Lebanon through the term of his successor, Charles Helou. A highly qualified former ambassador and government official who nevertheless lacked a strong personal political base, Helou had to work with a government, army, and even parliament that still held allegiance primarily to Chehab. As a result, Chehabist methods of government, which included a central role for the army's Deuxième Bureau, continued to prevail under Helou, and Chehab remained a powerful behind-the-scenes figure in government affairs.

Opposition to Chehabist methods and dominance continued to grow, however, gradually weakening the authority of the president, who controlled neither the political forces dominating his government nor those opposing it. In these circumstances, the growing polarization of Lebanese politics, following the 1967 Arab-Israeli war, over the role to be permitted the Palestine Liberation Organization (PLO) in Lebanon confronted the country at a time of increasingly weak central authority. A combination of anti-Chehabist politicians, significantly strengthened in the 1968 parliamentary elections, and pro-PLO figures, notably Kamal Jumblatt—all of whom opposed the "pervasive" role of the Deuxième Bureau—finally managed to unite to defeat Elias Sarkis, the Chehabist candidate, in the 1970 presidential elections. With the election of Suleiman Franjieh, a traditional political figure, as president, the Deuxième Bureau was purged of its Chehabist elements, the authoritarian aspects of Chehabist rule were brought to an end, and Lebanon quickly returned to its traditional patrimonial style of politics.

The overturn of Chehabist dominance occurred, however, at a time of increasing disintegrative pressures on the Lebanese political system. Whether a continuation of Chehabist-style government could have averted Lebanon's slide into civil war, two years after Amir Fuad Chehab's death in April 1973, will forever remain a matter of speculation. The election as president in 1976 of Elias Sarkis, one of Chehab's closest aides and the defeated Chehabist candidate in 1970, indicated that many believed that only a return to Chehabist methods and policies could restore order and civility in Lebanese politics. By this time, however, it was too late. The disintegrative pressures on the Lebanese political system of which Amir Fuad Chehab through his years as armed forces commander, president of the republic, and *eminence grise* of the Helou regime, had proved the master, now had overcome the central authority of the state; and central authority proved impossible to reassert.

With the failure of the Sarkis government to reestablish central government authority and to resume the state-building activities that were the central theme of Chehabist policies, Chehabism appeared finally to have been overcome as a political trend in Lebanon. Nevertheless, as Lebanon continued to flounder in relative political anarchy and civil violence in the 1980s, the historical memory of the Chehabist period as the high point of independent Lebanon's stability and prosperity loomed increasingly larger. As the scion of one of Lebanon's most historic and notable families, Amir Fuad Chehab, more than any other political leader, had provided a model of stable leadership and steadiness of purpose that was not forgotten but nevertheless seemed impossible to reassert in the fractious environment of Lebanese politics.

BIBLIOGRAPHY

Cobban, Helena. *The Making of Modern Lebanon*. London: Hutchinson, 1985.
Freiha, Adel A. *L'armée et l'état au Liban, 1945–1980*. Paris: Librarie generale de droit et de jurisprudence, 1980.
Gordon, David C. *The Republic of Lebanon: Nation in Jeopardy*. Boulder, Colo.: Westview Press, 1983.
Hudson, Michael C. *The Precarious Republic: Political Modernization in Lebanon*. New York: Random House, 1968.
Rabinovich, Itamar. *The War for Lebanon, 1970–1985*. Ithaca, N.Y.: Cornell University Press, 1985.
Salibi, Kamal S. *The Modern History of Lebanon*. London: Widenfeld & Nicholson, 1965.
———. "Lebanon under Fuad Chehab 1958–1964." *Middle Eastern Studies* 2 (April 1966): 211–226.
———. *Crossroads to Civil War: Lebanon 1958–1976*. London: Ithaca Press, 1976.
Ziadeh, N. A. *Syria and Lebanon*. Beirut: Librarie du Liban, 1968.

MAX L. GROSS

D

MOSHE DAYAN (1915–1981) was chief of staff of the Israel Defense Forces and later served as defense minister and foreign minister of the State of Israel. In each of these roles he had an important impact both on Israel and on the Middle East. Moshe Dayan was a controversial but charismatic leader, who raised strong feelings and had many supporters and rivals.

Moshe Dayan was the firstborn of Shmuel and Devora Dayan. He was born in Kibbutz Degania on May 2, 1915, to parents who were active members of the Hapoel Hatzair (Young Worker Movemment), the forerunner of the Israel Workers Movement (MAPAI). Dayan grew up in Nahalal, where he met Ruth, his first wife, in 1937. As a child Dayan suffered from many illnesses, including trachoma and pneumonia. Also as a child he had his first contacts with Arabs of the neighboring El Mazrib tribe, where he had a friend, Abd Abedat, who was his playmate. Among his deepest early memories was of the sight of Degania burning after an Arab attack on April 24, 1920.

Dayan was one of the first to join the Palmach (assault unit organization) when it was established, enlisting on May 18, 1941, and served under Orde Wingate in his night squads. From 1939 to 1941, Dayan was detained by the British in Acre when he was caught training in southern Lebanon (then Syria) but he was released in order to take part in an allied venture against the Vichy French in Syria in 1941. On June 7, 1941, Dayan headed a squad of Haganah (Defense) forces, who joined the British in an operation intended to destroy bridges in Syria. During an assault on a police station, Dayan used his binoculars in order to locate French positions. He was wounded by a bullet and he lost his eye. Consequently, Dayan had to leave the Palmach and was assigned to staff work in the Haganah. In this capacity he coordinated work with the British against pro-Nazi groups in the region.

During Israel's War of Independence in July 1948, Dayan was made the commanding officer of Jerusalem while it was under siege. In that capacity he took part in informal negotiations with King Abdullah ibn Hussein* of Jordan, whom he met a number of times. Dayan was instrumental in reaching ''the informal agreement'' concerning the border of the no-man's land in Jerusalem which became operative on December 1, 1948. It became formal in April 1949 during the armistice negotiations which took place in Rhodes, where Dayan served as a member of the Israeli delegation.

Between 1950 and 1953, Dayan served as commander of the Southern and Northern Command of the Israel Defense Forces (IDF) and later as head of the General Branch of Operations in the General Staff (making him the second in rank in the IDF). On December 6, 1954, he was appointed as Israel's chief of staff. Those opposing Dayan's candidacy were concerned about his tendency to politicize military activity. He was nominated with David Ben-Gurion's* support after a stormy cabinet defense-committee meeting. This was the first time a chief of staff had been nominated without a unanimous vote of confidence of the Cabinet. In 1955, Dayan suggested to Ben-Gurion that Israel attack Egypt before the Egyptians learned to use the new weaponry secured in their arms deal with Czechoslovakia. The plan was rejected by the Cabinet but was enacted a year later with the cooperation of France and Britain. Dayan was discharged from the IDF in January 1958.

In the November 1959 elections Dayan was chosen as a member of the Knesset (Parliament) and became minister of agriculture in Prime Minister David Ben-Gurion's government. In 1963, due to a controversy over the Lavon affair—the question of who gave an order to undertake clandestine activity against Egypt—Ben-Gurion left his party and established another party called Rafi (Israel Workers List). After much hesitation, Dayan joined Ben-Gurion and Shimon Peres* (who served during this period as deputy defense minister) and became a member.

Moshe Dayan continued to serve as minister of agriculture under Prime Minister Levi Eshkol.* Dayan brought to Israeli agriculture methods of long-range planning and national allocation of resources such as water. He resigned from the cabinet on November 4, 1964, when Eshkol tried to prevent him from participating in the formation of defense policy.

Until 1967, Dayan worked in a fishing company, and also went briefly to Vietnam to observe and write about the war. In May 1967, President Gamal Abdul Nasser* of Egypt demanded the withdrawal of the UN Emergency Force from Gaza and Sinai. When he declared a blockade of the Straits of Tiran it became clear in Israel that a new round of the Arab-Israeli conflict was about to begin. Ceding to popular demand, Prime Minister Eshkol was forced to hand the defense portfolio to Dayan against his expressed will, which had been to turn it over—if at all—to Yigal Allon or Yigael Yadin. Dayan did not have time to change operational plans, as he was nominated on the first of June 1967 and the Six Day War started on the fifth. However, Dayan's nomination inspired the country with confidence and helped Prime Minister Eshkol to give the green light for a preemptive strike.

After the war, Dayan had to find ways to replenish the equipment and ammunition of the IDF, due to the French embargo on Israel. In this period he supported the research-and-development functions of the Ministry of Defense, and Israel started to produce the Gabriel and Shafrir missiles. In the area of policy toward the West Bank and Gaza, Dayan initiated the Open Bridges Policy, providing an infrastructure for coexistence.

When Prime Minister Eshkol died suddenly on February 26, 1969, he was succeeded by Golda Meir,* and Dayan remained as minister of defense. At the time of the 1973 war, Dayan delayed the mobilization of Israel's reserve forces, a fact for which he was widely blamed by the Israeli public. Nevertheless, Dayan continued to serve under Golda Meir's leadership after the elections of December 31, 1973.

When Golda Meir resigned on April 11, 1974, her successor, Prime Minister Yitzhak Rabin,* did not nominate Dayan as a member of his cabinet due to the public debate about Dayan's ministerial responsibility with regard to the Yom Kippur War. At this stage Dayan was regarded by his political colleagues—the former members of his party who served as ministers—as a political liability. In the period between 1974 and 1977, Dayan served as a regular member of the Knesset, and was active in archeological excavations.

When Menachem Begin* became prime minister after the May 1977 elections, he asked Moshe Dayan to join his government in the capacity of foreign minister. Dayan recounts that he accepted on the condition that he would be allowed to say that the final solution in regard to the West Bank was negotiable, and Prime Minister Begin agreed to this condition. Thus, Dayan served as foreign minister under Begin, a period during which he had a crucial role in the Camp David negotiations.

Dayan resigned in 1979 as he felt the differences of viewpoint and policy between himself and the prime minister in regard to autonomy negotiations were too large. On April 4, 1981, Dayan established a new party called Telem (Party for Political Revival), which had as one of its primary goals the support of Dayan's proposals on the occupied territories: a unilateral establishment of Palestinian autonomy in the West Bank and Gaza. The party secured two mandates in the 1981 Knesset elections.

On October 16, 1981, Dayan died from cancer. He left a second wife, Rachel, two sons (Assaf who is an actor, and Ehud, a member of a cooperative settlement) and a daughter, Yael, who is a writer.

Dayan had been a "loner" since childhood. This is corroborated by his hobby, archeological excavation, which was generally undertaken alone. Unlike his public image, he was cynical and contemptuous of the human want of togetherness. Contrary to his public charismatic image, Dayan was not an ambitious political leader. Izhar Smilanski, who was a close acquaintance of Dayan for many years, wrote in a eulogy of Dayan in Davar, on November 27, 1981, "Every one who knew Moshe Dayan has to remember the hours of melancholy, the boredom and the pessimism, the sitting on the fence and the surprising hesitation and unexpected fog."

Others have suggested that Dayan had a feeling of fatalism concerning the solution of the Arab-Israeli conflict, and that he foresaw unending belligerence between the two nations. Nevertheless, in his biographies and other writings, Dayan showed empathy toward the Arabs as individuals who fight their own liberation war. Nevertheless, he consistently denied Arab claims and argued that Israel's roots in the country stem from the Bible and that they cannot be refuted. His hesitation before taking decisive action was clearly and repeatedly felt. For instance, three weeks before the start of the Sinai Campaign, Dayan wrote in his *Diary of the Sinai Campaign*, "We are torn between our desire to postpone the call-up almost to the last moment before the opening of the campaign, and our need to give the units time to get organized."

In fact, Dayan initiated action in the area of defense but not as a foreign minister, where he mainly reacted to the ideas of others whom he represented. Apparently Dayan never wanted to become prime minister. This has been affirmed by numerous interviews with people who worked with him. Indeed, the typical reaction of Moshe Dayan to this suggestion was, "and then what?" which was a part of his pragmatic calculations and prudence in regard to every step that had to be undertaken. Dayan would hesitate before he would make a decision, weigh the risks, and try to avoid the need to decide if at all possible. For example, he offered to resign from every cabinet in which he was a member. He offered his resignation to David Ben-Gurion when the Cabinet decided to withdraw after the Sinai Campaign in 1956. Dayan resigned his office as minister of agriculture under Prime Minister Levi Eshkol. Golda Meir decided against his resignation twice during the Yom Kippur War. When he failed to convince Menachem Begin in regard to the meaning of autonomy as discussed in the Camp David Accords, he resigned again. Usually Dayan was convinced to stay, perhaps because he preferred to remain and influence the government from within.

Dayan was the initiator of the reprisal policy against infiltrators from Jordan and Egypt. Apart from the general goal of having peace at the borders and defending the settlements of new *olim* (immigrants), this policy had two strategic goals: to "teach" the Arabs that forceful offenses against the truce agreements would be answered by force, and to reintroduce a fighting spirit in the IDF by setting a model for imitation to the whole of the military according to the model of Unit 101—a special unit responsible for enacting reprisal policy.

Following the Czech-Egyptian arms deal of 1955, Dayan suggested that Israel should initiate a preemptive strike. This was not approved by the Israeli Cabinet. Hence, Dayan and Shimon Peres, inspired by David Ben-Gurion, tried to find another means to overcome the danger involved in the change of strategic balance in the region. The alternative was to find a power that would support Israel. It was suggested that Israel look for cooperation with England and France against Egypt. The Israeli leaders who took part in this diplomatic activity were mainly Ben-Gurion, Peres, and Dayan. The plans, which materialized a year later, were to be called the Sinai Campaign of 1956.

When he was ordered to withdraw from Sinai by a cabinet decision, Dayan wanted to resign his office. He was convinced to stay for another period as IDF chief of staff. After that conflict, one of his political concerns was the possibility that the Soviet Union would interfere in an armed conflict against Israel. This was one of the reasons for his objection to escalation by mobilization of the reserve forces on the eve of the Yom Kippur War in 1973.

Dayan became defense minister in the Six Day War as a result of public demand, and did not change the army plans that had been prepared during the tenure of Prime Minister Eshkol as defense minister and Yitzhak Rabin as chief of staff. Nevertheless, he enjoyed the public image of being responsible for the victory. After the hostilities ended, there was hope that peace talks would soon begin. However, the situation was to develop in a different way. There was Dayan's famous comment that Israel was waiting for a phone call from the Arabs to initiate the process, but it did not materialize. In his book, *Breakthrough*, Dayan affirmed that there were talks with King Hussein ibn Talal* of Jordan but that an agreement was not reached.

The opening of avenues of communication that had been closed since 1948 by the Open Bridges Policy was initiated by Dayan. This policy permitted people and goods to cross the border between Jordan and the West Bank and Gaza Strip. The policy was instrumental in decreasing the estrangement between Israel and some Arabs, though the situation of war continued to formally exist.

The 1967 cease-fire agreement was violated by Egypt, which inaugurated heavy artillery shelling of Israeli soldiers stationed on the Suez Canal. Prime Minister Golda Meir declared in the Knesset on March 17, 1969, that Israel would honor the cease-fire as long as it was reciprocally kept. The reason for this declaration was the War of Attrition in the spring of 1969. Dayan differed; he announced that an escalation of hostilities was inevitable, and called for preparations to be taken against an eventual war initiated by Egypt. Israel countered the War of Attrition (1969–1970), and a cease-fire was signed on August 7, 1970.

In 1972, President Anwar al-Sadat* of Egypt suggested peace in return for all the lands Israel had conquered in the Six Day War. Dayan defined his position by saying that he preferred Sharm-el-Sheikh without peace to peace without Sharm-el-Sheikh. However, he changed his mind at Camp David. Sharm-el-Sheikh is a strategic position on the southeast coast of the Sinai Peninsula used by Egypt to blockade sea travel to Israel's port of Eilat.

Conventional wisdom has it that when the Yom Kippur War was about to start, Dayan did not agree to mobilize Israel's reserve forces, as he thought this would escalate the crisis. Dayan's version differs. In Yacov and Kfir's *Conversations with Moshe Dayan*, he relates that he objected to mobilization of the reserves needed for an attack, but not to mobilization of reserves needed for defense. The Agranat Commission did not find the defense minister personally responsible for the failure. However, this was not accepted by the Israeli public. Dayan lost political influence and became a focus for public blame. The issue remained highly controversial thereafter.

Foreign Minister Dayan was the first to contact an Egyptian emissary when he met Sadat's envoy Dr. Hassan Tuhami in Morocco on September 16, 1977. There he left the impression that Israel was ready to return the whole of Sinai to Egyptian sovereignty in exchange for peace. When Sadat came to Israel, on November 19, 1977, the foreign minister kept a low profile, concentrating on the study of the Egyptian demands and attitudes rather than making declarations. During peace negotiations Dayan supported the idea that some sort of accommodation should be reached with regard to the question of joint Arab-Israeli rule of Jerusalem.

On December 2, 1977, Dayan met again with Tuhami in Morocco. This time he was authorized by Prime Minister Begin to suggest the arrangements for redeployment of the IDF and the autonomy plan for the inhabitants of Judea and Samaria (the West Bank) and Gaza. Tuhami declined the suggestions on the spot, replying that Israeli settlements should be removed from Sinai and the Palestinians' right for self-determination should be recognized. These were the questions that continued to haunt negotiations.

Dayan wanted Jordan to have a standing in the autonomy negotiations, and suggested this to Prime Minister Begin who incorporated this suggestion into his plan. During the Camp David summit, Dayan, along with Aharon Barak and Meir Rosenne (who were there in the capacity of legal advisers), was instrumental in convincing Begin that a difference existed between a temporary agreement on autonomy and a final settlement that would protect Israel from the establishment of a Palestinian state in the area. On the subject of the Palestinians, the Israeli delegation was determined to avoid a formula that might be interpreted as agreeing to the Palestinians' right to self-determination and statehood. Dayan and Barak proposed and influenced Begin to agree that the future of the Palestinian Arabs dwelling in the West Bank and Gaza would be determined at talks to be conducted between the Palestinians, Egypt, Jordan, and Israel.

It was Dayan's idea that the fate of the settlements in Sinai should be decided by the Knesset. Another contribution was a letter signed by Begin, Ezer Weizman, and Dayan, which became part of the supplements to the peace treaty. The letter was written on September 17, 1978, and proclaimed Jerusalem an indivisible city.

Dayan's sole personal meeting with Sadat at Camp David took place on September 14, 1978. The conversation was difficult, as President Sadat asked for a gesture from the Israeli negotiating team to help resolve difficulties in his staff, in Egypt, and with the Arab countries. Dayan answered that the idea of creating the large Israeli settlement of Yamit in northeast Sinai was his gesture, "but before going ahead with its construction we approached you and offered to hand back to you the whole of Sinai within the framework of a peace treaty and that idea, too, was mine. What was your reply? No peace, no negotiations, no recognition of Israel" (1981:172). Dayan was referring to the Khartoum Arab summit resolution of 1967.

As to autonomy for the Palestinian Arabs in the West Bank and Gaza (an autonomy which would not compromise Israel's demand for acknowledgment of its sovereignty of the West Bank area) an interesting conversation took place between U.S. Secretary of State Cyrus Vance and Foreign Minister Dayan during the Camp David peace negotiations: Dayan said that a clear distinction should be made between principles that are appropriate for the autonomy negotiations and those that are appropriate for peace with Jordan. Autonomy should be given to the people, and would not apply to the territory of the West Bank. Secretary Vance thought this would not be agreed to by the Egyptians (Dayan 1981).

Dayan's contribution to the peace negotiations was considerable. Dayan suggested self-administration for the Arab inhabitants in the West Bank and Gaza Strip. This, in fact, was a suggestion of autonomy for the people and the territory. Begin disagreed, and felt that Dayan's suggestion would create a precedent that deviated from what had been agreed on and signed, and would have a negative impact on Israel's security interests. Negotiations had to continue without changing the agreement. This difference was expressed during debates in the Knesset, and Begin carried the vote.

In 1979–1980, the PLO (Palestine Liberation Organization) strengthened its hold in southern Lebanon and continued its raids into Israel. This led the government, and especially Prime Minister Begin and Foreign Minister Dayan, to believe that the United States did not see the dangers involved for Israel. The IDF continued to cross the border in order to deter Syria, the PLO and the Lebanese militias. The Litani operation of 1978 was the model that was considered successful. Menachem Begin instructed the IDF not to permit the compromise of Christian minorities in Lebanon. This later became one of the considerations in the decision to launch the 1982 war in Lebanon.

The year 1979 witnessed a loss of credibility of the Likud government and a decrease of its support even among its own ministers. Both Ezer Weizman as minister of defense and Moshe Dayan as minister of foreign affairs resigned in 1979. Dayan resigned on October 2, 1979. The reason given was that his view in regard to autonomy negotiations did not represent the views held by the government. The new government established by the Likud in January 1981 included neither Dayan nor Weizman.

Dayan's general impact on Israel and the Middle East was substantial. In the early 1950s, Dayan was the initiator of the reprisal policy, needed to defend Israeli borders from infiltration. This, in turn, was one of the considerations that led Egypt to acquire weapons from the Soviet Union. This created a posture of influence for the USSR, that escalated into the Sinai Campaign.

In 1967, Dayan served as defense minister, and after the Six Day War he opened the bridges between Jordan and the West Bank, creating a flow of people and goods. If at this period Dayan believed that Arabs and Israelis could live side by side for decades, his ideas changed at the end of his life when he came to believe that Israel had to take unilateral action in order to keep its hold on the areas of Judea, Samaria, and Gaza.

During the peace negotiations, Dayan played an important role while applying his influence in order to moderate Prime Minister Begin's position. His final contribution as foreign minister was to stabilize the Middle East by his role in the peace negotiations that led to the Camp David Accords and the Egypt-Israel Peace Treaty of 1979.

BIBLIOGRAPHY

Works by Dayan:

Diary of the Sinai Campaign. London: Harper and Row, 1966.
Story of My Life. New York: Marlow, 1976.
Living with the Bible. New York: Morrow, 1978.
Breakthrough: A Personal Account of the Egypt Peace Negotiations. New York: Alfred A. Knopf, 1981.
With A. Schweitzer. *Israel: The Changing National Agenda*. London: Dover, 1986.

Other Works:

Dayan, Yael. *My Father, His Daughter*. New York: Farrar, Straus & Giroux, 1985.
Erez, Yacov, and Ilan Kfir. *Conversations with Moshe Dayan* (Hebrew). Tel Aviv: Ma'ariv, 1981.
Heichal, Gabriella. *Decision Making during Crisis: The Korean and the Yom Kippur Wars*. Stanford: Stanford files, 1984. Hebrew edition: *Ma'arachot*, forthcoming.
Lau-Lavie, Nathan. *Moshe Dayan: A Bibliography*. London: Valentine Mitchell, 1969.
Luttwak, Edward, and Dan Horowitz. *The Israeli Army*. New York: Harper and Row, 1975.
Reich, Bernard. *Quest for Peace: United States-Israel Relations and the Arab-Israeli Conflict*. New Brunswick, N.J.: Transaction Books, 1977.
Tevet, Shabtai. *M. Dayan Biography* (Hebrew). Tel Aviv: Shoken, 1972.
Yanai, Natan. *Moshe Dayan on the Peace Process and the Future of Israel* (Hebrew). Tel Aviv: The Defense Ministry Publishing House, 1988.

GABRIELLA HEICHAL

SULEYMAN DEMIREL (1924–) was undoubtedly one of the dominant politicians in Turkey in the second half of the 1960s and 1970s, and continues to have considerable influence. While prime minister in 1965–1971, in the mid–1970s and in 1979–1980 he played an important role in the attempts to solve Turkey's long-lived socioeconomic crises as well as its internal sociopolitical tension and violence. He was almost succesful in his efforts to solve the socioeconomic crisis, but failed to solve the latter problems, and as a result, the military intervened for the third time and took over the rule in the country. Demirel was also responsible for vastly broadening foreign-policy openings, initiated by the governments of Turkey during the first half of the 1960s, while remaining essentially faithful to the Western alliances.

Suleyman Demirel was born in 1924 in a village in the Province of Isparta, in Central Anatolia. He studied at the high school in Afyonkarahisar and then at the Istanbul Technical University, from which he graduated in 1949 as a hydraulic engineer. He entered government service in the early 1950s and worked in several departments including Electric Studies, Hydro-Electric Plants, and Dams; he finally became director of the State Hydraulics Administration during 1955 to 1960, a post in which he acquired a reputation for administrative as well as professional competence. He visited the United States twice for study and work, first in 1949–1950 and later in 1954–1955, as an Eisenhower Fellow for Study. While not actively involved in politics, he became a close personal collaborator of Prime Minister Adnan Menderes,* not only in his own hydrological field but also in general rural development schemes. In 1960, after the fall of Menderes, he left the civil service and established a private enterprise as a hydraulic consultant and representative of American and other foreign companies, among them the famous international firm Morrison-Knudsen. He also taught at the Middle East Technical University in Ankara.

In 1961 he entered politics as a member of the Adalet Partisi (Justice Party or JP), the successor to the dissolved Democrat Party (DP), while maintaining his private practice, which was prosperous. The sudden death of the JP leader, Ragip Gümüspala, in mid–1964, led Demirel to the decision to become an active politician and to suggest himself as a candidate to the party's leadership. His contender for this position was the deputy leader, Saadettin Bilgiç, a physician who also had worked in a professional capacity for government institutions. Demirel did not impress the public as an orator, but he had some knowledge of economics and administration. He was well regarded by the party's intellectuals and, most important, he was supported by most of the former DP members in the party. In November 1964, Demirel was finally elected chairman of the JP by a very convincing majority—1,072 to 552 for Bilgiç—a position he kept until September 1980, when the party was dissolved.

However, Demirel was not an assembly deputy, and he was unable to coordinate the JP group in the National Assembly until the elections in October 1965. Nevertheless, he negotiated with the small parties to overthrow the Ismet Inonu* government in February 1965, and was behind the establishment of the coalition government with JP list Senator Fuat Hayri Ürgüplü as prime minister and himself as deptuy prime minister. Although Demirel was the JP leader, he could not be appointed prime minister because he was not assembly deputy. Furthermore, he was inexperienced, and several months as deputy premier would make him more acquainted with government organization and activities. However, his move to overthrow Inonu's government and establish a new coalition government led by the JP, about eight months before the elections, immediately proved his political abilities, because what was necessary, among other things, was to hold the government in order to win the elections. The JP emerged victorious from the elections of October 1965, and Demirel was requested to form a government.

Demirel served as prime minister in the years 1965–1971, 1975–June 1977, July 1977–December 1977, and November 1979–September 1980. In the years 1971–1974 he was in the opposition while a government of technocrats ruled the country in the name of the army. Three times he led the opposition in the

Assembly against the government of Prime Minister Bulent Ecevit* of the Republican Peoples Party: 1974–1975, June–July 1977, and December 1977–November 1979. He was twice ousted from power by military intervention (in March 1971 and in September 1980), although these military takeovers were not directed specifically against him or the Justice Party.

Following the elections of 1965, Demirel became so powerful within the Justice Party that he could exclude his main opponents from the government. He continued to consolidate his leadership and to be reelected by an overwhelming majority as the party leader. There were two distinct groups within the JP: the moderate liberal faction, which was reform-conscious in its outlook, and the right-oriented conservative faction, which had certain religious inclinations. The former was known as the "sworn faction" because they had taken the oath early in 1966 to stand by Premier Demirel and not to allow either the extreme right or former DP members to drag the party into extremism and thus to the fate suffered by the DP. Demirel managed to remain above the factions and followed a flexible policy of his own, which was not in line with any faction. He owed his strength in the party to this independence and to the fact that by remaining above the factions he had become indispensable. However, during the first years of his leadership he strengthened the moderate faction and with its help successfully coped with the influence of the religious extremists and the extreme conservatives, and managed to isolate both groups. However, in the 1970s he gradually moved to the right as a result of pressures within the party and from outside, especially those of the small ultraconservative parties participating in his coalition governments. This change became evident following the establishment of his new party, the True Path Party, in 1983–1984 as a conservative rival to the so-called moderate Motherland Party of Premier Turgut Ozal.*

Demirel is sensitive to criticism and on several occasions caused the expulsion of active members and even deputies (including the deputy for Antalya and the deputy for Trabzon in 1967) from the party because of their personal criticism of him. However, he enjoyed general support in the party, and the party members remained loyal to him. Even after he was deprived of his political activity rights, they maintained a vigorous campaign to reinstate him as a political leader.

There is no doubt that Demirel was one of the dominant political figures in Turkey in the 1960s and 1970s, and remained influential in the late 1980s. He certainly played a major role, for better or for worse, in reshapinng Turkey's political, economic, social, and cultural life, whether in power or in the opposition, and his ideas in the political, economic, and social fields were of great importance.

In some respects Demirel followed Menderes. He believed in parliamentary democracy and freedom, and for him election by the people was a powerful principle that could not be replaced by anything else. He always complained that personal views and emotional attitudes were dominating political life, and demanded that the political parties, constituting the essential elements of the regime, should arrive at a common understanding concerning some fundamental

concepts of the democratic government and should consider the country's problems in accordance with the requirements of the regime and the general interests
of the country. He claimed that the real factor that enabled democracy to survive
was the state of law that granted rights and obligations, but that equally important
were two other factors: mutual tolerance and civilized acceptance. His main
problem was his personal conflict with the leader of the rival Republican Peoples
Party, Bulent Ecevit, a conflict that led to deep mutual enmity and did not enable
the two leaders to reach any understanding and cooperation even in times of
austerity; this was one of the major reasons for the decision of the military, in
September 1980, to seize power.

Demirel insisted that Turkey should learn how to live with freedom. Freedom
could not be abolished in order to fight abuses of freedom except when these
abuses threatened the security of the state and the regime. With these ideas in
mind, he tried to cope with the growing political violence in Turkey on the one
hand and the demands of certain groups and parties to introduce changes in the
structure and functioning of democracy on the other hand. Demirel expressed
his view that those people who had accepted the regime of the country as defined
by the constitution as secular, democratic, social-minded, and as a state of law
(and the laws issued accordingly) had no reason to demand the change in the
existing order. Demirel was, to a large extent, traditionalist in his views concerning culture and religion. One can say that he favored freedom of worship
and of conscience, respected traditional culture, and advocated national ideas—
all within the secular-minded state and based on the rule of the law. He reiterated
the importance of secularism, but at the same time promoted colleges for modern
prayer leaders and preachers and stressed the need to uphold the prestige of
servants of religion and the establishments that provided religious education.

He did not, however, hestitate, despite many protests even within his own
party, to change Ataturk's rule forbidding Turkey from participation in Islamic
organizations, and decided to send an official delegation to the Islamic Conference in Morocco in 1969, following the attempt to burn down the Aqsa Mosque
in Jerusalem. This step led later to a Turkish decision to become a full member
of this conference, and to agree to hold one of its plenary meetings in Istanbul.

This decision emerged as a result of Demirel's pragmatic foreign policy. He
was deeply concerned with two major problems: the Cyprus question and the
economic crisis which, after 1973, was closely linked with the energy crisis; he
tried to mobilize support for the Turkish cause in Cyprus and to obtain economic
and financial aid from any source available. Therefore, he gradually developed
the policy of shifting away from an almost exclusive U.S. orientation to a more
diversified and flexible approach with two major trends: alliances with Western
Europe mainly for financial and technical aid, and the Arab-Islamic orientation
both for political support and for economic aid and cooperation (the latter especially with the oil-producing countries).

Demirel believed in a liberal economy and in economic development through
the private sector rather than through government intervention. He considered

free enterprise the most important foundation of the country's development. He supported the enlargement of internal markets, the protection of Turkish producers and customers according to the rule of a market economy, and, at the same time, the adaptation of Turkey to the requirements of foreign markets in order to compete. Nevertheless, he also supported a social welfare state. Demirel expressed his hope that at the end of the century Turkey would reach the standard the German Federal Republic had reached in the 1970s.

Demirel's problem was that he faced many difficulties in implementing his ideas and could not cope with them: rapid socioeconomic changes; the energy crisis and the shortage in foreign currency; growing political violence; the pressures exerted by various political and social groups, including the intelligentsia, which was struggling for recognition and power; pressures from the coalition government's small parties (the fascist National Action Party and the fundamental religious National Salvation Party); the inability to come to terms with the main rival political party, the Republican Peoples Party, which led, among other things, to a deadlock in legislation; and the growing opposition within the Justice Party to his concessions to the small parties participating in his coalition government.

In March 1975, Demirel established the Nationalist Front Coalition Government based on four parties—the Justice Party, the National Salvation Party, the National Action Party, and the Republican Reliance Party (RRP)—with the slogan "a Rightist Front against the Left." Demirel maintained little control over the small partners and could not cope with the deep economic crisis mainly because of their nationalistic approach to any foreign suggestion to overcome the crisis. Banks all over the world stopped honoring checks of the Turkish Central Bank, and Turkey's economic and industrial activities were partially paralyzed. The elections of June 1977 increased the number of the JP's seats in the National Assembly from 165 to 189, but the winner was the RPP, with 213 seats. Demirel's opponents within the party left it in December 1977 and established an independent group in the Assembly, which helped the RPP to establish a government and to send Demirel and the JP to the opposition.

The JP emerged more consolidated after the crisis of December, and better prepared to try to regain power. Demirel skillfully and remorselessly exploited every mistake of Ecevit's government to bolster his party's position and his own influence within it. In October 1978, Demirel was reelected as the leader of the party by an overwhelming majority of 1,439 votes out of 1,550. The country continued to suffer from political violence and economic crisis, but neither Demirel nor Ecevit were ready to reconcile or to reach compromise even for the sake of rescuing the nation.

Following the landslide victory of the JP in the by-elections of October 1979, Demirel returned to power by forming in November a minority JP government which survived, thanks to the support of two small rightist parties, until the military takeover in September 1980. Its tenure was marked by bold economic reforms carried out by a new economic adviser, Turgut Ozal,* and aimed at liberalizing the economy via massive financial aid from the West, which encouraged both Demirel's economic reforms and foreign policy. However, the Assembly was paralyzed by the inability to elect a new president; legislation was backlogged; political violence continued with increasing intensity; industry and services were still, to a large extent, paralyzed because of strikes, shortages in the energy supply and foreign currency; and political parties and politicians continued their enmity and quarrels. Demirel was unable to overcome these problems although he tried, and the military, while taking over in September 1980, continued his bold economic policy by entrusting its implementation to his under secretary for planning, Turgut Ozal.

The military dissolved the political parties and banned all political activities of former leading politicians for ten years. Most of them obeyed the ban and kept a low profile, including Demirel, who refrained from all public activities and waited, as did other politicians, to see what kind of democracy the military regime was going to establish. Demirel tried in November 1981 to reach a rapprochement with his main opponent, Ecevit, and phoned him to offer his sympathy after the latter was sentenced to prison, but nothing came of it.

In 1983, when new parties were established to participate in the November elections, JP former politicians who were close friends of Demirel established with his consent the Grand Turkey Party with a program that resembled that of the former JP. The party was not approved by the military. However, another party, which was not eligible to participate in the November 1983 elections but at least was not banned—Doğru Yol Partisi (the True Path Party or TPP)—was joined by many of the former JP members, who turned it into a successor to the JP. The party managed to obtain its legal existence in September 1984, when the Supreme Constitutional Court failed to find enough evidence to ban it. During 1985–1986, Demirel made increasingly more public appearances in favor of the TPP, defying the ban on his political activities. He was also the behind-the-scenes figure who caused the election of Husamettin Çindoruk, former head of the JP Istanbul Branch, as the leader of the TPP. He even joined Ecevit in severely attacking the president, Kenan Evren, following the latter's indirect attack on former politicians by accusing them of causing harm to Turkey.

During 1987, Demirel and other politicians demanded the waiver of the ban on their political activities. Premier Turgut Ozal responded by holding a referendum on this demand. The referendum held on September 6, 1987, waived the ban by a marginal majority of 11,723,209 votes to 11,641,961. Demirel immediately returned to politics and was elected on September 8 as the leader of the TPP in place of Çindoruk. However, in the general elections held in November 1987, his True Path Party won 19 percent and 59 seats in the 450-seat Assembly, compared to 36 percent and 292 seats of Premier Ozal's Motherland Party and 25 percent and 99 seats of the Social Democrat Populist Party of Erdal Inonu. Nevertheless, Demirel decided to continue his deep involvement in the political life of Turkey.

Demirel and the Justice Party were the successors of Adnan Menderes and the Democrat Party. Demirel continued to promote the liberal economy and to strengthen the private sector, but he also tried hard to keep democracy in accordance with the 1961 constitution and to maintain normal and even good relations with the military. However, he could not cope with the continuing economic crisis, which developed as a result of external factors such as the oil crisis as well as internal ones such as the enormous urbanization process. He also could not cope with the sociopolitical tension and violence that developed as a result of his own policies: He made possible the unprecedented rise of political forces of both the right and the left in accordance with the 1961 constitution, which provided broad guarantees against the power of the state, because he saw the development of civil society vis-à-vis the state as a security guarantee for his own rule. He also enhanced the power of the extreme right by cooperating with both the extreme nationalist party and the extreme Islamic fundamentalist party in coalition governments and thus increased political polarization. The military takeover in September 1980 deprived him of his political rights; nevertheless, he managed to return to political activity with the aim of continuing to play an important role. There is no doubt that his liberal economic ideas of the 1960s and his economic policy of 1979–1980 did and still do prevail, as well as the main idea of his foreign policy—diversification of Turkey's orientations. While strengthening politico-economic connections with the West, he also improved relations with the communist countries where he managed to obtain cheap technology, and with the Middle Eastern and other Muslim countries, where he started to open new markets.

BIBLIOGRAPHY

Works by Demirel:

Demirel'in Büyük Hedefi, Yeni Bir Sosyal Mukaveleye Doğru (Demirel's Great Goal: Towards a New Social Contract). Prepared for publication by Uğur Gümüştekin. Istanbul: Birlik Matbassi, 1974.
Büyük Türkiye (Great Turkey). Istanbul: Dergâh Yayinlari, 1975.
Anayasa ve Devlet Ideresi (Constitution and State Administration). Istanbul: Göktürk Yayinlari, 1977.

Other Works:

Ahmad, Feroz. *The Turkish Experiment in Democracy 1950–1975*. Boulder, Colo.: Westview Press, 1977.
Dodd, Clement H. *Politics and Government in Turkey*. Manchester, England: Manchester University Press, 1969.
———. *Democracy and Development in Turkey*. Beverley, North Humberside, England: Eothen Press, 1979.

————. *The Crisis of Turkish Democracy*. Beverly, North Humberside, England: Eothen Press, 1983.

Karpat, Kemal H. *Turkey's Foreign Policy in Transition 1950–1974*. Leiden, the Netherlands: Brill, 1975.

Karpat, Kemal H. (ed.). *Political and Social Thought in the Contemporary Middle East*. New York: Praeger, 1982, pp. 396–399.

ARYEH SHMUELEVITZ

E

BULENT ECEVIT (1925–), former leader of the Republican People's Party (RPP) and prime minister; a major figure in recent Turkish politics. He played an important role in developing legislation which strengthened the labor union and was very popular with workers. His rise to prominence from the mid–1960s through the 1970s took place during a period of significant new political and social developments in Turkey and in Turkish foreign policy. In domestic politics, there was a steady drift toward ideological politics and growing polarization between the left and the right. An important feature of this new trend was the transformation of the RPP—the political organization that was founded by Mustafa Kemal Ataturk in 1923 to oversee his modernization program—from a centrist political force into an advocate of democratic socialism. The rise of ideological politics for the first time in the republic's history was accompanied by two successive setbacks in the consolidation of Turkey's postwar parliamentary democratic system. Both the 1971 and 1980 political crises resulted in military interventions. However, in each case there was a transition back to democracy following a period of direct or indirect military rule. Along with these political changes, the 1960s and 1970s witnessed vast migration to the cities from the countryside, significant advances in economic development, and growing socioeconomic disparities. In the realm of foreign affairs, Turkey's decision to send troops to Cyprus in 1974—in response to the then-ruling Greek junta's attempt to alter the island's constitutional status quo through force—was an important threshold in postwar Turkish foreign policy. While this decision was immensely popular at home, it proved to be a major source of strain in Turkey's relations with her NATO allies (North Atlantic Treaty Organization), especially Greece and the United States.

Bulent Ecevit, who played an important role either as a catalyst in bringing about some of these changes or in shaping the policy responses to them, was born in Istanbul on May 28, 1925. His parents belonged to the political and cultural elite of Ataturk's newly established republic. His father was a medical doctor and an RPP parliamentarian; his mother was an art teacher and an accomplished painter. Ecevit was educated at the American Robert College in Istanbul. After graduation in 1944, he joined the government's press and publicity agency in Ankara. From 1946 to 1950, he was stationed at the Turkish embassy's press attaché office in London. While in London, he studied Sanskrit and art history at London University.

Prior to his entry into politics, Ecevit's chief interests were literature and journalism. Beginning with his school days at Robert College, he wrote and translated poetry, literary essays, and art criticism. Over the years he has published his own poems as well as translations of works by T. S. Eliot and R. Tagore. He began his career in journalism in 1950 as a literary critic for the RPP's official daily newspaper *Ulus*. Subsequently, he served as its foreign news editor, managing editor, political director, and chief columnist. His journalistic career took him to the United States in 1954–1955 where he was a guest writer for the *Winston-Salem Journal* in North Carolina. He visited the United States again in 1957–1958 as a Rockefeller Fellow at Harvard University.

Evecit's position at *Ulus* brought him into close contact with the RPP's veteran leader, Ismet Inonu.* With Inonu's backing, Ecevit became an RPP candidate from Ankara in the 1957 parliamentary elections. Upon his election to the Parliament, Ecevit rose rapidly in the party's hierarchy, benefiting from close ties with both Inonu and a younger group of reformist intellectuals led by Turhan Feyzioglu. Following the 1960 military coup, Ecevit became a member of the constituent assembly which drafted the new 1961 constitution. He then served as Minister of Labor in Prime Minister Inonu's three coalition governments during 1961 through 1965.

Ecevit's ascendancy in the RPP's ranks continued in the latter part of the decade. In 1966, he was elected the party's secretary-general following a bitter factional fight with his former political mentor Feyzioglu. This influential position, coupled with Inonu's advanced age, enabled Ecevit to consolidate his authority and power over the party apparatus between 1966 and 1971. Ecevit captured the RPP's top leadership after a showdown with Inonu in the aftermath of the 1971 military intervention. Ecevit opposed Inonu's decision to support the military-backed government of Prime Minister Nihat Erim and resigned from his post in the party. The RPP congress, which was convened in May 1972 to resolve this dispute, supported Ecevit over Inonu. Upon Inonu's resignation, Ecevit was elected to the chairmanship of the RPP.

For the rest of the 1970s, Ecevit was very much at the center of the Turkish political stage. Along with his chief rival Suleyman Demirel,* leader of the center-right Justice Party (JP), he took turns as prime minister at the head of coalition or minority governments between 1974 and 1980. During these turbulent years, which witnessed protracted political and economic crises amid a bloody terrorist campaign, Ecevit became prime minister three times: twice as head of the coalitions that were formed between the RPP and minor parties (1974 and 1978–1979), and once in a short-lived RPP minority government that failed the confidence vote in the parliament (1977).

Following the 1980 military coup, Ecevit was briefly detained by the ruling officers who held him, together with Demirel and the leaders of the two extremist minor parties, personally responsible for Turkey's drift into terrorism and civil strife. Later, he was jailed three times and spent 173 days in military prison for violating the ban on political declarations. The ruling junta headed by General Kenan Evren dissolved all political parties and banned 240 politicians, including Ecevit, from politics for five to ten years. Despite this ban, Ecevit maintained a relatively visible political profile and remained vocal in his criticisms of the military regime. During the transition to democracy after 1983, Ecevit refused to join the newly formed Populist Social Democracy Party (SODEP) which sought to replace the RPP in the Turkish party system. Instead, he helped to organize a new Democratic Socialist Party (DSP) and delegated its leadership to his wife, Rahsan. In 1987, Ecevit became the DSP's chairman following a national referendum which lifted the ban imposed by the military on the former party elites. In the parliamentary elections held during the same year, the DSP failed to capture any parliamentary seats. Subsequently, Ecevit resigned from its chairmanship only to be reelected to the DSP's leadership a year later.

Bulent Ecevit's most important contributions to Turkey's domestic politics are related to his efforts to organize and mobilize the underprivileged groups in Turkish society. His political thinking and vision were strongly influenced by the social democratic movements of Western Europe, especially those that flourished in the Scandinavian countries. This influence is best seen in Ecevit's attempt to establish a mass-based social democratic party with close political ties to organized labor. It is also reflected in his program of redistributive economic policies, social welfare provisions for the needy, structural reforms in the countryside, and state-directed industrial modernization. While Ecevit aspired to lay the foundations for social democracy in Turkey, his political style and electoral strategies had more in common with populist ideologies and movements. Other prominent populist leaders in postwar Turkish politics such as Adnan Menderes,* leader of the Democratic Party and prime minister during the 1950s, and the JP's Demirel were particularly successful in the political mobilization and social integration of the rural masses. Ecevit's populism was directed primarily at the urban lower classes. Turkey's industrialization and rapid urbanization created a favorable milieu for the emergence of a new type of politician—someone who could, through eloquent oratory and personalist-charismatic leadership, offer hope to the millions who had migrated from the countryside to Istanbul, Ankara, and other major cities in search of better economic prospects. Ecevit successfully fulfilled this role in the early 1970s. His advocacy of social justice for the underprivileged and his promise to create a new and more equitable social order in Turkey met with an enthusiastic response from the urban lower classes.

Ecevit's first major achievement in Turkish politics concerned the provision of new political and economic rights for industrial workers. During his stay in England in the late 1940s, Ecevit had been impressed by the strength of the

British trade-union movement and its influence on government policy-making processes. He foresaw a similar role for organized labor in Turkey. His tenure as minister of labor from 1961 to 1965 provided Ecevit with the political authority to put his ideas into action. Hitherto, the labor unions in Turkey had played a relatively marginal role in politics. However, the 1960s witnessed significant changes with respect to working-class politics: The 1961 constitution lifted some of the sanctions against class-based politics, the concept of the welfare state received considerable attention from the reformist intellectuals and party elites, and rapid industrial development expanded the size of the urban work force. However, the single most important factor in the growth of the trade-union movement was the new labor legislation of 1963 which, for the first time in Turkish history, legalized strikes, lockouts, and collective bargaining. Ecevit played a key role in this important policy change. He lobbied for the new legislation within the RPP and in Prime Minister Inonu's coalition government, he worked closely with the leaders of the labor unions and employer's associations in drafting the new bill, and he assumed legislative leadership when it came before the Parliament. All in all, the granting of the right to strike to workers owed much to Ecevit's determination and leadership. It also proved to be a turning point in the evolution of organized labor in Turkey. Empowered with new rights and experiencing steady growth in their ranks, the two strongest trade-union confederations—politically moderate Turk-Is (Turkiye Isci Sendikalari Konfederasyonu—Confederation of Turkish Trade Unions) and the radical leftist DISK (Devrimici Isci Sendikalari Konfederasyonu—Confederation of Revolutionary Workers' Trade Unions)—became pricipal participants of interest-group politics.

His work on behalf of organized labor established Ecevit's social democratic credentials. It also provided him with a strong following among the workers. Both these factors contributed to Ecevit's efforts to move the RPP toward a democratic socialist platform. When Ecevit was elected as secretary general in 1966, the RPP faced serious electoral and organizational problems. In the 1965 elections, its votes declined by nearly 10 percent, and the party suffered a major defeat at the hands of its center-right rival, the JP. At the same time, the newly established Marxist Turkish Labor Party (TLP) threatened to make inroads into the RPP's organizational base among the party activists in the universities. To stave off the challenges from both the political left and the right, Inonu defined his party's stand as "left of center" during the 1965 election campaign. However, this last-minute effort failed to win over many voters. The RPP continued to be viewed by a large segment of the Turkish electorate as an elitist party that basically represented the legacy of the authoritarian one-party period (1923–1946), and the interests of the Kemalist Coalition which included bureaucrats, military officers, educated professionals, and, in Eastern Turkey, large landowners.

A decade later, the RPP's electoral strength and ideological orientation had changed considerably. Its votes rose from 27.4 percent in 1969 to 33.3 percent in 1973, and then to 41.3 percent in 1977. In the two nationwide parliamentary elections held during the 1970s, the RPP surpassed the JP both times, and finished first. This remarkable turnaround was largely the outcome of Ecevit's political leadership. By a series of tactical moves—for example, criticism of some aspects of Ataturk's reforms, opposition to military involvement in politics, recruitment of activists from the middle and lower classes—he managed to weaken, if not totally eradicate, the RPP's elitist image. More importantly, he succeeded in laying the foundations for a new electoral coalition based on workers and urban marginals in the cities, and poor farmers and rural workers in the countryside. Election results in 1973 and 1977 showed that the RPP had begun to attract large numbers of urban lower-class voters, especially those who migrated to the cities and lived in the *gecekondu* (squatter site) areas. To the millions who had come to the metropolitan centers in search of better economic prospects, Ecevit's promise to transform Turkey's socioeconomic order and to march toward a bright new era in the near future appeared to be a much-needed message of hope.

In addition to this new populist electoral appeal, the RPP under Ecevit's leadership displayed a far greater interest in leftist policies than had been the case a decade earlier. Along with an explicit antibusiness and anti-American orientation, the party leadership employed an increasingly radical rhetoric that was heavily oriented toward mass appeal to workers, small peasants, and urban marginals. The dominant themes in the party's democratic socialist platform included fundamental changes in the distribution of wealth and power, state ownership of heavy industry, government control of the marketplace, and greater independence in Turkish foreign policy. The RPP also emerged as the staunchest supporter of the liberal 1961 constitution and the individual, associational, and other civil liberties guaranteed within it. The party's commitment to political and social pluralism was reflected in its defense of democratic processes, human rights, and greater tolerance for the expression of ethnic and religious-sectarian interests.

While Ecevit was successful in his quest to attain power by transforming the RPP, his political career suffered a major setback as a result of his poor performance as prime minister during 1978–1979. Ecevit came into office with the promise of ending terrorist incidents, finding a solution to the country's economic crisis, and fulfilling his earlier pledge to improve the living standard of the lower classes. However, he was unable to make much progress on any of these pressing problems. Under his coalition government, which included the RPP along with two minor parties and the independents, the deterioration in Turkey's political and economic conditions continued. As prime minister, Ecevit was unable to provide the effective political leadership Turkey desperately needed during its most severe crisis in the postwar period. Ecevit's failure was partly due to the fact that the methods that he had used successfully to attain political power proved to be inadequate for crisis management and government leadership. His inability or unwillingness to reach an accommodation with JP's Demirel in order to defend Turkish democracy against its enemies from the extreme left and right was one of the major shortcomings of Ecevit's leadership in the late 1970s. However, his disappointing performance was also due to the constraints within which he operated. He did not have a stable parliamentary majority and he could not control two major political forces that he had helped to transform and strengthen, that is, the organized working class and the RPP. The trade union movement was badly split between Turk-Is and DISK. Neither was supportive of Ecevit's government; and DISK's radical strategies aimed at further polarizing political life. Similar divisive tendencies were at work within Ecevit's own political party as well. As Ecevit's coalition government faltered, the disputes between the RPP's various ideological and personalist factions became more accentuated. The task of managing a weak coalition government and a divided social democratic party without the aid of organized labor turned out to be extremely difficult. Ecevit's inability to fulfil the expectations that he had helped to raise through a decade-long populist politics significantly weakened his electoral support. After eighteen months in office, he was forced to resign when the 1979 by-elections resulted in a landslide victory for Demirel's JP.

In addition to his prominent role in Turkey's domestic politics, Bulent Ecevit had a significant impact on Turkish foreign policy. This was largely due to his decision to send Turkish troops to Cyprus in 1974 during the crisis on the island republic. In July 1974, a coup staged with the active involvement of Greece's military regime forced the Cypriot President, Archbishop Makarios, to flee from the island. Turkey regarded the coup and Markarios's replacement by Nicos Sampson as an attempt to achieve a de facto union with Greece. Given Sampson's previous involvement in violence against the island's Turkish minority, Ankara also viewed the coup as a serious threat to its conationals. Under the 1960 Cyprus Treaty of Guarantee, Britain, Turkey, and Greece were entitled to intervene, jointly or singly, to maintain the constitutional status quo. Ecevit responded to the crisis first by seeking a joint British-Turkish intervention. When the British government refused to become involved, he ordered the Turkish military to land its forces on Cyprus. Ecevit's decision had far-reaching consequences. At home, it added significantly to Ecevit's popularity and charisma. Abroad, the Turkish intervention on Cyprus ushered in a series of new developments. On the island, there was a de facto partition, with the Greek-Cypriots and the Turkish-Cypriots living under separate regimes in the south and the north, respectively. Turkey's action over Cyprus led to a worsening of Turkish-Greek relations. Initially, the Turkish intervention threatened to trigger a full scale war between two NATO (North Atlantic Treaty Organization) allies. Although this was averted, the Cyprus problem remained a major source of friction in Turkey's relations with Greece during the 1970s and 1980s. Finally, Ecevit's decision in 1974 created strains in the Turkish-American alliance. Bowing to the pressure from the Greek-American lobby, the U.S. Congress suspended all military aid and sales to Turkey in 1975. Ankara responded by suspending American base facilities in Turkey. Although it was later lifted by President Jimmy Carter, the arms embargo seriously undermined the trust the Turks had placed in Turkish-American ties.

Ecevit's efforts to secure greater independence for Turkey from what he viewed as its excessive dependence on the United States in regional and international affairs also had significant political implications. One of his first policy actions as prime minister in 1974 was to end the ban on the cultivation of opium poppies which had been imposed by the previous military-backed Ankara government under some pressure from Washington. Later, when he ordered Turkish troops to Cyprus, he disregarded the pressure from the United States to reach a non-military solution. Again, he was partly motivated by his desire to show Turkey's independence from America. The intensification of the Greek-Turkish feuding and the U.S. arms embargo further strengthened Ecevit's belief concerning the need for new directions in Turkish foreign policy. When he became prime minister again in 1978, Ecevit announced that Turkey would restructure its foreign policy according to a new national security doctrine. The central theme of this new formulation was that Greece posed a greater threat to Turkish national security than the Soviet Union. Consequently, Ecevit argued that Turkey should lessen its dependence on NATO and the United States, seek closer ties with the Soviet Union and the Warsaw Pact countries, expand its relations with the Arab nations and the Third World, and seek to achieve self-sufficiency in weapons by developing its own defense industry. Although Turkey had already made some readjustments in its foreign policy by the mid–1970s, Ecevit's views carried the premise of fundamental changes with far-reaching implications for NATO and Turkish-American bilateral relations. However, the gravity of Turkey's crisis during his tenure as Prime Minister, and the strong opposition of the armed forces to Ecevit's "new national security doctrine," prevented Ecevit from introducing new radical policies in Turkey's foreign relations.

BIBLIOGRAPHY

Works by Ecevit:

Bu Duzen Degismelidir (This Social Order Must Change). Istanbul: Tekin Yayinevi, 1975.
Ataturk ve Devrimcilik (Ataturk and Revolution). Istanbul: Tekin Yayinevi, 1976.
Dis Politika (Foreign Policy). Ankara: Ajans Turk Matbaacilik Sanayii, 1976.
Siirler, Siir Cevirileri, Yazin ve Sunat Yazilari (Poems, Poetry Translations, Articles, and Essays on Art). Ankara: n.p., 1976.

Other Works:

Ahmad, Feroz. *The Turkish Experiment in Democracy 1950–1975*. Boulder, Colo.: Westview, 1977.
Dodd, Clement Henry. *The Crisis of Turkish Democracy*. North Humberside, Eng.: Eothen Press, 1983.
Harris, George S. *Turkey: Coping with Crisis*. Boulder, Colo.: Westview, 1985.
Rustow, Dankwart A. *Turkey: America's Forgotten Ally*. New York: Council on Foreign Relations, 1987.

Saglamer, Kayhan. *Ecevit Olayi* (The Ecevit Phenomenon). 3 vols. Istanbul: Belge Yay-
    inlari, 1974–1975.

                                                                   SABRI SAYARI

LEVI ESHKOL (1895–1969) was a leading figure in Israeli politics and the
organized labor movement for more than four decades both before and after
Israel achieved independence in 1948. He was a friend and close political ally
of David Ben-Gurion* and served in a number of government positions including
minister of agriculture and development, minister of finance, minister of defense,
and prime minister. He led Israel through the 1967 Arab-Israeli war and its
immediate aftermath.

With the resignation and departure from public office in June 1963 of David
Ben-Gurion,* the patriarch of modern Israel and its prime minister, the awesome
responsibility of filling the office held by this luminary fell to Levi Eshkol. Born
Levi Shkolnik in the shtetl of Oratovo, a railway junction in the Kiev district
of the Ukraine, on October 25, 1895, he was to remain Israel's third premier
until his death from a heart attack in February 1969 at the age of 73. It was
during his tenure in high office that Eshkol led the state through one of its most
traumatic periods since the birth of the nation in 1948. During the period of
May 15 to June 5, 1967, Egypt and Syria, with material and diplomatic support
from the Soviet Union, placed the security of Israel at risk. It fell to its prime
minister to direct the course of action to remove the threat and to insure the
continued security of the state and the nation.

Eshkol's early life fit the traditional pattern of a Jew in the pale of settlement
of the Russian Empire. Segregated culturally as well as socially, most Jews
turned inward, which was reflected in their basic education. Thus it was the case
for the young Eshkol, whose education was bound by the languages taught and
spoken—Yiddish, Hebrew, and Russian. Up to the time of his bar mitzvah,
education was by tutor, the local rabbi. While Eshkol wanted to continue his
education in the school in Odessa, which was then well known to the Jews of
Eastern Europe, there were no vacancies. Instead, a position was found in the
Hebrew college preparatory school in Vilna, Lithuania, at the fifth or sixth form,
where he went to study for two years. These were formative years, and it was
also during this period of study that Eshkol came into contact with Yosef Sprin-
zak, one of the early Jewish pioneers in Palestine, who had come to Vilna to
recruit other young Jews to further the Zionist effort. The idea of emigrating to
Palestine was appealing to Eshkol, although he met with resistance from his
family when he informed them of his plans. Indeed, Palestine at that time existed
essentially as an idyllic dream of Jewish Zionists, since few Jews actually lived
there and it was part of several Ottoman Turkish administrative provinces.

In January 1914, at age nineteen, Eshkol set out on foot from his home as
part of a contingent representing the youth organization, Hapoel Hatzair (the
Young Worker), to the port of Trieste, where he boarded a tramp steamer bound
for the Palestinian port of Jaffa, and unwittingly became a part of the Second

Aliyah (immigration to the Holy Land). He carried with him only the barest essentials in a knapsack, but had an enormous sense of enthusiasm. Within a month he arrived in his new homeland and made his way on foot to the Jewish settlement at Petah Tiqva. At first he served as a common farm laborer and watchman, but he soon became involved in the building of a pumping station. In the evenings he served as a cashier of the workers' kitchen, which he also managed. Soon thereafter he was elected to the Workers' Agricultural Council of Petah Tiqva. His organizational talents were readily recognized by others, and in August 1914 he was invited to develop other collective settlements at Atarot, on the Ramallah road north of Jerusalem, a project that was later to fail. Then, in the late spring of 1915, Eshkol traveled with several companions to Rishon le-Zion, the site of the famed Rothschild vineyards. There he and his comrades contracted to operate one of the farms, and there he met Rivka Marchak, whom he was to marry. By 1924, however, the marriage had failed and they agreed to separate; this was formalized three years later. A daughter, Noa, was conceived from the relationship.

When World War I broke out, the British organized young Jewish males into a military unit, the Jewish Legion. Eshkol entered military service of the Jewish Legion and for two years served in the fortieth Batallion of the Royal Fusiliers, emerging with a mediocre military record. Upon demobilization in 1920, he and fellow combatants helped to create Degania Bet, one of the country's first *kibbutzim* (collective settlements).

In December 1920, a convention of labor Zionists was held in Haifa with Eshkol in attendance. Out of this meeting came the Histadrut, the General Federation of Jewish Labor in Palestine, and Eshkol joined the executive board. During the next decade Eshkol was dispatched throughout Europe and to the Socialist International on various missions for the Histadrut. His work with the organized labor movement was a firm foundation for his involvement in the left-of-center political party, Mapai (Mifleget Poalei Yisrael, the Workers' Party), which was founded in 1929 and which elected Eshkol to its Central Council, where he served as both party secretary and member of the Central Committee. David Ben-Gurion was to become a powerful figure in the party and with him Eshkol was drawn into the vortex of party power. In the years to come, Eshkol would be viewed as a political appendage to Ben-Gurion because of the parallels in their careers as well as their friendship, but their personas were quite different. Ben-Gurion was always the theorist, the visionary, while Eshkol was the pragmatic activist with the capability for compromise.

Life for the early Zionists in Palestine was made difficult not only by the harshness of the land but also by the unreceptiveness of the Palestinian Arab community, a feeling that was frequently manifested in violence. Protection was afforded the Yishuv (the Jewish community in Palestine) by a self-defense organization, the Haganah, to which Eshkol's advice was applied first as a financial adviser and then as an arms procurer. It was also during this period that he met a fellow Russian emigré, Elisheva Kaplan, whom he took as his second wife in

1928 and with whom he had three daughters, Dvora, Tamar, and Ofra. Elisheva died of cancer in 1959.

With the rise of Nazism and fascism in Europe in the 1930s, Zionist leaders in Palestine began a program to save as many coreligionists as possible. In 1934, Eshkol was dispatched to Germany, where he remained for three years as the director of the Settlement Department of the Palestine Office in Berlin, and later as an agent for the Hechalutz pioneer organizations in Germany, Poland, and Lithuania.

By 1940 he had returned to Palestine and to Degania Bet. Unable to enter military service—he was forty-five years old—and since the Histadrut found little work for him, he went back to the kibbutz where he served as director of the Mekerot Water Board as well as remaining on the high command of the Haganah. In 1942 he was a part of the executive committee of the Jewish Agency for Palestine, the central Zionist organization. There Eshkol served as the director of its settlement department in charge of aliyah and placement of immigrants on various kibbutzim. Two years later came an important political appointment as the secretary-general of the Tel Aviv Labor Council, which also added to Mapai's political power among workers' organizations in this urban center.

The emergence of the State of Israel in 1948 was accompanied by the first major Arab-Israeli war. Eshkol was unable to take part as an active combatant but nevertheless contributed to the overall war effort. His experience with security during the prestate period provided the background to his appointment as the director general of the Ministry of Defense after the Declaration of Independence was issued on May 14, 1948. With the formal establishment of a Jewish state, Levi Shkolnik became Levi Eshkol. A series of shifts followed thereafter. One of the first objectives of the government was to get immigrants onto the land. Eshkol was appointed head of the Land Settlement Department of the Jewish Agency in 1949, and thus the problem of land and people fell under his purview. In this position he showed tremendous daring and imagination, and went far to utilize Israel's few resources for maximum gain. One such solution was borrowed from the Greek experience. Eshkol had seen years ago in Greece what had been done there for their compatriots who had been expelled from Turkey. Given only the essential building materials, the individuals themselves were expected to do much of the actual building of homes.

In 1951 he entered the Cabinet as the minister of agriculture and development, and the following year as the minister of finance, a post in which he served for eleven years. It then became his responsibility to pay the war debt and to come up with funds to upgrade the military. It was also during this time that he became deputy prime minister and chairman of the Cabinet's economic committee. The country's trade deficit was astronomical, and the availability of foodstuffs was a problem not far behind in priority. The solution was found in the export of citrus fruits and industrial goods, and by 1954 the worst of the economic danger was over.

Money was sought and came in from external sources other than trade. State bonds were issued, the United Jewish Appeal brought in hard currency from Diaspora Jews, and West Germany paid reparations and restitution payments to individual Jews living in Israel. Eshkol remained in the government as minister of finance and helped to develop a small oil industry. A twenty-year master economic plan was announced to develop the country's mineral wealth and enhance a fledgling chemical industry. At the same time, private industry was expanded and overseas trade was greatly encouraged. In this vein Eshkol introduced legislation in the Knesset in the summer of 1959 which would exempt foreign investors from taxes in an attempt to attract foreign capital.

In February 1962, Eshkol again took the initiative to deal with the country's economic woes by strengthening its relationship with Europe. A policy was instituted to increase exports and bring about an accommodation with the European Common Market. The plan, however, was not particularly well received by industrial workers since it called for the devaluation of the Israeli pound. This was followed in January 1963 with an announced wage and price freeze, an increase in tax rates, and a reduction in government social outlays.

Eshkol's contributions to Israel's economic development are clearly only one dimension of his involvement in state affairs; politics was to become another. His ties to the popular but controversial Ben-Gurion made an ugly impression in Israeli politics in 1953. In an abrupt and somewhat theatrical move, Ben-Gurion announced in November 1953 that he needed a rest because of what he referred to as "spiritual fatigue," although in reality it was because he had simply failed to get the government to accede to a particular set of proposals. He thereupon retired from active public service and moved to a kibbutz at Sde Boker in the Negev ostensibly to promote settlement in the southern part of Israel. However, it was also a time, Ben-Gurion thought, that favored a new generation of leadership, a circulation of elites catering to a younger cohort group. Although many Israelis thought Eshkol was a leading contender to be Ben-Gurion's successor, Mapai leaders, with Eshkol's acquiescence, selected the "Old Man's" arch rival, Foreign Minister Moshe Sharett. Early in 1955, Ben-Gurion rejoined the government as the minister of defense after the sudden resignation of Pinhas Lavon, who had held that post.

Pinhas Lavon had been eased out of the Defense Ministry in February 1955 because of the failure of a covert intelligence operation in Egypt. Much of the blame for the failure was placed on Lavon, who subsequently sought exhoneration. Lavon's role was essentially a political one, but at the same time he was a major player in the Mapai party. Ben-Gurion saw the entire matter as one of national security. Eshkol was more concerned with party unity and the maintenance of political stability. In addition, Ben-Gurion deeply resented the fact that Eshkol had not lined up solidly behind him in the maelstrom of internal political-party politics, which in turn produced a great deal of bitterness. Ben-Gurion strove to get to the truth of the matter to determine whether Lavon had in fact been derelict in his duties, whereas Eshkol, who was appointed to the investigative Committee of Seven, believed the entire truth could not be determined, and that even if it could, the event was so sensitive that it could not be discussed publicly. Nevertheless, Ben-Gurion was furious; in his view, a person could not compromise on principle. Eshkol, from his perspective, saw a darker intent behind Ben-Gurion's platitudes. Largely because of the Lavon affair, Ben-Gurion was unable to form a coalition that was acceptable to Mapai. In addition, Ahdut Haavoda (Unity of Labor) and Mapam (Mifleget Poalim Meuchedet—the United Workers' Party) refused to join. Ben-Gurion thereupon resigned for the second time on January 31, 1961.

Between the time of Ben-Gurion's resignation and the national elections in November 1961, both Eshkol and Ben-Gurion sought to reclaim party unity. There was a pragmatic decision to put the Lavon affair aside in order to gain an electoral victory, which was, indeed, to occur. There was now a new four-party government bringing in three center labor parties but dominated by Mapai and under the direction of Ben-Gurion as prime minister with Eshkol remaining as minister of finance; it was approved by the Knesset on November 2, 1961. Ben-Gurion's unswerving fervor for determining the culpability of the Lavon incident would not abate, and he undertook a number of steps in late 1964 to bring details of the episode out in public. The controversy created sufficient dissent within Mapai for Ben-Gurion again to announce what was to be his final resignation on June 16, 1963, thus bringing down the government that had lasted only two and a half years. With the full backing of Ben-Gurion, who was now out of government service, Israel's President Zalman Shazar formally designated Eshkol as prime minister on June 19, 1963, after the secretariat of the major party, Mapai, had voted for the move. Within a week the formalities had been concluded, and Eshkol traded the portfolio of minister of finance for the prime ministership, assuming along with it the title and function of the minister of defense, a dual appointment that was a carryover from the Ben-Gurion era. Within a week Eshkol created a "Government of Continuity," but it also was of short duration as the prime minister resigned on December 14, 1964, once again as a consequence of a dispute with Ben-Gurion over the conduct of the investigation in the Lavon matter. In any case, Eshkol was asked by the president to return to create a new government, which he did several days later.

Among the political turmoil that was already considered traditional fare in Israel, Eshkol sought to balance domestic demands while dealing with international developments. One of his first objectives domestically was to develop the Negev. Large numbers of Oriental and Sephardic Jews were emigrating to Israel and would not be readily absorbable in either the urban centers or the other developed regions of central or northern Israel. Israel's foreign policy was to be dominated by the continued pursuit of friendly relations with Western Europe and the United States, to include a cautious approach at rapprochement with West Germany that went as far as establishing formal diplomatic relations. The attempt to establish normal relations with West Germany revived unhappy memories in Israel and complex negotiations in West Germany, whose government was somewhat fearful of the reaction in the Arab world. Israel's relations with Asia and Africa also were expanded. Also during this time Eshkol announced to the Knesset (on May 17, 1965) a major new Arab-Israeli peace proposal. The plan, however, was rejected by the leaders of the Arab world and reflected in their national presses.

Ben-Gurion assumed that Eshkol would serve merely as a caretaker premier. When that assumption proved false, in July 1965 Ben-Gurion created his own splinter political party, Rafi (Reshimet Poalei Israel—Israel Workers List) along with Moshe Dayan* and Shimon Peres.* In this way Ben-Gurion thought his handpicked successor, Dayan, would assume office on his coattails. Ben-Gurion then turned also on his long-time friend and colleague Eshkol with vehemence, declaring that he was unfit to govern.

In the elections held in 1965, Ben-Gurion ran for election at the head of his new party, which was explicitly anti-Eshkol. Mapai took 43 seats in the Knesset (out of a total of 120) while Rafi won only 10. The sweetness of Eshkol's electoral victory, however, was balanced by the harsh reality that came with an economic slowdown in the country. The hesitancy to take corrective—but un-popular—measures was followed by the realization that some kind of action had to be taken; when something finally was done it was an overreaction. Immigra-tion, always a serious concern to Israel's domestic strength, reached its lowest level since 1948. In addition, unemployment was reaching 10 percent of the labor pool. Then came the crisis situation that preceded the outbreak of war in the summer of 1967. All in all, disorder characterized the Israeli political and economic scene. Rafi's electoral loss, the seemingly mismanaged economy, and unbalanced social scene fed the more aggressive Israeli political elements. Per-haps as a means to diffuse discontent, the attacks on Eshkol by the opposition increased. Contemporaneously, the Palestinians and the Syrians resumed violent incursions and other similar acts from both Jordan and Syria. Eshkol was hence forced to accede to the demand for harsh retaliatory measures by the military.

On the domestic scene, the institutional structure of Israel's agriculture was sufficiently sound to permit pressure for increased output. Eshkol had developed a well-tuned administrative team in both the Cabinet and the Prime Minister's Office. It was during this period that Eshkol married for the third time, on March 3, 1964, to Miriam Zelikovitz.

All else was put aside when on May 27, 1967, Egyptian President Gamal Abdul Nasser* moved a large number of his troops and material into the eastern Sinai desert, accompanied by aggressive rhetoric and the demand for the removal of the United Nations peace-keeping forces from the Sinai. Nasser also announced the closing of the Straits of Tiran to Israeli-bound shipping. The closure of the Straits of Tiran, which governs the sea lanes into the Gulf of Aqaba and the approach to the Israeli port of Eilat, was a *causus belli*.

The reaction in Israel was one of concern. Although Eshkol would later be condemned for what appeared to be inaction in the face of provocation, it was he who saw insufficient military preparation to the Egyptian threat; on May 11 he ordered his chief of staff to mobilize the army reserves. The situation in Sinai came before the Cabinet on May 27, the solution to which resulted in a split decision, nine to nine. Eshkol held the crucial tie-breaking vote; his critics argued that in this "period of waiting" he failed to display leadership by calling for a vote and forcing the issue to a policy decision. However, from Eshkol's point of view, in lieu of Western support to keep the international shipping lanes open, Israel would have to take unilateral corrective action, and he was uncertain of the country's capacity to do so. Eshkol's rationale essentially was that Israel's reliance on the United States was, of course, not only a necessary security blanket but also a means to influence the Europeans to provide Israel with more weapons. In addition, it was the time factor that was crucial, particularly for planning purposes. Nevertheless, delay without action was viewed by much of the public as well as segments of the military as inaction. The perceived lack of action by the Cabinet was followed by other pressures to include a late-night visit to Eshkol's residence by the Soviet ambassador who demanded to know Israel's intent towards Egypt, implying the potential for Soviet intervention. Eskhol also received a note from American President Lyndon Johnson cautioning Israel against overreaction and urging restraint. Another Cabinet meeting was held the following day, at which time it was voted to exhaust all political possibilities and to postpone any military initiative.

A broadcast to the nation was made on May 28. Eshkol had rushed to the radio station directly from the Cabinet meeting, was given an almost illegible, hand-written statement to read, and was immediately put on the air live. Not known for his speech-making delivery under the best of circumstances, his performance was poor and he gave the impression of weariness and weakness, not characteristics the people of Israel looked for at this particular time. In a statement to the Knesset on May 29, Eshkol described the situation as "grave."

Out of this apparent lack of clear direction, the need to broaden the ruling government's coalition became even more apparent. The opposition began a demand for a Government of National Unity and agreed to continue to accept Eshkol's leadership only if defense affairs were handled by someone else. Public opinion in Israel as well as within the ranks of Eshkol's own party looked to Moshe Dayan. Eshkol agreed to bring Dayan back into the government as minister without portfolio, maintaining his control over the Defense Ministry. The only stalwart supporter of Eshkol at this time was Golda Meir,* who would ultimately be his successor. Opposed by the political forces of Mafdal (Miflagah Datit Leumit—the National Religious Party), the Herut-Liberal Bloc, and the majority of Mapai, plus the personalities of Shimon Peres and Yigael Yadin, Eshkol was forced to give up the Defense portfolio to Dayan on June 1. The national sense of emptiness was filled by Dayan when several days later in an interview with the Western press he announced that Israeli security was strictly a domestic matter and it was not expected that either American or British boys would be asked to die for the sake of Israel.

War broke out on June 5 and resulted in an Israeli military victory. The war also brought additional territory to include East Jerusalem, but did not bring peace. The contentiousness of Israeli politics played havoc with any attempt to deal with policy matters such as the Occupied Territories. Dayan, because he was taken into the government prior to the war in 1967 as minister of defense, assumed the role of providing a military government in the Occupied Territories, requiring the daily establishment of rules and regulations as well as their inter-pretation. This daily practice often ran counter to the more broadly based policy-making organs of government headed by Prime Minister Eshkol. While Eshkol was the head of the ruling Labor Party, Dayan had considerable influence as a popular hero of the war and as someone influential among the military.

The territory gained as a result of Israel's military successes was now the subject of the politicians' negotiations and their varied motivations, whether ideological, patriotic, or some other combination. There was also external pres-sure. An Arab summit conference in Khartoum, Sudan, on September 8, 1967, concluded that no lasting peace agreement could be reached with Israel. Eshkol was forced then to take the position that the cease-fire lines would remain in place for the forseeable future. Eshkol was not deterred from seeking a formal peace agreement, and worked strenuously to get the support and attention of regional actors and beyond. In October 1967 he contacted Soviet Premier Anatoly Kosygin. The following month, a proposal was proffered to Jordan's King Hus-sein ibn Talal,* and the following month, a five-point peace proposal was made public. Similar efforts were frequent throughout 1968.

Peace and land were the two main policy considerations subsequent to the 1967 war. Both ideas were interdependent but had separate considerations. Both Britain and the United States urged Israel to assume the initiative in offering the olive branch to the Arab states as a means of breaking the deadlock. Eshkol embarked on a policy move using his Foreign Minister Abba Eban to put forth various proposals in the United Nations for a mediated settlement. Without a formal settlement with its Arab neighbors Israel's cordial ties to the United States and, to a lesser extent, to Europe required strengthening. The overriding concern was national security, even more so than controlling an unstable economy.

Still another issue, and one that had been close to Eshkol for years, was immigration. In June 1968, Eshkol took advantage of a coalition government of his own making and created a new government ministry for immigration and absorption, a function previously handled by the Jewish Agency of the World Zionist Congress. Yigal Allon was chosen to head this new office, and it was seen by many as an attempt by Eshkol to guide the Israeli political process to accept his personal choice for a successor. Without consulting his cabinet, Eshkol named Allon as his deputy premier.

Eshkol had been a Zionist-Socialist since his youth, with labor unity an abiding concern. As a member of the major political party, Mapai, he saw the party's fortune ebb and flow as groups split off or alternative organizations were created. In summer 1963, Eshkol began talks with Yitzhak Tabenkin of Achdut Haavoda to help create labor unity; they came to fruition in 1965 with the electoral coalition of Mapai and Achdut Haavoda to create the Alignment (Maarach). By January 1968, the prime minister was able to announce the creation of an Israeli Labor Party (Mifleget Haavoda), consisting of Mapai, Achdut Haavoda, and Rafi, which held the country together and confronted both defense and economic problems. It was also an important preparatory move prior to the November 1969 elections, in which the new Maarach or alignment emerged with Mapam now a partner. The outcome of this series of developments, however, was never to be known to Eshkol.

On February 6, 1969, Levi Eshkol died of a heart attack after a period of brief illness. Allon was chosen by the Cabinet to be the caretaker prime minister until a new government could be formed; at the recommendation of the Central Committee of Mapai, Golda Meir was chosen as his successor.

BIBLIOGRAPHY

Works by Eskhol:

B'ma'aleh Ha-derech (On the Way). Tel Aviv: Ayanot Publishers, 1958.
B'havlei Hisnalut (In the Pangs of Settlement). Tel Aviv: Am Oved, 1966.
The State Papers of Levi Eshkol. Ed. Henry M. Christman. New York: Funk & Wagnalls, 1969.

Other Works:

Bar-Zohar, Michael. *Embassies in Crisis: Diplomats and Demagogues Behind the Six-Day War.* Englewood Cliffs, N.J.: Prentice-Hall, 1970.
Brecher, Michael. *The Foreign Policy System of Israeli: Setting, Images, Process.* New Haven, Conn.: Yale University Press, 1972.
Medding, Peter. *Mapai in Israel.* Cambridge: Cambridge University Press, 1972.
Peres, Shimon. *From These Men: Seven Founders of the State of Israel.* New York: Wyndham Books, 1980.
Prittie, Terence. *Eshkol: The Man and the Nation.* New York: Pitman, 1969.

SANFORD R. SILVERBURG

F

FAHD BIN ABD AL-AZIZ AL SAUD (1921–   ) is both the head of state and prime minister of Saudi Arabia. However, he is not an absolute monarch due to the constraints imposed on him by the royal family. It is the king's responsibility to ensure and maintain a consensus among the factions of the family. King Fahd is also the highest legal official, serving as the "commander of the faithful," and has given himself the title of the Guardian of the Holy Mosques.

King Fahd bin Abd Al-Aziz Al Saud (literally Fahd, son of Abd al-Aziz, of the House of Saud), is the seventeenth ruler in the line from Muhammad bin Saud, and fifth king of Saudi Arabia. He was born in Riyadh in 1921, the eleventh son (eighth to survive to adulthood) of King Abd al-Aziz ibn Saud,* known in the West as Ibn Saud. King Fahd is tall—over six feet in height—and of heavy build. Of a family known to shun the spotlight, he is a very private person, but one who truly likes people and likes to be liked. He is also a doting father and devoted family man.

The Al Saud is divided into a number of collateral branches, each stemming from a descendant of Muhammad bin Saud. The ruling branch, descendants of Abd al-Rahman, Fahd's grandfather, are called the Al Abd al-Rahman. The princes of this branch are titled His Royal Highness (HRH). Members of the other branches are titled His Highness (HRH).

Fahd's father, King Abd al-Aziz, had many wives, though in accordance with Islamic law he never had more than four at one time. He married many of them for political reasons. Fahd's mother, Hassa bint al-Sudayri ("bint" means daughter), is from the powerful and princely Sudayri family of Najd (central Arabia), which is closely allied politically and by marriage with the Al Saud. She had seven sons, of whom Fahd is the eldest. An imposing woman in her own right, she reportedly demanded and received daily visits from her sons whenever they were in residence in Riyadh.

The seven blood brothers maintain a very close relationship, political as well as familial, and often act as a single group in royal family convocations as well as in national politics. In addition to Fahd, the brothers are Sultan, the minister of defense and aviation; Naif, the minister of the interior; Ahmad, the vice minister of the interior; Salman, the governor of Riyadh; Turki the former vice minister of defense; and Abd al-Rahman. In the West, they are sometimes called the "Sudayri Seven." At home they are called "Al Fahd," or House of Fahd, after Fahd, the oldest.

Fahd was educated by private tutors (as was the custom for all Abd al-Aziz's sons) in the Quran, Islam, the basics of mathematics, and geography, as well as the traditions and lore of the desert society that was his heritage. In later years, he privately undertook the study of English as well as subjects required for the public administration of the kingdom.

As a young man, Fahd quickly demonstrated a flair for the subtleties of family and national and international politics, as well as for public administration; he developed a reputation for hard work as well as hard play. In 1945, at the age of twenty-four, he accompanied his older brother and Foreign Minister Prince (later King) Faisal bin Abd al-Aziz Al Saud* to San Francisco for the convening of the United Nations. The visit not only broadened his horizons beyond the bounds of Saudi Arabia, but also made a lasting impression of the UN's value as an important body for shaping international consensus in the cause of world peace. Indeed, consultation (*shura*) and consensus (*ijma*) are age-old institutions in the Arab world; they are hallmarks of the Saudi political process and basic elements of Fahd's political decision making both domestic and foreign.

Shortly before Abd al-Aziz's death in November 1953, a new cabinet was formed with then Prince Fahd as the first minister of education. Prior to that time, public education was administered as an office of the Finance Ministry. Education in general in Saudi Arabia was rudimentary, and the curriculum was largely traditional and religious. In later years, the king recalled that when he first became education minister there was only one secondary school and a total of only thirty-five thousand students in the country. Today there are over twice that many students pursuing university degrees alone. To a very real degree, the "education explosion" Saudi Arabia experienced in the 1970s and 1980s was made possible by the groundwork for a national education system laid by Fahd in the 1950s.

The period from the mid–1950s to 1962 was one of political uncertainty in Saudi Arabia. By 1958, overspending and poor administration had reduced the kingdom to near bankruptcy. In March of that year, King Saud's brother, Prince Faisal, had been granted administrative powers to restore order to the kingdom's finances, public administration, and foreign policy. On December 21, 1960, Saud again reasserted his authority, creating a new cabinet, and Faisal retired to private life. Fahd, who was one of the strongest supporters of Faisal's modernization and development programs, did likewise.

In 1962, King Saud's poor health and the Egyptian-supported revolution in neighboring Yemen contributed to another crisis atmosphere. On October 17, Saud resigned as prime minister in favor of Faisal. Two weeks later, Faisal created a new cabinet; Fahd was appointed minister of the interior, a position he was to hold until Faisal's death in March 1975.

On November 2, 1964, Saud was obliged to abdicate in favor of Faisal (Saud died in February 1969); and in March 1965, Faisal named his brother Khalid as heir apparent and deputy prime minister. (The term crown prince is in a literal sense inappropriate in Saudi Arabia since the Al Saud, adherents of the strict Hanbali School of Islamic Law and the puritanical Wahhabi revival movement, eschew crowns or hats of any kind.) On October 17, 1967, Fahd was designated second deputy prime minister and second in line to the kingship.

The death of King Faisal at the hand of a deranged nephew on March 25, 1975, made Prince Fahd not only the heir apparent but the de facto chief administrative officer of the kingdom as well. As deputy prime minister, he relinquished the Interior portfolio.

Fahd's relationship with King Khalid has been widely misunderstood in the West. Khalid was a quiet, shy person with serious health problems who disliked the administrative details of running the kingdom and left this task primarily to Fahd. He was not, however, merely a figurehead; he was the final arbiter on all the kingdom's major policy decisions. The two worked well as a team during the tumultuous years of the 1970s, when increased oil wealth and expanded development plans went hand in hand.

When Khalid died on June 13, 1982, Fahd was named king. His half-brother, Prince Abdallah, head of the National Guard, was named heir apparent and deputy prime minister, and his full brother Sultan, minister of defense and aviation, was named second deputy prime minister and next in line of succession.

There is no hard-and-fast rule of succession in Saudi Arabia nor in Islamic political theory, which forms the basis of the Saudi constitutional system. Nevertheless, there is a preference in Saudi Arabia for succession to pass from brother to brother in order of seniority, provided the designee is morally and mentally capable in accordance with Islamic law and receives the consensus of the leadership. The leadership, in Saudi Arabia, is of course dominated by the royal family, but formally includes the religious leadership and other notables as well. On succession, this group, called Ahl al Aqd wall Hall (the People Who Bind and Loose), gives its formal approval, following which a *fatwa* (an Islamic legal opinion) is issued, giving the succession Islamic legal sanction. King Fahd is therefore not an absolute monarch in the Western sense but is bound by Islamic law and the consensus of the royal family and other notables. His style of rule is to lead by forming and proceeding from consensus.

In terms of domestic policy, the king follows in the tradition of Faisal, seeking to modernize the country physically while maintaining the traditionalist Islamic character of its society. From his days as education minister, Fahd has always been a great promoter of economic and social development. Both as heir apparent and as king he has fully supported the Saudi Economic Development Plans, which have transformed the kingdom from a medieval principality to a country possessing some of the most modern infrastructure in the world.

At the same time, neither Fahd nor his royal brothers and cousins have ever believed in pushing Saudi Arabia's very traditional, conservative society into the modern age faster than it was capable of going without creating social or political dislocations. Fahd is keenly desirous of preventing secularization from accompanying modernization. Saudi Arabia's political, social, and even economic institutions are based in Islam, and the political leadership is determined to keep it that way. The secularizing influences of modernization are of course inevitable, and for Fahd, the real question has not been how to prevent them totally but rather how to keep the basically Islamic society of the kingdom intact and prevent the type of cataclysms that swept the shah of Iran from the throne from occurring in Saudi Arabia.

The king also follows the traditional Saudi foreign policy orientation, the first priority of which is safeguarding the Islamic world and Islamic way of life. Saudis feel a special responsibility to protect the Islamic way of life as keepers of Islam's two holiest sites, Mecca and Medina.

Indeed, more Saudi human resources and more Saudi financial resources outside defense go into the administration of the annual *Hajj* (pilgrimage to Mecca) than into any other activity, domestic or foreign. Literally hundreds of millions of dollars have been spent expanding and beautifying the Haram Mosque in Mecca, the Prophet's Mosque in Medina, and other holy sites; in creating the infrastructure to handle the food, sanitation, transportation, and instruction of the nearly two million *Hajjis* (pilgrims) who visit each year; and in ensuring that this massive event is conducted with as much efficiency and reverence as is humanly possible. Each year, Fahd and other senior members of the government move to Mecca for the Hajj, personally greeting the foreign dignitaries from Islamic countries that are making the Pilgrimage.

In the Saudi view, there are three main threats to the Islamic world: communism, Zionism, and revolutionary Islamic fanaticism. In fighting communism, which is equated with atheism and thus antithetical to Islam, Fahd has long been a staunch supporter of close ties with the United States. The United States is not only the political and military bulwark of the Free World against communism, it is also basically a Christian, monotheistic society in harmony with Islam. (Islam recognizes Christianity, Judaism, and Zoroastrianism as the other revealed religions.) In the 1970s, Fahd spearheaded an effort to create a "special relationship" with the United States, not only in the spheres of politics and security but in economic cooperation as well. During a visit to Washington, D.C., in June 1974, he and U.S. Secretary of State Henry Kissinger announced the creation of a U.S.-Saudi Joint Commission on Economic Cooperation to be jointly headed by the U.S. secretary of the treasury and the Saudi minister of finance. Despite the vagaries of the international oil market with its current glut, and U.S. rebuffs of Saudi arms requests in the mid–1980s, which caused the Saudis to look elsewhere for much of its arms and defense contracting, that commission is still in existence.

The main problem for Fahd in maintaining close relations with the United States, from his perspective, is its unswerving support of Israel. Because Islam recognizes Judaism, Saudi policy professes not to be anti-Jewish but rather anti-Zionist, and Zionism is seen as a secular political doctrine that has been forced on the Arab world, and particularly on the Palestinians, against their will. The Saudis also have a deep religious attachment to the Aqsa Mosque in Jerusalem, the third holiest site in Islam after Mecca and Medina.

Fahd's approach to the Arab-Israeli problem has basically been to pursue self-determination for the Palestinians as a way to assuage the injustice to them caused by the creation of Israel. That done, he believes that all the states in the region, including Israel, can live in peace.

Fahd has long hoped that the United States, in the cause of Middle East peace, will bring this about by pressuring Israel into recognizing a self-governing Palestine. He did not believe that the Camp David Accords would accomplish this, however, and on August 7, 1981, he announced the Fahd Plan. Noteworthy in the plan was Point 7, "Affirmation of the right of all states in the region to live in Peace." Although Israel was not specifically mentioned, its right to exist in peace side by side with a Palestinian state was implicitly recognized.

The Fahd Plan failed to win an Arab consensus in 1981, but in September 1982, the Fez Plan, which was drawn basically from the Fahd Plan, was adopted by the Arab League Summit. Thus, the official Arab position on Middle East peace is a moderate position crafted by Fahd.

Although Saudis espouse the fundamentalist Hanbali School of Islamic Jurisprudence, the most conservative of all the Sunni Islamic schools, they are particularly concerned by the rise of the politically revolutionary brand of Islam practiced by the Iranian republic and various militant fundamentalist groups in the Arab and Islamic world. These groups are seen not as devout Muslims but as political fanatics threatening to use violence against all those who do not agree with their heretical interpretation of Islam. In this context, the Mecca Mosque incident of 1980 in which Iranian sympathizers took over the mosque was particularly sobering, and Fahd as well as other Saudis were outraged at the Iranian-orchestrated political uprising at the Hajj in 1987.

So great has been this threat to regional stability that Fahd realigned his Gulf policy to support Iraq against Iran in the Iran-Iraq war, and in the spring of 1988 broke off relations with Iran. In a very real sense, Saudi Arabia under Fahd seeks to protect the Islamic world from threats on both the left and the right.

BIBLIOGRAPHY

Bligh, Alexander. *From Prince to King: Royal Succession in the House of Saud.* New York: New York University Press, 1984.
Long, David E. *The United States and Saudi Arabia: Ambivalent Allies.* Boulder, Colo. : Westview, 1985.
Niblock, Tim (ed.). *State, Society and Economy in Saudi Arabia.* London: Croom Helm, for the Exeter Centre for Arab Gulf Studies, 1982.

Nyrop, Richard F. (ed.) *Saudi Arabia: A Country Study*. 4th ed. Washington, D.C.: U.S. Government Printing Office, 1984. American University Foreign Area Studies series.

Safran, Nadav. *Saudi Arabia: The Ceaseless Quest for Security*. Cambridge, Mass.: Belknap, 1985.

Shaw, John A., and David E. Long. *Saudi Arabian Modernization: The Impact of Change on Stability*. The Washington Papers, no. 89. New York: Praeger, for the Georgetown University Center for Strategic and International Studies, 1982.

DAVID E. LONG

FAISAL BIN ABD AL-AZIZ AL SAUD (1906–1975). The role of King Faisal is often overlooked in studies of Saudi Arabia, despite its great importance for the country and the region. Most scholars emphasize either the pre-Faisal era (characterized by the unification of Saudi Arabia), or the post-Faisal era (characterized by growing Saudi importance in oil and financial matters), thus ignoring the crucial link that Faisal's rule provided. Faisal's leadership was instrumental not only in insuring the regime's survival in the midst of serious threats, but also in transforming Saudi Arabia into one of the most stable and influential countries in the region.

Faisal was born on April 9, 1906, at a time when his father, Abd al-Aziz ibn Saud,* was steadily expanding his control in Central Arabia. When Faisal's mother, Tarfah, died in 1912, he was raised by his maternal grandfather, Sheikh Abdullah bin Abd al-Latif al-Al Sheikh. Sheikh Abdullah was a leading *alim* (religious scholar) who had tutored King Abd al-Aziz previously, and a grandson of Muhammad ibn Abd al-Wahhab, the founder of the Islamic unitarian movement, which gave religious legitimacy to Saudi rule. Faisal's childhood was thus spent in obtaining a religious education that left its imprint on Faisal's perceptions and beliefs.

To this religious background was added an early experience in assuming political tasks. Faisal commanded the Saudi forces in Asir in 1920 and led the Saudi assault on the western region of Yemen in 1933. A more important experience was gained in numerous visits to foreign countries, which accustomed Faisal at an early age to both modern and different ways of life. At age thirteen, Faisal led a Saudi delegation to Britain and France, among other European countries. Faisal was thus the first Saudi prince to travel in and become familiar with the West, and he visited Western Europe again in 1926 and 1932. He also was the first Saudi official to visit the Soviet Union, where he was sent by his father in May 1932.

Faisal's responsibilities expanded greatly as a result of his father's conquest of Hejaz in 1926. King Abd al-Aziz maintained the relatively complex and urban-based administrative system of Hejaz to administer the pilgrimage and its important revenues at the time. Accordingly, Faisal was appointed the viceroy of Hejaz and president of its consultative council in 1926. Additional responsibilities were given to Faisal when King Abd al-Aziz began to integrate the two regions of Nejd and Hejaz into a unified polity. Since the Hejazi administration was the principal vehicle in this effort, Faisal was appointed president of the newly established Council of Deputies in 1932. The Council of Deputies supervised all government agencies and was the antecedent of the Council of Ministers. Faisal had to exercise considerable authority at the time as King Abd al-Aziz continued to spend most of his time in Nejd while the Council of Deputies and other government agencies were located in Hejaz.

Faisal's responsibilities during his father's lifetime included the areas of foreign policy as well. He became the first Saudi minister of foreign affairs in 1930. Faisal's great interest in foreign-policy issues led him to maintain that post until his death in 1975, except for a two-year period during King Saud's rule. It was in his official capacity as minister of foreign affairs that Faisal visited the United States and met President Franklin Roosevelt in 1943. Faisal also led the Saudi delegation to the San Francisco conference of April 1945 which established the UN and signed the United Nations Charter on June 26, 1945, making Saudi Arabia a founding member of the United Nations. During the UN discussions over Palestine in 1947 and 1948, Faisal joined other Arab officials in opposing the partition resolution and criticizing the use of American influence in passing it.

To meet the growing complexity of administering the state as a result of the commercial production of oil, King Abd al-Aziz increased the number of ministries and established the Council of Ministers in 1953. These new structures were not yet operational when King Abd al-Aziz died on November 9, 1953. Saud bin Abdul Aziz, the eldest living son of the late king, assumed the throne, while Faisal became crown prince. The Council of Ministers was convened for the first time in March 1954. Faisal was soon appointed president of the Council of Ministers on August 15, 1954. The period of cooperation between Saud and Faisal was short-lived, however, as it soon became apparent that the succession arrangements were problematic.

Several factors had made the rivalry between Saud and Faisal seem almost inevitable at the time. Succession to the throne was not yet sufficiently institutionalized, especially because King Abd al-Aziz was the founder of Saudi Arabia. There was also considerable confusion about the actual separation of powers between the king on the one hand and the crown prince and president of the Council of Ministers on the other. In addition, there was substantial difference in the background and experience of the two brothers. Saud's background was mainly in tribal and military affairs; his travels began at an older age and were fewer than those of Faisal. Saud's previous authority as viceroy of Nejd had been limited by the direct involvement of King Abd al-Aziz in the administration of Nejd, while Faisal had enjoyed greater autonomy in his position as viceroy of Hejaz. It was only natural that Saud and Faisal would develop different styles of rule and different views of the world.

The problem of succession was further exacerbated by the presence of foreign threats to the Saudi rule at the time. The late 1950s and early 1960s were years of upheaval in the region as the Suez War, the Egyptian-Syrian union, the overthrow of the Iraqi monarchy, and the civil war in Yemen indicate. Thus, the Saudi royal family wisely considered any incompetence by the king, or lack of suitable health for that matter, as intolerable at this critical juncture of the region's history.

The result was a process of gradual takeover of power by Faisal that lasted almost six years, which indicates Faisal's preference for gradualism even in the most crucial of issues. The process began in 1957 when Faisal distanced himself from King Saud's policies by leaving the country for a long period of time. Saud's growing problems convinced him of the wisdom of reappointing Faisal to the presidency of the Council of Ministers in March 1958. King Saud's unwillingness to relinquish his authority led him to form a new cabinet under his presidency in 1960, which lasted less than two years. In 1962, Faisal was not only reappointed to the presidency of the Council of Ministers but also assumed all effective powers as the viceroy. This arrangement was formalized in November 1963 by a decision of a council of senior princes supported by a *fatwa* (religious ruling) from *ulama* (religious scholars). Finally, a similar decision called on King Saud to abdicate the throne in favor of Faisal, who became the third king of Saudi Arabia as of November 2, 1964.

Faisal's assumption of power in the kingdom owed a great deal to his ability to win the support of both the royal family and the religious elites. The Saudi royal family appreciated Faisal's leadership qualities as well as his efforts to maintain a balance of power within the family. Of great importance in this regard were Faisal's appointments in 1962 of some of the most able of his brothers to important posts. These included the appointment of Khalid bin Abd al-Aziz as deputy president of the Council of Ministers, of Fahd bin Abd al-Aziz Al Saud* as minister of the interior, of Abdullah bin Abd al-Aziz as president of the National Guard, and of Sultan bin Abd al-Aziz as minister of defense. Faisal's well-known piety and his ability to defend the traditional system of his country in the face of the growing wave of secular Arab nationalism also won him the support of the Saudi religious elites.

The process of power consolidation in Faisal's hands ran parallel to the process of domestic reforms he initiated. Faisal's long experience in domestic administrative bodies contributed to his ability to lead and strengthen the Council of Ministers, transforming it into the supreme government institution in Saudi Arabia, and increasing both the powers of the state and his own powers at the same time. One might consider Faisal's assumption of power and his domestic reforms as two sides of the same coin, disproving the notion that only revolutionary regimes are capable of removing unqualified leaders and launching ambitious reforms. Faisal's approach to reform was based on evolutionary and steady changes while preserving as much as possible the traditional and religious pillars of society. While such an approach might be slower than other more revolutionary approaches, it usually insures the irreversibility of reforms.

When Faisal was reappointed to the presidency of the Council of Ministers on March 24, 1958, he found the country on the verge of financial bankruptcy.

Despite an increase in the state's oil revenues, the absence of regular budgeting and extravagant spending had resulted in the incurrence of substantial debts and a marked depreciation in the Saudi currency. In response, Faisal established orderly budgeting and auditing arrangements, reduced the spending of government and the allowances of the King and Royal Family members to a minimum, and gained Saudi membership in the International Monetary Fund and the International Bank of Reconstruction and Development. Within eighteen months the country's financial system was sound again, with foreign currency reserves increasing substantially, the Saudi currency regaining its value, and a surplus replacing the deficit.

A much wider reform effort was launched when Faisal announced a ten-point program in 1962, following his assumption of effective control over the kingdom. The program covered a wide range of issues including the abolishment of slavery, modernization of the administration, the reorganization of religious and judicial institutions, the introduction of labor and social-security legislation, the utilization of natural resources, the building of infrastructure, and the establishment of the consultative council and local government system. With the exception of the local government system, all these reforms were implemented systematically throughout the 1960s. Thus, while considerable progress was made in the fields of administrative and social reforms, no dramatic changes were made in the basic political structure of the kingdom.

In implementing these reforms gradually, Faisal was able to overcome considerable societal and religious opposition. When the introduction of a nationwide program of female education was met by the objection of religious groups in 1963, Faisal insisted on the quick implementation of the program. However, he made female attendance of schools voluntary rather than compulsory, appointed a well-known alim to head the female education agency, and insured the sexual segregation of schools. The result was that over a quarter of a million women were enrolled in Saudi schools by 1975. Faisal reacted to a similar opposition to the introduction of a national television station in 1965 by two measures. On the one hand, he ordered the security forces to confront those fanatics who attempted to storm the station. On the other hand, he devoted several hours of daily broadcasting to religious programs, convincing the prominent religious elites of the usefulness of the new medium.

Faisal managed to strengthen the powers of the state and the royal family in the reform process. When the Grand *Mufti*, the highest religious and judicial authority in the country, died in 1970, Faisal abolished the post, replacing it with two separate and less autonomous institutions. The Ministry of Justice was established to integrate the Saudi judiciary into the government, while the Council of Senior Ulema, comprising seventeen members appointed by the king, was established to serve the king in his need of religious opinions or approvals. In the field of public administration, Faisal established the Public Administration Institute to offer training programs to civil servants and systematic review of administrative reforms. This contributed to the replacement of traditionally minded civil servants with modern, educated ones. The control of the government over the schools, the media, the judiciary, the religious institutions, and the bureaucracy was utilized to foster a sense of loyalty to and identification with the regime among the citizens of the different regions of the country.

The resulting consolidation of government power was put to use by Faisal's introduction of one of the most innovative developments in the kingdom: the five-year development plans. Faisal established the Central Organization of Planning in 1968 with the aim of preparing a coherent plan that would include all government reforms, projects, and expenditures for a five-year period. The first plan was drawn up in 1970 with three major goals: retaining the fundamental values of the society, preparing the economy for economic diversification in the postoil era, and increasing the defensive capabilities of the country. The Central Organization of Planning gained more powers when its president was appointed minister of state and a member of the Council of Ministers in 1971.

Despite the ambitious expenditure envisioned in the plan, the vast increase in the state's oil revenues in 1973 necessitated revising the plan and expanding its scope. Such revision in turn resulted in high inflation rates and the presence of bottlenecks in critical areas of the economy. While it took some time before these shortcomings were overcome, the fact remains that the development plan had made possible the rational utilization of the growing state revenues in building an impressive infrastructure with far-reaching effects.

One of these effects was a further confidence by the regime and an unprecedented level of political stability. The vast expansion in transportation facilities and communication networks, for instance, contributed considerably to the process of national integration and enabled government authority to reach the most remote of areas of the vast kingdom. Another example is the significant increase in the size of public administration that accompanied the developmental drive. By offering excellent employment opportunities, the regime successfully sought the cooptation of the growing number of well-educated Saudis.

When the first five-year development plan was completed in 1975, a second plan was drawn up with wider scope and greater expenditures. King Faisal died before its actual implementation, but he left his successors a solid base of reform efforts and an impressive experience in development planning.

Faisal's contributions in the area of foreign policy were even more impressive than his domestic reforms. The two areas were strongly related, since Faisal's reforms at home contributed to his ability to preempt the external challenges to Saudi rule. Faisal gave the foreign policy of Saudi Arabia three major characteristics it had lacked but desperately needed before: an ideological base, the maintenance of a crucial balance, and a high degree of consistency. Faisal's foreign policy was based on his interpretation of Islamic ideology, which conveniently named Zionism and communism as the main enemies of Islam. In fact, Faisal was convinced that Israel and the Soviet Union were natural allies working together, and regarded Israel as the primary source behind the growing influence of the Soviet Union in the Arab World. The West, however, was considered a natural ally in the joint Islamic-Christian struggle against communist atheism. In this context, American support to Israel was seen as a Zionist design to weaken Arab-American relations and to undermine the Islamic-Christian alliance.

Such an abstract ideology in turn justified the maintenance of a difficult balance between Saudi Arabia's identification with common Arab causes, especially the Palestinian cause, on the one hand, and Saudi relations with and reliance on Western countries, especially the United States, on the other. Accordingly, Faisal never allowed Saudi ties with the United States to go as far as permanently jeopardizing Saudi ties within the Arab World or vice versa. He was thus able to maintain a remarkable degree of consistency in the orientation of the Saudi foreign policy throughout the 1960s and early 1970s, despite the successive changes in regional and global settings during these years. Faisal was not a man of dramatic initiatives or sudden fluctuations in diplomacy, unlike many Arab leaders of that period.

The Saudi foreign policy in the 1950s reflected the domestic uncertainties surrounding the succession arrangements at the time and King Saud's lack of experience in foreign-policy matters. The Saudi foreign policy in the mid–1950s ran parallel to that of revolutionary Egypt, as the two countries joined efforts in opposing the policies of the Hashemite Kingdoms of Iraq and Jordan, especially their design to control Syria. When the dispute over the Buraimi Oasis weakened Saudi-British relations, King Saud found it also appropriate to join the Egyptian President Gamal Abdul Nasser* in advocating neutralism and opposing the Baghdad Pact. Recognizing the dangers of Nasser's revolutionary radicalism and growing popularity, however, King Saud revised his policies and went to extremes in the opposite direction, allying himself with the Hashemites, opposing the union between Syria and Egypt in 1958, and advocating the Eisenhower Doctrine in the Middle East. It was in this context that the Syrian security chief, Colonel Abdul Hamid Sarraj, made the allegation that King Saud had attempted to bribe him to undermine the Egyptian-Syrian union and to assassinate Nasser. This allegation, while never proven, was used by the influential Egyptian media to undermine Saudi prestige in the region, which reached its lowest level ever. This in turn convinced King Saud of the wisdom of leaving foreign-policy matters to Faisal.

In the early and mid–1960s, Saudi Arabia became actively involved in the Arab cold war. The Arab world was polarized into two opposing camps, with Faisal leading the conservative camp and Nasser leading the revolutionary camp. The rising wave of Arab nationalism and Nasserism had endangered the very existence of Arab monarchies at the time, especially in Jordan and Saudi Arabia. However, Arab nationalism as advocated by Nasser or the Arab Socialist Baath Party, the ruling party in Syria and later in Iraq, was problematic to Faisal not only because of political survival considerations, but also because of objective political-culture differences among different Arab countries. On the one hand, Saudi Arabia had not been subjected to direct colonial rule as had been the case in Egypt or Syria. Thus, while Faisal considered the territorial status quo in the

Arab world as a result of a natural historical development, Nasser and the Baath saw it as an artificial design initiated and maintained by colonial powers. On the other hand, Saudi Arabia did not have religious minorities or cosmopolitan cultures, unlike Egypt and Syria. The Saudi perception of Arab nationalism emphasized its Islamic component, while regarding secularism and socialism as ideologies alien to Arab Muslims.

The Arab cold war was markedly intensified by the civil war in Yemen between 1962 and 1967. The overthrow of the Yemeni monarchy and the assumption of power by Yemeni Nasserites were crucial issues to Faisal, who considered the Arabian Peninsula as a natural power base for Saudi Arabia. Nasser had sent thousands of his troops to support and insure the survival of the revolutionaries in Yemen. Faisal refrained from direct Saudi participation in the actual fighting inside Yemen, rightly recognizing the disparities between the Saudi and the Egyptian military capabilities, and the difficult geographical and tribal settings of Yemen, which made Nasser's tactics very frustrating and ultimately self-defeating. Faisal thus emphasized giving considerable assistance to Yemeni tribes supporting the monarchy, and strengthening Saudi ties with the United States. He also launched a diplomatic campaign, advocating Islamic solidarity as an alternative to Nasser's Arab nationalism, and visiting fellow Muslim conservative regimes such as Jordan, Morocco, Tunisia, Iran, Pakistan, and Turkey. Parallel to these efforts, Faisal left the door open for peaceful solutions to the problem, encouraging Arab mediators and meeting President Nasser several times. The intensity of the crisis was thus reduced, although its end had to await the Saudi-Egyptian rapprochement in 1967.

The humiliating Arab defeat in 1967 put an end to the crisis in Yemen and to the Arab cold war in general. Faisal's rapprochement with Nasser was based on two important effects of the outcome of the war. Since Israel occupied the holy city of Jerusalem, came close to Saudi Arabia's borders, and received unlimited American support, Faisal had to be concerned with Israel's future designs against the Arabs. In addition, Faisal saw in the defeat of Egypt a chance for attempting to influence Nasser's future policies, to weaken the Soviet presence in the region, and to moderate the views of Arab radicals. It was in this context that Saudi Arabia became the principal financial supporter of Egypt, and later of Syria and the Palestine Liberation Organization as well.

Saudi influence in the region increased accordingly. Faisal succeeded in convening the first Pan-Islamic Summit Conference in Rabat in 1969, which marked the first occasion of systematic Islamic support for the Arab struggle against Israel. Saudi Arabia also became an influential participant in Arab summit meetings, such as the Cairo Summit of 1970, which was convened to defuse the crisis in Jordan.

When domestic developments in the early 1970s brought more moderate elements to the leadership of both Egypt and Syria, King Faisal strengthened Saudi ties with the two countries. Faisal's major concern was that a just solution to the Arab-Israeli conflict was essential if the radicalization of the whole Arab

World was to be avoided. Accordingly, Faisal sought a more evenhanded American policy in the region, warning that American relations with Saudi Arabia would be undermined if total American support for Israel continued. In his declarations and statements in early 1973, Faisal linked the oil policy of Saudi Arabia to the conflict with Israel for the first time. The American administration, however, saw no need to change its Middle East policy, failing to take Faisal's remarks seriously.

It was in this context that Faisal led the use of the Arab oil as a political weapon following the outbreak of the 1973 war and the American supply of weapons to Israel. The Arab oil producers announced a monthly reduction in oil production and a total embargo of oil sales to the United States in support of the Arab goals in the war. However, when the United States began its peace efforts in the region, Faisal actively supported such an undertaking, for he considered the United States the only country capable of extracting the needed Israeli concessions.

Both the rise in Saudi Arabia's oil revenues and its active involvement in the Arab-Israeli conflict contributed to Saudi Arabia's assumption of a leading role in regional politics. Saudi Arabia became the principal mediator in inter-Arab conflicts, attempting to minimize the growing differences between Egypt and Syria. The mid–1970s saw Saudi Arabia enjoying considerable influence within the Arabian Peninsula as well. The common desire to prevent Iranian or Iraqi hegemony in the Persian Gulf drew the small Arab principalities of the Gulf closer to Saudi Arabia than ever before, while the need for financial assistance convinced the leaders of Republican North Yemen of the wisdom of good relations with Saudi Arabia. Faisal also played a leading role in strengthening Afro-Arab relations, offering substantial assistance to Black African countries, and visiting five of them in 1973.

Faisal's rule came to a sudden end when he was assassinated by a young nephew on March 25, 1975. As Saudi investigations did not prove any organized conspiracy, the assassin was tried and executed. The very smooth succession that followed testifies to Faisal's success in consolidating and institutionalizing the rule of Al-Saud. In fact, Faisal's successors felt secure enough to make the release of all political prisoners—some of whom were convicted military conspirators—their first decision. The new Saudi leaders saw no need to make any fundamental change in Faisal's domestic and foreign policies, preferring to build on the solid base he had established.

While Faisal's impressive achievements were certainly facilitated by unintended developments such as Nasser's defeat in 1967 and the rise in oil revenues in 1973, his leadership qualities were essential for providing the regime with the stability and confidence it needed. Central to Faisal's success was his unique ability to balance different trends and satisfy seemingly conflicting demands without losing sight of the basic direction of policy. This can be seen in both Faisal's domestic and foreign policies. In the former, he combined the preservation of traditional values with material improvements and social progress. In the latter he combined the ideological commitments of inter-Arab politics with the practical necessities of Saudi-Western relations.

BIBLIOGRAPHY

Beling, Willard A. (ed.). *King Faisal and the Modernization of Saudi Arabia*. Boulder, Colo.: Westview Press, 1980.
Bligh, Alexander. *From Prince to King, Royal Succession in the House of Saud in the Twentieth Century*. New York: New York University Press, 1984.
Al-Farsy, Fouad. *Saudi Arabia: A Case Study in Development*. London: KPI, 1986.
Huyette, Summer Scott. *Political Adaptation in Saudi Arabia, a Study of the Council of Ministers*. Boulder, Colo.: Westview Press, 1985.
Lacey, Robert. *The Kingdom, Arabia and the House of Saud*. New York: Avon Books, 1981.
Niblock, Tim (ed.). *State, Society and Economy in Saudi Arabia*. New York: St. Martin's Press, 1982.
Al-Yassini, Ayman. *Islam and Foreign Policy in Saudi Arabia*. Montreal: McGill University Center for Developing Area Studies Paper, 1983.

RAYED KRIMLY

FAROUK (1920–1965) was king of Egypt, sovereign of Nubia, the Sudan, Kordofan, and Darfur (ruled April 28, 1936–July 26, 1952). The son of King Ahmad Fuad I and Queen Nazli Sabri, he was born in Cairo on February 11, 1920. He was appointed chief scout of Egypt in 1933 and prince of the Said in 1934. Farouk succeeded to the Egyptian throne on the death of his father under a regency council until his eighteenth birthday, by the Muslim calendar. He took the constitutional oath in July 1937 and received the rank of field marshal of the Egyptian Army. He married Safinaz Dhu al-Fiqar (Faridah) in January 1938 but divorced her in 1948; he then married Narriman Sadiq in May 1951. Farouk abdicated his throne in July 1952 in favor of his son, Ahmad Fuad II (born January 1952), and spent the rest of his life in exile. He died in Rome on March 17, 1965.

Farouk's father Fuad I (ruled 1917–1936), had acceded to Egypt's throne late in life. He could only have done so with the support of the British, who needed an ally in Egypt on the death in 1917 of Husayn Kamil, whom they had installed to replace *Khedive* (viceroy) Abbas II (ruled 1874–1914) and whom they had suspected of intriguing against their interests. Fuad, too, feared that the former khedive might return to power or somehow obtain for his son, Prince Abd al-Munim, recognition as heir to the Egyptian throne. Fuad married late in life too, and the birth of Farouk gave him great joy. He carefully groomed the prince for the succession, and no luxury was denied to the boy. Because all the other children born to Fuad and Nazli were girls, playmates were brought in for Farouk, but he played more often with the palace servants. Fuad's royal duties left him little time or energy to devote to his son, and so Prince Farouk grew up in the company of people who deferred to his every whim. Although he became the leader of the Egyptian Boy Scouts at thirteen, he was given no chance to develop self-reliance or to face challenges. He was tutored privately. His mother resisted sending him away to school, but at fifteen he was sent by his father to England for further schooling. Rejected by Eton, Farouk applied to the Royal Military Academy at Woolwich, but failed its entrance tests and had to undergo a year's cramming while attending classes twice a week as a gentleman cadet.

Fuad's death on April 28, 1936, ended Farouk's formal education. In principle, his family, the British, and the leading politicians all agreed that the boy king should go back to school in England. In practice, everyone feared that he might be subjected to undesirable influences and decided that his presence in Egypt, with the three-man regency that would reign during his minority, would help steady the country. At this time, parliamentary government had just been restored after five years of virtual palace dictatorship, and the 1936 Anglo-Egyptian Treaty had just replaced the British protectorate over Egypt. As king, however, Farouk had no one to check his excesses—neither his mother, his tutors, Britain's ambassador, Sir Miles Lampson, nor Egypt's most popular politician, Mustafa al-Nahhas,* the leader of the strongly nationalistic Wafd Party. He snubbed his tutor, neglected his studies and gymnastic exercises, and took to racing his sports cars, consorting with his servants, and playing practical jokes. At the same time, however, he paraded his patriotism and piety, worshipped at a different mosque each Friday, and made a triumphal tour of upper Egypt. His popularity soon eclipsed that of Nahhas and other Egyptian politicians. On his eighteenth birthday (by the Muslim lunar calendar), he took the constitutional oath of office and soon was competing with the Wafd for power. Nahhas tried to cut his allowance, control his palace appointments, and limit his public appearances. To intimidate their opponents, both sides resorted to paramilitary groups: Young Egypt (a right-wing nationalist group often called the "Green Shirts") backed the king, while the Wafd had its "Blue Shirts." In December 1937, a popular demonstration near Abdin Palace gave Farouk the necessary pretext to replace Nahhas's Wafdist government with a pro-palace cabinet made up of politicians from the other parties. A rigged election, boycotted by the Wafd, gave those parties control of Parliament in April 1938.

The king then ruled as well as reigned in Egypt, but without the experience or the breadth of contacts needed to govern wisely. The veteran politician Ali Mahir (who was anti-British), Farouk's mother, and Farouk's former tutor, Ahmad Hasanayn, competed in exercising influence over Farouk. Soon after his eighteenth birthday (by Gregorian reckoning), he married Safinaz Zulfiqar, whom he renamed Faridah. The wedding occasioned great rejoicing throughout Egypt, and Farouk was arguably the most popular ruler Egypt had ever known. He was first member of his family who could make a formal speech in Arabic. When he visited a mosque on Fridays, he would often lead the congregation in worship, a prerogative of the *caliph* (temporal and spiritual head of Islam); indeed many Egyptians wished to revive the caliphate (abolished by Kemal Ataturk in 1924) and give the position to Farouk. The people and the politicians adored him; only later did they realize that they had spoiled him.

The outbreak of World War II raised other concerns. When the British declared war on Germany, after Hitler's attack on Poland in September 1939, they wanted Egypt to follow their example under the terms of the 1936 Anglo-Egyptian Treaty. King Farouk and his ministers, while professing support for Britain's war aims, demurred. The treaty allowed the British to send additional troops to Egypt in wartime to defend the Suez Canal. Nonetheless, the Egyptians were not obliged to declare war, and they hardly feared a German victory if it would free them of the British occupation. Farouk's Italian ties were notorious, and the British believed him to be in contact with Hitler. The British government and Ambassador Lampson considered deposing him, but hesitated, for to do so would flagrantly violate the 1936 treaty and open a rift between the Egyptian and British armies. Meanwhile, Nahhas was pressing for new elections that would return the Wafd to power. Ambassador Lampson had surprisingly good relations with the head of Egypt's most popular nationalist party, while the king and his advisers kept shuffling their cabinets to exclude the Wafd and to keep Egypt out of World War II. However, when General Erwin Rommel and his German troops took control in Libya and started pushing back the British in late 1941 just as the Japanese were seizing Britain's possessions in Southeast Asia, the continued control of the Suez Canal became vital to the British Empire's survival. Lampson's patience with Farouk and his anti-British advisers had been exhausted. On learning that the king was about to appoint Ali Mahir as prime minister, the ambassador handed Farouk an ultimatum, demanding that he appoint a Wafdist government that would uphold the 1936 Treaty. He must either accept Nahhas or abdicate his throne. Farouk tried to unite Egypt's leading politicians in opposing British interference. They favored a coalition government under Nahhas, but Nahhas insisted on parliamentary elections and a cabinet consisting entirely of Wafdists. Backed by British troops and tanks, Lampson entered Abdin Palace and demanded Farouk's abdication. At the last minute Hasanayn persuaded him not to sign the instrument but to let Nahhas appoint the ministers he wanted.

The events of February 4, 1942, as they have come to be known among both Egyptian and Western historians, marked a major change in Anglo-Egyptian relations and in Farouk's political and personal behavior. The Wafd party was seen as an instrument of British rule in Egypt, and indeed it did cooperate closely with the British but not to the extent of declaring war on the Axis powers. King Farouk, becoming ever more indifferent to politics, devoted himself to the pursuit of pleasure. Princess Shevikiar, Fuad's estranged first wife who had returned to Egypt after many years in exile, had taught him to play cards for money and introduced him to Princess Fatimah Tusun, with whom he had an affair. By this time, his marriage to Faridah was going sour, and he took to pursuing female companionship in night clubs and at parties. A car accident in 1943 caused him to suffer some broken bones. He spent a long convalescence in a British army hospital, and many Egyptians thought that maltreatment by doctors there caused a glandular disorder, which made him act in eccentric ways. Only in October 1944, when he finally could dismiss Nahhas (after several vain attempts), did his outlook improve. Rebutting a Wafdist member of Parliament after his 1944 Speech from the Throne, Farouk succinctly stated his political philosophy: "My good pasha, don't you know that the will of the people emanates from my will?"

In early 1945 Egypt hosted the Arab leaders as they put the finishing touches on the League of Arab States, and Farouk also met with both Winston Churchill and Franklin D. Roosevelt. While random acts of violence took the lives of a prime minister, the British Minister of State in Cairo, the Egyptian general who had helped Britain during the war, and the pro-British finance minister, Farouk was confident about his own popular support. Egypt had declared war on the Axis powers in time to become a charter member of the United Nations, but in spite of its association with the victorious Allies, Egypt still remained under foreign occupation. Extremist groups, such as Young Egypt, the fundamentalist Muslim Brothers, and the communists, were gaining supporters, as the king's ministers seemed unable to persuade the British to leave. In January 1946, Farouk invited the able, highly authoritarian politician, Ismail Sidqi, to form a government. Large-scale riots broke out in Cairo and were crushed, with heavy casualties. Siqdi negotiated with the British government to revise the Anglo-Egyptian Treaty, but his claim that the British recognized the union of Egypt and the Sudan under King Farouk set off riots in Khartum and disclaimers in London. British troops did withdraw from Cairo and Alexandria, but only into the Suez Canal zone, which became the largest army base outside the communist bloc. Farouk asked Sidqi's successor to take the Sudan issue to the United Nations, which decided not to back Egypt's claims or to contest the Anglo-Egyptian condominium in the Sudan. Late in 1947, the Palestine problem became Egypt's overriding concern, as the United Nations General Assembly voted to partition the former British Mandate into Jewish and Arab states despite the unanimous opposition of the Palestinian Arabs and the Arab countries. The Arab governments had promised to fight any attempt to establish a Jewish state, but it was not clear that Egypt could or would make a major military commitment. Egyptian army leaders viewed their troops as inadequately trained and supplied, but the popular pressure (especially from the Muslim Brothers) demanded Egypt's intervention in Palestine. Susceptible to flattery by Arab journalists, and perhaps fearing that Egypt's abstention would backfire if the other Arab armies defeated the Jews, Farouk committed his troops to fight for Palestine. They lost. Their defeat was due in part to military incompetence and government corruption, but also to the king's love affair with the film star Camelia (Lilianne Cohen), who was a secret agent for the Israelis. The officers never forgave Farouk for this humiliating debacle in Palestine, and it was the officers who eventually overthrew him.

In November 1948, King Farouk finally divorced Queen Faridah, a very unpopular move and one that he regretted ever after. Now grotesquely overweight and desperately lonely, Farouk sent his Italian servants far and wide to find him new female companions. Egyptian men feared taking their wives to public places where the king might see them and try to seduce them. His excesses became the source of idle gossip among all the classes and in every country. National morale was so shattered by the defeat in Palestine that Farouk appointed a strongman government in 1949 to clean out the revolutionaries. The Muslim Brothers and Young Egypt were purged, but not too effectively, for Farouk still feared the Wafd even more. A caretaker cabinet containing politicians of all the parties paved the way for a general election in 1950, and once again the Wafd won a majority of the seats in the Chamber of Deputies; however, its share of the popular vote fell below 50 percent for the first time. Not just Egypt's king, but its whole political system was on trial.

By this time, most Egyptians and foreigners believed that the monarchy would soon be overthrown. King Farouk and Prime Minister Nahhas, equally demoralized, were now being driven together by attacks from the revolutionaries, whom they could not purge. Nahhas tried to distract the people by attacking Britain's occupation of the Suez Canal and the Anglo-Egyptian condominium over the Sudan, but new economic problems brought on by the Egyptian government's failure to sell the 1951 cotton crop enflamed popular resentment. Farouk's second marriage, to a sixteen-year-old commoner named Narriman (followed by a three-month European honeymoon) did not improve the king's reputation at home (as he apparently had hoped it would). The leaders of Egypt's minority parties sent him a strongly worded warning to purge his palace staff of dishonorable men. Nahhas took the king's side and, at his instigation (but not Farouk's), Egypt's Parliament voted to abrogate the 1936 Anglo-Egyptian Treaty and the 1899 Treaty setting up the Sudan condominium, proclaiming Farouk king of Egypt and the Sudan. The British dug in for a long struggle, and soon Egyptians were fighting eighty thousand British troops in the Suez Canal zone. On January 25, 1952, the British in Ismailia attacked a base used by auxiliary police, killing fifty Egyptians and injuring one hundred. The next day, demonstrations in Cairo turned into riots. The rioters got out of control and began burning hotels, restaurants, shops, and clubs patronized by foreigners. Farouk, who was hosting a party to celebrate his son's birth, did not order the police or the army to stop the fires until much of central Cairo had been destroyed. A day later he ousted Nahhas and appointed a caretaker cabinet. With Cairo under curfew most of that spring, Farouk appointed four ministries in succession, while Egypt's condition grew worse.

Although a secret cabal of Egyptian army officers had long plotted against Farouk, they had feared challenging him directly. They decided to strike after Farouk vetoed their election of General Muhammad Nagib as president of the Officers Club and named his brother-in-law as war minister despite his notorious ignorance of defense matters. The military coup, carried on during the night of July 22, was greeted with great relief by the Egyptian people, and the officers decided neither to retain the king nor to try him but to demand his abdication (in favor of his son) and to exile him from Egypt. Farouk and his immediate family were allowed to sail on the royal yacht to Naples, carrying as much of his property as the boat could hold. In 1953 the officers declared Egypt a republic.

The ex-king, abandoned gradually by his friends and family, spent his last years in exile, dying in a night club (beside his latest girl friend) when he was forty-five. After a funeral in Rome, his body was flown to Cairo and buried in the Rifai Mosque.

Farouk had an intelligent and inquisitive mind. He was able to charm most Egyptians and foreigners whom he met. In his youth, he symbolized Egypt's hope for a national renaissance. He suffered, however, from various physical disorders, a lack of formal education and mental discipline, and an inability to distinguish good from bad counsel. As a result, he was unable to lead the Egyptian people to the achievement of their national goals: independence from Britain, constitutional government, economic development, and primacy within the Arab world. Although Farouk failed as king, no one in those times could have ruled Egypt easily. When he returned from England to succeed his father he had no enemies; when he left Egypt, he had no friends.

BIBLIOGRAPHY

Anis, Muhammad Ahmad. *4 Fabrayir 1942* (4 February 1942). Beirut: al-Mu'assasah al-arabiyah, 1972.

Evans, Trefor E. (ed.). *The Killearn Diaries, 1934–1946*. London: Baron, 1972.

Flower, Raymond. *Napoleon to Nasser: The Story of Modern Egypt*. London: Tom Stacey, 1972, pp. 164–169.

Grafftey-Smith, Laurence. *Bright Levant*. London: John Murray, 1970, pp. 230–236.

McBride, Barrie St. Clair. *Farouk of Egypt*. London: Robert Hale, 1967.

McLeave, Hugh. *The Last Pharaoh*. London: McCall, 1969.

Moore, Austin L. *Farewell Farouk*. Chicago: Scholar's Press, 1954.

Morsi, Leila, "Farouk in British Policy." *Middle Eastern Studies* 20, no. 4 (October 1984): pp. 193–211.

Neguib, Mohamed. *Egypt's Destiny*. New York: Doubleday, 1955.

Ramadan, Abd al-Azim. *al-Sira' bayn al-Wafd wa al-Arsh 1936–1939* (The Contest Between the Wafd and the Throne). Beirut: al-Mu'assasah al-arabiyah, 1979.

Salim, Jamil. *Qira'ah jadidah li-hadith 4 Fibrayir* (A New Reading of the 4 February Incident). Cairo: Dar al-Sha'b, 1975.

Smith, Charles D. "4 February 1942: Its Causes and Its Influence on Egyptian Politics and on the Future of Anglo-Egyptian Relations, 1937–1945." *International Journal of Middle East Studies* 10 (1979): 453–479.

Warburg, Gabriel. "Lampson's Ultimatum to Farouk." *Middle Eastern Studies* 11, no. 1 (January 1975): 24–32.

ARTHUR GOLDSCHMIDT, JR.

ALLAL AL-FASI (1910?–1974) was one of the rare historical figures who combined the skills of scholarship, oratory, and statesmanship. A man of action and ideas, with a career that spanned nearly fifty years, he was a poet, a leading proponent of the Salafiya movement, and a forward-looking thinker applying the lessons of the twentieth century to the theory and practice of Islam. He taught at the Qarawiyin University in Fez, was one of the most important nationalist activists and leaders in Morocco, and was a symbol of Morocco's *Istiqlal* (In-

dependence) Party. Later he was leader of the party for seventeen years after
Morocco's independence, a member of parliament and a minister, and a crusader
for causes as diverse as constitutional monarchy, Greater Morocco, Arabization
and Islamic education, women's rights, and a Palestinian homeland.

Born to one of the leading religious and intellectual families of Fez, Allal al-
Fasi grew up in an atmosphere permeated with Islamic tradition and opposition
to the French penetration of Morocco. In 1908, members of his family participated in the drafting of a constitution that was presented to Sultan Mulay Hafid.
His father, Abdelwahad al-Fasi, was born in the mid–1870s and became a
professor at the Qarawiyin University and secretary of its committee of overseers.
His father's brothers also held high positions as ambassador, minister, and *qadi*
(religious judge). His father owned property in Fez, was a close friend to several
high officials of the *makhzen* (royal entourage), and married Lalla Radya, widow
of a wealthy Fasi merchant and daughter of one of the city's more important
families of *shurfa* (descendants of the Prophet Mohammed). Shortly thereafter,
Allal was born in one of the finest homes in the Andalusian quarter of the city.
The young boy received a traditional Quranic education beginning at age five.
Two years later his mother died; his father soon remarried, and young Allal
became very attached to his stepmother Aicha al-Marnisiyya.

Allal's father and his father's friends became involved in the early 1920s in the
founding of the free schools—the schools were not tuition-free, but were free of
French control and provided a "modern" Islamic education. Allal attended and
then later taught at the Nasiriya school, so called because it was housed in a *za-
wiya* (headquarters of a religious brotherhood) which had once belonged to the
Nasiriya brotherhood. Later he attended the Qarawiyin University, where he was
awarded the title *alim* (scholar) and became a teacher in 1930. Two years later, as
a result of his political activities, his certificate as an alim was revoked under pressure
from the French, who also prohibited him from continuing to give his highly popular
course on the life of the Prophet Mohammed.

Early in his education, Allal al-Fasi reported that he began to see a need for
reforms in Islam as practiced in Morocco. His interests went further, however,
and by the age of fifteen he wrote a poem expressing growing nationalist feeling.
It read in part, "How is it after fifteen years that I am still playing? . . . And I
belong to an unfortunate nation which has not found the means to live life as it
wishes" (Alami 1972:41).

While a student at the Qarawiyin he became a leader of a group of students
opposed to one of the university's lecturers, Abdel Hay al-Kittani, who was the
leader of a Sufi order and a collaborator with the French. This group of students
formed a secret Students' Union dedicated to Islamic purity. They worked for
reforms in the university's curriculum, improvement of student life, and organized gatherings that brought them into contact with the students at the elite,
French-language College Mulay Idriss, attended by the sons of the Fasi commercial elite. This contact was to have enormous importance later as the Moroccan
nationalist movement drew heavily on those two elements—the traditionally ed-

ucated graduates of the Qarawiyin, and the more Western-oriented graduates of Lycée Mulay Idriss and its counterparts in Rabat and elsewhere. During this period Allal also helped to found a clandestine monthly publication that was circulated in mimeographed form to students in Fez and other towns in Morocco.

In 1928, Allal became a public figure when he was one of the coauthors of a protest note to the governor of Fez demanding an end to a French plan to divert the waters of Wad Fez to irrigate French *colon* (settler) farms. He also helped organize protest meetings and delivered fiery speeches against the plan. The experience he gained in 1928 came into play two years later when the French prevailed upon the young Moroccan Sultan Mohammed bin Yusuf to issue the *Berber Dahir*—a decree permitting Morocco's Berber population to use Berber customary law instead of Islamic law. Allal became one of the principal organizers of a campaign based in the mosques of Fez, Rabat, and Salé to foment protest demonstrations. Allal and several of his companions were detained for two weeks in the wake of these protests, but detention did not deter them. A member of a delegation sent to petition French Resident General Lucien Saint, he was one of the delegation members who was refused entry. On his return to Fez, Allal and several others in the delegation were arrested and exiled to the city of Taza for a period of two months.

Upon his release, the young activist resumed his former activities. Two of the other protest leaders, Mohammed el-Wazzani and Ahmad Belafrej, moved to Paris to attempt to influence French opinion, while Allal stayed behind in Morocco, organizing protests and offering his lectures on the Prophet's life at the university. Far from simple biography, however, in Allal al-Fasi's hands the course became a vehicle for the religious and political views embodied in the Salafiya movement and his own political ideas as well. The French were worried by this young firebrand and the audience he attracted. Consequently, they conspired with more traditional Sufi-oriented scholars at the Qarawiyin to put pressure on the administration to silence him. When this failed, the resident general announced promulgation of a *dahir* (decree) in May 1933, banning Allal and two other lecturers. Despite protests the order held, and Allal left for France within four months.

During a seven-month stay in Paris, Allal worked closely with Ahmad Belafrej and made contact for the first time with students from Algeria, Tunisia, and other parts of the Arab world. However, a new resident general, Henri Ponsot, permitted Allal to return to Morocco and tried to coopt him by making his father a judge and offering the young leader the position of minister of justice. Not only did he refuse, but he resumed his course at the university. Very quickly Ponsot put pressure on the Sultan to prohibit the lectures. When this failed, he ordered the Sheikh al-Qarawiyin to do so.

Now Allal turned to political organizing full time. Together with the other young nationalists, he created the Kutla al-Amal al-Watania (National Action Bloc), the first Moroccan nationalist party, which was founded in May 1934. In fact, the Kutla was really the public manifestation of clandestine movements founded in 1930 through 1932 with cells in Fez, Rabat, Kenitra, Salé, Casablanca, Safi, Marrakesh, Tangier, and Titwan in the Spanish-controlled northern zone. The structure of these organizations, which persisted in secret until 1944, closely resembled the structure of the Communist Party of France, with each cell an autonomous, self-contained unit, linked only to the "mother cell" in Fez, which was headed by Allal al-Fasi. The principal activities of the clandestine nationalist movement in the early 1930s were achieving support for the free schools, publishing two papers (one in Paris, the other in Fez), preparing the Plan of Reforms, organizing the alumni of the lycées in Fez and Rabat as political action groups, and organizing demonstrations in favor of Sultan Mohammed bin Yusuf (who the nationalists were adopting as a symbol and thereby winning over to their cause). By 1934, the sultan was beginning to be won over, and held his first significant meetings with the nationalists when Allal returned from France.

By far the most significant nationalist document of this period was the Moroccan Plan of Reforms, which ran to more than 130 pages. Its preparation, which took more than a year, was a closely guarded secret until the Arabic edition was released in Cairo in September 1934. The French edition was published in Paris in November and presented to the authorities. The release of the document, which was rejected by the French, marked the beginning of a new tactic as the nationalists now tried to reach a wider audience among the Moroccan public. In 1936, as the Popular Front government rose to power in France, the Kutla launched a series of mass meetings demanding fundamental democratic rights. After assemblies in Fez, Salé, and Casablanca in the first half of November, Allal and other nationalist leaders were arrested. This led to outbreaks of mass protests in all the main towns organized by the cell structures that had been in place since early in the decade. As a result, Allal and the other detainees were released.

This period marked the emergence of Allal al-Fasi as the paramount leader of the Moroccan nationalist movement. His election at the Kutla's October 1936 convention as its president infuriated fellow nationalist Mohammed Hassan al-Wazzani, who bolted the movement a few months later. Friends and associates, including Shakib Arslan, the Lebanese leader based in Paris, tried to heal the rift, but without success. Ahmad Balafrej emerged as the new number-two leader in the movement. Under his direction, membership in the Kutla boomed early in 1937, so that by the time the French forced its dissolution it counted more than sixty-five hundred card-carrying members in the French zone alone—twenty new cells had been created in a few months' time. So successful were the nationalists in expanding their popular base that in March 1937 the French forced the Kutla to dissolve. Because it was based on the previous clandestine structure, however, the group secretly reconstituted itself almost immediately as the National Party for Realizing the Reform Plan. At this group's first national meeting in April 1937 in Rabat, the schism between Allal, who wanted to continue expanding the movement's popular base, and al-Wazzani, who wanted to go back to the earlier approach of the small pressure group, became final. Actually, the return to clandestine activity had narrowed the gap between their approaches, and the real cause of the split had more to do with rivalries for power and the clash of personalities between two strong and ambitious leaders.

Throughout this period the nationalists had not demanded independence but rather reform of the French administrative and political system in Morocco. They wanted greater civil, educational, and political rights for Moroccan Muslims, and only the most radical individuals even spoke about eventual independence. Even the acute crisis in the fall of 1937, which led to Allal al-Fasi's arrest and exile, did not change the movement's reformist goals.

In September 1937, demonstrations erupted in Meknes to protest a French plan to divert water from the city's main supply to irrigate four nearby colon farms. Mass arrests in Meknes led the National Party to call for protest demonstrations, which were held in Casablanca, Fez, Rabat, Oudja, Marrakesh, and Meknes itself. Demonstrations continued throughout September and October, culminating in a clash with police in Khemisset on October 22, 1937. As a result, Allal, Ahmad Mekouar, Umar Abdeljelil, and Mohammed Lyazidi were arrested on October 25. Ultimately Allal was flown to exile in Gabon, an exile that lasted nine years until after the end of World War II. The arrests touched off a new wave of demonstrations, which the French brutally suppressed. With its leaders jailed and exiled, the National Party dwindled in importance—the French had succeeded in destroying it as a viable political force by decapitating it.

For Allal, the nine-year exile was an interminable frustration. Cut off from his nationalist colleagues, he played little if any part in the events of those years. Until early 1941, he was kept in a village in southern Gabon. Later he was transferred to Brazzaville in the French Congo. When Charles De Gaulle, leader of the Free French came to Brazzaville in 1942, it was suggested that Allal write to him expressing his support. Allal refused to do so unless De Gaulle would recognize Morocco's right to independence. De Gaulle rejected this condition, and Allal was moved to the village of Maiama, fifty miles from Brazzaville, where he remained in detention until after the end of the war.

Allal's demands mirrored the changing position of the nationalists. Indeed, some time during the period between Allal's arrest in November 1937 and the fall of France to the Nazis in June 1940, the nationalists' demands evolved from reforms to independence. This took concrete form on January 11, 1944, with the issuance of the Istiqlal (Independence) Party manifesto. In the space of the year since his January 1943 return from exile, Ahmad Balafrej had succeeded in reconstituting the dormant movement. While the concrete platform of the party still stressed reforms, the goal was now independence.

Up on his release from exile, Allal returned to Fez in June 1946 to a rousing welcome, but he stayed only a few months. In May 1947 he arrived, unannounced, in Cairo, which was to become his base for the next nine years. There he worked openly as the Istiqlal's representative to the League of Arab States, rallying support for Moroccan independence. In May 1948 he was elected general

secretary of the Committee for the Liberation of the Arab Maghrib, and throughout his stay he wrote articles for the local press and delivered public lectures
designed to mobilize mass support. He traveled extensively to seek support for
Moroccan independence, including a visit to the United Nations as part of the
Moroccan delegation in 1952. He also represented the Istiqlal Party at the 1955
Bandung Conference of Non-Aligned Leaders. When the French deposed and
exiled Mohammed V and his family on August 20, 1953, Allal immediately
went on Radio Cairo to declare his (and the Istiqlal's) support for the monarch.

Once Morocco had regained its independence in 1956, Allal returned to his
homeland. He had actively participated in the movement throughout, and was
readily acknowledged as a major figure on the Moroccan political stage. On
March 26, 1956, he arrived in Rabat and called on King Mohammed V,* completing the reconciliation with Morocco's leadership. However, the unity was
short-lived. Within the Istiqlal two distinct factions emerged—a traditionalist
group based around Allal, and a more radical group based around Mehdi Ben
Barka. In addition, Mohammed V clearly wanted to play a central role rather
than the ceremonial one that many in the party would have preferred. These
clashes led to the breakup of the Istiqlal in 1959 and its ultimate move into the
role of loyal political opposition to the king and his government. The schism in
the party occurred in January 1959, leading to the creation of the Union Nationale
de Forces Populaires (UNFP) in September. In January 1960, Allal was elected
president of the Istiqlal, and in July 1961 he joined the government as minister
of Islamic affairs. However, he and his fellow Istiqlal ministers resigned in
December 1962, and the party joined the opposition. In particular, Allal and the
party took forceful positions on Moroccanization of the economy, Arabization
of education, and recovery of Moroccan territory in colonial hands. For many
years he showed visitors a map of Greater Morocco, including not only Sidi
Ifni, Ceuta, Melilla, and Spanish Sahara, but also the Tindouf region in Algeria,
and Mauritania. In 1961 he took a strong position against Mauritanian independence from France, asserting Morocco's claim to sovereignty there, and he
opposed establishment of diplomatic relations with the desert country of Mauritania in 1969. Until his death in 1974, Allal remained an outspoken proponent
of Morocco's territorial claims to Spanish Sahara and Tindouf.

In 1962, Allal was elected to parliament, where he led the minority Istiqlal
deputies until King Hassan II* dissolved the body and declared a state of exception ending parliamentary government following the March 1965 Casablanca
riots. In 1970, when the king proposed a new constitution, Allal led the Istiqlal
into joining forces with the UNFP in a new *Kutla Watania* (National Bloc) to
boycott the constitutional referendum and subsequent parliamentary elections.
For the next two years the opposition maintained its unity during negotiations
with the palace that failed to achieve consensus. In 1972 they again campaigned
against a new constitution (still in force today) that was proposed by Hassan II.
As a result of this boycott, the opposition played a limited role in affairs of state

until after the 1975 Green March. The Green March was a November 1975 demonstration organized by the Moroccan government in which several hundred thousand unarmed civilians walked toward the former Spanish Sahara and small groups crossed into what was then Spanish territory. It underscored Moroccan nationalist resolve to gain the territory. In the meantime, Allal al-Fasi passed from the scene. He died of a heart attack suffered during a visit to Rumania while he was meeting with President Nicolai Ceaucescu on May 13, 1974.

Allal al-Fasi's long and illustrious career as a nationalist leader, politician, and statesman represents only a small part of his contribution to Morocco and the Arab/Islamic world. In addition, he was a mature thinker and scholar of distinction who was in many ways equally at home with the ideas of Islam and Europe. He drew his ideas from sources as diverse as the Quran, Jamal al-Din al-Afghani, Mohammed Abduh, Voltaire, Montesquieu, Dostoevsky, and Tolstoy. The roots of his ideology were in the Salafiya, or neo-Salafiya, movement, which was a continuation of the religious revivalism in Morocco dating back to the end of the eighteenth century. It was a movement that looked back to the roots of early Islam while blending in the experience of subsequent generations. Its purpose was the strengthening of Muslim peoples and their regeneration through a return to Islamic values. On this base, which he absorbed at the Qarawiyin in his youth, Allal constructed a political philosophy that has been described as a combination of nineteenth-century liberalism and rationalism with twentieth-century religious socialism of an egalitarian type.

In politics, Allal al-Fasi was a liberal democrat, in economics he was a socialist, and in religious matters he was a progressive conservative. He believed that "Islam is movement" (Rosenthal 1965; 158). In his writings, especially his *Al-Naqd al-Dhati* (*Self-Criticism*), published in Cairo in 1952, he dealt with a broad range of topics including Islam ("right and useful in and for every age and place"(ibid.: 156)), the West (positively critical), politics and administration (he favored popular participation and consultation), monarchy (it should be constitutional), democracy (he wanted "true democracy"), women's rights (they should have full political rights), law (*sharia* [Islamic law] should be supplemented by other doctrines to form Moroccan Islamic Law), economics (he advocated a form of socialism), and Moroccan society (its unity is based on Islam, the Maliki rite, and the Arabic language).

His overall attitude was based on a liberal interpretation of sharia. To Allal, sharia was the norm and any reform would involve full implementation of the sharia in public, private, and social affairs. Education therefore should be compulsory and Islamic in content and character, but with no compulsion for religious minorities, who should study their own religious traditions.

Allal clearly had carefully studied Western societies and history as well as the Islamic experience. As a result, his contribution was one that melded certain elements of the Western experience to Islam and its roots to create the basis for a modern Islamic and Moroccan reality.

BIBLIOGRAPHY

Works by al-Fasi:

al-Naqd al-Dhati (Self-Criticism). Cairo: n.p., 1952.
The Independence Movements in Arab North Africa. Trans. H. Z. Nuseibeh. Washington,
    D.C.: American Council of Learned Societies, 1954.

Other Works:

Alami, Mohamed el. *Allal el Fassi, Patriarche du nationalisme Marocaine*. Rabat: Ar-
    rissala, 1972.
Cohen, Amnon. "Allal al-Fasi: His Ideas and His Contribution Towards Morocco's
    Independence." *Asian and African Studies* (Jerusalem) 3 (1967): pp. 121–164.
Gaudio, Attilio. *Allal el Fassi, ou l'histoire de l'Istiqlal*. Paris: Alain Morceau, 1972.
Rosenthal, Erwin I. J. "Allal al-Fasi." In Erwin I. J. Rosenthal, *Islam in the Modern
    National State*. Cambridge: Cambridge University Press, 1965, pp. 154–178.

JEROME B. BOOKIN-WEINER

G

PIERRE GEMAYEL (1905–1984) (al-Jumayyil) will long be remembered as the founder and paramount leader of the Lebanese Phalanges (al-Kataeb al-Lubnaniah), a paramilitary youth organization that he later molded into the single most powerful independent political force in Lebanon. He played a significant if not crucial role in the struggle for Lebanon's independence from French rule in 1943. He transformed the Kataeb into a political party, and later led it in the fall of 1958 to reassert Maronite prerogatives following the brief civil war of that year, thus taking the party to national prominence. As a cabinet minister under President Fuad Chehab,* he pushed through important reforms, and was most instrumental in enacting social security legislation. In 1967 he joined two other conservative Maronite leaders in the Tripartite Alliance (Hilf Thulathi) to prevent socialist and revolutionary trends in the Arab world from spilling over into Lebanon. Dismayed by the failure of the Lebanese state in 1969 and 1973 to impose its authority by armed force in the face of claims by the Palestine Liberation Organization (PLO) to extraterritorial rights, Gemayel formed an armed Kataeb militia to act as a surrogate of the state. His most momentous impact on Lebanon came in 1975 when, galvanized by fears of an alliance between the Lebanese left and the PLO, he reacted in such a way as to precipitate the very outcome he feared, and set in motion a chain of events that escaped his control and culminated in a devastating civil war which consumed Lebanon and laid to rest, perhaps forever, the formula for confessional coexistence that he had held so dear.

Although the presidency of the republic eluded Pierre Gemayel's grasp, he became the father of two presidents. His youngest son, Bashir, became the first commander of the Lebanese Forces, the combined Maronite militias, in 1976. Defeating his rivals, Bashir became the most influential Maronite figure, over-shadowing his father. In 1982 Bashir emerged as the uncontested candidate for the presidency, but was assassinated barely three weeks after his election, before he could be inaugurated and just eight weeks short of his thirty-fifth birthday.

The elder son, Amin, virtually inherited the office from his brother at the age of forty. He enjoyed far broader support than Bashir, and went on to serve a full six-year term at the head of an ineffectual administration which he tried but failed to fashion into a full-fledged government of the country. When he left office on September 23, 1988, Parliament was unable to elect a successor, Lebanon was saddled with two rival governments, and not only the state but society itself was threatened with fragmentation.

Pierre Gemayel was the architect of the family's fortunes. Tall, gaunt, and ramrod-straight, with deep worry lines etched into his brow and cheeks, he was punctilious and courtly, although given to occasional dismaying bluntness. He was a commanding patriarchal figure who aroused veneration among his predominantly Maronite followers.

Pierre Gemayel was born on November 2, 1905, in Bikfaya, a mountain village eighteen kilometers from Beirut. His ancestors were said to have moved to the small Maronite village around 1545. One was granted the hereditary title of *sheikh* (chief) by Amir Bashir II Chehab (1794–1840); another, Philippe Gemayel, was elected patriarch of the Maronite church in 1795.

Pierre's father, Amin Gemayel, was a medical doctor by profession. His mother was a Greek Catholic from Beirut, the daughter of a commercial agent. Dr. Gemayel was active in the Society of Saint Vincent de Paul, which had connections in Paris with Arab nationalist and anti-Turkish groups. He had to flee Lebanon when the Ottomans restricted the autonomy of Mount Lebanon on the eve of World War I. He sought refuge in Mansourah, Egypt. The family, which consisted of Pierre, his brother, two sisters, and his mother, joined Amin as soon as they could.

The Gemayels returned from Egypt in the autumn of 1918, after the British and French troops had occupied the coast of Lebanon. Lebanon and Syria were placed under French mandate, and the French created the state of Greater Lebanon in 1920. The Gemayels took up residence in Saifi, and then moved to Ashrafieh, the eastern, predominantly Christian sector of the capital, Beirut.

Pierre went back to school. He later enrolled in the Jesuit-run St. Joseph University where he excelled at soccer, boxing, college wrestling, and cycling. He founded a Catholic youth soccer club, and then a Lebanese national soccer federation. He failed to qualify for admission to medical school, but was accepted in the school of pharmacy. He graduated with a *licence* (bachelor's degree) in pharmaceutical chemistry from the French Faculty of Pharmacy and Medicine of St. Joseph University and put in a training stint at Cochin Hospital in Paris but finished his training at his uncle's pharmacy in Beirut. He then opened his own pharmacy at Martyrs' Square in the commercial center of Beirut, and continued to do business there until the area was destroyed during the civil war in the late 1970s.

Pierre married his cousin, Geneviéve Elias Gemayel, also a native of Bikfaya, whom he had gotten to know during his stay at Mansourah. The marriage took place on August 5, 1934, and lasted until Pierre died fifty years later. The couple had four daughters, Madeleine, Jacqueline, Claude, and Arzé; as well as two sons, Amin, who was born on January 22, 1942, and Bashir, the youngest child, who came into this world on November 10, 1947. Both male children were born in Bikfaya. The first three daughters married businessmen, and the fourth daughter, Arzé, became the general superior of a Franciscan order of nuns, the Cross of Lebanon.

In 1936 Pierre Gemayel was designated by the Lebanese Football Federation as one of its two representatives at the Olympic games in Berlin. He was impressed by the discipline, order, and national zeal he witnessed there. While in Berlin, he also met Oberto Chris, who introduced him to the Sokols (Falcons), a Czech gymnastic society founded in 1862, which relied on physical education to inculcate the spirit of patriotism.

Gemayel hit on the idea of copying the discipline of the Nazis and Sokols in a Lebanese youth organization. On November 5, 1936, he and four others, Charles Helou, Georges Naccache, Chafiq Nassif, and Emile Yared, formed the Lebanese Phalanges. The founding of the organization was proclaimed on November 21, which then became the date for anniversary celebrations. Despite the paramilitary nature of the Kataeb—its khaki shirts, strong sense of nationalism, and dedication to a single charismatic leader—it was not a fascist organization, and neither then nor later, when it evolved into a political party, did it espouse a totalitarian ideology.

From a political perspective, the creation of the Kataeb was a response to the emergence of movements advocating pan-Arab or pan-Syrian unity, notably Antoun Saadeh's Syrian Social Nationalist Party (Parti Populaire Syrien), which had a strong appeal to many Greek Orthodox Lebanese. The Kataeb tended to identify Arab or Syrian nationalism with Islam; Lebanese nationalism was its formula for preventing the Christians from being overwhelmed by the surrounding Arab sea. The Maronites, unlike other Christian sects, view Lebanon as their one and only homeland.

Pierre Gemayel, in refining and propagating Lebanese nationalism, was also helping to bring about a social transformation. With the demise of the Ottoman empire, the coming of the French Mandate, and the country's transition from an isolated mountain refuge for Maronites and Druze into an expanded Lebanese republic, which included the predominantly Sunni Mediterranean coast, the largely Shiite Beqaa valley to the east, and Jabal Aamil to the south, the Kataeb served as an agent of social mobilization, offering new patterns of behavior and a new identity to replace the old psychological and social commitments that were being eroded. The Kataeb continued to play this role over the next four decades, for the Maronite community in particular, as the country went through a rapid modernization process. However, modernization did not erase sectarian or communal orientations, but led to their compartmentalization. This meant that sectarian and nonsectarian orientations and commitments could coexist within the same individual; whether particularistic or universalistic tendencies would be activated depended on the situation.

Gemayel was chosen to head the Kataeb because, unlike the other founders, he was not partisan toward either of Lebanon's leading Maronite politicians (Bishara al-Khouri or Emile Eddé), he had the required charisma and dedication, and he was willing to devote his time unstintingly to the organization. Over the years he seldom failed to attend weekly meetings, and his leadership was so effective that few challenged his authority; he almost invariable had his way despite the elaborate democratic decision-making structure the Kataeb was to acquire. Throughout the rest of his life, his name was synonymous with chief of the Kataeb.

The Kataeb's disciplined membership and paramilitary organization allowed it to play an important supporting role during the struggle for independence from France in the period of 1937 through 1943, and it emerged from the struggle endowed with a nationalistic mystique. The Mandate authorities banned the Kataeb, along with other paramilitary organizations, on November 18, 1937, and seized the organization's headquarters. In defiance of the ban, Gemayel led a Kataeb rally in Martyrs' Square to mark the organization's first anniversary. French Senegalese troops fired on the demonstrators, killing two and wounding seventy, including Gemayel. The Phalangist chief was jailed, but widespread strikes and demonstrations broke out and Gemayel was released. Boosted by these events, membership in the Kataeb rose to twenty-one thousand by 1938.

The Kataeb collaborated with the Najjadeh, its Muslim counterpart, in protesting food shortages and unemployment under Emile Eddé's government in 1941. This brought the government down, but the French authorities again banned the Kataeb. In spite of this, membership climbed to thirty-five thousand in 1942 when the Kataeb decided to admit women to its ranks.

On June 8, 1941, the Free French proclaimed Lebanon's independence. The Lebanese constitution was restored on March 25, 1943, and the new parliament met on September 21, 1943, and elected Bishara al-Khouri president. Riyad al-Sulh was appointed prime minister. However, the newly appointed French délegué-général, Jean Helleu, rejected the demand for an immediate termination of the mandate. On November 8, 1943, Parliament unanimously passed a bill effectively ending the Mandate. President Khouri signed the bill into law. Helleu reacted by placing Khouri, Sulh, and other leading political figures under arrest. He suspended the constitution, dissolved parliament, and appointed Emile Eddé president.

The Kataeb and the Najjadeh again joined forces to organize a nationwide strike, along with other Muslim and Christian groups. Riots ensued. A twenty-four hour curfew was clamped on Beirut. Two members of the Sulh cabinet escaped to the village of Bshamoun and set up a government in exile. The highly disciplined cadres of the Kataeb and the Najjadeh proved invaluable in facing French troops, organizing demonstrations, and acting as a go-between with the government in exile. Gemayel and twenty-three other Kataeb members were arrested, and thirty were wounded. The French finally relented and released the president and his cabinet, as well as the Kataeb members. On November 27,

1943, five days after the country's independence, a presidential decree was issued officially recognizing the Kataeb in appreciation of its services.

Pierre Gemayel wholeheartedly embraced the 1943 National Pact, the formula for coexistence among Lebanon's various communities, under which the Muslims renounced their desire to be incorporated in the Arab fold, and the Christians gave up their reliance on France. A democratic form of government was established, based not on majority rule but on a quota system whereby sectarian representation was embodied in the structure of government itself, seats in Parliament were allocated in a six to five ratio favoring the Christians, the top posts in the government were assigned to the various sectarian groups (for instance, the president would always be a Maronite Christian and the prime minister a Sunni Muslim), and the whole edifice depended on cooperation among the elite representing the communities that had entered into the bargain. The principles of the National Pact were incorporated in the Kataeb ideology and expanded the understanding of Lebanese nationalism.

In 1951 Gemayel ran for a parliamentary seat representing the Metn district, but lost to Pierre Eddé in a very close election. However, the first successful Kataeb candidate was elected that year. Membership declined to 23,500 by 1952. On May 29, 1952, the Kataeb officially registered as a political party, with Gemayel as its president. On February 21, 1956, its name officially became Hizb Al-Kataeb Al-Lubnaniah, the Lebanese Social Democratic Party.

Gemayel joined the swelling opposition to President Khouri near the end of his second term. However, Gemayel and the Kataeb were supportive of Khouri's successor, Camille Chamoun,* who was president from 1952 to 1958. Chamoun manipulated parliamentary elections to ensure the defeat of his opponents and to pack parliament with his supporters. This resulted in an armed rebellion led by the Druze leader Kamal Jumblatt,* the Sunni leader from Tripoli, Rashid Karami,* and several others. Chamoun was supported in this early but small-scale civil war by the Syrian Social Nationalist Party (SSNP), the Kataeb, Raymond Eddé's National Bloc, and an Armenian party called Tashnaq. It was widely rumored that the president was planning to overturn a recent constitutional amendment that prevented him from running for a second term. Gemayel and other Chamoun supporters saw the problem primarily as a case of Syrian and Egyptian meddling in Lebanon's affairs. The army remained neutral and most of the fighting on behalf of Chamoun was carried out by the SSNP. The Kataeb's military role in the affair was quite limited; in fact it was little more than keeping some vital roads open and protecting commercial centers. It was not involved in any major battles. Gemayel was criticized for supporting a corrupt regime and overlooking electoral fraud in his zeal to ward off foreign intervention.

After the 1958 civil war ended, Faud Chehab assumed the presidency and Rashid Karami formed a cabinet that was viewed as sympathetic to the former rebels. At that point Gemayel led the Kataeb in what came to be known as the counterrevolution. Following the kidnapping of a journalist working for Kataeb party organ *al-Aamal*, Gemayel called for a general strike on September 22. The assassination of another party official exacerbated the situation. The Kataeb set up barricades and brought activity in Mount Lebanon and Beirut to a virtual stand-still. When Karami's eight-man cabinet was announced, the Kataeb viewed it as leaning toward the rebels and therefore a violation of the agreement under which the civil war had ended. Bitter sectarian fighting ensued for three weeks. The conflict was resolved on October 14 when a new four-man cabinet was formed with Karami as premier but which also included Gemayel as deputy premier and minister of education, agriculture, and public works, and Raymond Eddé.

This ushered in a new era for the Kataeb. The party had emerged as the principal champion of Christian interests at the national level. Membership, which had declined to 26,500 in late 1954, swelled to 62,000 in 1959. In a 1959 by-election in Jezzine, the Kataeb party candidate defeated the local favorite, breaking the party's streak of bad luck at the polls. The party was often victorious in the elections after that. Six of its seven candidates were elected in 1960, most notably Pierre Gemayel, who handily defeated Pierre Eddé this time to become a deputy for Beirut. Four of the party's nine candidates were elected in 1964, and all nine were elected in 1968, including Gemayel, who was victorious both times. His leadership of the party was an important factor in its success at the polls. He provided the charismatic leadership that worked well in his patrimonial and quasi-traditional society. Gemayel was both a traditional Maronite leader, the champion of Christian communal causes, and a modern party leader and reformist cabinet member who was to try to broaden the appeal of the Kataeb and transform it into a truly mass party.

Working under a reformist president, the Kataeb entered on a reformist period of its own, with the party advocating social and economic measures that would benefit workers and the underprivileged groups in Lebanese society, many of which were not Christian. This was justified by the conservative wing in the party as a prophylactic measure against revolution, while the liberal wing saw it as an attempt to win over the Muslims and give them a stake in the system, transforming transnational loyalties to national ones.

Pierre Gemayel served as minister of finance (1960–1961); minister of health (1961); minister of public works (1961–1964); minister of communications and public works (November 1964-July 1965); minister of the interior (April-December 1966); minister of the interior, tourism, health, and posts, telegraphs and telephones (1968); as well as minister of public works and transport (November 1969–1970); in addition to the portfolio of education, agriculture, and public works that he kept for two years, until May 1960.

Gemayel, who was an advocate of social security legislation, was instrumental in securing the passage of a Lebanese social security code, which was promulgated on September 26, 1963, but actually implemented on May 1, 1965. He and the party were also supportive of the Green Plan to aid farmers. He was in favor of a new labor law, in principle including the right of unions to collective bargaining.

Support for the party came from various sectors and groups including students, small landowners, bureaucrats and civil servants, and lawyers and other professionals, although by the mid–1960s about 40 percent of party members were blue-collar or agricultural workers and small farmers.

The party was an important agent for socializing a significant sector of the Maronite community, from which it drew 80 percent of its membership. Furthermore, there is a direct relationship between the salience of threats to the Lebanese system and party membership; as the threats increased, membership rose, and as the threats declined, so did the number of Kataeb. After the sharp rise in the wake of the counterrevolution, it declined to 48,000 in 1960 and slid down further to 36,000 in 1964, but it jumped again to 63,500 in late 1967 and to 65,000 in 1971 as the perceived Palestinian threat arose. These factors, in addition to the successes the Kataeb had scored through the use of its paramilitary arm in the struggle for independence and in the counterrevolution, encouraged Pierre Gemayel to adopt a more confrontational attitude.

Following the 1967 Arab-Israeli war, the PLO rose to prominence and began operating out of Lebanon as well as Jordan. This invited Israeli retaliatory raids, which were disruptive for Lebanon and, Pierre Gemayel argued, highly counterproductive. Although in principle he supported the right of the Palestinians to wage guerrilla warfare to regain their homeland—after all, Gemayel was an ardent nationalist—he could not accept claims by the PLO to extraterritorial rights, and the infringements by the PLO on Lebanese sovereignty stirred Gemayel into action. Furthermore, the support of sizable sections of the Lebanese public for the PLO was predicated on sentiments of Arab nationalism, which ran counter to the Lebanese nationalism to which Gemayel had dedicated his life. To top it all, these events coincided with the activation of "progressive" leftists trends in the Arab world combined with anti-Western sentiments.

Fear of the emergence of leftist-revolutionary trends among Lebanon's Muslims prompted Gemayel to enter into what came to be known as the Triple Alliance with Camille Chamoun and Raymond Eddé, the two other most prominent Maronite leaders. The alliance lasted from 1967 to 1970. Following an Israeli raid on Beirut airport in which thirteen Lebanese aircraft were destroyed, the Triple Alliance convened a conference in the mountain resort town of Brummana during March 7–9, 1969. Lebanon awaited the outcome of the conference while it seemed as though the country were sitting on a powder keg. The explosion did not come then, although the Triple Alliance threatened to take matters into its own hands and resort to civil disobedience in the face of the incapacitation of the government. Gemayel wrote in *al-Aamal* on May 29, 1969, that "certain political figures in this country were trying to change the Lebanese system and create in its place a socialist state on the model of Syria, Algeria and Iraq. The Alliance will not allow such change to take place." From April to October 1969, friction between the Lebanese army and the PLO led to clashes which gave birth to the Cairo Agreement of November 1969. Gemayel found the agreement, which sanctioned but regulated PLO use of Lebanese territory to carry out raids against

Israel, highly distasteful. Following the eviction of the PLO from Jordan, the organization made Lebanon the base for its operations. The situation deteriorated. Ironically, the attempt by the PLO not to repeat the "mistakes" of 1970 in Jordan led to an equally disasterous outcome.

Gemayel and other Maronite leaders were particularly fearful of a linkup between Lebanese leftist and Arab or Syrian nationalist groups and the military arm of the PLO. The Kataeb assumed the role of guardian of the state and its members came to perceive themselves as vigilantes or auxiliaries. The Kataeb trained and equipped a militia, with the tacit approval and occasional help of the state, in anticipation of a confrontation. In a memorandum to President Suleiman Franjieh in February 1973, Gemayel warned that Marxists were trying to take over the country, adding that "should the state fail in its duty or weaken or hesitate, then, Mr. President, we shall ourselves take action" (Stoakes 1975: 222). Further clashes between the army and the PLO resulted in an amendment to the Cairo Agreement which came to be known as the Melkart Understanding.

The lines were drawn for a confrontation between left and right. On February 25, 1975, an incident took place that some regard as the true beginning of the civil war. A large trawling concern, called Protean and headed by Camille Chamoun, had been granted extensive fishing rights off the Lebanese coast. Fishermen in Sidon demonstrated against the concessions that had been granted to Protean. The fishermen clashed with government troops, and the leader of the demonstration, Maaruf Saad, who was the mayor of Sidon, was mortally wounded. His death touched off violent demonstrations in which Palestinian commandos joined with radical Lebanese militiamen to thwart the Lebanese army. The Kataeb staged noisy demonstrations in support of the army.

A later incident, on April 13, 1975, is more generally accepted as the spark for the civil war. That Sunday, armed men in a speeding car fired on Gemayel's entourage while the Phalangist leader was attending church in the Christian suburb of Ain al-Roumaneh. Gemayel's bodyguard and two others were killed. In retaliation, Kataeb militiamen ambushed a busload of Palestinians and their sympathizers passing through the suburb. Twenty-seven passengers, mostly Palestinians, were killed. Barricades went up in the capital and the fighting started in earnest. The civil war had begun. Gemayel at first refused to surrender those responsible to the authorities, precipitating the resignation of the Cabinet.

The National Movement, led by Kamal Jumblatt, tried to isolate the Kataeb politically. This had the unfortunate result of breaking down communications at a critical juncture. When Karami was finally asked to form a cabinet, neither Gemayel nor Kamal Jumblatt were represented, although they were on the newly formed national dialogue committee. The Kataeb received support from the traditional Maronite leaders, and the National Movement obtained Muslim support. This helped transform the conflict from a political into a sectarian one, and also helped complicate the solution to the problems at hand. Gemayel spoke repeatedly of a communist conspiracy and reaffirmed support for the 1943 National Pact. He voiced opposition to partitioning the country.

Although the Kataeb was doing most of the fighting on the Christian side, Gemayel showed greater willingness to compromise and clearer political vision than his allies. On December 16, following a visit by Gemayel to Damascus, the Kataeb acknowledged in a statement the need for fundamental and comprehensive reform in political, economic, and social matters. It also accepted the Cairo Agreement, but insisted on the return of law and order as a precondition for reform. Gemayel's conciliatory position was overshadowed by his followers' actions: On December 6, Kataeb rank and file massacred two-hundred Muslims in the streets of Beirut in retaliation for the killing of four Kataeb leaders.

The fighting that had been going on in the suburbs spread to the hotel district. Apparently in an attempt to force the entry of the army into the conflict, the Kataeb bombarded and virtually demolished the old commercial center in the capital. This was to have far-reaching implications, as business activity moved to regional centers, helping to bring about the division of the country into areas dominated by sectarian militias. The Kataeb overran the Christian Palestinian refugee camp at Dubai and the slums of Karantina and Maslakh.

On January 31, 1976, Gemayel joined with Chamoun, Franjieh, and Charbil Kassis, the superior of the Maronite Monastic Orders, to form the Front for Freedom and Man in Lebanon. This grandiose title was later simplified to the Lebanese Front. The alliance, however, further reduced the chances of reconciliation as decision making relating to political matters was shared by men with narrower interests and greater intransigence. Already, on November 25 of the previous year, Aasem Qansu, head of the pro-Syrian Baath Party, was quoted in the press as saying that Gemayel and the Kataeb were the victims of Chamoun, Franjieh, and the ultraradical Guardians of the Cedars.

Gemayel also accepted the compromise solution put forward by Syria, which Franjieh announced on February 14, 1976, providing for an even division of seats in Parliament between Muslims and Christians, and the election of the prime minister by Parliament rather than his appointment by the president. This may have been acceptable to traditional Muslim leaders, but it was rejected by the National Movement, which demanded total deconfessionalization (secularization) and kept pressing for a military solution. Syrian military intervention in Lebanon in the summer of 1976 put an end to any hopes of a victory by the National Movement.

Meanwhile, Pierre Gemayel was being eclipsed by his youngest son, Bashir. Bashir had graduated from St. Joseph University with a degree in law and political science in 1971. He was named political director of the Kataeb office in Ashrafieh in 1972. He was deputy commander of the Kataeb militia during the siege of the Palestinian refugee camp of Tal al-Zaater, and was promoted to commander in chief of the Kataeb Military Council on July 13, 1976, when his predecessor was killed in the fighting. Bashir was therefore in command when the camp fell soon thereafter. This was a significant victory that elevated him to national prominence. The battle for Tal al-Zaater also convinced the Christian militias of the need for a unified command structure. When the militias belonging to the

Kataeb, the National Liberal Party, the Guardians of the Cedars, and the Tanzim joined to form the Lebanese Forces, on August 30, 1976, Bashir became head of the Joint Command Council.

Thus Bashir rose to prominence ahead of his elder brother by forming his own power base. Although the Kataeb appeared to dominate the Lebanese Forces, being its largest component, this is misleading. The actual ties between the Lebanese Forces (which were independent) and the Kataeb were often weak or informal. There was also a demographic shift, as more fighters now came from Beirut working-class suburbs rather than from Mt. Lebanon. The Lebanese Forces also included Ansar al-Kataeb, largely consisting of militiamen who had been displaced by the fighting and had an ax of their own to grind. These troops owed direct loyalty to Bashir, not Pierre. An important change had taken place in the structure of command as well. Whereas the old traditional leaders in the Lebanese Front nominally controlled the Lebanese Forces, the young militia commanders in fact made their own decisions, although they paid lip service to their elders. In this sense, Bashir was supreme.

Bashir differed politically from his father and the older generation of leaders in that he was convinced that the National Pact was dead and buried. He said it should not be resurrected, and that it was time to set up a second republic. Bashir was ruthless in eliminating opposition to his authority within Maronite ranks. In 1978 he subdued Franjieh's militia, which resulted in the death of Tony Franjieh, the former president's son. He then took on Chamoun's militia, the Tigers, which he brought into line without much difficulty. He turned to the Israelis for support in an alliance which his father regarded with misgivings but which he accepted as necessary to get the Syrians out of Lebanon. Following the Israeli invasion of 1982, Bashir emerged as the sole candidate for president. He began to distance himself from the extremist positions he had staked out earlier, which were replete with the mystique of the "Christian Resistance." He appeared to be searching for policies that might be acceptable to all Lebanese.

Bashir was elected president by a scant majority of one vote in Parliament on August 23, 1982, but was assassinated on September 14 by an explosion at the Kataeb office in Ashrafieh, which also killed twenty-six others. He was survived by his wife, Solange Toutounji, and one child. Another child, a daughter, died in an earlier failed attempt on Bashir's life. Bashir's followers still revere him and consider him a martyr.

Amin, the eldest son, was elected president with the support of seventy-seven of the eighty parliamentary deputies who attended the session. He enjoyed far broader but less intense support than his brother and this support was to evaporate with time as hope gave way to disappointment.

Amin graduated with a master's degree in law from St. Joseph University in 1966. He opened a law practice and then was elected to Parliament, taking over the seat representing the Metn district that had been vacated by his uncle's death. He was reelected in 1972. Unlike Bashir, he went to the trouble of maintaining good relations with the Muslims, hence the optimism in the early days of his administration. He had also risen primarily in the political rather than the military branch of the Kataeb, having served in the political bureau as well as the militia.

Amin tried to live up to what the Kataeb had always said a president should be, stressing dedication to principle rather than compromise. He tried to reassert presidential power, which the Kataeb had always said had been eroding since independence, but he chose the wrong time to do this, as a strong presidency would have meant victory for one side over the other, and was therefore resisted. Whereas his father had turned to the Syrians for help and his brother to the Israelis, Amin chose the Americans.

Amin depended on U.S. political, economic, and military support to shore up the central government, rebuild the army, and reconstruct the economy. He even concluded an agreement with Israel that, with American help, could have served as the nucleus of a peace treaty. However, his innocence regarding the limits of American interventionism and Syria's ability to oppose the process led to retreat on almost all fronts. He was forced to abrogate the treaty with Israel, lost the Shouf region, and witnessed the disintegration of the army and the redivision of the capital.

Amin Gemayel embarked on a new strategy in 1984, consisting of a rapprochement with Syria, a national unity cabinet at home, government by consensus, and a bid to coopt militia leaders. A package of reforms was envisaged, involving devolution of central authority to elected local councils in the provinces, a one-to-one ratio in Parliament for Muslims and Christians, and a drive to secure the withdrawal of all remaining Israeli forces. The formula did not work. He faced a rebellion by the commander of the Lebanese Forces, Elie Hobeika, who, in a bid to outdo Amin Gemayel, signed an agreement with the Amal and Druze militias in Damascus on December 28. The tripartite agreement provided for constitutional changes including devolution of power from the president to the prime minister, who would be chosen by parliament. Hobeika's gambit failed, and he was ousted.

Amin ended his presidency in September 1988 by appointing the Maronite commander of the army prime minister in view of the inability of the parliament to elect a Maronite president. This left the country with two competing cabinets, since the Sunni prime minister refused to resign in favor of a Maronite. Thus, Amin's presidency, far from constituting a strong central government, brought Lebanon closer to partition than it had ever been.

Pierre Gemayel died on August 29, 1984, from a heart attack. He was serving as a cabinet minister at the time in Rashid Karami's cabinet, trying to shore up support for his son among Maronite ranks and to find a compromise formula that would resurrect the formula for confessional coexistence in Lebanon.

Pierre Gemayel has a list of considerable achievements to his credit, not least of which was building and leading the closest thing to a modern political party in Lebanon. However, he did not appear to realize the dangers he was courting, and the fact that modernization unleashes forces that can get out of control. Perhaps he did not realize the fragility of Lebanon's political system, which depended on cooperation among the elite rather than on strong institutions. He, along with others, also appears to have been the victim of the survival of traditional sectarian orientations and narrow parochial loyalties alongside universal values.

BIBLIOGRAPHY

Work by Gemayel:

Mawaqef wa Ara' 1975–1980 (Positions and Opinions 1975–1980). Beirut: Dar al- Amal Lilnashr, 1982.

Other Works:

Deeb, Marius. *The Lebanese Civil War*. New York: Praeger, 1980.
Entelis, John P. *Pluralism and Party Transformation in Lebanon—Al Kata'ib, 1936– 1970*. Leiden: E. J. Brill, 1974.
Gemayel, Amin. *Peace and Unity, Major Speeches 1982–1984*. Gerrards Cross, Eng.: Colin Smythe Ltd., 1984.
———. "The Price and the Promise." *Foreign Affairs* 63 (Spring 1985): 759–777.
Gemayel, Bashir. "The Liberation of Lebanon." *Middle East Review* 15 (Fall/Winter 1982–1983): 70–74.
———. "Geopolitique au Proche-Orient." *Herodote* no. 29–30 (April/September 1983).
Gilmore, David. *Lebanon, the Fractured Country*. New York: St. Martin's Press, 1983.
Khalidi, Walid. *Conflict and Violence in Lebanon: Confrontation in the Middle East*. Cambridge, Mass.: Harvard University Center for International Affairs, 1984.
Nantet, Jacques. *Pierre Gemayel*. Paris: Editions Jean Claude Lattes, 1986.
Randal, Jonathan C. *Going All the Way: Christian Warlords, Israeli Adventurers and the War in Lebanon*. New York: Viking Press, 1983.
Snider, Lewis W. "The Lebanese Forces: Their Origins and Role in Lebanon's Politics." *The Middle East Journal* 38 (Winter 1984): 1–33.
Stoakes, Frank. "The Supervigilantes: The Lebanese Kataeb Party as a Builder, Surrogate and Defender of the State." *Middle East Studies* 11 (October 1975): 215–236.

JENAB TUTUNJI

H

GEORGE HABASH (1926-   ). The story of George Habash largely reflects the unfolding of Palestinian political history between 1948 and 1988. For the two decades following the establishment of Israel, Habash, like many other Palestinians, entrusted the Arab regimes with the task of liberating Palestine. However, after the Arab countries' defeat in the June 1967 war, he formed the Popular Front for the Liberation of Palestine (PFLP), with its strategy of popular warfare and its Marxist-Leninist leaning. By 1988, Habash endorsed the establishment of an independent Palestinian state in the West Bank and Gaza Strip and the convening of an international conference for the resolution of the Arab-Israeli conflict.

George Habash, the leader of the PFLP, was born in Lidda, Palestine, to a middle-income Greek-Orthodox family in 1926. His father was a grain merchant. Habash attended high school in Jerusalem, where his academic performance was outstanding. In fact, he was one of ten students to receive a scholarship to the American University of Beirut (AUB) in 1936. After earning a bachelor of science degree in biology, he joined AUB's medical school in 1944. Seven years later he graduated as a medical doctor. The exodus of his family after the establishment of Israel in 1948 compelled the young Habash to become involved in politics.

Between 1948 and 1951 he became active in the Firm Tie society, a literary organization at AUB. During those years, Habash came in contact with two of his closest future associates: Hani al-Hindi, a Syrian Arab nationalist, and Wadi Haddad, a Palestinian Christian and the mastermind of the Palestinian aircraft hijackings in the late 1960s and early 1970s. Together with other Arab intellectuals, in the early 1950s the three men formed the Arab Nationalist Movement (ANM). The ANM advocated Arab unity, anticolonialism, and the reconstruction of Arab Palestine. The ANM also extended support to Egypt's president Gamal Abdul Nasser.* Habash and his colleagues believed that Nasser held the key for uniting the Arab world and liberating Palestine.

In 1956 Habash moved to Jordan and opened a clinic for the free treatment of the poor in Amman. His political agitation, however, led to his arrest by the government in 1957; after his release, Habash went to Damascus where he opened a similar clinic. However, in 1963 he was expelled to Lebanon. Habash's strong pro-Nasser stands were behind the expulsion order.

By 1964, signs of disunity within the ANM surfaced. A left-wing trend led by Wadi Haddad and Muhsen Ibrahim, a Lebanese Arab nationalist, was crystallizing. The collapse of the United Arab Republic of Syria and Egypt in 1961 and Nasser's failure to check Israel's plan to divert the Jordan River in 1964 weakened the faith of the ANM younger generation in the Egyptian president's ability to unite the Arab world. The launching by Fatah (Yasser Arafat's* own organization within the PLO) of military operations against Israel was an additional sign of their increasing disillusionment of Nasser's leadership. To conquer such challenges, Nasser established the PLO as a vehicle to buttress his influence throughout the Arab world in general and among the Palestinians in particular.

In response to these developments, Habash did not think at the time that independent Palestinian military action was a viable option. The Palestinians were not strong enough to liberate their land. Habash continued to believe that the recovery of Palestine was a collective Arab responsibility entrusted to Arab conventional armies, and that Nasser held the key for the liberation of Palestine.

Despite his unshaken belief in Nasser, Habash did not ignore the challenges resulting from the rise of a left wing within the ANM, the establishment of the PLO, and the Fatah military operations. Those events prompted Habash to establish the National Front for the Liberation of Palestine (NFLP) as a separate grouping within the ANM. The NFLP was not intended to be a substitute for the Arab collective war efforts or for Palestinian mass mobilization. The infrequency and irregularity of the National Front's military operations inside Israel prior to 1967 pointed to Habash's belief in the superiority of the Arab standing armies.

The shattering military defeat of the Arab armies by Israel in the June 1967 war brought about a fundamental change in Habash's political thinking. The defeat of the armies of Egypt, Syria, and Jordan, and the loss of significant territories to Israel dissipated Habash's old illusions about the capacity of those regimes to reconstruct Arab Palestine. On the contrary, these very same governments were perceived by Habash as a threat and as an obstacle to the Palestinian struggle against Israel.

One of the primary manifestations of Habash's intellectual transformation was his adoption of Marxism-Leninism. In the few months after the June 1967 war, Habash believed that a political and social revolution in the Arab world was a precondition to the liberation of Palestine. He contended that a guerrilla warfare modelled after the Viet Cong experience in South Vietnam, class struggle, the presence of a strong political party, mass mobilization, and self-reliance made up the linchpin for the revolutionary transformation of the Arab world. According to Habash, the workers and the peasants constituted the core of the new ''revolution.'' These two groups were expected to lead the Palestinians in a military struggle and to formulate the revolution's political and military program.

While assigning a major role for the workers and the peasants, Habash was also careful not to alienate the sizable Palestinian petit bourgeoisie. However; in view of the vacillating nature of this class, Habash did not give it any prominent role in the struggle or in the formation of the political ideology and program of the revolution.

Habash identified four enemies confronting the Palestinian people: Zionism, imperialism, Arab reactionary regimes, and, to a lesser extent, the Arab petit-bourgeoisie government of Syria and Egypt. By contrast, he regarded the communist countries, the Third World national liberation movements, and radical groups in the West as the natural allies for the radical Palestinians. The governments of Jordan and Saudi Arabia were particularly subjected to bitter denunciation and were regarded as agents for imperialism and enemies of the Palestinian armed struggle. Thus, the toppling of such governments came to be a primary task for Habash's new revolution. It was for this reason that Habash and his followers sought a military showdown with King Hussein ibn Talal* of Jordan in September of 1970.

Though Habash did not treat Egypt and Syria with the same degree of hostility, he considered the two governments as petit-bourgeoisie regimes and asserted that Nasserism was not a revolutionary regime but rather a reformist movement. Habash was particularly critical of the Syrian government for its refusal to allow the Palestinian commandos to attack Israel from within Syria. His deteriorating relationship with the Syrian government led to his imprisonment between February and November of 1968.

According to Habash, not all the Arab regimes were hostile to the Palestinian commando groups. Libya, Iraq, South Yemen, and Algeria were said to be progressive governments and supportive of the Palestinian military struggle. The ideological orientation of these four countries was also close to the ideology of the working class.

Between 1967 and 1973, Habash tried to translate his revolutionary rhetoric into tangible actions. He first sought to unite the different existing Palestinian commando groups. In December of 1967, Habash formed the Popular Front for the Liberation of Palestine (PFLP) from three separate groupings: the Heroes of Return, the Youth for Revenge, and the National Front for the Liberation of Palestine. In February of 1968, the leader of the PFLP met with Khalil al-Wazir from Fatah to unite the fighting forces of their two organizations. However, the reluctance of the PFLP to fight in the al-Karameh battle on the east bank of the Jordan against the Israeli army in March of 1968 and the growing rivalry between Fatah and the PFLP kept the two organizations apart.

In August of 1968, the PFLP introduced the technique of hijacking civilian aircraft in their fight against Israel, the West, and the conservative Arab governments. Habash's longtime associate, Wadi Haddad, was the architect of the hijackings. Initially, the PFLP followers attacked Israeli civilian planes on the grounds that these were used to transport Israeli soldiers and military equipment. In 1969 and 1970, the hijackings were extended to include West European and American carriers. The attack on such airplanes was in part carried out to protest American and West European support to Israel and in part to obtain the release of PFLP prisoners from European jails. Habash claimed that his organization did not aim to harm civilians but to publicize the Palestinian cause.

Aside from these justifications, considerations of power politics were also behind Habash's organization's involvement in airline hijacking. The growing rivalry between Habash and Yasser Arafat for the control of the Palestine Nationalist Movement was one of these political considerations. The publicity and visibility associated with each of these hijackings increased the credibility and the prestige of the PFLP among the Arab and Palestinian masses alike. Coming at the heel of the 1967 defeat, the PFLP's hijacking found an emotional appeal among many Palestinians.

By the early 1970s, the usefulness of Habash's revolutionary rhetoric was seriously questioned. Using Jordan as a staging ground for the PFLP's military operations led ultimately to a major military confrontation with the Jordanian army in September of 1970 and to the expulsion of the PLO's troops from Jordan in the summer of 1971. Prior to these events, Habash was certain that his followers, equipped with their revolutionary slogans, would topple King Hussein's regime. He hoped that in the case of any major confrontation to the Jordanian army, the progressive Arab countries would come to his aid. He was also confidant that the Jordanian soldiers of Palestinian origin would side with their fellow Palestinians within the PLO. None of these expectations, however, came to fruition.

Aside from this, Habash's PFLP was subjected to a number of splits soon after its formation. In October of 1968, Ahmad Jabril, a Palestinian who served as an officer in the Syrian army, broke away from the PFLP and formed the Popular Front for the Liberation of Palestine-General Command (PFLP-GC). In February of 1969, another split occurred when Nayef Hawatma, a Jordanian and a longtime associate of Habash, founded the Democratic Front for the Liberation of Palestine (DFLP).

Despite the publicity that the hijackings brought to Habash's PFLP, in the long run such activities proved to be counterproductive and harmful. The hijacking of Israeli and Western aircraft to Jordan, Egypt, Syria, and Algeria was very embarrassing to the governments of these countries. Such activities compelled King Hussein to eventually terminate the Palestinian military presence in his country without any serious opposition from the Arab states.

The PFLP's hijackings also increased the tension within the PLO and deepened the gap between Habash and Arafat. Even within the PFLP itself, some voices began to question the usefulness of hijackings, arguing that such a technique was not a Marxist revolutionary tactic. During the third convention of the PFLP in March 1972, Habash himself acknowledged that hijacking was counterproductive. Nonetheless, Wadi Haddad, who was in charge of the PFLP's external military operations, continued such terrorist activities.

As a consequence of its overemphasis on Marxism-Leninism, Habash's PFLP did not enjoy a wide following. Habash's adherents consisted mainly of discontented intellectuals and professionals. His Marxist orientation was incompatible with the dictates of Islam and Arab nationalism. In this context, Arafat's narrow focus on Palestinian nationalism was more mundane than Habash's sophisticated Marxist thinking. Indeed, in 1974 Arafat's pragmatism won him Arab recognition and endorsement at the expense of the more radical Habash.

Habash failed to translate the slogan of people's warfare into long-term, sustainable political gains. His revolutionary slogans neither liberated Palestine nor toppled the Arab regimes. On the contrary, the rise of Habash and other Palestinian radicals brought about an alliance between Nasser and his former adversaries in Jordan and Saudi Arabia.

Finally, the political, military, and economic outcomes of the 1973 October War further diminished Habash's new thinking. The war restored to the Arabs their fighting honor and dignity, and proved that the initiative for the resolution of the Palestinian question was the prerogative of the Arab governments. The vast economic opportunities that were brought about by the increase in the price of Arab oil lured young Arabs and Palestinians alike away from Marxism.

Following the 1973 October War, it was widely believed that a diplomatic solution to the Palestinian question was possible. This optimistic reading of the situation required some basic adjustments in Palestinian traditional stands. The convening of an international peace conference, the establishment of the West Bank–Gaza Strip Palestinian state, and the reconciliation between Jordan and the PLO were necessary moves for such a diplomatic solution.

Habash and his followers refused to change their attitudes with regard to these issues. They did not believe that the October War had changed the balance of power in the Middle East in favor of the Palestinians. For this reason, the PLO's participation in an international peace conference would not serve the interests of the Palestinians. What was worse from Habash's perspective was the fact that such an international conference would be convened in accordance with United Nations Security Council Resolutions 242 and 338. He opposed both resolutions because they called for the recognition of Israel within secured borders. In his opinion the continuation of military struggle should be the only course of action open to the PLO.

Habash was also opposed to the formation of a West Bank–Gaza state and to any reconciliation with Jordan. He linked an improvement of relations with Jordan to the downfall of the monarchy and the establishment of a democratic nationalist regime. Habash's views were in sharp contrast with the efforts of the majority of the Arab countries to bring about reconciliation between Jordan and the PLO.

Despite the compromise resolution of the twelfth session of the Palestine National Council (PNC) concerning the establishment of "a national authority" on any "liberated part of Palestine," Habash rejected the establishment of a "ministate" in the occupied territories. He remained committed to the goal of establishing a secular democratic state in all of Palestine.

Habash's opposition to such a small state rested on a number of grounds. First, the establishment of such an authority would mean making peace with Israel and the cessation of military struggle. Second, such a state in the occupied territories would be "reactionary" because of its close ties with the conservative Arab regimes and the "imperialists." Third, in view of the poor economic resources of the West Bank and Gaza, the economic viability of such a state was highly questionable. Finally, Habash's objection to the proposal of a Palestinian state was motivated by his fear that such a solution would not address the grievances and rights of those Palestinians who had lost their land in 1948.

Habash's opposition to the creation of a national authority was not an absolute one. The formation of a "revolutionary authority" that would not come about as a result of a diplomatic solution but rather from the pursuit of military struggle was acceptable. The goal of such an authority would be the establishment of a secular state in all of Palestine through the continuation of military struggle.

To register his opposition to any Palestinian participation in an international peace conference, the formation of a West Bank–Gaza state, or the normalization of relations with Jordan, Habash withdrew his representatives from the PLO executive committee and the central council on September 26, 1974.

Together with the pro-Iraq Arab Liberation Front, the PFLP-GC, and the Popular Struggle Front, Habash's PFLP formed the Rejectionist Front. The four organizations pledged to work toward correcting Arafat's "deviationist" policies. The Rejectionist Front lasted from 1974 to 1978. During this period, Habash presented a challenge to Arafat's diplomatic moves. This was the second time after the 1968–1970 period that the leader of the PFLP seriously opposed Arafat's leadership of the PLO.

However, the late 1970s witnessed a number of developments that led to a limited reconciliation between Arafat and Habash in 1979. The 1975–1976 Lebanese Civil War, the coming to power of the Likud bloc as a result of the 1977 Parliamentary elections in Israel, and the signing of the Camp David Accords and the Egypt-Israel Peace Treaty in 1978–1979, facilitated the normalization between Arafat and Habash. During the fifteenth session of the PNC in 1981, the PFLP representatives rejoined the PLO's Executive Committee and Central Council.

Following Israel's invasion of Lebanon and the dispersal of the PLO's troops to several Arab countries in 1982, Habash chose Damascus as the new headquarters for his organization. Between 1982 and 1985, fundamental differences arose between Habash and Arafat concerning the many issues that confronted the PLO. Habash differed with Arafat over the significance of Ronald Reagan's initiative, diplomatic coordination with Jordan, and reconciliation with Egypt. Despite the presence of such differences, Habash sought to maintain the unity of the PLO.

Habash gave a categorical rejection to the Reagan initiative, regarding it as an extension of the Camp David Accords. He denounced the initiative for its refusal to appropriate any role for the PLO and for its opposition to the establishment of a Palestinian state. In a Radio Monte Carlo interview on April 8, 1983, Habash criticized the Reagan Initiative when he asked: "Will it realize our rights of return, self-determination, and the formation of an independent Palestinian state? The answer is clear. . . . If we accept the Reagan plan will the land come back to us, will settlements stop? Why don't we then learn from the history and the truth behind the Zionist movement?"

Habash also opposed the Jordanian-PLO dialogue, which aimed at finding a diplomatic solution to the Palestinian problem through the confederation of a future West Bank–Palestinian entity with Jordan. He appealed to Arafat to make a categorical rejection of the Reagan plan and to end his dialogue with King Hussein in favor of the continuation of military struggle and the gathering of the dispersed PLO groups into Lebanon.

The improvement of the PLO's relationship with Syria was by far a more important task for Habash than the dialogue with King Hussein. Syria's proximity to Israel and its support of the Palestinian cause were valuable assets to the PLO in its war against Israel. The withdrawal of PLO forces from Lebanon after 1982 made it mandatory to establish close ties between the PLO and Syria. In this context, Habash warned that the Palestinian revolution could not afford to become a "refugee revolution."

Habash adopted a neutral stand concerning the split that took place inside Fatah in the spring of 1983. He called on Arafat and his opponents within Fatah to reconcile their differences through peaceful means. Habash accepted the demand by Fatah rebels to introduce reforms into the PLO.

In the wake of the growing rift between Arafat and Syria, and Arafat's expulsion from Damascus in June of 1983, Habash coordinated his political stands with Nayef Hawatma, the leader of the Democratic Front. Under the auspices of Syria, a joint leadership for the two organizations was established on June 26, 1983. In October 1984, the unity between the two fronts broke up in view of Habash's unyielding opposition to Arafat's effort to convene the seventeenth session of the Palestine National Council (PNC).

The convening of the PNC in Amman in November 1984 against Habash's wishes, and the subsequent signing of a joint agreement between Arafat and Hussein for joint diplomatic coordination in February of 1985 further deepened the opposition of the PFLP's leader to Arafat. Habash condemned both moves and demanded the ousting of the PLO's chairman. Habash was particularly apprehensive of the Arafat-Hussein agreements calling for a confederation of the occupied territories with Jordan and the formation of a joint Jordanian-Palestinian negotiating team. In his opinion, these two provisions conceded the PLO's exclusive role of representing Palestinian interests and compromised the Palestinians' right to return and form an independent state. Habash contended that the accords transformed the Palestinian question into a Jordanian internal matter and a question of borders between Israel and Jordan. In an interview with the BBC Arabic Service on February 14, 1985, he described the accords as a "dangerous and a qualitative turning point in the path of liquidationist solutions and a serious deviation from the nationalist course of the revolution."

Together with the PFLP-GC, the Popular Struggle Front, al-Saiqa, and Fatah dissidents, Habash formed the Palestine National Salvation Front in Damascus on February 22, 1985. With the support of Syria, the front posed itself as an alternative to Arafat's leadership of the PLO. However, the suspension by King Hussein of his dialogue with Arafat in February of 1986, Arafat's abrogation of his agreement with King Hussein in April of 1987, and the convening of the eighteenth session of the PNC in Algiers during the same month led to a reconciliation between Habash and Arafat. Habash accepted the PNC's resolutions, which called for the formation of an independent West Bank–Gaza Palestinian state, the convening of an international peace conference to resolve the Arab-Israeli dispute, and the PLO's participation in such a conference. The uprising that erupted in the occupied territories in 1987–1988 further improved relations between Arafat and Habash. Following King Hussein's severance of legal and administrative ties between Jordan and the West Bank, Habash favored the establishment of a Palestinian government in exile to fill the political vacuum.

Despite the limited size of his organization within the Palestinian Nationalist Movement, Habash's presence left a deep imprint on the PLO's policies and orientation. Though he was unable to impose his ideas on the PLO as a whole, Habash along with Hawatma constituted the real political opposition within the Palestinian Nationalist Movement. Both men served as a system of checks and balances inside the PLO's political institutions, modifying and even obstructing the endorsement of undesirable policies by Arafat.

The support Habash enjoyed among Palestinian and Arab intellectuals, the support that his organization received from Palestinian refugee camps in Lebanon, and his own charismatic leadership accounted for the PFLP's political weight within the larger Palestinian National Movement. These three factors allowed the PFLP to wield an influence within the PLO that was incommensurate with its numerical size.

Despite his numerous challenges to Arafat's policies and leadership, the outside threats to the PLO's integrity always compelled Habash to reconcile with Arafat to preserve the unity of the Palestinians. Habash's challenge was also attenuated over the years by a number of advantages that Arafat enjoyed. Arafat's narrow focus on Palestinian nationalism, his organization's superior capabilities, and his overall Arab and Palestinian legitimacy gave Fatah a decisive edge over the PFLP. Furthermore, Habash's Christian background and his radical slogans further limited the appeal of the PFLP.

Habash's constant emphasis on ideological issues made him the leading theoretician of the Palestinian Left. Despite this it is wrong to assume that the leader of the PFLP remained rigid in his political stands. The Habash of the late 1980s is not the same revolutionary Habash of the late 1960s. By the late 1980s, Habash had accepted, although reluctantly, the formation of a West Bank–Gaza state and the PLO's participation in an international peace conference. Such political stands had been unthinkable a decade and a half earlier.

BIBLIOGRAPHY

Ajami, Fouad. *The Arab Predicament: Arab Political Thought and Practice since 1967.* Cambridge: Cambridge University Press, 1981.

Becker, Jillian. *The PLO: The Rise and Fall of the Palestine Liberation Organization.* New York: St. Martin's Press, 1984.

Ben-Rafael, Eliezer. *Israel-Palestine: A Guerrilla Conflict in International Politics.* New York: Greenwood Press, 1987.

Cobban, Helena. *The PLO: People, Power and Politics.* Cambridge: Cambridge University Press, 1984.

Cooley, John J. *Green March: Black September and the Story of the Palestinian Arabs.* London: Cass, 1973.

Gresh, Alain. *The PLO, the Struggle Within: Towards an Independent Palestinian State.* Trans. A. M. Berrett. London: Zed Books, 1985.

Muslih, Muhammad Y. "Moderates and Rejectionists within the Palestine Liberation Organization." *Middle East Journal* 30 (Spring 1976): 127–140.

Sahliyeh, Emile F. *The PLO after the Lebanon War.* Boulder, Colo.: Westview Press, 1986.

EMILE SAHLIYEH

HASSAN II (1929–   ). King Hassan II of Morocco (Moulay al-Hassan ben Mohammed al-Alaoui) was born in the Royal Palace in Rabat on July 9, 1929. He was the first son of the Moroccan monarch Mohammed V* and Lalla Abla, and was named for his great-grandfather, Hassan I (ruled 1873–1894). Hassan's father had become sultan of the Sharifian Empire, which was then ruled as a French protectorate, in 1927. Upon the death of his father, Crown Prince Hassan became king of Morocco on March 3, 1961. As the head of state in a country strong in its sense of identity and traditions, Hassan's reign has witnessed the emergence of Morocco as a dynamic regional power. Hassan, who sees Morocco as a bridge between East and West, has jealously advanced Morocco's interests. He has welded the territory of the Spanish Sahara to Morocco—a matter that has yet to be resolved. Hassan survived dramatic attempts on his life in 1971 and 1972, has weathered occasional storms of domestic unrest, and has created a distinctive parliamentary system that retains broad everyday power and, ultimately, all the power in the throne. By virtue of his sense of duty, his deep sense of loyalty to his people, his long reign, his skills as an orator and politician, and his ability to cloak the exigencies of the present in the mystique of the past, Hassan plays the rare role of the successful and powerful twentieth-century monarch.

Hassan's career as king began with his childhood education. His personality, often described as forceful, bold, and innovative, was forged by the emerging realities of the Morocco of his youth. Hassan was schooled in the Rabat Royal

Palace by French and Moroccan governesses and tutors. His father organized traditional religious training for him by establishing a koranic school in the Palace. The Imperial College, founded in Rabat in 1942, brought together a select group of Moroccan youth, including Hassan's brother Moulay Abdullah and his sisters, for Hassan's secondary education. In 1948, Hassan enrolled at the Centre d'Etudes Juridiques et d'Economie Politique in Rabat and in his November 18, 1952, Throne Day speech, Mohammed V announced that Hassan had received his law degree from Bordeaux.

Hassan's public life can be traced to August 1931, when his father took him on a month-long tour of France that was organized around the Paris Colonial Exposition. At age five, Hassan was baptized ''Prince of the Atlas'' as ceremonial head of the Moroccan Boy Scouts—a group that was to play an understated role in the independence movement. Hassan was in attendance at the first World War II encounter between Franklin Roosevelt and Winston Churchill in Anfa, a Casablanca suburb, in January 1943.

Although Hassan was to play a role in the Moroccan independence movement, it was a role performed in the large shadow of his father and other political leaders who were instrumental in achieving independence through the work of the Istiqlal (Independence) Party. Founded in December 1943 with the declaration of an independence manifesto, the Istiqlal became the main organizing body in the independence movement; the Alaouite throne subsequently became the symbolic representation of Moroccan independence. As such, the part played by the sultan and his family cannot be overestimated. Particularly important in developing antagonisms between the French rulers of the Moroccan Protectorate and the Moroccan population was the sudden exile of the royal family. Accused of fomenting revolution against the French, the sultan and his family were exiled on August 20, 1953, first to Corsica, and from January 1954 until October 1955 to Madagascar. French attempts to create a new sultan out of Mohammed Ben Arafa al Alaoui in connivance with the pasha of Marrakech, Thami al Glaoui, was a disaster for the protectorate. Serving as his father's secretary throughout the period of exile to Madagascar became a time of testing Hassan's maturity.

As the French came to realize they had made a profound mistake by exiling the repository of Moroccan tradition, the shaky attempts to legitimize their substitute Moroccan leaders began to fall apart and the Liberation Army began to rise up in the countryside. When the government of Edgar Faure came to power in February 1955, new perspectives on Morocco came into play, and a series of events cascaded the country toward full independence. Mohammed V and Hassan were returned to France on November 1; the principle of Moroccan independence was established on November 6; and the sultan and his family reentered Morocco in triumph on November 16. Mohammed V formed the first Moroccan government in December 1955, and independence was officially declared on March 2, 1956. Hassan was twenty-six.

Hassan thus grew to manhood within the French colonial experience. His country had undergone dramatic and lasting transformations in a single generation, the essence of which were the imprint of French methods of education and administration, and the enduring legacy of French economic links. His thought had been hewn by French critical thinking. At the same time, the sense of a united Arab World had been given substance by the rise of Nasserism and the Arab League—movements that fascinated some in the struggle for Moroccan independence, but held no attraction for the Alaoui family. Hassan's later international policies, often cast in the light of geostrategic thinking, reflect a relentlessly logical mind. Hassan has a side to him that radiates rationality and a sense of progress, yet, much like the country he came to represent, Hassan retains a strong sense of Moroccan traditions and its a personal exponent of Islamic values. Hassan is thus full of seeming contradictions and ambiquities, an individual with qualities much like the arbitrary categories often ascribed to Morocco, with its "modern" and "traditional" sectors. He is, however, no split personality. Hassan has emerged, like many successful Moroccans of his generation, with an ability to span the divergent philosophies available to him. As king, Hassan is a person unable to ignore the challenges of his age.

In the first years of independent Morocco, Hassan's public image was better known in the rarefied atmosphere of the Morocco that was a playground for the international set than in the Morocco that was a needy nonaligned country set adrift by the French in their effort to save Algeria and her one million French settlers. However, Hassan was occupied by serious work. Entrusted with organizing the Royal Armed Forces (FAR) in 1956 and officially named crown prince by his father in 1957, Hassan led the FAR (which many called "Hassan's Boys") into battle in eastern Morocco and the Tafilalt to quell rebellions that had emerged over who was to run the country—the Istiqlal or the throne. In April 1958, Hassan took the FAR into the newly liberated southern zone of Tarfaya. Rebels in the Rif were crushed by February 1959. He spearheaded relief efforts following the Agadir earthquake in February 1960. In the welter of postindependence politics, Mohammed V named him deputy premier in May 1960. Hassan headed the Moroccan delegation to the UN General Assembly in the fall of 1960, during which he met with Khrushchev. Hassan's "procommunist" votes on China, the Congo, and Cuba attracted Western attention. Soviet President Leonid Brezhnev's 1961 visit resulted in the cementing of relations between Morocco and the Soviet Union. Western diplomats saw Hassan in this period as pursuing a calculated policy aimed at appeasing left-wing opposition at home and improving Morocco's position in the African and Middle Eastern political arenas. At home, Hassan's successes under the guardianship of his father served to enhance his reputation and provided a springboard for his sudden accession to the throne.

After five years as head of independent Morocco, Mohammed V died on February 26, 1961. At age thirty-two, Hassan ascended the throne on March 3, a day since celebrated as Throne Day. Apprenticed to the office by his father, Hassan's enthronation was unchallenged in Morocco. The legitimacy of the Alaouite monarch is solid. Hassan is the twenty-first Alaoui to rule Morocco and a thirty-fifth-generation descendant of the Prophet Mohammed. The Alaoui family descends from the Prophet through Ali, the Prophet's cousin and, as husband of Fatima, the Prophet's daughter, the Prophet's son-in-law as well. They are thus "Alaoui"—through Ali. The Moroccan Alaoui hearth is the southeastern region of the country, the Tafilalt, and the Alaoui consider the town of Rissani (adjacent to the ruins of Sijilmassa) their ancestral home. As descendants of the Prophet, the Alaouis are a *shorfa* (honorable) family; their male members carry the honorific first name "Moulay" as a token of their shorfa status. Hassan is a ninth-generation descendant of the first Alaoui to rule over Morocco, Moulay Rachid (1666–1672). Through the Alaouis' status as shorfa, Morocco was traditionally identified as the Sharifian Kingdom, and the word *sharif* (descendant of the Prophet) is associated with many elements of royal life.

Other components of Hassan's makeup link him to the Islamic community more broadly. He, like all Alaouite monarchs, is considered the "Commander of the Believers" (*amir al-muminin*), a protocollary title of the caliphs of early Islam employed by the dynasties of Morocco since the Marinids took on the title in the 1300s. In this sense, the king of Morocco is also the head of faith of his subjects; Hassan actively fills the role of religious head of state. He combines his political and spiritual functions freely, appearing frequently in public as the spiritual leader of his people. The annual "Ceremony of Allegiance" (*bayaa*) on March 4—the day after Throne Day—illustrates the potent spiritual role played by Hassan. Allegiance to the king is renewed publicly by thousands of Moroccan notables in a ceremony recognizing both his secular and his sacred qualities. What is truly remarkable is Hassan's ability to reinvigorate such traditional ceremonies, and in so doing, reinforce his power and legitimacy in an age in which unmitigated monarchs have become virtually extinct. Hassan's talents in making use of the past to serve the present are keys to understanding not only the nature of his rule, but Morocco itself.

Hassan's rule can be characterized as dominated by a series of protracted issues—most notably the development of a parliamentary system and the incorporation of the Spanish Sahara—that have been punctuated by dramatic events: major public demonstrations in 1965, 1981, and 1984; and attempts on his life and the throne in 1971 and 1972. Other issues—such as Maghribi state relations, the Moroccan role in the Arab-Israeli conflict, the place of the French in the Moroccan economy and of French language in the schools and administration, and corruption in public life—have played distinctly subordinate roles in the Moroccan drama. Underlying them all is the broader sweep of social forces in the country: strong demographic growth, rapid urbanization, rural-urban migration, and un- and underemployment, worker migration overseas, rising aspirations, and the development of the social and economic infrastructure. The impact of the prolonged drought of the 1980s might equally be added to this list. Nonetheless, Morocco has been a largely successful country since 1961, with a general sense of public progress over the period. Cries of doom over the compound nature of Morocco's problems have been allayed, or at least successfully postponed. Morocco ranks poorly in many economic and social indices, but Moroccans point to tangible improvements in their lives and recognize that tremendous strides have been made since their independence. The stability brought to Moroccan life through the long rule of Hassan II is directly responsible. Hassan has played the part of the classical "good" king in that he has created conditions that have allowed Moroccan life to flourish. He is, however, every inch an autocrat. Despite the conservatism and rigidity of the Moroccan political system and large areas that lie out of bounds—such as criticism of the king and the concept of the monarchy—the allegiance and enthusiasm shown Hassan are genuine. However the intensity of such feelings ebbs and flows with the currents of Moroccan life, and there have been times when Hassan's stock has been life-threateningly low.

In an interview with *Le Nouvel Observateur* (April 4, 1986), Hassan stated that "the first duty of a head of state, his most elementary duty, is to neutralize his country's adversaries to the maximum and to gain for himself the maximum number of friends." This sentiment is echoed not only in Hassan's foreign policy, but in his orchestration of domestic policies as well.

The search for a parliamentary system, rooted in the participation of political parties that have evolved from the Istiqlal and from the king's own interests, has occupied center stage in Hassan's ongoing search for a system that fits both his needs and aspirations and those of his country. Initiated from the throne, the system is premised on preserving the king's power and ensuring the accession to power of the next Alaouite generation. Hassan's first step toward parliamentarianism was the promulgation of a constitution in 1962. Since Mohammed V's dismissal of his ministers on the basis of political demagoguery in May 1960, government had been personally directed from the throne. The constitution and the December 1962 referendum endorsing it were opposed by the opposition party, the UNFP (Union Nationale des Forces Populaires, founded in 1959 by Hassan's former math teacher at the Imperial College, Mehdi Ben Barka, as a left-wing offshoot of the Istiqlal), and the UMT (Union Marocaine de Travail, founded in 1955 as the first distinctly Moroccan labor union). Another party, the Mouvement Populaire (MP), was founded by Mahjoubi Ahardane in 1957 and is commonly referred to as the Berber Party due to its close association with rural issues and the Berber population. The constitution, written by Hassan and his staff—in particular Ahmed Reda Guedira, his long-time right-hand man—preserved most of the prerogatives of the king and continued his right to name and dismiss the prime minister and ministers of state, although they had to be drawn from within the Parliament. Overall law-making responsibilities were vested in the Parliament through the prime minister, thus diluting Hassan's power.

The elections of May 1963 resulted in a split between the Istiqlal, the UNFP, and the Front pour la Défense des Intérêts Constitutionelles (FDIC), a party founded only two months earlier to represent the king's interests and forestall an Istiqlal victory. In any event, the FDIC failed to win a majority, seven of the nine government ministers lost, and a delicate game of ruling through coalition governments ensued in which a number of cabinets designed by Parliament proved ineffective. During this period, while Hassan began to strengthen his base among local-level rural leaders, the hierarchy of traditional tribal leaders including the *muqaddems* and *sheikhs*, who lay outside the modern administrative apparatus. Hassan's failed gambit with a constitutional monarchy was thus balanced by developing support for the throne in the countryside.

On evidence that has never been made public, Hassan had 130 Casablanca UNFP leaders arrested on July 16, 1963, for organizing a plot against the throne. Among those sentenced in March 1964 was the parliamentarian-in-exile Mehdi Ben Barka. Ben Barka, whose UNFP had called for land reform and whose impulses were essentially antimonarchical, had fled the country following the 1963 arrests. He was thus tried and sentenced to death in absentia. Unlike those who had remained in Morocco and were pardoned by Hassan at the time of the Aid al-Kabir feast in April 1965, Mehdi Ben Barka remained a thorn in the king's side. In one of the more intriguing episodes of modern Moroccan history, it appears that Hassan's interior minister, Mohammed Oufkir (a Berber World-War-II veteran who had been Hassan's bodyguard during the exile to Madagascar), and his head of state security, Ahmed Dlimi, arranged with the Paris police and French secret services to lure Ben Barka from Geneva to a house in the Paris suburbs where the former head of the UNFP was tortured and murdered by Oufkir and Dlimi. The role played by Jacques Foccart, French minister of state for African affairs, as the go-between for Hassan's henchmen and the French police, was never elucidated; in the Paris trial that followed, in November 1966, little light was shed on the affair. Hassan refused to extradite Oufkir so that he could testify; Dlimi appeared so late that a new trial—which was never held— was ordered. De Gaulle—often cited as Hassan's role model—was so angered by "l'affaire ben Barka" that relations were broken with Rabat and not restored until the month following De Gaulle's death in November 1970. The resultant loss of French foreign aid was a severe blow for Hassan, and the king turned to the United States for economic, military, and food aid. Some have suggested that Ben Barka was eliminated because he had simply gone too far, had refused to play the Rabat game of politics within the limits set by Hassan, and, perhaps most importantly, had refused to apologize for his actions.

A low-intensity border war with independent Algeria broke out in October of 1963 (the War of the Sands), resonating with the same ideological differences between Hassan's Morocco and socialist Algeria that have bedeviled their relationship over most of the postcolonial period. When Parliament first convened in November 1963, it met in an atmosphere in which the king's prestige had been enhanced by his conduct of the border war and in which the inherent weaknesses of the Parliament were to prove inescapable. Finally, following riots in Casablanca, Fez, and Marrakech in March 1965, Hassan suspended (but did not dissolve) Parliament in June. Pulled between liberal tendencies and authoritarian impulses, Hassan's first round of experimentation with parliamentarianism was over. He ruled through declaration of a state of emergency until 1970. Political activity came to a halt. Hassan appointed a new government and issued a three-year economic plan the day after he suspended Parliament. In March 1968, Hassan revived a form of representation employed by his father: a consultative assembly appointed by royal decree.

In search of direct support from the population, Hassan's government issued a new constitution in 1970; again, it was voted on in a national referendum and, this time, both the Istiqlal and the UNFP boycotted it and the subsequent parliamentary elections by forming a united "National Front" of opposition in reaction to the nonconsultative nature of the constitutional process. They failed in this effort, foiled by Hassan's reliance on a broad array of "independents"— politicians who were often UNFP or Istiqlal members but who had been encouraged to run on tickets representing the throne. In this instance, the legislature was reduced to a unicameral house, and a high voter turnout elected a two-thirds majority of "independents"—representatives friendly to the king. The 1970 constitution broadened the powers of the king by making him the supreme representative of the nation, thereby placing him above the legislature and granting him wide powers to govern by decree. The constitution further allowed the king to send a bill back to the House for a second reading on his own authority and forbade any debate on royal pronouncements. Parliament met from October 1970 until December 1971. Hassan's third constitution—by which Morocco has been ruled since—was promulgated on March 15, 1972. It enlarged the number of representatives elected by popular vote from one half to two thirds. No parliamentary elections were held, however, until a spirit of renewed political cooperation and liberalization of public life took hold following the Green March (the march of 350,000 Moroccan civilians into the Spanish Sahara to serve notice of Moroccan claims to the territory in November 1975). Parliamentary elections were held in 1977, but those parliamentarians did not actually meet until October 1983. New parliamentary elections were held on September 14, 1984.

By the 1980s, the Moroccan political spectrum had broadened to twelve parties, but the king's will had been institutionalized by the continuing invention of loosely organized parties designed to assert the throne's interests in Parliament. Thus Hassan's creation of a Moroccan constitutional monarchy has been a process that has generally depreciated the roles of the political parties even as political parties have proliferated. The road has also been marked by periods of royal dictatorship. On the other hand, the experiment has provided Moroccans with numerous opportunities to vote—albeit in elections often "cooked up" on the spot—and a sense of participating in an evolving process. At the same time, the post–1983 Parliament has met on a regular basis and has carved out areas of deliberation and legislation for itself of considerable substance in the regulation of commerce and industry. It may be that a fluid equilibrium has been reached between the throne, the people, and their aspirations for representative government. What really matters in Morocco is the evenhandedness by which government is perceived to act.

Some twenty years after its independence, like Morocco itself, Hassan seemed to recover his balance and began to truly lead. He survived two coup attempts, and in 1975, he rallied the nation behind him on the issue of the Spanish Sahara. Both coup attempts and the king's leadership on the Sahara illuminate his personality and the problems of his rule.

The coup of Saturday, July 10, 1971, took place at the oceanside palace just south of Rabat, Skhirat. Hassan's birthday party was interrupted by gunfire at two o'clock in the afternoon. Hassan and a handful of the eight hundred guests— who had been playing golf, swimming, and enjoying a buffet lunch—quickly took refuge in the throne room. The coup was a plot directed by the chief of the Royal Military Household, General Mohammed Medbouh. After the episode was ended, the trusted Minister of the Interior Mohammed Oufkir was immediately elevated to head defense and purge the officer corps of the disloyal. The episode worked largely to Hassan's favor: His control over the army was strengthened, and his miraculous escape from danger began to work in the public mind as proof of the king's powerful *baraka* (a charismatic power to produce blessings and general goodwill). His derring-do in the affair became legend. The whole affair was played out again—this time in the air—the next summer.

Hassan took advantage of the attempted coup to announce a series of reforms during Ramadan (November) 1971. Capturing the most attention was the crackdown on corruption. Six former ministers were arrested for kickbacks. Warrants were sworn out for the arrest for corruption of a half-dozen well-placed Jews— initiating an exodus of Jews from the country as important as that caused by any other single event in postindependence history. Hassan held out the new constitution as a reward for the people.

Returning from a private visit to France on September 16, 1972, Hassan's Boeing 727 was attacked by rebel Moroccan F–5 fighter planes just inside Moroccan airspace. Refusing to follow the rebels' instructions, the plane was fired on but managed to land as planned at Rabat. Legend has it that Hassan took command of the situation by getting on the plane's radio and, pretending to be a pilot, radioed the rebels that "Hassan is dead." This was not sufficient to allay the rebels' doubts, however, and the F–5s bombed the Rabat airport after the plane had landed and its passengers had rushed inside. The king ran outside and flattened himself in a grove of trees. Saved by a combination of skill, quick thinking, and, once again, luck, the king's appeal—simply as a rugged survivor— rose dramatically. Again, the truth was simple: As Hassan wrote (1978:153– 54), "The calamity had been caused by the vaulting ambition of one man, on whom I had bestowed many benefits"—Oufkir. Oufkir, who had perhaps been privy to the 1971 plot, committed suicide, it was announced, that same day.

These two episodes, so closely linked in time and personalities, had a resounding effect on Hassan. He emerged stronger from them, exerting his will to "Moroccanize" (impose 51-percent Moroccan ownership) French landholdings and businesses in the spring of 1974 and throwing over fifteen hundred members of his old foes in the UNFP (now reincarnated as the Union Socialiste des Forces Populaires or USFP), in jail. A prominent Marrakechi Muslim fundamentalist who had warned Hassan about corruption was thrown in jail and then into an insane asylum in 1974 for three and a half years. Relations with Valéry Giscard d'Estaing's France warmed, and became closer than at any time since before the Ben Barka affair. Hassan was clearly building friendships among the wealthy and powerful in anticipation of a time when he would need them. That time came in November 1975.

In a move that has been likened to Mao's "Long March," Hassan called on 350,000 Moroccan citizens to gather at the border of the Spanish Sahara in late October 1975 and prepare to walk in, unarmed, to exert their national claim to the territory as Moroccan terra irredenta—a claim rejected by the World Court in October. On November 6, armed only with the Koran and swathed in green, the color of the Prophet, they marched in. Remarkably, the move worked. Spain withdrew, abandoning the territory to Morocco and Mauritania. Morocco took the northern two thirds of what the world began to call the Western Sahara and remains territory in dispute as of 1989. Mauritania renounced its claim to territory in 1979, leaving Morocco the entirety. In the meantime, the organization of the Front for the Liberation of Seguiat al Hamra and Rio de Oro (the two provinces of the territory), popularly known as the *Polisario*, had emerged as an active military opposition to the Moroccan presence in the Western Sahara. Hassan, however, had pushed ahead with programs of economic development and re-population of the territory. By the mid–1980s, the territory's capital, Laayoun, had blossomed into a town of 250,000 people replete with a 35,000-seat stadium and a Club Mediterranée.

The territory was being forcibly welded to the rest of Morocco, one reason for which was its treasure trove of phosphate and iron-ore deposits. Already the world's leading phosphate exporter and the country's number one export earner, Hassan had taken his cue from Middle Eastern oil-rich states and had increased the price of Moroccan phosphates four times between the fall of 1973 and mid–1974. With a price slump underway in 1975, the economic motivation to take the Spanish Sahara was strong—heady development projects announced in the meantime needed to be financed. Moroccan claims of irredenta rode roughshod over the indigenous population's call for a plebiscite, and, with Spain's government in disarray upon the death of Franco, Morocco occupied the territory. What has occurred since has shown that Hassan did not necessarily overplay his hand, but he did encounter unexpected difficulties that have dominated his ability to rule and resulted in new Moroccan alliances both at home and abroad.

Foremost among these has been the constant alliance of Moroccans—political parties and the public alike—behind Hassan in his quest for a Sahara united with Morocco. The nation saw its military budget increase from 1.4 billion Moroccan dirhams in 1975 to 5.2 billion dirhams (504 million dollars) in 1985. The war in the Sahara occupied some 45 percent of the Moroccan budget in 1981 as the size of the FAR rose from 45,000 before the war to 150,000 in 1985 (versus some 21,000 for the Polisario). In 1978, the U.S. government estimated the daily cost of the Saharan war at one million dollars per day. At the same time, the foreign debt of Morocco grew to 13 billion dollars by the end of 1985, and its debt ratio was near 100 percent—the highest in the world. Morocco's 120 to 150-million dollar annual assistance from the United States in the 1980s was supplemented by strong assistance in outright grants and low-interest loans from Saudi Arabia and the UAE (United Arab Emirates), amounting to nearly 1.5 billion dollars in 1982. With the fall in the price of oil in world markets, these became severely diminished after 1986.

Hassan's bind was relieved by a series of military successes in the Sahara itself and his chessboard game of North African and African politics that bought Morocco time and friends. Hassan's dispatch of troops to Sese Seko Mobutu's endangered Kolweizi province in May 1977 brought him an undying friend in cobalt-rich Zaire, neatly tied into Morocco's cobalt resources and Hassan's ability to express himself on the nature of the Soviet threat to African and Middle Eastern geologic resources. This move bought time through solid relations with an anti-Polisario bloc in the Organization of African Unity, which ultimately seated the Polisario in November 1984. Morocco and its allies then walked out of the OAU (Organization of African Unity), resulting in the paralysis of the organization for several years to come. After many years of sharp discord, Hassan II met with Libya's Muammar Qaddafi* in August 1984 to inaugurate a two-year "Arab-African Union" that served to neutralize Libya's long-standing support for the Polisario and reduce Morocco's military burden in the Sahara. Although Hassan broke once again with Libya on August 29, 1986, Hassan's unyielding Saharan policies led to a new mix of Maghribi politics by 1988, when Algiers and Rabat announced a renewal of diplomatic relations in May (after a twelve-year absence) and leaders of all the Maghribi states—Algeria, Libya, Mauritania, Morocco, and Tunisia—met at the Arab League Summit in Algiers in June. Hassan arrived with an entourage of hundreds by boat from Tangier. An "era of good feeling" may be said to have ensued: In August, Hassan agreed to hold a plebiscite in the Sahara on the basis of the 1974 resident population, and in December 1988, he agreed to face-to-face talks with the Polisario, an organization previously described as "phantom" by the Alaouite throne. In all, if Hassan's long gamble in the Sahara proves redeemable, Hassan will have nearly doubled the size of his country and, once again, proved his skill at negotiating domestic and international politics to benefit the long-term interests of Morocco. In this risky game, Hassan will have proved himself to be an Alaouite monarch of undoubted resources, and may well have parlayed his *baraka*, skill, and genes into the next generation of Moroccan politics.

Hassan plays his role with considerable monarchical bravura. Hassan II has positioned Crown Prince Moulay Mohammed, his firstborn son (born September 6, 1963) into the mainstream of the public life of the throne. Early in his reign, it was not known if Hassan was married until the birth of his daughter, Lalla

Meriem, on August 26, 1962, in Rome. It was then presumed that Hassan had married in the period between his father's death and his accession to the throne (February 26–March 3, 1961). In any case, he married Lalla Latifa, a woman from an important Berber family and known only as the "wife of his majesty." His second son, Moulay Rachid (born 1968?), also captures prominent public attention. Both sons have had educations carefully organized around select classes at the premier national university, Universite Mohammed V in Rabat. Other daughters, Asma (born December 1965) and Hasnaa (born November 1967), have played an occasional role in public life. Lalla Meriem's September 1984 marriage to Fouad Filalli, a twenty-eight-year-old investment banker from Fez whose career in New York symbolizes the understated role of the Crown in international business, occupied all the hotel rooms in Fez and the front pages of Moroccan newspapers for a week. The Crown, as it is often called, is a significant business affair in Morocco. Hassan has often been identified as the richest man in Morocco (worth 500 million dollars in 1975), and his numerous relatives, after three hundred years in Rabat, are worth a good deal as well. Hassan lives in any one of seven palaces—Rabat, Skhirat, Casablanca, Fez, Ifrane, Marrakech, Agadir—at any given time of the year. Like the sultans of the past, he travels with his government from palace to imperial palace. Marrakech (winter) and Rabat-Skhirat, however, are his favorite palaces, and golf occupies his leisure time at both. American golf pros, in particular Claude Harmon, have worked to improve the king's game; Robert Trent Jones designed golf courses associated with the palace. Especially well known is the Dar es Salaam Golf Club near Rabat, where the Trophée Hassan II tournament is held every autumn. Hassan is also a noted fancier of Arabian horses. The king is known for his Cardin suits and his addiction to American cigarettes. His love for his late brother, Moulay Abdullah, and his sister, the Princess Aisha, who is important in the Moroccan women's movement as well as the independence movement, is well known in Morocco. Hassan typically addresses his citizens as "my dear people," and, depending on his need and mood, may scold like a father or instruct like a professor. Hassan has employed the world's best designers and chefs to organize the royal household. He occasionally visits a French chateau he bought in the early 1970s. He maintains a private jet at Orly ready to fly the necessary to Morocco. His telecommunications system is the equal of that of any in the world—though he may have trouble getting in touch with the remote parts of his country. In a country in which a tiny percentage of the population controls a vast majority of the wealth, Hassan is indeed king.

   Hassan's direct role in Middle Eastern politics has been limited, as his distance from the theater of conflict might suggest. Eighteen hundred Moroccan infantrymen sent to Syria in May 1973 fought in the Golan Heights in the 1973 October War. Hassan has been head of the Al Qods (Jerusalem) Committee of the Islamic Foreign Ministers since its founding in 1979. The king, whose skills in Arabic are often recognized as the strongest of any Arab leader, has played a backstage role in the formulation of Middle Eastern political initiatives, variously as the host, president, and mediator at meetings and summits of the Arab League, the Islamic Foreign Ministers Conference, and the Al Qods Committee. Hassan played a key role in arranging Sadat's visit to Jerusalem in 1977 through a behind-the-scenes series of meetings with Israeli Foreign Minister Moshe Dayan* and Prime Minister Yitzhak Rabin.* Israeli technical assistance has aided Hassan in the Sahara war, and Mossad services in Rabat have served the king to inform on his adversaries both at home and abroad—operations that would shock Moroccans were they well known. In a surprise initiative in July 1986, Hassan hosted the visit of Israeli Prime Minister Shimon Peres* to his Ifrane palace for talks on Palestinian sovereignty. Although these led nowhere in particular and earned Hassan a fair amount of vitriol from hard-line states, the global perception of his role as a mediator in the Israeli-Arab conflict has brought him wide recognition as a man of peace—an attribute that has served him well in his own conflict in the Sahara.

BIBLIOGRAPHY

Work by Hassan II:

The Challenge: The Memoirs of King Hassan II of Morocco. Trans. Anthony Rhodes. London: Macmillan, 1978.

Other Works:

Ashford, Douglas E. Political Change in Morocco. Princeton, N.J.: Princeton University Press, 1961.
Aubin, Jules, and Jim Aubin. "Le Maroc en suspens." In Annuaire de l'Afrique du Nord 1964. Paris: CNRS, 1964.
Berque, Jacques. "Tradition and Innovation in the Maghrib." Daedalus 102, no. 1 (Winter 1973): pp. 239–250.
Deeb, Mary-Jane. "Inter-Maghribi Relations since 1969: A Study of the Modalities of Unions and Mergers." Middle East Journal 43, no. 1 (Winter 1989): 20–33.
Eickelman, Dale F. "Royal Authority and Religious Legitimacy: Morocco's Elections, 1960–1984." In Myron J. Aronoff (ed.) The Frailty of Authority. Political Anthropology series no. 5. New Brunswick, N. J.: Transaction Books, 1986, pp. 181–205.
Leveau, Remy. Le fellah marocain: Defenseur du trône. Paris: Presses de la Fondation Nationale des Science Politiques, 1985.
Parker, Richard B. North Africa: Regional Tensions and Strategic Concerns. New York: Praeger, 1984. A Council on Foreign Relations Book.
Tessler, Mark A., and John P. Entelis. "Kingdom of Morocco." In David E. Long and Bernard Reich (eds.) The Government and Politics of the Middle East and North Africa. 1st ed. Boulder, Colo.: Westview Press, 1986, pp. 382–406.
Waterbury, John. The Commander of the Faithful: The Moroccan Political Elite—A Study in Segmented Politics. New York: Columbia University Press, 1970.

Zartman, William I. *Destiny of a Dynasty: The Search for Institutions in Morocco's Developing Society*. Columbia, S. C.: University of South Carolina Press, 1964.

JAMES ANDREW MILLER

HUSSEIN IBN TALAL (1935-   ). His Royal Majesty King Hussein ibn Talal of Jordan, grandson of Sharif Hussein of Mecca, became Jordan's monarch in August 1952 at the age of seventeen, and formally assumed the throne the following year after reaching the age of majority. His uninterrupted tenure makes him the longest ruling monarch in the world. His reign has witnessed the social and economic development of Jordan. Despite the loss of the West Bank and Jerusalem as a consequence of military defeat during the 1967 Arab-Israeli war, Jordan, under King Hussein, has been an important Arab world actor and a major player in the efforts to resolve the Arab-Israeli conflict.

King Hussein enjoys a rich and noble heritage. Hashem, a scion of the distinguished Quraish clan of Mecca and the founder of King Hussein's Hashemite family, was the Prophet Muhammad's great grandfather, and by tradition King Hussein is a direct descendant of the Prophet through his daughter, Fatima. In recent times, the Hashemites have again played a historic role in the Middle East. By the mid-nineteenth century, they were considered to be the most prominent religious and political family in Mecca, the capital of the Hejaz and center of Muslim pilgrimage. In 1908, Sultan Abdul Hamid II appointed the Hashemite leader Sharif Hussein ibn Ali, whom he thought to be loyal to the Ottoman Empire, *amir* (prince) of Mecca. From this base, the sharif and his very able sons, in league with the British but in the name of Arab nationalism, led the great Arab Revolt against the Ottoman Empire during World War I.

At the resolution of this conflict, Ali, the grand sharif's eldest son and heir apparent, remained in Mecca. In Damascus, his second son, Faisal, was originally made viceroy with responsibility for Syria and Transjordan. In 1920, the General Syrian Congress declared him king of the United Kingdom of Syria. However, basing its action on the secret wartime Franco-British Sykes-Picot Agreement, the French army soon removed him. Then, after an engineered plebescite, the British installed him as king of Iraq. Following these events, Abdullah ibn Hussein,* Sharif Hussein's third son and grandfather of King Hussein, entered Transjordan with the intent of marching to Damascus to reclaim the throne for the Hashemites. Thwarted in this aim, in 1921 he became amir of Transjordan with the acquiescence of the British.

Thus, for a brief period, Hashemites ruled the Hejaz, Iraq, and Transjordan. In 1925, Amir Ali ibn Hussein who had replaced his father in Mecca, lost the throne to the forces of the House of Saud as the Kingdom of Saudi Arabia was being pieced together in the Arabian Peninsula. The young King Faisal II, grandson of Faisal I, was killed in 1958 as the Hashemite rule in Iraq was terminated. Consequently, by mid–1958, King Hussein was the only remaining Hashemite monarch. However, other members of his family maintain an active role in public life.

When King Hussein was born in 1935, the Amirate of Transjordan had existed for only fourteen years. The country was a small, poor, sparsely populated, little-known backwater in the Middle East. At the time, Talal ibn Abdullah, King Hussein's father, was crown prince. His mother, Zein, an intelligent, perceptive woman, was from a collateral branch of the Hashemite family. Due to Talal's ill health—he was schizophrenic—the Jordanian leadership realized that Prince Hussein would be the next real inheritor of the throne. His grandfather, Amir Abdullah, specifically undertook to tutor him in statecraft, including him in many official meetings and even requiring him to translate upon occasion.

Despite his immediate family's meager means—his parents could not even afford him a bicycle—he was provided with a broad, although abbreviated education. In Amman his classes at an Islamic school and Kuliyat al-Matran (the Bishop's School) were augmented by special tutorials in Arabic and religion. Later, at the junior- and senior-high-school level, he attended the prestigious Victoria College in Alexandria where he greatly expanded his education and worldview as well as developing his love for sports and camaraderie with his fellow students. When Hussein was thirteen, a series of momentous events occurred in the Middle East that were to profoundly affect the young prince's future rule in Jordan. These were the creation of the state of Israel on Transjordan's western border, the Jordanian army's occupation of the West Bank, and, two years later, the West Bank's inclusion in the Hashemite Kingdom of Jordan, an act that would not only increase the size of the state, but also triple the population of the country as over eight hundred thousand Palestinian refugees and residents of the West Bank were added to Transjordan's mere four hundred thousand citizens.

On July 20, 1951, angered by Abdullah's secret negotiations with Israel, a Palestinian assassinated King Abdullah in Jerusalem's most famous Muslim shrine, Haram al-Sharif. The young prince, standing by his side, narrowly escaped death himself as a bullet deflected off a medal on his chest. Prince Hussein immediately became the next in line to the throne as his virtually invalid father was crowned king. In consideration of his royal future, Prince Hussein's education was shifted to England where he joined his cousin, Crown Prince Faisal of Iraq, at Harrow, an elite school for future leaders of Britain and the British Empire.

His life again changed on August 11, 1952, when, due to his illness, the Jordanian Parliament relieved King Talal of his duties and passed the crown to Prince Hussein. Not having reached his majority, a regency council ruled Jordan for a year as the new monarch completed his formal education. At the direction of his uncle, Sharif Hussein Nasser, he spent this period at Sandhurst, the British military academy equivalent to America's West Point. After a year of being treated and acting like an ordinary cadet, King Hussein returned to Amman where he assumed the throne in May 1953.

King Hussein, a man short of stature but deep of voice, acts and is treated very much like a king. Not an intellectual, but serious and intelligent, he is thought at times to be moody. However, for a leader of a small country buffeted by major Middle Eastern forces beyond his control, he retains a consistent moderation in his policies and the expression thereof. When he was young he had a passion for fast cars and airplanes, giving him a playboy image. As he has aged, he has not lost his physical prowess or his love for sport, but the image has dissipated. His direct intervention in several military crises during the early years of his reign proved his physical and psychological courage in a very public way and gave him an image of bravery that has served him well.

Contributing to the development of his character and personality were a few individuals who tutored and advised him over the years. The most important, it is said, was Amir Abdullah, who taught him what it was to be an Arab king and a Hashemite. His father's influence lasted only until his teenage years, but his mother's steady and conciliatory advice continues into the 1980s. Other Hashemites close to King Hussein were Sharif Nasser in the early years; Abdul Hamid Sharaf, a former prime minister, in the middle years; and Zaid bin Shakir, who is currently head of the Jordanian Arab Army. Since the late 1960s, his younger brother, Crown Prince Hassan, has grown in importance, not only as a sibling and heir to the throne but also as a serious adviser and a leader in his own right of the Jordanian social- and economic-development process. Prince Hassan is different from his brother. He is an intellectual with a degree from Oxford University and four books to his credit. Like his brother, he is quite visible in Jordan, frequently giving speeches at conferences on a wide variety of subjects.

Nonfamily mentors who were close, especially in the first two decades of King Hussein's reign, were five men who at various times held the prime ministry, two of whom lost their lives while in office. The latter two were Haza al-Majali and Wasfi Tal, who were assassinated respectively in 1960 and 1971; the other three were Said Mufti, Sameer Rifai, and Bahjat Talhouni. Habis al-Majali, an early protégé of Amir Abdullah and later head of the Jordanian Arab Army for many years, was also a steady and loyal friend and adviser. Outside of Jordan, one can cite President Dwight D. Eisenhower of the United States, a sort of father figure for the king, and Egypt's President Gamal Abdul Nasser* in the period following the 1967 Arab-Israeli war, which was a true disaster for both of them.

King Hussein has had four wives. In 1954, in an arranged match, he married Sharifa Dina, a distant and older cousin from Cairo. Despite the birth of a daughter, the couple proved to be incompatible and divorced after only eighteen months of marriage. In 1961 the king married again, this time to the daughter of a British military attaché, Princess Muna. This union produced two boys and three girls. Although King Hussein wrote of pleasant domestic bliss during these years, the marriage ended in divorce in 1972. In 1973 the king married a third time, to Alia Tuqan, the daughter of a prominent Nablus, West Bank, family. They had two children, a boy and a girl. This reportedly happy marriage ended tragically in 1977 when Queen Alia died in a helicopter crash. In 1978 King

Hussein married a fourth time to Lisa Halaby, the daughter of Najeeb Halaby, an Arab American and former chairman of Pan American Airways. Renamed Queen Noor, she and the king have four children, two boys and two girls.

Potential succession to King Hussein has been somewhat problematic. When Princess Muna bore the king a son in 1962, he was declared the crown prince. However, because his mother was not Arab, this was not a settled matter. Indeed, in 1965, while Prince Hassan was still at Oxford University, the Jordanian constitution was changed, making him the crown prince. He is the youngest of the three sons of Talal. The middle son, Muhammad, was passed over because he is known to be ill like his late father. This change of royal succession assuaged the local desire to have a purely Arab inheritor to the throne, and it placed an heir in line who was capable of assuming the crown should something happen to King Hussein in troubled times. It is said that the Queen Mother Zein had much to do with this decision. In 1974, Hussein and his Arab wife, Queen Alia, had a son, Prince Ali, who was placed in line to follow Crown Prince Hassan.

Crucial to King Hussein's reign are the attributes that give him legitimacy in the eyes of the Jordanians. The weight or saliency of these factors vary to some degree among the Jordanian socioeconomic groups. First, having led the Arab Revolt against the Ottoman Empire, the Hashemites have a special claim on the origins of Arab nationalism. King Hussein has clearly inherited this strong feeling for and sense of duty toward the larger Arab nation, which he frequently invokes in his public speeches. His view of Arab Nationalism, however, is not the ever-ephemeral search for political unity often called for by other Arab leaders, especially in the 1950s and 1960s, but rather a desire for strong cultural, social, economic—and at times, political and military—relations among the Arab states and peoples to make the whole more than the sum of its parts.

Second, King Hussein also claims legitimacy on the basis of his special relationship to Islam, that is, his being a direct descendent of the Prophet Muhammed. This religious relationship and the king's public attentiveness to religious issues and leaders are especially meaningful to the more traditional and religious Jordanians.

A third factor that buttresses the king's legitimacy is the perception that he is honestly interested in, and, very importantly, able to deliver on socioeconomic development. Most admit that King Hussein and his brother, Prince Hassan, have played crucial roles in creating a favorable climate for development efforts, and have been able to secure considerable financial resources to sustain them. This development process is high on the Jordanian public's agenda. It is frequently a subject of discussion in conferences, at ceremonial meetings, in the press, and on radio and television. From the mid–1970s on, Jordanians have increasingly enjoyed the benefits of this development. At the minimum it has helped coopt many people to the regime, especially some of the Palestinians of the middle class, some of whom otherwise might not have been so disposed. For many it has simply increased their loyalty. Some from the poorest classes, as well as those oriented towards radical Islamic fervor, would be the least likely to be influenced by this process.

The fourth attribute that reflects well on King Hussein's rule is the high degree of personal freedom and security enjoyed by his citizens. When Jordanians compare their lot to that of people in neighboring countries, their situation is viewed quite positively. Basically, as long as a citizen, whether of East Jordanian origin or Palestinian, is not threatening the state or causing disorder, he or she can proceed with business without undue interference. There are limitations though; King Hussein and Amir Abdullah before him have not allowed great degrees of political freedom or participation, and the security forces have been known to be very strict.

Fifth, King Hussein's very longevity in the face of adversity and regime-challenging crises creates respect. Remarkably, by 1988, his thirty-five years on the throne had made him the longest ruling monarch and head of state in the world. In a sense this durability and success breeds success. Another set of attributes is that the king is personally attractive, speaks beautiful Arabic, enjoys an image of strength of character and physical courage, and has an attractive family with many children. In addition, Jordanians like seeing the leader of their small and not inherently wealthy state dealing on their behalf as an equal with the leaders of the Middle East and the world.

Throughout the history of their rule in Jordan, the Hashemites have had an uneasy relationship with democratic institutions. The Parliament, which does exist, has been closely controlled in elections and performance. Due to the loss of the West Bank in 1967, there has been no general election since that date. Moreover, the Parliament was suspended by the king from 1974 until 1984, when it was recalled. In more recent years, by-elections have been held to fill vacant seats. In essence, King Hussein relates to members of Parliament more as representatives of their constituencies rather than as a collective with authority and responsibility. The Cabinet, accordingly, while responsible to Parliament, is in actuality more responsive to the king. High-level policy and national direction emanates from the palace, and the cabinet is a technical executor thereof.

When setting the course for the state, King Hussein considers the interests and needs of a series of constituencies. While not a conclusive list, and not necessarily presented in the order of importance, they would be: the Hashemite family; the East Bankers (the Transjordanians), especially the bedouin and the tribes; the military, which is heavily manned by the latter two groups; the Palestinians living in the East Bank and, to a lesser extent, those on the West Bank; the leaders of the other Arab states; and world leaders, especially those of the West. In this manner, King Hussein looks to a series of ever-widening concentric circles as he considers Jordan's policies and reacts to the never-ending pressures and counterpressures from the Middle East.

King Hussein's rule is marked by two major historical phases. The first two decades were dominated by crises and threats to the throne stemming from inside and outside the country. Radical Arab nationalism brought riots to the streets, challenges from his own prime minister in 1956, destabilization by the larger, stronger Arab states, and the devastating loss of the West Bank to Israel in the June 1967 war. While surviving, and often relying on the loyal military, King Hussein helped put in place the bases for development. Some of the essential infrastructure was constructed, and, most importantly, the school system was built so that the vast majority of the population could attain education. Also, the king removed the last vestiges of British rule when he relieved Lieutenant General Sir John Bagot Glubb as commander of the army and proceeded to Arabize the officer corps. In a parallel manner, he shifted Jordan's key reliance on assistance from Great Britain to the United States as the former's role in the world diminished and the latter's grew.

The second phase, starting about 1974, is distinguished by a calmer political situation internal to Jordan, much more rapid development fuelled by funds derived from the oil boom in neighboring states, and improved relations with most of Jordan's Arab neighbors in a relatively less radical regional political atmosphere. By the beginning of this period, the king and his regime had consolidated and institutionalized their internal control via the security and military forces, and had put behind them the tumult caused by the Palestinian guerrilla presence that had dominated the 1968–1971 period. King Hussein's heavy investment in education paid off handsomely as the country was able to provide skilled and educated Arab labor to its newly super-rich oil-producing neighbors as well as to attract funds—free, concessional, or in the form of remittances—for its own development process. It is said that of all the Middle Eastern countries that benefited from this oil wealth, only Jordan wisely invested the majority of its development funds. Despite his problems with the Palestinians, King Hussein has come to be a respected leader in most Arab capitals. Indeed, he has hosted two Arab summits in Jordan in 1980 and 1987, events that would have been unimaginable in Amman a decade earlier. Even though only in his fifties, King Hussein is becoming an elder statesman of the region.

With respect to the king's style of leadership, one can observe two seemingly contradictory trends. On the one hand, his executive freedom has diminished with time. Namely, he is less free today to decide and act unilaterally. Rather, to some degree he must seek to persuade and convince people of the wisdom of his course. This shift results from the very change in Jordan. When King Hussein came to power, the country was poor, uneducated, and relatively simple in its class and socioeconomic structure, and in this comparatively unsophisticated atmosphere, the bedouin and tribal soldiers and officers would follow their king virtually blindly, giving him considerable license to act on his own. By the late 1980s, the citizens had become much more complex and educated, with a college or polytechnic degree commonly held. Accordingly, the average citizen, including the soldier, albeit still loyal, needs to know why, and not just what to do.

On the other hand, King Hussein has grown tremendously in stature. In the early years he had to contend with older politicians. If he wanted to pursue a particular policy or make a decision not to their liking, he often had to argue his case and use various forms of personal pressure. Today, he certainly listens widely and seeks out advice, but once he decides or formulates policy it is not disputed, the other leaders accept it. Nevertheless, the policy must be explained to the educated, more complex Jordanian society.

Another long-term trend in the king's rule is his attempt to be moderate and centrist. As a corollary, he does not seek out enemies, and he does not try to make enemies or hold grudges against people. Thus, after times of internal challenge to the throne, his regime has not executed the challengers. (His vigorous quelling of the violent Palestinian challenge to the regime in 1970 does not break this pattern, rather, that was an exercise in actively defending his rule in a time of civil war.) Some challengers have been sent to prison or exiled, but many have been brought back and given positions of some trust. The king has not followed either radical or overly conservative social, economic, or cultural policies. A certain amount of tolerance is granted, but not so much as to disturb the society's norms. Furthermore, adjusting these limits according to the feelings of the time is not unknown.

The king's relations with the Arab World follow a similar pattern. As leader of a small, not intrinsically strong country, and in accordance with his perception of Arab nationalism, he attempts to maintain positive relations with the other Arab states. It can also be argued, however, that he is following a strategic policy for the survival of his country as he consistently attempts to maintain acceptable if not close ties with a majority of the strong Arab states. That his pursuit of these broad aims does not always succeed is demonstrated in recent years by Jordan's frequently strained relations with Syria's Hafez al-Assad* and Libya's Muammar Qaddafi.* In addition, the king probably resents the wealth of the kings and princes to the south and east from whom he must repeatedly request funds. Finally, he seeks positive relations with the West. For years, he has sought a closer political and military relationship with the United States, but has been continually frustrated by the terms of the U.S. relations with Israel. Nevertheless, his country maintains strong ties with America, especially in economic and educational terms.

BIBLIOGRAPHY

Works by Hussein:

Uneasy Lies the Head: The Autobiography of His Majesty King Hussein I of the Hashemite Kingdom of Jordan. New York: Bernard Geis Associates, 1962.
My War with Israel. As told to and with additional material by Vick Vance and Pierre Lauer. New York: William Morrow and Co., 1969.
"Reflections on an Epilogue: *Al-Takmilah* to the Memoirs of King Abdullah Ibn Al-Hussein." *Middle East Journal* 32, no. 1 (Winter 1978): 79–86.

Other Works:

Abidi, Aqil. *Jordan: A Political Study, 1948–57*. London: Asia Publishing House, 1965.
Aruri, Naseer H. *Jordan: A Study in Political Development (1921–1965)*. The Hague: Martinus Nijhoff, 1972.
Day, Arthur. *East Bank/West Bank, Jordan and the Prospects for Peace*. New York: Council on Foreign Relations, 1986.
Gubser, Peter. *Jordan: Crossroads of Middle Eastern Events*. Boulder, Colo.: Westview Press, 1983.
Jureidini, Paul A., and R. D. McLaurin. *Jordan: The Impact of Social Change on the Role of Tribes*. New York: Praeger, 1984.
al-Mady, Munib, and Sulayman Musa. *Ta'rikh al'Urdun fi al-Qarn al-'Ishrin* (History of Jordan in the Twentieth Century). Amman?: n.p., 1959.
Morris, James. *The Hashemite Kings*. New York: Pantheon, 1959.
Rustow, Dankwart A. *Hussein: A Biography*. London: Barrie and Jenkins, 1972.
Shwadran, Benjamin. *Jordan: A State of Tension*. New York: Council for Middle Eastern Affairs Press, 1959.
Snow, Peter. *Hussein: A Biography*. Washington, D.C.: Robert B. Luce, 1972.

                                                              PETER GUBSER

SADDAM HUSSEIN (1937-   ) rose through the ranks and held various positions in the government, military, and Baath party during his long career in politics before becoming president of Iraq in 1979. Even prior to his accession to the presidency he exercised considerable influence in the regime of President al-Bakr. During the 1980s Hussein presided over Iraq's eight-year war with Iran, and guided its economic development and reconstruction in the post-war era.

Saddam Hussein was born on April 28, 1937, to Sabha Tulfah al-Masallat who had lost her husband just before the birth, at the home of her brother, Khayr Alla Tulfah, in the village of Tikrit, situated on the bank of the Tigris some 150 kilometers north of Baghdad. According to his semiofficial biography, his parents were "poor peasants." Since he became president in July 1979, the official version has been that, on his mother's side, Hussein is connected to the family of the Prophet Muhammad.

When he was still a baby his mother married her brother-in-law, al-Hajj Ibrahim al-Hasan, and mother and son moved to Saddam's stepfather's mud hut in the village of Uja, not far from Tikrit. When he was ten, Saddam decided to go to school. This was a somewhat unusual ambition for a poor country boy, and his family tried to dissuade him, but he ran away to his maternal uncle's home in Tikrit, where he attended primary school for six or seven years. In 1955 he started his secondary studies in Baghdad. There he participated in antigovernment disturbances in 1956. In 1957 the young Saddam Hussein joined the underground Baath party as a low-ranking member.

On July 14, 1958, the monarchy was toppled by an army headed by General Abdul Karim Qassem.* For a few months the Baath party was allowed to operate legally, but very soon it clashed with General Qassem: while the Baath, in unison with the Nasserist Colonel Abdul Salam Arif, sought unity with Egypt and Syria (the United Arab Republic), Qassem was adamant about preserving Iraq's independence.

In fall 1959, the party chose Saddam to be one of a small group assigned to assassinate General Qassem. The assassination attempt that took place on October 7, 1959, failed. Hussein, though wounded by a bullet, managed to get to the Syrian border. In Damascus he was given a hero's reception by the Baath leadership there. This was when he met the cofounder and chief ideologue of the party, Michel Aflaq* for the first time, and his party career really took off. Aflaq promoted him to full membership in the party, a rare honor. From Damascus he moved to Cairo where, in 1961, he graduated from high school and enrolled in law school, but never seriously engaged in his studies.

On February 8, 1963, General Qassem was toppled by a coalition of the Baath Party and Nasserist officers. Saddam returned immediately to Baghdad, where he became involved in internal security. His natural ability to cope with difficult situations and to fend for himself, which had been developed during his childhood on his own, proved extremely useful in the chaotic situation that reigned in Baghdad during the Baath rule. At this time he also married his maternal cousin, Sajida, daughter of Khayr Alla Tulfah and sister of Adnan Khairallah, minister of defense from 1977 until his death in 1989.

Soon after the Baath party came into power it split between leftists, rightists, and a centrist group, which was headed by the then prime minister (and Hussein's relative from Tikrit), Brigadier General Ahmad Hasan al-Bakr. Saddam Hussein joined Bakr's faction. In late 1963, the rift between leftists and centrists (or "rightists," as the leftists called them) extended also to Syria, and this was the beginning of the rivalry between the Bakr-Hussein faction in Iraq and Hafez al-Assad's* faction in Syria. On November 18, 1963, the Nasserist president, Abdul Salam Arif, who until then had been no more than a figurehead presiding over an essentially Baath regime, removed the Baath from power.

In the fall of 1964, the Baath party planned a coup d'état against President Arif, but the plan was exposed and the police rounded up the culprits. The official version is that when Hussein was tracked down in Baghdad in October 1964 he defended himself with his pistol until he ran out of ammunition. He was then arrested, but in July 1966 he escaped. By then, most of the other party leaders had already been freed. According to Hussein's own version, while in prison he spent much time in contemplation over the reasons for the party's failure to stay in power and in planning for the future. To better understand the ways of a true revolutionary, he also took to reading Lenin.

On July 17, 1968, the Baath ousted from power President Abd al-Rahman Arif (who had succeeded his younger brother, Abdul Salam Arif, after the latter was killed in a helicopter crash in April 1966). While this coup d'état was made possible mainly by the help of a few non-Baathi army officers, who held key positions under Arif, the civilian Saddam Hussein was the key figure in removing, on July 30, 1968, the two more ambitious and dangerous of the four officers who had been instrumental in toppling the Arif regime. This second coup d'état within less than a fortnight placed power squarely in the hands of the Baath party, under President Ahmad Hasan al-Bakr.

In November 1969, Saddam Hussein became assistant secretary general of the party and deputy chairman of the highest decision-making institution, the Revolutionary Command Council (RCC). He owed this promotion in part to his success in purging the army of anti-Baathi officers and in establishing an effective and ruthless internal-security apparatus, but no less to his distant family ties and close political relations with President Bakr, who was also chairman of the RCC.

Between 1969 and 1971, Saddam managed to out-maneuver and remove from power his and Bakr's two most formidable opponents inside the party leadership and the RCC. General Salih Mahdi Ammash (minister of the interior and deputy prime minister) and Lieutenant General Hardan Abd al-Ghaffar al-Tikriti (minister of defense and deputy prime minister). Even though Hussein could not control the army without President Bakr and did not enjoy sufficient popular support, from the early 1970s on he became the main influence behind all the major political and economic decisions in Iraq.

On July 16, 1979, Bakr was forced to resign and Hussein became president and chairman of the RCC. A major purge took place and many of the new president's rivals in the party were executed. Since the mid–1970s close to 250 booklets have been published in Hussein's name, relating to current affairs and delineating his political theory. Since he became president in 1979, Hussein has been the object of a personality cult unparalleled in modern Iraqi history.

Saddam Hussein and Sajida have five children. The eldest son, Udayy, is married to the daughter of Izzat Ibrahim, Saddam's most faithful lieutenant. Udayy was, until late 1988, head of the Iraqi Olympic Committee. In November 1988 Saddam decided to have him tried for the murder of a bodyguard, and he resigned from all his posts. His other son, Qusayy, is married to Lama, daughter of General Mahir Abd al-Rashid, a Sunni Arab from Tikrit, who during much of the war commanded an army corps in the south and was Iraq's most illustrious field commander. Since the summer of 1988, however, Abd al-Rashid has been under house arrest, and Qusayy and Lama are separated. Saddam's daughter Ghard is married to Brigadier General Hussein Kamel Majid, the acting minister of heavy industry and war industry in 1988 (and earlier commander of Hussein's bodyguard), who is a paternal cousin of Saddam Hussein. Hussein has two other daughters: Rana, married to another cousin, an army major, and his youngest child, Hala. Iraq's minister of defense, Adnan Khayr Alla, is Hussein's maternal cousin, and the two leading figures in internal security are relatives: His paternal cousin, Ali Hasan al-Majid, is director of public security, and General Fadil al-Barrak, head of general intelligence, is a member of his tribe. One of the reasons for Hussein's longevity, despite a great number of attempts on his life, is the fact that he placed a substantial number of people who hail from his tribe and hometown in sensitive positions in internal security and, according to some reports, among his bodyguards.

Hussein is the chief architect of the existing political order in Iraq, wherein the regime rests essentially on three pillars: the army, which Hussein and his supporters have managed to turn into a docile tool, the various internal security bodies, and the civilian party. Through the effective use of all three pillars Hussein has managed to stabilize the rocky political system in Iraq. This stabilization, however, came at the price of a regime that is totalitarian in the extreme and is a continuous reign of political repression unparalleled even in the violent political history of modern Iraq. The result is that, while General Qassem's regime lasted less than five years; the first Baath regime lasted for eight months, and that of the Arif brothers some four and a half years, the second Baath regime has lasted for twenty years and, despite the eight-year war with Iran, seems stable.

Within a few months after the party came to power, the army was purged of two to three thousand officers who were regarded as potentially dangerous to party rule. This purge was conducted by Reserve Captain Taha Yasin Ramadan (in 1988, first deputy prime minister and commander of the Popular Army, the party militia) under the supervision of Saddam Hussein. At the same time, the party encouraged young Baathis to enlist and go through officers' courses, and their promotion was guaranteed. Then again, near the commander of every field unit down to the level of battallion the party has placed political commissars, who acquired the nickname "the watchful eyes of the party," to make sure that units do not march on the Republican Palace as was often the case in republican Iraq. This practice severely affected the efficiency and professionalism of the officer's corp. During the war, and after Hussein felt that he had the army under control, policies were reversed. The commissars, whose understanding of military affairs was very limited, lost much of their power, and young officers who proved themselves in battle were promoted over those veteran Baathi officers who did not show much promise.

Another aspect of the advent of the civilian party at the expense of the army was that, while in 1968, the highest policy-making body, the RCC, consisted entirely of army officers, already by early 1972, six out of nine RCC members were civilians, and in 1988 only one out of nine members of the RCC was a career army officer. Army officers were gradually excluded from political power in lower institutions, and the army officers' corps increasingly became a professional body with very little involvement in politics. This process, set in motion by Saddam Hussein in 1970 and supervised by him since, was a reversal of the process of the militarization of Iraqi politics that had been started in 1958. To assert his personal supremacy over his army officers, the civilian Hussein had President Bakr promote him to full general in 1976. When he became president in 1979, he was made a field marshal.

Another means through which Hussein secured the party's rule over the Iraqi political system was through a thick net of security organizations that became his personal stronghold. These organizations were aimed, in the first place, to expose and destroy the real and perceived enemies of the party: Nasserists, communists, Monarchists, Shii fundamentalists, and others. However, through his control of these organizations, Hussein managed to impose his rule over the party leadership itself and eventually to eliminate his enemies within it.

Finally, since he became the assistant secretary general of the Iraqi branch of the party in 1969, Saddam Hussein started a long-term campaign of expanding the party. In 1968 there were probably no more than 1,000 full members in the party and between 5,000 and 10,000 lower-rank members. While the number of full members increased slowly, that of lower-rank members expanded very rapidly. By 1976 the number of members of the party militia alone had reached 100,000. Upon Hussein's ascendancy to the presidency in 1979, a massive recruitment campaign was initiated for the party and the popular army. The result was that in 1987 the number of members in the popular army was more than 690,000, and the number of party members in the various ranks was over a million and a half, that is, some 10 percent of Iraq's total population.

The party and its militia became major socializing and indoctrinating agents: Upward mobility became increasingly dependent on membership in the party, and political discussions in the party cells an important vehicle through which the regime delivered its messages to a large number of households. Even though the popular army was never ordered to confront rebellious army units (which was supposed to be its main task), its very existence may have served to cow opponents of the regime. The existence of such large, active, and highly disciplined organizations is unique in Iraqi history, and in the Arab world it has a parallel only in Syria.

During its first years in power, the aims and means of the Baath Party in the Arab arena were reminiscent of those of Gamal Abdul Nasser* between 1955 and 1964. The aim was to achieve hegemony in the Arab world. The means were a vicious propaganda campaign against all neighboring countries and an effort to foster Baathi revolutions there. Iraq's main thrust was aimed against Syria and the Gulf States, but even Egypt under Abdul Nasser himself was not excluded. Saddam Hussein himself called on the Egyptian leader, a few months before his death in September 1970, to step down because he had failed the Arab nation in the June 1967 Six Day War. Indeed, all the Arab regimes were accused of being either treacherous (such as Syria under the rival Baath faction), impotent, or tools in the hands of American imperialism, as all had betrayed their duty in Palestine.

The first blow to this ambitious Arab policy came in September 1970 when Iraq broke its promise to the PLO to defend them against King Hussein ibn Talal's* troops, fearing that it could lead to the elimination of the Iraqi dispatch force in Jordan and to the downfall of the Baath regime in Baghdad. For the first time, the radical Baath regime had to recognize its limitations in "fulfilling its duty" in Palestine. Indeed, in early 1971, Iraq evacuated its forces from Jordan and, thus, widened the gap between the party's short-term promises and its actual capabilities.

A few months later, in November 1971, Iraq was again reminded of its limitations, when Iran annexed three strategic islands in the southern Gulf. Iraq failed to mobilize Arab support: indeed, by 1971 the Baath regime had managed to turn itself into the pariah of the Arab world. Saddam Hussein's reaction was very similar to that of Nasser in 1964, following his failure to foster Nasserist revolutions in other countries. Instead of confrontation he turned to cooperation with the existing regimes and toned down (though never completely relinquishing) the call for popular socialist revolutions. The only exception was Syria. On the Iraqi side it was Saddam Hussein, more than anyone else, who kept the embers of the rivalry between the two Baath regimes glowing. In this he found his match in Syria's Hafez al-Assad. (Obsessed with internal security, Hussein was wary of Syrian penetration into the Iraqi party.) Another change introduced by Hussein was that, like Nasser in the mid–1960s, in the late 1970s he, too, never relinquished his commitment to "the liberation of Palestine" but, much like Nasser, he postponed this dream for a more distant future. In the meantime, he explained, Iraq should concentrate on solving its own political problems at home and in the Gulf, and on development. Only later would it turn again to "radiate" its influence in the Arab world.

An area where Hussein made a major contribution toward bridging the gap between the party's theory and the needs and capabilities of the Iraqi state was that of Arab unity, the most important of the party's triple slogans (unity, liberation, socialism). Between the late 1960s and early 1970s, Iraq failed in its attempts to overthrow neighboring regimes (and thus to bring about "revolutionary" unity under Iraqi guidance) as well as in sporadic (and not very convincing) attempts to unite with existing ones. Under Saddam's guidance, the Baath regime changed course. They admitted that, in the first place, there was a need to postpone the application of Arab unity. Second, they rejected emphatically the notion (preached by the party, but never attempted in its practice in Iraq) of egalitarian and amalgamative unification. Instead, the concept of a loose federation that would preserve the existing Arab peoples was developed. This enabled them to turn to the development of Iraqi nationalism, based on Iraq's ancient Mesopotamian heritage. Even though intertwined with Arabism, the new credo fully legitimized the local political identity.

The search for the ancient Mesopotamian roots of the Iraqi people also served another purpose: to promote internal Iraqi unity. By returning to Babylon, as well as to the early Islamic period that preceded the Sunni-Shii cleavage, the regime hoped to create a common denominator for all Sunnis, Shiis, and Kurds. Yet another symbol of Iraqi internal unity serves the person of Hussein himself: He is depicted as the son of all parts and communities of Iraq (he appears wearing alternately Kurdish and Arab headgears, Arab *abaa'a*, and the army uniform), and he appears on emblems and posters side by side with Nebuchadnezzer, or hugging early Islamic war heroes who liberated Iraq from the Persian yoke, thus symbolizing the continuity of Iraqi history.

On the more practical level, since the oil boom of 1973–1974, investments in the underprivileged Shii south have been substantially increased. Finally, since the mid–1970s, in addition to the mobilization of large numbers of Shiis to the lower ranks of party membership (compulsorily, according to the opposition), a growing number of Shiis have started to appear in the highest echelons of the political system where previously only Sunni Arabs could be found. This included the RCC, the regional leadership of the Baath party, the government, and the middle and upper-middle echelons of the party and state apparatus. During the war, the same phenomenom also occurred in the senior command of the army. The Shiis of Iraq are still far from achieving equality with the ruling Sunni (and often Tikriti) elite, yet a process of incorporation of the Shiis into the apparatus of state and party is underway. Saddam Hussein is responsible for these developments more than any other single person in Iraq. In the same way it was his decision in the first place that those measures would be accompanied with severe repression of the Shii religious opposition to the regime. This combination of reward and punishment produced some results, at least in the sense that during the war there was no large-scale Shii revolt and there were no reports of defection of whole army units, some of which consist of 70 percent Shiis. Regarding the Kurds, however, not even such first steps were made, and Hussein's solution to their insurrection so far has been almost entirely in the realm of repression: massive bombardments, including the use of chemical warfare, and evacuating the population of the Kurdish countryside (where it was always easier to keep a revolt flowing) to the big urban centers of the Kurdish area and settling them there.

Soon after the Baath Party came to power, in the spring of 1969 Iran clashed with Iraq over sovereignty rights in the Shatt al-Arab waterway. In late 1971 the crisis was exacerbated when Iran annexed the three strategic islands in the Gulf. Hussein's means of compensating for Iraq's strategic inferiority were very similar to those adopted by the monarchy before him: Instead of King Faisal I and Nuri al-Said's* elusive Union of the Fertile Crescent, Saddam sought the support of his Arab neighbors except for Syria. In 1972 he improved relations with Sadat's Egypt, in 1974 he started mending his fences with the Gulf Arabs, and in 1976 he started a rapprochement with Jordan. During the Gulf war Iraq's ties with these pro-Western Arab states, including Anwar al-Sadat's (and later Hosni Mubarak's*) Egypt, became particularly close.

Clearly, Iraq's geostrategic needs took precedent over party doctrine in Hussein's policies. These policies justified themselves fully. The Gulf Arabs lent Iraq some thirty-five billion dollars during the war, and, along with Jordan, they provided Iraq with badly needed logistical routes, and Egypt provided Hussein with war materials and over one million workers.

Where the monarchical statesmen relied on British support against Iran, Saddam Hussein engineered a Treaty of Friendship and Cooperation with the USSR in April 1972. Under the war conditions he went one step further, and in November 1984 he resumed full diplomatic ties (which had been severed by Arif in June 1967) with another superpower, the United States. While the USSR supplied Iraq mainly with arms and credit, the United States provided it with credits and diplomatic support in the United Nations, imposed an effective arms embargo against Iran, and sent its navy to the Gulf, which seriously hampered the Iranian war effort. Finally, Saddam Hussein was behind Iraqi-French negotiations starting in 1974 to supply Iraq with a huge atomic reactor (seventy-five megawatts), which was far beyond Iraq's needs for research.

On March 6, 1975, after he had reached the conclusion that all his solutions were either insufficient or required more time to mature, it was Saddam Hussein who signed the Algiers agreement with the shah of Iran, Mohammad Reza Pahlavi.* In return for peace inside Iraq and on its border, he was ready for a humiliating concession when he gave up Iraq's sovereignty over the Shatt al-Arab east of the navigation line. After Iran stopped all support for the Kurdish revolt, the revolt crumbled within months, never fully to recover, not even during the Gulf war when Iran resumed its support. This was a major achievement in the struggle between the central government and the Kurdish population: the Kurdish revolts had haunted all the regimes since General Qassem's days. Thus, the same person who, when he needed time, had been the chief driving force behind the most important political concession to the Kurds in Iraqi history, the agreement in March 1970 to establish Kurdish autonomy, was also the one who dealt the Kurdish movement its death blow.

In the face of strong opposition at home and vitriolic attacks from Damascus against his readiness to concede Iraqi and Arab territory, Saddam Hussein remained staunchly committed to the Algiers agreement in its broad lines (and to the Shah) until Ruhollah Khomeini's* ascendency in Tehran in February 1979. By so doing he gave his Iraqi people another lesson in political realism that may prove useful in the peace talks after the war.

On September 17, 1980, Saddam Hussein declared that the Algiers agreement was null and void in response to Khomeini's support for the Kurds, his incitement of the Shiis, and his attacks on border towns. Five days later Hussein's armored divisions rolled into Iran. From the first days of the war it was identified with his person, as it was officially called Saddam's *Qadisiyya*, after the battle in Iraq in which the Muslim Arabs defeated the Zoroastrian Persians in 635 A.D. Before long, Saddam Hussein realized that his ambitious aims of toppling Khomeini and achieving hegemony in the Gulf could not be achieved, and he changed them: He suggested troop withdrawals in return for peace and noninterference, and left the issue of sovereignty over the Shatt al-Arab unclear, implying readiness for a new compromise. At the same time, Iraq started a massive operation of force building, relying on fire power and logistics where Iran relied on enthusiasm and human forces. Thus, for example, between 1980 and 1988, Iraq's regular army was augmented from twelve to over fifty divisions. The huge resources and arms supplies needed for carrying out this strategy were guaranteed by Hussein's foreign and Arab policies that, with the exception of Syria, managed to neutralize enemies and turn neutral countries like the United States into friends, often at the expense of party ideals.

Hussein, who brought his country to the brink of disaster, managed to save it from total destruction and defeat, but not from heavy losses: Iraq's economy was in a shambles, and it lost close to 1 percent of its population in mortalities alone. Hussein's next test will be the transition from war to peace. As Hussein has seen it since the mid–1970s, Iraq should aspire to Third World and Arab leadership, and the Arabs should aspire to become a world superpower like America and the USSR, Western Europe, Japan, and China. This will be achieved in the first place through civilian development and military aggrandizement in Iraq, and then through pooling together all the Arab resources.

To provide more working hands, Hussein gave unprecedented incentives to Iraqi women to work outside their homes. This was accompanied with improving their education and legal status. To increase the number of Iraqi citizens, he made it easier for other Arabs to naturalize, but more importantly, he gave far-reaching incentives to Iraqi families to bring up many children, and encouraged his people to marry young. Since the mid–1970s, Iraq's economy has been given an unprecedented push forward, using the new oil money. The main thrust has been in those areas where quick success was guaranteed and the achievements could show most clearly: oil and mining, the petrochemical industry, and massive irrigation projects. Hussein also gave a major push to education in Iraq: At the expense of quality, he increased the number of school children threefold and of students in higher education almost fivefold between 1970 and 1985, and since 1978–1979, he has conducted a sweeping campaign to eradicate illiteracy.

During the war, the need to streamline the Iraqi economy became particularly acute: Iraq ran out of reserves and could no longer afford waste and inefficiency. Here, too, it was Hussein who decided, contrary to party doctrine, to dismantle agricultural and consumer cooperatives and privatize some sectors of the economy. A side effect of these steps was the creation of a large stratum of private entrepreneurs, particularly contractors and merchants, who see in Hussein personally the best guarantee for their continued prosperity. Hussein made sure, however, that the main assets and thus the country's main sources of income, the oil wells and the phosphate and sulphur quarrying, as well as the large industries, remain in the hands of the government. This way he secured the central government's (and his own) hold over Iraq's economy and society.

BIBLIOGRAPHY

Baram, Amazia. "Saddam Hussein, A Political Profile." *The Jerusalem Quarterly* no. 17 (Fall 1980): 115–144.
———. "Mesopotamian Identity in Bathi Iraq." *Middle Eastern Studies* 19 (October 1983): 426–456.
———. "The Ruling Elite in Bathi Iraq 1968–1986: The Changing Features of a Collective Profile." *The International Journal of Middle Eastern Studies* 24 (November 1988).

Batatu, Hanna. *The Old Social Classes and the Revolutionary Movements of Iraq*. Princeton: Princeton University Press, 1978.

Farouk-Sluglett, Marion, and Peter Sluglett. *Iraq since 1958, from Revolution to Dictatorship*. London and New York: Routledge and Kegan Paul, 1987.

Iskandar, Amir. *Saddam Hussein, the Fighter, the Thinker and the Man*. Paris: Hachette Realities, 1980.

Khadduri, Majid. *Socialist Iraq: A Study in Iraqi Politics since 1968*. Washington, D.C.: The Middle East Institute, 1978.

Marr, Phebe. *The Modern History of Iraq*. Boulder, Colo.: Westview, 1985.

Matar, Fuad. *Saddam Hussein, the Man, the Cause and the Future*. Beirut: n.p., 1981.

Moss-Helms, Christine. *Iraq: Eastern Flank of the Arab World*. Washington, D.C.: The Brookings Institution, 1984.

AMAZIA BARAM

I

IDRIS I (1889–1983). Muhammad Idris was instrumental in the struggle for Libyan independence, and as head of the Sanusiya order served as a nationalist leader in that struggle. During the period between the two world wars Idris bargained with the Italians, the British, and the Egyptians for the establishment of an independent Libya. He came to an understanding with the British regarding the future of Libya after World War II, and in November 1949 the United Nations drafted a resolution to grant Libya its independence. Independence became a reality in December 1951 and Idris took the title of King Idris I. He pursued policies which focused on economic development and maintained good relations with Britain and the United States from which Libya received economic and security assistance.

Libya has been described as a child of the United Nations because its independence was first enunciated by the UN General Assembly in 1949. Its draft resolution stated that Libya, which was to include the three provinces of Tripolitania, Cyrenaica, and Fezzan, was to become an independent and sovereign state before January 1, 1952. Most of the major Western powers and the Arab states, as well as the Soviet Union, had an input in that declaration. Amir Muhammad Idris was then chosen by the Libyan National Assembly to become Libya's first ruler.

Muhammad Idris bin Muhammad al-Mahdi bin Muhammad bin Ali al-Sanusi al Khattabi al-Idrisi al-Hasani was the grandson of the founder of the Sanusiya movement, an Islamic revivalist movement the influence of which spread throughout North Africa, the Sahel, and beyond into large parts of sub-Saharan Africa, in the nineteenth century. By the end of the century, the Sanusiya movement was in complete control of Cyrenaica, although that region remained under nominal Ottoman sovereignty.

Muhammad Idris was born in 1889 in Jaghbub, in Cyrenaica near the Libyan-Egyptian border. His mother, Aisha bint Ahmad bu Sayf, was the fifth wife of Muhammad al-Mahdi, the eldest son of the founder of the Sanusi order. Muhammad Idris did not inherit his father's leadership of the Sanusiya. It went instead to an older cousin, Ahmad al-Sharif, who headed the resistance against the Italian occupation. During the period between 1913 and 1914, his bedouin forces inflicted heavy losses on the Italians.

By the outbreak of World War I, however, the conditions in Cyrenaica had deteriorated significantly, with famine, epidemics, and plagues following years of warfare. The government at the time, the Ottoman Porte, which had supported the Sanusi resistance, attempted to use it to fight the British forces in Egypt during the war. Unwillingly, Ahmad al-Sharif acquiesced and suffered a major defeat at the hands of the British. Vanquished and humiliated, he then turned over the leadership of the Sanusi Order to Muhammad Idris, and left Libya, never to return.

Sayyid Muhammad Idris had not approved of his cousin's involvement against the British in Egypt, and as early as 1914 had made his position clear. That stand assured him of British support during the next decades as he sought the ouster of the Italian forces and the leadership of Cyrenaica. Muhammad Idris's approach to the Italian problem was also different from that of his cousin. With the British acting as mediators, he opened negotiations with the Italians in July 1916, and by the spring of 1917 both parties had agreed on peace terms. Those included Muhammad Idris's control over Cyrenaica, which was in the process of becoming an autonomous region. An independent republic was declared in Tripolitania in 1918, and by the end of World War I, separate statutes had been issued for the two provinces. Each was to have its own parliament and local councils, with the Italians exercising very limited control over Cyrenaica and Tripolitania.

By 1920, however, both provinces were rejecting all forms of Italian control over their affairs, and Italy was unable to enforce its sovereignty over those territories. In October 1920, the Italians recognized Sayyid Muhammad Idris as hereditary *Amir* (ruler) of Cyrenaica and head of some of the inland oases, in exchange for abiding by the 1919 statutes regarding Italian sovereignty in the area.

The political climate was changing in Italy, with the Fascists consolidating their power domestically and eventually adopting a very different type of policy toward their colonies. The Libyans themselves were divided, especially in Tripolitania, over the issue of leadership. Arab-Berber fighting broke out in 1921 and the Berbers eventually sought the protection of the Italians on the coastal areas of Libya. Divided and feuding, the Tripolitanians turned to Muhammad Idris of Cyrenaica for assistance against the growing power of the Italians. In April 1922, they offered him help in extending his amirate to Tripolitania as well as to the rest of Libya, which he eventually accepted.

By then it was too late, however, as Guiseppe Volpi, the new governor sent to Tripolitania, had begun a major military operation to reestablish Italy's control over the whole country. Muhammad Idris realized very soon that there could no longer be a peaceful compromise with the new Fascist government in Italy that would make it possible for him to share power with the Italians in Libya.

Consequently, he opted to go into exile to Egypt, in October 1922, where he remained for the next three decades.

It took Italy nine years to conquer Libya, during which thousands of soldiers fought and died. Although the Cyrenaican northern lowlands were "pacified" early on, the Italians met with strong resistance in the Jabal al-Akhdar region of Cyrenaica. There an elderly sheikh, or tribal leader, Umar al-Mukhtar, who officially represented the Sanusi Order, led his forces in guerrilla raids against the Italians. It was only in 1931 that he was ambushed, caught, and publicly hanged at Suluq. With his death, the Libyan resistance came to an effective end in Cyrenaica.

Throughout those years of conflict, the Sanusi Order was the principal target of attack by the Italian forces. The *zawiyas* (cells) of the Sanusiya and the mosques were closed, the local Sanusi leaders were arrested, the property of the order was confiscated, and the Kufra oasis, the last stronghold of the movement, was bombed. Those actions generated a great deal of support for the Sanusiya in Libya. The order thus became the closest thing to a nationalist movement, as Libya never had an organized nationalist movement that fought for the country's independence. Muhammad Idris, as head of the order, was thus perceived as the symbolic leader of the fight for Libya's independence. The Egyptian government, however, did not permit him to play a very active role in the politics of his country so as not to antagonize the Italians with whom Egypt had good relations. However, his advice was often sought by those who carried on the fighting, and it was freely given.

It was only after World War II broke out that Muhammad Idris saw his opportunity to free Libya. With British support, he gave his approval to the formation of a Sanusi force under British command that would be used in fighting the Axis powers in Libya. In return, he asked—in the name of those Cyrenaican and Tripolitanian leaders who had agreed to this idea—that once the war was ended, Libya would become internally independent, be headed by a Muslim Libyan leader acceptable to the British, and become a British protectorate until the time when it was ready to assume full and complete independence. Although the British never formally accepted those conditions, they eventually formed the basis of Anglo-Libyan relations in the immediate aftermath of the war. It was not until 1947, when the Big Four powers signed a peace treaty with Italy, that the question of Libya's independence could be raised. Furthermore, it was only in November 1949, after prolonged negotiations concerning the fate of Libya, that the United Nations drafted a resolution to grant Libya its independence.

On December 24, 1951, Libya became independent and Muhammad Idris took the title of King Idris I of Libya. The following day in Benghazi, the first government of independent Libya was formed, headed by Mahmud Bey al-Muntasir. In the first decade of independence, King Idris's main objectives were to preserve the unity and integrity of the nation; to obtain aid to help build the state; and to ensure the security, independence and territorial integrity of Libya.

To achieve these goals, the king embarked on a foreign policy that was initially successful but ultimately led to his demise.

After having applied to the United Nations for membership, the Libyan government opted to join the Arab League in March 1953 to gain recognition and support in the region. This decision was also prompted by Arab and, more significantly, Egyptian pressure. Egypt hoped that through the Arab League it could play a more significant role in influencing the new Libyan administration.

King Idris was wary of Egyptian intentions. To safeguard Libya's independence, he signed a twenty-year Treaty of Friendship and Alliance with Great Britain in July 1953. In addition to considerable financial assistance, the treaty ensured the protection of Libya's territory from foreign aggression by providing for the passage and movement of British air and land forces in Libya, and the supply of equipment and arms to the Libyan army. The military base and military facilities obtained by the British were a further deterrent to any regional power with hegemonic ambitions over Libyan territory. When the Arab League offered Libya an annual grant of four million Libyan dinars to reject or amend the treaty, King Idris refused. The generous offer from the Arab states would have compensated Libya for the loss of revenues from the base and from British economic assistance and obviated the necessity of granting military facilities to any foreign power.

Libya was very poor, and the king's ability to obtain economic and financial assistance was vital for the state's survival. The primary objective of Libya's Treaty of Friendship with the United States, which was signed in September 1954, was economic. While the United States kept the Wheelus Military Base outside Tripoli and retained its troops and military equipment in Libya, the king received substantial compensation.

When the French attempted to sign a treaty with the Libyans similar to the British and American treaties, it was turned down. The Libyan prime minister argued that it was unnecessary because the military alliance with Britain and the treaty with the United States were sufficient to provide for the protection of the country and the financing of the greater part of Libya's economic development.

To protect its alliances with the Western powers and to avoid regional interference in its domestic affairs, the king chose a policy of neutrality in the inter-Arab conflicts between the more radical states and the more conservative ones. Although publicly King Idris supported all the Arab causes and Libya voted along with other Arab states in the United Nations, in fact, little else was done.

Nevertheless, it was almost impossible to remain completely uninvolved in the affairs of the Arab world. The Suez Canal crisis of 1956, for instance, affected Libya directly. Despite the fact that the Libyan government supported Egyptian President Gamal Abdul Nasser's* nationalization of the Suez Canal, an action that could have eroded British support for Libya, and asked Britain for guarantees that it would not use its bases in Libya to attack Egypt, the king faced serious domestic and regional criticism. In Tripoli demonstrations broke out in support of Nasser and condemning the tripartite attack on Egypt. The demonstrators demanded the breaking off of relations with France and Britain and threatened to attack the British forces stationed in Libya. Egypt intervened directly in the domestic affairs of Libya by encouraging the disturbances, distributing arms, and promoting attacks on American and British military installations. Although the king was able to weather that storm without having to break off relations with his Western allies or suffering further retaliation from Egypt, this crisis was the precursor of more serious events to come.

With the new revenues from the oil that began to be exported in the early 1960s, domestic opposition to the king's foreign policy in the region became more vocal. Young Libyans imbued with the ideals of Nasserism saw the new wealth as a means of ridding Libya of the foreign military presence. They also felt that they could then become more involved in the affairs of the Arab world. The king, fearing the consequences of such an involvement, would not make any fundamental concession to those demands.

In January 1964, students began to demonstrate in Benghazi against an Israeli proposal to divert the waters of the Jordan River and in support of an Arab summit in Cairo to discuss countermeasures to the proposal. The Cyrenaican Defense Force that was sent to maintain law and order in Benghazi during the demonstrations shot an undisclosed number of students, further exacerbating the situation and leading to riots all over the country. Although the situation returned to normal, these events demonstrated to the Libyan government the precariousness of its "neutral" foreign policy in the Arab world.

Nasser exploited the incident, and in a speech in February 1964 called for the closing of the British bases in Libya. He implied that the Libyans would be traitors if they did not do so because there were no guarantees that the American and British bases would not be used against the Arabs in the event of a war with Israel. That speech forced the Libyan prime minister to assert publicly that Libya would not extend or renew its military agreements with Great Britain and the United States after they expired. The king disapproved of that statement and a few days later, as a sign of his displeasure, announced that he was abdicating on grounds of ill health. However, a strong show of support by Libyan crowds demanding that he remain in power convinced him that he still had the support of his people, so he withdrew his abdication.

The 1967 Arab-Israeli war was perhaps the single most important event in the demise of King Idris. When the war broke out in June 1967, not only students but also large mobs of Libyans began rioting in Tripoli and Benghazi, attacking the British embassy and burning U.S. British armored trucks and cars. Port workers boycotted British ships, and oil workers went on strike despite government appeals to return to work. Although under enormous regional and domestic pressure to sever its diplomatic relations with Britain and the United States, the king refused to do so.

It was becoming apparent that the Libyan government was having increasingly less control over its foreign policy. It was being pulled irrevocably into Egypt's political sphere of influence, and there was little it could do. Furthermore, the

Western bases were no longer a deterrent to external intervention in Libya, but had themselves become a liability to the state. They were the focus of anti-Libyan propaganda that had fuelled domestic upheavals and undermined the legitimacy of the Libyan government.

To placate those who criticized Libya for its behavior during the war, King Idris and his cabinet began following a new course of action in foreign policy. It was agreed that the treaties with Britain and the United States would not be renewed. Second, Libya became, by the end of August 1967, a major aid donor to the states that had suffered most in the war, and third, Libya decided that it could no longer rely on others to protect it and so embarked on an ambitious plan to build its armed forces. It also began acquiring an ultramodern defense system produced by the British at the cost of 1.4 billion dollars. All these measures, however, did not quell the criticism from all quarters against the Libyan administration. By the time the 1969 coup took place, it had been expected both inside and outside Libya.

When Idris I first came to power he faced a country divided into three distinct regions: Tripolitania, Cyrenaica, and the Fezzan. Each had its own local leaders and viewed the other regions with a great deal of suspicion. His first task, therefore, was to ensure the survival of the state by reducing possible sources of conflict and enhancing the interest of individuals in all the provinces in being first and foremost Libyan citizens.

The first step taken by the National Assembly was to stipulate that Libya would have a monarchical and federal system of government. Federalism was to allay the fears of the Cyrenaicans and the Fezzanese that the Tripolitanians would dominate the new government and that they would not have a say in their own affairs. In 1963, however, Libya was declared a unitary state so that the oil wealth that was generated primarily in Cyrenaica could be more equitably distributed throughout the country. Those two stages in the evolution of the Libyan political system ensured that at the outset potential conflict between the provinces was reduced, and at a later stage that it was in the interest of the Tripolitanians and the Fezzanese, at least, to unite under one system so that they could share in Libya's new oil revenues.

The second step was to draft a constitution that would define, among other things, the powers of the provincial governments and those of the federal government. It was finally agreed that all matters concerning national defense, foreign affairs, public health and education, justice, and finance should be dealt with by the federal government as they affected the whole political system. Most other matters were left under the jurisdiction of provincial governments.

The Libyan constitution also defined the powers of the king. He was declared a constitutional monarch, but was given such extensive prerogatives that he was in effect the supreme power in the land. Neither the Supreme Court nor the prime minister could directly challenge him, and he remained inviolate. His personal style of rule was low-key and behind-the-scenes. He never made public statements, and chose to remain above any private, local, and regional conflicts and competitions that took place in Libya. He became the ultimate arbiter in such conflicts and his decisions were final.

In 1952, elections took place. As suffrage was not a universal right, only 140,000 Libyans voted. The National Congress Party, whose membership was urban and middle-class, and which was planning to play a major role in national politics, failed to get much support. Consequently, it claimed that the elections had been rigged and its members demonstrated rather violently in Tripoli. The police were sent in, dozens of people were killed, and the leaders were arrested. From then on, organized opposition to the government was suppressed and all but disappeared under the monarchy. The only form of opposition was spontaneous and temporary. These measures were aimed primarily at preventing the emergence of regional conflict, but they resulted in the stifling of the first flicker of democracy in Libya.

Despite the modern structure of the state, government was in effect in the hands of the king and his immediate entourage, with the provinces headed by local notable families on good terms with the king. It was at its best a benignly despotic state that worked relatively well, assuring its citizens of protection from outside interference and enough development aid to begin the building of Libya's infrastructure.

The export of oil in the early 1960s brought enormous revenues and with them new expectations and many changes in this small, traditional society of just over a million people. Although average incomes rose tenfold between the time of independence and 1963, the poorer Libyans, especially in the rural areas, were not getting any of its benefits. On the other hand, a few, especially those among the king's entourage, were reaping huge profits from the oil revenues and spending conspicuously. Furthermore, although the king was investing in development projects all over the country, many were long-range projects that began producing results only after Muammar Qaddafi's* coup. There were also massive and costly projects that were built, including a new capital in Bayda in the heart of Cyrenaica, that were viewed as an attempt by the king and his people to benefit his region at the expense of the rest of Libya. Consequently, the perception among the young and more educated citizens, was that the monarchy was not doing enough for Libyans and that the benefits of the oil wealth were not being equitably distributed. Nasser's inflamatory speeches also helped in creating a mood of discontent in Libya during the 1960s.

Despite criticisms directed against the foreign and domestic policies of King Idris I, his legacy has lasted to this day. He did maintain Libya's independence in the only way it could have been maintained in view of the very limited resources at his disposal in the 1950s. At a time when Libya was considered one of the poorest countries of the world, he was also able to provide Libyans with development assistance from foreign donors, which helped build schools and health clinics, and ensured Libyans of some basic necessities. Idris I also managed to keep the country together and to prevent regional conflict from erupting, despite major difficulties. Today's Libyan identity may be said to have been formed, at least in part, during the monarchy.

It was only in the aftermath of the oil boom that the situation began to unravel. One cannot say with certainty that another leader would have been able to cope more effectively given the rapidity with which the changes took place both domestically and regionally. Perhaps a younger, more vigorous leader might have been able to adapt better, but the king was old and sick and no longer interested in the day-to-day running of the country. However, despite the accusations of squandering the nation's wealth, Idris I did set up a welfare system to help alleviate the plight of the poor. The education system grew enormously during his reign, and Libya's major universities were set up under the monarchy. Agricultural-development and land-reclamation projects were started under the king and later pursued by Qaddafi. Housing plans were also made during those years, but only few saw the light before the king's ouster.

On September 1, 1969, Idris I was overthrown in a bloodless coup while he was abroad for health reasons. He then went back to Egypt, an exile for the second time, where he died in May 1983.

BIBLIOGRAPHY

Anderson, Lisa. *The State and Social Transformation in Tunisia and Libya 1830–1980*. Princeton, N.J.: Princeton University Press, 1986.
Deeb, Mary-Jane. *Libya's Foreign Policy in North Africa*. Boulder, Colo.: Westview Press, 1989.
Evans-Pritchard, E. E. *The Sanusi of Cyrenaica*. Oxford: Clarendon Press, 1949.
First, Ruth. *Libya the Elusive Revolution*. Baltimore: Penguin Books, 1974.
Khadduri, Majid. *Modern Libya: A Study in Political Development*. Baltimore: Johns Hopkins University Press, 1963.
Pelt, Adrian. *Libyan Independence and the United Nations: A Case of Planned Decolonization*. London and New Haven: Yale University Press, 1970.
Salem, Salaheddin Hassan. "The Genesis of Political Leadership in Libya, 1952–1969." Ph.D. diss., George Washington University, Washington, D.C., 1973.
Villard, Henry S. *Libya: The New Arab Kingdom of North Africa*. Ithaca, NY: Cornell University Press, 1956.
Wright, John. *Libya: A Modern History*. Baltimore: Johns Hopkins University Press, 1982.
Ziadeh, Nicola A. *Sanusiyah: A Study of a Revivalist Movement in Islam*. Leiden: E. J. Brill, 1968.

MARY-JANE DEEB

ISMET INONU (1884–1973) served in a number of positions under Mustafa Kemal Ataturk, including foreign minister and prime minister. Inonu was Ataturk's choice as successor, and was elected president the day after Ataturk's death in 1938. He led the Republican Peoples' Party for thirty-five years and during his leadership of Turkey he initiated a multi-party democratic system and led the country through periods of drastic challenge and change.

Following a great national hero is not an easy role. Some of those cast in such a situation have merely continued in the paths already set out and have made little mark of their own on history. Others have felt impelled to denigrate their illustrious predecessor, to try to undo some of his accomplishments in order to escape fading into insignificance. The Turkish Republic was fortunate that its progenitor, Mustafa Kemal Ataturk, was succeeded by a man who chose another, more constructive way: to complete what his chief had not—and could not—do. Ismet Inonu, Ataturk's long-intended successor, opted as his centerpiece to inculcate democracy not merely in form but also in substance. That was an achievement for which Ataturk was not temperamentally suited, for it meant a willingness to acquiesce in one's own political defeat.

Born in September 1884, Inonu started as a military officer, rising to general soon after moving into the political arena. Serving first as foreign minister, then prime minister, and finally president after Ataturk's death, he eventually presided over the transition to a multiparty regime in the aftermath of World War II. Following his defeat in the 1950 elections, he languished in opposition for a decade before reemerging as prime minister from 1961 to 1965. He led Turkey's reformist Republican Peoples' Party (RPP) from Ataturk's death in 1938 until just before his own demise in 1973. At that time, he was buried in a place of honor in Ataturk's mausoleum complex, and is generally regarded as Turkey's second most important leader of the Republican era.

Inonu built his illustrious career on intelligence and discernment combined with caution, loyalty, perseverence, and the ability to appear nonthreatening to his chief. However, in addition to these virtues of an able number-two leader, his success also reflected a remarkable receptivity to new ideas. Starting from a narrow military framework, he continually enlarged his view. This willingness to learn remained pronounced even in his eighties, when he was faced with new and complex political challenges growing out of a military takeover that threatened the achievements of his lifetime. His uncommon sensitivity to the outside world was all the more striking because from an early age Inonu had suffered from a serious hearing loss, so severe that it degraded his speaking voice and contributed to his notable lack of charisma.

An intellectual bent and studiousness marked Inonu from his youth, but his qualities of leadership and statesmanship developed only gradually. The scion of a middle-level bureaucratic family in the Ottoman Empire, he entered the military school system at the age of eight, and in due course completed the military school, at that time the usual route for those of modest means and undistinguished lineage to move into the elite. The hallmark of this educational regime was an exposure to foreign instructors, providing him with his first taste of Western models for the solution of problems. Inonu took especially to foreign languages, French and German, which he saw as the route of access to this rich Western lore. At the same time, like many of his colleagues, he was greatly influenced by Japanese successes in the Russo-Japanese War of 1905, reinforcing his conviction that Western learning could be effectively applied by non-Europeans.

From the first, Inonu showed that he valued this education by an intense dedication to academic success. He crammed for his hardest subjects during vacations, a practice he continued in military school. As a result, this reserved and retiring youth graduated as a lieutenant in 1903 at the head of his class. He was immediately assigned to the staff college, the institution through which all those destined for senior command had to pass. Again his meticulous preparation saw to it that he was first in his class on graduation in 1906.

Inonu emerged from staff college as a captain, but he had yet to distinguish himself through more than study. He had formed the usual bonds with classmates; indeed, some of his most loyal supporters dated from that experience. Inonu's respect for a fellow staff-college upperclassman, Fethi Okyar, who was far more politically minded, served after graduation to draw him into the secret Committee of Union and Progress then being organized within the army with the aim of forcing political change on the sultan. However, Inonu did not play a prominent role in the Young Turk revolution of 1908; he is said to have sympathized with the faction of Union and Progress that included Ataturk and that advocated taking the army out of politics in 1909. In any event, Inonu centered his own career on professional military matters for the next decade.

In the years immediately after leaving the staff college, Inonu acquired a senior patron, Ahmet Izzet *pasha*. This general was impressed with the captain's grasp of military maneuvers in joint exercises of the First and Second armies. As a result, in 1910 Inonu was posted to the campaign to put down rebellion in the Yemen. Here he had his first occasion to demonstrate his tenacity as a negotiator, successfully reaching an accord with the formidable Imam Yahya.* Thereafter, thanks to his patron, he was in 1913 assigned to Enver pasha's headquarters in Istanbul. Nevertheless, Inonu did not get drawn into Young Turk politics. While he progressed to lieutenant colonel by the start of World War I, he was still generally advancing in lockstep with others of his class.

The war did not do for Inonu what wars often do for survivors: that is, assure him rapid promotion. War's end found him only a full colonel. While he did not distinguish himself in military action as Ataturk had done in repelling the British landing at Gallipoli, Inonu did set the seal on his career by establishing close ties at this time with Turkey's future leader, serving under Ataturk's command on the eastern and then the southern fronts. These were not successful campaigns, yet they provided a chance to hone tactics. Even more important, Inonu was able to demonstrate his loyalty and perseverance in difficult times, traits that Ataturk clearly valued.

Fortunately for Inonu, the Turkish struggle for independence after World War I was based in the first instance on the military establishment and not the civilian elite. Thus he had the proper credentials for the inner circle. Nevertheless, he remained in Istanbul for almost a year after May 1919, when Ataturk left for Anatolia to organize rebellion against the sultan and resistance to foreign invaders. That was a time when Ataturk needed reliable agents and supporters in the Istanbul apparatus. Inonu served for brief periods in critical personnel posts in Istanbul, but the extent of his activity on behalf of the nationalists has not been established. Once the British troops occupied Istanbul, however, he was summoned to Ankara. Here Ataturk made him commander of the nationalist forces as chief of the general staff, a ministerial post during the exigencies of wartime. Despite the fact that four generals outranked him, these senior commanders accepted this highly unusual violation of normally sacrosanct seniority. Inonu's appointment, however, may have sown the seeds of future political rivalry with Fevzi Cakmak, whose duties as wartime minister of defense overlapped with those of Inonu.

The new chief of the general staff proved a good general, winning some important engagements against the Greeks in the campaign of delaying actions to slow their advance into Anatolia. However, Ataturk himself took personal command of the decisive battle in the struggle for independence to break the Greek lines and rout the enemy. Hence, Inonu emerged from this war with the credit of being a capable assistant rather than of being the architect of victory on the battlefield.

With the military phase of the conflict over, Inonu was drawn into civilian politics. Negotiations with the European powers to confirm the Turkish triumph were too important to entrust to Ataturk's political rivals, who had, for reasons of national solidarity, occupied leading posts in the wartime government. Thus the nationalist chief picked his trusted subordinate to go to Lausanne as foreign minister to negotiate according to a strictly limited mandate. Here Inonu displayed a dogged tenacity, infuriating polished European statesmen by exploiting his deafness, continually making them repeat their complicated formulations. Then, rather than exceed his mandate, he returned to Ankara without an agreement early in 1923, a tactic that allowed the Turks to wear down their opponents and in the end to win essential points. Nonetheless, the calculus of how far to bend was Ataturk's; Inonu was celebrated merely for his brilliant execution thereof.

This record of loyal service paved the way for assignments of greater responsibility. When political troubles threatened Ataturk's grip in 1925, the nationalist leader again turned to Inonu, who at age forty-one was made prime minister. It was clear that Ataturk selected him not only as a trusted subordinate but also as a tough, no-nonsense figure who would impart discipline to the political arena. Ataturk had had his fill of rivals in major political posts, as they constantly tried to limit his authority; the Kurdish revolt of 1925 offered a chance to make a clean sweep, a plan for which Inonu's qualities appeared providential. Indeed, the new prime minister performed so effectively in imposing a one-party regime and in backstopping the key social reforms Ataturk believed Turkey must experience that he allowed Inonu to serve as prime minister virtually without a break for over a decade until just before his chief's death in 1938.

Respect for the government as the guardian of the people animated Inonu's approach during these years as prime minister. He believed intensely in the secularizing, Westernizing, modernist reforms that made up Kemalism (Kemal Ataturk's doctrine), although his family had been religiously conservative and he had in 1916 married Mevhibe, a girl from a similar background. Nonetheless, his military training had convinced him of the responsibility of the government to modernize society. He was thus in the forefront of those who embraced the radical alphabet reform promulgated by Ataturk as well as the restrictions on dress to undercut Islamic influence in Turkish society. Such extreme devotion to reform was to cast Inonu as a special champion of new controversial educational experiments that would end by giving his opponents a convenient target for attack.

A second facet of Inonu's approach that was to have major consequences for Turkey's development was his commitment to the state as the agency to direct economic activity. Like other nationalists, he was profoundly affected by the European economic control over Turkey that had been imposed at the end of the nineteenth century and by the exploitative nature of foreign commercial enterprises in this atmosphere. If anything, he went even further than Ataturk in accepting the state's role in the economy.

Starting in the late 1920s with a campaign to nationalize the railroad network, which was owned by Europeans, Inonu soon became the strongest exponent of this etatist policy of establishing quasi-public enterprises to manage the commanding heights of Turkey's economy. His commitment to central planning by the early 1930s complemented his dedication to state economic activity; he was a major and active supporter of the Kadro movement to create a nationalist philosophy for Kemalism compounded from socialist and even fascist elements. Alone of the major Kemalist leaders, he wrote an article for the *Kadro* journal praising Kadro as a third way between capitalism and communism. Commitment to a strongly state-directed economy remained his point of view to the end of his life. It also established Inonu as the bitter rival of Celal Bayar, who in the 1930s joined the cabinet as the economic czar of Turkey with the aim of turning the etatist approach launched by Inonu into a "vitamin treatment" for private enterprise.

Inonu was celebrated for loyalty to his chief, but an even more basic leitmotif was his great caution. Indeed, when loyalty and caution collided, it was the latter that prevailed. This was demonstrated in his public break with Ataturk in 1937 over Turkish foreign policy. As prime minister, Inonu was technically responsible for the conduct of government business; Ataturk as president was constitutionally only the symbolic leader and not legally accountable for the implementation of policy. Nonetheless, Ataturk actually ran the country, and the inherent conflict of powers was resolved by Inonu's unquestioning deference to his leader.

However, when the issue of possible involvement in war was raised at the Nyon conference of September 1937, at which the Europeans met to deal with the problem of unidentified submarines in the Mediterranean, Inonu's innate caution came to the fore. He was unwilling to take the risk of agreeing to hunt down these submarines, at least until Turkey had consummated an alliance with Great Britain. Ataturk felt no such restraint and personally ordered the Turkish negotiator to sign the accord binding Turkey to action. When Inonu questioned whether his chief had given orders to the delegate from the dinner table where alcohol was served, he was taking on the president at two sensitive points: Ataturk's uncontrolled drinking and his fearless foreign policy. Ataturk responded by asking for and receiving Inonu's resignation in September 1937.

Although Inonu remained out of the government until his chief died the following year, he used this time to good advantage. Adding English to his roster of foreign languages, he began extensive readings in British parliamentary process. He may have been brought to this topic by the circumstances of his own dismissal, but British political thought had a pervasive influence on Inonu. It confirmed in him a determination to see Turkey move away from its single-party regime to a representative democracy based on direct elections. It was at this time that he evidently conceived an understanding of the need for a multiparty system, an understanding that lay behind his promise to liberalize Turkey's political life soon after being overwhelmingly elected president the day after Ataturk's death.

The Turkish parliament turned to Inonu as the all-but-unanimous choice for president in 1938 because he had been seen for so long as the anointed successor that few felt confident in the hands of his rival and Ataturk's last prime minister, Celal Bayar. In contrast to Bayar, Inonu had the foreign experience that suggested he would be able to negotiate the shoals of the gathering war; perhaps equally important, as a former general Inonu had the strong support of the military establishment, whereas Bayar, a life-long civilian, did not.

Inonu wasted no time in removing his rivals, whom Ataturk had placed in strategic positions in the government to make sure that no one else could get a solid grip on power. From the first, however, the new president signalled that he was willing to accept political liberalization in due course. To prepare for this eventuality, in his first major address he called for the creation of village teacher-training schools. This venture would eventually roil the political landscape and offer a target for opponents who feared communist infiltration of the educational system, and it would be dismantled by the Democrats in the 1950s, although education of the masses would remain a continuing commitment of Republican Turkey.

For the most part, however, innovations had to wait, as Inonu, who feared the uncertainties of military conflict, devoted himself to keeping Turkey out of World War II. While personally sympathetic to the Allies, he set such a high price in demands for military equipment and support to move against the Axis that in effect he prevented Turkey from being drawn into the fighting. Only when it was necessary to act in order to qualify for a seat in the United Nations did Inonu finally allow Turkey's formal declaration of war against Hitler's Germany.

Having assured that Turkey would successfully survive World War II, Inonu made good on allowing opposition parties to organize. His willingness to liberalize reflected a recognition that his austere personality did not elicit the general adulation Ataturk had boasted. Moreover, he clearly believed that by allowing party competition he would have a stronger claim on support from the Western democracies, support he felt particularly was needed in view of the Soviet territorial demands levied on Turkey at the end of the war by Stalin. However, although Inonu favored allowing the opposition to organize, he faced persistent objections from a conservative wing within his own party. To satisfy these hard-line elements within his own organization, he called snap elections in the summer of 1946 to catch the nascent opposition parties off balance.

Inonu's last four years as president saw him carefully shepherding political life toward more normal party competition. He outmaneuvered rather than forced out the conservative opposition within his party, and gradually led the bureaucracy to a more nearly neutral stance between the two major parties. When elections in 1950 ended in a sweeping victory by Celal Bayar's Democrat Party, Inonu was disappointed at the strong rejection by the electorate. Nonetheless, he faced down restive generals who apparently proposed quashing these contests to allow the Republican Peoples Party to remain in power. Inonu personally, therefore, is due the lion's share of credit for a successful transition to multiparty democracy, a system that has, despite some intervals of military intervention, nonetheless become the norm for Turkey.

Inonu's service as opposition leader in the 1950s was not unequivocally positive. His personal relations with Bayar and the new prime minister, Adnan Menderes,* rapidly deteriorated. Lacking a critical mass in Parliament after the major defeat in 1950 and the even more thorough trouncing in 1954, Inonu was not able to influence the course of politics during the decade of Democrat Party rule. Even with the larger representation that the RPP gained in 1957, he could not find ways for constructive shaping of policy. Indeed, hotheads in his party added to the bitterness of the clash with the Democrat Party. With a growing threat that the RPP might itself be closed down, Inonu sent ambiguous signals to the army not to obey illegal orders from the Democrat Party regime. That set the stage for the fall of Bayar and Menderes, who were ousted by a military junta in 1960, although Inonu almost certainly did not approve of the military moving to overthrow the civilian regime. Indeed, there is convincing evidence that he considered the 1960 military takeover an unwelcome development that deprived him of an almost sure victory had elections been held as scheduled.

The 1960–1961 period of military rule posed for Inonu the problem of getting the army back into the barracks. He used his prestige as a former general and Ataturk's right-hand man to forge links with the senior officers. After a purge of the revolutionary junta by its less radical elements, his pressure was influential in getting the ranking officers to begin the course of elaborating a new constitution and returning to elected government. Benefiting from the advantage of a long-established organization, his party emerged the strongest in elections in 1961, although as a result of the introduction of proportional representation (a system that Inonu himself favored to guarantee his party a major political role), it was not able to garner a majority in Parliament. With parties sympathetic to the former Democrat Party strongly represented in the assembly, Inonu was the generals' choice to serve as prime minister to prevent retaliation against the junta and to lead the country back into stable multiparty politics.

Inonu was successful in fostering this transition. In the process, in 1962 and again in 1963 he overcame two abortive coups led by a former military school commandant. He was forced to operate in coalition with difficult partners at the head of a procession of shaky governments, but his prestige and clear vision kept the process on track.

He was not even swayed from his course by an intense foreign-policy crisis with the United States over Cyprus in 1964, a crisis that caused permanent damage to Turkey's key bilateral relationships with Washington, D.C., and eventually impelled a major change in Turkey's whole foreign-policy construct. Despite these unsettling results for Turkey, the Cyprus controversy showed Inonu to be a resourceful diplomat. His military establishment had pressed for an invasion of the island to restore the position of the Turkish minority, which under heavy pressure from the Greek community, had taken refuge in enclaves. With his usual caution, Inonu was apparently unenthusiastic about this venture. He thus readily bowed to American pressure not to send Turkish troops to Cyprus, although he sharply rejected the extremely stern letter from President Lyndon Johnson threatening Turkey with dire consequences if it went through with invasion plans. Inonu made a special visit to Washington, D.C., on the heels of this exchange to extract assistance from the United States, which assigned former Secretary of State Dean Acheson to an effort that was almost successful in mediating a solution to the Cyprus issue.

Inonu never generated enthusiastic popular support, and as time passed after the 1960 military takeover, the need to propitiate the armed forces appeared to lessen. Moreover, the Justice Party, the political organization that had emerged to represent the former Democrat Party voting constituency, began to drain supporters from the smaller parties that had blossomed in the confusion of the immediate postrevolutionary era. Thus coalition politics became increasingly troublesome for Inonu: His coalition with the Justice Party broke down after only a few months; a second government formed with two smaller, right-of-center parties limped along through the second abortive coup in 1963; and the minority government he then put together collapsed after the Cyprus confrontation with the United States shook Turkey's traditional foreign-policy orientation. By early 1965, Inonu's steady hand no longer appeared essential to guarantee civilian rule, and it was clear that he had lost his ability to assemble a majority in Parliament. Thus, when his minority government was defeated on a budget vote in February 1965, he left the prime ministry for the last time.

An important part of Inonu's legacy was to encourage an end to the view inherited from the one-party era that opposition was inherently disloyal. He thus devoted considerable energy to binding up the wounds of the period of military rule. To this end, he had strongly objected to the execution of Menderes by the junta on the eve of the 1961 elections, and once prime minister, he presided over a gradual rehabilitation of the Democrat Party deputies who had been incarcerated by the military rulers. The capstone of this process was his support for the pardoning of Celal Bayar in 1966 and the personal, public reconciliation of these two ancient enemies against the evident wishes of the ranking generals.

Inonu was less successful in inculcating a democratic spirit into his own party. After his old and trusted friend Refik Saydam died in 1942, he was never again comfortable with a number-two leader in the party. As a result, a procession of figures occupied the second-in-command post of party secretary general. The final incumbent in the position, Bulent Ecevit,* served as an Inonu protégé in the effort to bring down Turhan Feyziglu, who had been bold enough to suggest that Inonu was too old to remain at the head of party and government. However, as Ecevit grew stronger within the organization, his relations with his chief deteriorated, and Inonu, after seeing his slate defeated in a final contest over party posts in 1972, resigned from the party's leadership a few months short of his eighty-eighth birthday. He left a party that in some ways found it difficult to recover from this leadership crisis.

Inonu's legacy of multiparty democracy has been buffeted by a period of military rule since his death in 1973, but the roots put down during his era ran deep, and even the military rulers in power in 1980 accepted the need to return to elected government once disorder had been ended and a more workable constitution had been elaborated. All the individuals involved, from the military to civilian politicians of almost all stripes, acknowledged that an elected regime was the only legitimate form of rule for Turkey; this universal recognition owes much to Inonu's patience and skill. Thanks to Inonu's accomplishment, it is unlikely that a military career will ever again provide the route to power for leaders of major Turkish political parties, as it did for Ataturk and Inonu.

In the economic realm, Inonu's ideas of reliance on the state have not stood the passage of time well. The classical Turkish formula of import substitution behind high tariff walls to make Turkey largely independent of the world economy did not work. Since 1980, the Turks have rejected much of this mentality and the system it required in favor of an export-led economy with a greater role for private initiative. However, although the kind of etatism that Inonu favored has largely been disavowed, the concomitant commitment to greater government responsibility for social justice lives on—not as the dominant strain in contemporary Turkey, but as a motivating force for the social democratic party in which Inonu's son Erdal was been a prime mover. One day this Social Democratic Populist Party may indeed win power, and if it does, Ismet Inonu's approach of emphasizing government responsibility is likely to play a larger role.

BIBLIOGRAPHY

Ahmad, Feroz. *The Turkish Experiment in Democracy, 1950–1975*. Boulder, Colo.: Westview Press, 1977.

Aydemir, Sevket S. *Ikinci Adam*. 3 vols. Istanbul: Remzi Kitabevi, 1966–1968.

Harris, George S. "Political History of Turkey, 1945–1950." Ph.D. diss., Harvard University, 1956.

Karpat, Kemal H. *Turkey's Politics: The Transition to a Multi-Party System*. Princeton: Princeton University Press, 1959.

Lewis, Bernard. *The Emergence of Modern Turkey*. 2d ed. London: Oxford University Press, 1968.

Logoglu, Osman F. "Ismet Inonu and the Political Modernization of Turkey 1945–1965." Ph.D. diss., Princeton University, 1970.

Tamkoc, Metin. *The Warrior Diplomats*. Salt Lake City, Utah: University of Utah Press, 1976.

Toker, Metin. *Ismet Pasayla 10 Yil (1954–1964)*. 4 vols. Ankara: Akis Yayinevi, 1966–1969.

Webster, Donald. *The Turkey of Ataturk*. Memsha, Wisc.: George Banta, 1939.

GEORGE S. HARRIS

ISA BIN SULMAN AL-KHALIFAH (1933–). Sheikh Isa bin Sulman became the eleventh member of the al-Khalifah family to rule Bahrain on his confirmation as *amir* (ruler) of the country by the family's senior sheikhs on December 16, 1961. The ensuing quarter century has proven a momentous period, both for the ruler and for his small but strategically located island nation. Sheikh Isa's reign has seen the islands' independence from British imperial control, a marked expansion in the size and scope of the country's central administrative bureaucracy, and the gradual displacement of petroleum production as the predominant sector of the Bahraini economy. These changes have generated periodic outbreaks of social unrest and political disorder that have shaken the foundations of al-Khalifah authority, but the regime has so far managed to contain these challenges, due in large part to the unimpeachable reputation and political acumen of the amir.

Sheikh Isa was born on June 4, 1933, and named for his great-grandfather, who had died the previous December after holding the title of amir for almost fifty-four years. Little is known of his childhood and adolescence. He appears to have been educated by a succession of British tutors and family retainers, and to have accompanied his father, Sheikh Sulman bin Hamad, on a number of trips to India during his youth. As his first official act, Sheikh Isa led a deputation of Bahraini notables to Baghdad in June 1953 to represent the Al Khalifah at the coronation ceremonies for Iraq's King Faisal II. Two years later, in the company of one of the most prominent merchants on the islands, he and his brother Sheikh Khalifah visited the United States and Europe for an extended period of time.

In 1956, Sheikh Isa was appointed by his father (who had been confirmed as amir in 1942) to the post of president of the municipal council of Bahrain's largest city, Manama. This appointment came at a particularly crucial time, following as it did three years of widespread political disturbances between the country's Sunni and Shii communities that precipitated the mass resignations of the Shii members of the council. Elections to replace these representatives had to be cancelled due to continuing unrest in the city. The disorders culminated in the emergence of a liberal nationalist movement on the islands during 1954; the leadership of this movement called itself the Higher Executive Committee and prevented a second attempt to hold elections for the municipality by systematically intimidating prospective candidates. Consequently, Sheikh Isa took over a skeleton council consisting entirely of Sunni notables with close personal ties to the ruling family. As a way of restoring popular support for the work of this body, the municipality under his direction created a free-trading area at the city's port. This and other related policies laid the groundwork for the resumption of open elections, which took place in 1958.

At almost the same time, the ruler appointed Sheikh Isa to the country's newly formed Administrative Council. This committee was headed by the ruler's great-uncle, Sheikh Abdullah bin Isa, and was charged with discussing and carrying out a limited range of public matters, not including financial and foreign affairs. Despite its rather restricted purview, the council represented the seed from which Bahrain's central bureaucracy germinated during subsequent decades. It also constituted the most significant forum in which members of the ruling family met with influential commoners to deliberate issues of mutual concern. Along with his position on the council, Sheikh Isa served as acting president of the government's education committee during his brother Sheikh Khalifah's recurrent absences from the islands.

Throughout 1957, Sheikh Isa began to play a more prominent role in Bahrain's political and economic affairs. In early November he took an active part in the events surrounding the country's first Development Week. He presided over the opening of the new Manama public school; and he personally threw the switch inaugurating electrical service to the agricultural village of al-Budayya.

On January 31, 1958, the amir confirmed his son's growing stature within the ruling family by designating him heir apparent. The following month, Sheikh Isa accompanied his father and a delegation of senior government officials to Saudi Arabia to meet with King Saud bin Abd al-Aziz. This visit produced a treaty whereby the two rulers delimited the marine boundaries separating their respective domains while providing for the equitable division of any revenues derived from petroleum production within a formerly disputed offshore area. Later that summer, Sheikh Isa personally presented title deeds to some 360 villagers for lands surveyed by the Department of Rural Affairs. The heir apparent then paid an official visit to London, accompanied by his brother Sheikh Khalifah. He returned to oversee the opening of a unified water-supply network for the cities of Manama and Muharraq, having taken charge of the newly created water-supply department earlier in the year.

Over the next two years, Sheikh Isa assumed greater responsibility for the day-to-day management of Bahrain's internal and external affairs as the amir suffered a series of debilitating heart attacks. At some point during this period he became acting head of the al-Khalifah family council, a position that enabled him to distribute the revenues from oil production and other favors among the members and retainers of the clan. Sheikh Sulman bin Hamad passed away on November 2, 1961. Following a mourning period of forty days, Sheikh Isa succeeded to the office of amir on December 16 with the unanimous consent of the al-Khalifah. He ended the year by presiding over the opening of two large-scale development projects initiated by the late ruler: the new terminal building at the airport outside Muharraq and a high bridge connecting the country's two main islands.

During his first years as ruler, Sheikh Isa continued to pay close attention to urban affairs. The improvement of roads and parks throughout Manama was accelerated under his supervision, while the government distributed deeds to both urban and rural lands to individual citizens in the amir's name. To mark the second anniversary of his accession, the ruler laid the foundation stone for the state's most ambitious housing project up to that time, the new community lying midway between Manama and ar-Rifa, and designated Isa Town. In addition, the amir increased both his personal and his administration's annual contributions to the Department of Shii Religious Endowments (*awqaf*) for use in repairing mosques and schools and in drilling wells for use by the islands' disparate Shii villages.

As it became increasingly clear that the smaller Arab amirates would be unable to agree on an acceptable form of union in the wake of Britain's withdrawal from the Gulf, Sheikh Isa took steps to create an autonomous government apparatus for Bahrain during the late 1960s. In 1968 he decreed the formation of a national guard under the command of his son Sheikh Hamad, who graduated from the British military academy at Mons in England that spring; on January 14, 1969, he created a Department of Foreign Affairs under the directorship of his uncle, Sheikh Muhammad bin Mubarak. A year later, the amir reorganized the Administrative Council, transforming it into an appointed cabinet and giving his brother Sheikh Khalifah the title of prime minister. Finally, on August 14, 1971, he declared Bahrain an independent state and applied for membership on its behalf in both the United Nations and the Arab League. The next day he signed a treaty of friendship with the British Resident in the Gulf, Sir Geoffrey Arthur, that reportedly committed the two governments to mutual consultation in time of need but also made Bahrain responsible for its own defense and foreign relations.

At the end of the country's first year of independence, the amir decreed that elections would be held for twenty-two members of a forty-five-member Constituent Assembly charged with drawing up a draft constitution for the amirate. This decision did not meet with unanimous approval on the part of the senior members of the al-Khalifah. Several prominent sheikhs worried that the promulgation of a constitution would encourage the population to question the legitimacy of autocratic rule and would provide a platform for more radical groups demanding wholesale changes in the country's political and social structure. The ruler, while acknowledging these objections, nevertheless pushed forward with plans to hold the elections. From his perspective, constitutional government implied no general conception of popular sovereignty or democratic rule. When the turnout for these elections proved surprisingly large and a number of prominent critics of the regime won seats in the Assembly, the amir moved to silence those who had opposed the elections on the grounds that they would be stacked in favor of the al-Khalifah and its closest supporters by reshuffling the Cabinet and cutting back on the number of appointed representatives. These moves produced a final body composed of twenty-two elected members and nineteen unelected ones.

The draft constitution that resulted from this Assembly's deliberations was approved by the ruler on June 2, 1973. It included provisions that fixed the terms of any final constitution for the ensuing five years, guaranteed de jure equality for women and formal recognition of the right of trade unions to organize, reaffirmed the role of the Cabinet as the primary administrative organ of the government, and mandated further elections for a National Assembly. The second election took place in December of that same year, ushering in a turbulent twenty months of parliamentary politics on the islands. When, in August 1975, members of the Assembly began to openly criticize the public-security ordinance imposed by the regime and the state's close ties to the United States, the prime minister tendered the resignations of the Cabinet. Sheikh Isa accepted these resignations and formally suspended the Assembly, but then reinstated the Cabinet and granted it "full legislative powers." This action enabled government ministers to continue to propose legislation and submit it to the amir for his approval.

By all accounts, Sheikh Isa is an exceptionally tolerant and level-headed chief of state. He has a reputation for moderation in both public and private matters. This quality allows him to serve as the symbol of al-Khalifah paternalism: It is the amir who presides over the open court (*majlis*), which is convened regularly at his country palace outside ar-Rifa. At these courts, as well as at those courts for women held by his wife, Sheikha Hessa al-Khalifa, any Bahraini citizen can petition the ruler personally to redress a grievance or tender a request. It is also the amir who officiates at ceremonial occasions such as the opening of the recently established national bank or the ground breaking for the causeway linking the islands to the eastern coast of Saudi Arabia, and it is of course the amir who hosts visiting dignitaries and represents the regime at the annual meetings of the heads of state of the Islamic Conference Organization and the Gulf Co-operation Council.

However, in addition to providing a paragon of autocratic beneficence, Sheikh Isa epitomizes the pragmatic, if not actually reformist, wing of Bahrain's dominant social coalition. His consistent support for the controlled introduction of new technologies and social services patterned along Western lines has succeeded in improving the daily lives of the great majority of the amirate's population, while he has at the same time avoided alienating the more conservative members of the al-Khalifah and their political allies. Even his severest critics tend to deride his physical appearance and personal eccentricities rather than accusing him of outright despotism or insensitivity to the needs of his subjects. Consequently, the character of his reign has substantially enhanced the regime's ability to survive successive waves of social discontent and even short periods of open rebellion.

Sheikh Isa's exercise of the powers and duties of the office of amir epitomizes the transformation in al-Khalifah rule over Bahrain that has taken place in the last four decades. During the 1930s and 1940s, British advisers took responsibility for the country's most important political and economic affairs, leaving for the ruler only such ceremonial tasks as welcoming visiting dignitaries and paying official calls on neighboring heads of state. However, with the rise of a liberal nationalist movement on the islands in the years following World War II, Bahrain's rulers have adopted a variety of Western administrative structures and procedures as a way of channelling oil revenues into social welfare programs designed to broaden the regime's bases of support. Sheikh Isa, in his capacity as head of the Manama municipal council, played a pivotal role in this effort to reconsolidate the country's dominant coalition. By the late 1960s, the growing managerial expertise of the senior sheikhs of the al-Khalifah enabled them to create the political institutions necessary for Bahrain to emerge as an independent state in the wake of Great Britain's withdrawal from the Gulf. Furthermore, despite persistent objections within the ruling family concerning the pace of institutional change on the islands, Sheikh Isa has managed to contain the shocks that have characterized recent Bahraini politics through a unique combination of deft administrative measures and subtle appeals to traditional authority.

BIBLIOGRAPHY

Anthony, John Duke. *Arab States of the Lower Gulf: People, Politics, Petroleum.* Washington, D.C.: The Middle East Institute, 1975, ch. 2.

Bulloch, John. *The Persian Gulf Unveiled.* New York: Congdon and Weed, 1984. pp. 5–7.

Lawson, Fred H. *Bahrain: The Modernization of Autocracy.* Boulder, Colo.: Westview, 1989.

Nakhleh, Emile A. *Bahrain: Political Development in a Modernizing Society.* Lexington, Mass.: D. C. Heath, 1976.

FRED H. LAWSON

ABD AL-FATTAH ISMAIL (1939–1986) exerted a strong influence on the People's Democratic Republic of Yemen (PDRY, South Yemen) for almost twenty years in his role as ideologue and general secretary of the ruling party. Unpopular with many because of his dogmatic adherence to Marxism-Leninism and his insistence that it be rigorously applied in the still-tribal country, he nevertheless inspired strong loyalty within the political system and led a faction that was either dominant or that closely circumscribed the activities of another dominant faction.

Ismail was born in the North Yemeni district of al-Hujariyah, but like many of his contemporaries, migrated south to Aden in search of better opportunities. He attended Aden Technical College and became a schoolteacher; in 1957 he secured a job (apparently as a teacher) at the British Petroleum refinery in Aden, but quickly found his true vocation as a union activist and revolutionary organizer. He was one of the founders of the National Liberation Front (NLF) in South Arabia.

In its inception a mainstream pro-Nasser organization, nationalist and socialist, the NLF espoused Yemeni unity like most other Yemeni groups; unlike most others, it insisted on the need and desirability of armed struggle. It was initially (and largely remained) oriented toward the tribal territories, and these two characteristics contributed greatly to its eventual victory. Ismail, then, was somewhat of an oddity in this group, but he played an important role. As an urban worker, dogmatically radical (reputedly the only Marxist among the NLF leadership in the early days), committed to the importance of violence and a tightly knit organization, not beholden to any tribal group (because of his North Yemeni origins), he was able to build an organization capable of attracting Aden's workers away from the more moderate, union-based, People's Socialist Party (PSP).

His urban base and radical ideology gained him a place in the NLF's negotiations with Egypt. In August 1965, the Egyptians had brokered the unification of South Arabia's progressive forces under the leadership of the PSP. This had been rejected by the NLF's in-country leaders of the struggle, the "secondary leadership," of which Abd al-Fattah Ismail was a member. The Egyptians then forced another conference where, after applying great pressure (even subjecting Ismail and his colleagues to house arrest for several months, as well as threatening to cut off all support for the NLF), they announced another merger. Once back on their home ground, Ismail and his colleagues rejected this arrangement as well, and continued the struggle despite the hostility of Cairo and a lack of support in the international arena.

By November 1967, the NLF had easily established itself as the dominant force in the tribal areas. More importantly, Ismail's organization had defeated the PSP in a series of bloody battles in Aden (and had for a few weeks taken and held the Crater district of Aden against the British army). Britain recognized the internal balance, and handed over power to the NLF when it withdrew. Abd al-Fattah Ismail's contribution was recognized by his appointment as the minister of culture, guidance and Yemeni unity in the moderate first government of independent South Yemen. However, his activities in the radical left-wing faction, particularly at the Fourth Congress of the NLF in March 1968, where he attacked the approach of the moderate faction and demanded revolutionary internal and external policies (for example, the noncapitalist path of development, village soviets, a people's militia, and the creation of South Yemen as a center for international revolution), caused his dismissal in 1968. He was taken back into the regime when the moderates needed help against tribal unrest and external pressure, and after a year of developing a stronger power base, was instrumental in the overthrow of the moderates in June 1969. In the radical new South Yemeni regime, Ismail gained the potentially dominant position of general secretary of the NLF.

However, other power bases were significant, particularly the tribal, personal, and government organizations (as well as elements in the NLF) that were loyal to President Salim Rubay Ali,* with whom Ismail competed until 1978. The two men and the factions they personified did not disagree fundamentally on the changes needed in South Yemen: agrarian reform in the direction of cooperatives or collective and state farms; nationalization of major economic institutions; dilution of the position of the military through the creation of people's militias; the struggle against imperialism and the reactionary governments in the Arabian Peninsula; and realignment of the PDRY with the socialist countries. However, they did disagree on the instruments to be used to achieve these reforms, the choice of socialist allies (the Soviet Union or China), the pace of transformation, and, of course, which faction was to be in charge.

In this struggle, Ismail was consistently the more dogmatic, the more insistent that policies conform to "scientific socialism," even when this contributed to economic stagnation and political isolation. Even the promise of vast economic aid from Saudi Arabia did not entice him from his anti-Saudi stance or from his support for the overthrow of a now-conservative North Yemeni government. He was quick to align himself with the USSR. In this he went beyond the desire for economic aid to the state sector and military assistance against real and imagined threats on the PDRY's borders (a desire shared by virtually all South Yemenis); he was insistent also on close political links between the two countries, particularly on the development of organic ties between the Communist Party of the Soviet Union (CPSU) and the "vanguard party" he wished to build in the PDRY.

It was the nature of this party and its function in society that provided the focus for the continuing power struggle. Ismail insisted on the need for a ruling party in the mold of the CPSU, highly centralized, bureaucratic, and tightly controlled. This was to be a party that was not merely one of several working parts of the political system but its driving force, penetrating all significant institutions of society, guiding them, and ensuring that they functioned in accordance with the wishes of the party leadership (and, in practice, of its dominant faction).

Ismail was not strong enough to immediately overcome Rubay Ali's opposition to his vision of the party; however, the widespread agreement among the factions on the desirability of "scientific socialism" and close ties to the Soviet Union gave him an advantage. Moreover, the failure of Salim Rubay Ali's more pragmatic policies in the mid–1970s to ameliorate the PDRY's dismal economic conditions, and the enhancement of the USSR's positions in the region after its intervention in the Horn of Africa in late 1977, created favorable conditions for Ismail. By the spring of 1978 his faction had won out, and plans to create the vanguard party were announced. However, Rubay Ali continued to resist, and after a bizarre spasm of violence in June in which North Yemeni President Ahmad al-Ghashmi was killed by a South Yemeni bomb, Rubay Ali was arrested and executed, and his followers were purged.

Within four months the vanguard party, the Yemeni Socialist Party (YSP), had been organized with the help of Soviet and East European advisers. It was a bureaucratic party on the Soviet model, with primary organizations in all parts of society and a Central Committee, all tightly controlled by a Politburo (of which Ismail was named general secretary—in December he also became president of the country). The party affirmed its determination to be the leading force in the PDRY, guided by the principles of scientific socialism stringently applied. It also affirmed close party ties with the CPSU.

In general, relations with the Soviet Union grew closer, partly because of the Ismail faction's predilections, and also because of the threatening attitude of the moderate Arab governments concerning the bomb attack and the ensuing violent transfer of power. The closeness was by no means universally popular, however, and for eighteen months the Soviet–South Yemeni relationship interacted with the domestic situation with particular intensity. The Soviet Union was the sole supplier of military aid and advice, and this was no doubt welcomed in the PDRY generally and in the military in particular. Soviet and East European advisers were attached to all major institutions, and while they kept a low profile, they could not be invisible. Their unpopularity grew especially because of their connection with the planned economy which was continuing to perform poorly; supplies of basic goods, including some foodstuffs, were often scarce. Soviet economic aid was perceived as being inadequate and of poor quality, and in the important fishing sector Soviet captains were widely believed to be taking more than their agreed share.

Popular lack of enthusiasm for the Soviets created complications for Abd al-Fattah Ismail, who was personally far less popular than Salim Rubay Ali had been. He had a stiff, bookish manner, seemingly remote from the problems of daily life, and appeared preoccupied with theoretical Marxism. He was blamed for the increasingly visible material privileges of party and military officials. His unpopularity was not diminished by his refusal (unique among South Yemeni leaders) to participate in public prayers, even if only on official religious occasions; South Yemen, for all its ''scientific socialism'' had not espoused atheism, and Islam continued to play an important role in people's lives. Opposition to Ismail quickly developed in the political elites, particularly among those who continued to see some answers to South Yemen's economic problems in more pragmatic policies. Prime Minister Ali Nasser Mohammed* allied himself with Defense Minister Ali Antar (both of whom had important tribal connections) and began to cut into Ismail's authority.

Ismail was constrained by his very strong commitment to his unpopular domestic policies, and he attempted to sustain his support by pursuing contradictory foreign policies: closer relations with the Soviet Union; resumption of dealings with Saudi Arabia; and support for the North Yemeni armed dissident movement, the National Democratic Front (NDF), which had its headquarters in Aden and was a participant in the PDRY's political system. The Soviets approved of the first and second policies, the Saudis of the second. The third was not only demanded by Ismail's natural radical constituency, it was his preference as well, for he had not given up the desire to unify the Yemens under radical aegis. The moderate aspects of his policy ran afoul of this support for the NDF as the latter's fight in North Yemen was transformed into a brief inter-Yemeni war in February 1979, which for a time appeared likely to expand as the United States seemed to threaten intervention.

Ismail (and indeed South Yemeni politicians of all stripes) looked to the Soviet Union for protection; Moscow responded with gestures of support: a high-profile visit in May 1979 of several of its newest warships, the granting to the PDRY of observer status in the Council of Mutual Economic Assistance (the first Arab country to achieve this position), a visit by Soviet Premier Aleksei Kosygin in September (the first and only visit by a top Soviet leader to the PDRY), and the signing of a twenty-year Treaty of Friendship and Cooperation during Ismail's visit to Moscow in October. These signals of Soviet support benefited Ismail in the short run, and he reciprocated with strong support in the United Nations and the Islamic world for the Soviet invasion of Afghanistan.

However, by the spring of 1980, the close relationship had become to some extent a liability that allowed the more pragmatic of his colleagues to step up their opposition to him. As before, the difficulty was that the Soviet connection (as well as radical South Yemeni policies regarding North Yemen and Afghanistan) was constraining the possibility of substantial aid from a conservative Arab countries and the West. The South Yemeni economy continued its poor performance, and Soviet aid continued to be less than desired and needed. Aden experienced more food shortages and cuts in its electricity supply; the Soviets were identified with both the organization of agriculture and the glacial pace of construction of power stations for Aden. Ismail (and the Soviets) could thus be blamed for economic and administrative shortcomings, and this served to unite a range of opponents, many of whom were concerned primarily with tribal politics or angered at their exclusion from the seat of power by Ismail and his compatriots of North Yemeni origin. In April 1980, while Ismail was out of the country, the "out" factions in the Politburo combined to force his resignation, which was accepted by a narrow margin by the YSP Central Committee.

The Soviets argued unsuccessfully on behalf of Ismail, but quickly bowed to reality and then offered him exile in Moscow. There he stayed, in a style befitting a retired head of state, for approximately five years. Nevertheless, as the power struggle again developed in Aden in 1984, there were reports of him being allowed to meet South Yemeni figures who were opposed to the new leader, Ali Nasser Mohammad, and to openly meet Arab politicians visiting Moscow. Mohammad was forced to allow Ismail to return in early 1985 to take up a position in the YSP Central Committee Secretariat. Analysts have been divided on the Soviet role in his return; some have judged that Moscow encouraged or even forced it, either to help strengthen the YSP or to protect Soviet interests in the face of Mohammad's growing pragmatism; however, a reversion to Ismail's previous domestic and foreign policies would not have been in Moscow's interests, and Ismail's return may have been generated solely by the changing internal balance of power in Aden and abetted by sympathizers in Moscow (itself in the midst of another succession).

In any case, Ismail's return heated the South Yemeni power struggle to a boil. At the Third Congress of the YSP in October 1985, he and his followers and allies forced Ali Nasser to relinquish his majority in the Politburo, although not in the Central Committee. From that point the regime was deadlocked, with Ismail's faction apparently confident it would take over power shortly. On January 13, 1986, the tension reached the breaking point at a meeting of the Politburo. Ali Nasser Muhammad's bodyguards opened fire on his opponents, and in the ensuing battle Ismail was fatally wounded.

Abd al-Fattah Ismail left an indelible mark on the PDRY. He was the driving force behind the development and maintenance of tight multidimensional ties with the Soviet Union. He was also the driving force behind the creation of the Yemeni Socialist Party, the "vanguard party" which, although it is riven by severe tribal and factional cleavages, has retained its authoritarian, quasi-Marxist orientation and its leading role in society. Despite the demonstrable failure of both these factors to advance South Yemeni development, they are likely to continue to dominate the PDRY's future.

The author wishes to thank the Advisory Research Committee, Queen's University, for its support in the preparation of this article.

BIBLIOGRAPHY

Abir, Mordechai. *Oil Power and Politics*. London: Cass, 1974.
Gueyras, Jean. "South Yemen, Cuba of Arabia." *Le Monde*, February 27 and 28, 1979.
Katz, Mark N. *Russia and Arabia: Soviet Foreign Policy toward the Arabian Peninsula*. Baltimore: Johns Hopkins University Press, 1986.
Lackner, Helen. *P.D.R. Yemen: Outpost of Socialist Development in Arabia*. London: Ithaca Press, 1985.
Mylroie, Laurie. *Politics and the Soviet Presence in the People's Democratic Republic of Yemen: Internal Vulnerabilities and Regional Challenges*. Rand Note N–2052. Santa Monica, Calif.: Rand, 1983.
Novik, Nimrod. *Between Two Yemens: Regional Dynamics and Superpower Conduct in Riyadh's 'Backyard.'* Tel Aviv: Tel Aviv University, Center for Strategic Studies, 1980.
Page, Stephen. *The Soviet Union and the Yemens: Influence in Asymmetrical Relationships*. New York: Praeger, 1985.
Peterson, John E. *Conflict in the Yemens and Superpower Involvement*. Washington, D.C.: Georgetown University Center for Contemporary Arab Studies, 1981.
Stookey, Robert W. *South Yemen: A Marxist Republic in Arabia*. Boulder, Colo.: Westview, 1982.
Yodfat, Aryeh. *The Soviet Union and the Arabian Peninsula*. London: Croom Helm, 1983.

STEPHEN PAGE

J

JABIR AL-AHMAD (1926–) has ruled Kuwait since 1977. In his years of rule, Sheikh Jabir has seen Kuwait through a series of foreign-policy crises, all with major domestic implications. The final chapter on Sheikh Jabir is yet to be written; however, his record, as it stands today, suggest that in foreign policy he has been able to do remarkably much with little. At home, his record is mixed. While his policies have brought Kuwait a good deal of stability in an unsettling time, this stability has often been bought at the price of political participation.

Sheikh Jabir was born in Kuwait in 1926, the third son of Ahmad al-Jabir, who ruled from 1921 through 1950, all of Jabir's childhood. As a child, he saw his brothers, cousins, and uncles all assume positions of importance. Nonetheless, while born to opportunity, he was not assured the throne. Kuwait, like the other Gulf monarchies, lacks a tradition of primogeniture. It took many years for Jabir to come to power.

Jabir's early years were a time of radical change. In the 1930s, the Japanese invention of cultured pearls destroyed the local pearling economy, bringing economic crisis to Kuwait. The school Jabir attended, the Mubarakiyya, was forced to close from 1931 to 1936, owing to a lack of funds, and Jabir's education was continued with tutors. It was in the midst of this economic crisis in the 1930s that oil was discovered. The destruction of the old pearling economy and the creation of a new oil-based economy caused serious political dislocation. The interwar period was consequently a time of some political uncertainty when royal family (Sabah) power was being challenged, unsuccessfully, by the merchant class. The first merchant uprising had occurred shortly before Jabir's birth, in 1921, over the accession of his father. The second occurred in 1938, when a group of merchants formed a legislative council, leading ultimately to a confrontation with the *amir* (ruler), which the merchants lost. The thirties were also a period of serious dissension within the ruling family. Jabir came of age watching his father struggle constantly to keep power from his cousin, Abdallah al-Salim al Sabah,* who succeeded Ahmad on his death in 1950.

By the time Jabir became amir, he was already in his fifties and commanded considerable experience in the three most important state institutions: security, finance, and oil. From 1949 to 1959 Jabir directed security at Ahmadi, the small city that grew up around the oil operations. During this period Jabir began to develop a political following. By the early 1950s, the British government, with an eye for such things, noticed Jabir as possible amir material. In the 1950s, a period of Arab nationalism and some domestic turmoil, Jabir was championed by many as a safe progressive, a younger sheikh, sympathetic to some of the Nasserist ideology but unlikely to introduce radical change. Jabir's attempts to develop this base did not go unchallenged. In 1959 the amir appointed Jabir director of the Finance Department, with a mandate to bring the new state institutions under central financial control. Jabir took his job seriously, which put him at odds with the amir's leading adversaries, Fahd al-Salim and Abdallah Mubarak, who refused to submit their accounts. In the end, of the three only Jabir survived politically. In the course of the struggle, as head of finance Jabir meanwhile made his reputation as an opponent of unrelegated government fiefdoms.

The position of finance director also involved Jabir in negotiations with British Petroleum and Gulf Oil. He thus acquired foreign-policy experience, serving as liaison between the oil company and the amir. During this period, Jabir also established the Kuwait Fund for Arab Economic Development, one of the earliest foreign-aid programs, giving him regional foreign-policy experience. In these years he acquired a reputation for hard work, attention to detail, and punctuality.

In 1962, in the crisis atmosphere following independence and a threatened Iraqi invasion, amir Abdallah put to rest a decade of speculation by naming an heir apparent, his brother Sabah. In some ways Sabah was an unusual choice. His nomination broke a pattern, set by the previous three amirs, of alternation between the Jabir and Salim lines of the ruling family. Had Abdallah chosen from the Jabir branch, as many expected, then Jabir al-Ahmad was the most likely choice. However, Jabir enjoyed some popular support from the younger and more educated population, a group whose pro-Nasserist bent troubled the ruling family. Perhaps more critically, Jabir still lacked family seniority. Abdallah's brother Sabah, a low-key but experienced and steady figure, was less controversial, and his nomination was well received. This was a difficult time for Kuwait; continuity, not controversy was needed. Jabir had to wait. Meanwhile, departments became ministries and Jabir became Kuwait's first finance minister.

In 1965, amir Abdallah died and Sabah became ruler. Jabir, passed over for succession before, now became prime minister and crown prince, returning the alternation to the Jabir line. The decision was controversial—it took six months for the family to officially name Jabir. For all the controversy, however, the practical implications of the succession were few. Sabah's rule, following the heady days of development and oil under Abdallah, was a period of consolidation. Under Sabah, as prime minister Jabir quietly assumed increasing control of Kuwait's administration, especially during the amir's extended absences abroad and, toward the end, in the absences enforced by illness. By the time Jabir formally assumed power, he was exercising it. In these years he played a particularly important role in constructing Kuwait's investment and diversification policy, building on his experience as finance director. He also continued Abdallah's policy of rapid expansion of social services.

In December 1977, Sheikh Sabah died and Jabir became amir. His first task was to consolidate power. To accomplish this, he turned to two sets of allies: his factions within the ruling family and his popular base. The consolidation of factional power centered on Jabir's choice for crown prince. There were several possibilities. The first was that Jabir, like Abdallah, would dispense with the historical alternation between the Jabir and Salim lines and name a close relative. The leading choice was his brother and close adviser, foreign minister Sabah al-Ahmad who, as of the late 1980s, has become one of the most powerful figures in Kuwait. The other possibility was a candidate from the Salim side. One contender was Jabir Ali, who had held important cabinet posts and enjoyed substantial beduin support. Jabir Ali had been a challenge to Jabir for some time now. He had, for example, pressed for the separation of the crown prince and prime minister posts, both of which Jabir al-Ahmad held. The amir was determined to restrain Jabir Ali.

The last and, to Jabir, the best choice was another candidate from the Salim side, Saad Abdallah, minister of defense and the interior. In a volatile family council in which Jabir Ali's supporters reportedly walked out, the amir named Saad crown prince and prime minister in early 1978. Having deferred to the Salim line in this choice of heir apparent, Jabir moved quickly to name his own brothers to the state's highest positions: Sabah became foreign minister and deputy prime minister; Khalid, minister for palace affairs, Nawaf, interior minister; and Mishaal, chief of police. The youngest brother, Fahd, choosing glory over power, became head of Kuwait's Soccer Association, taking the team to the World Cup finals.

At the popular level, the amir consolidated power by actively continuing state support for social services (education and health care) and continuing to use the state as employer of last resort of Kuwaitis. As this last policy had the unintended effect of proliferating government departments, the amir also introduced a set of administrative reforms, a policy that allowed him to consolidate power within the state apparatus.

These policies benefited Kuwaitis in general, but Kuwaiti society is highly stratified. Jabir has had to adopt policies to deal with each line of stratification. Some groups define themselves socially, by communal origin. For example, a distinction is made between the historically settled and historically beduin families. The most important communal distinction is between the majority Sunnis, who have always dominated political and economic life, and the minority Shias, comprising perhaps 20 percent of the national population. The Iranian revolution, a Shia revolution, gave Kuwait's Shias a focus for long-standing political grievances. Perhaps more importantly, it led Kuwait's ruling Sunnis to adopt discriminatory policies in the hopes of preventing political organization along sectarian lines, but with the actual consequence of exacerbating Shia grievances. Increasingly, Kuwaiti as well as expatriate Shias have been implicated in political violence in Kuwait. In 1987, members of two important Kuwaiti Shia families—Bahbahani and Dashti—were arrested in connection with oil-installation bombings. The Bahbahani arrest is noteworthy in part because of the higher social standing and royal family ties that this family has enjoyed.

Some groups define themselves economically, by class. The merchants are one such well-defined political group. Many are also socially distinct, members of Kuwait's purported first families, who arrived in the eighteenth century. The leading merchants were historically a politically volatile group, and Sheikh Jabir was, like his predecessors, careful to appease them with economic support and promises that he would not fundamentally alter Kuwait's economic system, with its free-market enclaves for the merchants. One unintended consequence of this policy was to encourage the formation of the Suq al-Manakh, the unofficial stock market that grew up in response to old merchant family domination of the official stock market. When the unofficial market crashed in 1982, it left 92 billion dollars in postdated checks and the country in recession.

In general, however, most of amir's potential opponents and allies do not define themselves economically. Kuwait depends almost exclusively on oil and investments, revenues that are paid directly to the state. As a result, Jabir has at his disposal substantial funds, which his opponents lack, and which he can and does use for political purposes to reward allies and to placate potential enemies such as the merchants and the working class. One strategy that Jabir inherited from his predecessor was that of preventing the emergence of a politically volatile working class by relying heavily on foreign labor, workers who could be deported at the first sign of political action. Given Kuwait's small population, this strategy made sense. However, relying on foreign labor had unfortunate political consequences of its own.

Kuwait relies so heavily on expatriates that Kuwaitis are now a minority in Kuwait. According to the 1985 census, Kuwaitis are only 40 percent of Kuwait's population, 680,000 out of 1,016,000. Rulers have always considered the nonnationals a potential threat. Most nonnationals are politically quiescent since their primary purpose in Kuwait is to earn money, and the price for political activism is deportation. Although most nonnationals stay a short time (40 percent stay for under five years), those who do stay constitute a potential threat. The most active expatriates are Arabs, comprising 63 percent of the nonnationals. They share with Kuwaitis a language and elements of a common culture. From these shared elements grow a sense of political entitlement. Historically, Kuwait's 350,000 Palestinians have been particularly active. In the 1950s, Yasser Arafat* helped found Fatah, the core of the PLO, in Kuwait. Kuwait's expatriates also provide other states with the necessary entry into Kuwaiti politics. Today Iranians, Iraqis, and Lebanese are well-represented among those arrested for political violence.

Given these constraints, the amir's first goal and most successful accomplishment in domestic politics has been to maintain political stability. Other accomplishments, and they are not minor, include the preservation of economic and social rights in an era of falling revenues. The price for political stability and economic well-being has been political participation. Jabir has adopted an increasingly hostile attitude toward the National Assembly, which was established shortly after Kuwait's independence. Jabir's attitude toward the body has always been mixed. In 1976, shortly before Jabir came to power, Sheikh Sabah suspended the Assembly. Jabir inherited the suspension and initially defended it, citing the dangers of anarchy. He later reversed himself, however, reconvening the Assembly in 1981. However, the 1985 elections brought in a more vocal opposition than the government wanted. The amir found it increasingly difficult to reconcile the Assembly's positions with his own policies, and in 1986 he suspended the body. Reasons for the dissolution included dissent within the ruling family itself, which was Jabir's most important constituency. This was prompted by Assembly attacks on Sabah ministers, including the justice minister, who was forced to resign in 1985, and the oil minister. Jabir has also cited the Gulf war and the presence of external forces aiming at destabilizing Kuwait. With the Assembly's closure went many attendant political rights, such as assembly and expression. Ultimately unable to reconcile the preservation of political and civil rights with political stability, the amir turned increasingly away from participatory institutions and toward repressive ones.

In foreign policy, the amir has been more successful. No sooner had Jabir come to power, then he was confronted with a political problem of apparently overwhelming proportion: the Iranian revolution of 1978–1979 and then, in 1980, the Iran-Iraq war, which was virtually on his doorstep. These events gave rise to a series of domestic problems involving both expatriates and Kuwaitis. The amir has had to face a series of attacks on the state: attacks on the U.S. and French embassies as well as government offices in 1983, the hijacking of Kuwait Airways planes in 1984 (and again in 1988) in an effort to free the seventeen men convicted in the 1983 attacks, a 1985 near-fatal attack on the amir's motorcade, and attacks in 1986 and 1987 on oil installations. Kuwait's vulnerable geographic position—a small state, dangerously wedged between Iraq and Saudi Arabia, almost at the front of the Gulf war—gives it few foreign-policy options. Kuwait cannot control its environment, its only hope is to manipulate it.

For most of his rule, the central problem facing Sheikh Jabir was the Gulf war. Jabir aligned Kuwait firmly with Iraq, providing financial and logistical support. This policy was dictated primarily by geographic necessity—Iraq is closer. However, Kuwait has also had problems with Iran. Kuwait refused Ruhollah Khomeini* entry after his deportation from Iraq in 1977. After the revolution, Kuwait feared revolutionary ideas would diffuse into Kuwait via its Shias. In the course of the war, these fears became real. Kuwaiti installations and tankers were the target of Iranian missiles on several occasions. These factors convinced Jabir to take a position firmly behind Iraq. Still, Jabir was careful to limit support to finance and logistics, for example denying Iraq facilities on the Kuwaiti islands of Warba and Bubiyan.

One unintended consequence of this pro-Iraqi position was to predispose Kuwait to play a more active role in Egypt's repatriation into the Arab world because of the military support Egypt could offer. Egypt's presence at the Islamic Summit in Kuwait in 1987 was one of the first steps toward its wider regional acceptance. Historically Kuwait has been a strong rhetorical and financial supporter of the Palestinians. It paid substantial amounts to the confrontation states after 1967 and 1973, and to those involved in the Palestinian uprising in 1988. Jabir is mindful of the large Palestinian community in Kuwait, a community with a history of political activism. In 1988 the police had to forcefully break up pro-Palestinian demonstrations. Nonetheless, Jabir is even more mindful of the war practically on his border.

Sheikh Jabir's most dramatic foreign-policy moves have involved playing off the United States and the Soviet Union. Kuwait, always modestly pro-American, was also first among the Gulf sheikhdoms to establish diplomatic relations with the Soviets. In 1965, Jabir's first official trip as prime minister took him to China and the Soviet Union. Since the war, Jabir has actively encouraged the superpowers to reenter the Gulf in the hope that their presence would bring an end to hostilities and, in the meantime, offer some protection to Kuwait's tankers. Kuwait's request for protection, however, received little response from the United States until Jabir thought to turn to the Soviets, prompting the United States to reverse its decision and, in 1987, to move to reflag Kuwaiti tankers.

The U.S. reflagging was a diplomatic coup for Jabir. He managed to invoke massive U.S. support for his tankers without renouncing anything substantial in the way of national sovereignty—technically the United States was not protecting Kuwaiti vessels but rather reflagged, U.S.-registered ships. Other factors contributed to Kuwait's success, but Jabir's political skill in recognizing and exploiting the particular local dimension of U.S.-Soviet rivalry played a key role. Still, the policy was not without costs. Domestically, it was seen as a sign of increasing dependence on the United States, in a state that publicly values nonalignment. This opposition contributed to Jabir's reluctance to allow more open dissent. Crown Prince Saad has publicly stated that he will not allow the United States to base forces in Kuwait. The policy also met with less than complete enthusiasm from the other Gulf states.

Of all the policies to flow from the war, Jabir's consistently hard-line policy against releasing the seventeen men jailed in connection with the 1983 bombings has been the most popular at home. The government has rejected repeated demands for their release, from Lebanese kidnappers and, most recently, from hijackers in the 1988 Kuwait Airways flight from Bangkok to Kuwait.

Monarchies, like democracies, have established succession mechanisms, and these is no reason to believe that Kuwait's would not work were Sheikh Jabir to die. Indeed, the issue has received renewed attention since the nearly successful attack on the amir in 1985. As matters now stand, Saad will succeed Jabir. As in the past, the real struggle will likely occur over the naming of the crown prince. If Saad follows tradition, he will name an heir apparent from the Jabir line. Even assuming a smooth succession, however, there is likely to be much jockeying for power as the Jabirs strive to preserve their positions and as Saad tries to do what Jabir did, to place his own family members in positions of power. Among the Jabirs likely to be fighting for power are Jabir's well-placed brothers, among them Sabah Ahmad. Jabir, who has married several times, has many children and they, too, could be expected to become more politically involved. Sheikh Jabir, however, is in his sixties; Saad is only four years younger. Jabir may well live and rule for many years, with his most notable policies yet to come.

BIBLIOGRAPHY

Abu-Hakima, Ahmad Mustafa. *The Modern History of Kuwait*. London: Luzac & Co., 1983.
Burke's Royal Families of the World. Vol. 2. *The Middle East and North Africa*. London: Burke's Peerage, 1980.
Crystal, Jill. *Oil and the State in the Gulf: Rulers and Merchants in Kuwait and Qatar*. Cambridge: Cambridge University Press, forthcoming.
Daniels, John. *Kuwait Journey*. Luton: White Crescent Press, 1971.
Dickson, H.R.P. *Kuwait and Her Neighbors*. London: George Allen & Unwin, 1956.
Freeth, Zahra, and Victor Winstone. *Kuwait: Prospect and Reality*. London: George Allen & Unwin, 1972.
Ismael, Jacqueline. *Kuwait: Social Change in Historical Perspective*. Syracuse: Syracuse University Press, 1982.
Rush, Alan. *Al-Sabah: History and Genealogy of Kuwait's Ruling Family: 1752–1987*. London: Ithaca Press, 1987.
al-Sabah, Y.S.F. *The Oil Economy of Kuwait*. London: Kegan Paul, 1980.

JILL CRYSTAL

KAMAL JUMBLATT (1917–1977) was a politician with wide and diverse interests who fascinated both his enemies and his followers by his eagerness to acquire knowledge in a wide range of subject areas. He was a maker and breaker of governments, a dialectician who perceived politics as a game and revolution as a calculated adventure. He played a maverick role in Lebanon which made him visible and active in inter-Arab affairs, a role that was acknowledged by most Arab leaders.

Kamal Jumblatt was born in the village Al Moukhtara (The Selected) in the Shouf Mountains. His father, Fouad Jumblatt (1885–1921), studied at the American University of Beirut but was unable to complete his undergraduate studies due to illness. He was appointed by the Ottomans as the administrator of the Shouf, and he served as governor (*kaimakam*) of the Shouf during the French mandate. In 1921 Fouad Jumblatt was assassinated. After his assassination, Nazira Jumblatt, Kamal Jumblatt's mother, assumed a prominent role in a society traditionally ruled by men. For thirty years *Al Sit* Nazira (Lady Nazira), as she was usually called, played an important role in maintaining the prestige, power, and influence of the Jumblatt family within the Druze community. Al Sit Nazira's role was undoubtedly crucial particularly during the period of the French Mandate of Lebanon. She was accused of being a French accomplice by her opponents, though none of the accusations were substantiated. Nevertheless, she helped to keep the Druze of Mt. Lebanon out of the reach of the revolt of the Druze of Jabal Al Arab in Syria against the French authorities between 1925 and 1927.

In 1926 Kamal Jumblatt was sent by his mother to attend the Institute of Aintura (a Catholic mission) for his primary and secondary education. During his primary education he met Fouad Rizk and Emille Tarabye, both of whom later became prominent figures in the Jumblatts' Progressive Socialist Party. Although Jumblatt was inclined toward sufism and wished to become a priest during his years at Aintura Institute, his mother convinced him to give up that wish, which could have undermined his prospects of leadership in the Druze community. Upon his graduation from Aintura in 1937, he went to the Sorbonne in Paris and received two degrees, one in psychology and the other in sociology and ethics, in 1938. During Jumblatt's stay in France he had his first contact with the communist youth movement which was very active at that time and which influenced his political thought. Years later, in a speech he delivered in 1966, he said that he was impressed by the French communist youth activism in helping the needy and the poor.

In his early years, Jumblatt showed little interest in politics. In his book *Pour un Socialisme Plus Humain* (For a More Humane Socialism) he explained that at the beginning of his life he had two wishes. The first was to become a physician and practice medicine in a remote area in Africa; the second was to embrace the priesthood. However, the death of Hikmat Jumblatt (the leader or *zaim* of the Jumblatt faction since the death of Fouad Jumblatt, Kamal Jumblatt's cousin and brother-in-law) and his mother's forceful role helped determine his future destiny. After returning to Lebanon in 1938, Kamal attended the French Law School in Beirut. In the same year he established several workshops in Al Moukhtara in which employees worked an eight-hour shift as opposed to the standard twelve or more hours per day, were paid above-average wages, and also received food stocks. He wanted to establish a socialist experiment, for which he was called the feudal socialist lord. This was one of the first signs of Jumblatt's socialist inclinations.

In 1942, one year after his graduation with a law degree, Hikmat Jumblatt died. Kamal was the most likely successor. Hikmat had been a member of the National Bloc, a parliamentary caucus headed by Emile Eddé, father of parliamenterian Raymond Eddé. Kamal following in the footsteps of his cousin Hikmat, joined the National Bloc and won on its election ballot, thus gaining a parliamentary seat in 1943. During this period the young Kamal's political philosophy diverged from that of his mother. While she was close to Bishara al-Khouri, the first president following Lebanon's 1943 independence, Jumblatt chose to distance himself by joining the National Bloc, the political party that opposed the Constitutional Bloc established in 1934 by Bishara al-Khouri.

His first public expression of his political thoughts came in 1941, during a brief speech in the presence of French General George Catroux after the defeat of Vichy government troops in Lebanon. In that speech Jumblatt spoke with great sympathy about the condition of the peasants, and also raised the slogan that freedom and independence for individual citizens and the community are only attained when bread and labor are guaranteed along with justice and dignity. During the 1941–1949 period, Jumblatt's political thinking became more influenced by socialist thoughts in a manner that alarmed Sit Nazira. Dismayed by her son's socialist tendencies, she appealed to Sheikh Abdallah Al Aleily, a distinguished linguist and Sunni clergyman, because she feared that Kamal would lose the leadership of the Druze community if he continued to challenge the very basis of traditional Lebanese politics on which the Jumblatt leadership was based. Sheikh Abdallah told her that socialism as a modern trend would not only help preserve his role as a leader, but might even extend it to a larger populace. Al Aleily was one of Jumblatt's friends and cofounder of the Progressive Socialist Party in 1949.

After he was elected to the Lebanese Parliament in 1943, Jumblatt started maneuvering as an opposition leader with unconventional thinking. In his first speech in Parliament, delivered in October 1943, he outlined the basic foundations on which he felt the newly independent Lebanon should be anchored. Jumblatt emphasized Arab nationalism as the only guarantee for Lebanon's independence. He also emphasized that this was the first time the inhabitants of *Grand Liban* (Greater Lebanon)—Sunni, Shiite, Druze, and Christians—acknowledged their allegiance to that country instead of the *Petit Liban* (Little Lebanon) of Mount Lebanon. One year later, he lobbied the Parliament to introduce an income tax bill. He argued then that the progressive income tax was fair because it progressed with the increase of income. Jumblatt believed that private property had a social function; therefore, any surplus from the need of a family or individual should be owned by the society.

Jumblatt's political action style was influenced by Gandhi's political philosophy of direct action. In his life style, morality, and political activism, Jumblatt attempted to set a positive example for his followers. As a consequence, his followers called him "the teacher," (*al-Moualem*). Moreover, the philosophy of direct action became a party policy. For example, party members were instructed to help the poor in building their houses and constructing irrigation channels for the peasants' lands, inter alia, in order to put forth an ideal example for society. The 1943–1948 period of Jumblatt's life was mainly characterized by factional politics and political experimentation. Jumblatt began to emerge as the most prominent vocal critic of the political regime and henceforth placed himself on the left of the Lebanese political spectrum.

In 1945, the young leader concluded that Lebanon's political strife was a direct consequence of the sectarian nature of the Lebanese political system that had been established in 1943. In the same year, Jumblatt advocated a solution to the crisis that was a radical political reform consistent with modern secular democratic principles as established by the French revolution of 1789. During that period the country had been witnessing the emergence of political opposition to the regime, and clashes between Christians and Muslims had intensified. As a consequence, political freedoms were banned by the government. A year later, in 1946, Jumblatt established the National Liberation Bloc, which included prominent Lebanese leaders such as Abd Al-Hamid Karami (father of Prime Minister Rashid Karami,* who was assassinated in 1987), Alfred Nakash, Omar Beihum, Abdallah Al Aleily, and others. The main objective of the bloc was the reform of the political system through two main avenues: amending the constitutional voting laws and enhancing the freedom of the press. Regarding Lebanon's foreign policy, Jumblatt's bloc advocated close economic and political cooperation with members of the Arab League, especially with Syria due to its historical ties with Lebanon, and neutrality or nonalignment in Lebanon's international relations. Jumblatt was strongly opposed to signing any agreements with France as a precondition for its withdrawal in 1946.

Jumblatt's vocal opposition to the Lebanese political system became more radical during 1946. He started to express deep frustration about the possibility of political reform within the political system. He said that "corrupt" elements within the Parliament frustrated attempts of deputies desiring political change and reform. Thus, Jumblatt thought that reform was impossible in Lebanon if pursued within the parameters of the political process. Although he contemplated resigning his parliamentary seat in order to follow a different course of action, he gave up that idea after certain political groups allied with President al-Khouri's Constitutional Bloc tried to expel him from parliament. Instead, Jumblatt threatened to use force to retain his seat.

In 1949, Jumblatt established the Progressive Socialist Party (PSP), a secular Lebanese political party. The party was the synthesis of a decade of political experimentation. Jumblatt attempted through the establishment of the PSP to transcend his main base of popular support, which had been restricted to the Druze community. He envisioned the party as the ideal modern vehicle to reach out to all Lebanese communities. The establishment of the party was one of Jumblatt's major achievements; the PSP was destined to play a key role in Lebanese politics in years to come. Under the leadership of Kamal Jumblatt, the PSP attracted people, mainly the intelligentsia, from different religious backgrounds. Among the 1949 party leadership only Jumblatt was a Druze; six members were Christians and one was Sunni.

During the 1950s, Jumblatt's main achievement was the establishment of the Socialist Patriotic Front (SPF). The front succeeded in bringing about the resignation of president Bishara al-Khouri in 1952, and in the same year, the SPF candidate Camille Chamoun* was elected to the presidency. However, the newly elected Chamoun broke his commitments to the reform program under which he had secured the Socialist Front's support. Soon after Chamoun's defection, the front collapsed, and Jumblatt called for the establishment of a new opposition bloc, called the Popular Front.

The Popular Front included the PSP and several opposition figures, and adopted the program of the previous front: It advocated the secularization of the state, primarily through the abolition of sectarian representation in public office. The front also advocated the enhancement of political freedoms. Economic reform, economic planning, and the neutrality of Lebanon's foreign policy were also on the front's political agenda.

The 1950s were a turbulent decade in the Middle East due to increasing superpower competition, which led to polarization in the area. Consequently, the polarization was reflected in Lebanon's political groupings. President Camille Chamoun, championing a pro-West foreign policy, was eager to join the Baghdad Pact in 1955, and in 1957 he announced his acceptance of the Eisenhower Doctrine. Moreover, since the rise of Gamal Abdul Nasser* in Egypt in 1952, leftist opposition groups, primarily Nasserites, started to advocate a stronger pan-Arab anti-Western political line. Thus, regional and international tensions provided a favorable atmosphere for an internal crisis that lacked only a detonator. The detonator came in the form of the 1957 parliamentary elections. In that election most opposition candidates lost their parliamentary seats to Chamoun's supporters. The opposition led by Jumblatt attributed its loss to electoral fraud. What further compounded the problem was Chamoun's attempts to seek another term in office, which required a constitutional amendment. Thus, the internal, regional, and international stages had been set for a showdown.

Hostilities broke out in the Lebanese capital, Beirut, as well as in the north, the south, and the Shouf Mountains. Military confrontation took place between Chamoun's supporters and the militia formed by the opposition. Large parts of the Shouf fell to rebel forces commanded by Jumblatt's PSP. The revolt lasted six months, and in July 1958 the American Marines intervened at the request of President Chamoun. The revolt, in which Jumblatt played a leading role, ended in a political compromise under which Chamoun gave up the idea of a second term and the army commander, General Fuad Chehab,* was elected as the new president.

Chehab and Jumblatt had overlapping political agendas and shared some common views regarding political reform. Accordingly Jumblatt engaged in a policy of constructive engagement with the new regime in an attempt to advance his reform plan. President Chehab introduced some important administrative reforms. The establishment of the Council of Civil Service was an attempt to modernize and upgrade the quality of public employees and to introduce the criterion of recruitment on merits instead of the sectarian quota system. Jumblatt saw those changes as a step to modernize the state and also as an important attempt to curtail the influence of the "traditional bosses" who manipulated the government-employment process to serve their clientele and to perpetuate the boss-client relationship. After three years of constructive engagement, and after serving in the government of Prime Minister Saeb Salam (a Sunni political boss) as minister of education, Jumblatt concluded that attempts to modernize the political system from within were futile. He came to that conclusion after he failed to convince other cabinet members to embark on a reform plan similar to the one carried out in the Ministry of Education. In January 21, 1961, Jumblatt wrote in the PSP weekly magazine *Al Anba* that the Lebanese capitalists were using the state's apparatus to impose their own class hegemony over the masses. He added that some sectarian feudal bosses (a reference to traditional leaders) encouraged sectarian tensions to abort the development of public political consciousness, thus diverting the public's attention from achieving their socialist goals.

This political stand earmarked the end of Jumblatt's short-lived constructive-engagement policy (1958–1961), and the resumption of another course of active opposition. It is important to mention here that in the 1960 parliamentary election, the PSP won twelve parliamentary seats from a total of ninety-nine, that is, about 13 percent of the total seats. The twelve PSP winning candidates were six Christians and six Muslims; eight came from the Shouf, two from the Biqa, and two from Beirut. The PSP Parliament members formed a parliamentary bloc called the National Struggle Front. Jumblatt's political behavior after 1961 was influenced by several regional and international factors. The breakdown of the Syrian-Egyptian alliance in 1961 was perceived by the Lebanese leader as a serious setback to pan-Arabism and the Arab socialist movement. Consequently, Jumblatt conceived that a new regional configuration of forces was in the making which was detrimental to the achievement of his reform program. However, perhaps as a rule, spontaneous popular movements are not usually as rational and calculative as Jumblatt maintained. In the 1960s Lebanon was witnessing an upsurge in a popular movement demanding social, economic, and political reform. Student demonstrations became a daily ritual. The Arab defeat in the June 1967 war, however, was seen by Jumblatt as another setback that had upset the regional balance of forces in favor of the conservative forces at both the regional and national levels. However, the defeat of the Arab regimes' forces by Israel brought into existence the Palestinian armed resistance. Jumblatt thought that the emergence of the Palestinian resistance could help in correcting the balance in favor of the forces of change following Nasser's decline. That was one of the main causes behind Jumblatt's efforts to form an alliance with the Palestinian resistance.

The appearance of the Palestinian resistance in Lebanon brought a new volatile element to the Lebanese theater. In April 1969, the first military showdown took place between Palestinian forces and the Lebanese army. As a result, supporters of the Palestinian resistance in the Lebanese left took to the streets on April 23, 1969, and clashed with police forces in protest of government policies toward the Palestinians. Through these developments a new polarization process began to occur between supporters and opposers of the military operation of the Palestinians from the Lebanese soil. The polarization took place along sectarian as well as ideological and political lines. Following the ''April incidents,'' as they were commonly referred to in Lebanon, Jumblatt was appointed minister of the interior in Prime Minister Rashid Karami's* government. During Jumblatt's one-year service as minister of the interior, he formulated the Bill of Party Organization and Associations, under which several leftist parties were legalized, such as the Syrian Social National Party and the Lebanese Communist Party. Jumblatt resigned in 1970 to concentrate on the PSP after the party had suffered from a decline in public support in the 1968 election as reflected in its loss of four of the twelve parliamentary seats it had won in the 1960 election. Until his assassination in 1977 he did not occupy any cabinet portfolio. Perhaps the 1970–1977 period was the most fruitful and complex of Kamal Jumblatt's political career. During those years he became the most outspoken and prominent leader of the Lebanese left, and a distinguished politician in Arab and Third World affairs.

In 1972 Jumblatt received the Lenin Medal from the Soviet Union for his role championing world peace, and in 1973 he chaired the Arab Joint Front Participating in the Palestinian Resistance. He also participated in the 1966 Afro-Asian Solidarity Conference.

The Two Years War (1975–1976) was another important test of Jumblatt's leadership abilities, especially since the outcome of that civil war would decide the future of the Lebanese political system. In his book *I Speak For Lebanon*, Jumblatt described this war as a historic opportunity to transform the confessional and outdated institutions of Lebanon into truly secular and democratic ones. For Jumblatt, the chairman of the leftist PLO alliance, the civil war was a revolution, and for him "revolution is an unforgiving affair, it is like life itself, a calculated and deliberate adventure" (1982:15). As a result of this "adventure," Syrian troops entered Lebanon to prevent the imminent victory of the leftist-PLO alliance in 1976.

Jumblatt strongly opposed the Syrian intervention in Lebanon; shortly before his assassination he conferred with President Hafez al-Assad* of Syria to express his position, highlighting the importance of an independent, democratic, unified and secular Lebanon. In Jumblatt's view, those principles were incompatible with the Syrian regime's objectives in Lebanon. Shortly after that meeting, on March 16, 1977, Jumblatt was assassinated in the Shouf, a few miles from his village of al Moukhtara. This brought Jumblatt's revolution to a dramatic end.

The assassination of Kamal Jumblatt was considered by the leftist alliance (the Lebanese National Movement) to be a grave blow due to his central role in bridging the differences between the various parties and factions. He had played an essential part in keeping the alliance afloat in a highly fragmented political environment. Criticism of Kamal Jumblatt falls into two general categories. The first is that he was a dreamer, a utopian thinker who did not grasp the social and political realities of Lebanon. Critics claim that this explains why his dream for change was not achieved. The second criticism raised is that Jumblatt sought the elimination of sectarian representation (a key point in Jumblatt's political agenda since the 1940s) and embarked on a line of opposition for personal rather than national motivations: As a Druze, he did not qualify for the presidency of the republic, a position traditionally held by the Christian Maronites. Thus, the argument is made, Jumblatt's political life was strongly motivated by his personal ambition to become president.

Nonetheless, both types of critics agreed that Kamal Jumblatt was one of the greatest thinkers and political leaders in modern Lebanon and the Arab world. Perhaps one of his greatest legacies was the creation of a distinguished political school manifested in his party ideology, which represented a new form of socialism, molded with Jumblatt's idealism and realism. The contradiction between idealism and realism was never resolved. Moreover, another important legacy is his reform program, which remained the main political platform of the Lebanese left.

BIBLIOGRAPHY

Works by Kamal Jumblatt:

Pour un Socialisme Plus Humaine (For a More Humane Socialism). Beirut: n.p., 1973.
Robou Karn Min Al Nidal (A Quarter of a Century of Struggle). Beirut: Progressive Socialist Party Republications, 1974.
I Speak for Lebanon. London: Zed Press, 1982.

Other works:

Binder, Leonard (ed.). *Politics in Lebanon*. New York: John Wiley & Sons, 1966.
Hudson, Michael. *The Precarious Republic: Political Modernization in Lebanon*. Boulder, Colo.: Westview Press, 1985.
Khalil, Khalil Ahman. *Thourat Al Amir Alhadith* (The Revolution of the Modern Prince). Beirut: Dar Almatbouat Al Sharkiya, 1984.
Suleiman, Michael. *Political Parties in Lebanon*. Ithaca, N.Y.: Cornell University Press, 1967.

NAZI RICHANI

WALID JUMBLATT   (1949–) inherited from his father the heavy burden of leadership in the Lebanese quagmire. As the leader of the Progressive Socialist Party, with one of the largest military forces in Lebanon, Walid Jumblatt secured for himself a critical role in the redrawing of the geo-political map of his country and served as a significant force in waging war and making peace in Lebanon.

Walid Jumblatt was born in Al Moukhtara, Lebanon, on August 7, 1949. He received most of his primary and secondary education at the International College in Beirut. He then attended the American University of Beirut, where he received a B.A. in Political Studies.

During the lifetime of his father, Kamal Jumblatt,* Walid did not play any significant political role. However, during the 1975–1976 Lebanese Civil War, Walid became engaged in military training and fighting, but without assuming any official responsibilities in the Progressive Socialist Party (PSP), the party founded by his father in 1949. However, in 1976, shortly before the Syrian intervention, Walid assumed military responsibilities in the Shouf area. After Kamal Jumblatt's assassination on March 16, 1977, Walid, his only son, succeeded him. This seemed logical in a society strongly attached to its traditional practices. At Kamal Jumblatt's funeral, Walid was given the mantle of authority. The traditional cape (*Abaat*), the symbol of obedience to the leader, was placed on his shoulders by Sheikh Al Aql (the highest spiritual leader of the Druze) as a gesture that his community had chosen him to be the successor. His sudden ascension to the ranks of power is strikingly similar to that of his father. Perhaps the abrupt rise to power following an assassination had become characteristic of the Jumblatt family as both his father and his grandfather were assassinated.

Jumblatt's ascendance to the chairmanship of the Progressive Socialist Party was not smooth. Immediately after the assassination of Kamal Jumblatt, Farid Jubran (a Christian Catholic), the vice president of the party, became the interim president. Soon after there was a debate about how to facilitate the transition process without jeopardizing the Druze popular support of the PSP. In less than a month, the debate came to an end and the party had yielded to tradition. The party was concerned about maintaining Druze support, which constituted a substantial majority of the PSP rank and file. Eventually, Walid Jumblatt became the president of the PSP. During the same period, a simultaneous debate was taking place behind the scenes for the chairmanship of the leftist alliance known as the Lebanese National Movement (LNM). Soon afterward, Walid Jumblatt was chosen to lead the LNM.

Between 1978 and 1982, Walid Jumblatt had to deal with the complexities of a dismembered country largely under Syrian and Israeli influence. On another front, Jumblatt had to face several challenges to his leadership within the Druze community (his main base of political support) particularly from the Arsalan Druze feudal faction (Jumblatt's maternal uncles). Walid tried to establish his leadership in the vacuum created by his father's assassination. Walid Jumblatt's primary concern in the 1977–1982 period was to consolidate his power and bring the Druze community under his leadership. Druze support was essential for him if he was to play a national role in the Lebanese arena.

Walid Jumblatt followed an active policy of opposition to the regime of President Elias Sarkis (1976–1982). Following in his predecessor's footsteps, he advanced a political reform program, "The Intermediate Reform Plan," which was formed in 1975 by the LNM. After the 1978 clashes between the Syrian "Arab Deterrent Forces" and rightist militias in the eastern suburbs of Beirut, a realignment process took place. An uneasy alliance emerged between former foes: the LNM-PLO and the Syrians. The alliance was dictated by regional and international conditions, particularly after the signing of the Camp David Agreement by Egypt and Israel in 1979. Syria's hope for a negotiated settlement through which it might recover the Golan Heights (occupied by Israel in the June 1967 war) faded in light of the new regional balance of forces established after Camp David. The realignment of forces created a condition of political and military stalemate that remained without serious challenge until the eve of the 1982 Israeli invasion. The Lebanese left wing did not recover from the military and political setbacks of 1976 or from the loss of its most prominent leader, Kamal Jumblatt, in 1977. Under the chairmanship of Walid Jumblatt, the Lebanese left was searching for a political agenda that would accommodate the established correlation of forces in Lebanon since the 1976 Syrian intervention.

However, a new challenge to Walid Jumblatt's leadership was posed by the Israeli invasion of Lebanon in June 1982. The 1982 war brought the Lebanese National Movement formula to its eclipse. On October 30, 1982, Jumblatt declared the suspension of the LNM alliance, paving the way for a new set of alliances dictated by changing political conditions in the aftermath of the Israeli invasion. In Jumblatt's opinion, the LNM formula did not suit the evolving situation.

Like many other Lebanese leaders, Jumblatt surprised by the intensity and thrust of the Israeli invasion, which they had thought would not exceed a forty-kilometer limit. The Progressive Socialist Party forces, as well as many other units of the leftist-PLO alliance, failed to put up a serious fight against the invading forces. As a result, the Israeli forces were able to occupy the Shouf Mountains—including Jumblatt's hometown, Al Mukhtara—without meaningful resistance. Soon after the invasion, the Israelis tried to persuade the Druze community, particularly the clergymen, to collaborate with the occupying forces. The Israelis used two main tactics to achieve their objective. First, they used persuasion, drawing on notables from the Druze minority of Israel, such as their spiritual leader Amin Tareef and the Parliament member Amal Nasser Eddine. Second, they permitted the deployment of the right-wing militias (Lebanese forces, who were predominantly Maronites) in Druze areas, knowing that these militias and the Progressive Socialist Party had been in a state of war since 1975. Thus, the Israeli approach could be called a carrot-and-stick policy, whereby they used the ''carrot''—the Druze of Israel—to persuade the Druze of Lebanon to collaborate, and also used the ''stick''—the right-wing militia—to push and enhance the process of collaboration. That Israeli policy was a failure as the forthcoming events proved; in particular, the Druze under the leadership of Jumblatt were instrumental in undermining the May 17, 1983, Israel-Lebanon agreement. Walid Jumblatt had to reckon with the Israeli occupying forces and also had to deal with the threat posed by the right-wing militia. Jumblatt's tactic during that period was to eliminate the immediate threat posed by the right-wing Christian militias. Jumblatt was able to achieve that objective by maintaining a good relationship with the Syrian regime, which directly and indirectly supplied most of the PSP's weapons and ammunition. In July 1983, Jumblatt launched a vigorous campaign against President Amin Gemayel's attempts to sign a peace treaty with Israel. Eventually, the left-wing alliance and their allies—primarily the Shiite Amal movement—succeeded in bringing the treaty of May 17 to an end after the PSP forces overran the right-wing militia's position throughout the Shouf mountains. The defeat of the right-wing militias in September 1983 and the disintegration of the central government army in Beirut after February 6, 1984, had created a new balance of forces in the country unfavorable to the camp who wanted the treaty. Meanwhile, Israel had started withdrawal of its forces.

After the Mountain War, as it is referred to in the Lebanese lexicon, Jumblatt became one of the strongest leaders of Lebanon. His credentials as a political leader appeared to be indisputable. Walid Jumblatt emerged an indispensable element in the Lebanese formula for making both war and peace. Since September 1983, the PSP has gained control of the entire Shouf, Aley (with the exception of Souk Al Gharb), and parts of the Maten. In the PSP-controlled areas, the party has set up civil administrations to carry out the daily services for the community. Moreover, the PSP has established its own judiciary system and police force, in addition to its own regular army. The PSP has also introduced changes in the educational curriculum, particularly at the elementary and intermediate levels in history and civil education. The PSP tried to extend its power to the western quarters of Beirut, but this eventually led to severe street confrontations between the PSP and the Amal Shiite Movement, which ended in February 1987 after the redeployment of Syrian soldiers.

After 1984, Jumblatt occupied the position of minister of tourism and public works in Prime Minister Rashid Karami's cabinet, until Karami was assassinated in 1987. Jumblatt's visibility in the Arab and international communities has increased in the last few years. He has maintained his party's links with the socialist parties of Europe through the Socialist International, of which the PSP is a member. Moreover, Walid Jumblatt preserved the historical links between the PSP and India. Moreover, the PSP developed good relations with the non-aligned movement and with Afro-Asian liberation movements. Jumblatt also has cordial relations with the Soviet Union and the socialist bloc in general. The socialist countries provide the PSP with student scholarships in addition to political support and military assistance.

Walid Jumblatt belongs to the new young generation of Lebanon's political leaders. Leaders such as President Amin Gemayel (son of Pierre Gemayel,* founder of the Phalange Party), Dory and Dany Chamoun (sons of ex-President Camille Chamoun*), Samir Jaja, and Nabih Berri (the last two are not descendants of traditional political families) share three general characteristics. They all belong to the post–1943 generation of Lebanon's independence. The second is their political pragmatism, and, finally, those leaders rose to power during or after the 1975 civil war.

Walid Jumblatt, like the other new pragmatic leaders, is still entangled with the ideological legacies of his predecessors. What remains to be seen is how those young leaders will reconcile the ideological legacies of their predecessors and their own political brand of pragmatism. Walid Jumblatt's pragmatism rests on three main guiding principles. The first is the need to consolidate his power and influence in the predominantly Druze districts of Shouf, Aley, and southern Maten. These areas became Jumblatt's main military power base, and consequently helped him to extend his political influence to new geographical areas. During the 1980s, the PSP registered some successes in Sidon and Tripoli, two predominantly Sunni districts. Jumblatt sought to reactivate the PSP in Tripoli, particularly after the 1987 assassination of premier Rashid Karami, the main political leader of Tripoli.

Similarly, Walid Jumblatt, following in the footsteps of his predecessors, focused on Sidon in drawing his alliances. Nowadays, Jumblatt is a close ally of Mustafa Saad, one of Sidon's most influential leaders. It seems that Jumblatt's relative failure to forge a stable alliance with the Shiites has reinforced the importance of enhancing his relationships with the Sunni of Tripoli and Sidon.

The second guiding principle has been to maintain a relationship with the Lebanese left wing, particularly the Lebanese Communist party. However, it has been apparent that this relationship vacillated greatly during the 1983–1987 period, which may be attributed to the pragmatist line followed by Jumblatt. In a conversation with the author early in 1987, Jumblatt said that the Lebanese left wing, in general, has lost ground to sectarian and fundamentalist groups, which in turn has led to a new configuration of forces, particularly in the aftermath of the 1982 Israeli invasion. This perspective partially explains Jumblatt's flirtation with the Amal Movement and the *Hizb Allah* (Party of God) during 1983 through 1987.

However, as events later showed, the PSP-AMAL alliance proved to be an easy and shaky one. In February 1987, the PSP joined forces with the left and fought fierce battles against Amal on the streets of Beirut. Thus, Jumblatt once again succeeded in retaining his traditional alliance with the Lebanese left wing.

The third guiding principle is to check the Syrian regime's attempts to confiscate the margin of manueverability that Jumblatt has tried to secure. It is usually assumed by the Western media that Jumblatt is a satellite to Syria, an assumption that is quite inaccurate. Jumblatt's strategy since he took over after his father's assassination has been two-pronged: On one hand, he has attempted to maintain a working relationship with Syria as the only viable Arab alternative with strong influence in Lebanon; on the other hand, he has sought to cultivate other regional alliances—with Libya and the PLO for example—to check the Syrians and to gain a margin of maneuverability.

Finally, the Progressive Socialist Party under Walid Jumblatt has been largely reduced to a militia with little distinction from other military formulations operating in Lebanon. Attempts have been made to correct that trend, especially in the party conference held in summer 1987. However, some party officials said to the author that these attempts were insufficient to return the party to political responsibility and thus curtail the influence of the military lieutenants. In effect, several leading members of the party became inactive in the last few years as a result of the military ascendancy within the party, which has been transformed into a military organism that bears little resemblance to the political party he inherited from his father, Kamal Jumblatt.

BIBLIOGRAPHY

Azar, Edward, et al. *The Emergence of a New Lebanon: Fantasy or Reality?* New York: Praeger, 1984.

Cobban, Helena. *The Making of Modern Lebanon*. London: Hutchinson, 1985.

Khalaf, Samir. *Lebanon's Predicament*. New York: Columbia University Press, 1987.

NAZI RICHANI

K

RASHID KARAMI (1921–1987). In mid-twentieth-century Lebanon, the political requirement that the prime minister belong to the country's Sunni Muslim community has restricted access to the office for about 20 percent of the population. The majority of Lebanon's Sunni population lives in its three principal coastal cities—Beirut, Sidon, and Tripoli—and political leadership among them traditionally has been wielded by a few rich, urban commercial families. Tripoli's Karami family was one such leading Lebanese Sunni Muslim family, and Rashid Karami, its senior member from the 1950s through the 1980s, made himself the master of the political system of which he became a part. Ten times he served as prime minister between 1956 and the time of his assassination in June 1987. More than any other Lebanese Sunni politician, he made himself the indispensable politician without whose cooperation and support little could be accomplished in Lebanon.

Born in 1921 and raised during the period of the 1920–1941 French Mandate for Syria and Lebanon, Karami received a French education, graduating from the College des Frères in Tripoli. For higher studies, however, he was sent to Egypt where he studied in the Faculty of Law at the University of Cairo. Obtaining his license to practice law in 1947, he did so for four years prior to being elected as deputy in 1951, when he took the seat of his late father, Abdul-Hamid Karami (1890–1947).

Karami's political orientation and the source of both his strength and weakness in Lebanese politics rested on his heritage as the scion of a traditional, notable Syrian-Lebanese family. Possessing great inherited wealth based on ownership of extensive properties in the Tripoli area, the family used its riches to forge powerful patron-client relations in the city. This patronage made the family powerful politically, and its concomitant national political influence enabled the Karamis to augment their wealth as well as to deliver services and patronage to a never-expanding, loyal body of political clients. Such was the essence of traditional politics in Syrian-Lebanese society, where effectiveness at delivering patronage rather than one's views on issues was the basis of political power and influence.

Unlike his father, Abd al-Hamid Karami, who during the French Mandate had favored union with Syria rather than Lebanese independence, Rashid Efendi (or simply al-Efendi, as he was commonly called) followed the lead of Riyad al-Sulh of Sidon, independent Lebanon's first prime minister (1943–1951), and supported the concept of Lebanese independence. This commitment probably reached maturity after the forcible confiscation of properties of other members of his class in Syria during the early 1960s.

Despite his support for an independent Lebanon, however, Karami remained a staunch Arab nationalist and unwaveringly supported the view that Lebanon was an Arab country whose duty was to support and maintain solidarity with various pan-Arab causes. This policy orientation often brought him into conflict with various Maronite politicians, but kept him in favor with various Arab regimes having influence in Lebanon, especially Syria and Egypt. Other Sunni figures, such as Saeb Salam of Beirut, tended to hold the office of prime minister when Saudi influence was preeminent within the Lebanese government.

Karami emerged into prominence in Lebanese politics during the 1956 Suez crisis when, together with two other prominent Sunni political figures, Saeb Salam and Abdullah Yafi, both of Beirut, he championed the claims of Gamal Abdul Nasser's* Egypt to nationalize the Suez Canal. At the same time, Karami, then serving his first appointment as prime minister, resigned and withdrew support from President Camille Chamoun* when the latter refused to break off relations with Great Britain and France for their military intervention in Egypt. Soon, Karami, Salam, Yafi, and other political opponents of Chamoun, including the Druze leader Kamal Jumblatt,* joined forces to form a National Front to defeat pro-Chamoun candidates in the 1956 parliamentary elections. In the elections, however, it was mainly opponents of the president who lost their seats in Parliament, including Yafi, Salam, Kamal Jumblatt, and the Shia leader Ahmad al-Assad of al-Taybeh; Karami retained his seat. The electoral defeat of these prominent political figures who, like Karami, normally could not be defeated in a "fair" election, soon led to a collapse of the Lebanese political system and the crisis of 1958. When it was over, Karami, who had supported the insurrection against President Chamoun, was ideally placed to be called on by Chamoun's successor, General Fuad Chehab,* to attempt to heal the breach that had been opened in Lebanese politics. For this purpose, the new President Chehab asked him to serve as prime minister.

Under the slogan, "no victor, no vanquished," Chehab and Karami worked effectively to restore civil order in Lebanon after the 1958 crisis. Chehab's policy of giving Muslims a larger share in the government enabled Karami to appear a stronger Muslim prime minister than Lebanon had previously known, while Karami's respect for the prerogatives of the Maronite president—rather than challenging them as other Muslim politicians tended to do—enabled him to retain Chehab's favor. Under the leadership of the two men, a fair degree of political stability was restored to Lebanon, and significant economic and infrastructural development also gained momentum in all parts of the country.

Karami's stature as Lebanon's preeminent Sunni politician continued under President Charles Helou (1964–1970). Under Helou, Karami was in many ways the effective ruler of Lebanon during his tenure as prime minister. He continued to consult Chehab on major issues, and Helou, without a political base of his own, was unable to distinguish himself in any way from the Chehab-Karami alliance that continued to dominate his government.

During Helou's regime, however, new pressures began to emerge that once again would tear Lebanon apart politically. Following the 1967 Arab-Israeli war, the growth and consolidation of an independent Palestine Liberation Organization (PLO) among Lebanon's two to three hundred thousand Palestinians gradually divided the Lebanese into two major opposing camps. On the one hand were those, mainly Christians and most traditional politicians, who while supporting the Palestinian cause nevertheless feared the extension of the Arab-Israeli conflict to Lebanese soil and opposed the PLO role in Lebanon. On the other hand was an emerging cadre of new political activists, mainly non-Maronites, who were disillusioned with Lebanon's rigid, established political system, which denied them an effective political role, and who believed the Lebanese government should actively support the PLO and favored its growth as a potential ally in restructuring Lebanon's political system.

The growing division in Lebanese politics actually abetted Karami's political influence and placed him in the position of appearing as the indispensable politician. A firm supporter of the PLO and Arab causes in general, Karami nevertheless upheld Lebanese independence and the sectarian political system that was the basis of his own political power and influence in Lebanese society. He was therefore trusted by Lebanon's traditional politicians not to compromise too much with those who sought radical political change, even while he championed the right of the PLO to organize and defend itself on Lebanese soil. In these circumstances, Karami pursued a role as mediator rather than confrontationalist, a role that augmented his political influence.

Issues reached a head in early 1969, following the Israeli raid on Beirut International Airport on December 28, 1968. Conducted in retaliation for several Palestinian hijackings of Israeli aircraft in Europe, the raid had the impact of polarizing the emerging trends in Lebanese politics and inaugurated the long crisis that finally deteriorated into civil war in 1975. As prime minister, Karami committed the Lebanese government to a policy of recognizing "the legitimate right of the Palestinian people to struggle for the liberation of their homeland" (Salibi 1976:39), even while he sought a formula that would preserve Lebanese independence and sovereignty and limit the impact of Israeli reprisals. The correct formula, he believed, was embodied in the concept of *tansiq* (coordination) between the Lebanese government and the PLO. He advanced this formula throughout 1969 as pressures to crack down on the PLO became increasingly strong from one side of the Lebanese political spectrum, and as neighboring

Arab regimes and the newly emerging left wing in Lebanese politics exerted equally strong pressures to support the PLO and to mobilize against Israel.

When in May 1969 President Helou publicly criticized the PLO for not respecting Lebanese sovereignty, Karami abruptly resigned as prime minister. Karami's move provoked an eight-month crisis that ended only when his concept of tansiq had been formally enshrined in the Cairo Accord between the PLO and the government of Lebanon in November. The technique of resignation proved effective because no other Sunni politician could be found to form a new government, and it gradually became clear that the established political system could be maintained only if Karami's concept of providing a formula to legitimize the PLO's presence and activities in Lebanon were adopted. The Cairo Accord, therefore, was mainly a result of Karami's stubborn adherence to principle as well as his determined efforts to mediate a very difficult problem. The accord became the symbol of his political influence, and as long as it endured his continuing role as mediator between the PLO (along with its Lebanese supporters) and the traditional political establishment was ensured.

Despite its apparent resolution of a fundamental issue that had come to dominate Lebanese politics, however, the Cairo Accord itself continued to be a divisive issue. As a result of the PLO's success in obtaining a legal basis for its incorporation in Lebanon, the so-called left wing in Lebanon also gained in strength, alarming those who championed the traditional political system, particularly Maronite leaders, who also began to mobilize their supporters in defense of the status quo. Increasing violence between Israel and the PLO over Lebanon's southern border also had the impact of making especially South Lebanon a more violent place, leading many Lebanese to begin losing faith in the capability of the government to provide them with security.

Growing dissatisfaction with the Chehabist regime of Helou and Karami, but most particularly with the hated *Deuxième Bureau* (military intelligence), which the regime had used to keep a close eye on opposition groups in Lebanon, led to the defeat of Elias Sarkis, the Chehabist candidate in the 1970 presidential elections. The election instead of Suleiman Franjieh of Zghorta, near Tripoli in North Lebanon, spelled a temporary end to Karami's role as Lebanon's premier Sunni politician. Under Franjieh, who sought to appoint weaker and more compliant Sunni prime ministers, the strong center in Lebanese politics Karami had provided was missing, and the continuing polarization of Lebanese politics proceeded apace, finally erupting in hostilities in April 1975.

Only when it was clear in May 1975 that the open warfare that had erupted in Beirut was not going to be halted short of drastic political measures did Franjieh finally call on Karami to resume his post as prime minister. Karami remained in office until December 1976, and throughout the civil war remained the central Lebanese political figure seeking to mediate the conflict. Karami kept the Ministry of Defense portfolio himself and thereby kept command of the army, but to create the strongest possible cabinet he appointed as interior minister former President Camille Chamoun, a powerful political rival with whom he had hardly spoken since 1958 and who also controlled a militia involved in the hostilities. At the same time Karami deliberately excluded Phalange Party leader Pierre Gemayel* and Druze leader Kamal Jumblatt,* who controlled the principal militias engaged in the fighting.

Although Karami's efforts produced a cease-fire that held through the summer of 1975, the resumption of fighting in September plunged Lebanon into an abyss of conflict from which it had not emerged by the time of his death more than a decade later. Refusing to order army intervention to halt the fighting because the army might be accused of taking sides in the conflict, or worse, because it might split (as it eventually did) along partisan lines, Karami demonstrated his earnestness by installing himself in October 1975 in the old Ottoman Serail (government house) in downtown Beirut. From there he called on the Cabinet and other political leaders to join him, stating that he would not leave until peace had been restored.

The effort did not produce the desired result, but it did start a process of negotiations, involving both Syria and the PLO, that in February 1976 produced a seventeen-point Constitutional Charter that was accepted by President Franjiyah on behalf of the government. A key provision of the charter was its adoption of a fifty-fifty Christian-Muslim formula for representation in Parliament, as opposed to the traditional six-to-five ratio in favor of the Christians that had prevailed since independence.

The Cairo Accord of 1969 was the first milestone in Lebanon's political evolution to have been due primarily to Karami's tenacious mediation efforts; the 1976 Constitutional Charter was the second, although it remained unimplemented due to the lack of an overall peace settlement. Grudgingly accepted, if at all, by Lebanon's conservative Maronite politicians because it retained a sectarian basis for the distribution of political power in the country, the charter continued to be opposed by the "progressive" forces led by Kamal Jumblatt, who continued to insist on a total abolition of Lebanon's sectarian political system. Despite the compromise the charter represented, therefore, fighting continued until it was forcibly suppressed by Syrian military intervention in the summer of 1976.

Although Karami had played a major role in involving Syria as a negotiating partner to help achieve a mediated Lebanese settlement, in the end Syria entered Lebanon in force to pursue goals of its own, to the dismay of Karami, who soon resigned from playing any central role in Lebanese politics for the next several years. Despite Syrian support for Elias Sarkis—a man with whom Karami would have worked closely a few years earlier—to succeed Franjieh as president in 1976, Karami interpreted Syrian actions in support of the right-wing Maronite leaders and against the PLO and the Lebanese left wing as aimed at reviving the prewar political status quo in Lebanon, primarily for the benefit of Syria, on whom a newly revived Maronite hegemony would be dependent. Consequently, together with Kamal Jumblatt and Raymond Eddé, he refused to attend

Sarkis's inauguration in September 1976, and after resigning as prime minister, he spoke out frequently against the government.

Challenges to Karami's political preeminence in Tripoli by such new ideological groups as Farouk Muqaddam's Nasserist 24 October Movement, other Lebanese National Movement groups, and the fundamentalist Islamic Tawhid Organization preoccupied his energies during the presidency of Elias Sarkis (1976–1982). Nevertheless, Karami managed to remain the respected and central mediator of the turbulent politics of his city during the late 1970s and early 1980s.

Before he left the center stage of Lebanese politics, however, Karami had one more act to play. In May 1983 he joined an odd assortment of Lebanese political figures—including former President Franjieh, Walid Jumblatt,* Communist Party leader Georges Hawi, Baath Party leader Asim Qansu, and Syrian Socialist National Party leader Mahmud Abdul-Khalek—to form a "National Salvation Front" to resist implementation of the May 17, 1983, agreement between Israel and Lebanon that had followed Israel's 1982 invasion of Lebanon. When the agreement collapsed of its own accord following the unilateral withdrawals under fire of both Israeli and U.S. forces beginning in late 1983 and early 1984, Karami once again found himself the key Sunni politician needed by Lebanon's new president, Amin Gemayel, to form a new government.

Despite considerable erosion of his political base in Tripoli due to continued bitter fighting in that city, Karami, now sixty-two, remained Lebanon's most prominent Sunni politician. However, the government he now was called on to lead and the society that government claimed to represent were far different from those he had served just eight years before. The Maronite president was no longer the strong figure that his predecessors had been prior to the civil war. In addition, the continuing conflict in Lebanon had ceased being primarily a struggle between those defending the country's established political status order and those who were trying to transform it. Rather, it had become more complex, with struggles within each sectarian community abetting those between the various communities. Moreover, the Israeli invasion had effectively weakened the PLO and the Lebanese left wing as viable political forces in Lebanon.

In these circumstances, Karami once again sought to construct as strong a cabinet as possible. It consisted of a mix of respected traditional political figures as well as new ones who, like Shia leader Nabih Berri, controlled important forces on the ground but who were also committed, like Karami himself, to the principle of an independent Lebanese state. Militant extremist groups, such as the Maronite Lebanese Forces and the Shia Hizbollah, remained outside of central government authority, however, leading Karami once again to involve Syria in the Lebanese mediation process. By the end of 1985 the result was the so-called Tripartite Agreement signed by Elie Hubayka on behalf of the Lebanese Forces; Nabih Berri, leader of the Shia Amal militia; and Walid Jumblatt, representing his own Druze community and his Popular Socialist Party (PSP) militia.

After the Cairo Accord and the 1976 Constitutional Charter, the 1985 Tripartite Agreement was a third milestone that had nearly been reached as a result of Karami's unceasing efforts to reconcile the minimum demands of Lebanon's disparate and competing political factions. In this case, he facilitated an agreement in which neither he, as representative of Lebanon's relatively unarmed Sunni Muslim community, nor the elected president of the Republic were signatory partners. He had come to realize that peace would be restored to Lebanon only by the consent of the country's dominant militias; with Syrian support, they alone had the power to dominate the extremist groups. Only in this way could the guns be silenced so that the political evolution of Lebanon could proceed in the corridors of power—a process in which he was a master—rather than on the battleground of the streets—in which it had become clear that no Lebanese was a master.

The agreement required that Syrian-supported Hubayka and Berri dominate their respective militias and sectarian communities; however, this was something neither proved able to do. The failed Tripartite Agreement proved to be Karami's last major initiative for a comprehensive settlement of Lebanon's complex civil war. In August 1986, Syrian troops once again entered West Beirut to restore order. In 1976 it had been President Franjieh who had requested them on behalf of the Lebanese government; now it was Karami who had done so over the objections of President Gemayel. Continued intra-Maronite fighting, intra-Shia fighting, intra-Palestinian fighting, Shia-PLO fighting, Druze-Shia fighting, and Muslim-Christian fighting, together with a continuing hostage crisis involving more than twenty European and American kidnapped civilians, had created conditions in Beirut that made outside intervention virtually inevitable. Karami preferred Syrian intervention to that by any other country.

The invitation symbolized his own failure, however, as well as his declining political influence. That the tide was turning was also symbolized by the May 21, 1987, vote in the Lebanese Parliament formally abrogating both the May 17, 1983, Israel-Lebanon Agreement and the 1969 Cairo Accord. Stubbornly refusing to affix what should have been his pro forma signature to a bill passed by the Parliament, Karami clung to the principles in which he believed and which symbolized the powerful role he had played in Lebanese politics for nearly three decades. It was to cost him his life. His assassination by a bomb placed under the seat of his helicopter occurred on June 1, and within days the bill was signed by his successor. Although his assassin was not officially identified, the reason for the assassination was at least circumstantially clear.

Karami can easily be criticized for not having been a fully successful politician. Neither the Cairo Accord, the 1976 Constitutional Charter, nor the 1985 Tripartite Agreement succeeded in resolving Lebanon's continuing crisis, although each possessed the potential for doing so. Following his death, none of these agreements remained in effect as elements of Lebanese law. It can also be argued that Karami's resolution to prevent conflict was more apparent than real and that his role helped to promote conflict and violence in Lebanon rather than to resolve it. He can also be criticized for lacking strong leadership in that his political orientation was a middle-of-the-road philosophy that neither strongly defended Lebanon's traditional political system nor effectively incorporated the demands of those who sought to transform it. Finally, he also can be criticized for pursuing public office primarily for personal status and private gain, because such goals were indeed aspects of the traditional Lebanese political system of which he was a part, and it was this system he sought to defend.

Karami was a unique Lebanese politician. His values were those of the liberal, democratic political culture that Lebanon had known through the early years of his political career, and he resisted being attracted by the radicalism that overtook so many of his political colleagues. Although like most prominent political figures in the dangerous Lebanon of the late 1970s and the 1980s he traveled with a retinue of armed bodyguards, Karami never raised a militia. Rather, he relied on the peculiar feature of the Lebanese political system that assigned the office of prime minister to a member of his religious community to guarantee him a political role. In fulfilling this role, he sought to be a mediator rather than a fighter. Such a role was an exception in Lebanon rather than the norm. That Karami failed in his quest to lead Lebanon toward a settlement that would enable the country to conduct its politics more peaceably was more an indication of the overwhelming nature of the issues than of his ineptitude or lack of conviction. Schooled in Lebanon's traditional politics, Karami applied his skills in an effort to preserve Lebanese independence and restore the shattered balance among its contending factions. The results of his major mediation efforts proved unenduring, providing only temporary reprieves from the forces—both internal and external—that ultimately consumed him. More than any other Sunni politician, however, Karami was able to play an indispensable role that few others in Lebanon were positioned to play.

BIBLIOGRAPHY

Cobban, Helena. *The Making of Modern Lebanon*. London: Hutchinson, 1985.
Deeb, Marlus. *The Lebanese Civil War*. New York: Praeger, 1980.
Gordon, David C. *The Republic of Lebanon: Nation in Jeopardy*. Boulder, Colo.: Westview Press, 1983.
Hudson, Michael C. *The Precarious Republic: Political Modernization in Lebanon*. New York: Random House, 1968.
Rabinovich, Itamar. *The War for Lebanon 1970–1985*. Ithaca, N.Y.: Cornell University Press, 1985.
Salibi, Kamal S. *The Modern History of Lebanon*. London: Weldenfeld & Nicholson, 1965.
———. *Crossroads to Civil War*. London: Ithaca Press, 1976.

MAX L. GROSS

KHALIFAH IBN HAMAD AL THANI (1932–). His Highness Sheikh Khalifah ibn Hamad Al Thani has been the *amir* (ruler) of the State of Qatar, a wealthy Arab sheikhdom in the Persian Gulf, since 1972. His reign has been one of rapid economic growth fueled by substantial petroleum and natural gas resources. He has promoted the modernization of the government's administrative structures, the diversification of the economy, and the strengthening of the independence and distinct identity of the state. He has also supported cooperation between the Arab states of eastern Arabia. His lifetime, however, has spanned a period of Qatar's history that began in great poverty and regional tensions.

Qatar is a peninsula jutting into the Persian Gulf off the east coast of Saudi Arabia between Bahrain and the United Arab Emirates. Its flat, stony, barren surface is relieved occasionally by man-made gardens and irrigated farms; otherwise, the main features are the capital of Doha on the east side of the peninsula, where the majority of the state's two hundred thousand people live, and a few small towns and settlements along the coasts and dotting the interior. Qatar's economic livelihood was based on the Persian Gulf pearl industry. The industry's collapse after 1930 threatened Qatar's economic survival. The country's economic salvation was the discovery and exploitation of its large petroleum and natural-gas resources.

The Al Thani clan first migrated to Qatar from Najd in Arabia in the late eighteenth century, but they only began to gain prominence in Qatar in the mid to late nineteenth century, during the reigns of Sheikh Muhammad ibn Thani and his son Sheikh Jasim, the current ruler's great-grandfather. These men were both skilled pearl merchants and wily diplomats. Sheikh Muhammad often served as liaison for Qatar affairs between the Al Saud of Nejd and the Al Khalifah of Bahrain. In the 1850s and 1860s, Sheikh Muhammad and Sheikh Jasim also occasionally mediated between the tribes in Qatar and the Al Khalifah rulers of Bahrain, who held suzerainty over Qatar at that time. To establish and preserve Qatar's independence between the 1870s and World War I, Sheikh Jasim, as ruler, successfully crafted a foreign policy that struck a balance between the ambitions of the British and Ottoman empires in eastern Arabia, and reduced the influence of Bahrain. Sheikh Jasim was succeeded by his son Sheikh Abdallah.

Sheikh Khalifah was born in 1932, during the reign of his grandfather, Sheikh Abdallah, in al-Rayyan, a village to the west of the capital, Doha. Sheikh Abdallah succeeded his assassinated uncle, Sheikh Ahmad, as the governor of Doha in 1906, and then was chosen to be ruler of Qatar by the Al Thani family when his father, Sheikh Jasim, died in 1913. Sheikh Abdallah, who ruled Qatar from 1913 to 1949 and lived until 1956, had three sons; his second son, Hamad, was his favorite.

Sheikh Hamad ibn Abdallah Al Thani (1898–1947) never became the official ruler of Qatar, but he exercised an increasing amount of authority from the mid–1930s until his untimely death in 1947. The source of Sheikh Hamad's power was not only his status as Sheikh Abdallah's favorite son, but also a political agreement with the British government signed in May 1935 in which the British, among other things, recognized Sheikh Hamad as heir apparent. As a result of that agreement, and with the consent of the Al Thani family council, Sheikh

Hamad and his sons, including Khalifah, gained a position of superiority in the line of succession over other Al Thani claimants. This caused tension in the family since it was not the tradition of the Arab tribes of the peninsula to automatically acquiesce to prearranged patrilineal lines of political succession.

Sheikh Khalifah received a traditional education from tutors. Although he was the fourth of eight sons, he became his father and grandfather's favorite. When Sheikh Hamad died in 1947, Sheikh Khalifah was too young to become heir apparent, and his grandfather, Sheikh Abdallah, reasserted his own authority as ruler rather than designate his eldest son, Sheikh Ali, the new heir apparent. Sheikh Abdallah hoped to stay on as ruler until Sheikh Khalifah came of age and could rule. By the late 1940s, however, Sheikh Abdallah was too old to rule effectively. In 1949, in the wake of agreement to an off-shore oil concession with Superior Oil Company (a concession area later acquired by Shell Oil Company), the revenues of which Sheikh Abdallah intended to monopolize, the Al Thani family, with British knowledge and support, deposed Sheikh Abdallah and installed his eldest son, Sheikh Ali, as ruler.

Sheikh Ali's reign (1949–1960, died 1974), however, was fettered from the outset by a family agreement, reaffirmed upon his accession as ruler, requiring the line of succession to return to the *ayyal* Hamad (the sons of Hamad) after Sheikh Ali's reign. As a result, competition for power, influence, and money intensified during the 1950s between the ayyal Ali and the ayyal Hamad and their supporters. Succession was always the long-term issue, but on a more immediate level, family members were concerned about the distribution and expenditure of the growing state revenues and family allowances. It was during this period that Sheikh Khalifah began to acquire some administrative experience. He served jointly with his cousin, the ruler's son Sheikh Ahmad ibn Ali, as a judge on the civil court, and in the late 1950s Sheikh Khalifah became director of education.

Sheikh Ali's government began to use some of the new oil revenues to build schools, hospitals, roads, distribution systems for water and electricity, and other basic infrastructure improvements in Doha and in many smaller towns and villages. By 1960, however, Qatar was on the verge of bankruptcy and the Al Thani family, with British support, forced Sheikh Ali to abdicate in favor of his son Sheikh Ahmad. Again, the ayyal Hamad had been skipped over in the line of succession, but this time Sheikh Khalifah's branch of the family gave its consent to Sheikh Ahmad's succession on the condition that Sheikh Khalifah be designated crown prince and deputy ruler. Sheikh Khalifah soon added many other duties and government portfolios, to the point where he became the de facto if not the de jure ruler of Qatar.

Sheikh Khalifah's growing grip on power in Qatar during the reign of Sheikh Ahmad (1960–1972, died 1977), was due in large measure to his seriousness and capacity for work. This was in sharp contrast to Sheikh Ahmad, who spent most of his time (up to eleven months each year) out of Qatar at his villas near Geneva or in Dubai (he was married to the daughter of Sheikh Rashid, the ruler of Dubai) or on hunting trips in Iran and Pakistan. Moreover, Sheikh Ahmad's expenses absorbed more than half of Qatar's oil revenues.

In November 1960, soon after Sheikh Khalifah had become crown prince, he was appointed finance minister, which gave him direct responsibility for financial and petroleum affairs. In addition, he was responsible for the state's development plans, organizing the administrative system, proposing laws and decrees, carrying out the function of chief justice, and supervising the work of the other departments of government, which had grown to over thirty by 1970 when a provisional "constitution" led to a reorganization of the government. He was appointed chairman of the board of directors of the Monetary Commission of Qatar and Dubai in March 1966. In June 1969 he became the head of the Department of Foreign Affairs, which reflected Britain's loosening of direct control over Qatar's foreign policy in light of Britain's decision to leave the Gulf.

The British decision in 1968 to withdraw from the Gulf by 1971 precipitated a three-year period of intense negotiations between Qatar, Bahrain, and the seven emirates of the Trucial Coast. Sheikh Khalifah played a major role in the negotiations for the Federation of Arab Emirates, which resulted in the creation of the United Arab Emirates in 1971. On July 7, 1968, as part of the negotiations, Sheikh Khalifah was appointed president of the Provisional Federal Council. The following year the council was converted into a cabinet, and on October 21, 1969, Sheikh Khalifah was appointed federal prime minister. Throughout the negotiations, Sheikh Khalifah, together with his Egyptian legal adviser, Dr. Hassan Kamel, were constant advocates of a Gulf federation, but disagreements between the rulers over the division of federal power led Bahrain and then Qatar to declare their independence in 1971 rather than join the new United Arab Emirates. Even so, Sheikh Khalifah had established his credentials as a fervent supporter of Gulf regional unity, and had also even more fully solidified his position as the effective ruler of Qatar.

During the federal negotiations, Qatar drafted a Provisional Statute (sometimes referred to as a constitution), which was promulgated on April 2, 1970. This law provided for the possibility of Qatar joining a new federation should one be established. More importantly, the new statute reorganized the government, established a cabinet, and added the office of prime minister to Sheikh Khalifah's duties as deputy ruler. On May 29, 1970, Sheikh Khalifah formed his first government under the new statute, and took control of its Finance and Petroleum portfolios.

As Sheikh Khalifah acquired more power, the ruler, Sheikh Ahmad, became even less attentive to the government. When Qatar declared its independence on September 1, 1971, Sheikh Ahmad did not even bother to return home from Geneva. With independence came full responsibility for foreign affairs, which Sheikh Khalifah assumed with the new Foreign Ministry portfolio that had been created on September 3, 1971. While Sheikh Khalifah's duties and responsibilities grew, the ruler's eldest son, Sheikh Abd al-Aziz, minister of health, began to assert his claim to succeed his father as ruler. The rise of this potential rival and the growing administrative problems that resulted from authority being divided between an absent ruler and the deputy ruler, led Sheikh Khalifah with family support, to depose Sheikh Ahmad on February 22, 1972; Ahmad was on a hunting trip in Iran at the time. This "coup" became known as the "corrective movement."

As ruler, Sheikh Khalifah immediately instituted financial and administrative reforms. He abolished the infamous "four-quarters rule" whereby three fourths of the country's oil revenues had gone to the family: one quarter to the amir, a second quarter to the Al Thani princes, and a third quarter to a reserve fund controlled by the Al Thani family, with only one quarter transferred to the state treasury. He established Qatar's first ten-year development plan (1972–1982), appointed new members to the Council of Ministers, and implemented the long-promised plan for a Consultative Council (Majlis al-Shura). This council had been established by decree in 1964 and its members appointed (all from the Al Thani ruling family), but it had never met. Sheikh Khalifah radically changed the composition of the council by appointing notables from other important tribes, communities, and merchant families, as well as some younger individuals who represented the new generation. Although truly consultative and not legislative, the council provides an outlet for debate on proposed laws, budgets, and government policy.

The membership of the Council of Ministers also reflects Sheikh Khalifah's efforts to bring all branches of his family and other important families into the decision-making institutions of the government. The difficulty with this approach is that when vacancies occur they must be filled by another member of the same branch of the family. For example, when Sheikh Abd al-Rahman ibn Saud ibn Abd al-Rahman Al Thani, minister of justice, died on March 2, 1975, the minister's position was not filled. No suitable candidate could be found from that branch of the family, which has dominated Wakra, the main town between Doha and Qatar's oil-export port at Umm Said and its environs since the late nineteenth century. A similar problem exists at the Foreign Ministry. This portfolio was given to Sheikh Khalifah's younger brother, Sheikh Suhaym, in 1972. Sheikh Suhaym considered himself a prime candidate for crown prince or at least prime minister, after the "corrective movement" of 1972, but he never realized his ambition. When Sheikh Khalifah decided to appoint his eldest son, Sheikh Hamad, as heir apparent, crown prince, and minister of defense in 1977, Sheikh Suhaym was disconsolate and refused to attend meetings of the Council of Ministers. He continued to believe he deserved better treatment until his death in 1985. Since then, the Foreign Ministry portfolio has remained open, with the duties being covered by the minister of state for foreign affairs, Sheikh Ahmad ibn Sayf ibn Ahmad Al Thani. Similarly, the Ministry of Commerce, held by Sheikh Nasir ibn Khalid ibn Ahmad Al Thani until he died on August 2, 1986, has remained open. Sheikh Nasir is from another branch of the family known as the ayyal Ahmad, which long held pretensions to the throne due to the fact that their patronymic, Sheikh Ahmad ibn Muhammad, had been de jure ruler of

Qatar from 1893 until his assassination in 1906. Nonetheless, Sheikh Khalifah's attention to these family issues has helped him maintain broad support for his rule.

Although his three predecessors were forced to abdicate their position, this is an unlikely scenario for Sheikh Khalifah. In fact, it is often said that if an election for ruler were held in Qatar, Sheikh Khalifah would win because his dedication to the development and welfare of his country exceeds that of any of the other likely candidates.

The sheikh has his critics. He is criticized by some for monopolizing power, for insufficient commitment to political power-sharing through an elected parliament, and, in particular, for relying too closely on long-time foreign advisers. Many of the department heads from the 1960s remained in their jobs even after the 1970 reorganization and the 1972 coup since they had originally been Sheikh Khalifah's appointees. The Council of Ministers created a new level of bureaucracy on top of the old departmental structure, but it did not immediately eliminate the "old guard." Over time, however, the process of Qatarization, strongly promoted by Sheikh Khalifah, has replaced many of the foreign personnel with Qataris.

On the positive side, the economic and development policies of Sheikh Khalifah have gained him a reputation as a prudent steward of Qatar's resources. Under Sheikh Khalifah, Qatar has been less prone than some of its neighbors to spend money on conspicuous projects with marginal value to the society. Sheikh Khalifah has also continued to promote the idea of Gulf cooperation, even if Gulf unity remains elusive. He is a strong supporter of the Gulf Cooperation Council (GCC), and worked for Gulf cooperation in such fields as a Gulf Common Market long before the GCC was established. In foreign affairs he has maintained close and friendly relations with Saudi Arabia but also correct relations with Iran despite the long Iran-Iraq War in the 1980s. He has also attempted to improve relations with Bahrain, even though their historic border dispute remains unsolved. Even within the family he has settled differences between the various branches and mended relations with his cousin Sheikh Ahmad in 1975. Many of Sheikh Ahmad's relatives have returned to Qatar and are active and successful in commerce. Sheikh Khalifah is one of the most secure and respected rulers in the Gulf.

BIBLIOGRAPHY

Anthony, John Duke. *Arab States of the Lower Gulf: People, Politics, Petroleum*. Washington, D.C.: Middle East Institute, 1975.

Abu Nab, Ibrahim. *Qatar: A Story of State Building*. Doha, Qatar: n.p., 1977.

Nyrop, Richard F. (ed.) *Persian Gulf States, Country Studies*. Washington, D.C.: U.S. Government Printing Office, 1985.

Peterson, John E. *The Gulf States: Steps Toward Political Participation*. The Washington Papers, no. 131. New York: Praeger, 1988.

State of Qatar, Ministry of Information. *Speeches and Statements by His Highness Sheikh Khalifa bin Hamad Al Thani*. Doha: 1976.

Sadik, Muhammad T. and William P. Snavely. *Bahrain, Qatar, and the United Arab Emirates: Colonial Past, Present Problems, and Future Prospects.* Lexington, Mass.: Lexington Books, 1972.

                                                                                STEVEN R. DORR

RUHOLLAH KHOMEINI (1902–1989). Ayatollah Ruhollah Musavi Khomeini was in two respects the man of the 1979–1989 decade. He was the only leader of a nation-state who combined religious and temporal authority. He was also the only leader who consistently challenged the accepted norms of the international community of states. The world viewed his passing from the scene with as much surprise as it did his meteoric rise to power.

Khomeini was born on September 24, 1902. The title *Ayatollah* (the Sign of God) denotes the highest scholarly religious standing a Shia Muslim cleric can achieve. Very few Ayatollahs are acknowledged by the Shia community as the "source of imitation," or the "model" (*marjae taqlid*). Khomeini was recognized as such a model rather late in life. Many of his followers addressed him as the *Imam*. In the Twelver Shia tradition, this title is ordinarily reserved for the twelve historical Imams, who are considered to be the spiritual successors of Muhammad, the Muslim Prophet, through his cousin and son-in-law Ali, the first Imam. The twelve Imams are considered to be *Masum* (infallible). This characteristic was not regarded to be applicable to Khomeini. The title of *Hajj Aqa*, denoting one who has performed the religious obligation of pilgrimage to Mecca, and that of *Sayyed*, indicating one who is a descendant of Ali's son Husain, the historical third Imam, were often used in addressing Khomeini before the Iranian Revolution.

His first name, Ruhollah (the Spirit of God), is a common name in spite of its lofty religious meaning. His last name, Khomeini, comes from his birthplace, the town of Khomein, which is about two hundred miles south of Tehran, Iran's capital city. Khomeini's father, Mustapha Musavi, a leading cleric, was murdered there only five months after Ruhollah's birth. The child was raised by his mother, Hajar, and aunt, Sahabeh, both of whom died when Ruhollah was about fifteen years old. In 1928 he married the daughter of a high-ranking cleric named Ayatollah Muhammad Thaqafy Tehrani. They had two sons and three daughters. Khomeini's first son, Hajj Sayyed Mustafa, first studied religious subjects with his father and then with Ayatollah Sayyed Muhammad Burujerdi, who was then the model cleric in Iran. Sayyed Mustafa was later exiled to Najaf in Iraq and was allegedly killed by the late Shah Mohammad Reza Pahlavi's* security agents. The younger son, Hajj Sayyed Ahmad, studied at first in a secular high school and later joined the ranks of religious students at the holy city of Qom. He was quite active and influential in Iranian politics behind the scenes after his father seized power from the Shah's regime.

The murder of his father, the untimely deaths of his mother and aunt, and the assassination of his son had a profound impact on the formation of Khomeini's character. Two of his personality traits were attributed directly to the impact of the loss of life of his close relatives. There were reputedly his steely resolve and his single-mindedness, which were amply demonstrated by his long struggle against the Shah's regime both in Iran and while in exile.

His interest in political activism partly reflected the nature of his education, the examples of several generations of leading religious leaders, and his own personal experience in Iranian politics. Khomeini began his studies in 1908 at the age of six. He first learned to read Persian texts and the Koran, the holy book of the Muslims, in Arabic. Subsequently, he was taught Islamic jurisprudence by his older brother, Ayatollah Murteza Pasandideh. The most important part of his education was completed under the tutorship of Ayatollah Abdul Karim Haeri-e Yazdi, the model for many devout Iranians, first in Iraq and later in Qom.

The subjects that Khomeini studied went beyond the traditional fields. Although thoroughly versed in such subjects as *Sharia* (Islamic law), *Fiqh* (jurisprudence), and *Usul* (legal principles), he questioned the stifling rigidity with which most of the *ulama* (religious scholars) interpreted these. His keen interest in reason alongside revelation emerged in his study of ethics and philosophy. Although, like his teacher, he was not a political activist during his student days, his political quietism during the dictatorial and anticlerical rule of Reza Shah was a matter of tactical prudence rather than subservience to the shah's rule. It was no coincidence that he was the first religious scholar to challenge Reza Shah's blind secularism. The challenge was occasioned after the Shah's 1941 abdication of the throne by an anti-clerical tract, *Assrar-e Hezar Saleh* (Secrets of a Thousand Years), written by a disciple of Ahmad Kasravi, Iran's leading nationalist historian. In response, Khomeini wrote *Kashf-e Assrar* (Discovery of Secrets), refuting that tract point by point.

While example of his teacher, Ayatollah Haeri-e Yazdi, taught him political prudence, those of two other teachers taught him the need for political activity on the part of religious leaders under appropriate circumstances. Ayatollah Muhammad Kazem Khorasani, the teacher of his teacher and the author of the renowned *The Sufficiency*, was an activist religious leader during the Iranian Constitutional Revolution (1905–1911). The tripartite coalition of the Bazaari merchants and artisans, the modern-educated intellectuals, and the *ulama* that led to the granting of the constitution of 1906 broke down soon thereafter, resulting in a serious split among those religious leaders who supported the constitution and those who opposed it. Khorasani was a supporter of the constitution, while Sheikh Fazlollah Nuri was its arch opponent. Khorasani called Nuri a non-Muslim while Nuri called Khorasani an atheist. Although after the Iranian Revolution Ayatollah Khomeini praised Nuri, before the revolution, Khomeini, like Khorasani, accepted the constitution, as evidenced by his book *Kashf-e Assrar*. The constitution provided for the religious supervision of legislation by means of a Theocratic Committee, which was empowered to veto any man-made law that was considered to be un-Islamic.

Besides Khorasani, another religious leader who must have influenced Khomeini was the teacher of the teacher of his teacher. Sayyed Mohammad Hasan Shirazi taught Khorasani, who taught Haeri-e Yazdi, who taught Khomeini. Shirazi was the first Iranian religious leader to oppose monarchical policies that he considered inimical to the interests of the Iranian people and Islam. In 1890, the Iranian ruler Naser ed-Din Shah capped his ruinous financial and economic foreign policies by granting a sweeping tobacco concession to the British, jeopardizing the interests of millions of Iranians, whether the cultivators, the sellers, or the buyers of tobacco. The Tobacco Uprising, the protest movement of the Iranian people against the monopoly control of tobacco by a foreign concessionaire, was led by Shirazi. As " the model jurisprudent" at the time, he issued a *fatva* (religious opinion) in December 1891, prohibiting the use of tobacco "in whatever fashion" because it "is reckoned war against the Imam of the Age [*Saheb-e Zaman*]—may God hasten his advent!" (Mottahedeh 1985:217–218). Every smoker of tobacco in any form stopped smoking and the shah was forced to cancel the concession in January 1892.

For Khomeini, the Tobacco Uprising and the Constitutional Revolution were more than momentous historical events. They were the embodiment of the examples set by generations of religious leaders who had risen to positions of political leadership in the fight against the abuse of power by incumbent secular rulers. Just as these events had provided the opportunity for Shirazi and Khorasani to lead the Iranian people in the struggle for freedom from internal tyranny and external domination, other events in the 1960s gave Khomeini a chance to stake his claim to religiopolitical leadership of the forces opposed to the Shah's regime.

First, he rose in opposition to the Local Council Elections decree issued by the cabinet of Assadollah Alam in the wake of the shah's dissolution of the *Majlis* (Parliament). According to Sayyed Hameed Ruhani, a principal biographer of Khomeini, at the initiative of Khomeini the two other grand Ayatollahs of Qom—Golpayagani and Shariatmadari—met with him to discuss the decree and to send telegrams to the Shah and his prime minister, protesting against the un-Islamic and unconstitutional nature of the decree. The three grand Ayatollahs condemned the decree because, in the ceremony of mandatory oath taking, it substituted any "holy book" for the "holy Koran." It also gave suffrage to women at a time when no one enjoyed freedom, and it was issued in the absence of the Majlis. In a separate telegram, Ayatollah Khomeini told the Shah that the ruler was "surrounded by the sycophants and slaves who would attribute all anti-Islamic [*khalaf-e din*] and unlawful acts to the person of His Majesty" (Rouhani n.d.:155–156). In a much harsher telegram, Khomeini strongly advised Prime Minister Alam "to obey God Almighty and the Constitution, to fear the consequences of deviation from the holy Koran, from religious injunctions and from the law, and to refrain from endangering the life of the country" (ibid., 156–157). In the face of vehement opposition led by Khomeini and supported by many bazaari merchants and artisan guilds, Alam was forced to withdraw the bill.

The second event of the early 1960s that was used by Khomeini to assert political leadership was occasioned by the shah's call for a national referendum regarding his White Revolution. The principal feature of the shah's revolution was the land reform program. The opposition of prominent religious leaders to land reform stemmed from the fact that it threatened their vested interest in the revenues of the lands they held and used for religious educational purposes. Conscious of this opposition, the Shah, in a major speech in Qom on January 3, 1963, tried to divide the ulama by depicting some as the proponents and others as the opponents of land reform. He criticized the latter for allegedly being "preoccupied with the appearance rather than the substance of the religion" (Ramazani 1964:28). However, his ploy backfired. Khomeini, Golpayegani, and Shariatmadari joined together to condemn the Shah's call for a referendum. More importantly, on the same day that the Shah spoke in Qom, Khomeini for the first time attacked the Shah's person. In the shah-ulama conflict over the Local Council Elections decree, the shah had belittled the three grand Ayatollahs by calling them *Hojatolislam*, a rank lower than that of Ayatollah. Khomeini now retaliated by simply calling His Majesty "Mr. Shah." The next day Khomeini was arrested. The people rose up in protest the following day, June 5 (the historic 15 *Khordad*). The Shah's police crushed the uprising in Tehran, killing many demonstrators. Subsequently the Constitution of the Islamic Republic of Iran identified this event as "the great and bloody Islamic revolution in June 1963 which in truth was the starting point of the blossoming of this glorious and widespread uprising [the Iranian Revolution in 1979] which established and confirmed the centrality of the Imam Khomeyni as the Islamic leader."

The third event that Khomeini used to gain political leadership and challenge the Shah's regime was occasioned by the grant of diplomatic immunities and privileges to the American military personnel in Iran. In 1964, the U.S. government extended a two-hundred-million-dollar credit to Iran for the purchase of arms. This had to be approved by the Parliament, which coincidentally had to approve the Pentagon's demand for a "status of forces agreement." In the eyes of the public, the two issues became linked. The shah and the United States were seen as having colluded to impose capitulatory privileges on the Iranian people for the benefit of the American military personnel and their dependents. In a stinging declaration, Khomeini characterized the relevant bill passed by the parliament as "the document of the enslavement of the Iranian nation." It placed the Iranian nation "under American bondage," he charged. "I declare," Khomeini said, "that this shameful vote of the Houses of the Parliament is contrary to Islam and the Koran and hence illegal; it is contrary to the will of the Islamic nation. . . . The world must realize that all the difficulties faced by the Iranian nation and the Muslim people are because of aliens, because of America." The Shah's regime exiled Khomeini, who first resided in Turkey briefly and then lived in Iraq for almost fifteen years before triumphantly returning to Iran.

Khomeini rose to the position of the supreme leader in postrevolutionary Iran by taking advantage of the factional diversity of the Shah's opposition. The anti-

Shah political movement that Khomeini had led consisted of a wide variety of forces. They spanned the whole spectrum of revolutionary politics, from the extreme right to the extreme left. No neat categorization of the hundreds of such political groups and subgroups is possible. Generally speaking, at the center of the political spectrum were the religious and secular nationalists who formed the backbone of the Provisional Revolutionary Government (PRG) under the leadership of Prime Minister Mehdi Bazargan. To the extreme left of center were religious and secular socialists such as the Mujahedin Khalq and the Tudeh Communist Party, respectively, and to the extreme right were the Shia fundamentalists represented by the Islamic Republican Party (IRP). Each of these forces wanted to engineer a new state in its own exclusivist image. Thus, upon the seizure of power by the revolutionary militia in February 1979, a factional struggle for power replaced the anti-Shah alliance of diverse forces.

Khomeini set himself the task of engineering an Islamic state in his own image. He had outlined the bare bones of such a state in a collection of lectures delivered in Najaf while in exile and published as a book in 1970 under the title Islamic Governance (*Hokumat-e Islami*). While rejecting both the sovereignty of the monarch and the rule of the people by the people, he introduced therein the key concept of Rulership of the Jurisprudent (*Velayat-e Faqih*). In spite of political opposition, he formally established an Islamic Republic headed by just such a ruler on April 1, 1979, "the first day," as he put it, "of a Government of God" (*New York Times*, April 2, 1979).

Although Article 56 of the Islamic Constitution of Iran states that the "absolute ruler of the world and humanity is God and He alone has determined the social destiny of human beings," Article 5 provides that in the absence of the Twelfth Imam, the Faqih (jurisprudent) will exercise divine authority. The absence of any fixed term of office and any checks and balances make the authority of the Faqih nearly absolute. Could such unlimited authority lead to some kind of dictatorship? Loyalist constitutional lawyers of Iran say it could not, on the ground that the Faqih must enjoy, according to both Islamic principles and Article 109 of the constitution, such attributes as piety, knowledge of Islamic laws, courage, resourcefulness, and administrative and leadership abilities. Anyone with such qualifications, they argue, has nearly reached "the state of infallibility" (*maqam-e essmat*) and hence can do no wrong. Furthermore, they argue, Article 111 of the constitution provides for the removal of the Faqih from his position of leadership if he loses one of the qualifications mentioned above. Finally, they say, both the Shia tradition and the constitution require that the Faqih must enjoy "the confidence of the majority of the people."

How, in practice, did Khomeini attain such an exalted position? The concept of the rulership of the jurisprudent was not new in Shia tradition, but it had never been actualized before Khomeini. In his efforts to make himself the supreme ruler of the Islamic Republic, he first threw his weight behind the secular and religious nationalists at the center of the political spectrum. On February 5, 1979, he appointed Mehdi Bazargan as the prime minister of the PRG, which largely represented the Liberation of Iran Movement and the National Front. Although some bazaari merchants and shopkeepers as well as ulama supported these groups, the bulk of their support came from the modern-educated intelligentsia. After the fall of the PRG on November 6, 1979—two days after the seizure of the American embassy by "the followers of the Khomeini Line"— Khomeini threw his support behind the Shia fundamentalists. He hailed the seizure of the U.S. embassy as the beginning of the "second revolution," which he considered to be better than the first one, which had resulted in the fall of the shah. By shifting his support from the religious and secular nationalists at the center of the political spectrum to the Shia fundamentalists at the extreme right, Khomeini in effect appropriated all the instruments of power wielded by the Shia fundamentalists, including thousands of local autonomous committees (*Komiteh*), the revolutionary courts, and the Revolutionary Guards. The vehicle of appropriation was the IRP, which also controlled the Revolutionary Council, the legislative arm of the revolution before the election of the Majlis.

Khomeini's third major move toward supreme leadership was the dismissal of President Abul Hassan Bani-Sadr on June 22, 1981. This so-called "third revolution" represented the final successful effort of the Shia fundamentalists to take complete control of the Islamic government. However, the Shia fundamentalists had never been a monolithic whole. They had been united by their common goal of monopolizing all power against the revolutionary forces at the center and the left of the political spectrum, but once that goal seemed to have been achieved, the latent polarization between the two groups surfaced. Khomeini characterized this polarization as the emergence of two ways of thinking, whereas Hashemi-Rafsanjani referred to it in terms of two main factions.

The two schools of thought represented the classical division in Shia religio-political thought and action. Khomeini knew both schools and had no objection to their coexistence as long as the competition between the two did not harm the Islamic-Iranian national interest. On the one hand, there had always been those Shias who were quietist and others who had been activist and even revolutionary. His own teacher, Ayatollah Haeri-e Yazdi, for example, had been only an expedient quietist in the sense that he kept himself out of political activity during Reza Shah's anticlerical dictatorship. In effect, he practiced a kind of "dissimulation" (*taqiya*) of his real belief in the face of danger. On the other hand, the teacher of his teacher, Khorasani, and in turn his teacher, Shirazi, had been active in the Tobacco Uprising and the Constitutional Revolution respectively. In a sense, Khomeini himself may be said to have been more of a quietist than an activist at first, when he accepted both the 1906–1907 Constitution and the idea of a limited monarchy. He later turned activist and finally revolutionary.

Before the Shah's overthrow, he assailed, as a revolutionary leader, the extensive powers of the Shah and the state in the name of the supremacy of Islamic law. However, after the seizure and consolidation of power, he sought, as the head of the state, to expand the powers of the state. Toward that end, Khomeini's fourth major move as the supreme leader of the Republic was to abolish the IRP. Although it had served him as the principal instrument of consolidation of power, by 1987 it had become so polarized that he abolished it on May 2 of that year. Although by this act Khomeini in effect threw his weight against the religious and business interests that dominated the IRP, he presumably was acting in the Islamic-Iranian national interest by crushing the incipient infighting between the conservative and radical factions that had sapped the IRP of its vitality.

Institutionally, vested religious and business interests were largely reflected in the twelve-member Council of Guardians created by the constitution to avoid conflict between the "precepts of Islam and the Constitution" (Article 91). This council, therefore, could block any act of the Majlis that is considered to contradict the Sharia. Just as the conservative interests prevailed in the council, the reformist or radical interests dominated the Majlis. Conflict between the two groups was inevitable. Legislative bottlenecks proliferated as the council blocked social and economic bills passed by the Majlis regarding such vital issues as land reform, taxation, control of profits and prices, nationalization of foreign trade, better distribution of goods and services, and so forth. In a simplified sense, the division on socioeconomic issues was between the free-marketeers and the etatists, the latter insisting on the more intensive intervention of the state in the economy. The battle, however, was fought in the garb of *Fiqh* (Shia jurisprudence) and the issue was joined in terms of the interrelationship between state authority and Sharia injunctions.

No wonder, then, that Khomeini's fifth and final move to consolidate and further expand his own powers and those of the republic took the form of decreeing categorically the absolute supremacy of the state and its head, the Faqih, over the Sharia. On January 1, 1988, President Ali Khamenei expounded on the religiolegal limits of governmental authority. In a surprising public rebuttal on January 6, 1988, Khomeini in effect expanded for the first time the already nearly unlimited powers of the Faqih under the constitution. He called it "absolute rule by the Faqih." In the key paragraph of this far-reaching opinion, he told President Khamenei:

The ruler is authorized to demolish a mosque or a house which is in the path of a road, and to compensate the owner in cash. The ruler can close down a mosque if need be, or can even demolish a mosque which is the source of harm [*zarar*] if its harm cannot be eliminated except by demolition. The government is empowered to unilaterally revoke any lawful agreements with people if the agreement contravenes the interests of Islam and the country. It can prevent any matter, whether religious or secular, if it is against the interests of Islam. The *hajj* [pilgrimage], which is foremost among divine obligations, can even be temporarily prevented if it is contrary to the interests of the Islamic country. (Foreign Broadcast Information Service, *Near East & South Asia*, January 7, 1988)

The hitherto frustrated socioeconomic radicals took heart, and Prime Minister Hussein Musavi latched onto the decree to seek the implementation of those bills that had been approved by the Majlis and vetoed by the Council of Guardians. To him and like-minded technocratic social-welfarists, it seemed that the government now enjoyed the kind of power that was needed to address the burgeoning social and economic problems of the country. He believed that this decree, particularly as applied to legislation regarding laborers would enable him to review the bills and proposals in the Majlis and find solutions to many problems. The conservative faction considered Khomeini's decree a major blow to their interests, but Khomeini considered it to be in Iran's Islamic and national interests. In effect, Khomeini had finally made himself the absolute ruler of Iran by divine right through the Prophet and the Imams. This move seemed to run counter to the Shia tradition of respect for the plurality of jurisprudential opinions, but it also seemed to be fully compatible with the ethos of the ancient Iranian political culture which was accustomed to absolutism, authoritarianism, and even despotism. The same ethos that made it possible for the Shah to declare himself the *Shahinshah* (King of Kings) made it possible for Khomeini to present himself as the *Faqih al-Fuqaha* (jurisprudent of jurisprudents).

The passing of Khomeini on June 3, 1989, marked the end of the Khomeini era of the Iranian Revolution. None of the "model" clerics who survive him combine his kind of charisma and political experience. President Ali Khamenei was chosen to succeed him by more than four-fifths of the members of the Assembly of Experts present. One of the constitutional amendments approved by referendum on July 28, 1989, removed the requirement that the Iranian leader should be a "model" Ayatollah. Khamenei was thus made Iran's supreme leader. The simultaneous election of Hashemi-Rafsanjani as president further insured a smooth transition of power after Khomeini's death. Should this power configuration endure, the chances are that Iran's future domestic and foreign policies will be guided more by the national interest than by ideological purity.

BIBLIOGRAPHY

Amir Arjomand, Said. *The Turban for the Crown: The Islamic Revolution in Iran.* New York: Oxford University Press, 1988.

Bakhash, Shaul. *The Reign of the Ayatollahs: Iran and the Islamic Revolution.* New York: Basic Books, 1984.

Davani, Ali. *Nehzat-e Rouhaniyun-e Iran.* Bonyad-e Farhangi-e Imam Reza, n.d.

Milani, Mohsen. *The Making of Iran's Islamic Revolution: From Monarchy to Islamic Republic.* Boulder, Colo.: Westview Press, 1988.

Mottahedeh, Roy. *The Mantle of the Prophet: Religion and Politics in Iran.* New York: Pantheon Books, 1985.

Rajaee, Farhang. *Islamic Values and World View: Khomeyni on Man, the State and International Politics.* New York: University Press of America, 1983.

Ramazani, R. K. "Church and State in Modernizing Society: The Case of Iran," *The American Behavioral Scientist,* January 1964.

Ramazani, R. K. *Revolutionary Iran: Challenge and Response in the Middle East.* Baltimore: Johns Hopkins University Press, 1986.

Rouhani, Hamid. *Nehzat-e Imam Khomeini.* Tehran: Entesharat-e Rah-e Imam, n.d.

R. K. RAMAZANI

M

SADIQ AL-MAHDI (1936–   ) (al-Sayyid al-Sadiq al-Mahdi, Sadeq el-Mahdi) has been prime minister of Sudan from July 1966–July 1967 and from May 1986 to June 30, 1989, when he was ousted by Sudanese military forces in a lightning coup. Born into the country's most famous family and educated in Sudan and England, he has at various times been a prominent politician, a leader of government, a "holy man," and a noted academic and scholar. This diversity of activity and his well-earned reputation bespeak not only Sadiq's broad and unusual talents but also mask a number of operational difficulties and shortcomings in his brilliant career.

He was born in 1936, a great grandson of Mohammed Ahmed, who had proclaimed himself to be the *Mahdi*, (the rightly guided one), a messianic figure in Islam, especially prominent in Sufi movements throughout the nineteenth century A.D. During the 1870s and 1880s this religiopolitical movement unified most tribes of the Upper Nile Basin against Egyptian-Ottoman misrule, and thus formed a foundation for the subsequent political entity known today as Sudan. Sadiq's grandfather was the legendary Imam Abd al-Rahman M.A. al-Mahdi who led the *mahdiyyah* sect—also known as *ansar*—for more than fifty years, and who was one of the most prominent nationalist leaders during the Anglo-Egyptian Condominium (1899–1955). He also founded the Umma Party in March 1945 as the political expression of the ansar; and he was succeeded as Umma Party and *imam* (spiritual leader of the sect) by his son Siddiq, Sadiq's father, upon his death on March 24, 1959.

Siddiq's leadership of Umma and ansar was short-lived. He had been unalterably opposed to military rule—General Ibrahim Abboud's junta had seized power in November 1958—and in the eyes of some observers, had literally worried himself to his death on October 2, 1961. Following that unforeseen event, the two leadership functions were separated for the first time: The imamate was given to Siddiq's younger brother, el-Hadi, while the presidency of the Umma Party fell on is twenty-five-year-old son, Sadiq.

Sadiq had received his first substantial education at the then-private Comboni College, a secondary school run by Catholic clergy in Khartoum, and subsequently studied at St. John's College, Oxford. He later returned to Oxford University on many occasions as visitor, guest lecturer, and, in 1983, as fellow at St. Anthony's College. Even a casual observer could easily notice Sadiq's analytical skills, remarkable vocabulary in Arabic and English, and obvious erudition as a public speaker; this was clearly a tribute to his excellent education and innate intelligence.

This combination of family and academic background propelled Sadiq's early political career with a rapidity that was heretofore unknown in Sudan and that was envied by more than a few. For example, as president of the Umma Party he was the youngest leader ever of a major political organization. At the same time it should be noted that membership in the Mahdi family entailed some complications as well. One need only recall the intermittent competition with his uncles over leadership functions. In addition, he acquired as brother-in-law one of his later fiercest personal and political rivals, namely Dr. Hassan A. al-Turabi.

After the October 21 revolution in 1964 terminated military rule, Sudan experienced one of its most turbulent phases in the subsequent six-month transition period. Some new radical groupings joined older antiestablishment forces and threatened to push the country into serious political and economic crises. Sadiq's leadership of the ansar and his negotiating skills in dealing with other parties contributed significantly to the triumph by the forces of moderation leading up to parliamentary elections in April 1965. During these elections his party won the largest number of seats. Sadiq himself had to wait another year until he reached thirty, the minimum age for deputies, at which time he won a by-election and, within a few days, ascended to the position of prime minister.

At the time many observers had high hopes for Sudan's future under the dynamic leadership of young Sadiq. However, the legendary infighting within and among Sudanese parties undid the new prime minister within a year, as it has done before and since to other would-be leaders. Sadiq was undermined in part by the envy of his older rival, Ismail al-Azhari, leader of the coalition National Unionist Party and the country's first prime minister and elder statesman, who played on similar envy by older Umma Party politicians and religious notables. In part he also fell victim to his own inexperience in controlling intraparty rivals and ambitious coalition partners. In the end, he lost both the premiership (to a temporary coalition of former allies) and his parliamentary seat during the next election in 1968. The latter loss can be ascribed to a certain amount of complacency, a bitter lesson that was to haunt him for a long time. The former loss, however, seemed to result from a sadly common trait of Sudanese politics: a joint effort by lesser figures to frustrate successful leadership.

Some might argue that Sadiq was simply too young for a political elite used to revering elder statesmen in a very traditional society. Others could point to misgivings by conservative forces about Sadiq's imaginative approaches to

Southern leaders. Sadiq's proposals for resolving the North-South conflict on an equitable basis may have been too much too early for some; although President Jafar Mohammed Nimeiri* made it the blueprint for his own effort a few years later, leading to the successful Addis Ababa Accords of March 1972, which ended seventeen years of civil war and gave regional autonomy to the South.

In fact, many observers believe that Nimeiri's decision to seize power in May 1969 was accelerated by the prospects of a large political groundswell in early 1969 which would have returned Sadiq al-Mahdi to the country's highest office, but this time within the framework of a presidential system à la the United States.

As it turned out, Nimeiri seized power, installed a military regime, and outlawed all political parties. Along with other parliamentary leaders, Sadiq al-Mahdi was arrested and imprisoned. He was charged with high treason, but managed to escape later and fled into exile, at various times in Libya, Saudi Arabia, and Great Britain. He became one of two cofounders of the national opposition to Nimeiri's junta and often attacked the May Regime from abroad as consisting of "illegitimate usurpers."

Over the years, more than a dozen coup attempts were launched against Nimeiri's rule, one of the most spectacular (and nearly successful) of which was directly sponsored by Sadiq al-Mahdi in July 1976. Throughout the sixteen years of military dictatorship, Sadiq was mostly in exile, but he intermittently returned to Sudan. Several times he was arrested, only to become free again. In late 1977, he was invited to join the government and its only legal party, the Sudan Socialist Union (SSU). He briefly agreed, but soon withdrew his participation because certain alleged promises had not been kept. Whether in or out of the country, and whether free or in prison, most political observers agreed that Sadiq al-Mahdi was the obvious alternative to General Nimeiri as leader of Sudan.

The collapse of the junta on April 6, 1985, opened the door for the return of democratic government via a transitional regime that was to prepare the country for elections in April 1986. Once again Sadiq al-Mahdi played a major role in rallying not only his own political forces but also a constellation of civilian politicians who were mutually bent on preventing possible intervention by other military elements, who may have harbored dim views about the prospects of civilian government. As the transitional period proceeded and the country was wracked by economic crises, rebellion in parts of the South and the first-ever Sahelian drought of major proportions, the prospect of parliamentary government under Sadiq al-Mahdi became brighter with each passing week as the Umma leader launched a massive and well-organized election campaign. This major effort, carried out under most difficult circumstances, yielded electoral victory for the now reconstituted Umma National Party, which won 100 of 233 contested districts and swept its leader into the office of prime minister in May 1986. He has held this position ever since (at the head of two coalition governments) along with the Defense portfolio (from June 1986 on).

By late 1988, the prime minister faced a familiar set of issues, namely, the need to maintain a stable coalition government; revitalize the economy; obtain foreign assistance for economic development, humanitarian efforts (for example, drought and refugee relief), and national-security purposes; contain or eliminate the rebellion in parts of the South led by the Sudanese Peoples Liberation Movement (SPLM) and army (SPLA) under John Garang; and resolve the long-standing constitutional issue concerning the nation's legal system.

The latter problem is closely intertwined with the broader issue of Sudanese identity within an Afro-Arab context. The current and most specific manifestation centers around the role of *shariah* (Islamic) law. One version was introduced by former president Nimeiri in September 1983, an act that provoked much consternation and displeasure abroad, and among non-Muslims and many educated Muslims at home. Sadiq al-Mahdi had been more vociferous than any other well-known politician in his opposition to these laws (to the point of landing once again in prison). During the preelection transitional period he stated first and often in public that these ''September laws'' should be repealed, and vowed to do so if elected. To the surprise of many, both at home and abroad, he has not as yet carried out this promise. On the contrary, after reconstituting his government in May 1988 by including the previous opposition National Islamic Front (NIF), he agreed to defer repeal of these laws. Perhaps under pressure from his new coalition partners who, after all, had been instrumental in bringing about the 1983 legislation, and who have been ideologically committed to further Islamization of the state, Sadiq's government introduced a bill to Parliament in September 1988 whereby an ''alternative'' set of ''true'' Islamic laws would become the basis for Sudan's constitution. After strong pressures from many quarters both pro and contra, the draft proposal was temporarily withdrawn and referred to committee.

These events illustrate some of the conflicting political pressures that Sadiq has had to face perennially, resulting not the least from the multiplicity of his roles (for example, as statesman, politician, and religious leader), but also from an occasional personal tendency to waver in the face of pressure. Addressing first the conflict resulting from these multiple roles, one must recall that Sadiq al-Mahdi's political base in the Umma Party is directly tied into his relationship with the ansar movement.

As is generally the case in the Middle East and North Africa, religious and temporal leadership of a community are usually granted to a single person, and frequently to one institution as well. This was also true for the followers of the Mahdi movement until the death of Siddiq al-Mahdi in 1961. Because his son Sadiq was judged to be too young at age twenty-five to assume both leadership functions on one hand, and because there had been some dispute about the intended system for succession from the late, great Imam Abd al-Rahman on the other—whether father to son or senior to next senior surviving son of Abd al-Rahman—the two functions were divided between Sadiq and his uncle Imam al-Hadi. This division worked to some degree but was not wholly satisfactory.

After all, the Umma Party early on drew its membership almost entirely from followers of the mahdiyyah, and it stands to reason that their spiritual leader would wish to involve himself in their political fortunes. Similarly, when Umma chief Sadiq needed mass support, as in street demonstrations against communists and leftists in early 1965 or in violent opposition to the Nimeiri regime such as in 1970 and 1976, he would call on the ansar by using religious symbols. The ansar came and responded every time. It would seem unrealistic not to expect some turf battles and jealousy under such circumstances.

A major incident of this kind occurred during Sadiq's first premiership, when his formal coalition partner but political rival, Ismail al-Azhari (of the NUP) undermined the ruling Umma-NUP coalition by inducing Imam al-Hadi into opposition to Sadiq in a successful vote of no confidence in Parliament. This maneuver not only cost Sadiq his premiership in 1967, but indirectly led to the political chaos of the following two years which enabled Nimeiri's military faction to seize power in May 1969.

When this government cracked down on the ansar as its most potent opponent, invaded their headquarters on Aba Island in March 1970, and killed thousands of ansar including Imam al-Hadi, the issue of the imamate arose once again. Sadiq was exiled to Egypt but claimed his murdered uncle's mandate. Most ansar seemed to accept this development, and still seem to up to this day, but a certain number of traditionalists disagreed and swore allegiance to al-Hadi's younger brother, Ahmed. For the record, a similar splinter group emerged after Nimeiri's demise within the Umma Party around the person of Wali al-Din al-Hadi al-Mahdi, son of the late Imam al-Hadi.

Though once important, these internal disputes no longer constitute a significant challenge to Sadiq's present leadership among the ansar. More problematic is the inherent conflict between the multiple roles that Sadiq must perform in order to be successful. He needs to appeal to his ansar base for political support in elections, yet he must also quite inevitably disappoint some of these traditional supporters if he is to make the new Umma National Party truly national—rather than sectarian, and hence regional—and achieve solutions to some of the country's major problems, such as ending the rebellion on terms acceptable to non-Muslims, and in general, modernizing the nation. Thus far, he has been unable or unwilling to accommodate these conflicting demands along the lines that he had envisioned.

This general predicament is somewhat reflected in Sadiq al-Mahdi's considerable writings and in many of his public lectures abroad. It is worth noting that he has lectured frequently at many of the world's leading universities in Britain, the United States, and throughout the Middle East. Examples of topics he has addressed include "The Islamic Idea and the Modern State," "Contemporary Revolution in the Arab World," "Afro-Arab Conditions," "You Ask about the Mahdiyyah," and "Islamic Punishment and Its Place in an Islamic Order." In the United States he addressed and subsequently published writings on such topics as "Islam and Revolution in the Middle East and Northern Africa" and "Development and Politics in the Modern Sudan."

Like many Sudanese leaders before him, Sadiq al-Mahdi enjoys making his own foreign policy. He would appear to be well qualified to do so, given his extensive travels during the past thirty years and his frequent dialogues with foreign leaders and other public personalities on the international lecture circuit.

Early on in his second administration (1986) it became clear that Sadiq wanted to reverse the Cairo-Washington axis orientation practiced by Jafar Nimeiri from the mid–1970s to the mid–1980s. In agreement with the transitional regime of 1985–1986, Sadiq's Sudan no longer participates in "Operation Bright Star" (joint military exercises with the United States and Egypt) nor grants access to its basing facilities for U.S. forces. It also has replaced the Nile Valley Integration Project of Nimeiri with a vaguer "brotherhood charter."

To underline his departure from Nimeiri's policies, Sadiq al-Mahdi visited Libya before Egypt, Persian Iran before Arab Iraq, and the Soviet Union before the United States. Whereas these gestures were primarily made for symbolic purposes—to signal independence, rather than alignment—the next set of foreign-policy directives was entirely pragmatic: Closer ties were forged with Saudi Arabia and other GCC (Gulf Cooperative Council) states in the hope of attracting desperately needed economic assistance, and a reassessment of relations with neighboring states was undertaken. Like his predecessor in the transition, Sadiq al-Mahdi argued persuasively for the need to maintain dialogues with potentially dangerous regimes in Libya and Ethiopia to prevent their support to anti-Khartoum rebels, especially in southern and western Sudan.

As examination of his record as a statesman yields the following preliminary results: Ethiopia still supports John Garang's Sudan Peoples Liberation Army, but Libya no longer does so, and, in fact, it has been the first state to grant significant economic and military aid to Sudan after the fall of Nimeiri. The United States has reduced its economic assistance every year (except for humanitarian aid), while Saudi Arabia has stepped up its help. Sadiq al-Mahdi was able to use his good offices to reduce tensions between Egypt and Libya; but he was less successful in his mediation between Iraq and Iran, and in his earlier efforts to obtain the release of American hostages in Tehran in January 1980.

An overall balance sheet reveals an extraordinary personality with political, religious, and academic attributes rarely seen anywhere, and virtually unparalleled among his contemporaries in the Middle East. He built the Umma Party into the most successful political organization ever known in Sudanese politics, and was the major architect of its electoral victories in 1965 and 1986. Toward this effort he acquired substantial backing from Great Britain and the United States in the 1960s and 1980s, while receiving support from Libya and Saudi Arabia in the 1970s. In this connection it must also be noted that he bears some responsibility for the electoral defeat in 1968. His personal rivalry and intermittent hostility toward NIF leader Dr. Hassan A. al-Turabi has been an enigma in domestic affairs, and his relationship with Egypt on the foreign-policy front been similarly characterized by dynastic rivalry, suspicion, and intermittent hostility. His relationship with southern Sudanese political leaders has been stigmatized by the Mahdi label, because many Southerners presume a continuation of imperial designs shown by Mahdists one century ago. However, he has repeatedly, at least on paper, designed plans that would grant the southern Sudanese perhaps more genuine autonomy than any other prominent leader.

Perhaps it can be argued that Sadiq al-Mahdi's greatest assets have also been his very real handicaps. His analytical skills, political experience, and charismatic appeal have for twenty years made him Sudan's best hope for guiding the nation forward intelligently under democratic auspices. When these very qualities frightened his factionalized and sectarian enemies into counteralliances, he has not been particularly adept in coaxing them into a more productive stance. As a result, he has often appeared paralyzed. The observer cannot help but wonder whether this may be due to some confusion on his own party, as to whether he should be the head of a factional party, the country's governmental leader, an almost mystic "holy man," or—in a flight from the confusions of Sudan's demographic, geographic, economic, and political complications—an Oxford don.

BIBLIOGRAPHY

Works by al-Mahdi:

Yas alŭnaka an al-Maydiyyah (You Ask about the Mahdiyyah). Beirut: Dar al-Qadayah, 1975.
Ahădith al-Ghurbah (Discussions of Alienation). Beirut: Dar al-Qadayah, 1976.
"The Concept of an Islamic State." In Altaf Gauhar (ed.), *The Challenge of Islam.* London: The Islamic Council of Europe, 1978.
"The Economic System of Islam." In Salem Azzam (ed.), *Islam in Contemporary Society.* London: Longmans, 1982.
"Islamic Society and Change." In John Esposito (ed.), *Voices of Resurgent Islam.* New York: Oxford University Press, 1983.
al-Uqŭbăt al-shariyyah wa mawqihah min al-nizăm al-ijtimăi al-islămi (Islamic Punishment and Its Place in an Islamic Social Order). Cairo: Zahra lil-ilăm al-arabi, 1986.
Turăth al-Sŭdăn (Sudan's Heritage) (series). *Jihăd fi sabŭl allah* (Struggle in the Path of God), *Jihăd fi sabŭl al-istiglăl* (Struggle for Independence), *Jihăd fi sabŭl al dŭmŭqrătiyyah* (Struggle for Democracy), *Thawrah 21 Oktŏber* (The Revolution of 21 October [1964]). Khartoum: Government Press, n.d.

Other Works

Bechtold, Peter. *Politics in the Sudan.* New York: Praeger, 1976.
Holt, P. M., and M. W. Daly. *The History of the Sudan from the Coming of Islam to the Present Day.* New York: Longmans, 1988.
Malwal, Bona. *People and Power in Sudan.* London: Ithaca Press, 1981.

PETER K. BECHTOLD

GOLDA MEIR (1898–1978) was for more than forty years a member of the inner circle of the Histadrut (the National Labor Federation), Mapai Israel Workers Party, and the Labor Party. She earned a reputation for doing whatever job was necessary—with political craft and selfless devotion. As a seventy-year-old matriarch, she was brought out of retirement in 1969 to become Israel's fourth prime minister. This big, strong-chinned woman, whom David Ben-Gurion once called "the best man in my cabinet," looked more like a warm doting grandmother than an astute political leader with enormous prestige inside her political party. Blunt and often unyielding in her ways, she nevertheless remained acceptable to all factions. With enormous energy and resolve, she led Israel through the 1973 war.

Golda Mabovitch (later Meir) was born on May 3, 1898, in Kiev, Russia. Her father was a skilled carpenter who seldom had a regular job. Her mother, Bluma, gave birth to eight children, three of whom survived. The family was pitifully poor. In 1903 Golda's father moved the family to Pinsk and then emigrated alone to the United States with plans to bring his family later. Pinsk was a celebrated center of Russian-Jewish life, but Golda's childhood memories highlighted pogroms and atrocities committed against the Jews. Three years later, her mother took her three daughters to America, joined their father, and settled in Milwaukee. The sisters enrolled in school and Golda's mother opened a tiny grocery store that barely survived. At age eleven, she organized a group of girls from her school to raise money for textbooks, and she made her first public speech.

Golda completed elementary school when she was fourteen and was valedictorian of her class. Her ambition was to become a teacher and she fought with her parents to continue on to high school instead of going to work immediately. She entered high school in 1912. When her mother tried to marry her off at age fifteen, she managed to escape to Denver where she joined her sister Sheyna. Sheyna's apartment had become a center for Russian Jewish immigrants who, like Sheyna, had come to Denver for treatment of tuberculosis at the Jewish Hospital for Consumptives. Golda's circle now included a collection of anarchists, socialists, and Zionists, who spoke mostly in Yiddish, and often about new Jewish settlements in Palestine. She also met Morris Meyerson, an immigrant from Lithuania, who loved poetry, art, and music. In 1913, at age sixteen, Golda fell in love with Morris. When her father requested her to come home, she did so, reentered high school, and graduated in 1916. Her parents were now more comfortable and active in the community. During World War I, the small Mabovitch house became a depot for Jewish boys enlisting in the Jewish Legion to fight with the British Army in the hope of liberating Palestine. It also became a small center for socialist Zionists. Zionism began to fill Golda's life.

As a teenager, Golda was a determined, courageous, energetic person. On weekends and afternoons she taught Yiddish at the Jewish Center in Milwaukee. In 1917, she organized a protest march to dramatize the anti-Semitic pogroms in Russia and received some national publicity. At age seventeen she joined the Poalei Zion (Workers of Zion) Party. She was now determined to marry Morris and move with him to Palestine, but feared that she might have to choose between Palestine and Morris, who lacked her indomitable will and Zionist concerns. For a brief period she found work in Chicago in a public library. The Balfour Declaration of November 1917 and its promise of a Jewish homeland in Palestine persuaded Morris Meyerson to agree to emigrate with Golda. They were married in December 1917.

Speaking English and Yiddish fluently, Golda traveled on speaking tours for the Socialist Zionists. In 1918, she was chosen to be a delegate from Milwaukee to the first national convention of the new American Jewish Congress. Her political career began here. She was already a gifted orator with an emotional and direct manner of speaking that could hold an audience spellbound. In 1921 the Meyersons moved to New York City to prepare for emigration to Palestine. The journey was a succession of nightmarish disasters, finally ending in Tel Aviv, in the autumn of 1921, one year after the founding of the Histadrut, the national federation of labor, which later played a major role in Golda's political career.

The Meyersons' first application for membership in *kibbutz* (collective settlement) Merhavia was rejected because the kibbutz did not want married people yet and did not think that a young American woman would work hard at chicken farming. They were permitted to come on trial in the autumn of 1921. There was little to eat and living conditions were quite primitive. Golda was happy in Merhavia, but Morris was plagued by the grimness and lack of privacy. As a delegate to the kibbutz conference in 1922, Golda met key Zionist leaders, including David Ben-Gurion* (the general secretary of the Histadrut), his closest associate Yitzhak Ben-Zvi (later the second president of Israel), Israel Tabenkin (the principal ideologue of the kibbutz movement), Levi Eshkol* (who became the third prime minister of Israel), Berl Katznelson (a dominant intellectual figure of Labor Zionist), Zalman Shazar (later president of the State), and David Remez, who became Golda's mentor in Zionist affairs.

When Morris became ill in 1923, the Meyersons moved to Tel Aviv where Golda secured a job as a cashier in the Public Works and Building office (later, Solel Boneh) of the Histadrut. David Remez then offered her a job in the Jerusalem branch of this office. They lived for four years in a shabby corner in Mea Shearim, an old orthodox quarter of Jerusalem, where their two children, Menachem and Sara, were born. Life in Jerusalem was difficult. Golda's pay was frequently held up for lack of funds, and she spent her time caring for her babies and washing clothes in a nursery in exchange for school fees. Then, in 1928, through Remez, she became secretary of the Women's Labor Council of the Histadrut in Tel Aviv. By this time the Meyerson marriage was failing, although Golda worked hard to be a mother to her two children, mending their clothes, cooking at night, occasionally going to the movies with them, and feeling guilty about traveling abroad without them.

In her new position, Golda became a leading member of the Histadrut. When Mapai (Labor Party) was formed in 1930 by the merger of Ahdut Haavodah and Hapoel Hatzair (Young Workers), she quickly became a major figure in the new party. Between 1928 and 1932, she traveled often in the United States and

Europe to advance Labor Zionist programs. From 1932 to 1934, she served as
an emissary from Palestine to the Pioneer Women's Organization, primarily to
help raise funds for training young women for work in Palestine.

She returned to Tel Aviv in 1934 and was invited to join the Executive
Committee of the Histadrut. She now rose rapidly in the Labor hierarchy. She
participated in the controversies following the murder in 1933 of Chaim Arlo-
zoroff, a leading personality of Labor Zionism, and in the growing friction
between the left and right wings of Zionism. Her experience in the 1930s in
dealing with various aspects of immigrant absorption, which had become the
central issue of Zionism, proved to be excellent training for her assignment as
Minister of Labor beginning in 1949. She also had intensive experience as a
labor negotiator with the British concerning the working conditions of Histadrut
members employed in building British army camps in Palestine. She worked
closely with Ben-Gurion, who was then heading the Jewish Agency in Palestine.
In 1937–1938, in the debate over partition of Palestine into separate states for
Arabs and Jews, she opposed partition because the proposed Jewish ministate
was too small. She later wrote in her autobiography, *My Life*, that she and many
of her party colleagues were wrong: "Ben-Gurion, in his greater wisdom, arguing
that any state was better than none, was right" (p. 167).

In the intensifying struggle against the British in Palestine from 1939 to 1948,
she fought for unlimited Jewish immigration, demanded that the British permit
Jews to enlist to fight against the Nazis, and worked to strengthen the Jewish
economy and social structure in Palestine in order to absorb a larger immigration.
From the record of this period, she learned that "no foreign government would
ever put the same value on Jewish lives as we did" (*My Life*, p. 163). In 1946,
when the British arrested all the members of the Jewish Agency Executive and
the Vaad Leumi (National Jewish Council) that they could find in Palestine,
Golda became head of the Political Department of the Jewish Agency, replacing
Moshe Sharett (then Shertok), who was imprisoned in Latrun. Ben-Gurion escaped arrest because he was on a mission abroad.

The year 1946 was a time of great decisions. The British had refused U.S.
President Harry Truman's appeal for the immediate admission of one hundred
thousand refugees from the Nazi concentration camps. The Anglo-American
Committee of Inquiry was formed and held hearings in Palestine in March and
April, with Golda testifying for the Histadrut. In May the Anglo-American
Committee recommended that one hundred thousand immigrants be admitted to
Palestine at once and that restrictive regulations governing land sales be abolished. The British rejected the recommendations. On June 29, the Mandatory
forces imprisoned more than three thousand Jews and did great damage in Jewish
settlements. Their intention to destroy the Haganah (the Jewish defense organization) was thwarted when its leaders were tipped off. As the head of the
Political Department, Golda unsuccessfully urged Chaim Weizmann*, then in
residence in Palestine, to issue a statement of policy adopting civil disobedience
toward the government of Palestine.

In 1947 the battle against Jewish immigration turned into open warfare. When the British opened detention camps in Cyprus for illegal immigrants, Golda negotiated with the authorities to permit orphaned children and families with children under one year of age to be granted priority for inclusion in the list of 750 given entry visas every month to Palestine. From June to September 1947, she was preoccupied with conferences with members of the United Nations Special Committee on Palestine (UNSCOP), which recommended partition of Palestine in its report of August 31. In the meantime, the road from Tel Aviv to Jerusalem had become a fierce battleground and Jerusalem was under seige by Arab forces. The UN voted on November 29, 1947, to endorse partition, and Golda went to the United States in January 1948. For six weeks she helped raise fifty million dollars through the metropolitan Jewish federations. In the six months before the Declaration of Independence was proclaimed on May 14, 1948, she met twice secretly with King Abdullah ibn Hussein* of Transjordan to dissuade him from joining the Arab League in attacking Jewish Palestine. Her efforts failed. Although Jerusalem was besieged, she managed to get to Tel Aviv to attend the Independence ceremony and sign the Proclamation.

In early June 1948, Golda was appointed Israel's first minister to Moscow, but was unable to take up the appointment for several weeks because she was hospitalized with a broken leg suffered in an automobile accident in New York City. In her seven months in Moscow, she personified Israel for Soviet Jews. Ben-Gurion wanted her back in Israel to serve as Minister of Labor. She returned to Israel in April 1949 to take up this post, which she held until 1956 when she began a decade-long tenure as foreign minister under Ben-Gurion and Levi Eshkol. She characterized these years as "the most satisfying and the happiest of my life" (My Life, p. 256). Her principal function was to effect the absorption of hundreds of thousands of immigrants who flocked to Israel from 1948 to 1953. She initiated large-scale housing and road-building programs and vigorously supported unlimited immigration, despite the dreadful conditions under which most immigrants lived during the early years of statehood.

She also went on repeated fund-raising trips to the United States, Europe, and South America. She worked with the American Jewish leader Henry Montor, and Eliezer Kaplan, Israel's first minister of finance, to create the concept of the State of Israel Government Bond, and took up the task of developing support for it. The first Israel Bond campaign was launched in May 1951. She also participated directly in the development of the first National Insurance Bill in January 1952 and the National Insurance Act of 1954, which established Israel's social security system, the maternity benefits program, and other welfare measures. However, her work in finding jobs, clothes, housing, and medical care for immigrants was her major achievement as minister of labor. By 1952, immigration had begun to taper off to about one thousand per day, and she was active in the program of population dispersal, which sent new immigrants directly to new development areas and border villages all over Israel, with an emphasis on agricultural production. She became a familiar sight inspecting building sites and new settlements.

When she succeeded Moshe Shertok as foreign minister in 1956, she Hebraicized her name. Now Golda Meir, she was already a familiar figure on the international scene. She frequently addressed the General Assembly of the United Nations and effectively conveyed the moral aspects of Israel's interests. Her direct, emotional style contrasted sharply at times with the intellectual sophistication of senior ambassadors. As foreign minister she attempted to increase Israel's inventory of defense weapons to balance Czech and Soviet arms flowing into Egypt under Gamal Abdul Nasser.* After Nasser nationalized the Suez Canal in July 1956, the plan for an Anglo-French assault on the Suez developed. The Suez war began on October 29, 1956, and was over by November 5. With astonishing speed, the Israeli Defense Forces had captured the Gaza Strip and the Sinai Peninsula and had cleaned out the nests of Egyptian *fedayeen* (commandos). A third of the Egyptian army had been broken, but the Anglo-French attack on Suez failed. Pressure from the United States and the UN forced Israel to withdraw from the Sinai Peninsula in 1957.

Another significant achievement was the extension of Israeli aid to African nations as a critical way of strengthening Israel's international position, particularly in Ghana, Liberia, Senegal, the Ivory Coast, and Nigeria, which she often visited. From 1958 to 1973, about five thousand Israeli advisers assisted African countries in developing programs in agriculture, hydrology, regional planning, public health, engineering and construction, tourism, medical services, and community services.

In the fourth Knesset (Parliament) elections in 1959, Ben-Gurion, now seventy-four, again headed the Mapai-led coalition government, but strife in the party developed as he attempted to bring several young men into leadership positions. The Lavon affair, which stemmed from an Israeli intelligence failure in Cairo in 1955 while Pinchas Lavon was minister of defense, came to dominate domestic politics. After ten members of the Cabinet, including Meir, approved a report that exonerated Lavon, Ben-Gurion refused to accept the report and resigned as prime minister in January 1961. In the elections that followed, Mapai lost five seats. Despite demands that Ben-Gurion be replaced, he remained prime minister until June 1963, when he resigned in defeat. In 1965 Meir joined with Sharett, Sapir, Eshkol, and Eban to oppose Ben-Gurion, Moshe Dayan,* and Shimon Peres* on the Lavon affair. Ben-Gurion then resigned from Mapai and formed the RAFI party (the Israel Labor List), thus marking the end of the Ben-Gurion era in Israeli political life. He was bitter toward Golda, whom he had trusted completely for thirty years.

Because of ill health, Golda was not active in the campaign for the Knesset elections of 1965. She resigned in January 1966 and was succeeded as foreign minister by Abba Eban. Because of her enormous popularity in Mapai, she was prevailed on to accept appointment as general secretary of the party. In that position, Golda was Prime Minister Eshkol's closest adviser. Apart from the Six

Day War in June 1967, internal party issues dominated Israeli politics. In January 1968, Golda was instrumental in facilitating the union of Mapai, RAFI, and Ahdut Haavodah to form the Israel Labor Party. In the post–1967 period, this spectacular consolidation led labor to a more militant posture on the future of the West Bank. After serving for two years as general secretary, she retired briefly from public life.

After Eshkol's death in February 1969, party leaders—except for Moshe Dayan and Shimon Peres—beseeched Golda to succeed Eshkol. She was told that she was "the only one with enough authority, experience, and credit within the party to be acceptable to almost everyone" (*My Life*, p. 377). When she became Israel's fourth prime minister in March 1969, Golda was seventy years old. She retained the National Unity Government that Eshkol had constructed. In the Knesset elections at the end of October, the Labor Party won 56 seats (out of 120). Installed again as prime minister, she maintained the national unity government. However, when the new Gahal right-wing party under Menachem Begin refused to accept the American peace initiative and withdrew from the cabinet coalition early in 1970, she reformed the government.

In this euphoric post–1967 period, Golda Meir resolutely resisted initiatives to negotiate with the Palestinians. In December 1971, President Richard Nixon received her in Washington, D.C., at a time of mounting tension between the two countries. She succeeded in obtaining the president's approval of further arm shipments to Israel.

As minister without portfolio in the governments of Eshkol, Meir, and Yitzhak Rabin* from 1967 to 1977, Israel Galili constructed an active program of Jewish settlements in areas of the West Bank not occupied by the Palestinians. The new doctrine, which Meir supported, provided that Israel would remain in the occupied territories and would establish many small settlements and a few urban centers. Israel would convert unpopulated Arab territory into a defensive network, and it would establish military corridors to deter Arab aggression and safeguard Israeli settlements. The Jordan River was conceived as a permanent strategic border. There would be no annexation. Eventually, Jordanian sovereignty over the West Bank and Gaza would be encouraged to develop local self-government, and all local government machinery, including the Jordanian structure, would remain in operation.

On the diplomatic front, until the outbreak of the Yom Kippur War in 1973, there was almost total immobility. Her inner circle appeared to be secure and confident, despite the intensification of infighting in the ruling circle, especially over the position of Moshe Dayan. The Meir government was not sensitive to world opinion; it dismissed American pressure to return to the pre–1967 borders; and it underestimated the challenge of Arab radicalism. Her government saw little possibility of a serious Arab challenge during the period from 1969 to 1973, and hence Israel was insufficiently prepared for the war of 1973. Her greatest challenge in fifty years of public service came during the first ten days of the war, when Israel's survival hung in the balance. Her courage and inner strength were critical in turning defeat into a costly military victory.

The 1973 election, which was postponed until December 31, was affected by a series of disasters that undermined the standing of the Labor Party. The Meir-Dayan-Galili regime was bitterly attacked for courting disaster in the Yom Kippur War. Meir, who had begun her service as prime minister with one war, now ended her term with another. She was drained and deeply distressed by the savage infighting in the Labor Party. Following the election, in early 1974 she had great difficulty forming a government with Dayan as minister of defense. Now seventy-five, she decided she could not continue. She announced her resignation to the Knesset early in April. For two months she headed a caretaker government until Yitzhak Rabin was able to complete his cabinet and obtain the support of the Knesset in June. During that final two-month period, the Preliminary Report of the Committee of Inquiry headed by Supreme Court President Simon Agranat cleared Meir and Dayan of direct responsibility for Israel's unpreparedness for the 1973 war.

For half a century, Golda Meir's career was marked by unshakable determination, physical and emotional stamina under stress, and deep suspicions both of Arab objectives and of major-power guarantees of Israel's security. She was utterly convinced that Israel must depend as much as possible on her own resources. Above all, she was a courageous, determined political leader with a granite-like nature. She perceived her world in strong, stark colors that ruled out shades of gray. She died on December 8, 1978.

BIBLIOGRAPHY

Work by Meir:

My Life. New York: G. P. Putnam's Sons, 1975.

Other Works:

Arian, Alan (ed.). *The Elections in Israel 1969*. Jerusalem: Jerusalem Academic Press, 1972.
Arian, Asher (ed.). *The Elections in Israel 1973*. Jerusalem: Academic Press, 1975.
Herzog, Chaim. *The Arab-Israeli Wars: War and Peace in the Middle East*. New York: Random House, 1982.
Safran, Nadav. *Israel the Embattled Ally*. Cambridge, Mass.: Belknap Press of Harvard University Press, 1978, 1981.
Spiegel, Steven L. *The Other Arab-Israeli Conflict*. Chicago and London: University of Chicago Press, 1985.
Syrkin, Marie (ed.). *A Land of Our Own: An Oral Biography by Golda Meir*. Philadelphia: Jewish Publication Society, 1973.
Yaniv, Avner. *Deterrence without the Bomb: The Politics of Israeli Strategy*. Lexington, Mass.: Lexington Books, D. C. Heath and Company, 1987.

MARVER H. BERNSTEIN

ADNAN MENDERES (1899–1961) was one of Turkey's leading politicians in the second half of the 1940s and especially in the 1950s, when, as prime minister, he was directly responsible for the major political, economic, and sociocultural changes in Turkey's internal affairs, as well as for the major changes in Turkey's foreign policy, and indirectly responsible for the developments that occurred in the years following the 1950s. As an advocate of liberal economy, he reshaped the socioeconomic structure of Turkey, strengthening the ties between the rural and urban societies and laying the foundations for the emergence of a strong middle class. However, he also made certain steps that caused severe crises in the economic, social, and internal political realms, which finally caused the army to seize power. As an ardent supporter of the West, he managed to plant Turkey deeply in the Western camp and to tighten its relations with the United States and the Western European states. However, while entirely identifying Turkey with the West, he managed to maintain cordial relations with the communist camp and its leader the USSR.

Adnan Menderes was born in 1899 in Aydin (the Aegean region of Anatolia) to a large landowning family. He studied at the American College in Izmir. He spoke English well and, therefore, was considered to understand the Americans better than other Turkish politicians. Later, while an assembly deputy, he improved his education by studying law at Ankara University. However, he never really entered the practice of law, and as a result he has been classed as an agriculturalist, because both his general background and his livelihood revolved more about his position as a large landowner than about his legal work. As a reserve officer he was sent in 1916 to Syria but, becoming ill, he was transferred to Izmir, where he served until the end of World War I. A year later, in 1919, he joined the irregular military units (*çeteciler*), which maintained a guerrilla warfare against the Greek Army in western Anatolia in the War of Independence (1919–1923). There he met Celâl Bayar, at that time one of the commanders of those units. He entered politics in the late 1920s with already well-defined ideas of supporting democracy and liberal economy, and, therefore, became very active as the Aydin Organization's chairman in the establishment of the Free Republican Party, which was formally launched by Ali Fethi Okyar in August 1930. In its program, its wide support in western Anatolia, and its active functionaries, this party was a precursor of the Democratic Party and its successors: the Justice Party and lately the True Path Party, both led by Suleyman Demirel.* Following the decision of the Free Republican Party to abolish itself in December 1930, Adnan Bey, with an outstanding reputation as an eminent politician, joined the ruling Republican Peoples Party and was elected deputy to the fourth National Assembly in 1931. While a deputy in the fifth National Assembly (1935–1939), Adnan changed his family name from Ertekin to Menderes—the Turkish name of the river Meander, which irrigates, among others, the province of Aydin including his own fields.

He soon started to express his opposition to the étatist policy of his party, especially after the death in 1938 of the founder and leader of Republican Turkey, Mustafa Kemal Ataturk, the initiator of that policy. In the seventh National Assembly (1943–1946), Menderes voted on three occasions against his party's government, and in May 1945, when Turkey joined the United Nations, he began the process that finally caused the split in the Republican Peoples Party (RPP) and the expulsion of a group led by himself and his three associates: Celâl Bayar, Mehmet Fuat Köprülü, and Refik Koraltan. Menderes declared that Turkey had committed itself to democratic principles by ratifying the United Nations Charter, and with his three friends proposed a number of legal reforms that would guarantee those rights and liberties included in the charter. The proposals were rejected both by the party and by the National Assembly. The group published the proposals and criticized the totalitarian line of the RPP in Ahmet Emin Yalman's newspaper, *Vatan*, the main publication supporting democracy. Consequently, Menderes and his friends were expelled from the RPP in September 1945.

President Ismet Inonu* continued the process of democratization, nevertheless, and led to the establishment of multiparty democratic regime. This move enabled Bayar, Köprülü, Koraltan, and Menderes to officially establish a new party—the Democrat Party (DP)—on January 1946. Despite the DP's defeat in the elections of July 1946, in which the party managed to win only 61 seats in the Assembly, Menderes and his colleagues continued to prepare the party for the next elections concentrating, mainly on the organization of the party and on a consistent propaganda campaign against the ruling party, especially in the social, economic, and religious fields. Those efforts were fruitful: In the general elections of May 1950, the DP won 396 seats in the Assembly, while the ruling party, the RPP, won only 68. Celâl Bayar was elected president of the Republic and Adnan Menderes was appointed the prime minister. He did in fact reach the Premiership after serving as deputy for twenty years, but without any ministerial experience. This did not prevent him from winning the elections of 1954 and 1957 and remaining prime minister for a decade until he was deposed and arrested following the military takeover in May 1960. Menderes's ten-year Premiership was a decade of achievements and changes both in Turkey's internal affairs and in its foreign relations, but it also was a decade of regression of the political, legal, and social rights of the citizens, and of deterioration in the economic realm as well as in relations with some countries.

For Menderes, joining the Western institutions was an unequivocal and un-debated subject. He considered Turkey a European country and an active member of the Western democratic camp in opposition to the eastern Soviet-communist camp. He therefore made every effort to join the Western defense alliance and to establish a pro-Western defense alliance in the Middle East. In July, two months after gaining power, he offered troops to the UN forces fighting in South Korea. Then he led the negotiations that resulted in Turkey's becoming a full-fledged member of NATO (North Atlantic Treaty Organization) in February 1952. He tried to continue the foreign policy of Ataturk, advocating security and stability in the two neighboring regions of Turkey in the northwest and the southeast: the Balkans and the Middle East. In the Balkans he reached a Non-Aggression and Friendship Pact with Greece and Yugoslavia in 1953. In the Middle East he was active in 1954–1955 in establishing a defense pact (the

Baghdad Pact), in which Iraq, Britain, Pakistan, and Iran were also full-fledged members. Although relations with Greece deteriorated because of the Greek riots in Cyprus and the attack by Turks on Greek citizens and property in Istanbul and Izmir, and although Iraq left the Baghdad Pact following a military coup d'état in July 1958, the Menderes government managed to overcome these crises. In 1959, Greece, Turkey, and Britain signed an agreement that at that time solved Cyprus's crisis and provided independence to the island. In the same year the United States responded to the remaining members of the Baghdad Pact (now Central Treaty Organization-CENTO) and signed a bilateral defense accord with each of them. The United States found in Menderes an ardent supporter and a leader it could rely on and trust, while Menderes found in the United States a big brother of Turkey who was at times ready to extend military and financial aid to strengthen his own regime. Following the military coup d'état in Iraq in 1958, Menderes decided to intervene militarily, and it was only through the most vigorous U.S. arguments that he was dissuaded from doing so. Thereafter, a large, long-sought loan from Turkey's Western allies was forthcoming, which did much to shore up the country's economy and to improve Menderes' political stature.

Relations with the Soviet Union remained, to a certain extent, tense, with some intermissions. Nevertheless, it was in 1953 that the USSR relinquished all claims on Kars and Ardahan in northeastern Anatolia and all requests for participation in the administration of the Straits. Furthermore, in the same year an agreement was signed with the USSR on the building of the Serdarabat Dam near Iğdir on the border near the Black Sea.

Three major factors played an important role in the consolidating of Menderes' political power and his socioeconomic programs: (1) the exercise of a liberal economy with minimal intervention of the state, except the field of development, which was extensively promoted; (2) attention to the voters' interests even if they were contrary to his political and socioeconomic ideas; and (3) his fear of losing power eventually led him to return to authoritarianism.

Menderes' economic goal was to bring the country to the level of the industrial states of Western Europe in productivity and standard of living within a meaningful time. However, to obtain such a goal he needed at least several decades and severe economic measures, which could cause his party the loss of votes, especially in the rural areas where the party maintained its main support. Therefore, Menderes could not cope with the economic crises and made numerous concessions, especially on the eve of elections, which only enhanced the crises; he did this only to stay in power. The economic crisis of 1955 caused political and economic restlessness, which culminated in the riots of September 6–8 in Istanbul and Izmir against the Greek citizens and, to a certain extent, against other non-Muslims; and to the attempt to unseat Menderes in December. The fact that the authorities did not intervene to end the riots for about three days led to the conclusion that Menderes was interested in diverting the restlessness against targets other than the government, and was using the Cyprus Crisis as a means for diverting the people in those cities against the Greek citizens and their premises. The riots, it seems, developed into proportions far beyond the original plan and intentions, and led Menderes' opponents within the DP to criticize Menderes for not carrying out his promises. Nine party members were expelled and ten resigned. This "group of nineteen" organized a new splinter party, the Freedom Party. However, Menderes managed to dismiss several of the more controversial ministers by promising to pay more attention to the economic problems, and to emerge much more powerful than before. The economic crisis continued, but Menderes seemed unwilling to contain the deterioration. Only in mid–1957, after another economic breakdown did he take drastic measures, but immediately before the elections of October 1957 he increased crop subsidies, declares a moratorium on farmers' debts and other concessions, all of which were tantamount to "buying" the vote.

However, no one can ignore the great changes that occurred under Menderes in the socioeconomic field despite the continuous economic crisis, or perhaps because of it. During the decade of Menderes' rule, the important process of the peasant economy's integration into the national economy was started; this occurred as a result of the construction of a nationwide highway system, which opened up the hinterland and improved the connections between the rural and the urban areas. It also substantially enhanced the urbanization process, especially in the big cities. Undoubtedly again the need of the peasant vote to keep Menderes in power was one of the main reasons. Furthermore, peasants were relieved of taxation, and provinces whose peasants supported government policies enjoyed government favors, especially modernization. Moreover, Menderes courted the peasants by relaxing restraints on religious ceremonies and prayers, and those he favored were provided financial aid for building mosques. Menderes could in this way also count on the support of the urban masses because large parts of these masses were peasants moving to the urban areas. He also started housing schemes, but never managed to cope with the speedy development of the huge slums (*gecekondu*) around the big cities. Another important change was the new and swiftly growing class of entrepreneurs and merchants in the cities and towns as a result of the DP favoring private enterprise over state enterprise. This growing class endorsed Menderes and his party.

With the support of the peasants, the urban masses, and the emerging new middle class, Menderes could secure an overwhelming majority in any freely competitive elections. Nevertheless, Menderes soon restored to restrictive policies that at least in retrospect did not seem necessary for victory at the polls. Following roughly three years of good feeling, political life grew increasingly bitter and taut. Menderes started to pursue a path that could lead only to a return to authoritarianism and a reversal of the democratic progress that had so strenuously been achieved. He pushed through the legislature a succession of laws designed to strike down public criticism, cripple the opposition parties, and bring the administrative and judicial branches of government firmly under party control. University autonomy was seriously undermined by a law issued in July 1953 forbidding university faculty members to engage in political activities, and by government-instigated actions against certain of the more politically minded faculty members in 1956.

As of December 1953, Menderes' government started to limit the political activities of the rival political parties. First, most of the assets of the RPP, the most formidable rival, were confiscated by the government, closing the People's Houses and seizing the party's newspaper press. Second, in 1954, following the elections in which Kirshehir Province returned the only assembly deputies elected from the Republican National Party, as a punishment, the Menderes government redefined the boundaries of the province, lowering the status of Kirshehir from that of provincial capital to district capital. Third, in June 1956, a bill limiting the holding of public political meetings was approved. Fourth, in September 1957, on the eve of the elections, a law was approved that made political coalitions in elections illegal. The parties were also practically barred from access to the state radio, and Menderes managed to make it almost impossible for the opposition parties to engage in free electioneering.

Severe limits were also gradually laid on the freedom of the press by a series of stringent press laws. In March 1954, a law was passed prescribing heavy punishment for news reporters whose writing was deemed harmful to the political or financial prestige of the state, or which invaded private life. The power of the government over the press was increased by certain amendments introduced to that law in June 1956, which among other things obliged the newsmen to prove what they had written in all cases. As a result, hundreds of journalists and editors were sentenced to imprisonment for certain periods, and freedom to discuss public issues was to a large extent curtailed.

Even the landslide victory of Menderes in the elections of May 1954 (the DP won 503 seats out of 541) did not end his fears or stop his strict measures to secure himself in power. Only two months after the elections the impartiality of the civil service and the independence of the judiciary were challenged by a law giving the government the power to discharge civil servants, professors, and most judges without the right to appeal. Civil servants who failed to toe the party line were dismissed and judges handing down decisions not to the liking of the regime were forced to retire or were transferred. Also, according to the law, the retirement of judges after twenty-five years' service became mandatory. This law enabled Menderes and his government to bring loyal persons to the administration and the courts. This system of favoritism and protection was also introduced in the military. Menderes promoted officers freely, no doubt hoping thereby to gain in popularity, but he chose officers for the top commands because of fidelity to the prime minister and his party, not merit. During the DP decade (1950–1960), the social and economic status of military officers declined because as a fixed-income group they were adversely affected by inflation, while the status of the manufacturers and shopkeepers rose.

Menderes seems to fear the fixed-income group—the civil servants, the military, the judges, and so forth in contrast to farmers, manufacturers and merchants. Menderes' attitude is best illustrated by his fears of the workers. The DP program included a promise to the workers to grant them the right to strike and collective bargaining. He never implemented this promise because he feared not only the political use of the strike, but also its possible impact on wages and prices. He in fact did not need to court the workers, because at least a part of them, the rural emigrants and the traditionalists, were considered supporters of the DP.

There was an opposition to the antidemocratic measures of Menderes within the DP. This was expressed almost entirely in DP meetings and not in the voting in the National Assembly. Moreover, the opposition that was manifested through Assembly votes included disagreement with policies other than the government antidemocratic proposals. Only at the end of 1955 was there much criticism of the severe punishments given the newspaper reporters. Twenty-eight DP deputies left (or were expelled) and established a new party—the Freedom Party. Menderes was still powerful and the splinter party could not emerge to become a real threat to the DP. In the elections of 1957, the Freedom Party won only four seats in the Assembly. There was also certain tension between Menderes and the president, Celâl Bayar, who was, with Menderes, among the founders of the DP. The tension had started already in the beginning of the 1950s when Menderes substantially reduced the role of the presidency and increased the powers of the premiership. However, neither one dared to appear openly against the other for their own sake as well as that of the party.

However, Menderes lost some of his popularity within the party and among the citizens, and this first came to the surface in the general elections of 1957. The DP was again victorious and won 424 seats in the Assembly, but the main opposition party, the RPP, won 178 seats and other parties won 8. Menderes became more authoritarian in ruling the party and the country, and at the same time made every effort to regain popular support and to secure his leading position. In February 1959 he survived an airplane crash at the Gatwick Airport (London) in which most passengers were killed or injured. Menderes immediately used this accident to enhance his prestige and influence by stressing that Allah had saved him for the sake of the Turkish nation. Later he established the mass "nonpolitical organization" called the Fatherland Front (Vatan Cephesi). It seems that he wanted to have an organizational home in the event he finally felt compelled to bolt from the DP.

At the end of 1959 and the beginning of 1960 Menderes faced stubborn resistance to his growing authoritarianism from members of the semiautonomous institutions that he had tried to suppress—the political parties, the press, university faculty and students, the judiciary, and the bureaucracy. Under this pressure Menderes was compelled to invoke force and ordered infantry units to suppress meetings of the political opposition parties and the student protest demonstrations (demanding "freedom") that followed, and to impose martial law on Istanbul, Ankara, and Izmir. The military refused to be used and chose as the lesser evil to violate its already well-established and obviously essential tradition of political neutrality, and to intervene. The officers involved in the conspiracy against Menderes knew that he was going to move against them and were convinced that they had no other choice.

The military takeover occurred on the night of May 27, 1960. Menderes and other DP leaders were arrested and later were put to trial. The DP was banned and later in September 1960 it was abolished. Menderes was found guilty of violating the constitution, of abusing power in the anti-Greek riots, of suppressing the opposition and the students' demonstrations, and of misusing secret funds. He was also found guilty in connection with the attempted murder of the opposition leader Ismet Inonu and the attempt to employ troops in order to prevent Inonu from attending his party's congress in Kayseri in April 1960. Menderes was sentenced to death by the Supreme Military Court on September 15, 1960, but his execution was delayed by a "suicide attempt" and was carried out on September 17, 1961, over the protest of several of Turkey's allies, including the United States, and of the RPP's leaders. The military did not dare spare Menderes for fear of his possible return to power. The 40-percent vote against the new constitution in the Referendum of 1961 indicated, despite the trial, that Menderes still enjoyed popular support, and served as a warning to the military to refuse him mercy.

There is no doubt that Menderes contributed to the development of the private sector, which later became a major factor in expanding Turkey's industry and in improving and broadening Turkey's services. He started to close the gaps between the rural and urban economies and societies; this later enhanced the urbanization process as did the improvement of the socioeconomic conditions in the rural area. He was responsible for the concessions made on account of secularism, although he was careful not to exceed certain bounds and confined himself only to concessions in the field of Islamic worship. However, he did eventually begin to use Islam as a political weapon, especially when economic problems started to cause a drop in his mass support. However, Menderes' ambitions and fears of losing power became unrestrainable, ultimately dragging the country into a severe dictatorship in which an opposition to his rule became an openly dangerous venture, a dictatorship that finally brought the army—which until that time had been painstakingly kept out of politics—to power, initiating a tradition of military takeovers in Turkey. On the other hand, Turkey's governments after 1960 continued, to a large extent, to exercise his pro-Western foreign policy and his liberal economic ideas.

BIBLIOGRAPHY

Work by Menderes:

Menderes Diyor Ki (Menderes Says That). Prepared for publication by Sükrü Esirci. Istanbul: Bahar Matbaasi, 1967.

Other Works:

Ahmad, Feroz. *The Turkish Experiment in Democracy 1950–1975*. Boulder, Colo.: Westview Press, 1977.

Karpat, Kemal H. *Turkey's Foreign Policy in Transition 1950–1974*. Leiden, The Netherlands: Brill, 1975.

Robinson, Richard D. *The First Turkish Republic: A Case Study in National Development*. Cambridge, Mass.: Harvard University Press, 1963.

ARYEH SHMUELEVITZ

MOHAMMED V (1909?–1961). When Mohammed bin Yusuf was born in 1909 in Fez, Morocco, no one could imagine the central role he would play in his country's history. At the time of his birth, Morocco was going through the pangs of the crises that led to the signing of the Treaty of Fez on 30, March 1912, which gave France a protectorate over the country. By the time of his death in 1961, Morocco, under his leadership, had emerged from the era of foreign domination to become an important player among the newly independent states of Africa and the Arab-Islamic world.

The future sultan's birth was such an unimportant event that we have no record of its exact date, and, in fact, even the year of his birth is not entirely certain. He was the third son of Mulay Yusuf, brother of Sultan Mulay Hafid, who was to sign the Protectorate Treaty with France in 1912. In the tumult that followed the treaty, his father was selected in 1912 to replace his uncle as sultan, yet the young prince remained a minor figure. He moved from his birthplace in Fez to the Royal Palace in Rabat, where he received a traditional education and was viewed as a most unlikely ruler. Nonetheless, on his father's death in 1927, Morocco's French overlords anointed him as the new sultan, in large measure because they expected him to be more malleable and easier to control than his older siblings. What neither they nor the Moroccan religious, commercial, and intellectual elite could foresee was that the young sultan would ultimately emerge as the symbol of Moroccan national resistance to French control, the leader of Morocco's struggle for independence, and the first king of modern Morocco.

Before his selection as sultan in 1927, the young prince had led a rather unexceptional life. As a young boy, we are told, he played in the streets of Fez with the children of the city. As he grew older, he took part in court ceremonies and was presented to the legendary French Resident General Marechal Lyautey in 1924. Two years later his father took him along on a trip to France, and later the same year he was married. When his father died in November 1927, the *ulema* (learned men) of Fez elected him Sultan of Morocco—and the French "protectors" played a major role in this selection.

On his accession to the throne, the seventeen-year-old Mohammed V was ill-prepared for his ultimate role. As a member of the Alawi dynasty, he was invested with a measure of legitimacy because of his *sharifian* (descended from the Prophet– background—the Alawis are descendants of the Prophet Mohammed and enjoy special prestige as a result. Under the guidance of his teacher Si Mammeri (promoted to chamberlain) and grand vizier Mohammed el Mokri (who had already served a quarter century in the imperial entourage), Mohammed V began to learn about the power he now held, the limits placed by the French on that power, and, above all, about the country and people he was to rule and lead.

Slowly he began to emerge from his shell, but his political emergence would take nearly two decades. In July 1928, he traveled to France again, where he was received by President Gaston Doumergue at the Elysée. Surrounded by French officials in Morocco, he took up tennis, the French game of *boules* (a form of lawn bowling), and horseback riding, sports he continued to enjoy until his death. These were not the only signs of an emerging modernism in Mohammed V. When his first son, Moulay Hassan,* was born in July 1929, he called on a midwife with modern training rather than a traditional midwife to attend the birth. As his children, including his daughters, grew, he insisted that they receive a modern education, and he organized the College Imperial for them and the children of other leading figures in Rabat. While his wife was never seen in public, his two sons and four daughters became increasingly public figures, usually clad in Western clothes.

However, his first venture into the political arena came on May 16, 1930, when he acquiesced in the French decision to issue the famous Berber *Dahir* (edict) granting Berber customary law supremacy over Islamic law among Morocco's Berber population. Designed to divide Moroccans along Arab-Berber lines, in many ways this act led to creation of the modern Moroccan nationalist movement. It unified Berbers and Arabs alike in opposition to what all perceived as an attack on Islam, one of the pillars of Moroccan unity and identity. Many young nationalist activists saw the young sultan as the fulfillment of French desires for a pliable figurehead who could be manipulated for French ends. However, the protests engendered by the issuance of the Berber Dahir became the first lesson for Sidi Mohammed in the politics of Morocco under French rule, and he began to understand the issues he and his fellow compatriots faced.

Despite their disappointment that the sultan had agreed to the Berber Dahir, the nationalists set out to win Mohammed V over to their cause. In 1933, they demanded creation of Throne Day in commemoration of his accession to the throne on November 18. They organized popular demonstrations, punctuated with cries of "Long live the Sultan!" when he visited Fez in 1934, and they occasionally managed to meet with him when the French and el Mokri would permit. While Mohammed approved of the nationalists' Plan of Reforms in 1934, including its assertion of the sovereignty of the sultan, he did not approve of the violent demonstrations that took place around the country three years later in the wake of a French plan to irrigate four *colon* (settler) farms near Meknes with water from the city water supply. As a result, when the French proposed exile for the two principal nationalist agitators, Allal al-Fasi* and Mohammed Hassan el-Wazzani in October 1937, he raised no objections.

It was during World War II that Mohammed V began to assert his independence and show signs of the leadership he would later exhibit in guiding his people to independence. First he proclaimed his loyalty to France when it was attacked by the Germans. After the fall of France, the French authorities in Morocco pledged their loyalty to the Vichy regime under Maréchal Philippe Pétain, and Sidi Mohammed reaffirmed his loyalty to France. When Resident General H. Nogues then proposed that he implement the anti-Semitic Nuremburg laws when the Vichy government imposed them in France itself, Mohammed V flatly refused, saying that Morocco's Jews were his subjects, whom he must protect. After the Allied Operation Torch landing in Morocco on November 8, 1942, he was received twice by U.S. President Franklin D. Roosevelt during the Casablanca Conference in January 1943. While there is some dispute as to how strongly Roosevelt intimated that the United States would back Moroccan aspirations for independence after the war, there is little doubt that the meetings, also attended by Mulay Hassan, had a great impact.

In 1943, the Moroccan nationalist movement, in some disarray since 1938, reconstituted itself under the leadership of Ahmed Balafrej. On January 11, 1944, Balafrej and his collaborators issued the Istiqlal (Independence) Party manifesto, which demanded independence for all Morocco "under the protection of His Majesty Sidi Mohammed bin Yusuf." However, the sultan did not rush to support the nationalist claims, telling his viziers in the presence of Resident General Gabriel Puaux that "the word independence must disappear from the hearts and the mouths" (Julien 1978: 191). Repression of the nationalists followed, with the key leaders arrested, Balafrej deported to Corsica, and protest demonstrations brutally suppressed. Nevertheless, the nationalists did not despair of winning over Sidi Mohammed.

In February 1945, he was deeply moved to see the crowds, organized by the Istiqlal, acclaiming his entry to Marrakesh with cries of "Long live the King! Long live the nation!" The buildings along his route also were festooned with nationalist slogans. The French expected the supposedly malleable Mohammed bin Yusuf to condemn the slogans. Instead, his response was to assure listeners in Marrakesh that "everything that saddens you saddens me too. Everything you hope for, I hope for too" (Landau 1957: 46). The meaning was not lost on the Istiqlalis, who began to see Mohammed V as a potential ally. In subsequent meetings in Paris with Charles de Gaulle, leader of the Free French, the Moroccan Sultan pressed for concessions. One of the most important was the recall of the French Resident. When he was replaced by Erik Labonne, prospects for reconciliation began to look good. Labonne began by opening the prisons and allowing leaders such as Allal al-Fasi to return to Morocco after a nine-year exile in Gabon. Nonetheless, it would be two more years before Mohammed V spoke out again.

During the war, Mohammed V had acquired a new set of goals. Now he wished to play a significant role in Morocco and the world. Many of his advisers told him that to do so he must visit the international city of Tangier, passing through the Spanish zone. Such a visit would demonstrate the unity of the country—broken up into two Spanish zones, a French zone, and the international city of Tangier—under the sultan. Although the French were troubled by the prospect of such a visit, Labonne consented and reviewed the text of Mohammed

V's remarks before departure, adding a passage extolling the virtues of the Protectorate.

A few days before the sultan's scheduled visit to Tangier, there was a violent incident in Casablanca on April 7, 1947, where Senegalese troops massacred eighty-three Moroccans and wounded several hundred more before the police finally intervened. Throughout Morocco people were horrified and blamed the French—some even thought it a deliberate provocation designed to make the Sultan abandon the Tangier visit.

Sidi Mohammed decided to omit any favorable reference to France from his remarks in Tangier, but, in French eyes, this was not his only sin in Tangier. He used the occasion to speak of the "legitimate rights of the Moroccan people." Then on April 12, taking full advantage of the presence on journalists from around the world gathered for his visit, he declared that "It goes without saying that Morocco—being a country attached by solid bonds to the Arab countries of the East—desires to strengthen those bonds ever more resolutely, especially since the Arab League has now become an important factor in world affairs" (Landau 1957: 46).

After twenty years of watching, listening, and bending, Mohammed V had finally shown that inside there was a man of steel who was ready to become the symbol of the Moroccan struggle for independence, which he did. As a result, Mohammed V was able to strengthen the legitimacy of the Moroccan monarchy and reinforce its role in Moroccan political life.

The most immediate consequence of the Tangier speech was the recall of Labonne. In his place the French sent General Alphonse Juin, a hard-line military man from Algeria, who was granted vast powers by the authorities to deal with the situation and the sultan. Over the next four years, Juin and the French increasingly came to see Mohammed V and his son Mulay Hassan as the cause of their problems in Morocco. During a visit to France in 1950, the sultan presented a series of demands to the French government. The French expressed willingness to make mild reforms (which caused them problems with the colonialists) but refused to discuss the crucial issues of the sovereignty of the sultan and the abolition of the Protectorate.

From 1951 until Moroccan independence in 1956, the country endured a series of crises that thrust the sultan onto center stage. In December 1950 and January 1951, Mohammed V's growing assertiveness brought him into conflict with both Juin and Thami el Glaoui, pasha of Marrakesh and a strong ally of the French. On December 21, 1950, Glaoui attacked the sultan during an audience, blurting out "You are not the Sultan of Morocco, you are the Sultan of the Istiqlal," whereupon Sidi Mohammed ordered him to leave the palace forthwith. Glaoui and the French then rallied local Moroccan officials in the south against the sultan. In January 1951, Juin demanded that the monarch either denounce the Istiqlal or abdicate, which he refused to do. Finally, on February 25, 1951, Juin had the palace surrounded with tanks, Glaoui brought Berber tribesmen to the gates of Rabat, and Abdel Hay Kittani mobilized the Sufi brotherhoods in an attempt to force Sidi Mohammed to either capitulate or abdicate. In the end, the sultan capitulated and signed documents agreeing to Juin's demands. However, he explained, he had signed to avert a bloody confrontation. Because he had signed under duress, he did not consider the document legally binding.

The sultan continued, in his Throne Day speech for example, to press for full sovereignty. In October 1952 he issued a statement calling for an arrangement permitting Moroccans to govern themselves "by means of a representative parliament and a constitutional government of a modern democratic character," a proposal the French rejected. In December, the murder of Tunisian labor leader Ferhat Hachad led to a sympathy strike in Casablanca which ended in clashes between workers and the police resulting in scores of deaths and injuries. Brutal repression followed. The next year would see the French succeed in deposing Sidi Mohammed.

Once again using Thami el Glaoui and Abdel Hay Kittani, the French maneuvered to remove the sultan, with the crisis coming to a head in mid-August 1953. When Resident General A. Guillaume (who had replaced Juin two years before) returned to Rabat on August 13, he presented Sidi Mohammed with an ultimatum to sign all the decrees he had refused to sign for years. Meanwhile Glaoui and Kittani were mobilizing their supporters to support the French, oppose the sultan, and facilitate his deposition in favor of his elderly uncle Mulay Ben Arafa. Glaoui organized a march of his tribal followers (with a great deal of French logistical support), and on August 20, 1953, Mohammed bin Yusuf and his two sons Mulay Hassan and Mulay Abdallah were taken from Rabat to exile—first to Corsica (where they were later joined by the rest of the family members) and then to Madagascar. Mulay Ben Arafa was proclaimed sultan.

Sidi Mohammed's deposition and exile served to make him a martyr in the cause of Moroccan nationalism and reinforced his popularity among the masses. In the wake of the events of August 20, the Istiqlal and others organized resistance, including armed resistance, terrorism, and an economic boycott; by April 1954, for example, sales of tobacco had declined over 78 percent. The French soon realized they had created a bigger problem than they had already had. After the outbreak of the Algerian Revolution in November 1954, finding a solution became increasingly important.

After trying a number of tactics, the French finally opened talks with the nationalists at Aix-les-Bains in September 1955. By this time the level of violence in Morocco had increased markedly. On October 1, the French forced Mulay Ben Arafa to step aside in favor of a four-member Throne Council. Later in the month, with the violence continuing and even with Thami el Glaoui calling for the sultan's restoration, the French had little choice. On October 31, Mohammed V arrived with his family in Nice and was received as a sovereign. Within twenty-four hours he was in Paris receiving Thami el Glaoui (after making him cool his heels for several hours while he met with other less important figures) who reportedly prostrated himself before the sultan four times. On November 17, 1955, the sultan returned to Morocco to a tumultuous welcome.

Now there were the new challenges of organizing the affairs of state for full independence in March, and then the tasks of getting Spain to relinquish control of its zones in order to reunify the country. Disparate political forces, harnessed together in the drive for independence had to be kept in harness, a task that proved impossible. In his five years as king of Morocco after independence (he discarded the title "sultan" in favor of the more modern "king"), Mohammed V continued to show his mettle. He deftly maneuvered through a thicket of political groupings to emerge as the paramount political figure in the country. In fact, in his last months he removed the prime minister and served in that capacity himself, with his son and heir Mulay Hassan* as deputy prime minister.

After independence, Mohammed V increasingly stressed Morocco's African and Asian ties. He traveled widely, saw himself as a mediator in the disputes among his Arab brethren to the east, and hosted a January 1961 meeting in Casablanca that led to the formation of the Organization of African Unity. When he died on the operating table of unexpected complications from minor surgery on February 26, 1961, he was planning a trip to the Muslim states of south Asia.

Mohammed bin Yusuf was a seminal figure in Moroccan history. His role as a symbol of Moroccan nationalism secured the position of the monarchy in postindependence Morocco. Whereas earlier Alawi sultans had rested their legitimacy on their sharifian origin and their military might, now the king added to his religious role the roles of national leader and reunifier of the state. Though raised in a traditionalist environment and almost invariably appearing in public in traditional attire, he was anything but a traditionalist. By educating his children in both the fundamental precepts of Islam and the fundamentals of modern Western learning, and by encouraging his daughters to play an active role in public life, he set examples that many citizens of Morocco have followed.

BIBLIOGRAPHY

el Alami, Mohamed. *Mohammed V, histoire de l'independance du Maroc*. Rabat: Editions A. P. I., 1981.
Julien, Charles-André. *Le Maroc face aux imperialismes, 1415–1956*. Paris: Editions J. A., 1978.
Lacouture, Jean. *Cinq hommes et la France*. Paris: Seuil, 1961.
Landau, Rom. *The Sultan of Morocco*. London: Robert Hale Ltd., 1951.
———. *Moroccan Drama, 1900–1955*. San Francisco: American Academy of Asian Studies, 1956.
———. *Mohammed V, King of Morocco*. Rabat: Morocco Publishers, 1957.

JEROME B. BOOKIN-WEINER

ALI NASSER MOHAMMAD (1939–   ) was named president of South Yemen in April 1980. He continued his predecessor's policy of close relations with the Soviet Union and Eastern Europe, but also sought to improve relations with Saudi Arabia. He strove to improve relations with North Yemen and reached a political working arrangement with Yemeni president Salih.*

Ali Nasser Mohammad was in many ways the most enigmatic of the triumvirate that dominated the People's Democratic Republic of Yemem (PDRY or South Yemen) following its independence in 1967. A primary-school headmaster under the British rule, he apparently did not play a role in the actual fighting, but became a member of the military office of the National Liberation Front (NLF) in the struggle for independence. He is not mentioned as one of the secondary leadership that kept the NLF on the path of armed struggle, nor was he prominent in the radical wing of the NLF during either its attempt to transform the party in 1968 or its successful coup (the "Corrective Movement") in June 1969. He remained a member of the NLF's General Command during its brief moderate phase and was appointed minister of local government in April 1969. Nevertheless, his radical credentials must have been acceptable, his tribal connections useful, and his organizational and administrative skills in the military valued, for in July 1969 he was appointed minister of defense. His task was to remake the South Yemeni armed forces, to replace the British-trained officer corps, and to create a "people's army" which, under the watchful eyes of political commissars, could not only defend the revolution against the external enemies then threatening its frontiers (emigré forces based in North Yemen and Saudi Arabia) but also act as an agent of socialist transformation within the PDRY. In the course of this process he oversaw the military's full transition to Soviet weapons.

Mohammad was made prime minister in August 1971 (while retaining the Defense portfolio), thus becoming the junior member of the ruling triumvirate with Salim Rubay Ali* (the PDRY's President) and Abd al-Fattah Ismail* (the general secretary of the NLF). In this colorful and ideologically charged company, he often seemed invisible. Nonetheless, he turned out to be a survivor, with skills and political instincts that made him acceptable to the various factions and that enabled him not only to survive the often violent twists of South Yemeni politics but even to rise to the top. He was a Marxist-Leninist (in the South Yemeni context) and reliably pro-Soviet (apparently in part out of conviction but also in recognition of the PDRY's weakness). He was also a bureaucrat, concerned with the orderly building and functioning of government and society, and appreciative of the need for a party that could facilitate these goals. He was thus acceptable to the Ismail faction (probably on sufferance) and to the Soviets. At the same time, within this political framework he was a pragmatist, preoccupied with economic development and the population's standard of living, and concerned lest too vehement an attachment to a radical ideology alienate the population and potential donors of foreign aid. This made him acceptable to the populist and increasingly pragmatic Salim Rubay Ali and to the Soviets, who viewed with some concern both Rubay Ali's Maoist tendencies and Ismail's dogmatic determination to apply Marxist-Leninist principles regardless of South Yemeni social and economic realities. Finally, he was of the Dathina tribe, by tradition important in the military in both the pre- and postindependence eras; this tribal affiliation made him valuable to both camps.

The fact remained, however, that he was overshadowed within the regime by the other two leaders until 1978; to maintain his position, he had to ally himself with one or the other. When either or both espoused a policy, he could not block it; thus, for example, the nationalizations of the early 1970s went ahead, although he would likely have warned of their deleterious effect on foreign investment and aid and on levels of remittances from expatriate workers. However, he probably drew some strength from his successful dealings with the Soviets, who after mid–1972 committed themselves to the preservation of the PDRY with a diverse economic aid program and a large military program, and advisers (co-ordinated with Eastern Europeans and Cubans) spread throughout the important institutions of the system. Ali Nasser visited the Soviet Union more often than his colleagues, and met with all the senior Soviet political figures; he was the first South Yemeni to be honored with a meeting with Leonid Brezhnev (March 8, 1973).

As the power struggle between Rubay Ali and Ismail intensified between 1974 and 1978, Ali Nasser Mohammad apparently was able to maintain some measure of neutrality. It is probable that he was sympathetic to Rubay Ali's more prag-matic foreign policy which, implicitly abandoning the revolutionary strategy toward the PDRY's neighbors, included rapprochement with North Yemen and the opening of relations with Saudi Arabia; the goal of this policy, it is clear, was to attract large-scale economic aid. That Ali Nasser was not considered by Abd al-Fattah Ismail to be entirely reliable was indicated by his loss of the Defense portfolio in October 1977. On the other hand, Ali Nasser would certainly have disapproved of Rubay Ali's individualistic ruling style, and he was probably in favor of the creation of a strong party; this, in company with his own ad-ministrative skills allowed him to retain enough of the confidence of the Ismail faction to permit him to align solidly with it in the spring of 1978.

Thus, in the upheaval of June 1978, Mohammad did more than survive. Even after Ismail consolidated his power by adding the presidency of the PDRY to his position as general secretary of the new Yemeni Socialist Party (YSP), Ali Nasser was acknowledged as a member of a duumvirate. It seems reasonable to see this as a tactical move by Ismail. He needed a known moderate and pragmatist to assuage some of the domestic anger at the summary execution of the popular Salim Rubay Ali and even more so the outrage of most of the Arab world at this and the related assassination of YAR (Yemen Arab Republic) President Ahmad al-Ghashmi. Ali Nasser probably smoothed the way for South Yemen's reconciliation with the Arab world at the Baghdad Conference in November 1979, and may even have been the one who persuaded Ismail to moderate his stance and agree to visit Saudi Arabia.

Nevertheless, factional politics are endemic to South Yemen, and Abd al-Fattah Ismail's antitribalism and dogmatic domestic policies, which were widely blamed for the PDRY's continuing dismal economic record, quickly made pos-sible a coalescence of more pragmatic forces (and those with a greater concern for continuing tribal sensibilities) around Ali Nasser Mohammad and the dynamic minister of defense, Ali Antar. This coalition made rapid progress in shifting the balance within the regime against Ismail, and although he attempted to bolster his position by moving the PDRY even closer to the USSR with the signing of a twenty-year Treaty of Friendship and Cooperation, his status had declined enough by April 1980 for his opponents to gain the support of "his" vanguard party and remove him.

The desire had again arisen to ameliorate the domestic economic situation with foreign aid from the conservative oil states and the West. Events in the Persian Gulf region had made the conservative oil states less concerned about the Soviet presence in South Yemen. However, domestic controls in the PDRY were a factor discouraging investment, as was the Ismail faction's support for the overthrow of the YAR government. Ali Nasser Mohammad, who managed to exclude Ali Antar from formal power by securing all three top positions (general secretary of the YSP, president and prime minister) moved to relax some of the domestic controls, and to defuse the inter-Yemeni conflict completely.

On the latter issue there is no reason to think that Mohammad, like Rubay Ali and Ismail, would not have welcomed a new revolution in North Yemen leading to a "Marxist-Leninist" government and Yemen unity, probably under YSP tutelage. Yemeni unity has entered the mythology of both countries and has been a potent legitimizing slogan of all leaders (although none has been willing to sacrifice power or the social system to achieve it). Unlike Ismail, however, Ali Nasser had a secure (tribal) power base in South Yemen and little emotional or ideological attachment to defeating the reactionaries and tribalists. Thus he was involved in most of the numerous efforts at negotiated unity agreements, whether piecemeal or comprehensive. In October 1972, after a brief border war between the two Yemens, he negotiated an agreement to unify them within a year. Joint committees were established to work out the details, but unification did not progress; each government continued to host, and to a greater or less extent encourage, groups that aimed to destabilize or overthrow the other government. Under Ismail the PDRY gave extensive assistance to the National Democratic Front (NDF), the amalgam of North Yemeni opposition groups that the Ismail faction had had a hand in creating. The activities of the NDF (which controlled substantial pieces of YAR territory) and of the YAR military led to the outbreak of another border war in February 1979, after which the two governments again signed a unification pact. Nevertheless, Ismail's continued support of the NDF ensured that unification again went no further.

However, when Ali Nasser Mohammad gained power, his more pragmatic approach offered hope for the reduction of tensions and even for unification. He first had to contend with hard-liners still in the YSP Politburo, and the NDF prospered even as the unity committees were meeting, and after high-level inter-Yemeni meetings had been institutionalized and a draft joint constitution had been drawn up in December 1981. It was only in May 1982, after the North Yemeni armed forces had dealt the NDF several defeats and the PDRY had suffered devastating floods, that Ali Nasser was able to curb the transborder flow of assistance. Relations then warmed, and in the summer Mohammad and YAR President Ali Abdullah Salih* toured Arab capitals attempting to forge a unified Arab response to Israel's invasion of Lebanon. They continued to meet frequently. Nevertheless, little of substance was accomplished. The idea of unity, while emotive, ignored the deep differences in the economic, political, and social development of the "two parts of the motherland." However, Ali Nasser's stress on peaceful unification did help to achieve a radical reduction of inter-Yemeni tensions, which was no mean achievement.

Other foreign-policy moves, such as the agreement to establish relations with Oman in 1982 after fifteen years of vituperation—and, until 1976, years of support for guerrilla movements in Oman—pleased the Gulf Arab states; on the other hand, there were disturbing inconsistencies (such as the signing of the Tripartite Agreement in 1981 with Ethiopia and Libya and the backing of Iran in the Gulf War) which perhaps were to be explained by the continuing volatility of the political situation in Aden.

On the whole, however, Ali Nasser's foreign policy did assist him in his quest for diversified sources of foreign aid and investment. By 1985, after measures against the private sector had been relaxed, remittances from South Yemenis working abroad began to expand, and some West European companies had begun to operate in South Yemen (including in the all-important oil-exploration sector). The economy as a whole showed signs of recovery, and living standards rose.

Nevertheless, as always the improvement benefited some citizens more than others, and conspicuous consumption and corruption grew, often to the benefit of Ali Nasser's tribal and political supporters. Despite (or because of) his rapid accretion of the top positions in the country, an opposition faction coalesced, comprised of tribalists, those of stronger ideological conviction, and those of North Yemeni origin. This disparate group (in which Ali Antar played a leading role) was encouraged by some indications of Soviet disquiet at the direction of Ali Nasser Mohammad's policies, despite that country's welcome of his policy of regional accommodation. The USSR's concern may have been aroused by the backsliding in his home governorate of Abyan, where some collective farms were being disbanded. It was probably also alarmed by his invitation to Western oil companies, fearing they might succeed where the Soviets had thus far failed, and give Ali Nasser new options.

Whatever their reasons, the Soviets provided the catalyst in Ali Nasser Mohammad's downfall in January 1986, which was caused by the return of Abd al-Fattah Ismail in early 1985 (something Moscow could easily have prevented). The power struggle in Aden had heated up in 1984, with Ali Nasser being criticized for his more pragmatic foreign policy (his *Riyalpolitik*, in the local humor), and accused in June at a YSP Central Committee plenum of downgrading the importance of ideology. Members of the opposing factions were added to the Politburo, which first forced the return of Ismail and then in February 1985 demanded the resignation of Ali Nasser from the prime ministership.

Factional violence was only narrowly averted in the summer. At the third YSP Congress in October 1985 Ali Nasser was forced to accept a "compromise" that would mean the end of his dominance (and, given the growing bitterness of the dispute, probably also the end of his political career if not his life): His faction was given a majority on the Central Committee, while the other faction had a majority on the more powerful Politburo. The new majority reportedly began to insist on personnel changes, which would presumably have weakened Ali Nasser's position further. Rumor had it that he would be deposed shortly.

In this charged atmosphere, Ali Nasser Mohammad evidently struck first; accepted wisdom has it that at a Politburo meeting on January 13, 1986, his bodyguards opened fire, killing Ali Antar and other leading figures of the op- position factions outright and fatally wounding Abd al-Fattah Ismail. Vicious fighting spread quickly throughout the city and then its environs as some of the tribes most closely connected to the leaders became involved. The armed forces divided, but the tank corps joined the anti-Mohammad forces and proved to be the deciding factor. Ali Nasser had not remained in Aden, but had gone to his home base in Abyan. On January 18 (while the fighting was still fierce) he flew to Ethiopia; whether this was to seek assistance or, as he later claimed, in response to an invitation to fly to Moscow for mediation talks, it was a serious mistake. His supporters fought for their lives for another few days, and then several thousand fled with their families to North Yemen.

The new South Yemeni leadership, under the technocrat and former prime minister President Haydar Abu Bakr al-Attas and YSP General Secretary Ali Salim al-Bid, a long-time Ismail loyalist, declared a general amnesty for the fighters. However, they resisted all pressure from neighboring states and the Soviet Union to include Ali Nasser. He and eighteen of his close associates were sentenced to death in absentia in December 1987.

Ali Nasser Mohammad presided over the most prosperous and peaceful period in the PDRY's short history, yet eventually he fell, succumbing to (and himself contributing to) continuing personal rivalries and the endemic ideological and tribal cleavages of South Yemeni society. Nevertheless, with the help of changing regional and global conditions, he appears to have set the country on a sustainable moderate course; his successors have not moved to alter it in any significant measure. Ironically, it is Ali Nasser himself who is the most unsettling factor in the near term, living in exile in North Yemen, isolated by that government from his followers in the camps on the border but a threat nevertheless to the still-unstable political system in the PDRY.

The author wishes to acknowledge the support of the Advisory Research Committee, Queen's University, in the preparation of this article.

BIBLIOGRAPHY

Cigar, Norman. "State and Society in South Yemen." *Problems of Communism* 34, no. 3 (May-June 1985): 41–58.

———. "South Yemen and the USSR: Prospects for the Relationship." *Middle East Journal* 39, no. 4 (Autumn 1985): 775–795.

Halliday, Fred. "Catastrophe in South Yemen: A Preliminary Assessment." *MERIP Reports* (March-April 1986). Vol. 16 No. 2 pp. 37–39.

Hawley, David. "Aden's Uneasy Peace." *Middle East Economic Digest* Vol. 31, No. 10 (March 7, 1987): 4–5.

Katz, Mark N. "Civil Conflict in South Yemen." *Middle East Review* 19, no. 1 (Fall 1986): 7–13.

Mylroie, Laurie. *Politics and the Soviet Presence in the People's Republic of Yemen: Internal Vulnerabilities and Regional Challenges.* RAND Note N–2052. Santa Monica, Calif.: RAND Corporation, 1983.

Page, Stephen. *The Soviet Union and the Yemens: Influence in Asymmetrical Relationships.* New York: Praeger, 1985.

Perera, Judith. "The Rise and Fall of Ali Nasser Mohammad." *The Middle East* no. 137 (March 1986): 5–6.

Pollock, David. "Moscow and Aden: Coping with a Coup." *Problems of Communism* 35, no. 3 (May-June 1986): 50–70.

Wenner, Manfred W. "The 1986 Civil War in South Yemen: A Preliminary Assessment." In B. R. Pridham (ed.). *The Arab Gulf and the Arab World.* London: Croom Helm, 1988.

STEPHEN PAGE

MOHAMMAD REZA PAHLAVI (1919–1980). During his reign the Shah carried out a national development program (the White Revolution) that included infrastructure development, the eradication of diseases such as malaria, and the establishment of literacy programs. In foreign policy, the Shah strengthened his ties with the west and improved the military to become the major political-military force in the Persian Gulf.

He was known at the height of his grandeur as His Imperial Majesty, Mohammad Reza Pahlavi, *Shahanshah, Aryamehr*, or King of Kings and Light of the Aryans. He came to that august stature through being the first son born to Reza Kahn, then the senior Iranian officer in the Cossack Brigade, the most powerful military force in Iran. Reza Kahn staged a coup in 1921 with the help of an Iranian journalist, Seyyed Zia ed-Din Tabataba'i, and became minister of war in the new Cabinet. It did not take Reza Shah long to oust Zia and become prime minister, nor much longer to oust the last shah of the Qajar dynasty and, in 1925, to crown himself Reza Pahlavi and his six-year-old son crown prince.

Reza Shah was determined to provide his son with a manly education to prepare him for assuming the throne. He had a palace specially prepared for the boy, staffed entirely by males with the exception of a single governess. He then forcibly separated the boy from his mother, his older sister, and his twin sister, Princess Ashraf, so that the crown prince would not succumb to a feminine atmosphere. In 1921 he married a second wife and, astoundingly in the Iran of that day, aroused the wrath of his first wife. She refused to accept the new wife or to ever again share her bed with her husband. He moved out shortly thereafter.

Taking away her son may have been Reza Shah's way of punishing his ex-wife, but it proved devastating for the young boy, who quickly fell victim to a series of debilitating and nearly fatal illnesses. He was close to death at least once and came to believe that his recovery from each of his illnesses was the result of divine intervention. He believed that he had been saved by the Lord for a higher purpose, namely kingship.

In 1931, the crown prince was sent to Switzerland in the company of a small number of Iranians of his own age to serve as companions, a Persian tutor to insure fluency in his native tongue, and a private physician to attend to his sickly condition. After a year of preparatory work, the boy entered the Le Rosey secondary school, from which he graduated in 1936. Only then did he return to Iran. By his own admission, his Swiss education was of great importance in introducing him to the values of the West, but it was also a personal nightmare involving years of loneliness and isolation.

When the crown prince returned to Iran, he was enrolled in Tehran's Military Officers' School and began to receive day-to-day instructions from Reza Shah on the duties of a king. To complete his preparation for the throne, Reza Shah found a suitable bride for his son—the sister of King Farouk* of Egypt. Mohammad's marriage to Queen Fawzia proved a disaster. She did not speak Persian and the Shah did not speak Arabic. The newlyweds conversed in French. Queen Fawzia found Tehran backward and provincial after cosmopolitan Cairo, and the Shah's family found his Arab bride an unfit choice for the Iranian crown prince. Divorce was not long in coming, but not before the birth of a daughter. The Shah married again to an Iranian bride, Soraya Bakhtiar, the child of a German mother and an Iranian tribal leader. That marriage was reportedly considerably more gratifying, but no offspring were produced, which was the official explanation for the divorce that followed. Finally, the Shah married Farah Diba, who was referred to as Empress Farah Pahlavi. In 1960 she gave birth to her first child, a son, Reza II, who was later officially designated crown prince. Three more children were subsequently born. Empress Farah joined the Shah when he went into exile and remained with him through the bitter end of his life.

In short, by the standards Reza Shah had held, he had fully prepared his son for kingship. The boy was raised to become a "man," he was taught Western knowledge and values, he was trained as an officer in the Imperial Iranian Armed Forces, and he was married to a bride who linked him to an important Middle Eastern ruling house. But the Shah did not develop qualities of leadership. The Shah could command, but not lead, he could inspire fear but never commitment. He could not make the most difficult decisions, and lacked the ruthlessness and hardness a ruler must have. Toward the end he refused to order the Iranian armed forces to suppress the revolution through violence.

Despite these deficiencies, the Shah ruled Iran for thirty-seven years until virtually all the Iranian people rose in a spectacular revolution to demand his ouster and the destruction of his dynasty. He fled his country in January 1979, and lived as a pariah. However, even from exile he was to exercise considerable influence on international politics.

By the fall of 1979 the cancer that had first been diagnosed in the early 1970s appeared to have taken a substantial turn for the worse. President Jimmy Carter relented and granted the Shah asylum in the United States. The Shah flew to New York from Mexico for medical treatment. Iranian radicals used the Shah's entrance into the United States to stage what amounted both to a coup in Iranian politics and an act of international lawlessness. A group of Tehran University students, encouraged by Ayatollah Ruhollah Khomeini* and other clerics, stormed the American embassy on November 4, 1979 and seized its occupants. Simultaneously, the government of the Islamic Republic was forced to resign. The radicals used the occasion to impose a drastic Islamic regime on the country. In addition, they held fifty-two American citizens captive for 444 days. Only after the inauguration of U.S. President Ronald Reagan did the Iranians free their captives. By then, the Shah had long since left the United States and died. At the end of his life, President Anwar al-Sadat* of Egypt had welcomed the Shah to Cairo where, undergoing one last cancer operation, he died in lonely disgrace in August 1980. To this day, his remains are interred in Cairo's al-Rifai mosque, awaiting the day when political conditions in Iran will allow his return to the soil he considered sacred.

A story widely told in Tehran toward the end of the revolution captured the extent to which the Iranian people had determined the Shah to be their enemy. In the fall of 1978, in the midst of the revolution, the Shah received his last state visitor, Hua Kuo Feng of the People's Republic of China. The story has it that in their private conversations the Shah asked Hua if there were any dissidents within the People's Republic. The Chinese leader owned up to their existence. "Well," pressed the Shah, "just how many dissidents are there in China?" Hua guessed that there might be thirty or even thirty-five million of them. "Interesting," the Shah mused. "That's the same number we have in Iran." The point of the story, of course, is that the total of thirty-five million dissidents was equivalent to the entire population of Iran. By the fall of 1978, in the months before the Shah's flight, it appeared as if the entire Iranian people had, indeed, turned against him. To understand how this came to be the case, it is useful to review the most significant event of each of the four decades in which the Shah was monarch.

The Shah came to the throne as a result of the overthrow of his father's rule. In August 1941 Russia invaded Iran from the north and Britain invaded from the south. The two states had grown fearful, following the German invasion of the USSR, of growing German influence in Iran and the possibility of a German dash through Russia across the Caucasus into a sympathetic Iran, thus depriving the Allies of Middle Eastern oil resources. In addition, the Allies needed a transit route free from German submarines to supply war materials to the Soviet Union. Iran was the obvious choice.

Without offering significant resistance, the Iranian army collapsed in the face of the coordinated invasion. With its collapse, and with British and Russian forces in Tehran, the allies were in a position to demand the abdication of Reza Shah. They replaced him as monarch with his son, the crown prince, an inexperienced young man of twenty-one. The chaotic years of World War II, characterized by the weakness of the throne, foreign occupation, economic disintegration, and savage attacks on the twenty-year rule of Reza Shah, highlighted the insecurity under which Mohammad Reza assumed him kingship. Supported by the occupying powers, who viewed him as a source of stability, and by many of the elite, including the military generals who had served his father, the Shah continued to maintain a tenuous grip on the throne while devoting his efforts to eliminating his many internal enemies.

His investiture set the tone of his subsequent rule and confirmed for many Iranians the wisdom of the central myth that Iran could never be an independent state in the face of the might of the great powers—that those powers would never allow Iran independence, which might conflict with their grand designs. The results, Iranians believed, were open and hidden conspiracies and plots by the great powers to continue their control over the destiny of Iran. Reza Shah, they believed, was only one aspect of that grand design. When he no longer served that purpose, he was removed. In his stead, it seemed to many Iranians, the great powers had imposed his son, a personally and politically weaker ruler, who would be more likely to allow the foreign powers to realize their ambitions. In short, Mohammad Reza Shah began his tenure in the decade of the 1940s perceived by many of his countrymen as an unwitting tool of foreign powers at the least. To his everlasting discredit in the eyes of his people, future significant events during his reign lent credence to the belief that he ruled at the sufferance of foreign governments and did so because he continued to serve their interests.

The most significant political event of the next decade of the rule of the Shah—the 1950s—was the crisis between the Shah and his prime minister. Mohammad Mossadegh.* In 1951, the Majlis, the Iranian Parliament, voted to nationalize the Anglo-Iranian Oil Company. The British retaliated and Iran was unable to sell the petroleum for which it now claimed complete ownership. Negotiations dragged on for months without progress toward a resolution. Eventually, diplomatic relations were broken off and Mossadegh decided to go it alone with an "oil-less" economy. Deprived of oil revenues and foreign exchange, Iran's economy shrunk while the population suffered from economic hardships.

Mossadegh demanded ever greater authority from the Shah in order to cope with the mounting economic crisis, while the Shah was increasingly pressured by his supporters to curb the excesses of the prime minister. In 1952, the Shah dismissed Mossadegh and appointed Qavam al-Saltaneh in his place, hoping to resolve the diplomatic impasse with Great Britain and the mounting domestic political and economic crises. Qavam had previously served as premier and had brilliantly outmaneuvered the USSR following World War II. Mossadegh's popularity, however, was at its peak, and thousands of demonstrators rioted in Tehran to protest his dismissal. The Shah had no option but to reappoint him. A direct confrontation between the Shah and his prime minister became inevitable.

In the following months, Mossadegh's position gradually weakened as many of his political allies defected. With the internal situation deteriorating and the Tudeh, the Iranian communist Party, becoming overtly more active, the British and the newly elected Eisenhower administration in the United States became concerned over what they perceived to be threats menacing Western interests. The intelligence agencies of the two states designed a coup d'état, enlisted the support of the Shah, and sent operatives into Tehran to set the process in motion.

As part of the scheme, the Shah formally dismissed Mossadegh, as was his constitutional prerogative, in August 1953. Mossadegh refused to accept his dismissal, however, instead arresting the officer who had presented him with the Shah's rescript. Panicked, the Shah fled the country, stopping in Baghdad and then traveling on to Rome. However, CIA (U.S. Central Intelligence Agency– operatives in Tehran pressed on with the coup, despite contrary orders from their headquarters in Washington, D.C. Street crowds were brought out of the bazaars of south Tehran to demand the return of the Shah. Units of the Iranian armed forces joined the pro-Shah demonstrators and tanks surrounded Premier Mossadegh in his home. General Fazlollah Zahedi, once a prisoner of the British because of his pro-German sympathies, had been selected by the British and American government to succeed Premier Mossadegh. With the arrest of Mossadegh, Zahedi was installed and the Shah and his Empress returned from abroad.

After the elimination of the most serious threat to his rule, the Shah began consolidating his personal power. One of the most important steps he took was to purge the armed forces officer corps. Hundreds of officers were dismissed or arrested, accused of membership or sympathy for the Communist Party. Although the purge was used as the occasion to oust officers loyal to Mossadegh, the vast majority of the ousted military personnel belonged to the "Officers Club" of the Communist Party. Next, the Shah turned to neutralizing communists and Mossadegh supporters throughout Iran. To do so, the Shah began to experiment with new forms of control. With the initial help of the United States, and later that of Israel, he established a secret police force responsible for both internal security and foreign intelligence, the State Security and Intelligence Organization, known by its Persian acronym, SAVAK. He also established competing political parties, both headed by court favorites completely loyal to him.

The most salient political event of the 1950s, then, was the competition for power between the Shah and his prime minister. Mossadegh was almost universally revered in Iran as a nationalist seeking to enhance Iran's independent control over its most valued national resource, oil. The reputation of the Shah was already suspect, in large measure because he had been brought to his throne by foreign powers. His struggle against Mossadegh seemed to confirm this evaluation. The role of the CIA in the 1953 coup, rumors of which began to appear in print in the United States, sealed that view of the shah.

The most salient political event of the decade of the 1960s did nothing to enhance the Shah's standing in the eyes of his people. The decade had begun with protests over the elections to the Majlis which had been blatantly rigged to return deputies committed to the Shah. The elections were cancelled. A new round of elections produced no more satisfactory results, but a Majlis was, finally, convened. When protest demonstrations were held in front of the Majlis, a Tehran teacher was killed. The government collapsed and the Shah appointed as prime minister Dr. Ali Amini, who was popular with the demonstrators for favoring limitations on the power of the throne and widely reputed to be devoted to civil liberties and possessed of profound personal integrity.

By the end of the year, however, Amini had failed to satisfy any section of the politically active population. He had been unable to induce the Shah to call new parliamentary elections, and was reduced to ruling by decree. He was able to do little to alter the political or economic priorities the Shah had established or to bring the National Front into political activities. In conjunction with the Shah's initial distrust of Amini, it was clear that his time was running out. Following a budgetary crisis, Amini resigned and the Shah asked his closest boyhood friend, Asadullah Alam, to form a new government.

With Alam's appointment, the Shah turned to securing his throne through a program of reform known as the "White Revolution," which included such measures as land reform, worker profit sharing, and suffrage for women. The White Revolution was submitted to the people of Iran in a referendum that was overwhelmingly approved.

In June of 1963, however, the newly established domestic tranquility was again shattered by three days of nationwide urban rioting, touched off by the arrest of Ayatollah Ruhollah Khomeini. Khomeini had first come to public attention in 1961 for his outspoken opposition to the rule of the Shah. Later, he criticized the Shah's land reform program and suffrage for women, and accused the Shah of being an agent for the international Zionist-Jewish conspiracy. Pictures of Khomeini covered the bazaars of Iran during the 1963 religious holidays of *Muharram*, a time of increased passions as the devout anguish over the martyrdom of Imam Husayn, son of Ali and grandson of the Prophet Muhammad. The Shah's authorities waited until the early morning hours of June 4 after the end of the holy days and then arrested Khomeini. Within hours, crowds of protesters began to form before the bazaars of Tehran and, by 10 A.M., the troops had opened fire. However, the riots went on, quickly spreading to several other cities. Only after several days of bloodshed was the army able to impose peace. The opposition claimed that many thousands had been killed by the troops of the Shah. The government, however, set the figure at less than one hundred.

The arrest of Ayatollah Khomeini and the violent suppression of the subsequent protest demonstrations was a third significant component of the evolving picture of the Shah that the Iranian people were beginning to develop. Many were already convinced that he had been installed by foreigners to serve their interests. The Mossadegh incident had convinced Iranians that Great Britain and the United

States played a key and even decisive role in his rule. The Khomeini arrest and subsequent suppression convinced many Iranians that the Shah was unalterably opposed to the clerics and thus to Islam itself. In addition, he was seen as increasingly ruthless and committed to ruling through repression, relying primarily on SAVAK and the power of the armed forces, to whose expansion and improvement he devoted major resources.

The most telling symbolic event of the decade of the 1970s was the Persepolis celebration that the Shah hosted in 1971. The Shah determined that the rule of Iranian kings had been consolidated some two and a half thousand years previously. To commemorate the twenty-five-hundredth anniversary of Iranian kingship, the Shah determined to provide appropriate ceremonies. The result was a gala party, extraordinarily expensive and equally offensive, finally, to the people of Iran. The heads of state of every country in the entire world were invited. Personalized living quarters, in the form of silken tents, were prepared for the guests. With the exception of Iranian caviar, all the food and the champagnes and wines were imported from France.

The formal ceremonies at Persepolis were meant to celebrate Iranian kingship. They focused on the pre-Islamic past when the institution of the Iranian monarchy had been established and then recalled each of the dynasties whose existence constituted the history of Iranian kingship. Nowhere was the role of Islam in Iranian life acknowledged, let alone honored. In addition, the celebrations drained massive amounts of funds, almost all of which were spent on foreign goods for the purpose of entertaining foreign dignitaries. Not only were the Iranians not invited, but because of the outbreak of terrorism in Iran with an attack on a rural police station in February of 1971, unusually intense security blanketed the entire country.

Persepolis had two major symbolic consequences. It reinforced the Iranian people's belief that the Shah's principal audience—the observers of the Iranian political drama whom he especially sought to impress—were foreigners and not the Iranian people. The drama on the stage concerned the Shah and his political elites. The audience was composed of the foreigners. There appeared to be little room for the Iranian people in the Pahlavi theater. A second consequence of the ceremonies was to become increasingly evident as the 1970s unfolded. The lavish, international celebration of an anniversary that was at best historically suspect, marked a new level of Pahlavi grandeur, but with each passing year, it became clear that the Shah had difficulty distinguishing between the grandiose and the merely grand.

His own grandiosity was marked in many ways. In May 1972, U.S. President Richard Nixon and his secretary of state, Henry Kissinger, visited Tehran to facilitate the Nixon Doctrine of inducing regional powers to serve as proxies for American power. They promised the Shah the right to buy any nonnuclear U.S. weapons system without congressional or Pentagon review, a privilege accorded no other foreign power. The Shah seized the opportunity to propel Iran into the status of regional military superpower.

The grandiosity of the Shah was further enhanced when he played a key role in the counsels of OPEC (the Organization of Petroleum Exporting Countries) at their Tehran meeting in December 1973. The Arab oil exporters had imposed an embargo against states that had supported Israel in the 1973 war. The Shah induced all OPEC states to end the embargo in exchange for a quadrupling in the price of oil. Not only did the Shah appear to be the leader of OPEC challenging the interests of the West, the principal oil consumers, but he drastically drove up the revenues accruing to Iran. In 1970, Iranian oil revenues were running at an annual rate of one billion dollars. By 1974, through a combination of higher prices and increased sales, Iran earned twenty billion dollars.

The expansion of the Shah's grandiosity matched that of the oil revenues and was evident in many ways. The Shah took to lecturing the West about the decadence of Western culture and society and the superiority of Iran. He began to suggest that Iran would overtake most Western countries and become as developed as Sweden by the year 2000. He took to avoiding the choking traffic jams and pollution of Tehran, to which the new oil revenues had contributed, by traveling solely by helicopter. The vision of the Shah's helicopter whirling above Tehran seemed to capture his personal remoteness and detachment from Iranian life.

One of the most telling examples of that grandiosity was to occur in the middle of the decade. The Shah abolished the Iranian calendar—the same calendar used since the beginning of Islamic history in most of the Islamic world. That calendar counted the days from the flight of the Prophet Muhammad from Mecca to Medina. In its place, the Shah replaced the Iranian calendar with the *Shahanshahi* or Imperial calendar, which was dated from the supposed accession to the throne of Cyrus the Great. The Iranian people were incensed. The Shah had destroyed their most fundamental method of ordering the world and used all the power of the Iranian state to forcefully impose the new date on every public or private letter, document, or publication.

The central themes that led the Iranian people to their revolutionary rejection of the Shah were already manifest at the inception of his rule. Each subsequent decade of that rule was marked by a crucial event that further elaborated them or brought new ones to the fore. These themes formed the basis of the beliefs the Iranian people held about the Shah. It was the combination of these themes that supplied the Iranian people with the energy to rise in revolution and successfully demand his ouster. By the inception of the revolution, those themes were made up of four principal components: (1) the Shah had been brought to the throne by foreign powers to serve their interests; (2) both to preserve his rule and to win the personally gratifying plaudits of foreigners, the Shah devoted himself to the service of those foreign powers, especially the United States; (3) the grandiosity of the Shah, bolstered by foreign support and vast financial resources, had grown to limitless proportions, putting the Shah out of touch with the realities of Iranian life; and (4) the Shah had come to believe that the principal impediment to the realization of his grandiose ambitions was the failure of the Iranian people.

These themes propelled the Iranian people to a deep sense of rage at the monarch whom they had come to believe had devalued them in the interests of his relations with the West and viewed them as what was principally wrong with Iran rather than its most substantial asset. The Shah's carping at the West during the 1970s and the increased power of the Iranian state did nothing to impress the Iranian people. These beliefs have continued to feed the evaluation of the Shah in the decade since the revolution and his ouster. In fact, however, the Shah made major contributions to the transformation of Iran. There is no doubt that from his investiture in 1941 to his flight in 1979, Iran experienced the most rapid economic growth and the most substantial cultural transformation in its history. Oil was clearly driving the Iranian economy. It accounted for almost 40 percent of the GNP in 1978. In the same period, it represented 77 percent of the revenues of the government and 87 percent of its foreign-exchange earnings. The fate of its oil revenues determined the fate of Iran's economy. From 1971 to 1978, Iran's GNP rose from 17.3 billion dollars to 54.6 billion dollars, while GNP per capita rose from 450 to 2,400 dollars.

The Shah used the oil revenues to force the transformation of Iran from a backward, isolated, and weak country with a largely illiterate population to a powerful state and society. The Shah presided over a booming economy characterized by rapid urbanization, substantial industrialization, the widespread dissemination of literacy and formal education, and the creation of a national economy with a country-wide communications infrastructure including radio, television, and telephone, as well as a network of contemporary roads, railroads, and airline services. Iran was rapidly being integrated into the world economy and into world culture as well. By the 1970s, the largest number of foreign students studying in the United States from any country in the world save Canada came from Iran. All these positive changes, which were propelling Iran into what once was referred to as modernity, had their costs. Those costs were frequently substantial, but there is little doubt that with the perspective of time and the diminution of the passions that led to the revolution, the Shah will come to be remembered more for his contributions to the modernization of Iran than has been the case during the first decade of the Islamic revolution.

BIBLIOGRAPHY

Work by Reza Pahlavi:

Answer To History. Briarcliff Manor, N.Y.: Stein and Day Publishers, 1980.

Other Works:

Abrahamian, Ervand. *Iran between Two Revolutions*. Princeton: Princeton University Press, 1982.
Arjomand, Said. *The Turban for the Crown: The Islamic Revolution in Iran*. Oxford: Oxford University Press, 1988.

Bakhash, Shaul. *The Reign of the Ayatollahs: Iran and the Islamic Revolution.* New York: Basic Books, 1984.

Bill, James A. *The Eagle and the Lion: The Tragedy of American-Iranian Relations.* New Haven: Yale University Press, 1988.

Sick, Gary. *All Fall Down: America's Tragic Encounter with Iran.* New York: Random House, 1985.

Stempel, John D. *Inside the Iranian Revolution.* Bloomington, Ind.: Indiana University Press, 1981.

Zonis, Marvin. *The Political Elite of Iran.* Princeton: Princeton University Press, 1971.

Zonis, Marvin, and Daniel Brumberg. *Khomeini, Iran, and the Arab World.* Harvard Middle Eastern Papers, Modern Series. Cambridge: Harvard University Center for Middle Eastern Studies, 1987.

MARVIN ZONIS

MOHAMMAD MOSSADEGH (1882–1967). For many Iranians, Mohammad Mossadegh's twenty-seven month rule from April 1951 to August 1953 is one of the more controversial periods in contemporary Iranian history. Throughout his political career, Mossadegh had one preeminent political preoccupation: a thorough opposition to foreign intervention and interference in Iran. An old-fashioned liberal, he believed neither in ideological dogma nor in the use of coercion in government. Nonetheless, Mossadegh has remained one of the most enigmatic personalities in contemporary Iran.

Born to a prominent family in Tehran on June 16, 1882, Mossadegh's political career spanned more than fifty years and has had a lasting impact on Iranian politics. At the age of sixteen, he began working for the Ministry of Finance of Khorassan province where he was responsible to the central government for the accounts and taxes of the province. He resigned from his post after some ten years so that he could continue his education and embarked on a journey to Europe. Ultimately he reached Paris, arriving there in March 1909. He obtained his doctorate in law in May 1914, the first Iranian to obtain a doctorate in this subject.

Mossadegh returned to Iran in 1914 and was invited to join the School of Political Sciences in Tehran. Before becoming governor general of Fars province in 1920, Mossadegh wrote several books: *Procedural Order in Civil Courts*, *Capitulations and Iran*, and *The Limited Liability Company in Europe*. According to one source, his second book generated opposition from the British Legation, which accused Mossadegh of having German sponsors. Not surprisingly, the British acrimony and animosity toward Mossadegh would make him a spokesman for the anticolonial and nationalist forces, who perceived him as a leader determined to challenge long-held British interests in the Iranian petroleum industry.

Mossadegh's rise as a nationalist leader coincided with Reza Khan's accession to power in 1921. His supporters urged him to come to Tehran from Fars in order to take part in the *Majles* (Iranian Parliament) elections. It was as a deputy to the Fifth Majles in 1925 that Mossadegh spoke and voted against Reza Khan's plan to declare himself the Shah of Iran. His opposition to Reza as Shah (1926–

1941) is fundamental to the understanding of his political thought. First of all, Mossadegh was not opposed to all aspects of Reza Shah's rule. In fact, in the beginning, he believed Reza Shah had started with good intentions and had genuine concern for Iran's future in the turbulent twentieth-century world. Mossadegh felt the Shah was being sidetracked by his sycophantic and greedy entourage who wanted the Shah to become a dictator so that their economic interests would be protected. In his memoirs, Mossadegh described his opposition to Reza Shah in constitutional terms, questioning the legality of Reza Shah's attempt to become an authoritarian ruler. The 1905 Iranian Constitution, Mossadegh argued, was meant to stop the emergence of authoritarianism. During the debate on a single-article bill for the change of dynasty in the Majles, Mossadegh made the following speech against the motion: "The honorable gentlemen know that I speak out of principle, and not because of any personal feelings. . . . Today, in the 20th century, is it possible that anyone can accept that a constitutional country can have a governing king? . . . If we call him king, prime minister, and governor, as well as everything else, this is idolatry and cult of personality and a return to complete tyranny and authoritarianism" (1988). Despite Mossadegh's opposition, the Majles voted (115 in favor, 5 against, with 30 abstentions) to legitimize the Pahlavi dynasty. Mossadegh served another term in the Sixth Majles, but Reza Shah saw to it that he was not elected to the Seventh Majles in 1928. During the next sixteen years, Mossadegh was arrested twice (1930 and 1940), and exiled to his home village of Ahmadabad near Tehran. Moreover, illness often weakened him during those years, forcing him to go to Europe for short periods to seek treatment.

Following Reza Shah's unceremonious departure from Iran in 1941, and the accession of his son, Mohammad Reza Shah* (1941–1979), Mossadegh resumed the second phase of his political career. He was elected to the Fourteenth Majles on January 22, 1944. The young Shah tried unsuccessfully to block his election, however, in a manner reminiscent of Reza Shah's dilemma, this action only enhanced Mossadegh's reputation, making him a hero in the eyes of the electorate. In the meantime, an Iranian politician by the name of Sayyed Zia Tabatabai was also elected to the Fourteenth Majles. Sayyed Zia had gained notoriety for his attempted coup of 1919, which was widely perceived to have been sponsored by the British government. His 1944 election was made possible through means of manipulation and tampering with the ballot box. As soon as the Majles was inaugurated, Mossadegh initiated a debate on the credentials of Sayyed Zia, making one of his most eloquent speeches and putting forward his views on constitutionalism and dictatorship. Attacking Sayyed Zia as the harbinger of dictatorship and corruption, he pointed out that Sayyed Zia had been in the service of British interests in Iran and had then been removed for twenty years, and should not be allowed to return to play the same role in a different era. Mossadegh relentlessly introduced documents to show that Sayyed Zia's election was fraudulent. In short, Mossadegh portrayed Sayyed Zia as an imposter who was capitalizing on his long banishment from Iran in order to be considered a martyr. Although Mossadegh was unsuccessful in expelling Sayyed Zia from the Majles, he nevertheless destroyed Sayyed Zia's reputation. Moreover, Mossadegh's hard-hitting speech captured the imagination of the younger generation of citizens who were becoming increasingly nationalistic and saw in Mossadegh the potential for implementing their aspirations.

Another political action that contributed to Mossadegh's national recognition was his battle against granting oil concessions to foreign powers. Since the primary means through which external influence was exerted in Iran involved oil and the exploration and exploitation thereof, the ultimate clash between Mossadegh and the foreign-controlled oil industry was inevitable. There was no more glaring example of foreign presence in Iran than the Anglo-Iranian oil company (AIOC) (until 1935, the Anglo-Persian Oil Company), and it was difficult for any other foreign power to obtain a toehold, much less any significant concession. Despite this, American as well as Russian companies were attempting to rival British interests. These attempts provoked anxiety on the part of the British government and the oil company. The rivalry reached its climax during the Allied occupation of Iran from 1941 to 1945. In order to counter this, Mossadegh proposed to the Majles that the government recognize oil as the country's most important economic and political power tool. He sponsored legislation curtailing the authority of the central government in the area of oil concessions and forbidding any cabinet to discuss an oil concession or any other concessions with a foreign government while foreign troops were on Iranian soil. This bill effectively terminated the American and Russian drives for oil concessions. Mossadegh's sponsorship of this legislation infuriated the Russians; his stand in effect hampered the Russian plan for an oil concession in northern Iran since by the end of 1945 they had not evacuated Iran. Mossadegh next prepared himself to confront the powerful AIOC, which had been active in Iran for four decades.

The AIOC had been the target of Iranian nationalists since the early 1930s. In November 1932, Reza Shah unilaterally canceled the D'Arcy concession (a sixty-year concession with exclusive privileges to explore for and develop petroleum over a five-hundred-thousand-square-mile area of Iran. Five provinces that bordered on the Soviet Union were exempted from this concession). A new agreement was signed in 1933 that provided a modest improvement in terms of revenues per ton received and guaranteed a minimum annual payment. The AIOC agreed to hire Iranian nationals in supervisory and technical positions, and not to interfere in internal Iranian affairs. The new concession covered one hundred thousand square miles, and the company was exempted from all taxes other than those included in the D'Arcy concession. Nevertheless, it was a victory for the British since the new concession extended for another sixty years (to 1993). This agreement temporarily blunted the nationalist drive. The latter would resurface in the 1940s when Allied forces occupied Iran. This time the nationalist forces found Mossadegh to confront the British in his drive for eradicating foreign domination of Iran.

In the elections for the Fifteenth Majles in 1947, the question of oil and national independence was the platform on which Mossadegh and his followers were elected. A mosaic of forces ranging from religious nationalist to social democratic and socialist movements emerged as the most vocal supporters of Mossadegh. The Shah and his entourage were concerned about instability and wanted to maintain the status quo. Mossadegh's supporters were loosely organized under the National Front, about two hundred delegates from a cross-section of parties and classes. They looked to Mossadegh for leadership and were united on the issue of nationalization.

In 1947, the Iranian government approached the AIOC to seek a revision in the 1933 oil agreement. Simple economics were sufficient to show that Iran was not getting a fair deal for its oil. The total dividends paid to Iran represented approximately 8 percent of the AIOC's net profit in 1948, whereas the British government was receiving about 30 percent in taxes. The Iranians referred to the agreement between American companies and Venezuela, according to which that country was receiving more than three times the amount paid to Iran. Finally, after much acrimony and confrontation, the Iranian government signed a new agreement (known as the Supplemental Agreement) on July 17, 1949. This pact provided for increases in the royalty from twenty-two to thirty-three cents per barrel. Premier Saed's government, which negotiated this pact, presented it to the Majles for ratification. However, the National Front mounted a vociferous opposition and was able to prevent its passage. The Majles sent the agreement to its twenty-two-member Committee on Oil for a complete review, and raised the possibility of nationalization. Mossadegh was the chairman of this committee. Not surprisingly, the Committee on Oil rejected the pact after Mossadegh forcefully pointed out the agreement's shortcoming, namely, the inability of Iran to inspect the AIOC books and accounts, and the absence of any control over the price of oil sold to Iran by the company. It is likely, given Mossadegh's character, that the revenue consideration was second in his mind to the political question of nationalizing the industry and terminating British influence in Iran.

By the early 1950s, Anglo-Iranian relations had deteriorated to the brink of a total break in diplomatic relations. The country had become polarized on the issue of nationalization, and those who called for calm and compromise were finding themselves isolated and labelled as "pro-British." Only four days after Prime Minister Ali Razmara spoke before the Majles in support of the Supplemental Agreement and in opposition to the idea of nationalization, on March 7, 1951, he was assassinated by an Islamic fundamentalist group. Frightened by the assassination, the Majles passed a bill to nationalize the oil industry a week later on March 15. Mossadegh was the prime mover behind this bill. He had not only succeeded in dominating the Majles, he had also become the most popular statesman in Iran. The shah had little alternative but to appoint Mossadegh as prime minister in April 1951. Thus, at age sixty-nine, frail and exhausted by decades of active life, Mossadegh began the third and final phase of his political career.

Mossadegh introduced his cabinet to the Majles on May 1, 1951, and stated that the foremost objective of his government was to seek the implementation of the nationalization law throughout the land. By July 1951, a charter was drawn up for the new state oil company, the National Iranian Oil Company (NIOC). The results were predictable. The British reacted angrily, arguing that the oil agreement was still valid because it had been accepted by the previous cabinet. To this Mossadegh replied, "Neither the Iranian Majles nor any other parliament in the world can restrict the right of its successors to legislate" (Diba 1986: 119).

Although there were many proposals and counterproposals throughout 1952, the positions of Britain and Iran remained essentially unchanged. The British organized an effective international boycott of Iranian oil. Iran's oil export income dropped from more than four hundred million dollars in 1950 to less than two million dollars in the two-year period from July 1951 to August 1953. In the meantime, a power struggle ensued between the shah and Mossadegh over the control of the military and the latters' request for extraordinary powers from the Majles. Mossadegh resorted to his populist tactic of resigning, but four days of street demonstrations forced the shah to call him back. Assured of his position, Mossadegh became increasingly authoritarian in an attempt to preserve his policies and programs. However, by now the United States had become increasingly concerned over the tensions between Britain and Iran.

U.S. President Harry Truman's Administration had become deeply worried about these events and the possibility of British military action against Iran. At first, U.S. Secretary of State Dean Acheson sought to placate the British while trying to convince Mossadegh to agree on a compromise solution. American leaders were convinced that a possible British military attack was not only unwarranted but also might serve as a pretext for Soviet intervention. The American pressure was successful. It held off a British military attack while President Truman sent his special envoy, Averell Harriman, to Iran to work out a compromise. However, the hard-line, inflexible position of the British, their determination to maintain their control over the petroleum industry, and Mossadegh's revolutionary stand on nationalization had expanded the chasm between the two protagonists beyond any compromise. The British were insensitive to changing times in Iran, and did not understand the political importance of Mossadegh's nationalization policy.

In the beginning, the Truman administration agreed with Mossadegh that sovereign states had the right to nationalize provided there was just compensation. When Mossadegh visited the United States from October 8 to November 18, 1951, a State Department team led by George McGhee produced a five-point proposal that Mossadegh found acceptable. The gist of this plan involved giving the Iranians control over the exploration, production, and transportation of oil, as well as a modest amount of compensation for the British for the AIOC's facilities and the formation of a joint Anglo-Iranian committee to determine the price. In mid-November 1951, Britain's new Conservative government, with

Anthony Eden as foreign secretary, refused even to discuss the proposal. George McGhee, who estimated that he spent over seventy-five hours in discussion with Mossadegh, was shocked by the news. According to one source, McGhee went to see Mossadegh and afterwards stated that Mossadegh had anticipated the British response. McGhee told Mossadegh that he no longer thought it possible to reach agreement with the British.

Mossadegh had made the best offer he could. The British intransigence only polarized the political atmosphere inside Iran. The British were determined to get rid of Mossadegh and his government, but they could not achieve this without the aid of the United States. The British government applied diplomatic pressure on the United States to shift its position. With the possibility of a Republican administration coming to power in Washington, D.C., the chances for this shift improved. President Dwight Eisenhower's Administration perceived the situation quite differently from that of his predecessor. The Republicans were more concerned with the growing power of the Iranian Communist Party and the denial of the rich Iranian oil reserves to the Western world. Furthermore, Eisenhower did not want to endanger European security, and viewed NATO (the North Atlantic Treaty Organization) as the lynchpin of U.S. anti-Soviet foreign policy.

The enigmatic nature of Mossadegh himself and his negotiating techniques, which were frustrating to the American diplomats, further exacerbated the situation. However, beside his personal convictions, Mossadegh's unyielding position was essential within the context of the social forces at work in Iran. The Communist Party was constantly agitating for a tough antiimperialist line against the West, while the National Front was even more divided between the secular liberal forces and the religious nationalists. The latter did not agree with Mossadegh's strong-handed approach toward the shah. Mossadegh had weakened his own position by demanding constitutional amendments that would have given him more power as prime minister. In the January 1952 elections for the Majles, Mossadegh moved to suspend election results in some rural areas because he felt the results would be unduly pro-shah. Later in August 1952, Mossadegh sought approval for a bill in the Majles that would have given him the power to draw up bills and execute government programs prior to parliamentary approval. These actions gave the impression that Mossadegh was becoming increasingly dictatorial in his methods.

The confrontation between the shah and Mossadegh was one of the factors leading directly to Mossadegh's final removal. Beginning in early 1953, the nationalist coalition collapsed when Ayatollah Abolghasem Kashani withdrew his support. The latters' religious credentials, along with his strident anti-British philosophy, had provided Mossadegh with solid political credentials in those days of nationalist upheaval. Another powerful politician, Mozaffar Baga'i, head of the Toilers' Party, also turned against Mossadegh. The Toiler's Party had an estimated five to seven thousand members. Its membership bridged the gap between the bazaar and the university even thought its basic constituency was rooted more in the former. These losses were a serious blow to Mossadegh; it effectively cut his connections with the lower middle classes and the Iranian masses. Mossadegh was forced to rely more heavily on the left and the communist Tudeh Party.

In a series of rapid political events, the confrontation between the shah and Mossadegh led to a flight from Iran by the shah on August 16. The CIA and the British intelligence organization MI6 organized demonstrations in support of the shah in the streets of Tehran. The operation was successful. The shah returned to Tehran on August 22, 1943. Mossadegh was forced to flee his residence and was arrested thereafter. The fall of Mossadegh marked the end of a century of passive American involvement and was the start of a new era of extensive American support for the shah that lasted until 1979.

Mossadegh was put on trial in November 1953, which lasted over forty days. In the court, Mossadegh defended his political actions, condemned the shah's rule, criticized the United States for its intervention, and praised democratic values. He was given a three-year jail sentence, after which he was exiled to his home village near Tehran. He died on March 5, 1967, as a result of a hemorrhage from an old ulcer. The progovernment press in Tehran gave a brief mention of his death. Foreign newspapers printed long obituaries. The *New York Times* tastelessly belittled him, emphasizing the fact that: "the old man held cabinet meetings while propped up in bed by three pillows and nourished by transfusions of American blood plasma. He favored pink pajamas, occasionally covered by a fawn-colored jacket, during these sessions" (March 6, 1967). These distorted images fail to provide an understanding of what Mossadegh meant to those who saw inspiration in his words and actions. One sympathetic source summed up Mossadegh's performance in his trial in a very poignant way: "He wept, laughed, went on a hunger strike, and once or twice fainted. And all the British and American mass media saw in all this heroic as well as skilled conduct by a man of seventy-two was, on the whole, the antics of a broken old fool. The Iranian people, however, saw it in an entirely different light; Mossadegh had lost some popular support before the coup.... But his unfair and illegal trial, and especially, his conduct both at the trial and in the appeal tribunal won him more support and admiration than he had ever enjoyed" (Diba 1986: 57). For many young Iranians who took part in the revolution of 1978–1979, Mossadegh's legacy provided them with not only a desire to pursue democratic objectives but also a strong feeling of resentment toward the United States for its interventionary policies of enhancing dictatorship in Iran.

The brief years of Mossadegh's rule have had a deep and lasting significance. His was the most determined attempt ever seen in Iran to create a government upheld by popular support, and to use it in order to obtain not simply an improved position within the imperial system but complete independence. His memory has remained in Iran as a symbol of independence. In the eyes of most Iranians, Mossadegh continues to be a beloved figure of enormous charisma. His very emotionalism and physical frailty (he was in constant poor health) endeared him to his people, who saw in him the embodiment of a weak and embattled Iran.

BIBLIOGRAPHY

Works by Mossadegh:

Le testament en droit musulman (Secte chiyite). Precedéd d'une introduction sur les sources du droit musulman. Ph.d. diss. Paris: Libraire Georges Cres et Cie., 1914.
Memoirs. Trans. by Homa Katouzian. Texas: Books Distribution Center, 1988.

Other Works:

Abrahamian, Ervand. *Iran Between Two Revolutions*. Princeton, N.J.: Princeton University Press, 1982.
Bozorgmehr, Jalil. *Mossadegh dar Mah'Kameh-e Nizami* (Mossadegh at the Military Tribunal). London: Jebhe Press, 1987.
Diba, Farhad. *Mohammad Mossadegh: A Political Biography*. London: Croom Helm, 1986.
Katouzian, Homa. *The Political Economy of Modern Iran*. New York: New York University Press, 1981.
Roosevelt, Kermit. *Countercoup: The Struggle for the Control of Iran*. New York: McGraw-Hill, 1979.
Zabih, Sepehr. *The Mossadegh Era: Roots of the Iranian Revolution*. Chicago: Lake View Press, 1982.

BAHMAN BAKTIARI

HOSNI MUBARAK (1928–   ) succeeded Anwar al-Sadat* as president of Egypt in October 1981 after Sadat was assassinated. Mubarak has presided over Egypt's return to the Arab fold after it was ostracized and isolated as a result of Egypt's 1979 peace treaty with Israel. Egypt under Mubarak has remained committed to honoring the terms of that agreement, while restoring its position in the Arab world. Under Mubarak Egypt has focused on improving Egypt's economic and social situation.

Unlike his two predecessors in the presidency, Gamal Abdul Nasser* (1952–1970) and Anwar al-Sadat (1970–1981), Hosni Mubarak's life before being appointed vice president in 1975 was entirely that of a professional military officer. While the former leaders were also military men, in fact both struggled politically in the cause of Egyptian nationalism and were members of the Free Officers movement, which took over the country in 1952.

Mubarak's own policies appear to be a synthesis of those of his two predecessors. Nasser inaugurated land reform and socialist measures that benefited peasants and workers alike. He did so, however, under authoritarian auspices and in the process failed to adequately institutionalize them via an authoritarian state and a single-government party. These measures have been indelible, however, as has his foreign policy of antiimperialism. Taken together, they constitute the Nasserist sentiment of today. The disastrous military defeat by Israel in 1967 led to less emphasis on socialism and a closer relationship to the Soviet Union. Sadat built on these tendencies and directed them into the positive Egyptian military performance in the 1973 war. Following the war, however, he directed

the economy toward a greater reliance on domestic and foreign private investment, and he moved foreign policy away from the Soviet Union and toward the
United States. His commitment of Egypt to the 1979 peace treaty with Israel
cemented his ties to the West and a market economy while at the same time
causing him to retreat from democratization as a result of intensified public
criticism of his policies and the political corruption of his regime. His assassination relieved Egypt of pent-up political pressures and provided for Mubarak's
ascendancy to the presidency.

Mubarak was born in the village of Kafr al-Meselha near Shebin al-Kom, the
capitol of Minufiyya Province on March 4, 1928. He was one of five children.
His father was an inspector in the Ministry of Justice. In this respect, then,
Mubarak is typical of the Egyptian post–1952 elite in his middle-class and often
provincial origins. He graduated from the Military Academy in 1949 after an
accelerated program of study, and from the Air Force Academy in 1950. As a
very junior air force officer in 1952, he played no role in the largely army Free
Officer takeover of the country in July 1952. He trained in L28 and TU16 Soviet-
made bombers, and in 1964 was put in charge of the training of Egyptians at
the Frunze military training center in Moscow. He then became commander of
various air bases including Cairo West in January 1966. Israel's invasion of
Egypt in June 1967 was preceded by a lightning attack on Egyptian air-force
bases resulting in the near total annihilation of the air force. After 1967 he was
commander of the Air Force Academy from 1967–1969. In 1969 he became air
force chief of staff and was made commander in chief of the air force in April
1971. In this capacity he was in command during the October 1973 war. The
air force played an important but not principal role in that war due to a greater
reliance on missile air-defense systems to cover the advance of the army in the
Sinai. Immediately after the war he was sent to Arab capitals to explain the
war's outcome. He was made air marshall in 1974, which anticipated his appointment as vice president in April of 1975.

As part of the process of detaching himself from Nasserism, Sadat appointed
Mubarak as vice president in 1975. As a non–Free Officer and a competent
professional officer, he replaced Kamal al-Din Hussein who had been a Free
Officer. In Sadat's characterization, he represented the new generation of "the
crossing," namely, the 1973 October War. The style of Sadat's leadership in
terms of a "big-picture" emphasis on diplomacy resulted in opportunities for
Mubarak to gain political experience. He was given the experience of presiding
over cabinet meetings and making international journeys; for example, he went
to China to seek replacement engines for Egyptian Soviet aircraft, he led the
Egyptian delegation at the Organization of African Unity meetings in 1975 and
1976, and in 1980 he met with U.S. President Jimmy Carter at the end of his
administration and also met incoming members of the new Republican administration. In addition, he had been made vice chairman of the National Democratic
(government) Party in 1976. What emerges from this background is a person

who in fact had significant administrative, political, and diplomatic experience before assuming the presidency.

Sadat had deliberately sought the support of religious groups during his tenure in office in order to strengthen his popularity. In sowing the wind, he reaped the whirlwind by creating a political atmosphere that led to his own assassination by such an extremist group on October 6, 1981. At the time of the assassination, Mubarak stood at Sadat's side on the reviewing stand and was slightly wounded in the arm. With great presence he remained dignified and in control while at the same time keeping his wounded arm out of sight. Mubarak had been appointed and not elected to the vice presidency and therefore after the death of Sadat he did not automatically inherit the presidency. Instead, under the Egyptian constitution, the speaker of the Parliament became acting president. An emergency meeting of the Parliament nominated him for president, and in October 1981 a plebescite approved his assumption of the office. His behavior on the reviewing stand was to characterize his presidency. He has been coolly competent and deliberate in reaching decisions. This has been accompanied by an ability to delegate authority. His style, however, was at first misunderstood and has remained uninspiring. Initially even his competency was in question.

This was revealed in a joke that circulated in the first months of his presidency: "On the Sudanese-Egyptian border, an official was confronted by three Egyptians who had lost their passports. The first was a woman who said she was Nagwa Fuad—Egypt's famous belly dancer. When asked to prove it by dancing, she did so and was allowed to enter. The second was a man who said he was Abd al-Halim Hafiz—Egypt's most famous singer. When asked to prove it by singing he did so and also entered Egypt. A third was a man who said he was President Hosni Mubarak. When asked what he could do to prove it, he replied, 'I can't do anything.' The official replied, 'You must indeed be the president,' and gave him permission to enter."

The question of competency has been answered in subsequent years by a style of deliberate and consultative domestic and foreign-policy decision making. What remains illusive, however, is the degree of his authority and control over Egyptian policies. Thus, after his accession to office he moved to distance himself from the repressive and corruption excesses of Sadat. In November 1981, he released from prison the five hundred non-religious political prisoners whom Sadat had arrested in September (one thousand religious prisoners remained to be released more slowly). They left prison and were received immediately in the president's office. In addition, he moved to hold highly publicized trials of corrupt figures, including Sadat's half-brother. These trials have had their intended effect of not attempting to stamp out very widespread corruption but rather working to restrain it and make it less excessive.

Mubarak inherited the peace treaty with Israel as well as the closeness of the relationship with the United States. He has remained scrupulously committed to the former and cordial to the latter. He also inherited, however, important criticisms of the peace treaty as having abandoned the Palestinians. Nonetheless,

Mubarak waited patiently for the final withdrawal of Israel from Egyptian territory in the Sinai in April 1982. Equally patiently, he has successfully pursued the diplomatically long-drawn-out Egyptian objective of establishing the validity of its 1914 boundary against Israeli claims at Taba at the head of the Gulf of Aqaba. While the treaty with Israel is adhered to, it has become a "cold peace" as the result of the shock effects of the Israeli invasion of Lebanon (two months after evacuating the Sinai), the Israeli implication in the Shatilla and Sabra Palestinian refugee-camp massacres in late 1982, and, beginning in December 1987, the *intifadah* (Palestinian uprising) in the West Bank and Gaza, which was accompanied by brutal Israeli repression. To balance the continued adherence to the treaty, however, and to mollify his critics, Mubarak has worked to return Egypt to the Arab fold after its nearly universal condemnation by the Arab world in 1979. He did this symbolically by condemning the Israeli invasion of Lebanon and recalling the Egyptian ambassador, by sending food and medical supplies, and by providing Egyptian naval unit escorts to the PLO (Palestine Liberation Organization) evacuation of Tripoli in 1983. In 1984 and 1985, he reopened relations with Jordan, and this plus the passiveness of U.S. policy after the failure of the U.S.-sponsored Lebanese-Israeli peace treaty of 1983 and the bombings of the U.S. embassy and marines provided Mubarak with the incentive to promote a peace process. This potential Palestinian ticket for readmission to the Arab state system was superceded by the turn of events in the Persian Gulf and the development of a tanker war. Egypt already had military supply, training, and agricultural-worker connections with Iraq. At the November 1987 Arab Summit in Amman, Jordan, Egypt's potential military role in the Gulf was affirmed, and as a result, all but Algeria, Syria, Lebanon, and Libya have subsequently resumed diplomatic ties with Egypt.

Ties with the United States have stabilized and normalized in spite of American policy. U.S. economic and military assistance to compensate Egypt for such lapses of aid from Arab sources as a result of the 1979 treaty has continued (a program so large that it is second only to that of Israel in the entire world). A major low point occurred over the 1985 *Achille Lauro* hijacking where on the one hand the Egyptians negotiated the release of the hostages, and on the other, the Americans hijacked an Egyptian aircraft carrying the captors to disciplinary action by the Palestine Liberation Organization in Tunis. This caused a quick, angry response in Egypt. American policy became inert only to belatedly be revived following Mubarak's visit to Washington, D.C., in early 1988. This was followed by repeated trips to the region by the American Secretary of State George Shultz and a result has been that the relationship has matured and become more equal.

In domestic political terms, there is little doubt that, unlike his predecessors who exercised authoritarian rule, Mubarak either does not wish to, or cannot. The ultimate question is whether Mubarak is in a position reactive to political forces at work in Egypt or whether he is able to manipulate them. It is clear that the military constitutes the bedrock of the system. It is said for example, that the appointive position of vice president has remained vacant since 1981 because deputy prime minister and minister of defense, General Abd al Halim Abu Ghazala, will not accept the post and will not allow anyone else to do so. In the major disturbances of January 1977 and the riot of the security police for economic reasons in February 1986, it has been the restrained intervention of the army that has saved the day. As the army expands into community action projects and produces electrical and electronic consumer goods (for example, refrigerators and televisions), it has become even more politically central under General Abu Ghazala. Furthermore, as deadly conspiracies are hatched from the right by Islamicists and from the left by organizations such as the Egyptian Revolution (under the leadership of Khalid Nasser, the eldest of Nasser's sons) Mubarak is heavily dependent on the Ministry of the Interior and the various intelligence services. In fact, it is possibly this reliance that has contributed to the continuation of Sadat's experiment with democratization. Mubarak has freed the press almost totally. This safety valve of opinion has served him well, and is especially well illustrated in the case of the 1984 and 1987 parliamentary elections which, while being significantly free, still had seemingly local inter-ferences. It has been the security apparatus that has drawn criticism and not Mubarak himself. His overwhelming reelection as president in October 1987, while not obviously stage-managed, probably reflects both his popularity and the public's perception of him as acceptable to both the military and security organizations. This is the atmosphere of Egypt's one-party-dominant version of democracy, which at least structurally resembles that of India and Mexico.

Mubarak's economic policy has reflected a complex of factors. There is first the inheritance from Sadat of the creation of a dual public- and private-sector economy. Rhetorically at least, Mubarak has attempted to compensate for Sadat's neglect of the public sector. This was especially the case prior to 1984, when he regularly took part in public dialogues on economic policy. As Egypt's indebtedness has increased, however, he has found himself having to respond to International Monetary Fund (IMF)–sponsored "reforms," namely, a greater role for the private sector in order to an an IMF–Paris Club agreement to postpone interest payments for ten years. In addition, further interim loans have been forthcoming (at the end of 1987 and in early 1988). In fact, his 1987–1992 Five Year Plan formally increases the investment role of the private sector. This IMF arrangement along with some increases in the "four pillars" of tourism, oil, the Suez Canal, and worker remittances—have brought a breathing spell to Egypt's economic problems.

Mubarak's personal position and the stability of Egyptian leadership remains precarious. Economically and politically, much depends on his diplomatic skill in the management of the external international and regional environment. Re-newed ties with the Soviet Union will at least symbolically balance an important economic and military technology reliance on the United States. Diversification of foreign economic assistance to include Europe and Japan as well as Arab Gulf support will also strengthen him. Cutting off such aid, however, or the return of workers from the Arab states and a dramatic reduction in their remittances as a result of a decline in oil revenues, would shock the system. Politically, Mubarak still needs to grasp the Palestinian "ticket" in order to relieve himself of major pressure from the clandestine ideological left and the religious right. Meanwhile he can placate some segments of this criticism by diplomatic activity and by at least verbally supporting the public sector and allowing the fuller expression of Islamic values. Ultimately, economic performance and the ability to provide policy accomplishments will be what is necessary to secure his leadership.

BIBLIOGRAPHY

Aly, Abdel Monem Said. "Democratization in Egypt." *American Arab Affairs* 22 (Fall 1987): 11–27.

Bianchi, Robert. "Egypt: Drift at Home, Passivity Abroad." *Current History* 85, no. 508 (February 1986), pp. 71–74, 82–83.

Cantori, Louis J. "Egyptian Policy under Mubarak: The Politics of Continuity and Change." In Robert O. Freedman (ed.), *The Middle East after the Israeli Invasion of Lebanon*. Syracuse, N.Y.: Syracuse University Press, 1986.

Cooper, Mark. *The Transformation of Egypt*. Baltimore: Johns Hopkins University Press, 1982.

Dessouki, Ali E. Hillal. "The Primacy of Economics: The Foreign Policy of Egypt." In Bahgat Korany and Ali E. Hilal Dessouki (eds.), *The Foreign Policies of Arab States*. Boulder, Colo.: Westview Press, 1984.

Hinnebusch, Raymond, Jr. *Egyptian Politics under Sadat*. London: Cambridge University Press, 1985.

Moore, Clement Henry. "Money and Power: The Dilemma of the Egyptian Infitah." *Middle East Journal* 40 (Autumn 1986), pp. 634–650.

Sonbol, Amira. "Egypt." In Shireen Hunter (ed.). *The Politics of Islamic Revivalism*. Bloomington, Ind.: Indiana University Press, 1988.

Springborg, Robert. *The Political Economy of Mubarak's Egypt*. Boulder, Colo.: Westview Press, 1988.

LOUIS J. CANTORI

N

MUSTAFA AL-NAHHAS (1879–1965) was Egypt's most popular politician from Sa'd Zaghlul's death in 1927 to the 1952 revolution. His name was virtually synonymous with his party, the Wafd. Coming from modest origins, without the large estates or family connections that helped other politicians rise to power, he was a capable organizer and an eloquent orator, but he often lacked tact and good judgment. A fierce rival to kings Fuad and Farouk*, he could always win any election that was not rigged by the palace or the rival parties. He was discredited, however, by the Egyptians' disillusionment with the 1936 Anglo-Egyptian Treaty, his acceptance of the premiership in February 1942 after the British ambassador's ultimatum to Farouk, and his failure to prevent the burning of Cairo in January 1952. The 1952 revolution ended his political career and Gamal Abdul Nasser's* populism and reform program eclipsed his reputation, but he and the Wafd kept some of their popular backing beyond the Nasser years.

The son of Sheikh Muhammad al-Nahhas (a lumber merchant), Mustafa al-Nahhas was born in Samanud on June 15, 1879. He was educated in Samanud and Cairo and received his degree from Khedivial Law School in 1900; he then worked as a lawyer in Mansurah. He was appointed judge in the National Court at Tantah in 1914, joined the Wafd (and became its secretary) in 1919, and was subsequently dismissed from his judgeship. He was exiled with Sa'd Zaghlul to the Seychelles in 1921–1923, and on his repatriation was elected deputy from Samanud to the first Chamber of Deputies in 1923. He served as communications minister in 1924, was elected deputy from Abu Sir Banna (Gharbiyah) in 1926, and was elected vice president of the Chamber of Deputies in 1926 and president in 1927. He was chosen to lead the Wafd after Sa'd Zaghlul's death in 1927. Mustafa al-Nahhas married Zaynab al-Wakil in June 1934. He was prime minister in 1928, 1930, 1936–1937, 1942–1944, and 1950–1952, and served in other posts including interior minister in 1928, 1930, 1936–1937, and 1942–1944; and foreign minister in 1942–1944. He led the Egyptian negotiating team for the 1936 Anglo-Egyptian Treaty (which he denounced in 1951), was arrested and tried after the 1952 revolution, and died in Cairo on August 23, 1965.

Nahhas seems not to have been politically active in his youth, but he backed the Nationalist Party of Mustafa Kamil and Muhammad Farid. At the end of World War I, when Sa'd Zaghlul was forming the delegation (the Wafd) to plead the cause of Egypt's independence at the post-World War I Peace Conference, the Wafd selected Nahhas to represent the Nationalists, although the Nationalists themselves had chosen others to represent their party. Dismissed from his judicial post in 1919, he became indispensable to Zaghlul as a youth organizer and went into exile with him to the Seychelles from 1921 to 1923. Both men were absent from Egypt while the 1923 constitution was being drafted, but they returned in time to turn the Wafd into a political party and to run for the Chamber of Deputies in the first national elections. Nahhas was the delegate from Samanud and became the minister of communications in the Wafdist cabinet of January–November 1924. Reelected in 1926, his appointment to a cabinet post was blocked by the objections of Britain's high commissioner, Lord George Ambrose Lloyd, but Nahhas was chosen as one of the two vice presidents by the Chamber of Deputies. He became its president in 1927.

When Sa'd Zaghlul died on August 23, 1927, Nahhas and Fathallah Barakat (Sa'd's nephew) were the main contenders for the succession. Barakat had a strong influence on the peasants, but was disliked by the palace, the British, and indeed by Zaghlul's widow, who preferred Nahhas. So, too, did many other Wafdists, who hoped they could influence Nahhas once he took power. Nahhas used the Wafdist majority in Parliament to undercut the negotiations then in progress for a definitive Anglo-Egyptian treaty to reconcile Great Britain's concern for its imperial communications with Egypt's demands for complete independence. King Fuad agreed to let Nahhas head a coalition government made up of Wafdists and Liberal Constitutionalists in February 1928, hoping that the Wafd would soon fall from power. Nahhas antagonized Britain by introducing a bill that would have barred the police from interfering in public meetings. Backed by the dispatch of British warships to Alexandria, High Commissioner Lloyd extracted a promise from Nahhas to put off consideration of the bill to the following session. Nahhas's reputation was tarnished by allegations that he and two other Wafdist lawyers had accepted a fee of 130,000 Egyptian pounds (about 650,000 dollars) to transfer guardianship over Prince Sayf al-Din's property from King Fuad to the prince's mother. These allegations, added to the sudden "resignation" of the leading Liberal minister, gave the king ample pretext to dismiss the Nahhas cabinet, appoint an exclusively Liberal Constitutionalist government, dissolve Parliament (which under Nahhas's leadership had become increasingly unruly), and suspend the 1923 constitution.

Out of power, Nahhas adopted an obstructionist stance toward the palace and its minority government, which agreed to a treaty that would have removed all British troops from Cairo and Alexandria. When a Labor government took power in Britain in 1929, it argued that an Anglo-Egyptian treaty was more likely to be upheld by the Egyptians if it were approved by a popularly elected government. Attempts to arrange a coalition of all major politicians failed, and King Fuad had to call for new parliamentary elections, in which Nahhas won a resounding majority. The Wafdists then rejected the Anglo-Egyptian treaty that had been negotiated by their opponents, and from March to May 1930 Nahhas led the Egyptian negotiating team in London, but the British refused to make any new concessions whereas Nahhas sought unlimited Egyptian immigration into the Sudan. Quarrels within the Wafdist delegation further discredited Nahhas, and the negotiations were broken off. Using his Wafdist majority in Parliament, Nahhas challenged King Fuad with a bill that would have punished any minister who violated the 1923 constitution. Fuad rejected the bill and Nahhas resigned in an effort to pressure him, but the king called his bluff and accepted his resignation. He also abolished the 1923 constitution, replacing it with one that took power from the popularly elected Parliament and gave it to palace politicians having no party connections or public backing.

Nahhas, his Wafdist disciples, and their Liberal rivals wandered for five years in a political wilderness. In 1935 the Italian conquest of Ethiopia made the British more eager to obtain a treaty that would ensure Egyptian support for their occupation of the Suez Canal, while it made the Egyptians aware of an imperialist threat that they feared even more than the British. The leading politicians formed a united front to demand a restoration of the 1923 constitution (which was detested by Fuad) and to negotiate an Anglo-Egyptian treaty. Shortly after King Fuad's death in April 1936, the Egyptian electorate chose, as usual, a large Wafd majority. Nahhas formed his third cabinet and headed the Egyptian delegation in the negotiations for the 1936 Anglo-Egyptian treaty. Nahhas believed that this treaty, which reduced to ten thousand the number of British troops that could remain in Egypt in peacetime and would transfer them to the Suez Canal zone as soon as adequate barracks could be built for them, would guarantee him a long period of popular rule in Egypt. In fact, his government's greatest accomplishment was to persuade the Western powers at the 1937 Montreux Conference to give up the Capitulations, treaties that had exempted Europeans in Egypt from its laws and taxes. The Nahhas ministry also secured an agreement under which the Suez Canal Company admitted two Egyptians to its governing board. The Wafdist cabinet set up Egypt's first military schools for aviators and mechanics, founded the staff college, and expanded the officers' academy by opening it to young men who could pass a competitive examination (thus admitting, among others, Gamal Abdul Nasser and Anwar al-Sadat*). The Wafdist government under Nahhas was, however, discredited by corruption, nepotism, and partisanship in the appointment of national and local officials, as well as failure to curb young King Farouk to compete with him for popular support. Some highly respected Wafdists left the party and later formed the "Sa'dist group," challenging Nahhas as the Wafd's leader. An ultranationalist movement known as Young Egypt or the "Green Shirts" tried to assassinate him in November 1937. Nahhas formed his own parliamentary group, the "Blue Shirts," which broke into the Sa'dist clubhouse to intimidate its members. Nahhas was backed by Britain's Ambassador, Sir Miles Lampson, but Farouk had the support of al-Azhar University, the rising Muslim Brothers Society, and Young Egypt. Student demonstrations in front of his palace gave Farouk the pretext to oust Nahhas's cabinet. A liberal-dominated coalition took power and held a rigged election in 1938. Nahhas remained out of power until 1942.

He remained a visible political figure, however, for Britain needed a strong proponent of its 1936 treaty once World War II broke out, underscoring Egypt's strategic importance. Both the British and the Egyptians believed that only the Wafd could win a freely contested election and that only Nahhas was willing to carry out the terms of the treaty. The British government and Ambassador Lampson came to believe that the king was irredeemably pro-Fascist and would have to be deposed. Farouk's hostility toward the Wafd and Nahhas was notorious, and any British bid to bring them back to power was sure to cause a confrontation with the palace. In early 1942, Germany's advance across Libya and Japan's capture of Britain's East Asian possessions rendered the British position in Egypt highly vulnerable. Lampson decided, therefore, to force the issue with Farouk, hoping to make him abdicate. Nahhas, like all the other Egyptian politicians, opposed British interference in Egypt's affairs, but he wanted to head a Wafdist government even if it took power behind British tanks. On February 4, 1942, Lampson demanded that Farouk either ask Nahhas to form a government or abdicate. The king reluctantly let Nahhas appoint a Wafdist cabinet. After this confrontation, Egyptians no longer could view the Wafd as a nationalist party. Soon Nahhas was challenged by his hitherto loyal lieutenant, Makram Ubayd. Encouraged by Farouk, Makram quit the Wafd and published his *Black Book* containing allegations that the Nahhas regime was corrupt. Without seeking British approval, Nahhas had Makram put under house arrest and then exiled to the Delta despite widespread popular protests. However, the British still needed Nahhas to support the Allies; they did not let his Wafdist cabinet fall until October 1944, after the Axis threat had receded.

Together with Fuad Sirag al-Din, his new lieutenant, Nahhas increased the Wafd's involvement in social issues. The wartime cabinet raised the minimum daily wage for farm workers, abolished fees for government elementary schools, lowered taxes on small landowners, strengthened the labor union laws, and established the first rural health centers. Nahhas's major accomplishment, however, was to move Egypt closer to Arab unity. Iraq's prime minister, Nuri al-Said,* was promoting an organic union of the Fertile Crescent states, one that would have excluded Egypt and Saudi Arabia. In 1943 Nahhas met individually with the leaders of the other Arab countries and in the following year convened a general meeting in Alexandria, where he proposed creating a League of Arab States. It would not be a union, a federation, or an alliance, but rather an organization that each Arab country might join without losing its sovereignty. The attending states signed a document called the Alexandria Protocol, urging cooperation among the Arabs and forming a committee to draw up a charter for the proposed Arab League. Nahhas fell from office one day after the protocol was signed, and others would reap the credit for his efforts, but he played a major role in bringing Egypt closer to pan-Arabism.

By the time Nahhas had regained a position from which to influence Egypt's politics, the country's ties to the Arab world had been confirmed by its participation in the 1948 Palestine War, albeit in a losing cause. The defeat had discredited King Farouk and Egypt's constitutional system generally, but the old order made one last bid for popularity by calling a general election for January 1950. Even though most of the Wafd's leaders had defected by this time, Nahhas's party won most of the seats in the Chamber of Deputies (but less than half the popular votes cast). The Wafd passed new laws to benefit poor people, notably one redistributing a million acres to landless peasants; but Nahhas's main aim was to persuade the British government to renounce the 1936 Anglo-Egyptian Treaty, leave its Suez Canal base, and hand the Sudan over to Egypt. He failed. Nineteen months of discussion left both sides frustrated, and Nahhas proceeded to abrogate both the 1936 treaty and the 1899 agreement that had established the Anglo-Egyptian Condominium over the Sudan. Britain did not flinch, but some one hundred thousand Egyptians stopped working for the British troops at the Suez Canal base, the remaining British teachers and civil servants in Egypt were summarily dismissed, and extremist youths, called *fidaiyin* (self-sacrificers), began harassing British forces. On January 25, 1952, a clash broke out between British troops in Ismailia and Egyptian auxiliary policemen acting under orders from the interior minister, Fuad Sirag al-Din. Over fifty policemen were killed, setting off protest demonstrations the next day. The demonstration in Cairo got out of hand, leading to the deliberate burning of most of the major hotels, stores, and clubs patronized by Europeans in the downtown area. King Farouk gave Nahhas emergency powers to quell the riots, but the next day he dismissed him.

The Cairo fire highlighted the breakdown of Egypt's political institutions: the monarchy, the parliamentary system, the Wafd, and indeed all the other political parties and movements. Six months later a cabal of army officers, nominally led by General Muhammad Nagib but in reality commanded by Colonel Gamal Abdul Nasser, seized control of the Egyptian government. Nahhas, vacationing in Europe, hastened back to Egypt, expecting to be asked to form a new government. Nagib and Nasser met with him at length before they decided against giving the Wafd the power that Nahhas was demanding. In September the parties were ordered to purge themselves of all old regime leaders. Nahhas defied the order, but the officers managed to split the Wafd. In January 1953 they seized the party assets and formed a single party, the National Liberation Rally. Nahhas and his wife, who the officers thought had taken over the Wafd, were arrested and tried. Nahhas was censured for condoning corruption among his colleagues; his wife was fined for rigging the Alexandria cotton market. Confined to their villa in Garden City, they lived out their lives in relative obscurity. Nahhas's funeral in 1965 attested to his lingering popularity, as thousands followed his bier to its final resting place, defying Nasir's efforts to downplay the Wafdist leader.

Nahhas was a tall, imposing man, extremely proud, an eloquent speaker, and a capable organizer. While personally honest, he sometimes failed to check the corruption of his colleagues. He could easily be influenced by fellow party members. As a party leader, he tended to become jealous of men as capable and popular as himself, and many of the best Wafdists left the party on that account. Due to his own humble background, he could appeal to poor people but often felt threatened by the power and status of the rich. His obstinancy made him a principled nationalist leader, but an uncompromising politician who at times needlessly offended his friends and foes. He never got along well with the palace and only occasionally could work with the British or with leaders of other political parties. Egyptians remember him better for his errors than for his accomplishments, but for some he was the very archetype of a prerevolutionary politician.

BIBLIOGRAPHY

Works by Mubarak:

"Foreword." In Roy Choudhury. *Egypt in 1945*. Calcutta: n.p., 1946.
"Anglo-Egyptian Negotiations." *Near East* 37 (April 3, 1930): 375.

Other Works:

Berque, Jacques. *Egypt: Imperialism and Revolution*. Trans. Jean Stewart. London: Faber, 1972, pp. 520–523.
Colombe, Marcel. *L'évolution de l'Egypte, 1924–1950*. Paris: G. P. Maisonneuve, 1951.
Current Biography 12 (July 1951); 451–453.
Deeb, Marius. *Party Politics in Egypt: The Wafd and its Rivals, 1919–1939*. London: Ithaca Press, 1979.
Gomaa, Ahmed M. *Foundation of the League of Arab States*. London: Longman, 1977.
el-Hadidy, Mohamed A. "Mustafa al-Nahhas: A Case Study of Egyptian Political Leadership." Ph.D. diss., London School of Oriental and African Studies, 1985.
Quraishi, Zaheer Masood. *Liberal Nationalism in Egypt: Rise and Fall of the Wafd Party*. Allahabad: Kitab Mahal, 1967.
al-Rafii, Abd al-Rahman. *Fi A'qab al-Thawrah al-Misriyah* (In the Aftermath of the Egyptian Revolution). 3 vols. Cairo: Maktabat al-Nahdah al-Misriyah, 1947–1951.
Ramadan, Abd al-Azim. *al-Sira bayn al-Wafd wa al-Arsh, 1937–1940* (The Struggle between the Wafd and the Throne). Beirut: al-Muassasah al-Arabiyah, 1977.
al-Said, Rifat. *Mustafa al-Nahhas: al-siyasi wa al-zaim wa al-munadil* (Mustafa al-Nahhas: Politician, Leader, and Fighter). Beirut: al-Muassasah al-Arabiyah, 1976.
al-Sayyid-Marsot, Afaf Lutfi. *Egypt's Liberal Experiment: 1922–1936*. Berkeley and Los Angeles: University of California Press, 1977.
Smith, Charles D. "4 February 1942: Its Causes and Its Influence on Egyptian Politics and on the Future of Anglo-Egyptian Relations, 1937–1945." *International Journal of Middle East Studies* 10 (1979): 453–479.
Terry, Janice Joles. *Cornerstone of Egyptian Political Power: The Wafd, 1919–1952*. London: Third World Centre, 1982.

Warburg, Gabriel. *Egypt and the Sudan: Studies in History and Politics*. London: Frank
    Cass, 1985.

ARTHUR GOLDSCHMIDT, JR.

GAMAL ABDUL NASSER (1918–1970), an Egyptian army officer who came
to power after leading a military coup against King Farouk,* was a figure of
outstanding importance in twentieth-century Egyptian history and in the immediate postcolonial era in the Middle East. When Nasser was born, Great
Britain not only occupied Egypt militarily but had established a Protectorate over
the country, thus beginning the integration of Egypt into the British Empire.
The Suez Canal was almost wholly owned and controlled by non-Egyptian
interests. Egypt itself had been ruled for almost two thousand years by non-
Egyptians. In the period after World War I, Egypt had a powerful monarchy
and a weak parliamentary regime, which Great Britain still dominated. By the
time of Nasser's death, Egypt was a fully independent state that had wrested
control of the Suez Canal in 1956. Israeli troops, however, were stationed on
Egyptian soil, and the limits of Egyptian autonomy from the world economy
were becoming clear. Internally, Nasser's importance can be gauged by his
policies ending all direct European control over the country, enacting a series
of land reforms, and nationalizing major industries. Internationally, Nasser's
importance can best be appreciated in terms of his role as a model for the
nonaligned movement in which new states sought to maximize their freedom of
action without regard to Cold War policy commitments.

The trajectory of Nasser's career is one of striking successes between his
assumption of the office of prime minister in 1954 until the early 1960s. Thereafter, Nasser's policies were increasingly less successful until the disastrous 1967
defeat by Israel undermined the capacity of the Egyptian state to pursue policies
independently of the United States and the Soviet Union and damaged Nasser's
own self-confidence.

Nasser was born in the village of Bani Morr in the Upper Egyptian province
of Asyut on January 16, 1918. For the most part, he received his primary and
secondary education in Alexandria and Cairo. Until 1936, entry into the military
academy and the upper ranks of the army were restricted so that lower- and
middle-class Egyptians could not undertake careers as officers. In 1936, negotiations between the nationalist Wafd party and the British government (which
still had troops stationed in Egypt) increased Egypt's independence somewhat,
and it became possible for middle-class boys to enter the Military Academy.
Nasser became a cadet in 1937. After graduation in 1938 he was assigned to
the Upper Egyptian town of Mankabad along with two other second lieutenants,
Zakaria Mohieddin and Anwar al-Sadat,* both of whom were to assume prominence in the Free Officers movement which brought down the royal regime in
1952. In 1941 Nasser became an instructor at the military academy, a post that
enabled him to meet other young officers. Nasser served as commander of the
Sixth Battalion in the 1948 Arab-Israeli war. His unit was besieged in the Faluga

salient in October 1949 and remained under siege until the conclusion of the armistice agreement between Israel and the four Arab states which agreed to sign.

On his return to Egypt after the war, Nasser began to organize young officers who, like himself, were dissatisfied with the social inequities of the royal regime and who came from lower- and middle-class backgrounds. By the end of November, Nasser had established the core of his movement. Among his early recruits into the movement of Free Officers were Abdul Hakim Amer, Abdul Latif Baghdadi, Kamal El-Din Husain, and Khalid Mohieddin. Shortly thereafter Anwar al-Sadat and Zakaria Mohieddin were coopted into membership.

Egypt was a country of deep social and political antagonisms during the first years of the 1950s. The Egyptian population was largely rural, and rural conditions were significantly worse than those in urban areas. Land ownership was highly concentrated before 1952. Fewer than 0.10 percent of landowners owned 20 percent of the land, while almost 95 percent of landowners shared 35 percent of the land. Most of these 2,642,000 small landowners owned less than one acre of land. Even these small landowners made up only a fraction of the total rural population of almost 14 million people. An even more urgent indicator of agrarian crisis was the continued growth of the landless in Egypt, who by 1950 accounted for 44 percent of the rural population. Wealthy landowners had great political power as well as economic advantage, and in consequence peasants, tenants, and agricultural laborers had very low incomes. These low incomes meant that malnutrition was widespread and so, consequently, were pellagra and lowered resistance to parasitical diseases.

The dramatic growth in the Egyptian population provided a large reserve for migration from the countryside to the cities during the period from Nasser's birth until 1952 and beyond. Life in the cities was attractive to peasants faced with high rents, low incomes, and poor nutrition, but it had severe problems of its own. Inflation was high in the late 1940s and unemployment increased after World War II. Even in the largest industrial establishments, wages were often low and working conditions poor. Unions were frequently repressed and workers were not encouraged to become more efficient or productive on the job.

The possibility of changing any part of the national economic or social life through peaceful political means was slim. The British in collusion with the king still contrived to keep the one party with a parliamentary majority and a commitment to the constitution—the Wafd—out of office. The Wafd itself suffered from institutional arteriosclerosis, and even after winning an absolute majority in the 1950 elections, was unable either to implement a coherent policy of social reform or to end the presence of British troops on Egyptian territory in the Suez Canal zone. On January 25, 1952, a confrontation occurred between British troops in the city of Ismailia in the Canal Zone and Egyptian police; fifty police were killed and more were injured. Political violence had become widespread, and included assassinations of several leading political figures. The zenith of violence was reached in a riot on January 26, during which fires were set in different parts of Cairo and the Wafd was dismissed from office yet again. Seemingly ungovernable, Egypt became a state waiting to collapse.

The military officers of lower-class background who entered the military academy after 1936 had the cohesion to make a coup when civilian political organizations lacked the capacity to bring down the old regime. Three thousand troops commanded by two hundred officers took control of the Army Headquarters in Cairo during the night of July 22–23, 1952, and brought a new military government to power. The new regime was committed to reforming Egyptian social and economic life. The army officers did not have a well-developed program before coming to power, but they did want to enhance Egypt's independence. Consequently, they believed that foreign control of Egypt had to be ended, that the Egyptian economy had to grow, and that the inequities in the Egyptian economy had to be resolved.

The first step was land reform. By September 7 the new regime had launched a land reform program designed to bring about a transformation of the countryside and a redistribution of power. Under the 1952 law, a ceiling of land ownership of two hundred acres per person was set. Land in excess of the maximum was bought in a forced sale at relatively low prices and redistributed to small tenants and farmers, with preferential distribution to those actually working the land that had been expropriated. The transformation of the countryside in terms of equality was remarkable. The middle-class peasantry came to dominate the countryside, which had previously been controlled by a tiny elite of wealthy non-residents. Almost in one stroke the power of a previously dominant rural social group was diminished if not destroyed, and the government found support among those who were previously economically and politically marginal. Successive land reform laws in 1961 and 1965 set limits of one hundred and fifty acres respectively.

Land reform by itself could not solve the problem of providing adequate living standards for the entire population of Egypt, however. The population was already too large and was growing too fast for there to be sufficient land to provide all Egyptians—even all rural Egyptians—with an economically viable holding. Only economic growth could help Egypt, and the project seized by the Nasser government to promote economic growth was the building of a gigantic new dam on the Nile—the Aswan High Dam. The High Dam would impound sufficient water to make year-round irrigation possible throughout Egypt as well as supplying power to electrify rural Egypt and allow the creation of new industries. Egyptian industry had to be stimulated for the Egyptian economy to provide incomes for all Egyptians. Stimulating the industrial economy required investment. Almost 60 percent of capital help in Egypt before 1952 was foreign-owned, and one of the most productive sources of revenue was the Suez Canal, whose tolls flowed primarily to bondholders in Europe rather than into the state coffers.

Nasser and the Free Officers did not nationalize the Canal or foreign-owned enterprises because of ideological predilection. Increasing the independence of the state rather than socialism was the intent of Nasser's program. In 1953 the regime hanged leaders of a worker's demonstration at the Kafr al-Dawwar textile plants outside Alexandria, thereby demonstrating that the military authorities were not committed to the left wing, the workers, or even a return of the parliamentary liberties of the previous regime. By late 1954 Nasser had become the supreme political authority in Egypt. Land reform broke the power of the landed aristocracy; the dissolution of the political parties and Parliament broke the power of the established urban middle class and any organized opposition; and Nasser had ousted the regime figurehead, General Muhammad Najib, and assumed the offices of prime minister and president.

Nationalization of the Suez Canal was Nasser's greatest foreign-policy triumph, but he was led to it primarily by the course of events in the international arena. The signature of the Baghdad Pact between Iraq and Turkey on February 24, 1955, presented Nasser with a profound challenge. On the one hand he could join a treaty aimed at restricting Soviet influence in the Middle East and increasing British and American influence in the region. On the other, he could assert the independence of Egypt as a state whose foreign policy reflected only the decisions of native-born rulers. The desirability of heightened independence remained a legacy of the colonial era. The possibility of greater independence increased sharply in 1955 as Nasser, along with other Third World leaders, began to bargain aggressively with the United States and the Soviet Union in the attempt to play one off against the other.

Between April 18 and April 25, 1955, Nasser was in Bandung, Indonesia, participating in the first important meeting of heads of state of the large non-Western states. Meeting with leaders of the Chinese, Indian, Indonesian, Yugoslav, and Ghanaian governments, Nasser's willingness to challenge the West increased dramatically. Bandung was the crucible from which emerged the doctrine of "positive neutrality," which meant that leaders of former colonies would look to the Soviet Bloc as well as the West for aid in pursuing state policies. Five months after his return from Bandung, Nasser announced the signing of an arms contract with Czechoslovakia. With another stroke of the pen, Nasser had destroyed an equilibrium. In 1952 it had been the internal equilibrium of rural power; this time it was the equilibrium of international power relations. With a supply of arms from Eastern Europe and the Soviet Union, Nasser was free of Western influence. No longer could Britain, France, or the United States inhibit Egyptian policymakers by refusing to sell them arms.

The response of the Western powers to the doctrine of positive neutrality was at best cool. Egypt was moving away from the close relationship with the West that had existed during the colonial era. Egyptian independence had the natural corollary of an increased willingness to challenge Israel whether directly or by supporting Palestinian guerrilla operations from Egyptian territory. Nasser had no intention of allowing the Palestinians to determine the course of Egyptian policy but he was willing to aid them in their struggle against Israel. Nasser clearly conceived of the Palestinian struggle against Israel as equivalent to the Algerian struggle against France, which he also strongly supported.

Difficulties arose in negotiations between Egypt and Britain and the United States regarding the financing of the High Dam project in 1956. In July, Britain and the United States withdrew from the project and were followed by the World Bank. In response, Nasser nationalized the Suez Canal and announced that profits from the canal would finance the High Dam and Egypt's economic independence. Israel, France, and Great Britain all had reason to oppose the increased independence of Egypt, and in the ensuing months the Suez Canal crisis unfolded. In November, Israel invaded Egypt and threatened the canal in a maneuver secretly arranged with Britain and France. The invasion allowed Britain and France to reoccupy the Canal Zone, but the plan miscarried due to U.S. and Soviet opposition, and the forces of all three countries had to withdraw.

Nasser and Egypt emerged from the Suez crisis with vastly enhanced prestige: State sovereignty over the Egyptian territory was supreme, the nationalization of the canal stood and with it the flow of funds into Egypt, the defeat of former colonial powers was manifest, and Israel was forced for the first time to withdraw from Arab territory. Even the High Dam—centerpiece of the new regime's hopes and plans—was to be built with aid from the Soviet Union. Nasser emerged from the Suez crisis as the supreme hero of the Arab world, and his regime became the focal point for popular aspirations for countries from Algeria to Iraq. Perhaps the only shortcoming from Nasser's point of view was that the troops of the United Nations Emergency Force (UNEF) were stationed only on the Egyptian side of the Israeli-Egyptian border. The presence of UNEF troops did, however, serve to ease the likelihood of provocations across the border and also allowed the two states to enjoy something of a modus vivendi.

The period between 1956 and 1963 marked the apogee of the Nasserist era. Nasser had become the most successful practitioner of positive neutrality. Not only had he emerged victorious during the Suez crisis, but in its aftermath he became the avatar of Arab nationalism and Arab unity. In 1958, the leaders of a weakened and coup-ridden Syria merged their state into the United Arab Republic, which was almost wholly under Egyptian control. Nasser himself was able to claim the bulk of the responsibility and hence the glory of the transformation of Egypt from a weak peripheral state to a central player in the Arab world and a major actor in international politics.

In the decade after 1956, Nasser became the symbolic representative of the Arab world—the bearer of its aspirations, hopes, and ideals. Nasser embodied Egypt, and Egypt symbolized the awakening of the Arab world and, in Nasser's words, its emergence as the center of the three circles of Arab identity, African identity, and Islamic identity. Nasser's popularity and perceived charisma developed to unprecedented heights in the Arab world, and millions of people listened to the broadcast of his speeches on the Egyptian radio station, "Voice of the Arabs."

Nasserist parties developed in Lebanon, Syria, Jordan, Iraq, and in the Arab states of the Gulf. The leaders of revolutionary regimes, especially in Iraq (after the 1958 overthrow of the monarchy) and in Syria defined themselves in relation to Egypt and Nasser. The mention of Nasser's name or the display of his photograph were implicitly a criticism of regimes that had not yet broken with their colonial past, had not yet embarked on programs of redistribution, or had not come face to face with Israel. Egypt increasingly became a "liberated zone" for Arab radicals and anticolonial revolutionaries, whether the Algerian National Liberation Front, Palestinian students, or republican army officers from the Gulf states. Egypt's welcoming posture toward Arab nationalism, expressed daily in her newspapers and broadcast on Cairo radio's "Voice of the Arabs," was accompanied, however, by a narrowing of formal political life in Egypt: Communists were in prison and many of the Muslim political activists had sought refuge in the conservative Gulf monarchies. While no cult of personality such as that surrounding Joseph Stalin or Mao Tse-Tung developed around Nasser, Egypt became a country with an ever narrower political life. The secret police, political prisons, and even concentration camps existed to keep political discourse within an extremely narrow framework. An atrophy of political and intellectual life developed in the climate of repression that began to descend.

What were essentially the costs of success—largely discounted by Nasser in the first decade of his regime—built up to overwhelm the positive balance of that first decade. Two kinds of costs overwhelmed Nasser. First were the growing strains on the Egyptian state as it proved unable to deliver on the expectations its earlier successes had raised. Second were the growing burdens of maintaining the position at the center of the Arab world and the world at large that Nasser had attained in the 1950s. Land reform ran out of steam by 1965 when the maximum area allowed owners was lowered to 50 acres. Although it might have been possible to lower ownership limits again, a point of diminishing returns had been approached. Industrial investment in large turnkey operations provided by the Soviet Union had occurred, notably in the Helwan Iron and Steel Complex, the High Dam, and the Nag Hammadi Aluminum plant, but overall labor productivity was low. In consequence, the Egyptian economy was not in a situation to provide satisfactory industrial or other urban work for those who left the rural areas.

Egypt under Nasser was not only the exemplar but also the protector of republican regimes. One such regime was that created in North Yemen. Consequently, after 1962, Egypt was pulled into a war in North Yemen that is often characterized as "Nasser's Vietnam" because of its cost in lives and equipment. This war pitted Nasser not only against the traditional ruler of Yemen but also against the Saudi royal family which backed the Yemeni Imam. As many as fifty thousand Egyptian troops were stationed in Yemen. The war continued until August 1967, and Egyptian troops launched a major offensive in August 1966 which included the use of poison gas.

The period between 1962 and 1967 appeared at the time to be one of deepening Egyptian commitment to socialism, nationalism, and radical revolutionary action. In retrospect it appears more as a period in which Nasser found himself enmeshed in unanticipated and unwanted strategic situations as a result of tactical initiatives. Nasser wanted to expand the base of the Egyptian economy in terms of heavy industry, yet the large-scale investment projects in the area of heavy industrial development were often themselves counterproductive in terms of developing outputs proportional to the capital invested. The decisions made by Nasser and his government to expand employment as the price for controlling the independent action of trade unions often led to poor performance in terms of productivity. Growing isolation from the West, due in part to the Yemen war, also led to foreign-exchange shortages.

The greatest disaster of the Nasser period, however, lay not in the domestic economy but in international relations. Nasser's penchant for tactical improvisation turned to disaster when it became the basis for a major strategic Israeli victory in June 1967. Although Nasser had warned throughout the early 1960s that war with Israel would be counterproductive without high levels of Arab preparedness and unity, he nevertheless found himself drifting toward war in early 1967. The drift to war was promoted by two distinct kinds of processes: One had to do with Arab-Israeli rivalry and conflict, and the other had to do with inter-Arab rivalry and conflict. Arab-Israeli conflict increased throughout the 1960s, although the direct conflict concerned Arab states other than Egypt. In mid–1964 Israel completed the National Water Carrier, which drew water from the Jordan river and the Sea of Galilee. The riparian Arab countries, Jordan and Syria, did not recognize Israel, and announced plans to divert the sources and tributaries of the water Israel used, and also to prepare for war should Israel intervene to prevent the diversion.

The Arab states also created the Palestine Liberation Organization and a Palestine Liberation Army, primarily as a way to preempt any independent organization by the Palestinians. Egypt administered the Gaza Strip in which one hundred fifty thousand Palestinians lived, but tightly controlled Palestinian political and military activity.

Searching for a foreign policy victory to defuse criticism from the Iraqi and Syrian regimes, Nasser believed that a demand for a withdrawal of UNEF troops in Gaza would suffice to put both Israeli and Arab critics in their places. Withdrawal of UNEF forces from Gaza would clarify Egypt's role as a sovereign power and warn Israel against military moves against Syria, yet would not force Nasser into a conflict that he did not believe his army was ready to fight. Unexpectedly, UN Secretary General U Thant removed the UNEF not only from Gaza but also from Sharm al-Shaikh on the southern coast of the Sinai Peninsula, thereby placing Israeli navigation to the port of Eilat once more under the direct control of Nasser. Nasser invoked a blockade of Eilat and Israel launched a preemptive war that shattered the air forces of the surrounding Arab states, and then occupied the Sinai Peninsula up to the Suez Canal once again as well as the West Bank of the Jordan and the Golan Heights on the Syrian border.

The basis of the Nasser regime was shattered, and Egypt took no major new initiatives domestically or internationally as long as Nasser lived. Paradoxically, however, Nasser may have been more popular in the last three years of his life than ever before. In a dramatic television speech broadcast on June 9, 1967, Nasser submitted his resignation publicly. Nasser said he intended to place the presidency in the hands of Zakaria Muhieddin who, although he was a Free Officer, was widely perceived as being right-wing and pro-American. Demonstrations, partly planned but increasingly spontaneous, broke out demanding that Nasser remain in power. Hundreds of thousands and perhaps millions of Egyptians participated. Nasser himself remained the vessel of popular hopes and aspirations. Nasser's closest associates in the revolution, however, including Field Marshall Abd al-Hakim Amer, who not only commanded the armies but was responsible for preparations for war, were humiliated. Amer committed suicide shortly afterward.

Nasser remained in power, but the years until 1970 were largely a holding operation. At a meeting of Arab heads of state in Khartoum in August 1967, Egyptian intervention in Yemen was finally ended and a unified Arab stance in relation to Israel was formed. At Khartoum, Nasser was authorized to seek a political solution to the issues involved in the Arab-Israeli conflict as long as there was no negotiation or reconciliation with Israel, and no recognition thereof. Widely perceived as indicative of Arab intransigence, the Khartoum declaration did suggest that a political solution was necessary and, when coupled with an evaluation of Nasser's speeches of the period, suggests the possibility of a prearranged solution with Israel emerging as a result of talks between the United States and the Soviet Union.

United Nations Security Council Resolution 242, calling for the exchange of land for peace, was approved in November 1967. It was accepted by Nasser and moved generally in the directions he had envisaged. He even accepted the English text despite its ambiguities over how much of the territory occupied by Israel would be returned and despite its reference to Palestinians only as refugees. Nasser accepted the mission of UN special correspondent Gunnar Jarring on behalf of the United Nations to try to prearrange peace, and held discussions with representatives of the Soviet Union and the United States which, as formally presented by U.S. Secretary of State William Rogers, was quite close to the peace agreement signed a decade later by Anwar al-Sadat and Menachem Begin.

Domestically, the regime was rocked by several crises, notably the mass demonstrations of workers and students protesting the light treatment meted out to those responsible for the disastrous war and the failure of the regime to advance further in the direction of redistribution. Increasingly, however, Nasser's attention was drawn once more to the international arena, where the effects of the 1967 defeat were most salient in the renewed occupation of Egyptian soil less than fifteen years after the British had been forced out. The issue of the Palestinians became key to a successful resolution of the effects of the war from Nasser's viewpoint. In 1969, Nasser negotiated the Cairo Agreement, which allowed the Palestine Liberation Organization led by Yasser Arafat* autonomy in the refugee camps. In September 1970, although he was ill and tired, Nasser also played a role in ending the battles between Jordan's King Hussein ibn Talal* and the Palestinians in Jordan. Nasser negotiated an end to the Jordanian blood-letting at a meeting of Arab heads of state that began September 22. On September 27, 1970 at 10 P.M. Arafat and Hussein signed an agreement to end the Black September. Shortly thereafter, Nasser, who had had heart attacks earlier, complained of chest pains. On September 28, 1970, at 6:15 P.M., Nasser died as a result of a massive heart attack.

In *The Philosophy of the Revolution*, Nasser set out an essentially populist and radical egalitarian social agenda coupled with an assertion that newly independent states of North Africa and the Middle East could readily overcome the legacy of borders drawn during the colonial era. The brotherhood of the Arab peoples was, in Nasser's view, a fundamental reality, while the state structures of the region were evanescent. During Nasser's lifetime, and given the remarkable record of his success in the first decade after coming to power, Nasser and Nasserism seemed on the verge of recreating the Middle East in the image of Arab unity and Arab socialism. In retrospect, however, Nasser and Nasserism as expressed in *The Philosophy of the Revolution* seem less like a blueprint for revolution or even for Arab nationalism than like a series of astute but fundamentally incoherent improvisations applied domestically and internationally. The institutional antagonisms between states and the national identities based on local communities remain like the rocks on which the enchanting vision of a single Arab ship of state under the captaincy of Nasser irrevocably foundered.

BIBLIOGRAPHY

Work by Nasser:

The Philosophy of the Revolution: Egypt's Liberation. Washington, D.C.: Public Affairs Press, 1955.

Other Works:

Abdel Fadil, Mahmoud. *Development, Income Distribution, and Social Change in Rural Egypt*. Cambridge: Cambridge University Press, 1975.
———. *The Political Economy of Nasserism*. Cambridge: Cambridge University Press, 1980.
Abdel Malik, Anouar. *Egypt: Military Society*. New York: Vintage, 1973.
Baker, Raymond. *Egypt's Uncertain Revolution under Nasser and Sadat*. Cambridge, Mass.: Harvard University Press, 1978.
Harik, Ilya. *The Political Mobilization of Peasants*. Bloomington, Ind.: Indiana University Press, 1974.
Kerr, Malcolm. *The Arab Cold War: Gamal Abd al-Nasir and his Rivals*. (3d ed.) London: Oxford University Press, 1971.
Lacouture, Jean. *Nasser*. New York: Alfred Knopf, 1973.

Vatikiotis, P. J. (ed.). *Egypt since the Revolution*. New York: Praeger, 1968.
Waterbury, John. *The Egypt of Nasser and Sadat: The Political Economy of Two Regimes*.
    Princeton: Princeton University Press, 1983.

                                                                    ELLIS GOLDBERG

JAFAR MOHAMMED NIMEIRI (1930–   ) ruled the Sudan longer than any
other leader since the country's independence in 1956, but the impact of his rule
has been entirely negative. One of the least qualified of all Sudanese leaders in
terms of intellect, education, and political experience, Nimeiri left his country
poorer, less productive, and more divided after his sixteen-year rule than at any
time in its modern history.

    In early 1989 the Sudan's external debt was estimated at twelve billion dollars
and the country was unable to meet debt-service payments. This crippling debt
was accompanied by a lowered standard of living, shortages and higher prices
on essential commodities, and general economic stagnation. Much of the economic crisis the Sudan faced in the mid- and late 1980s resulted from the heavy,
uncontrolled borrowing carried out by Nimeiri in the mid–1970s to finance
development projects. Many of the projects remained unproductive in the 1980s,
and some of the borrowed money disappeared into the pockets of corrupt government officials. Both the civil and the military service were so often purged
and so demoralized by corruption at the top that they ceased to perform in the
years following independence.

    Most injurious of all the harm done the Sudan by Nimeiri was the renewed
outbreak of civil war in the south. The greatest achievement of the Nimeiri era
came early in the regime with the attainment in March 1972 of the Addis Ababa
Accord, ending the country's seventeen-year civil war. Nimeiri squandered the
goodwill he and his colleagues had achieved with the southern Sudanese, broke
the promises he had made to the south, and, even after he saw war break out
again in early 1983, flaunted his indifference to southern sensitivities by his
adoption of an Islamic code in September of that year—an act that made reconciliation impossible.

    Nothing in Nimeiri's background foreshadowed his future preeminance in
government. He was born in 1930 in Omdurman, the old capital of the Sudan.
Nimeiri's family were Dongolawi, one of the major riverine tribes of the northern
Sudan (the tribe of the Mahdi—the leader of the Sudan's religious-nationalist
uprising in the nineteenth century), and one of the handful of tribes that had
traditionally supplied central political leaders. In a culture where one's family
and background are well known and important, Nimeiri came from an obscure
family with no previous background at the high levels of government. Fortunately
for him, the importance of family and tribal background had diminished considerably by the time he came to power.

    Nimeiri attended the Al Hijra Elementary School in Omdurman and the Wad
Medani Government School, where he was known as a fine athlete who was
active in swimming and soccer. He attended what is regarded as the finest

secondary school in the country, Hantoub, and following that, in 1949, entered the Military College, from which he was graduated in 1952 as a second lieutenant. He served in the Western Command, in Juba (southern Sudan) and served a tour of duty in Cyprus and West Germany. He studied at the United States Army Staff College in Fort Leavenworth, Kansas, in 1964–1965. He was posted to Gedaref in the east, and Torit in the south. At the time of the May 1969 coup he was in command of the infantry school in Gebeit in eastern Sudan.

Nimeiri was an easygoing, popular officer best known for his skill at soccer. Although in later years he attempted to portray himself as having been a fine scholar and a devout Muslim during his years as a student and a young officer, officers and others who knew him then agree that he was an indifferent student and showed no signs of being especially devout.

Nimeiri came to power by virtue of being the senior officer in a group that carried out the successful coup d'état on May 25, 1969, against an increasingly unpopular and ineffective democratic government. Although a larger group of officers—calling themselves the Free Officers in conscious imitation of Gamal Abdul Nasser's* group in Egypt—had been meeting secretly for some years, this group had decided in April 1969 not to go ahead at that time with the coup they had been planning against the strife-ridden parliamentary government that had come to power in 1965. A small group of officers within the Free Officers movement left the April meeting determined to move on their own. Three members of this group were in command of troops—Khalid Hassan Abbas led a tank corps, and Abu al Gasim Mohammed Ibrahim and Zein al Abdin Mohammed Ahmad led paratrooper units. Within this small group of young majors, Nimeiri was the only lieutenant colonel, and it was naturally assumed that he would assume the chairmanship of the Revolutionary Command Council (RCC) after the easy success of the coup.

During the first two and a half years of the new regime, Nimeiri was no more than the first among equals. In fact, some insiders in the regime regarded him, despite his position as chairman of the RCC, as distinctly inferior in power within the council to the brilliant, if enigmatic, Farouk Osman Hamadallah, or the two young military strongmen, Abu al Gasim Mohammad Ibrahim and Khalid Hassan Abbas. Nimeiri—and all the young officers of the RCC—were influenced by the one nonmilitary member of the RCC, Babikir Awadallah, a well-known and respected jurist, who had been brought into the planning for the coup before it occurred and who had been made prime minister and foreign minister upon its success. During the first two and a half years the new government was distinctly pro-Soviet in its foreign policy and directed toward nationalization and other moderately socialist ventures in domestic policies.

In July 1971, three members of the RCC who had been purged in 1970 led an abortive coup d'état that was strongly supported by the Sudanese Communist Party (which had been an ally of the new government at its inception in 1969). It was only after this three-day coup attempt that Nimeiri emerged as ruler of the Sudan and began a series of shrewd maneuvers that would propel him into a position of absolute power.

Interestingly, it was not Nimeiri who suggested that, following the abortive coup, the RCC should be disbanded and that he assume the presidency. It was Khalid Hassan Abbas, grief-stricken over the death of his younger brother during the coup attempt, who made the suggestion, and it was approved with very little discussion. A referendum was held, with Nimeiri the only candidate for the presidency; to no one's surprise, he won. This was the beginning of the end of the power of his colleagues from the now-defunct RCC. Slowly, over a period of four years, Nimeiri managed to strip away the power of the five of the six former RCC members who were still alive (three RCC members, Hashim al Atta, Babikir al Nur, and Farouk Osman Hamadallah had been purged from the RCC in 1970 and had led the July 1971 coup, following which they had been executed). By 1975 all but Abu al Gasim Mohammed Ibrahim had left the government under less than amicable conditions; some of the RCC members had been brought back into the government, but in distinctly subservient positions.

The greatest achievement of the seventeen years that Nimeiri was in office was unquestionably the March 1972 Addis Ababa Accord, ending the seventeen-year civil war. The new government had come to power promising a new approach to the southern conflict, and achieved the accord by using an astute mixture of military force and political concessions. No one would have imagined, during the heady days following this extraordinary achievement, that war would break out again more threateningly than ever only eleven years later.

Nimeiri's shrewdness in managing power within the government, first demonstrated by the way he defanged his former colleagues (by pushing them into a position where they resigned in anger), served him well in the years following his accession to the presidency in 1972. He was unhampered by the 1973 constitution, which granted him broad powers and set up a Parliament that was rarely more than a rubber stamp. Nimeiri's technique consisted of bringing into the government potentially powerful individuals but balancing two or more of them against one another. In this way, for instance, he played off against one another such potent figures as his old RCC colleague, Abu al Gasim Mohammed Ibrahim (who continued to have a strong following in the army and among southerners), and Sadiq al-Mahdi,* scion of the Mahdi family and political leader of the important Ansar sect. Sadiq al-Mahdi had opposed the new government since its inception, had been mostly in exile since the government's violent showdown with the Ansar in 1971, and was the leader, from exile, of the bloody but unsuccessful coup and invasion attempt of July 1976. Following mediation by several individuals, Sadiq al-Mahdi and Nimeiri reached a reconciliation agreement in 1977, under which the Ansar leader was to return to the Sudan and join Nimeiri's tame political party, the Sudanese Socialist Union, in exchange for unpublished reforms. The reconciliation was a brilliant success for Nimeiri because it tarnished Sadiq al-Mahdi's reputation without bringing about any reforms. Nimeiri fostered the natural rivalry between Sadiq al-Mahdi and Abu al Gasim, so that the two could never work together. In 1978, Sadiq al-Mahdi opposed Nimeiri's support of Egyptian President Anwar al-Sadat's signing of the Camp David Accords, and used this issue as a pretext to leave the powerless slot he had been given in the political party.

By the mid-1970s, al-Nimeiri's internal power balancing had propelled him into a position of genuine dictatorship. From this time on, no one but Nimeiri had real power in Khartoum. Power could only be achieved and wielded through an individual's influence on or approval by Nimeiri. From 1972 until 1976, Nimeiri was much influenced by his brilliant but opportunistic foreign minister, Dr. Mansour Khalid, who had pushed Nimeiri in the direction of national unity and development as the themes of his presidency during those years.

It was also in the mid-1970s that Nimeiri's lack of deep political conviction began to become clear. Never a committed leftist, he nonetheless—like most of the officers of the RCC—had followed a vaguely "socialist" line between 1969 and 1971, much influenced by prominent members of the Sudanese Communist Party who had been brought into the cabinet. After the abortive communist coup in 1971, Nimeiri was understandably resentful of what he regarded as his betrayal by the Soviet Union, and he became a great deal less hostile toward the West than he had been in the early years. Pleased by American offers of aid in the rebuilding of the southern Sudan after the 1972 Addis Ababa Accord, Nimeiri restored diplomatic relations with the United States (which had been broken off at the time of the 1967 Arab-Israeli war), while maintaining at least nominally normal relations with the Soviet bloc.

In the late 1970s, however, Nimeiri began to move clearly to the right. He became openly hostile to the Soviet Union and most of its allies, and dropped any pretense at nonalignment. He went so far, in his courtship of the United States, as to offer the United States bases in the Sudan—an offer that took the United States by surprise and caused shock in the Sudan and the Arab world.

Nimeiri's personal popularity had sunk significantly by this time as well. From at least 1980 on, jokes constantly circulated in Khartoum about his ignorance, his corruption, and the ineffectiveness of his government. Nimeiri himself began to lose contact with political realities. The first sign of this was the publication in 1978, in France, of a book about Nimeiri to be distributed by all Sudanese embassies, a book that rewrote the recent history of the Sudan to glorify Nimeiri to such an extraordinary extent that it could not be distributed in the Sudan. In the same year, Nimeiri published a book entitled *The Islamic Way: Why?*, which was believed to have been written by one of his aides. Nimeiri purged the last political figure with any possible following of his own—his old RCC colleague, Abu al Gashim Mohammed Ibrahim—in 1979.

There were a few signs, other than his book, of Nimeiri's coming religious revival, but some observers believe that his concern over his coronary artery deterioration, diagnosed by physicians at Walter Reed U.S. Army Hospital in Washington, D.C., prompted a kind of conversion experience in which Nimeiri rediscovered his Islamic roots. In September 1983, Nimeiri enacted a sweeping

Islamic code that abrogated tax laws, turned to Islam as the source of legislation, and called for traditional Islamic punishments. Soon even non-Muslims were sentenced to hand amputation for theft and flogging for possession of alcohol in Khartoum. Nimeiri's closest external allies, Egypt and the United States, were appalled, and tried to distance themselves from his regime. Other observers suggested that, having looked to the left for guidance and then to the right, Nimeiri had nowhere to look for new support but heavenward. Nimeiri's close new advisers were obscure Islamic mystics, and government ministers were ordered to lead their employees in daily prayers—or face dismissal. Even more ominous for the future of the Sudan was the renewed rebellion in the south, which had recommenced in early 1983 as a result of southern dissatisfaction with Nimeiri's southern policies and took on new strength with the enactment of the new Islamic code. Nimeiri seemed not to care, although the achievement of the 1972 reconciliation with the southerners had once been the proudest achievement of his government.

Even while the political situation reached this new low, the Sudanese economy was plummeting to a disastrous level. The drain of the expenditure on the war in the south and the loss of tax revenues because of the new Islamic code, coupled with high oil prices following the second oil shock of 1979 and the mounting external debt that was now coming to light—all these factors were fueling inflation and shortages that angered a population already disenchanted by Nimeiri's capricious policies. He had supported Egypt's peacemaking with Israel to the extent that the Sudan had followed Egypt into isolation in the Arab world, and this had been quite unpopular. His sudden and harsh enactment of Islamic law had alienated even devout Muslims, who felt it was wrongly applied.

Nimeiri had done everything within his considerable power to make sure that he was not removed from power by the force that had brought him to power: the army. He had alternatively purged and placated the ranking officers. He had established "military corporations" for import-export, retailing, and other services; these entities provided services for the military that were unavailable to the general population and provided extra income for ranking officers. Observers believed them to be simply a systematic means of corrupting the military. Officers who opposed his policies were purged.

It had not been possible, however, to remove all power from the army, which was still Nimeiri's source of power; nor was Nimeiri able to know the depth of resentment within the army caused by his treatment of it. On April 6, 1985, while Nimeiri was traveling outside the Sudan, his widely respected minister of defense, General Abdel Rahman Siwar al Dhahab, took power in the face of mounting strikes and massive demonstrations that had been prompted by the economic squeeze. The coup that toppled Nimeiri was far more than a palace coup; it was a change of government led by a conservative general of great integrity, who had taken power at the prompting of a broad-based coalition of Sudanese professionals. General Siwar al Dhahab ruled in conjunction with a civilian cabinet and, a little over a year after removing Nimeiri from power, he handed the power over to an elected civilian government.

Nimeiri was in Cairo when he learned of the coup. He ordered his plane to fly to Khartoum, but the pilot informed him that Sudanese air space was closed at government decree. The former president remains in Cairo, despite efforts by the transitional government and the successor democratic regime to get Egypt to return Nimeiri to Khartoum for trial. Many Nimeiri associates were imprisoned following public trials, including not only the very unpopular Dr. Bahauddin Mohammed Idris, who controlled access to Nimeiri for several years before his overthrow, but also the former RCC members (except for Abu al Gasim Hashim, who is in poor health, and Babikir Awadallah, who has lived in Cairo since leaving the government in the early 1970s).

The shadow of a military coup hangs heavily over the Sudanese democratic regime that was installed in 1986. Repeating the mistakes of the democratic governments of 1956–1958 and 1965–1969, the new government under Prime Minister Sadiq al-Mahdi seems to have learned nothing during the long years of the Nimeiri period. The Sudanese themselves expect that the military will step in as soon as it recovers from the trauma of its last adventure in politics, and they hope that this time their military rulers will actually attain the goals that have presumably motivated both previous military governments: efficient and effective leadership, economic stability, and an end to the bloody and futile civil war.

BIBLIOGRAPHY

Works by Nimeiri:

The Islamic Way: Why? Khartoum: Government Press, 1978.
The Islamic Way: How? Khartoum: Government Press, 1982.

Other Works:

Bechtold, Peter K. *Politics in Sudan: Parliamentary and Military Rule in an Emerging African Nation*. New York: Praeger, 1976.
Beshir, M. O. *Revolution and Nationalism in Sudan*. London: Rex-Collins, 1974.
History of the Sudan: Once upon a Time . . . Nimeiri. Tournai, Belgium: Afrique Biblio Club (Paris), 1978.
Holt, P. M., and M. W. Daly. *The History of the Sudan*. London: Weidenfeld and Nicolson, 1979.
Warburg, Gabriel. *Islam, Nationalism and Communism in a Traditional Society: The Case of the Sudan*. London: Frank Cass and Co., 1978.

SALLY ANN BAYNARD

O

TURGUT OZAL (1927–). The military coup of September 12, 1980, ushered in significant new developments in Turkish politics. Turgut Ozal's rise to national political leadership was one of these developments. A relatively unknown person who had spent most of his adult life in various government jobs as a technocrat, Ozal became the dominant civilian politician in Turkey during the 1980s. First as deputy prime minister in charge of economic affairs under military rule, and later as prime minister during the transition to democracy, Ozal gained international recognition for his efforts to restructure Turkey's economy. At the same time, Ozal played a key role in the redemocratization of the Turkish political system following the military's decision to hand power back to the civilians. Ozal also accomplished a goal that had eluded several other prominent Turkish politicians in the past: He formed a new political party that broke the near-monopoly that Turkey's two dominant parties had enjoyed during nearly three decades of electoral politics. In the area of foreign policy, Ozal's most important contributions concerned his efforts to achieve rapprochement with Greece, to gain full membership for Turkey in the European Community, and to give priority to economic factors in Turkey's regional and international relations.

Ozal is a native of Malatya, a city in southeastern Turkey, where he was born on October 13, 1927; to parents of modest means. His father started out in life as an *imam* or religious teacher. Following the establishment of the modern Turkish republic, he became a teacher in Turkey's secular school system. Later, he joined the state-owned Turkish Agricultural Bank, a job that required frequent moves to various provincial cities for the Ozal family. Ozal's mother was also a teacher. Ozal graduated from Instanbul's Technical University in 1950 with a degree in electrical engineering. After joining the Electrical Power Survey Administration (EPSA) in Ankara, he went to the United States in 1952 to study economics and engineering. Upon his return to Turkey in 1953, Ozal participated in several major hydraulic power station and electrification projects, which were carried out under the EPSA's supervision. While working at the EPSA, Ozal held a part-time teaching position at the engineering faculty of the Middle East Technical University in Ankara. In the aftermath of the 1960 military coup, Ozal joined a group of young technocrats and social scientists in setting up Turkey's first State Planning Organization (SPO).

During the 1960s and 1970s, Ozal's career benefited substantially from his position as a protégé of Suleyman Demirel,* leader of the Justice Party. Demirel had been Ozal's boss at the EPSA, and the two men had worked together in the State Planning Organization. When Demirel became prime minister in 1965, he appointed Ozal as his special technical adviser. Two years later, Ozal was put in charge of the SPO by the Demirel government. When Demirel launched his economic stabilization program in 1970, which included a major devaluation of the Turkish lira, Ozal was one of his key policy advisers. Turgut Ozal remained at the head of the SPO until the 1971 military intervention that ousted Prime Minister Demirel from office. Subsequently, Ozal went to work for the World Bank in Washington, D.C., where he spent two years as a special projects adviser and senior economist. Upon his return to Turkey, he successively served as the managing director of two large private business conglomerates—Sabanci Holding and Asil Celik—and a major employers' association. In 1977, Ozal made his first attempt to become involved in national politics. He became a candidate for the parliament from the Islamic fundamentalist National Salvation Party (NSP) in Izmir. His younger brother, Korkut, held a prominent position in the NSP's leadership ranks—a factor that influenced Ozal's decision to join the party. However, the NSP did poorly in Izmir, and Ozal failed in his bid for a parliamentary seat.

Following his return to power in late 1979 at the head of a minority government, Prime Minister Demirel again gave a key role to Ozal in economic policy-making. Ozal's appointment as undersecretary of the State Planning Organization came at a time when Turkey was in the throes of a severe political and economic crisis. While political terrorism and violence claimed an ever-increasing number of victims, the Turkish economy suffered from the effects of spiralling inflation, acute trade imbalances, rising foreign debt, growing unemployment, and labor unrest. Under Demirel's instructions and with the guidance of the International Monetary Fund, Ozal unveiled a major austerity and reform package in January 1980. Known as the January 24 Measures, Ozal's plan lay the foundations for the stabilization of the Turkish economy in the early 1980s.

The military coup of September 12, 1980, was a turning point in Ozal's career. Following the coup, General Kenan Evren's military administration asked Ozal to remain in charge of the economy as deputy prime minister. Ozal accepted the offer and continued to implement the economic austerity and reform measures that he had begun under Demirel. He resigned from his post in July 1982 in the wake of a financial scandal that shook the country's banking sector. When General Evren's military rule moved toward limited political liberalization by removing some of the restrictions on electoral politics, Ozal formed his own political organization, the Motherland Party (MP), in May 1983. Although no fewer than fifteen parties were set up, the armed forces permitted only three parties, including Ozal's, to participate in the parliamentary elections.

Ozal's second venture in politics was far more successful than his first. The 1983 elections, which were held under less than normal democratic circumstances, resulted in an upset victory for Ozal's MP while the military's favorite, the Nationalist Democracy Party, suffered a major electoral defeat. After becoming prime minister, Ozal assumed a central role in Turkey's transition from military rule to democracy. This process made considerable headway through two nationwide referendums, a parliamentary election, and a contest for local elective posts. Unlike those of 1983, the early elections that Ozal called in 1987 were conducted with the full participation of Turkey's main political forces. Despite a decline in its votes, the MP retained its parliamentary majority and Ozal returned to a second term as prime minister. By the end of 1988, he had been in office continuously for five years—a feat that was accomplished by only two other political leaders in postwar Turkish politics, namely, Adnan Menderes* and Suleyman Demirel.

However, Ozal's importance stems less from his durability in government than from his role as a leader who carried out significant changes in Turkey's economic and political life. In the realm of economics, these changes centered on two principal objectives: first, to get Turkey out of the economic paralysis it faced in the late 1970s, and second, to catch up with advanced industrial economies of the West through an ambitious modernization program. Ozal achieved remarkable success in normalizing the country's deteriorating economic and financial conditions. The stabilization program of 1980 was primarily designed to check the three-digit inflation rate, improve the foreign-exchange deficit, and end the shortages of basic consumer goods. Ozal's austerity measures, combined with his commitment to a more realistic exchange-rate policy, produced almost immediate results: Inflation began to recede, shortages were abated, and the atmosphere of imminent economic collapse dissipated.

After turning the economic tide, Ozal sought to find a solution to Turkey's economic malaise through a series of reforms. The most significant of these concerned changes in the country's trade regime. In addition to the abolishment of foreign-exchange controls, there was a major policy switch from import substitution to export promotion. While the government began a massive export drive by providing various incentives and subsidies to the exporters, it also proceeded to lift the restrictions on imports. Turkey's state-owned economic enterprises (SESs) constituted another major area of reform. To increase their efficiency and competitiveness, Ozal trimmed the state subsidies to the SESs and permitted them to raise the prices of their products through periodic adjustments to the prevailing market conditions. Finally, Ozal introduced measures that represented marked departures from established practices: New laws created a more favorable environment for foreign investment, privatization schemes opened up the possibility of an eventual transfer of state-owned industries and public works to private shareholders, and the elimination of excessive bureaucratic controls and procedures prepared a favorable environment for the operation of a market economy.

Several factors contributed to Ozal's achievements in restoring normalcy to the Turkish economy and in launching his ambitious economic-modernization program. First, the near collapse of the country's economy in the late 1970s created a suitable milieu for economic and financial reforms. The poor performances of the Demirel and Ecevit governments in managing the economy between 1974 and 1980 discredited both import substitution and statism as effective strategies of economic growth. Many people, especially among the influential business and military elites, were convinced of the need for a new approach to the country's economic plight. Second, save for the first eight months of 1980, Ozal implemented the initial phase of his stabilization program under an authoritarian military regime. The absence of possible opposition from political and social forces—left-wing parties, radical trade unions, students, and intelligentsia—provided him with considerable leeway in economic policy-making. Finally, international developments worked in Ozal's favor. The downfall of Shah Mohammad Reza Pahlavi* in Iran and the Soviet invasion of Afghanistan reinforced Western strategic concerns about Turkey's crisis. As a result, Ozal's stabilization and reform measures received substantial financial backing from Turkey's Western allies and from the international agencies. At the same time, an unforeseen regional development, namely the outbreak of the Gulf war, came as a boon to Turkey's economic recovery since both countries involved became heavily dependent on Turkish exports.

The performance of the Turkish economy during the early 1980s reflected the impact of the changes that were implemented under Ozal's leadership. Following its recovery, the economy experienced a relatively high growth rate. The most striking results were achieved in the promotion of exports, which more than tripled between 1980 and 1987. Although the Middle Eastern markets, especially Iran and Iraq, accounted for a significant part of this trend, Turkey's exports to the OECD (Organization for Economic Cooperation and Development) countries also grew at the remarkable annual rate of 20.2 percent between 1980 and 1985. Ozal's efforts to modernize and privatize the public sector had less striking but nevertheless significant results: The cutback of subsidies and the lifting of price ceilings forced the SESs to be more competitive, preparations were started to transfer some of the SESs to the private sector, and the bonds of several large-scale state properties—including the Bosporus Bridge in Istanbul—were sold to private shareholders. In general, the transformation of the country's economic infrastructure, financial institutions, and links with the world economy progressed at a rapid pace.

Despite these remarkable changes, Ozal's economic modernization program ran into serious problems in the second half of the decade. Beginning in 1985–1986, Turkey was once again faced with a runaway inflation which reached an annual rate estimated to be around 80 percent in 1988. The reemergence of inflation was primarily due to political considerations: Government expenditures, particularly those related to political patronage-oriented projects, rose sharply as Ozal sought to maintain his popular support in electoral contests. Although the Turkish economy continued to grow at an impressive rate and the country's export performance maintained its momentum, the steep inflation rate created widespread disillusionment in Ozal's management of the economy. Fixed income groups, retired people, and industrial workers whose salaries had been frozen were among the hardest hit by the spiralling inflation rate. Furthermore, the economic policies pursued by the governing Motherland Party worsened the gap between the rich and the poor as the latter experienced a drastic decline in their standard of living and real income. Although Ozal retained the confidence of the international financial community by fulfilling Turkey's external debt-servicing requirements, the country faced a growing debt burden. Ozal's problems in managing the economy were compounded by the transition from authoritarian rule and the reemergence of competitive politics. Political liberalization provided wider scope for opposition to Ozal's policies from rival political parties and organized interest groups.

Turgut Ozal's impact on Turkish politics was no less significant than his influence on Turkey's economy. He entered electoral politics in 1983 largely on the basis of his record as a technocrat and an economic policymaker, but in the course of the next few years, he emerged as a skillful politician and one of the most powerful leaders of modern Turkey. Turkey's return to democracy after 1983 was gradual, and the transition process was controlled by the military. Nevertheless, once the initial political liberalization began, Ozal assumed a central role in the restoration of democratic institutions and processes. Ozal's transition strategy gave primacy to three factors. First, he sought to establish a working relationship with the military. Although Ozal had worked as the military regime's "economic czar" from 1980 through 1982, the top military command resented his decision to form his own political party in 1983. However, Ozal managed to regain the officers' trust by preserving their control in policy-making on issues related to national security and by supporting the military against its critics over allegations of human rights violations.

Second, Ozal's transition strategy was based on gradually legitimizing the supremacy of civilian control in politics through elections and referendums. One of his first moves after coming to power was to hold local elections in early 1984. This was a critical step in the civilianization of the state apparatus, since most of the elected mayors and local officials had been replaced by retired military men following the 1980 coup. After 1984, the Turkish voters went to the polls in an early parliamentary election in 1987 and two referendums in 1987 and 1988. Ozal's main objectives in holding frequent electoral contests—which the referendums inevitably became—were to legitimize his own role in Turkish politics and to consolidate the MP's position as the leading party of the center-right. However, this strategy also included the legitimization of the institutions of electoral competition, interest representation, and executive accountability—

all of which contributed significantly to the redemocratization of Turkish politics in the 1980s.

The third component of Ozal's strategy was to organize a new political party that would be responsive to the new realities of Turkey's social and political life in the 1980s and beyond. His plan for this new political force was based on the premise that the majority of the electorate had become disillusioned with the traditional political parties and their leadership. Ozal believed that a new political organization, which shunned close identification with formal ideologies and sought to represent the interests of a broad social coalition of middle-class voters, would appeal to several different constituencies of Turkey's pre–1980 party system. These included the supporters of the center-right Justice Party (JP), the center-left Republican People's Party (RPP), the far-right Nationalist Action Party (NAP), and the Islamic fundamentalist National Salvation Party (NSP). The Motherland Party (MP) which Ozal launched in 1983 initially fulfilled his expectations. In the 1983 parliamentary elections the MP received the broad support of voters who had previously backed rival, and in some cases, ideologically opposing parties. In this respect, Ozal was the architect of a major realignment in Turkish party politics. The emergence of a political force that attracted new cadres and elites into its organizational ranks and received the support of a broad-based founding coalition contributed significantly to the democratization of the Turkish political system. Furthermore, by finishing first in several national and local electoral contests between 1983 and 1987, Ozal's MP brought about another important change in Turkish politics. Until 1980, newly formed parties in Turkey had consistently failed to become major players in party politics due to the strength of the two-party system. The MP's electoral successes in the 1980s marked a radical departure from this long-established trend of Turkish democracy.

Although Ozal remained the dominant personality of Turkish politics, developments in the late 1980s posed potentially serious challenges to his leadership. The problems of the Turkish economy, and especially the government's inability to check the rise of inflation, was an important factor in Ozal's declining electoral popularity. At the same time, Ozal continued to face a strong challenge from Demirel and his new True Path Party (TPP) for control of the center-right in Turkish politics. Demirel waged a relentless campaign against his former protégé, whom he accused of opportunism. Ozal's governing MP also encountered an increasingly radical opposition from the center-left Social Democracy Party (SODEP), which emerged as the second strongest political force in the party system. Finally, there were increasing signs of growing factionalism within Ozal's own MP. By 1987, a factional coalition of former NAP and NSP supporters appeared to have captured most of the MP's organizational network. This Islamic right-wing faction began to challenge Ozal on various policies while Ozal tried to maintain an intraparty balancing act by supporting the MP's liberal faction.

Ozal's bold leadership style and his efforts to integrate Turkey more fully into the world economy led to several important developments in Turkey's foreign relations during the 1980s. After years of conflictual relations, Turkey and Greece appeared to be headed for a rapprochement following a historic meeting between Ozal and the Greek Prime Minister Andreas Papandreou in early 1988. Ozal personally took the initiative in creating a favorable political atmosphere for a new era in Greek-Turkish relations. Despite the misgivings expressed by the opposition parties and the press in Turkey, he made several symbolic gestures in favor of Greece, and he became the first Turkish statesman to visit Athens in almost a quarter of a century. Although the major problems between two neighboring NATO states over Cyprus and the Aegean remained unresolved, the atmosphere of Greek-Turkish relations took a turn for the better in the late 1980s. In 1987, Ozal took another bold step in foreign policy when Turkey made a formal application to join the European Community (EC). His decision ended the long period of procrastination by the successive Ankara governments concerning the merits of Turkey's membership in the community. While the chances of Turkey joining the EC in the very near future seemed small, Ozal's initiative was an important signal that highlighted Turkey's commitment to Western Europe in terms of its long-term economic and political expectations. However, Ozal's tenure in office also witnessed a substantial expansion of Turkey's economic ties with the Middle East. While the export of Turkish manufactured goods to the Middle Eastern markets grew at a rapid pace, there was also a significant rise of banking and investment activities by the multilateral Islamic institutions in Turkey. Although Turkey did not yet emerge as the most important bridge between Europe and the Middle East in international economic relations—a goal that is highly valued by Ozal—his administration made significant progress toward attaining it.

BIBLIOGRAPHY

Work by Ozal:

"Turkey's Path to Freedom and Democracy." *Washington Quarterly* 10 (Autumn 1987):
    161–165.

Other works:

Aures, R., and T. C. Thompson. *Turkey: A New Era*. London: Longwood Publishing
    Group for Euromoney, 1984.
Harris, George S. *Turkey: Coping with Crisis*. Boulder, Colo.: Westview, 1985.
Heper, Metin, and Ahmet Evin (eds.). *State, Democracy and the Military: Turkey in the
    1980s*. Berlin and New York: Walter de Gruyer, 1988.
Mackenzie, Kenneth. *Turkey in Transition: The West's Neglected Ally*. London: Institute
    for European Defense and Strategic Studies, 1984.
Nas, Tevfik F., and Mehmet Odekon (eds.). *Liberalization and the Turkish Economy*.
    Westport, Conn.: Greenwood, 1988.
Rustow, Dankwart A. *Turkey: America's Forgotten Ally*. New York: Council on Foreign
    Relations, 1987.

                                                          SABRI SAYARI

P

SHIMON PERES (1923–) became Israel's eighth prime minister in 1984 after a career dedicated to public service. In addition to serving as prime minister he has held several other prominent government positions including defense minister, foreign minister, and finance minister. He was a protégé to David Ben-Gurion,* who appointed him director general of the Ministry of Defense. Peres rose through the ranks of the Labor Party, and in 1977 became the party's chairman and its nominee for prime minister in the *Knesset* (Parliament) elections of 1977, 1981, 1984, and 1988. He has been active in his pursuit of a negotiated settlement to the Arab-Israeli conflict, and is an advocate of territorial compromise in exchange for peace between Israel, the Arab states, and the Palestinians.

Shimon Peres (formerly Persky) was born August 1, 1923, in the town of Vishneva, Poland. Vishneva provided a thoroughly Jewish environment for Peres to mature in, from its homogeneous population to the schools in which the language of instruction was Hebrew. His parents observed Jewish laws and customs, and his grandfather encouraged Peres's interest in Judaism. This interest ultimately waned as he became more involved in Zionist activities. During his youth Peres devoted considerable amounts of time and energy to literature, especially the reading and writing of poetry.

The Zionist movement was active in Vishneva, and the Persky family was among those who sought to emigrate to Palestine. Because of British restrictions and the financial burdens associated with immigration, Yitzhak Persky emigrated to Palestine in 1931, leaving his wife and two sons behind. The family was reunited in Palestine two years later when Shimon Peres was ten years old.

Several youth movements representing differing ideologies were active in Vishneva. Shimon became involved in the largest of the movements, Hashomer Hatzair (Young Guard), and later joined Hanoar Haoved (Working Youth), which introduced him to the *kibbutz* (collective settlement) as a way of life. It was within these groups in Vishneva that Shimon Peres began to emerge as a leader. He utilized his verbal and written communication skills along with his talents as an able administrator and organizer to build an impressive reputation, which gained him recognition among leaders in the Zionist movement in Vishneva and later in Palestine. These included prominent Zionist figures such as David Ben-Gurion, Levi Eshkol,* Berl Katznelson, and Pinhas Lavon, all of whom were instrumental in Peres's advancement through the ranks of the political establishment in later years both in the Yishuv (the Jewish community and institutions in Palestine during the British Mandate) and the State of Israel.

By 1941, Peres had become a leader in the kibbutz movement in Palestine, and he continued his efforts within Hanoar Haoved to increase the size and organizational activities of the movement. He advocated the diversification of economic activity of the kibbutzim, outside of the traditional realm of agriculture, and into modern industrial production. This generated substantial opposition by many ideological purists, who believed that the concept of the kibbutz should be based solely on an agrarian society. In 1942, Peres joined Kibbutz Alumot (located in the Galilee region of northern Palestine) and he remained a member until 1957. It was here that Levi Eshkol approached Peres with an offer to work in the kibbutz movement's secretariat in Tel Aviv. Peres was appointed chairman of the Organization Department, which gave him the responsibility of forming new branches and increasing membership.

Peres was married to Sonya Gelman at Kibbutz Alumot on May 1, 1945. A special bond appeared to exist between them, and they were committed to each other through love, marriage, and friendship. They frequently turned to each other for advice and support during later and difficult periods in their lives.

Peres's military career began in the Haganah, the clandestine defense force of the Yishuv. He rose to the rank of position commander by his late teens, and in 1947, at the age of twenty-four, he accepted Levi Eshkol's offer to serve as director of manpower. Peres's responsibilities were far greater than his title would suggest. He was very active in the procurement and manufacture of arms for the Israel Defense Forces (IDF), the military forces of the newly proclaimed Jewish state, which was established on May 15, 1948. His successful efforts to develop and acquire arms both at home and abroad gained him recognition as one of the pioneers of Israel's defense industry. Peres viewed self-sufficiency in the area of weapons development and manufacture as an integral aspect of national independence, which would best provide for Israel's security and survival.

After Israel's War of Independence in 1949, Peres asked Prime Minister Ben-Gurion for a leave of absence to study abroad. Ben-Gurion granted the leave provided Peres continue his arms acquisition efforts in the United States, where he had chosen to study. Upon his arrival in New York in January 1950, Peres began lobbying the U.S. government for weapons. Due to the American embargo of arms sales to the Middle East, he was frustrated in his attempts to purchase weapons through official channels. Consequently he focused his efforts on raising funds from affluent Jews in the United States and Canada to finance his clandestine purchases of weapons on the international market.

Peres returned to Israel at the end of 1951, and in February 1952 he was appointed by Ben-Gurion to serve as deputy director general of the Defense Ministry. In October 1952, Peres replaced Zeev Schind as acting director general of the Defense Ministry. This swift promotion surprised few, who recognized Ben-Gurion's efforts to elevate several of his younger protégés to senior positions. Shortly after Peres's promotion, Moshe Dayan* was appointed to the position of chief of staff, a move that was opposed by the older generation of Mapai (Israel Workers Party) leadership, including Golda Meir* and Moshe Sharett. The older generation complained that Peres and Dayan often exercised authority beyond what their positions granted them. This was attributed to the special relationship they shared with Ben-Gurion, and the political protection that relationship afforded them.

During Ben-Gurion's tenure as prime minister between 1948 and 1963 (excluding 1954–1955, when Moshe Sharett held the post), Peres often acted on the "old man's" personal orders, which were known to few outside Ben-Gurion's inner circle. Ben-Gurion was a prophetic and visionary leader who relied on Peres's administrative and executive talents to translate his visions into reality. The range of Peres's operational activities was limited by the parameters of Ben-Gurion's vision. Peres was both openly criticized and quietly envied because of his relationship with Ben-Gurion. He frequently absorbed the brunt of criticism directed at him in lieu of Ben-Gurion or Moshe Dayan, who were generally immune from substantial personal criticism; Ben-Gurion due to his status as patriarch, and Dayan because of his recognition as a military hero.

As director general of the Defense Ministry, Peres continued his efforts to acquire high-quality weapons for the IDF. The geopolitical realities of the Middle East in 1955 led Peres to pursue close relations with Britain and France. Britain, France, and Israel shared the common political and strategic objective of limiting the growing power and influence of Egypt's Gamal Abdul Nasser.* Peres fostered the concept of a tripartite alliance against Nasser when he approached Britain and France for arms, and in 1956 he concluded purchases of major weapons systems from France including Mystère–4 aircraft. These efforts culminated in a coordinated military action against Egypt in November 1956. The IDF demonstrated its ability to integrate and coordinate its weaponry and manpower, and swiftly captured the Sinai Peninsula from Egyptian forces.

Peres spent much of his time fostering Franco-Israeli relations, and France remained Israel's primary supplier of major weapons systems until after the Six Day War of 1967. Peres generally conducted sensitive negotiations with French officials outside the channels of diplomacy, which often aggravated relations between Israel's Defense Ministry and its Foreign Ministry. Peres's efforts included getting France to provide Israel with an atomic reactor, which was located at Dimona and which became an integral part of the country's nuclear research and development efforts.

As director general of the Defense Ministry, Peres concluded arms deals and initiated sales of military equipment—both IDF surplus and arms manufactured in Israel—with states in Asia, Africa, and Latin America as well as Western Europe. These sales were important in the development of Israel's arms industry, which produces both for supply to the IDF and for export. Peres was instrumental in the creation of Bedek, which later came to be known as the Israel Aircraft Industries (IAI). In addition to military aircraft, Peres supported efforts to develop a variety of missile systems, combat seacraft, and civilian aircraft.

Peres's Knesset career began in 1959 when he was elected to Parliament as a member of the Mapai Party but continued to serve as deputy minister of defense. Peres was included in Ben-Gurion's cabinet, which gave him more of a role in policy debates, although the majority of his time was spent running the affairs of the Defense Ministry. He continued his efforts to expand and formalize the military-supply relationships with France and Britain and pursued closer relations with the United States.

In 1962, U.S. President John F. Kennedy's administration decided to sell the Hawk antiaircraft missile system to Israel, the first significant American sale of military equipment to Israel. More important, it was the beginning of the U.S.-Israeli military supply relationship, which continued to grow over the following years; the United States eventually (after 1967) became Israel's primary supplier. Peres concluded the deal for the Hawks, and met with President Kennedy during a trip to Washington, D.C., in April 1963.

Two months later, Ben-Gurion resigned and was replaced by Levi Eshkol as prime minister and minister of defense. Eshkol and Peres shared warm personal relations, and Peres agreed to remain in the government as deputy minister of defense. Tensions between the old guard and the young continued within Mapai, often producing caustic debate. Levi Eshkol, Golda Meir, and Pinhas Sapir controlled the four most important portfolios in the government: the premiership and the ministries of defense, foreign affairs, and finance. Peres, Dayan, and other disciples of Ben-Gurion were given more obscure and less influential positions.

Ben-Gurion's retirement from politics lasted only two years before he returned to the political arena in June 1965 as the leader of a new political party called Rafi (Israel's Workers' List). Ben-Gurion's decision to form the party resulted from several motivations, including his malevolence toward Eshkol and the old guard, and the poor treatment his followers were receiving. This was exacerbated by continuing problems from the Lavon affair of 1954, which pitted Pinhas Lavon against Ben-Gurion and their respective followers within Mapai against each other in a struggle over who should bear responsibility for a foreign policy and intelligence debacle that had taken place a decade earlier.

Peres resigned his position in the government to join Ben-Gurion and become secretary general of the new party. He managed the party's campaign efforts in the 1965 election, in a campaign that was characterized by frequent hostile attacks, many of which were directed at him. The Rafi Party won ten seats in the election of 1965. The government coalition did not include Rafi or any of its members. Ben-Gurion accepted the futility of his struggle with Mapai, and turned the leadership of Rafi over to Moshe Dayan. Ben-Gurion initially rejected the notion of a reunion with Mapai; however, Peres argued that Rafi had outlived its usefulness and that the time had come for reconciliation. In 1968, with no apparent outstanding issues between them, Rafi joined with Mapai and Ahdut Haavodah to form the Israel Labor Party.

Tensions grew along Israel's borders with Egypt and Syria during the spring of 1967, which heightened the potential for war. By May 1967, war appeared imminent after Nasser blockaded the Straits of Tiran and ordered the withdrawal of the United Nations Emergency Force (UNEF) from the Sinai Peninsula, which had been stationed in that area as a buffer force between Israel and Egypt after the Sinai Campaign of 1956. In Israel a Government of National Unity was formed in response to the crisis, and Moshe Dayan was appointed minister of defense. Peres negotiated on behalf of Rafi, and played an instrumental role in bringing about the "wall-to-wall coalition."

Although the Israeli victory over the Arab armies in the Six Day War of 1967 altered the geopolitical balance in the Middle East, it had little effect on domestic Israeli politics, and the Labor party continued its predominance in the Knesset elections of 1969 and 1973. During this period Peres held a variety of cabinet posts including minister of absorption, minister of transport, minister of information, minister of communications, and minister without portfolio, with responsibility for economic development in the occupied territories. Golda Meir, who succeeded Levi Eshkol as prime minister after his death in February 1969, kept Peres on the decision-making periphery by placing him in positions removed from defense and foreign policy. She seemed determined to exact political revenge on Peres for the years he had ignored her authority as foreign minister. The attacks that Peres and Meir launched against each other during the struggle between Mapai and Rafi further embittered their personal relationship.

The surprise attack by Egypt and Syria on Israel in October 1973 and the political and military failures associated with Israel's leadership before and during the Yom Kippur War carried a heavy political price for the Labor party. Although the electorate returned Labor to power in the Knesset elections of 1973, Prime Minister Meir and Defense Minister Dayan bore the brunt of public criticism. In April 1974 Golda Meir submitted her resignation, which brought down the government. This was the end of the reign of the "old guard," since Eshkol and Meir were gone from the political landscape and Pinhas Sapir refused to be a candidate for the premiership. Consequently, the two candidates who emerged were Peres, who was serving as the minister of information, and Yitzhak Rabin,* the minister of labor, former chief of staff, and former ambassador to the United States. Rabin was the preferred choice of the party establishment, many of whom still resented Peres's role in Rafi. Rabin won over Peres in a close vote by the Labor Party's Central Committee, but Peres's performance established him as the number two leader in the party. The new government was established in June 1974, with Rabin as prime minister and Peres as minister of defense.

Relations between Peres and Rabin were strained during the term of the government and often erupted into public recriminations. Disputes arose over domestic and foreign policy, the selection of personnel and the scope of their authority (for example; Rabin's appointment of Ariel Sharon in July 1975 as an adviser on security matters), and the chain of command and related procedures within the defense establishment. These debates were often conducted through the media, which contributed to the growing perception in Israel of a Labor party in disarray and torn by internal strife.

The greatest success for Peres and the Rabin government occurred between June 27 and July 4, 1976. An Air France aircraft en route from Tel Aviv to Paris was hijacked by Palestinian terrorists and taken to Entebbe Airport in Uganda. In return for the hostages, the hijackers demanded the release of forty PLO terrorists imprisoned in Israel and thirteen others being held in several European states and Kenya. Israel's leaders were confronted with the most serious terrorist incident since the Munich Olympics disaster in 1972. The government appointed a team of ministers (including Peres and Rabin) to deal with the crisis. Peres and Chief of Staff Mordechai (Motta) Gur were responsible for formulating a plan for a military rescue mission. After considerable debate, the rescue mission was approved and the commando force departed for Uganda. The mission was executed with minimal casualties to the hostages or the commandos. It provided a needed boost in morale throughout the ranks of the IDF, and helped restore public confidence in the military, which had been badly eroded by the failures of the Yom Kippur War.

The period prior to the Knesset elections of 1977 was characterized by controversy within the Labor party and by continuing animosity between Peres and Rabin. Peres formally announced his intention to challenge Rabin for the party leadership in January 1977. The showdown took place at the Labor Party convention the following month, where Rabin prevailed by a slim majority. However, a series of scandals, including the disclosure that Rabin's wife maintained bank accounts in the United States in violation of Israeli currency laws, led Rabin to resign from the chairmanship of the Labor Party in April 1977, just one month prior to the Knesset elections. Peres became the party's new leader and candidate for the premiership.

Despite Peres's efforts to prepare for the elections, for the first time in Israel's history a non-Labor-led government won a plurality of Knesset seats and succeeded in forming the government. This was the beginning of a seven-year period in which the Likud led by Menachem Begin* and later by Yitzhak Shamir* would form and lead the government coalition, and would formulate defense and foreign policy while Labor was in the opposition. Furthermore, it was the Begin government that continued the peace negotiations with Egypt. These efforts helped produce the historic trip of Egypt's President Anwar Al-Sadat* to Jerusalem in November 1977, the Camp David Accords in September 1978, and the Egypt-Israel Peace Treaty in March 1979.

Peres continued to play an active role in foreign affairs despite the fact that he did not hold a position in the government. He traveled abroad frequently and participated in a variety of international conferences such as those of the Socialist International. While abroad he often had the opportunity to meet with leaders of other states, which helped improve his image as a statesman. These meetings frequently did not have the prior approval of the prime minister or the foreign minister, which left Peres open to charges that he was conducting a personal foreign policy without formal authority.

In June 1977, Peres was elected Labor Party Chairman, and in addition to being the head of the opposition in the Knesset, he was responsible for preparing the party for the next election. This included a reorganization of the party's senior ranks, which helped rekindle the ongoing struggle for the leadership of the party. His chief opponents were Rabin and Yigal Allon, who was the preferred choice of the Ahdut Haavodah faction of the party. Allon's sudden death in February 1980 left Rabin as Peres's only opponent. Rabin's challenge was set back in December 1980, when the Labor Party voted by a large margin to retain Peres as party chairman and candidate for prime minister in the upcoming elections.

By the beginning of 1981, Menachem Begin and the Likud were experiencing difficulties that seriously threatened their electoral prospects. The economy was plagued by triple-digit inflation and excessive government spending, and the Likud leadership was unable to bring either under control. During this period, public opinion polls suggested that the electorate was going to return the Labor Party to office, possibly with an unprecedented absolute majority eliminating the need to form a coalition. However, the 1981 elections produced an even split of Knesset seats between Labor and Likud, the mandate to form the government was once again given to Likud, and Begin managed to secure a majority in Parliament. Despite continuing economic problems and a series of traumatic events associated with the war in Lebanon, the government remained in power until Begin's resignation in September 1983. Yitzhak Shamir, Begin's foreign minister, replaced him as prime minister and leader of the Likud Party until the next election in July 1984.

The 1981 election was Peres's second loss to Begin. Questions arose within the Labor Party regarding Peres's public image and his inability to lead the party to victory. However, in 1984 Begin was absent from the political scene and Israeli politics was entering a more pragmatic phase better suited to Peres's personality. The 1984 campaign focused more on issues and less on personalities.

Despite Begin's absence from the campaign, the continuing Lebanese quagmire, and inflation approaching 400 percent, Labor was unable to achieve a decisive victory in the election. Labor secured forty-four seats to Likud's forty-one, and although he received the mandate to form the government, Peres was unable to form a majority coalition. This was due in part to the distribution of seats in the Knesset among the thirteen other parties. This led to the formation of a National Unity Government (NUG), which was a new experiment in Israeli politics. Cabinet positions were divided evenly between the two major blocs in a balance of power. A rotation agreement was adopted which called for Peres to serve as prime minister for the first half of the fifty-month term while Shamir served as foreign minister. After twenty-five months, the two men switched positions for the balance of the term.

During his tenure as prime minister, Peres presided over Israel's withdrawal from Lebanon and confronted the economic problems with austerity measures that returned solvency to the economy. He conducted an active foreign policy that frequently led to disputes with his Likud partners regarding the scope of Peres's authority to act without explicit government approval. He was especially active in his efforts to bring King Hussein ibn Talal* of Jordan into negotiations regarding the future of the West Bank and Gaza Strip and their Palestinian inhabitants. Peres has been a long-time advocate of a "Jordanian option," which envisions limited Israeli withdrawal from the West Bank as part of an arrangement where Israeli security considerations are met while Jordan handles the administration of the area. Peres also supported the convening of an international conference designed to address outstanding issues between Israel, those Arab states willing to participate, and the Palestinians. Neither plan made any significant progress. Peres spoke for only half of Israel's government; the other half was adamantly opposed to the proposals, and Peres was constrained by the terms of the coalition agreement that required support by both Likud and Labor before changes in the status quo could take place. Furthermore, Hussein refused to come forward and enter into such negotiations.

Among Peres's successes was a summit meeting with King Hassan II* of Morocco in July 1986, which represented only the second time an Arab head of state had officially and publicly met with an Israeli prime minister. Two months later he met with President Hosni Mubarak* of Egypt to discuss outstanding issues in Egyptian-Israeli relations. Peres was active in exploring the possibility of reestablishing diplomatic relations with several Eastern Bloc nations, including the Soviet Union, and Israeli officials met with representatives of Eastern European states in negotiations toward this goal. Israel's "special relationship" with the United States improved considerably during Peres's tenure, a change from the tension that had frequently characterized relations during Begin and Shamir's tenure in office.

Peres proved himself to be a capable leader and overcame many of the negative images that followed him throughout his career. He upheld his party's commitment to the National Unity Government, which demonstrated that he placed national interests above narrow personal ambitions.

The 1988 Knesset election campaign focused primarily on foreign-policy issues, particularly the continuation of the peace process and the elements of a future negotiated settlement. After Peres had secured the nomination for the number one position on the party's election list, he launched an active campaign drawing clear distinctions between his vision of Israel's future and Shamir's, who was Likud's choice for prime minister. Labor's campaign focused on peace as the central theme. It was a risky strategy for Peres, especially in light of the Palestinian uprising in the West Bank and Gaza which erupted in December 1987 and continued for over a year. The *intifada* (uprising) bolstered the position of the right-wing parties prior to the election, since a majority of Israelis agreed with the law and order "iron-fist" policy employed by the government to restore calm in the territories. Peres relied on his ability to convince voters that he could negotiate a settlement that brought peace while providing for Israel's security requirements. His position was made clear in his comments: "We have an army that is so strong, we don't have to be afraid of peace . . . . We have to have the courage to decide what kind of country we will have . . . an Israel of endless war, or an Israel of peace" (*Washington Post*, October 23, 1988). Peres ran on a platform of hope for Israel's future, and characterized his opponent's platform as one based on fear.

As in the 1984 election, the 1988 election did not produce a clear victory for either Labor or Likud. Both lost Knesset seats to smaller and more ideologically defined parties on the extreme right and left of Israel's political spectrum. Fifteen parties received enough votes to gain Knesset representation, also similar to the situation in 1984. The religious parties did especially well, winning eighteen seats in the Knesset, which gave them the balance of power in the formation of a coalition. Shamir and Likud won forty Knesset seats, one more than Labor, and was given the mandate to form a coalition by President Chaim Herzog.

The Labor Party and Peres were disappointed by the results, as it initially appeared that Shamir would establish a coalition with the religious parties and other rightist parties. After several weeks of intense negotiations, Peres and Shamir reached an agreement to enter into a new coalition. Peres required that Labor be an equal partner to Likud in the government, and that the Cabinet seats be distributed equally between the two parties. The central difference between the 1988 coalition agreement and the 1984 agreement was that Shamir would serve as prime minister for the duration of the government. Peres accepted the position of finance minister, and it was agreed that Yitzhak Rabin would remain in his position as defense minister. The coalition agreement was similar to the 1984 agreement in requiring consent by both parties on controversial policy issues such as territorial compromise and the modalities of the peace process.

Questions remain as to whether the 1988 Knesset election campaign will be Peres's last campaign as chairman of his party. His departure will likely inaugurate a transition to a younger generation of Labor leaders. He discusses retirement at times, but believes he still has much to accomplish. After a lifetime of dedication and service to the State of Israel and the Jewish people, Shimon Peres believes that his greatest challenges lie ahead of him. It remains to be seen whether he can lead Israel into a new era of peaceful coexistence with the Arab States and the Palestinians, or if the next generation of Israel's leaders will inherit the same dilemmas that were passed on to Peres.

BIBLIOGRAPHY

Works by Peres:

David's Sling—The Arming of Israel. New York: Random House, 1970.
From These Men: Seven Founders of the State of Israel. Trans. Philip Simpson. New York: Wyndham Books, 1979.
"A Strategy for Peace in the Middle East." *Foreign Affairs* 58 (Spring 1980): 887–901.

Other Works:

Arian, Asher. *Politics in Israel: The Second Generation.* Chatham, N.J.: Chatham House, 1985.
Fein, Leonard J. *The Politics of Israel.* Boston: Little, Brown, 1967.
Golan, Matti. *Shimon Peres: A Biography.* Trans. Ina Friedman. New York: St. Martin's Press, 1982.
Herzog, Chaim. *The Arab-Israeli Wars: War and Peace in the Middle East from the War of Independence through Lebanon.* New York: Vintage, 1982.
Kurzman, Dan. *Ben-Gurion: Prophet of Fire.* New York: Simon and Schuster, 1983.
Laqueur, Walter, *A History of Zionism.* New York: Holt, Rinehart, and Winston, 1972.
Reich, Bernard, and Gershon R. Kieval (eds.). *Israel Faces the Future.* New York: Praeger, 1986.
———. *Israeli National Security Policy: Political Actors and Perspectives.* New York: Greenwood, 1988.
Sachar, Howard M. *A History of Israel: From the Rise of Zionism to Our Time.* New York: Alfred A. Knopf, 1979.

JOSEPH HELMAN

Q

QABUS BIN SAID (1940–   ). Since coming to power Sultan Qabus has introduced significant socioeconomic reforms and political changes in Oman. The health, welfare, and educational systems have been upgraded. He also has improved the infrastructure, building roads and an international airport, electricity generating plant, schools, hospitals, and low cost housing.

Qabus bin Said, sultan since 1970, is the fourteenth ruler from the Al Bu Said dynasty in an unbroken chain from the mid-eighteenth century, and the ninth sultan from the Al Said branch of the family. After a long period of decline in the Omani state, Qabus's father, Said bin Taymur* (reigned 1932–1970), was able to engineer a modest revival of the Al Bu Said fortunes. Responsible for pulling the country out of debt and presiding over the reunification of the coast and the interior in the 1950s, Said's parsimony at a time of growing development in neighboring oil states and his excessively autocratic style of governing led to increasing dissatisfaction in the 1960s, especially in the southern province of Dhufar. The seeming deterioration in Oman's domestic situation led Qabus bin Said to join forces with British and Omani groups to overthrow his father in July 1970.

Dhufar had been tenuously annexed to the Al Bu Said domains only in the nineteenth century. The coastal population is comprised of Arabs, mainly from the widespread Kathiri tribe, and the descendants of African slaves. The surrounding mountains, however, are the home of the seminomadic jibbalis, who speak several South Arabian languages related to but distinct from modern Arabic. Said bin Taymur regarded Dhufar as his personal estate and not part of the Muscat state, and sought to keep the province isolated and unchanged to an even greater degree than the rest of Oman. Attracted by Salala's congenial climate and the freedom it offered from the demands and pressures of Muscat, Said bin Taymur spent increasing amounts of time there and did not return to Muscat after 1958.

Qabus bin Said was born in Salala in 1940, the son of Said's second jibbali wife, (Said also sired two daughters). After being tutored in Islamic subjects in

Dhufar, he was sent to England for schooling near London at the age of eighteen. He subsequently attended the Royal Military Academy at Sandhurst and served seven months with the British Army of the Rhine. Following a world tour and a short period studying local government in the English Midlands, Qabus returned to Salala in 1964 and there was kept deliberately inactive and virtually under house arrest.

Two factors combined in the late 1960s to shake Oman's isolation and threaten the status quo: the discovery of oil in 1964 (production began in 1967) and the growing rebellion in Dhufar. Adamant in his belief that national independence depended on fiscal soundness, Said bin Taymur refused to embark on ambitious and costly development projects until he had the money in hand to pay the entire cost. Consequently, the tangible benefits from oil revenues were largely invisible to the general population, whose rising expectations were fueled by the dramatic transformation visible in other Gulf states, despite the fact that Said had initiated such development projects as the new port of Matrah (now known as Port Qabus), the Greater Matrah Master Plan, and some schools, hospitals, and roads.

At the same time, Said's extreme paternalism in Dhufar had produced scattered outbreaks of dissidence in the early 1960s. By 1965, the Dhufar Liberation Front was waging a serious guerrilla war and, in 1968, its leadership was taken over by Marxist elements, who renamed it the Popular Front for the Liberation of Oman and the Arabian Gulf (PFLOAG, and later PFLO). With the help of sanctuary in neighboring and newly independent South Yemen, and supplies and advisers from first China and then the Soviet Union, PFLOAG was able to exert total control over the Dhufari mountains and start threatening the coastal towns by 1970.

The deteriorating situation prompted several British officials in the Muscat army and government, together with a few Omanis, to discuss the sultan's removal. At the same time, Qabus's forced inaction, a pattern of treatment that Said had meted out to other educated family members, led him to conclude that his father was no longer capable of running the country, and caused him to join forces with the plotters in Muscat. Attacks in June 1970 on two army installations in northern Oman by the National Democratic Front for the Liberation of Oman and the Arabian Gulf, a small PFLOAG offshoot formed to expand the rebellion to northern Oman, forced Qabus and his associates to accelerate their plans. On July 23, 1970, the son of the governor of Dhufar (a boyhood friend of Qabus) and a British officer (a classmate of Qabus at Sandhurst who had been seconded to the Sultan's Armed Forces) led an assault on Said's palace in Salala. After a brief gun battle, Said capitulated and was flown to Bahrain for treatment of his wounds and then on to exile in London. Two weeks later, the newly proclaimed sultan, Qabus bin Said, entered Muscat for the first time ever and announced a new era for the country.

An immediate priority of the new sultan was to reverse his father's cautious approach to development and to launch the country on an immediate program of developing the infrastructure and social services. For the first time, the state became dedicated to providing schools, health-care facilities, water and electricity, telecommunications, and a growing road network. By 1976, sufficient groundwork had been laid for implementing the country's first five-year development plan. At the same time, the vast expansion of job opportunities and improved standards of living caused the return of many of the fifty to one hundred thousand Omanis who had gone elsewhere in the Gulf States to look for work. By the late 1980s, the capital region of Muscat-Matrah and its suburbs had been transformed into a major metropolitan area rivalling the capitals of the other Gulf states. Changes in the towns and villages of the interior, while not so dramatic, were equally significant in reinforcing the image of the state as a benevolent provider and Sultan Qabus as the agent of this transformation.

Within a week of the 1970 coup, a new government had been created. The country's first true Council of Ministers was established, with the sultan's uncle, Tariq bin Taymur, as prime minister. Unfortunately, Tariq's vision of an advanced constitutional monarchy, which was prompted by his education and residence in Turkey, India, and West Germany, clashed with the sultan's conception of his role. The tension between the two was further aggravated by unscrupulous advisers on both sides, and Tariq was forced to resign his position in 1971. Although the two were later reconciled, Tariq never again played more than a marginal role in the government until his death in 1980. The consequence was the emergence of a small government with the single figure of the sultan at the apex. The process of consultation with key family members, tribal leaders, and religious notables, which characterizes the political systems of other Arab Gulf monarchies, does not apply to Oman.

Nevertheless, within a few years the organization of the various ministries had been filled out. By the beginning of the 1980s, a new generation of ministers, who were younger, better educated, and relatively more technically qualified, had joined the cabinet. The state's most effective institution in 1970, the Sultan's Armed Forces (SAF), also continued to grow and develop. Having been trained as a military officer, Sultan Qabus took great interest in the development of both SAF and the Royal Oman Police.

A major spur to SAF's expansion was the continuing threat of the Dhufar rebellion. While the overthrow of Sultan Said had caused many moderate rebels to surrender and accept government amnesty and even official positions, the hard core continued to fight on. To combat PFLOAG, SAF was modernized, expanded, better armed, and better trained, with the considerable assistance of seconded and contracted British officers, while India, Pakistan, and Jordan also provided some personnel, and Jordan briefly sent army units and sold aircraft to the sultanate. The Shah Reza Pahlavi* of Iran was particularly helpful, providing up to seventy-five hundred troops; and Iranian air and sea cover was instrumental in clearing rebel activity from the coastal plain.

By December 1975, the mountains had been systematically cleared of guerrilla activity and the rebellion effectively came to an end. Government provision of jobs, wells, schools, and health clinics to the jibbalis ensured that the province would remain loyal. In the succeeding years, Dhufar was increasingly and probably irreversibly integrated into the rest of the sultanate. The numbers of Dhufaris in senior government positions continued to grow, helped no doubt by the Dhufari origins of the sultan.

In the succeeding years, Sultan Qabus tended to steer a moderate course in foreign policy. The long-standing relationship with Britain continued to be strong. British advisers were to be found in all branches of the government, and British seconded and contracted personnel filled key positions in the armed forces. In addition, the sultanate purchased the bulk of its military equipment from the United Kingdom. An agreement was signed with the United States in 1980 providing for American assistance in upgrading Omani military installations and providing some development aid in return for the U.S. right to prestock military equipment in Oman and use some bases on an occasional basis. The agreement was renewed for another five years in 1985.

Sultan Qabus also forged a policy of strengthening relations with nearby Arab countries, which had been virtually nonexistent before 1970. His rapprochement with King Faisal bin Abd al-Aziz Al Saud* in Riyadh in 1971 ended the traditional enmity between Oman and Saudi Arabia. In 1981, Oman became one of the six founding members of the Gulf Cooperation Council (GCC). Oman's dependence on foreign assistance in winning the Dhufar war and its geographic location on the southern shores of the strategic Strait of Hormuz generally led it to argue within the GCC for closer cooperation with the West in security matters. At the same time, it has been the most reluctant member in economic cooperation, fearing the competition from its more developed neighbors.

Ties to Jordan have been close, partly based on Jordan's willingness to assist Oman during the Dhufar war and partly due to the friendship between Sultan Qabus and King Hussein ibn Talal*. Oman was one of the few Arab countries not to break relations with Egypt following the Camp David agreement. Despite being an oil producer, the sultanate has never joined the Organization of Petroleum Exporting Countries (OPEC) or the smaller Organization of Arab Petroleum Exporting Countries (OAPEC).

By the 1980s, Sultan Qabus had become prepared to temper his country's conservative outlook with the pursuit of better links to the radical countries. Diplomatic relations were established and ambassadors exchanged with the People's Democratic Republic of Yemen (South Yemen) and the Soviet Union. Some Iranian military units remained in Dhufar up to the time of the Iranian revolution, and Oman, along with the UAE (United Arab Emirates), has attempted to maintain open lines of communication between the GCC and the Islamic Republic of Iran.

The impact of Qabus bin Said on Oman undoubtedly has been mixed. While he was indeed the instigator of a "new era," his style of governing remained extremely personalized, with an uncritical acceptance of the advice of a small circle of advisers and ministers. By the end of the 1980s, new generations of

Omanis were beginning to appear who had never known the old era and were thus unlikely to be as grateful or loyal to Qabus as the older citizens.

More immediately, there remained the question of succession. By the late 1980s, Qabus had neither produced a direct heir nor seemed likely to do so. Furthermore, he seemed unaware of the apprehension and uncertainty caused by his lack of a line of succession. The situation in Oman was far more acute than similar circumstances in Saudi Arabia or the Gulf emirates would have been for a number of reasons. First, other members of the small Al Said family were generally regarded as unsuitable choices to lead. Second, tribal and religious leadership had been rendered impotent since the events of the 1950s. Third, while Dhufaris were to be found in many top positions, their positions appeared to be tied to the presence of the sultan. Fourth, other members of the capital's elite were largely from merchant families either of recent arrival in Oman or of minority sectarian and ethnic backgrounds, as well as perceived as corrupt in some cases. Being unrepresentative of the Omani population, they were unlikely to command much loyalty.

BIBLIOGRAPHY

Graz, Liesl. *The Omanis: Sentinels of the Gulf.* London: Longman, 1982.
Hawley, Donald. *Oman and Its Renaissance.* London: Stacey International, 1977. 4th rev. ed. Atlantic Hts., N.J.: Humanities Press, 1987. Distr. Stacey International (London and New Jersey).
Khadduri, Majid. *Arab Personalities in Politics.* Washington, D.C.: Middle East Institute, 1981, pp. 241–287.
Peterson, J. E. *Oman in the Twentieth Century: Political Foundations of an Emerging State.* London: Croom Helm; New York: Barnes and Nobel, 1978.
———. "American Policy in the Gulf and the Sultanate of Oman." *American-Arab Affairs,* no. 8 (Spring 1984): pp. 117–130.
———. "Oman." In Michael Adams (ed.). *The Middle East.* New York: Facts on File Publications, Handbooks to the Modern World, 1988: pp. 329–339.
Pridham, B. R. (ed.). *Oman: Economic, Social and Strategic Developments.* London: Croom Helm, for the University of Exeter Centre for Arab Gulf Studies, 1987.
Townsend, John. *Oman: The Making of a Modern State.* London: Croom Helm; New York: St. Martin's Press, 1977.

J. E. PETERSON

MUAMMAR QADDAFI (1942–   ). Libya in the past two decades has attracted a great deal of attention in the West primarily because its rather controversial leader, Muammar Qaddafi. Seen in the early days as a somewhat romantic revolutionary figure, his behavior on the world political scene soon earned him the title of madman, and more recently that of dangerous terrorist. However, an analysis of his background, and of the domestic and external problems and issues with which he has had to deal, reveals a man quite different from his portrait in the international mass media.

Muammar Qaddafi was born in the spring of 1942 in the area of Sirte, on the Mediterranean coast of Libya. He was the only surviving son and the youngest child of a poor family belonging to the Qadhdhadhifa, an Arabized Berber tribe. He was brought up by his aging parents Muhammad Abd al-Salam Bin Hamad Bin Muhammad (also known as Abu Minyar), who was approaching sixty, and his mother Aisha, and by three older sisters who doted on him. In 1952, at the age of ten, he was sent to elementary school in the town of Sirte, where his schoolmates taunted him for being nothing more than a poor bedouin. He had to sleep in the neighborhood mosque, and could only return to his family, who lived miles away from the center of town, during the holidays. Four years later he moved, with his family this time, to the Fezzan province, where he attended the Sebha Preparatory School.

The five years he spent in Sebha, between 1956 and 1961, were his politically formative years. Dramatic economic and political changes were taking place in neighboring Egypt and had a profound impact on youth throughout the Arab world. The 1956 Suez Canal crisis saw the evacuation of the British forces from Egypt; Gamal Abdul Nasser's* agrarian reforms and broad nationalization undermined the power of the wealthy upper classes in Egypt, and a new more egalitarian social order began to emerge. The Egyptian leader's call for a united Arab world electrified the Arab youth, who saw in him a great charismatic leader.

Nasser became Qaddafi's model. Somewhat older than his classmates, he quickly assumed a leadership role in the Sebha Preparatory School and began organizing his school friends. It was there he created the first Command Committee, composed of many of those who would later become members of Libya's Revolutionary Command Council (RCC). He also led demonstrations against the French in Algeria, in protest against the assassination of Patrice Lumumba in the Belgian Congo, and in support of many of the anticolonial movements in Africa. Finally, he was expelled from school in 1961 for demonstrating against the breakup of the United Arab Republic, which had been the union between Egypt and Syria.

Qaddafi and his family left Sebha and moved on to Misrata, in Tripolitania, where he completed high school and took his qualifying exams to enter college. In Misrata he reestablished contact with many of his childhood friends from Sirte, with whom he promptly shared his new political ideas. Eventually, when they graduated in 1963, at least three youths from this group joined the Military Academy with him in Benghazi. There they created the nucleus of the Free Unionist Officers Movement, which was an organization aiming at overthrowing the Sanusi monarchy and taking over power in Libya.

The Unionist Officers had links with their civilian counterparts in other institutions of higher learning. The proximity of the Military Academy to the University of Benghazi allowed Qaddafi to enlarge his circle of friends, who by that time included most of those who would later become members of the RCC: Abd al-Salam Jallud, Bashir al-Hawadi, Abu Bakr Yunis, Mustafa al-Kharrubi, and Umar al-Muhayshi. Qaddafi also created a highly organized system of secret cells within the military, with a central committee that met regularly to discuss political matters.

After graduating from the Military Academy in 1965, Qaddafi was sent to Britain to attend an army school at Bovington Hythe in Beaconsfield, where he took a six-month signals course. On his return to Libya he enrolled in the University of Benghazi and majored in history. He never completed his studies, but was commissioned in 1966 to the signals corps of the Libyan army, and was posted in Gar Yunis at the barracks outside Benghazi. He was thus able to remain in regular contact with the network of friends and fellow officers that he had developed over the years, and to continue building the secret organization that enabled him to carry out the coup.

On September 1, 1969, a bloodless military coup overthrew the Sanusi monarchy. Little was known about the coup-makers except that they called themselves the Free Unionist Officers and that their slogan was "social justice, socialism, and unity." During the first three months of the coup there appears to have been a struggle for power between Qaddafi and his close associates, on the one hand, and an older group of high-ranking officers and civilians who had cooperated with Qaddafi in the coup, on the other. The latter, represented by members of the first postcoup cabinet, like Prime Minister Sulayman al-Maghribi, Defense Minister Adam al-Hawwaz, and Interior Minister Lieutenant Colonel Musa Ahmad, were strongly nationalist, and advocated the nonrenewal of the base treaties with the United States and Britain. They were not, however, antagonistic to the West, and wished to maintain good relations with Western powers. Regionally, they were more Arab-oriented than the previous regime, and spoke more openly of Arab causes. When it came to Egypt, however, they were cautious, and although offering to continue providing it with financial aid, they were unwilling to consider any form of bilateral unity project between the two countries.

In contrast to Maghribi and his colleagues, Qaddafi advocated radical change on both the domestic and foreign-policy levels. He fully endorsed Nasserism as a doctrine, and in flamboyant rhetoric denounced "world imperialism" and declared "revolution every day in every area" (Bayda Domestic Service, September 16, 1969, in *FBIS*, September 17, 1969). The showdown came in early December 1969 when a coup against the regime was announced. Qaddafi accused Defense Minister Adam al-Hawwaz and Interior Minister Musa Ahmad of being the major conspirators and had them arrested. The next day a constitutional proclamation was issued giving all powers to the Revolutionary Command Council and proclaiming it the supreme authority in the land.

Whether a countercoup did indeed take place or whether Qaddafi created the upheaval in order to rid himself of his troublesome colleagues as well as of a large number of high-ranking officers is debatable. The fact remains that in the confrontation, Egypt sided with Qaddafi. It provided him with the intelligence and the military backing he needed to enable him to succeed. According to diplomatic sources, Egyptian troops were sent to Libya at the time of the alleged coup, at Qaddafi's request. Thus, by adopting the Nasserist ideology, Qaddafi secured the support of the Egyptian authorities, who were interested in exercising their influence on Libya. In contrast to Maghribi, Musa, or Hawwaz, Qaddafi was willing to toe the line behind Egypt, evacuate the foreigners from Libya, and invite Egyptian forces in to replace them. In return, Nasser supported Qaddafi in his showdown with his more moderate rivals.

Over time, however, Qaddafi moved away from Nasserism and developed his own particular brand of socialism, which he called "natural socialism." His main tenets were propounded in his *Green Book*, published in three volumes between 1976 and 1978. His concept was based on a precapitalist form of economy that emphasized complete egalitarianism in society. Wage labor was to be abolished and workers were to become partners in industrial ventures. Land belonged to God and consequently could not be owned by individuals. Families could cultivate land and graze their cattle on it but could not claim indefinite ownership. Trade and commerce were exploitative and nonproductive activities that were to be taken over by the state to prevent the making of profit and the unnecessary accumulation of wealth by some members of the society at the expense of others.

Qaddafi's conception of Arab nationalism never differed very much from that of Nasser. He saw the Arab world as one nation extending from the Atlantic to the Persian Gulf, and linked by linguistic, cultural, ethnic, and historical ties. He advocated the unity of all Arab states economically, politically, and militarily, so that they could form a powerful bloc to meet the Israeli threat to the region. Furthermore, like Nasser he believed that the Arab world should remain nonaligned and should support not only the Palestinians but other "revolutionary" movements in the Third World.

Qaddafi's Pan-Islamism revolved around the notion of a loose union of all Muslim nations and peoples, in which the Arab world would play a central role in the revival of Islam. It was less politically oriented than Arab nationalism and focused more on spiritual union and religious reformism.

Unlike Nasser, however, religious reformism has been a central part of his ideology. He has emphasized that the Quran was the only source of *sharia* or Islamic law, and that those parts of the *hadith*, the Prophet's sayings, that did not conform to the Qur'an could be overlooked. He has viewed the Muslim Prophet Muhammad as a purely human intermediary between God and humanity, whose words could be challenged when they were not of divine inspiration. He has also taken the position that since the Quran was in Arabic, anybody could read and understand it, and that there was little need for *imams*, Muslim clergymen, to interpret it; thus he incurred the wrath of the traditional Libyan religious establishment. More recently, Qaddafi has taken a highly unusual position for a Muslim leader, stating that "the question of religion has nothing to do with politics," and taking a stand on a *de facto* separation of church and state (*Al-Safir* (Beirut), March 21, 1985, pp. 8–9).

Qaddafi's economic reforms went through a number of phases. The first, between 1969 and 1973, was characterized by the twin process of nationalization and Libyanization. Nationalization, in part or in whole, of the branches of international petroleum companies operating in Libya began to take place in late 1971. British Petroleum, Bunker Hunt, Occidental, Oasis, and eventually Shell were completely nationalized, while the Libyan Government's share in Mobil, Exxon, Chevron, and Texaco was increased to 51 percent. Qaddafi also raised the price of oil and decreased production.

The Libyanization of the branches of foreign banks operating in Libya also took place during that period. Insurance companies and all major companies providing basic infrastructural facilities such as electricity, public transport, and communication, suffered the same fate. The property of Italians was sequestrated, and foreign-owned industrial plants were taken over by the state.

During the second phase, 1973 to 1975, Qaddafi concentrated on building a power base for his regime by redistributing some of the oil wealth among the largest possible number of Libyans and providing them with much-needed social services. Expenditures on housing, water, electricity, transport, and communications constituted 67.3 percent of the total national budget during that period. Agriculture assistance, in part through agricultural cooperatives, was extensive, as was the state's support for the small-business sector, which had already begun receiving major subsidies and loans in the previous phase. Industry also received a big boost, and many new plants and factories were opened between 1973 and 1975.

Despite those transformations, the agricultural sector continued to face many problems including manpower shortages, the unavailability of water, and the remoteness of some areas from marketing centers. The new industrial policies were not cost-effective as they required the importation of raw material, capital goods, and skilled labor. Furthermore, the subsidizing of Libyan entrepreneurship was creating greater rather than less economic inequality in the society, with members of the ancient régime benefiting most from the new policies.

The Green Book heralded more drastic economic reforms. Workers were encouraged to take over and administer industrial and commercial enterprises. Tenants became owners of their homes, paying mortgages to the state rather than rent to the landlords. Public corporations replaced the private sector in foreign trade, and large government cooperatives became substitutes for the small retail traders. The government gradually stopped financing the private sector's entrepreneurs altogether.

Those reforms led to chaos and confusion in the economy. Abolishing the role of the private sector in domestic and foreign trade created unprecedented shortages of a number of basic goods and commodities. The new housing policy put a stop to private investment in construction, leading to a serious housing crisis. Finally, the takeover of businesses and industries by workers increased the inefficiency of those organizations, which were already suffering from a shortage of trained administrative personnel.

The phase between 1980 and 1987 was a very difficult one for Qaddafi. The fall in oil prices and the imposition of economic sanctions on Libya by the United

States and other Western powers further eroded Libya's economy. It became indebted, had to freeze or cancel many of its industrial and housing projects, and by the mid–1980s resorted to expelling tens of thousands of foreign workers, whom it could no longer employ or pay. Black-marketeering flourished as Libyans found ways of circumventing the state's Draconian economic measures. Smuggling of subsidized products such as rice, oil, and tea from Libya to neighboring states where they sold for higher prices further exacerbated existing shortages.

By 1988 Qaddafi had to face the fact that his reforms had failed: They had led neither to the development of the economy nor to the creation of a political base for the regime. There was strong opposition to his policies now, at all levels of society, and the 1980s witnessed more attempts at overthrowing him than at any other time. To survive politically Qaddafi has begun to change course. In the early months of 1988 he set free a number of political prisoners, and invited members of the Libyan opposition living abroad to come home, promising to return their confiscated property. Shopkeepers have also been gradually allowed to open up their stores and sell their products on the market.

After coming to power, Qaddafi abolished not only the monarchy but all political parties as well. Following the Nasserist model he first created the Arab Socialist Union (ASU) in July 1971, a mass party controlled by the state, which proved to be ineffective and was formally disbanded in 1975. In 1973 he instituted a system of basic popular congresses and popular committees at the local, regional, and national levels. Those committees were elected and their role was to take over the functions of the local government at the district level. They were also responsible for the running of state corporations, industries, and even universities.

There were problems, however; some of the elected members used their new powers to settle personal scores, for instance, and many were so inexperienced that they were incapable of running large state corporations and organizations efficiently. Consequently, in 1977 Qaddafi created watchdog groups, the revolutionary committees, to oversee the activities of the popular committees, creating more confusion and more conflict in domestic politics. Those committees have continued to exist up to the present despite the problems they created. The General People's Congress has been, by and large, little more than a rubber stamp for the government's policies, and has approved almost every major reform advocated by Qaddafi.

Qaddafi's foreign policy can be viewed as a pyramid made up of five overlapping levels. At the very top stands North Africa, which includes not only the Maghreb (Algeria, Tunisia, Morocco, and Mauritania) but also Egypt and Sudan, as well as Chad and the Western Sahara. At that level Qaddafi's foreign policy has been one of realpolitik. He has built a relatively large army and acquired an enormous arsenal to act as a deterrent to any external power with hegemonic ambitions on Libya. He has also made sure that he was always allied to one of three major regional powers: Egypt, Algeria, or Morocco, which have acted at different times as allies and protectors, and have offset potential threats from other powers.

His alliance with Egypt until 1973 was a major factor in helping him consolidate his power in Libya, and gave him the legitimacy he lacked domestically and regionally. The Hassi Masud defense treaty of 1975 with Algeria provided Libya with the regional ally that it had lost when relations between Qaddafi and Anwar al-Sadat* deteriorated in the aftermath of the 1973 Arab-Israeli war. The Arab-African Federation of 1984 with Morocco strengthened Qaddafi vis-à-vis the conservative Arab states, and took Libya out of its regional isolation after it was refused membership in the tripartite alliance of 1983 between Algeria, Tunisia, and Mauritania. Finally, Qaddafi's efforts to remain in control of the Aouzou strip in Chad and to have a say in the internal affairs of that country are based primarily on his fear of external intervention in Libya through its southern borders. It is a matter of security rather than one of ideology.

The second level of the pyramid is that of the Arab world east of Egypt. At that level, Arab nationalist ideology has played a significant role in determining Libya's foreign policy, especially with respect to the Arab-Israeli conflict. Qaddafi became a founding member of the Steadfastness and Confrontation Front, which was formed in December 1977 to oppose the peace negotiations with Israel, following Sadat's visit to Jerusalem.

Qaddafi's relations with other Arab states have often been ambivalent and full of contradictions. He has been openly critical of all traditional Arab regimes, attacking them publicly in the Libyan mass media; yet he deals with them when it suits his purpose. Although an Arab nationalist, he has supported Iran in its war with Iraq, and Ethiopia against Sudan under Jafar Mohammed Nimeiri.* He has supported opposition groups in almost every Arab country and yet has played the role of mediator between Arab states when they were in conflict. In the past year, Qaddafi has changed course and moved toward the position of the mainstream Arab states, supporting Yasser Arafat* and the PLO rather than the more extreme wings of the Palestinian movement, and distancing himself somewhat from both Syria and Iran. Again it is too soon to know if this is a serious change in Libya's foreign policy or if it is only tactical.

The third level of the pyramid includes all the states of the Islamic world in Africa and Asia. Qaddafi's foreign policy toward those states has been significantly although not exclusively determined by Pan-Islamic ideology. He has given economic assistance to many of those states, tying it to cultural agreements involving the teaching of Islam, the building of mosques, and the building of schools where Islam was taught. Uganda, Togo, Burundi, Niger, Mali, Gambia, the Central African Republic, and Gabon were some of the recipients of that aid in Africa; Pakistan, Indonesia, and the Philippines in Asia also benefited from Qaddafi's support of their Muslim populations.

Islam was not the only factor that determined Libya's foreign policy toward those countries. In the early 1970s, Qaddafi used economic aid to induce many African states to break relations with Israel and to vote with the Arab states at the United Nations. Support for states such as Uganda and Ethiopia was often a function of their strategic location with respect to Sudan and the waters of the Nile, and Qaddafi's aid and involvement in Niger, Mali, or Chad was linked more to considerations of security and the expansion of Libyan influence than to the support of their Muslim populations.

The fourth level of the pyramid is that of the Third World, which includes many of the states in the previous levels but also many that are neither Muslim nor Arab, in Latin America, Asia, and Africa. His "revolutionary socialism" has been the primary ideological determinant for his support of movements that have branded themselves "socialist," "revolutionary," or "antiimperialist," from Zaire to New Caledonia and Nicaragua. Again as in the previous cases ideology has not been the only consideration, and Qaddafi's use of ideological rhetoric to justify support for radical groups in Egypt, Tunisia, Morocco, or Mauritania has often been nothing but a smokescreen to dissimulate his real intentions to destabilize these states.

The last level of the pyramid includes the industrialized countries of both the Western and Eastern blocs. Until 1973, Qaddafi was critical of both capitalism and communism, and his Third Universal Theory was presented as an alternative to both systems. Although closer to the Soviet camp ideologically, he remained wary of its intentions in the world and disapproved of its approach to religion. After the Arab-Israeli war of 1973, and especially after Sadat's move toward better relations with the West, Qaddafi's ties with the USSR and the countries of the Eastern Bloc were strengthened significantly, while his relations with the United States deteriorated. Libya's relations with Western European countries, especially France, Italy, West Germany, and Austria, were better than those with the United States. They did suffer many setbacks over the years, however, because of a number of issues, including Qaddafi's support of terrorist groups in Europe, the conflict in Chad, and relations with Israel and the Arab world.

Libyan-Soviet relations have been determined by mutual interest, and have revolved primarily around the purchase of large quantities of weapons which have been payed for in hard currency and oil. Politically, Qaddafi has needed a strong ally to provide him with domestic and regional legitimacy, and to balance U.S. influence in North Africa. In the Soviet Union, Libya has been perceived as a counterpoise to Egypt, which it lost to the West, in a region that constitutes the southern flank of the NATO (North Atlantic Treaty Organization) forces in the Mediterranean.

The sharp drop in the price of oil in the early 1980s, and the inability of Qaddafi to pay the Soviets in hard currency, has curtailed the USSRs weapon sales to Libya and exacerbated the countries' relations. Libya has had to resort to bartering oil to pay some of its outstanding debts to the USSR and the Eastern Bloc countries. Despite Qaddafi's frustrations over the USSR's reaction to the U.S. bombing of Libya in 1986, he will no doubt continue to keep on good terms with it because the relationship is a strategic one for both the Soviet Union and Libya.

U.S.-Libyan relations have gone through a number of phases since the military coup of 1969. Until 1974, Qaddafi's criticism of U.S. policy in the Middle East, and in particular of its support for Israel, was not unlike that of other Arab nationalist leaders. It was only when Egypt moved closer to the United States after 1974 and Libya was left out in the cold by Sadat that Qaddafi began to fear for Libya's security. A strong Egypt supported by the United States and no longer at war with Israel might have hegemonic ambitions over Libya. It was then that Qaddafi moved closer to the Soviet camp and that his anti-Western rhetoric became more virulent.

Between 1975 and 1979, U.S.-Libyan relations were strained, and the United States adopted a policy that included the refusal to sell any arms or military hardware to Libya, and limited the export of other items that could be used for both military and civilian purposes. In December 1979, a month after the Iranian revolution took place, Qaddafi, emboldened by what he perceived as a decline of American influence in the Middle East, allowed Libyans to sack and burn the American embassy in Tripoli.

When Ronald Reagan was elected president in the United States in 1980, Qaddafi was chosen as the principal target of his antiterrorist policy. In retaliation for real or presumed acts of terrorism, the United States took economic and political measures to isolate Libya regionally and internationally, and to bring about the downfall of Qaddafi. Those measures culminated in the U.S. bombing of Tripoli and Benghazi in April 1986.

Qaddafi was able to turn the attack to his advantage domestically and regionally. He told the Libyans that the attack demonstrated that the United States was an imperialist power that threatened the security of Libya. Two years later, in June 1988, he was able to get a resolution passed by the Arab leaders at the summit in Algiers, condemning the U.S. attack on Libya. Qaddafi has now strengthened his position in the Arab world and is waiting, hoping to have better relations with the Bush administration.

Qaddafi took power in Libya in a bloodless coup, which he quickly transformed into one of the most radical socialist revolutions in the Middle East. It was a unique blend of Islamic reformism and precapitalist socialism based on his own bedouin and tribal experience. He was able to carry out those changes secure in the knowledge that his country had extensive oil reserves that could meet all its major development needs. After almost two decades it has become obvious even to him that the revolution has failed to achieve most of its principal goals.

The significance of this is that it mirrors the failure of socialism in other parts of the Arab world, the disillusionment of Arabs with revolutionary rhetoric, and the return of many to more traditional approaches to government and to social and economic relations. Islamic fundamentalism, on the one hand, and the search for more democratic forms of government, on the other, are some of the ways the Arabs have dealt with the changing political environment.

Qaddafi has also demonstrated how a small, underdeveloped Third World nation can attain an important stature and be perceived as a significant actor on the international scene. His flamboyant style, his unorthodox behavior, his espousal of radical causes, and his unerring skill in manipulating the mass media, have put Libya on the map. This in the long run may be one of the few lasting achievements of his legacy. Despite having squandered their wealth, Qaddafi has given the Libyans a stronger sense of identity and a greater awareness of their importance in world affairs.

BIBLIOGRAPHY

Works by Qaddafi:

The Green Book. Part One: The Solution to the Problem of Democracy 'The Authority of the People.' London: Martin Brian and O'Keefe, 1976.
————. *The Green Book. Part Two: The Solution to the Economic Problem 'Socialism.'* London: Martin Brian and O'Keefe, 1977.
————. *The Green Book. Part Three: The Social Basis of the Third Universal Theory.* Tripoli: Public Establishment for Publishing, Advertising and Distribution, 1978.

Other Works:

Anderson, Lisa. "Qadhdhafi and the Kremlin." *Problems of Communism* (September-October 1985).
Cooley, John K. *Libyan Sandstorm: The Complete Account of Qaddafi's Revolution.* New York: Holt, Rinehart and Winston, 1982.
Deeb, Marius K., and Mary-Jane Deeb. *Libya since the Revolution: Aspects of Social and Political Development.* New York: Praeger, 1982.
Deeb, Mary-Jane. *Libya's Foreign Policy in North Africa.* Boulder, Colo.: Westview Press, 1989.
El-Fathally, Omar I., and E. Monte Palmer. *Political Development and Social Change in Libya.* Lexington, Mass.: Lexington Books, 1980.
First, Ruth. *Libya, the Elusive Revolution.* New York: Africana Publishing Co., 1974.
Sicker, Martin. *The Making of a Pariah State: the Adventurist Politics of Muammar Qaddafi.* New York: Praeger, 1987.
St. John, Bruce. *Qaddafi's World Design: Libya's Foreign Policy 1969–1987.* London: Saqi Books, 1987.
Wright, John. *Libya: A Modern History.* Baltimore: Johns Hopkins University Press, 1982.
Zartman, I. William, and A. G. Kluge. "Heroic Politics: The Foreign Policy of Libya." In Bahgat Korany and Ali H. Dessouki (eds.). *The Foreign Policies of Arab States.* Boulder, Colo.: Westview, 1984.

MARY-JANE DEEB

ABDUL KARIM QASSEM (1914–1963) ended the rule of the Hashemite dynasty over Iraq in a bloody coup in 1958. While in power he steered Iraq toward closer links with the Soviet bloc and withdrew Iraq from the Baghdad Pact. Qassem implemented agrarian reform hoping to liberate the peasants from debt and end the prevailing feudal system. He sought to give women more rights in marriage, divorce, and inheritance.

Military opposition to the Hashemite monarchy of Iraq and its pro-Western policy can be traced to the early years of World War II. In 1941, a group of officers staged an unsuccessful anti-Western coup d'état. Despite its failure, strong feelings of Arab Nationalism and antiimperialism persisted among the army ranks and among segments of the Iraqi population. These feelings were strengthened by the successful Egyptian revolution of 1952 that abolished the monarchy and established a republic that became increasingly anti-Western in its policies.

Shortly after the Egyptian revolution, two secret Free Officers groups were formed in the Iraqi army. Their objective was to topple the Iraqi monarchy and reorient Iraq's foreign policy. Notable among these officers were Colonel Abdul Salam Aref and General Abdul Karim Qassem. The history of modern Iraq for a decade thereafter was affected by these two men. The two Free Officers groups joined forces in 1956, creating a strong, unified underground movement. The tripartite English, French, and Israeli aggression on Egypt that same year played a major role in bringing the groups together. Abdul Karim Qassem held the senior rank among the Free Officers, and because of this he was elected to head their Central Organization.

Abdul Karim Qassem was born December 21, 1914, in Mahdiyya, a poor quarter in the center of Baghdad. His father was a sunni Arab, but it is believed that his mother was a shia Kurd and that her family originally came to Baghdad from the northeastern part of Iraq near the Iran-Iraq border. Qassem's mixed sectarian origin may have played a role in his later political appeal to the shia.

Qassem came from a poor family. His father, according to some, was a grain and sheep dealer without a fixed profession or job; according to others, he was a carpenter. His early poverty certainly gave him sympathy for the poor and downtrodden. Qassem went to high school in Baghdad, where he was apparently an indifferent student, and taught in an elementary school for one year (1931–1932). Probably because it had greater status, he decided on a military career, and in 1932 he went to the military college. He graduated as a second lieutenant in 1934 and participated in a military expedition against rebellious tribes in the lower Euphrates.

In 1941 he became a staff officer after graduating from the General Staff College. The following year, while stationed in Basra, he and Abdul Salam Aref participated in publishing underground, antigovernment leaflets. During the war, he returned to Baghdad to teach at the Iraqi Royal Military Academy. In 1947, he was sent with the Iraqi Army to Palestine, where he participated in the Arab-Israeli War of 1948–1949; he was described by fellow officers as courageous. Like other Iraqi officers who participated in the conflict, he emerged bitter over the Arab defeat, much of which he blamed on the regimes in power. In 1950 he was sent to England for a training program at the senior officers school in Devizes. All these military achievements gave Qassem prestige and high status in the eyes of his fellow officers. Well before the 1958 revolution in Iraq which overthrew the monarchy and established the republic, Qassem was considered an honest loner. He was known also to be nervous, moody, and unpredictable, although capable of exercising much personal charisma. While many Free Officers advanced strong nationalist opinions, Qassem was more attracted to liberal ideas, and advocated moderate nationalistic views. Some authors believe that he was influenced by the ideas of the National Democratic Party, a center-left group advocating democracy and social reform.

While the Free Officers were engaged in their underground activities, Qassem was suspected by his superiors of being a member of the movement. He was called at least once to the Ministry of Defense, where he underwent some questioning, but he was not subjected to any further interrogation or charged with any misdoing. Ironically, by 1957 Qassem had become the chairman of the Central Committee of the Organization of Free Officers, and thus was in charge of making the important decisions in that organization. The main reason Qassem was elected chairman of the Central Committee lies in the fact that he was the senior Free Officer in the group. At its height, the Free Officers numbered 200 to 250.

When the Central Committee of the Free Officers decided to make limited contact with political parties in the National Front, Qassem chose to contact the National Democratic Party, an early indication of his leftist, reformist leanings. At least three times before July 1958, coup orders were given by the Command of the Free Officers, but all were subsequently cancelled. In July of that year, with great secrecy, Qassem and Aref staged their coup using several army units. Qassem and Aref were both stationed at Jalula, a base northeast of Baghdad when, on July 14, 1958, army units headed by Aref were ordered to Jordan in support of King Hussein ibn Talal.* Instead, they occupied central points in Baghdad—the central telecommunications unit; the Radio and TV Building, and the Ministry of Defense. A battalion of the Iraqi army encountered little resistance when it went to occupy the Royal Palace, where members of the family, including the young King Faisal and his uncle Prince Abd al-Ilah were summarily executed. The same fate was inflicted on Nuri al-Said,* who was killed the following day while trying to escape. Nuri was seen by the population as the strong man of the monarchy and the symbol of its pro-Western policies in Iraq; he was also the obstacle to closer ties to the United Arab Republic (UAR) led by Gamal Abdul Nasser.*

Qassem did not play an active role in occupying vital points in Baghdad; rather, he was the key coordinator in the military moves of the other commanders who marched toward Baghdad. In contrast to the revolution in Egypt, the Organization of the Free Officers in Iraq lost its cohesion and ceased to exist once the monarchy was felled.

Soon after the coup, signs of divergence between Qassem and Aref emerged; Qassem assumed political primacy as prime minister, while Abdul Salam Aref became his deputy and minister of the interior. Aref adopted strong Arab nationalist policies that were socially conservative and anti-Communist. He emphasized the need of Iraq to further strengthen ties to Nasser and the UAR. It was not long before Qassem, possibly to compensate, showed signs of allying with communists and leftists, increasingly adopting attitudes of "Iraq First" which were aimed at distancing Iraq more and more from the UAR. Both men encouraged street demonstrations by their followers.

When the rift between the two men became intolerable, Qassem relieved Aref of all his duties as deputy prime minister and minister of the interior and appointed him as ambassador to the Federal Republic of Germany. Aref left for Europe, but he never reached Bonn. Instead, he returned to Baghdad, whereupon Qassem arrested him on charges of plotting against him. Aref was tried in secret and sentenced to death, but Qassem commuted his sentence to life imprisonment. Thus Aref lived, ironically, to play a major role in the downfall of Qassem in 1963, and to become Iraq's president from 1963 to 1966.

It was not long before a special court was set up, headed by Fadil Abbas al-Mahdawi, a relative of Qassem's, to try high officials of the old regime. It soon came under pressure from the communists who, with their control of the masses, turned it into a sham and a mockery of justice. The defendants were ridiculed and insulted by the audience with the acquiescence and even participation of the judges and the public prosecutor. The court lionized Qassem and contributed to his conception that he had a sacred mission to serve the Iraqi people.

Before a year had passed, Qassem was portraying himself as the "sole leader" of Iraq. His photos were ubiquitous, and his speeches were printed and distributed everywhere in the country and even abroad. He encouraged the idea that the Iraqi revolution had been masterminded and executed by him alone.

Probably the most devastating policy he adopted, and one that was instrumental in antagonizing the Iraqi people, was his endorsement of communist groups and his acquiescence in their takeover of the streets, and of schools and colleges. The communists, who had played a minor role if any in the 1958 revolution, used the political tolerance that emerged after the revolution to enhance their power and to take control of popular street demonstrations. It is possible that Qassem saw in the communists a movement that represented the poor and deprived segments of the population. The communists saw in Qassem a leader with whom they could ally in order to achieve their objectives. While recognizing that they could only take power gradually, if at all, they sought to achieve their policies through Qassem. For nearly two years, the communists were in the ascendancy in Baghdad and elsewhere. In July 1959, for the first time since the end of World War II, communists participated in the government. Communists soon gained control of a number of the unions and professional organizations that proliferated in that period, among them the labor and farmers unions, and the federations for students, teachers, and women.

On March 7, 1959, nationalist army units in Mosul revolted against Qassem. The leader of the rebellion was Colonel Abdul Wahhab al-Shawwaf, commander of the Mosul Garrison. An early member of the Free Officers' group, Shawwaf resented Qassem's capture of the revolution and the leftist turn of his policy. His revolt coincided with a march on Mosul by a procommunist group, the Peace

Partisans, and was a reaction against it. The rebels also accused Qassem of endangering Iraq's relations with the UAR. However, the ill-prepared and poorly coordinated revolt was quickly put down by Qassem, and Colonel Shawwaf was killed. Hard on the heels of the revolt, the city of Mosul witnessed a massacre when the Peace Partisans and their supporters were given a free hand to kill those they suspected of being anticommunist or supporters of Shawwaf. Another massacre was committed in Kirkuk on July 14, 1959, when communist elements assembled in that city to celebrate the first anniversary of the 1958 revolution. These elements, attempting to enlarge their support and weaken their enemies, encouraged ethnic rivalry between the Kurds, some of whom were procommunist, and the Turkish population of Kirkuk, a relatively conservative and anticommunist segment of the population. The result was a series of atrocities, with several hundred Turks murdered or wounded.

Qassem condemned these communist acts, but the condemnation came too late to improve his image. The army itself was shaken and dismayed by the trial and execution of the officers who had participated in the Mosul revolt. A number of these were founding members of the Free Officers Organization, such as Midhat al-Haj Sirri, and were trying to reverse the leftward trend of the regime.

In foreign affairs, Qassem's policies were those of an Iraqi nationalist who focused on Iraq and made it a nonaligned country following positive neutrality. He was quite successful in cutting Iraqui ties to Great Britain, which had symbolized to Iraqis their submission to the West. Qassem froze Iraq's activities in the Baghdad Pact, and in March 1959 officially withdrew from it. For the West, the Iraqi retreat from the Baghdad Pact constituted a major defeat for its security interests and a decisive shift in the balance of power in the Middle East.

A second major shift in Iraq's foreign policy came in July 1958 when Qassem reestablished diplomatic relations with the Soviet Union. Recognition of other Communist Bloc countries followed. These ties were established ostensibly to keep a balance between East and West. In fact, however, Qassem shifted Iraq's foreign relations in the direction of the Communist countries by making the first arms purchases from the USSR and by seeking military and economic assistance—and advisers—from Communist Bloc countries. The arms purchases made Iraq partially dependent on the Soviet Union for its armaments, a trend that continued for the next three decades.

Qassem had an important impact on Iraq's social and economic structure. His most important legacy was in the area of agrarian reform. Before the 1958 revolution, Iraqi farmers were subjected to severe maldistribution of land and income. Some 45 percent of the landowners owned about 1 percent of the land, while less than 1 percent owned 55 percent of the land. Most of the farmers were tenants in debt to the landlord. The government, headed by Qassem, passed the first agrarian reform (Law No. 30 of 1958), with the object of liberating the peasants from debt and from the control of their landlords and of liquidating the feudal system. The law did not abolish private ownership of land; in fact, it was rather conservative. It limited land ownership to 1,000 *dunums* (250 hectares) for irrigated land in the central and southern regions and 2,000 dunums (500 hectares) for the rain-fed areas in the north. Treasury bonds with twenty-years' maturity were granted to compensate owners for expropriated land. Unfortunately, although much land was confiscated, the new regime lacked the mechanisms to redistribute the land and to support the new owners. As a result, agricultural production declined.

Qassem also attempted to improve the status of women. In December 1959, he revised the personal status code regulating family relations in a way that gave women more rights in marriage, divorce, and inheritance. The law did not survive intact after his regime. Qassem also encouraged the formation of the General Union of Iraqi Women. Although Iraqi women were considered well advanced compared to women in the rest of the Arab world, the fact that they gained their own federation was another important step in their advancement.

Qassem began by welcoming the Kurdish leader, Mustapha Barzani, back to Baghdad from exile, and the new regime recognized the Kurds as partners with the Arabs in the new constitution. It was not long, however, before Kurdish elements, headed by Barzani, and encouraged by the communists and by the weakness of Qassem, went into rebellion against the central government, starting in 1960. Qassem tried to weaken Barzani's movement by encouraging some progovernment Kurdish tribes to fight the Barzani forces which occurred from March 1960 through September 1961. When such efforts did not put an end to the rebellion, regular armed units were sent to the north, and the Iraqi air force bombarded Kurdish villages. Qassem's policies began a long cycle of warfare in the north that outlasted Qassem's regime by many years.

Initially, the Kurdish rebellion made some gains in the north. Barzani's forces denied certain roads and small towns to the Iraqi army, which, in turn, launched attacks against the Kurdish guerrillas. After nearly two years of inconclusive fighting, Qassem announced an end to the offensive in October 1961. However, armed clashes between the two antagonists continued. By July 1962, Mustapha Barzani seemed to be gaining the upper hand by expanding the territory under his control, although government forces were always able to hold the cities. The struggle between the Kurdish rebels and Qassem's troops continued to the end of Qassem's era. His inability to end the Kurdish rebellion was a major factor in weakening his regime. It is worth noting that Qassem was the first to recruit Kurds to fight other Kurds side by side with the regular Iraqi army. These "government" Kurds have become known as Fursan (Cavaliers). Such a practice was adopted and encouraged by succeeding Iraqi governments and is used today by the present rulers of Iraq.

Along with his procommunist policy and the Kurdish rebellion, Qassem's claim to Kuwait helped undermine his regime. He was not the first Iraqi to claim Kuwait, however. The Ottomans, at the end of the nineteenth century, nominated the sheikh of Kuwait as a *qaimakam* (county head) to be attached to the *vali* (governor) of Basra, but no official acceptance by Kuwait was made. Instead, in 1899 Kuwait signed an agreement with the British government making Kuwait a British protectorate. Following Iraq's independence in 1932, a movement emerged in both Iraq and Kuwait demanding a union between the two countries. However, the British soon put an end to this movement in Kuwait.

Thus it was not a total surprise to Iraqis when Qassem announced, immediately after Kuwait's declaration of independence in June 1961, that Kuwait was considered a part of the Basra governorate, and its sheikh a *qaimakam*. Tension in the area rose immediately. British troops landed in Kuwait to defend the newly independent country against a possible Iraqi attack. These troops were later replaced by units dispatched by the Arab League, and Iraq found itself isolated in the Arab world.

Qassem's failure to support his statements with any military action made it clear that he was not serious in his claims. Although Qassem summoned some staff officers and asked for military plans, they stalled for time, not only because such plans would be difficult to realize, but because they feared Qassem would become strong and it would become more difficult to eliminate him.

Despite this fiasco, Qassem was the first Iraqi leader to focus strongly on the Gulf. He was the first to call the Persian Gulf, the ''Arab Gulf,'' and under his leadership, Radio Baghdad started new propaganda programs aimed at the Arab Gulf sheikdoms then under British protection. From this time on, Iraq steadily increased its interest in the Gulf, until, in the 1970s, it became the major focus of its foreign policy.

One of the most important of Qassem's achievements was in the field of oil. In 1960, he signed Law Number 80, which began the process of breaking the hold of foreign oil companies over Iraq's oil production. The law confiscated all of the territory granted to the Iraq Petroleum Company (IPC) under its concession, except for the portion currently under production. For years this land had remained unexploited by IPC, an issue that had become a bone of contention with Iraqis. The National Iraqi Oil Company (NIOC) was subsequently established and the surplus lands were entrusted to NIOC for development. Law No. 80 prepared the way for the later nationalization of all foreign companies working in the field of oil, a nationalization completed in 1973.

Opposition to Qassem started soon after he became prime minister in July 1958. Arab nationalist elements were the first to criticize him because of his refusal to establish closer ties with the UAR. Such elements were found among both civilian and military groups. The civilian element was spearheaded by the *Istiqlal* (Independence) Party and the *Baath* (Renaissance) Party, an Arab nationalist party formed in Syria in 1947. Both parties had been represented in the cabinet formed immediately after the 1958 revolution, but their ministers resigned and joined the opposition in February 1959, after Qassem tilted toward the communists. The failed Mosul rebellion sharpened the frustration and alienation of the Arab nationalist contingent. The Baath party tried, on its own, to assassinate Qassem while he was driving in the streets of Baghdad on October 7, 1959. This attempt, too, was unsuccessful, although Qassem was wounded during the attack.

The Baath and other Arab nationalists were not the only ones opposing Qassem. Conservative and religious groups were antagonized by the spread of communist propaganda during his first two years. They also opposed his social programs, in particular the law that expanded women's rights. The religious establishment criticized Qassem and joined the Islamic Liberation Party, which was licensed for a short time before it went underground.

Elements of opposition were also working actively inside the army, preparing for the elimination of Qassem and a takeover of power. These efforts culminated in a successful military coup, led by the Baath, on February 8, 1963. There was a bloody street battle lasting almost twenty-four hours between Qassem loyalists on the one hand, mainly the military police and the communists, and the Bath and the Arab nationalists on the other. Qassem was captured and executed on the following day.

Despite his shortcomings, Qassem became a modern legend in Iraq. He ended the Hashemite monarchy; broke the hold of the West over Iraq; began social reform; and was the first Iraqi to rule over Iraq in more than one thousand years.

BIBLIOGRAPHY

Ali Ghalib, Sabih. *Qisat Thawrat 14 Tamuz wa-l-Dubbat al-Ahrar* (The Story of the July 14 Revolution and the Free Officers). Beirut: Dar al-Talia, 1968.
Batatu, Hanna. *The Old Social Classes and the Revolutionary Movements of Iraq*. Princeton: Princeton University Press, 1978.
Dann, Uriel. *Iraq Under Qassem, a Political History, 1958–1963*. New York: Frederick A. Praeger, 1969.
Iraq, Committee for the Celebration of the 14 July Revolution. *The Iraqi Revolution in its First Year*. Baghdad: Times Press, 1959, 1960, 1961, 1962.
Iraq, Ministry of Defense, Coordinating Committee for the Special High Military Court. *Muhakamat (Trials)*. Vol. 5. Baghdad: Ministry of Defense, 1958–1962.
Khadduri, Majid. *Republican Iraq: A Study in Iraqi Politics since the Revolution of 1958*. London: Oxford University Press, 1969.
Marr, Phebe. *The Modern History of Iraq*. Boulder, Colo.: Westview Press, 1985.
Penrose, Edith, and E. F. *Iraq: International Relations and National Development*. Boulder, Colo.: Westview Press, 1978.

LOUAY BAHRY AND PHEBE MARR

SHUKRI AL-QUWATLI (1891–1967) was one of the most important nationalist politicians of the French mandate era in Syria. He served as president of the Syrian Republic between 1943 and 1949, and again between 1955 and 1958. Born in Damascus in 1891, he grew up in the tumultuous final decades of the Ottoman Empire. He belonged to a Sunni Muslim family of prosperous merchants and landowners of the Shaghur quarter who made their fortune first in trade with Baghdad and the Arabian peninsula and then from agriculture. By the mid-nineteenth century, the Quwatli family had joined the social and political elite of Damascus.

Quwatli studied in a Catholic elementary school and then at Maktab Anbar, the elite government preparatory school in Damascus, before going on to Istanbul for advanced training in public administration. However, by the time he returned to Damascus, the Young Turks had come to power in Istanbul and imposed unpopular centralization and Turkification policies on the Syrian provinces in a desperate bid to hold the Ottoman Empire together. In the years immediately prior to World War I, many notables in Damascus and other Arab towns either lost or were denied the government posts they felt they deserved. Like other qualified young men of his generation from the Syrian upper classes, Quwatli was unable to secure a respectable post in the Ottoman provincial administration.

In Istanbul, Quwatli had already come into contact with members of the secret Arab nationalist society, al-Fatat, and joined its anti-Turkish leaders upon his return to Damascus. In 1916, with no stake in the Ottoman state, he joined the Hashemite-led Arab Revolt and participated with his al-Fatat comrades in underground activities against the Turks. Eventually he was arrested and jailed; in prison, he is said to have been tortured for months and even to have attempted suicide rather than divulge any secrets to the Turks. Reports of his heroism vaulted him into the limelight as a nationalist hero.

With the establishment of the Hashemite Prince (later King) Faisal's Arab government in Damascus at the end of World War I, Quwatli became an official in local administration, though he devoted most of his time to extragovernmental nationalist activities as a member of the recently established Arab Independence (*Istiqlal*) Party, the most radical of the nationalist groupings in Syria. Forced to flee Damascus during the French occupation of July 1920, he took up residence in Egypt, a country to which he would return often in his career.

The first half of the 1920s was marked by a confrontation between Syrian nationalists and the French, who received the mandate for Syria and Lebanon in 1920 (officially in 1922). After toppling Faisal's Arab government, the French separated Lebanon from Syria and then divided Syria into separate units along sectarian and regional lines. They centralized power in their own hands and adopted unpopular economic and political measures that caused serious discontent throughout much of the country and led to the Great Syrian Revolt of 1925–1927, the most significant rebellion of the 1920s in the Arab world.

In exile, Quwatli became an unofficial roving ambassador for the Hashemite-leaning Syrian-Palestine Congress, the principal Arab nationalist propaganda and fund-raising organization headquartered in Cairo. His connections with Shakib Arslan, the noted Arab intellectual and pan-Islamic activist, as well as his anti-French activities, caused the French to rank him as one of the most dangerous Syrians in exile.

During his exile, Quwatli grew increasingly hostile to the Hashemites on the grounds that they had collaborated with the British in order to secure their thrones in Transjordan and Iraq. He was greatly encouraged by the rise of Abd al-Aziz ibn Saud* and the Arabian tribal leader's easy and rapid conquest in the mid–1920s of the Hejaz, the traditional seat of Hashemite power. His family's historic trading relations with the Saudis enabled Quwatli to position himself as the main intermediary between ibn Saud and the Syrian-Palestine Congress during the Great Syrian Revolt. His ability to secure funds from the Saudis for the Syrian rebels enabled him and his Arab Independence Party comrades to challenge the pro-Hashemite leadership of the Congress. As the Syrian Revolt collapsed in late 1926 in the face of a reinforced French army of occupation, a wide rift developed between Syrian rebel leaders and exiles along pro- and anti-Hashemite lines. This schism was sufficiently pronounced by the end of the revolt to create permanent lines of division in the Syrian independence movement.

After the revolt, Quwatli resumed his pan-Arab activities in exile, supported by Shakib Arslan. However, with the French amnesty of 1930, he returned to Damascus. At first he kept a low political profile, devoting most of his time and energy to transforming fruit and vegetable processing into a modern industry. Depending at first on purchases of large quantities of fruit from the Quwatli orchards around Damascus, in 1932 he founded the Syrian Conserves Company, a major nationalist enterprise that employed two hundred workers, including many women, and which produced about twenty-five tons annually of processed fruits and vegetables for export to Palestine, Egypt, and Europe. The success of the Quwatli enterprise brought him much praise from nationalists and the sobriquet, the "Apricot King." Along with another nationalist-inspired enterprise, the National Cement Company, the Syrian Conserves Company became the pride of the principal Syrian nationalist organization of the French mandate era, the National Bloc.

The National Bloc, like the Wafd Party in Egypt and the Neo-Destour in Tunisia, was one of several broad-based groupings that appeared after World War I to spearhead the Arab independence struggles against the British and the French. The bloc was founded in 1927 and immediately adopted an evolutionary approach to the nationalist goals of Syrian unity and independence. The failure of the Syrian Revolt had convinced nationalists to drop armed confrontation as a strategy for winning French recognition; the bloc's more delicate tactics of mixing intermittent popular protest with diplomacy reflected its leadership's preference for an ideology that aimed at restoring the type of balance between foreign rule and local leadership that had been operative in late Ottoman times. While the revolt's collapse had chastened nationalist leaders, its fierceness and duration had also convinced the French government of the need to make some concession to the desire for self-government in Syria. A constitution was promulgated in 1930 and a parliament elected in 1932.

Although Quwatli disapproved of the National Bloc's moderate politics, he joined the organization in 1932, having become persuaded that this was the best way to insure it did not compromise Syria's future. He was instrumental in preventing bloc leaders in Damascus from accepting a most unfavorable treaty with France in 1933.

In that same year, a new political organization composed of younger radical pan-Arabists began to pose a challenge to the National Bloc. Known as the

League of National Action, its leaders included middle-class professionals, especially lawyers, who were increasingly disenchanted with the bloc's political ineffectiveness and its elitism. Many of the leaders had been educated in Europe in the 1920s and early 1930s, where they were inspired by the influence of radical youth movements in European politics. On their return to Syria, these young activists organized university and high-school students against the French, in the process stealing the bloc's thunder. Among bloc leaders in Damascus, only Quwatli commanded the League of National Action's respect for his uncompromising commitment to pan-Arabism and especially to the Palestinian cause.

Quwatli's influence with the league enabled him to widen his patronage network in Damascus and to challenge more moderate nationalists like Jamil Mardam, the principal architect of the bloc's policy of "honorable cooperation" with the French. At the same time, he was instrumental in persuading several important league members to join the bloc, which enabled him to closely monitor the radical tendencies of these younger nationalists.

Frustrated by its continued inability to relax French control over Syria, the National Bloc launched a paralyzing fifty-day general strike in early 1936, which caused the French government to recognize the necessity of coming to an agreement with the bloc. A nationalist delegation was invited to Paris to negotiate a treaty. At first negotiations did not go smoothly, but when the left-wing Popular Front came to power in June 1936, they reached a relatively swift and satisfactory conclusion. The terms of the treaty were hammered out, and it was agreed it would not come into force for three years. These years were to serve as a transitional period in which the National Bloc was permitted to govern and to share power with the French High Commission.

Shukri al-Quwatli had been one of the principal instigators of the general strike of 1936, though he did not go to Paris for the negotiations, preferring to remain in Damascus in charge of National Bloc operations. Soon after the return of the nationalist delegation, parliamentary elections were held, and Quwatli, like other bloc leaders, won a landslide victory. He joined the first National Bloc government of Prime Minister Jamil Mardam, and served as minister of defense and of finance. In government, he was the voice of pan-Arab interests, organizing support for the Arab rebellion in Palestine and opposition to French efforts to cede the Alexandretta district to Turkey. Within government and in National Bloc councils, he was recognized as the leading rival of the more moderate Jamil Mardam.

After Mardam became widely suspected of agreeing to new, unfavorable secret clauses of the Franco-Syrian Treaty, Quwatli resigned from government in early 1938, under pressure from his old Independence Party comrades. His departure made the Mardam government increasingly untenable and, one year later, Mardam himself resigned after the French government failed to ratify the treaty.

The transitional period, which ought to have led to the ratification of the treaty and to independence, was not allowed to run its course. In France, the quick decline of the Popular Front brought into power some leaders who had never believed in the policy of 1936. Furthermore, many who had believed in it changed their opinion, either because the prospects of another world war made it important that French authority should not be weakened in Syria and Lebanon, or else because events in Syria convinced them of the country's unreadiness for self-government. Similarly, the nationalists came to doubt the sincerity of French intentions, above all because the French ceded the northwestern district of Alexandretta to Turkey, but also because it became clear that the French Parliament would not ratify the treaty of 1936, even after the National Bloc government granted additional concessions to France. Meanwhile, the government's strength declined as suspicious minority communities, quietly encouraged by French agents, caused frequent disturbances, and radical nationalists attacked it on the grounds that it had compromised Syria's integrity and future as a politically independent state.

By the outbreak of World War II, nationalist fortunes were bleak. Although in Syria there was a certain sympathy with the Allied cause, there was clearly no great enthusiasm. Memories of the misery and starvation experienced during World War I were still fresh. The broken promises of the last war, the loss of Alexandretta, and the unratified treaty made Syrians from all walks of life wary of French intentions.

However, the Anglo-Free French invasion of Syria in 1941 introduced direct British influence into Syria and the possibility of reestablishing a more equitable balance of power between foreign rule and the nationalist leadership. Denied access to the French, who still preferred puppet leaders of their own choosing, the National Bloc sought British support for its return to power.

Shukri al-Quwatli emerged during the war as the leading nationalist politician in Syria. Jamil Mardam and two of his closest bloc associates had lost position and face in 1940, when they were accused of being involved in the assassination of Dr. Abd al-Rahman Shahbandar, a major nationalist opponent of the bloc leadership. After they fled Syria to avoid incarceration, Quwatli was virtually the only politician of national stature left in Damascus. However, the Free French refused to deal with Quwatli, accusing him of being in secret collusion with Nazi agents in Syria. To protest French policy, he went into self-imposed exile in Iraq, where the British had reinforced their position. Although they suspected Quwatli of pro-German leanings and recalled his strong involvement during the Palestinian rebellion of the late 1930s, the British also saw advantages in supporting an independent Syria. Not wishing to alienate their moderate Arab allies, including Quwatli's old friend, ibn Saud, who assured them that the Syrian leader's earlier ties to the Axis powers had been purely tactical, the British opted to apply pressure on the French to accept Quwatli's return. After the national elections of 1943, Parliament chose Quwatli as the first president of an "officially" independent Syria. It was another three years, however, before the French evacuated the country.

Independence brought about a fundamental change in the character of politics in Syria. The traditional position of nationalists, between distant ruler and local society, suddenly disappeared. The nationalists themselves became the government, and their actions were subject to a new set of rules. Their triumph was short-lived, however, because their control of political life was already being challenged by a growing professional middle class in the towns, and by army officers, many of them of rural origin.

Although Shukri al-Quwatli's remarkably untarnished reputation as a nationalist enabled him to meet some of the challenges to his leadership, in the end flaws in his political character got the best of him. Denied the opportunity during the French Mandate to acquire experience in government and to acquire statesmanlike qualities, as president he was incapable of controlling the financial excesses and political intrigues of some of his more wily National Party (as Quwatli had renamed the bloc in 1943) colleagues. It did not take long for his administration to become the focus of widespread criticism, scandal, and factionalism.

In 1949, Quwatli was deposed as president by the first military coup d'état in modern Syrian history. Once again he went into exile in Egypt. Government corruption, the absence of substantitive economic reforms, and the Syrian army's humiliating defeat at the hands of Israel during the Palestine war of 1948 all contributed to the military's intervention in Syrian politics.

Fierce inter-Arab rivalries governed Syrian political life throughout the 1950s. Pitted against one another were the Hashemite monarchies in Iraq and Jordan on one side, and Egypt and Saudi Arabia on the other. Quwatli's long-standing relations with the Saudis and the Egyptians and his hostility to the Hashemites determined on which side he stood. His five years in exile were spent colliding with his Arab patrons against the Hashemites and their allies in Syria, the People's Party. He owed his return to Syria in 1954, after the downfall of the military regime of President (Colonel) Adib Shishakli, to the support he received from Cairo and Riyadh.

Quwatli's long absence from Syria, the imposition of military rule, the rivalry of the pro-Hashemite People's Party, and the growth of three radical organizations—the communists, the Muslim Brothers, and the pan-Arabist Baath Party—had damaged the National Party's prospects in the new elections of 1954. However, when the office of the presidency became vacant the following year, Quwatli's name was put forth. He was not the strongest candidate—many recalled the corruption associated with his earlier term as president (1943–1949), and the army disliked him; still, he radiated a certain appeal as a hero of the independence movement, the conservative, propertied classes preferred him, and his opponent, Khalid al-Azm, was thought by some influential army officers to be too close to the Soviet Union. These and other factors enabled him to return to the office from which he had been dislodged six years earlier.

If Quwatli's first two terms in office (1943–1949) were widely regarded as unsuccessful, his third term was even more so. He returned to the presidency at the height of the Cold War in the Middle East. Syria had become the object of East-West rivalry and of an inter-Arab struggle between the pro-Western

Hashemite monarchy in Iraq and the nonaligned republican regime of Gamal Abdul Nasser* in Egypt. He was incapable of controlling these forces, let alone a hostile Syrian army, communists, and Baathists.

In the end, America's inability to distinguish between nonalignment and Soviet domination in the Arab world; coupled with the growth of popular anti-Western sentiments as a result of the Anglo-French-Israeli invasion of Suez in 1956, kept Syria from joining the American-supported Baghdad Pact, which had been formed in 1955 to halt the spread of Soviet influence in the Middle East. At the height of the Suez Crisis, Quwatli went to Moscow to seek Soviet support in the event of an attack on Syria. Shortly thereafter, Soviet arms began to flood the country. Quwatli's own political base was by then so weak that he was pulled along by the new, prevailing winds of radicalism and popular pan-Arab sentiments. He did not oppose Syria's union with Egypt in 1958, and resigned as president in order to allow Nasser to assume the presidency of the new United Arab Republic. For all intents and purposes, Shukri al-Quwatli's long and once distinguished political career had come to an end. He spent the remaining years of his life on the political sidelines watching the collapse of the Egyptian-Syrian union in 1961 and the coming to power of the radical pan-Arab Baath Party in 1963. By the time of his death in 1967, he could scarcely recognize the political system under which Syrians lived.

BIBLIOGRAPHY

Work by Quwatli:

Majmu at khutab (Collected Speeches). Damascus: n.p., 1957.

Other Works:

Gomaa, Ahmed M. *The Foundation of the League of Arab States: Wartime Diplomacy and Inter-Arab Politics 1941–1945*. London: Longman, 1977.

Hourani, Albert. *Syria and Lebanon: A Political Essay*. London: Oxford University Press, 1946.

Khoury, Philip S. *Urban Notables and Arab Nationalism: The Politics of Damascus, 1860–1920*. Cambridge: Cambridge University Press, 1983.

———. *Syria and the French Mandate: The Politics of Arab Nationalism, 1920–1945*. Princeton: Princeton University Press, 1987.

Longrigg, S. H. *Syria and Lebanon under French Mandate*. London: Oxford University Press, 1958.

Seale, Patrick. *The Struggle for Syria: A Study in Post-War Arab Politics 1945–1958*. London: Oxford University Press, 1965.

Tibawi, A. L. *A Modern History of Syria Including Lebanon and Palestine*. London: MacMillan, 1969.

al-Yunis, 'Abd al-Latif. *Shukri al-Quwatli*. Cairo: n.p., n.d.

PHILIP S. KHOURY

R

YITZHAK RABIN (1922–   ) is one of the most prominent military and political figures in modern-day Israel. He epitomizes the brashness and self-reliance
that many observers say sets apart the first generation of native-born Israeli
leaders from the older generation of Israel's founding fathers. Having joined the
elite Palmach (strike forces) unit at age nineteen, Rabin spent the next twenty-
six years in the military, rising through the ranks to become chief of staff in
1964 and one of the principal architects of Israel's lightning victory in the June
1967 war. He left the army shortly after the war to begin a new career as a
diplomat, serving for five years as Israel's ambassador to the United States.
Rabin later returned to Israel to succeed Golda Meir* as prime minister in early
1974, but his tenure as prime minister ended abruptly because of a scandal
involving a violation of Israel's strict foreign-currency regulations. By 1984,
Rabin had staged a political comeback as defense minister in the Labor-Likud
National Unity Government and became one of the government's most popular
ministers. At the same time, he bore the brunt of domestic and international
criticism for his handling of the Palestinian rioting in the West Bank and Gaza
Strip that began in late 1987. Despite his hard-line approach to the Palestinian
unrest, Rabin has consistently been a voice of moderation in Israel on broader
Arab-Israeli peace issues and a strong advocate of the imperative of trading land
for peace.

The son of Russian immigrants to Palestine, Rabin was born in Jerusalem on
March 1, 1922. He did not become a public servant by chance. He grew up in
a household where both his mother and father were prominent public figures in
Labor politics and active in the fight to secure a Jewish homeland. The example
set by his parents had a lasting impact. Rabin recounts how his mother, working
as a nurse, and father, a soldier in the Jewish Legion, met in Jerusalem two
years before he was born, drawn together by Arab attacks on the city's Jewish
Quarter. His father, Nehemiah, arrived in Palestine in 1918 from the United
States, to which he had fled thirteen years earlier from Russia. He was forced
to leave his native land because of his involvement in the Social Revolutionary

Party underground. Arriving in the United States penniless, Rabin's father became a tailor and trade-union activist. He received his indoctrination to Socialist Zionism in the *Poalei Zion* (Workers of Zion) Party, the first Socialist-Zionist party in the diaspora and a forerunner of the *Ahdut Haavodah* (Unity of Labor) Party in Israel. Nehemiah eventually came to Palestine as a soldier in the Jewish Legion and, after his discharge, resumed his trade-union activities as an organizer in Tel Aviv. He also became involved with the Histadrut labor federation.

Rabin's mother, Rosa, was also a prominent political activist. Born in Russia to a wealthy family with a flourishing lumber business, she was attracted to left-wing politics and revolutionary activities. However, she soon became disillusioned with Soviet communism and, although not a Zionist, found her way to Palestine in 1919. She spent her first few months on a *kibbutz* (collective settlement) in the Galilee. It was during a visit with an uncle in Jerusalem that disturbances in the city broke out and she met Nehemiah Rabin.

Rabin has described the atmosphere in his parents' household as "spartan," and has taken pride in the family's dedication to public causes. He has commented that his parents saw their public activity not as a way of furthering personal interests but as a duty owed to the community.

Young Rabin dreamed of attending a prominent agricultural training school and devoting his life to reclaiming the land, although he did not have a personal passion for agriculture. The return to the soil, and especially the establishment of collective settlements, was seen as a national duty in those days by youngsters like Rabin who had been raised on the principles of the Labor movement. Consequently, Rabin entered the prestigious Kadouri Agricultural School in the Galilee in 1937. After graduation in 1940, he moved to Kibbutz Ramat Yohanan near Haifa, where he and other young pioneers were to be trained to eventually establish a new settlement of their own. His pioneering career was cut short, however, by an encounter one night in 1941 in the kibbutz dining hall with a local *Haganah* (Jewish underground defense force) commander, Moshe Dayan.* After describing the dangers facing the country from Syria, which was then under the control of the pro-Nazi Vichy regime, Dayan invited Rabin to volunteer for the elite Palmach (strike forces) unit.

Rabin joined the Haganah at the end of May 1941, beginning a career that would last for twenty-six years. His first military operation was to cut telephone wires behind French lines in Lebanon in advance of invading Australian forces. Rabin was subsequently involved in other Palmach operations, including an attack in late 1945 on a British detention camp near Atlit in order to liberate several hundred "illegal" immigrants. Less than a year later, Rabin was arrested in a massive British sweep that netted most of the members of the Jewish Agency and thousands suspected of belonging to the Palmach, and he spent a brief period in a British prison. In October 1947, Rabin was appointed deputy commander of the Palmach by its commander, Yigal Allon.

One month before Israel declared its independence on May 15, 1948, Rabin was put in charge of the Palmach's newly created Harel Brigade and was assigned the task of eliminating Arab strongholds along the Tel Aviv-Jerusalem road. His unit was also instrumental in preventing the predominantly Jewish western part of Jerusalem from falling into Arab hands. Later transferred to the southern command, Rabin was involved in the final campaigns of the fighting to secure Israeli control of the Negev. Only three days after moving to the southern command in late August 1948, Rabin also decided to marry Leah Schlossberg, with whom he had been romantically involved since 1944. Their daughter, Dalia, was born in 1949 and their son, Yuval, was born in 1956. Rabin also had his first taste of international diplomacy while at the southern command when he was asked by Chief of Staff Yigael Yadin to join the Israeli delegation to the armistice talks with Egypt at Rhodes in early 1949.

Rabin's first experiences with war left a strong impression on him. Inconsolable with the vision of sending poorly equipped soldiers to face a more numerous and better-armed enemy, Rabin realized that Israel's only hope for survival lay in creating an army that was capable of defeating any future aggression with the fewest possible casualties. Rabin dedicated his military career toward that end, and held a variety of positions in the army during Israel's formative years, including head of the army's tactical operations division from 1950 to 1952, head of the training branch from 1954 to 1956, and commanding officer of the northern command from 1956 to 1959, whereupon he was appointed army chief of operations.

It was as chief of operations that Rabin first came into conflict with Shimon Peres,* who was then deputy defense minister. The conflict with Peres originated as a legitimate difference of opinion over who should determine the priorities in the acquisition and manufacture of arms. Rabin believed that the decision should be made by professional soldiers—the men who had to use the arms— rather than by civilians in the defense ministry, who only bought or manufactured the weapons. The conflict between the two men, however, was not merely professional. It developed into a bitter personal feud that steadily worsened and that eventually undermined both Rabin's effectiveness as prime minister and the Labor Party's electoral fortunes.

Rabin was appointed chief of staff in January 1964 during a critical period in Israel's history. After nearly eight years of relative quiet along Israel's frontiers, Rabin's tenure as army chief of staff coincided with growing Arab-Israeli tensions. During his first month in office, the Arab states held a summit meeting in Cairo and decided to take steps to thwart Israel's National Water Carrier program. They also decided to establish the Palestine Liberation Organization (PLO) and to support Palestinian terrorist attacks against Israel.

The situation along the armistice lines deteriorated thereafter as the Syrians stepped up artillery barrages on Israeli settlements in the Galilee and Palestinian guerrillas launched raids into Israeli territory. During this period, Chief of Staff Rabin devoted himself to the dual tasks of restructuring the army and acquiring more advanced weaponry in anticipation of a presumably inevitable clash with Israel's Arab neighbors. The war finally came in June 1967, after Egyptian

President Gamal Abdul Nasser massed troops along the border with Israel and announced a blockade of Israel's southern waterways at the Strait of Tiran.

Rabin's army won a decisive victory over Egypt, Jordan, and Syria in six days, radically transforming the situation in the Middle East. To a large degree, the victory of the Israeli army was the result of Rabin's efforts as chief of staff to upgrade the infantry, which had been neglected by his predecessors. However, his performance as chief of staff during the May-June 1967 crisis was tarnished by his incapacitation during a thirty-hour period from May 23 to 25, forcing Major-General Ezer Weizman, then chief of army operations, to assume many of Rabin's responsibilities. Rabin acknowledges in his autobiography, *The Rabin Memoirs*, that he returned from a series of meetings on May 23, "in a state of mental and physical exhaustion." He suffered "from a combination of tension, exhaustion, and the enormous amounts of cigarette smoke I had inhaled in recent days. . . . But it was more than nicotine that brought me down. The heavy sense of guilt that had been dogging me of late became unbearably strong on May 23" (p. 81). Rabin's sense of guilt was apparently brought on by his uncertainty about the wisdom of his decision to mobilize Israel's reserves. Was this a prudent move or did it escalate the war of nerves with Egypt to a point where neither Israel nor Egypt could back down? Was he endangering Israel's existence by leading Israel into a war when it was isolated and abandoned by the major Western powers? After a thirty-hour rest, Rabin returned to full activity, but stories of the chief of staff suffering a mental breakdown during one of the most fateful crises in Israel's history would haunt Rabin throughout his later political career.

In February 1968, Rabin arrived in the United States to take up his new position as Israel's ambassador. Going to Washington, D.C., was the realization of a much-cherished dream. Rabin believed that, in the wake of the June 1967 war, strengthening Israel's ties with the United States was the greatest political challenge facing the country, and he felt his background as chief of staff would help to accomplish that task. Rabin set four goals for himself as ambassador: ensuring the supply of arms to Israel; coordinating U.S. and Israeli policies on a political settlement in the Middle East in preparation for eventual peace talks; securing U.S. financial assistance for the purchase of arms and to strengthen Israel's economy; and securing a commitment from the United States to use its deterrent capabilities to prevent direct Soviet military intervention against Israel in the event of another Arab-Israeli war.

Rabin was appointed over the objections of many professionals in the foreign ministry, and spent five years in the United States as ambassador. It was a critical period in U.S.-Israeli relations as the United States launched a series of Middle Eastern peace initiatives that brought the two states' interests into conflict. Rabin played a key role in the almost constant bilateral consultations necessitated by the peace initiatives.

Throughout this period, Rabin's relations with the foreign ministry were less than harmonious. On more than one occasion he was criticized by other Israeli officials for the manner in which he performed his duties as ambassador. He was accused of not advising the Israeli Government about an impending U.S. initiative in June 1970 to restore the Egyptian-Israeli cease-fire, and he was later criticized for deliberately failing to communicate Israel's rejection of the proposal to the United States. Rabin wanted his government to soften the tone of its rejection to minimize the damage to U.S.-Israeli ties. He also suggested that Israel delay its response so as not to be the first party to reject the plan. Rabin was openly critical of the foreign ministry and its manner of conducting business, and claimed that in the long run he and his staff alone were responsible for preserving good relations with the United States.

Ambassador Rabin created a stir in the United States and in Israel in June 1972 for making remarks that were interpreted as a blatant attempt to interfere in U.S. domestic politics. In an interview on Israeli radio, Rabin commented that President Richard Nixon had gone farther than any of his predecessors in expressing support for Israel in his speech to Congress after his return from Moscow. Rabin thought he was simply stating a fact that he wished to bring to the attention of the Israeli public. The remark was interpreted by many in Israel and the United States, however, as an endorsement of President Nixon's candidacy for reelection.

In March 1973, Rabin returned to Israel expecting to be appointed to the Cabinet. No such job was waiting for him, however, and he had to delay his entrance into politics until after the next Israeli election, which was postponed from October until December 1973 because of the outbreak of war on October 6. Labor won the election, and Rabin was invited by prime minister–designate Golda Meir to join the new cabinet as defense minister because of Moshe Dayan's refusal to serve in the new government. Even before the *Knesset* (Parliament) had a chance to approve Meir's new government, however, Dayan suddenly announced his willingness to join. Since he was Meir's preferred choice for the defense portfolio, Rabin was shifted to the labor ministry. Rabin has commented that the post was less than he had hoped for but more than some of his colleagues had wanted for him.

Meir's government lasted barely one month. She resigned following publication of the Agranat Commission's interim report on the conduct of the government on the eve of the 1973 October War. The search for a new prime minister began and eventually focused on a choice between Rabin and Shimon Peres. On April 22, 1974, Rabin was chosen by the Labor Party central committee, but Peres's strong showing in the vote earned him the second-ranking post in the cabinet—the defense ministry—from which he tried to undermine Rabin's authority at almost every turn in the hope of becoming prime minister himself.

Rabin had few successes as prime minister, but those he had were significant. In the military arena, Rabin concentrated on rebuilding the Israeli army through the purchase of sophisticated weaponry and restoring its self-confidence, which had been shattered by the surprise of the 1973 October War. The successful raid at Entebbe airport in Uganda on July 4, 1976, which freed hostages held by Palestinian hijackers, helped to restore the army's and the nation's self-confidence.

In the geostrategic and political arenas, Rabin successfully negotiated a second disengagement of forces agreement with Egypt, which was brokered by the United States. In so doing, he established a reputation as a tough bargainer on vital national-security interests while simultaneously strengthening and formalizing the U.S. commitment to Israel's security.

Rabin's term as prime minister ended prematurely, largely by his own doing. In December 1976, he contrived a coalition crisis in order to bring down his government and force new elections. Rabin hoped that Labor would be able to capitalize on the scheduling of early elections and would score a large enough victory at the polls to extend his term in office and to consolidate his hold on the party leadership. What he did not know at the time was that he would not be the party's candidate for prime minister in the May 1977 election. One month before the election, he was forced to step down in disgrace after admitting that he and his wife had maintained an illegal bank account in the United States. His long-time party rival Peres was appointed acting prime minister, and was designated to head the Labor Party list in the election. Labor suffered a historic defeat at the polls.

For the next four years, Rabin found himself in the political shadow of Labor leader Peres, and the relationship between the two was highly contentious. Indeed, the ongoing rivalry between Rabin and Peres was a major factor contributing to Labor's inability to unseat Menachem Begin's* Likud bloc in the June 1981 election. Rabin challenged Peres for the party's leadership at its national convention in December 1980, but lost. He received the support of only 30 percent of the party's delegates, while Peres was supported by the remaining 70 percent. The acrimony between the two Labor leaders deeply affected the party's campaign, as Peres excluded Rabin from the proposed Labor government until the last minute when he was brought in to replace the dovish Haim Bar-Lev as minister of defense. The bickering within the Labor Party between Peres and Rabin reinforced the public's image of the party's internal disarray and seriously undermined its electoral appeal.

By 1984 Rabin had finally managed to bury the political hatchet with Peres, and staged a remarkable political comeback. He assumed the defense portfolio in the National Unity Government that was formed following the July 1984 election, and soon became one of the government's most popular ministers. His popularity stemmed largely from his tough talk and even tougher actions in dealing with the Palestinian *intifada* (uprising) that began in December 1987. Rabin's approach to the deteriorating situation in the occupied territories combined the two things public opinion polls indicated most Israelis wanted: the use of heavy-handed force to quell the Palestinian unrest, and the readiness to exchange territory for peace.

Despite his hard-line approach to the Palestinian uprising, Rabin has consistently maintained a moderate view on Arab-Israeli peace issues. For him, the key to a settlement of the Palestinian problem remains Jordan. It has been so for the past twenty years, and the unrest in the occupied territories had not changed this view. At the same time, he has said that he would be prepared to negotiate with any PLO official who renounced the Palestine National Covenant, accepted United Nations Security Council Resolutions 242 and 338, and stopped all acts of terror.

Rabin shared the Labor Party position that a peace settlement would be based on the existence of only two independent states, Israel and a Jordanian-Palestinian state east of Israel. Rabin's vision of a settlement also includes the unified and expanded city of Jerusalem as Israel's capital; the Jordan River as Israel's security border; significant border changes from Israel's pre–1967 lines, although the bulk of the West Bank and Gaza Strip would be included in the Jordanian-Palestinian state; and the provision that the majority of Palestinians living in the occupied territories would be included in the Jordanian-Palestinian state, and those living under Israel's control would have the choice of becoming Israeli citizens or remaining Jordanians. Above all else, Rabin holds to the view that, while the territories Israel has occupied since June 1967 constitute strategic depth in the event of war, the bulk of them are bargaining chips that must be exchanged for peace.

After decades in the military and political limelight, Rabin continues to play a pivotal role in Israel's ongoing search for peace and security. As a military leader, Rabin has been unyielding in his commitment to protecting the country's security, whether it has required formulating strategic plans for confronting Israel's external Arab enemies or adopting controversial tactics for quelling the Palestinian intifada. As a politician, however, Rabin's voice has been one of moderation as he has counseled his countrymen that ultimately a political solution must be agreed upon by the parties to the Arab-Israeli conflict and that Israel will have to compromise for peace.

BIBLIOGRAPHY

Work by Rabin:

The Rabin Memoirs. Boston: Little, Brown, and Co., 1979.

Other Works:

Aronson, Shlomo. *Conflict and Bargaining in the Middle East*. Baltimore: Johns Hopkins University Press, 1978.
Brecher, Michael. *Decisions in Crisis*. Berkeley: University of California Press, 1980.
Elon, Amos. "Governing is Harder than Conquering." *New York Times Magazine*, May 4, 1975 pp. 11, 40–50.
Golan, Matti. *Shimon Peres: A Biography*. London: Weidenfeld and Nicolson, 1982.
Kieval, Gershon R. *Party Politics in Israel and the Occupied Territories*. Westport, Conn.: Greenwood Press, 1983.

Reich, Bernard, and Gershon R. Kieval (eds.) *Israel Faces the Future*. New York: Praeger
     Publishers, 1986.
————. *Israeli National Security Policy*. Westport, Conn.: Greenwood Press, 1988.
Slater, Robert. *Rabin of Israel: A Biography*. London: Robson Books, 1977.

                                                                GERSHON R. KIEVAL

RASHID BIN SAID AL MAKTUM (1912–   ). Sheikh Rashid, ruler of the
amirate of Dubai and vice president and prime minister of the United Arab
Emirates (UAE), is an impressive figure who, with his rival Sheikh Zayed bin
Sultan Al Nuhayyan,* ruler of Abu Dhabi and president of the UAE, has dominated the federation since its creation in 1971. Born in 1912 and, thus, about
six years older than Zayed, Rashid has been either regent or ruler of Dubai in
his own right for almost fifty years, since 1939. In that time he has secured his
family's uncontested rule of Dubai and, through his energy and intelligence,
made it the model of a highly prosperous and well-run state. At the same time,
he has both provided critical support to the cause of federation and has played
the part of Zayed's nemesis in thwarting the latter's goal of achieving an effective,
centralized federal government.

Rashid and Zayed are an interesting contrast. Each belongs to a faction of the
Bani Yas tribal federation, but the faction of Rashid—the Al Bu Falasah—broke
away and left Abu Dhabi in the 1830s to establish its own state in Dubai. The
two amirates and their rulers have been rivals ever since, constantly clashing
over territorial and other issues. In the case of Rashid and Zayed, the rivalry is
made more acute by their contrast in personalities. Rashid, though the paramount
chief of the Al Bu Falasah, is a cosmopolitan merchant, disdainful of bedouin
culture, while Zayed embodies the values of tribal society and views the wealthy
merchant class with a certain inborn suspicion. Rashid displays the cunning and
bold flair of a confident businessman, while Zayed exemplifies the physical
courage and stoicism of a tribal chieftain. Rashid rules in conformity with a
bottom-line mentality, whereas Zayed governs with the open-handed liberality
of the desert.

Rashid's parents were a dramatic contrast—his father, Said, was withdrawn
and indecisive, while his mother, Hussah, was forceful and, in an almost totally
male-dominated society, was nonetheless the real embodiment of political leadership in Dubai for many years. On one occasion she is said to have led the
defense of Dubai against an attack from neighboring Sharjah, while her husband
and sons remained passive. Rashid seems to have inherited something of each
of these contradictory dispositions. In young manhood he is remembered as
having been a "cerebral type" whose actions reflected not only high intelligence
but also a measure of shyness and uncertainty. He was close to a circle of young
men, several of whom would become important merchants in Dubai. One of the
youthful activities Rashid most enjoyed was the recitation of poetry. Character-
istically, he would listen while his friends recited. Rashid received little formal
education; his practical education in commercial matters began with the long

hours he and his boyhood intimates spent at the Dubai customs house observing the activities of the merchants.

However, during the period of his regency, 1939–1958, when he exercised much of the political authority in Dubai, Rashid displayed the combination of subtlety and determination that has sustained his governance. When, shortly after World War II, he determined to construct an airport for Dubai in spite of the opposition of the British government's local political agent, he displayed tenacity and a clever mastery of the indirect approach in tricking the British into providing what he wanted. At a critical juncture in the fortunes of his ruling branch of the Al Maktum, he resorted to both trickery and ruthlessness. In 1939, under the aegis of a political-economic reform movement, two other branches of the Al Maktum schemed to reduce Said's authority. These were the Bani Rashid and Bani Suhayl, which had several times sought to depose Said and even to take his life. Both Rashid and his mother steeled his resolve to resist this challenge, and Rashid helped contrive a plot to foil it. The would-be usurpers were invited to Rashid's wedding, where the bridegroom's armed party attacked them, killing several. Members of the Bani Rashid and Bani Suhayl lines have since played a significant, subsidiary role in Dubai's politics, but there has never been any hint of renewed challenge to the rule of the Bani Hashar line. It was after these events, when Said's confidence as ruler had been shaken, that Rashid assumed significant responsibility for Dubai's affairs as regent to his father.

First as regent and, since 1958, as ruler in his own right, Rashid has devoted himself single-mindedly to the one all-consuming object of his career—building the economic strength and expanding the wealth of Dubai. Rashid's rule is based on no obvious political model; its proper paradigm is a large, efficiently run commercial enterprise. Indeed, he has been Dubai's leading merchant as well as its political leader. With his business pragmatism, Rashid adopted many of the innovations introduced by the reform movement he had defeated and turned them to his own use as a sound basis for Dubai's orderly development. Early in Rashid's regency, the first dispensary and first post office of the Trucial States (later the independent United Arab Emirates) were established in Dubai, and by 1949 the only hospital in the lower Gulf was opened in Dubai. In the 1950s, the port of Dubai was improved and expanded and a modern municipal administration was established to promote the city's rational development and growth with the active involvement of the private sector. Because of its practical benefits, education was encouraged and, in 1958–1959 the first girl's school in the area was founded.

While Rashid's political ambitions essentially have been contained by the borders of Dubai, his view of commerce has always been much more cosmopolitan. As a young man in the 1930s he already urged that Dubai welcome Iranian merchants who wished to settle there. Some of these were of Arab origin, though long resident in Iran. This open-minded approach to Dubai's development brought Indian as well as Iranian businessmen to Dubai, creating a highly sophisticated commercial community that had already made the amirate the wealthiest state in the lower Gulf before the advent of massive oil-export earnings in the 1960s.

Exploitation of Abu Dhabi's vast oil resources, beginning in 1962, had begun to bring it greater wealth than Dubai's as independence of the Trucial States from Great Britain in 1971 neared. This, combined with Abu Dhabi's far greater territory, made it inevitable that that state and Zayed, its ruler, would take the lead in seeking to draw the small states of the lower Gulf into some form of political union or cooperation. Rashid was persuaded of the practical necessity of forming a political federation with his neighbors once British protection was withdrawn. Thus, following the 1968 announcement of Britain's intention to withdraw from the Gulf, he was willing to set aside the animosity generated by long years of enmity between Dubai and Abu Dhabi and by the personal rivalry between the two leaders themselves, and join Zayed in forming a union of their two states, issuing a call for the other Trucial States to join them. This led eventually to the creation of the United Arab Emirates (UAE) in 1971, with Rashid agreeing to serve as vice president with Zayed as president. Further, Rashid aligned himself with Zayed in rejecting Ras al-Khaimah's demands for a greater voice in the federation as the price for his joining. Moreover, when an early test of federal authority arose in connection with an attempted coup in Sharjah, one of the UAE's member states, Rashid backed Zayed in quashing the attempted usurpation and installing in place of the murdered *emir* (ruler) a member of the Sharjah ruling family acceptable to the federal government.

However, if Rashid was prepared to cooperate for the greater good, there were clear limits to the extent of his cooperation and a considerable price exacted to secure it. Even as he was allying himself with Zayed to promote a union that would serve the common cause, he insisted that Abu Dhabi should receive no support in its territorial dispute with Saudi Arabia, a dispute that threatened to truncate the former's hinterland. In determining the division of political power within the UAE, Rashid was able to achieve a virtual equivalence of power with Abu Dhabi, despite the latter's far greater territorial extent, military power, and wealth. He assured critics that Dubai as well as Abu Dhabi must approve any substantive matter before it can be agreed to by the Supreme Federal Council (compromising the seven amirate rulers) and procured an equal number of votes in the Federal National Council (the UAE's advisory body). Further, his three sons were all granted important positions in the new federal government. This was testimony both to Zayed's commitment to securing essential support for the new union and his willingness to be magnanimous in his approach to Rashid, as well as to Rashid's determination to drive as hard a bargain as he could on behalf of Dubai.

Consistent with his position at the birth of the UAE, Rashid has since advanced the cause of Dubai single-mindedly, supporting the union when and to the extent that it appeared necessary to secure his own state's essential interests. Though most of the federal civil servants are from Dubai, Rashid regularly castigated the bureaucracy's inefficiency and decried the fetters it threatens to impose on

Dubai's thriving free-enterprise system. A champion of what might be called a "states' rights" approach, Rashid pressed for a loose federation against the strongly centralized federal government to which Zayed and many of the young, better-educated UAE citizens are committed. Thus Dubai has not pulled its weight in making the federation work, falling far short of the pledged 50 percent of its oil revenues to the UAE treasury and leaving the burden of financing the poorer emirates overwhelmingly to Abu Dhabi. Moreover, Rashid's insistence on emiral autonomy has prevented any meaningful unification of the federal military establishment, and his business-as-usual approach to Iran during the Iran-Iraq war undercut Zayed's more balanced federal policy.

Rashid's spoiler attitude within the UAE on this and other issues has had wider ramifications. Within the Gulf Cooperation Council (GCC), including Kuwait, Saudi Arabia, Bahrain, Qatar, the UAE, and Oman, it weakened attempts to act as an effective bloc in countering the threat of the Iran-Iraq war and trying to mediate its conclusion. Similarly, with respect to oil, Rashid's independent line has far-reaching consequences. In staying outside the Organization of Petroleum Exporting Countries (OPEC), he has exempted Dubai's oil production from that organization's quota system. With the decline in oil prices, Dubai has increased its production, placing Abu Dhabi in the difficult dilemma of either having to cut its own production to keep the UAE within its overall quota or maintaining its own production at the level perceived necessary to finance the federal government.

Rashid's independent course has provoked political crises within the UAE, notably in 1976 when Zayed's threat to resign the presidency was turned aside by formal commitments to strengthen the federal government, and in 1979 when a similar threat was overcome by Rashid's reluctant agreement to serve as prime minister. For seventeen years the UAE's constitution has remained provisional while the nature and scope of federal authority are debated. Despite cosmetic concessions to the "unionists," the "federalists," led by Rashid, have kept the federal government weak and stymied in its movement toward effective centralized power. While Zayed's later career has been largely devoted to championing wider Arab causes, partly because of his frustration in trying to realize his vision of the UAE, Rashid's unqualified promotion of Dubai's interests has never wavered, remaining unencumbered by a serious impulse to provide support to other countries or movements.

Rashid's legacy will be an efficiently run, free-enterprise state whose development, despite minimal territory and relatively modest resource endowment, has been a dramatic economic success story. Rashid has taken a number of major gambles, including such projects as the world's largest dry dock, a major new port facility, and the huge Dubai International Trade Center, each initiative derided as a useless extravagance by many outside critics and each, in the end, confirming his prescient judgment. The most telling proof of his ultimate success is that, since 1981, Rashid has been disabled by ill health to the extent that his eldest son and heir apparent, Maktum, together with his younger sons, has largely directed the affairs of Dubai with no discernible disruption or alteration of course. At the end of the Iran-Iraq War, with its links to Iran well maintained, Dubai was poised to handle the finances for Iranian reconstruction. The business of Dubai remained business.

BIBLIOGRAPHY

Abdullah, Muhammad Morsy, *The United Arab Emirates: A Modern History*. London: Croom Helm; New York: Barnes and Noble Books, 1978.

Anthony, John Duke. *Arab States of the Lower Gulf: People, Politics, Petroleum*. Washington, D.C.: The Middle East Institute, 1975.

Heard-Bey, Frauke. *From Trucial States to United Arab Emirates: A Society in Transition*. London and New York: Longman Group, 1982.

Kelly, J. B. *Arabia, the Gulf and the West: A Critical View of the Arabs and Their Oil Policy*. New York: Basic Books, 1980.

Khalifa, Mohammed Ali. *The United Arab Emirates: Unity in Fragmentation*. Boulder, Colo.: Westview Press, 1979.

Peck, Malcolm C. *The United Emirates: A Venture in Unity*. London and Boulder, Colo.: Westview/Croom Helm, 1986.

Zahlan, Rosemarie Said. *The Origins of the United Arab Emirates: A Political and Social History of the Trucial States*. London: MacMillan Press, 1978.

MALCOLM C. PECK

S

ANWAR AL-SADAT (1918–1981) was the third Egyptian president since the abolition of the monarchy in 1953. His eleven-year rule was characterized by dramatic changes such as making Egypt the closest ally of the United States among the Arab states, in direct contrast to Egypt under his predecessor Gamal Abdul Nasser. Sadat also transformed Egypt from the leading Arab state confronting Israel into the first Arab country to sign a peace treaty with that adversary. Furthermore, Sadat opened up the Egyptian economy and began the process of political liberalization.

Anwar al-Sadat was born on December 25, 1918, in Mit Abu al-Kum village of the Manufiya province in the Delta region of Egypt. He was the son of an Egyptian civil servant and a Sudanese mother. Until the age of seven he was brought up in Mit al-Kum by his grandmother. In 1925, he moved to Cairo where he attended primary and secondary schools. In 1936 he finished his secondary education by obtaining the General Certificate of Education.

Two interrelated developments took place in 1936 that were of paramount importance. First was the expansion of the Egyptian military beyond the eighteen-thousand-soldier limit imposed by the British government since 1882, in the wake of the Anglo-Egyptian Treaty of 1936, made Egypt more independent from Britain. Second was the opening up of the Military Academy to cadets not recruited from the upper classes, which hitherto had dominated the officers' corps. Anwar al-Sadat, like many others including Gamal Abdul Nasser, took advantage of this opportunity and enrolled in the Military Academy, graduating in 1938.

By 1941, Anwar al-Sadat was actively involved in clandestine political groups, one of which was the precursor of the Free Officers' Movement which was formed in the late 1940s, and which had links with the Muslim Brothers, led by Hasan al-Banna. Sadat's activism in anti-British clandestine organizations and his contacts with German agents resulted in his imprisonment in 1942. He escaped from prison in 1945 but continued his political activities through a series of assassinations against prominent politicians in cooperation with some leading members of the Muslim Brothers. Sadat was directly involved in the assassination in January 1946 of a former minister of finance, Amin Uthman Pasha, who was known for his pro-British leanings, and he was apprehended and remained in prison until he was released in August 1948. After unsuccessful attempts to work in business, journalism, and even acting, Sadat used his contacts with the head of King Farouk's Iron Guard, Dr. Yusuf Rashad, with whom he collaborated in the unsuccessful attempts against the life of the leader of the Wafd Party, Mustafa al-Nahhas,* to be reinstated in the army in 1950. It was also during the same year that he married Jihan Safwat Rauf, who was fifteen years younger than he. (Sadat's first marriage, which lasted for twelve years and ended in 1948, was a traditionally arranged marriage in which he fathered three daughters).

It was in the wake of the 1948 Arab-Israeli war that some disenchanted military officers organized themselves in late 1949 into the Free Officers' Movement (Harakat al-Dubbat al-Ahrar), which was led by Gamal Abdul Nasser. Nasser had drawn upon the army officers who had experience in clandestine anti-British organizations, and therefore it was not surprising that he invited Anwar al-Sadat to join the command of the Free Officers Movement in late 1951. Sadat's role in the military coup of July 23, 1952, was, at best, ambiguous. Sadat was informed of the imminent coup a few days ahead of time, and arrived in Cairo from al-Arish in Sinai, where he was stationed, on the eve of the coup. However, he went with his wife to the cinema and became involved in a brawl that ended up in a police station, thus establishing an alibi in case the coup would fail. Sadat was probably torn between two loyalties: On the one hand, he owed his return to the army to Dr. Yusuf Rashad, the head of the king's Iron Guard; and on the other hand, he owed his position in the command of the Free Officers Movement to Gamal Abdul Nasser. Sadat had already spent a total of five years in jail, and therefore he was determined to leave his options open and support the side that would prevail. Nevertheless, Sadat was the person who read the first proclamation of the Egyptian Revolution on the radio on the morning of July 23, 1952.

As Gamal Abdul Nasser began to consolidate his power in 1954, against the challenge posed by General Muhammad Naguib and those who wanted to return to civilian rule, and against the Muslim Brothers, Sadat decided that the only way of surviving was to side with Abdul Nasser. Throughout the eighteen years of Abdul Nasser's rule, Sadat had cultivated the image of the self-deprecating, unambitious, yes-man politician. Sadat was the only leading member of the Free Officers Movement to write the story of the Egyptian Revolution—*Revolt on the Nile*, published in 1957. Sadat played an important role in the Egyptian military intervention in Yemen in the wake of the military coup of September 26, 1962, but he never initiated policies, and the decision to commit such a large contingent of Egyptian troops in Yemen was taken by Abdul Nasser and the commander of the Egyptian Army, Field Marshal Abd al-Hakim Amir. The most prominent political position Sadat had occupied prior to his appointment as vice president in December 1969, was speaker of the National Assembly, largely a ceremonial post.

The June 1967 Arab-Israeli war, which was disastrous for Egypt, had undermined the power of Field Marshal Amir, the closest associate of Abdul Nasser, who was in charge of the military and who had allegedly committed suicide in August 1967. By 1969 the only members of the original command of the Free Officers Movement who were still alive or had not fallen out of favor were Husain al-Shafii (a nonentity), and Anwar al-Sadat, who became a close confidant of Abdul Nasser. The latter decided before leaving for Morocco to attend an Arab Summit to appoint Sadat as his only vice president on December 20, 1969.

When President Gamal Abdul Nasser died suddenly of a heart attack on September 28, 1970, Sadat became the president of Egypt. He was faced with a clique of what he called later "the centers of power" (Marakiz al-Qiwa), who were Ali Sabri, Sharawi Juma, Sami Sharaf, and, to a lesser extent, Muhammad Hasanayn Haikal (the confidant of late President Abdul Nasser and the editor of *al-Ahram* newspaper). None of these challengers had the prestige and status that Sadat had. As they were inexperienced in how to retain power after they had been used to act as Abdul Nasser's cronies, Sadat was able to outmaneuver them. Sadat wanted to revamp the Arab Socialist Union and oust Ali Sabri, but the latter, in cooperation with Sharawi Juma (the minister of the interior) and other cabinet ministers staged a collective resignation to precipitate a crisis. Sadat, in a very shrewd move, accepted their resignation, appointed Mamduh Salem as minister of the interior, and alerted his Republican Guard (al-Haras al-Jumhuri) to control the city of Cairo if the need arose. On May 15, 1971, Sadat became the uncontested master of Egypt, depicting those who had lost the power struggle as perpetrators of the police state. Sadat released a large number of political prisoners, and gave back properties to those who were under sequestration.

Sadat had pursued, in the period between 1971 and the October War of 1973, domestic and foreign policies that were at once a continuation of, and different from, those of Abdul Nasser. Sadat kept the one-party system of the Arab Socialist Union, but he weakened its somewhat monolithic structure by allowing more freedom at various levels of organization. He appealed to those who were ostracized politically or had suffered economically due to the imposition of the socialist measures of 1961–1964 under Abdul Nasser by giving them back their political rights and their private properties. Sadat also appealed to the Muslim Brothers, and began using the epithet "the believer" (*al-Mumin*), and to employ the first name "Muhammad" before Anwar. This was not surprising, as the main domestic challenge at that time came from the left, which included Nasserites and communists. After he had called 1971 "the year of decision" (Sanat al-Hasm) with respect to the Arab-Israeli conflict, Sadat let it pass without any action, and this led to a series of demonstrations and strikes in January 1972 by Egyptian students—the first major domestic challenge after the power struggle of May 1971.

In foreign policy, in April 1971 Sadat continued Nasser's legacy by forming with Syria and Libya the federation of Arab Republics, which was a modest step toward the Nasserite goal of Arab unity. On the other hand, Sadat satisfied those who were Egyptian nationalists first and foremost, by changing the country's name from United Arab Republic (by which it had been known since February 1958) to the Arab Republic of Egypt. Although Sadat continued to express his ideology in revolutionary and Arab Nationalist rhetoric, he cultivated relations with all Arab regimes and in particular with Saudi Arabia. Sadat's links to Kamal al-Adham, King Faisal bin Abd al-Aziz Al Saud's* brother-in-law and the head of Saudi Intelligence, antedated the 1970s. The Trilateral Alliance of Egypt, Saudi Arabia, and Syria was crucial for the successful planning of the October War of 1973. King Faisal was privy to the decision by Sadat and the Syrian President Hafez al-Assad* to launch a coordinated attack on Israeli forces on October 6, 1973. Another development which was a departure from Nasser's legacy was ending the role of the Soviet military advisers and technicians in July 1972, a move that boosted the morale of the Egyptian military and was instrumental in making Sadat appear more decisive in his policies.

Wars can make or unmake charismatic leaders, and the October War of 1973 was no exception. Sadat, who had been hitherto underestimated by both his friends and his enemies became suddenly "the hero of the crossing," a charismatic leader in his own right. The Egyptian Army fought better in the October War of 1973 than in the disastrous military encounters of 1956 and 1967. This very fact contributed to the cause of peace because the Egyptians became more willing to compromise and settle their differences with the Israelis. Sadat sought U.S. mediation in the disengagement agreements between Egypt and Israel following the October War. The role of Henry Kissinger, the U.S. secretary of state, in bridging the gap between Egypt and Israel, resulted in the Egyptian-Israeli Disengagement Agreement of January 1974, which Kissinger shrewdly negotiated separately from the Syrian-Israeli Golan Heights Disengagement Agreement of May 1974. Later, Kissinger was able to convince Egypt and Israel to sign the Disengagement Agreement of September 1975 (Sinai II); which virtually ended the state of belligerency between Egypt and Israel, and which was preceded by the reopening of the Suez Canal in June 1975.

The October War of 1973 had made Sadat more assertive in his domestic policies, and began the gradual, though nevertheless partial, dismantling of the economic and political system he had inherited from Gamal Abdul Nasser. The *October Paper* issued in April 1974 was a landmark in the new *infitah* (opening) policy with respect to incentives given to foreign capital and to Egyptian investors who had accumulated capital and wealth in the Arab oil-producing countries. However, the public sector (Nasser's legacy) was not subordinated to the private sector, let alone undermined.

The Arab Socialist Union (ASU) was gradually transformed into what was at that time called the Manabir (forums), which eventually crystalized into separate political parties of the center, right, and left. Sadat took the middle road and regarded the Center Party as his own; under different names, this party continued to dominate the political system. For instance, in the October 1976 parliamentary elections, the government party (then called the Egypt Party) won 280 out of a total of 352 seats. In January 1977, the Arab Socialist Union was formally abolished.

On January 20, 1977, Cairo, Alexandria, and other towns witnessed a wave of riots unprecedented since Sadat came to power, and caused by the reduction of subsidies on certain goods, some of which were necessities for the Egyptian household. The Egyptian government responded by rescinding the decision to lift subsidies. Sadat was particularly annoyed, depicting the rioters as "thieves." The impact of these events on the Parties Law of May 1977 was to make it even more restrictive than previously envisaged. Nevertheless, the Wafd Party of the pre–1952 period was able to get the support of a sufficient number of members of parliament to organize itself into a legal political party. The popularity of the Wafd Party rose dramatically, with a reported membership of over one million, which prompted Sadat to crack down on the party and its leaders in June 1978. From then on, Sadat became increasingly intolerant of opposition parties and political dissent; this reached its culmination with the rigged elections of the 1979 Parliament, the establishment of a loyal opposition (the Socialist Labor Party formed by Ibrahim Shukri), and the incarceration of practically all the prominent leaders of the political opposition in September 1981. Moreover, the last few years of Sadat's rule were marred by sectarian conflict between militant Muslims and the Coptic Christian minority, which was exacerbated by a personality clash between Sadat and the spiritual head of the Coptic community, Pope Shenouda.

Sadat surprised his fellow citizens as well as the world when he declared on November 9, 1977, in a speech to the Egyptian Parliament that his quest for peace was so strong that he would be willing to appear before the Israeli Knesset (Parliament) in Jerusalem to further the cause of peace in the Middle East. The reasons for Sadat's historic visit to Jerusalem on November 19, 1977, were basically threefold. First was the realization that his Arab partners (Syria and the Palestine Liberation Organization or PLO) in the negotiations with Israel under the rubric of the Geneva Peace Conference (which was initially convened in December 1973) were either not serious or not ready for the peaceful settlement of the Arab-Israeli conflict. After all, Sadat had waited in vain for over two years since the signing of the Israeli-Egyptian Disengagement Agreement of September 1, 1975, for his Arab partners to join the peace process. Sadat was convinced that President Assad of Syria did not want peace, and that the Syrian military intervention in Lebanon was not for the purpose of taming the PLO but to control it in such a manner that it would not be able to participate directly or indirectly in the peace negotiations. Second, Sadat was fully aware that his visit to Jerusalem would be historic, and that it would have been unthinkable to his predecessor Abdul Nasser, thus making it even more attractive to Sadat in his quest for immortality. Third, facing a Likud Cabinet in Israel for the first time, Sadat needed a dramatic move to reactivate the peace process.

The contents of Sadat's speech on November 19, 1977, were less important than the fact that Sadat was delivering it at the Israeli Knesset, and that the president of the leading Arab state, Egypt, was talking directly and publicly to Israeli leaders; this was unprecedented. Despite what Sadat called "the breaking through [of] the psychological barrier" between him and the Israelis, intensive mediation efforts by the United States and by United States president Jimmy Carter himself were needed to reach an agreement (the Camp David Agreements) between President Sadat and Prime Minister Menachem Begin in September 1978. The Camp David Accords comprise two parts. The first deals with Egyptian-Israeli relations; it involves Israel pulling out from the rest of Sinai, and an international peace-keeping force to be deployed in its wake. Egypt was to sign a peace treaty and normalize its relations with Israel, including full diplomatic representation. The Egyptian-Israeli Treaty was signed in March 1979, and Israel completed the withdrawal of its troops from Sinai in April 1982. The second part of the Camp David Agreements, which pertains to a comprehensive peace and to the autonomy of the West Bank and Gaza Strip, has been interpreted differently by the two sides, and has never been implemented.

The reaction of the vast majority of the Arab states to the Camp David Agreements was negative, leading to the suspension of Egypt's membership in the League of Arab States, and the severing of diplomatic relations between Egypt and all the members of the league except for Sudan, Oman, and Somalia. Sadat was ostracized in the Arab World, and was often depicted as traitor, while Sadat dubbed the rulers of most of the Arab states "dwarfs." Nevertheless, a few months before Sadat's assassination, Iraq, which was pressed in its war with Iran, bought weapons from Egypt and continued to provide employment for over one million Egyptians who were residing in Iraq. Similarly, Saudi Arabia took an unprecedented move in publicly formulating, in August 1981, what was called the Fahd Plan (with an input from the PLO), which was an indirect consequence of the Camp David Agreements.

The Egyptian-Israeli Peace Treaty brought some tangible benefits to Egypt, making it the second largest recipient of U.S. military and economic aid. U.S.-Egyptian relations have reached unprecedented levels of cooperation, a complete volte face when compared with the kind of relations that existed at the time when Sadat took power.

Sadat's assassination on October 6, 1981, eight years to the day from when he launched his October War of 1973 and while he was attending a military parade celebrating that conflict, was not a reaction to the peace treaty with Israel but more a consequence of Sadat's internal policies against the opposition, including militant Islamic groups such as al-Jihad, which was responsible for his assassination.

In Sadat's eventful life one can trace the evolution of the individual from the young military officer who was engaged in terrorist operations to the mature statesman who was praised for his historic actions whether of war or peace. In his autobiography, which is entitled in Arabic *al-Bahth An al-Dhat* (In Search of Identity), one can sense this evolution. Sadat was not looking for a national identity or a religious identity, because being an Egyptian and a Muslim were both taken for granted by him. What he was looking for was the kind of polity Egypt should be. Influenced by the Society of Muslim Brothers and fascist ideology in his youth, Sadat rejected the liberal and democratic system which had "prevailed" in Egypt prior to 1952.

Sadat was a member of the ruling elite during Nasser's era, but he was more often than not an observer on the sidelines rather than an active participant. He had gained wisdom by pondering the major events that had engulfed Egypt during that period. He had viewed the 1956 Suez War and the military intervention in Yemen as disasters, but he had kept his analysis to himself. Only when he had the opportunity, that is, after he came to power, did Sadat follow policies that were in harmony with his views. In 1972 he distanced himself from the Soviet Union and moved closer to the conservative Arab states. The October War of 1973 and its aftermath provided the opportunity to change Egypt's foreign policy in favor of the West and in particular the United States.

Sadat also paved the way for the economic and even political liberalization of the Egyptian polity. Nevertheless, he was never able to transcend the antiliberal and antidemocratic biases of his formative years. Sadat wanted to differ from Nasser by changing the domestic economic and political system, but he did not want to change it to the extent that he would become accountable and therefore could be voted out of power. In three major aspects Sadat's policies were a continuation of his predecessor's. First was the continued importance of the Egyptian Army as the backbone of the Sadat regime; second was the keeping of the inefficient public sector almost intact; and third was the system providing for large subsidies of basic food items and other necessary goods.

Sadat's greatest legacy, and one that will remain for many generations to come, was the retrieval of Egyptian territory that was lost during his predecessor's rule, and the first peace treaty to be signed between an Arab state and Israel. Sadat thus immortalized himself as an Egyptian nationalist and as a champion of peace in the Middle East.

BIBLIOGRAPHY

Works by Sadat:

Revolt on the Nile (orig. publ. in Arabic in 1954). New York: John Day, 1957.
In Search of Identity: An Autobiography. New York: Harper and Row, 1978.

Other Works:

Al-Baghdadi, 'Abd al-Latif. *Mudhakkirat 'Abd al-Latif al-Baghdadi* (Memoirs of 'Abd al-Latif al-Baghdadi). 2 vols. Cairo and Alexandria; Al-Maktab al-Masri al-Hadith, 1977.

Binder, Leonard. *In a Moment of Enthusiasm: Political Power and the Second Stratum in Egypt*. Chicago: Chicago University Press, 1978.

Deeb, Marius. *Party Politics in Egypt: The Wafd and Its Rivals 1919–1939*. St. Antony's Middle East Monographs no. 9, London: Ithaca Press. Published for the Middle East Centre, Oxford, 1978.

Hamrush, Ahmad. *Qissat Thawrat 23 Yulyu* (The Story of the 23 July Revolution). Vol. 4: *Shuhud Thawrat Yulyu* (Witnesses of the July Revolution). Beirut: Al-Mu'assat al-'Arabiya lil-Dirasat wal-Nashr, 1977.

Hinnebusch Raymond A., Jr., *Egyptian Politics under Sadat: The Post-Populist Development of an Authoritarian-Modernizing State*. Cambridge; Cambridge University Press, 1985.

Hirst, David, and Irene Beeson. *Sadat*. London: Faber & Faber, 1981.

Waterbury, John. *The Egypt of Nasser and Sadat: The Political Economy of Two Regimes*. Princeton, N.J.: Princeton University Press, 1983.

MARIUS DEEB

MUSA AL-SADR (1928–1978?). Al-Sayyid Musa al-Sadr (Moussa Sadr, Musa Sadre) is one of the most intriguing and fascinating political personalities to have appeared in the modern Middle East. He was an ambitious but tolerant man, whose controversial career had an enormous impact on the Shii Muslim community of Lebanon. He was a reformer who sought to improve the standard of living of the Shi'ites and unite them. He spoke out against the Maronite-dominated government for neglecting the south where a majority of the Shi'ites lived. Musa Al-Sadr was determined to force the government to acknowledge the grievances voiced by the Shi'ites, but his efforts were overtaken by the civil war. His admirers saw him as a man of vision, political acumen, and profound compassion, while his detractors remember him as a deceitful, manipulative political chameleon. In a society all too marked by pettiness, greed, and political cowardice, Musa al-Sadr was a towering presence (literally as well as figuratively, as he was well over six feet tall). Though he disappeared in 1978, he remains a vibrant presence in Lebanon, still inspiring his followers and dogging his enemies.

Musa was born in Qom, Iran, in 1928, the son of Ayatullah Sadr al-Din Sadr, an important Shii Muslim *mujtahid* (a Shii jurisprudent qualified to make independent interpretations of law and theology). In Qom he attended primary and secondary school and a Shii seminary, and then went on to Tehran University where he matriculated in the School of Political Economy and Law; the first mujtahid to do so. He did not intend to pursue a career as a cleric, but upon the urging of his father he discarded his secular ambitions and agreed to continue an education in Islamic jurisprudence (fiqh). One year after his father's death in 1953, he moved to Najaf, Iraq, where he studied under Ayatullahs Muhsin al-Hakim and Abdul Qasim Khui.

He first visited Lebanon, which was his ancestral home, in 1957. During this visit he made a very strong and positive impression on the Lebanese Shia, including his relative al-Sayyid Abdul Husain Sharaf al-Din, the Shii religious leader of the southern Lebanese coastal city of Tyre. Following the death of Sharaf al-Din in 1958, he was invited to become the *imam* (senior religious authority) in Tyre. In 1960 he moved to Tyre, with the active support of his teacher and mentor, Ayatullah Muhsin al-Hakim. He was granted Lebanese citizenship in 1963.

One of his first significant acts was the establishment of a vocational institute in the southern town of Burj al-Shimali (near Tyre), where Shii youths could gain the training that would allow them to escape the privation that marked their community. The institute was constructed at a cost of half a million Lebanese pounds (about 165,000 dollars) with monies provided by Shii benefactors, the Ministry of Education of Lebanon, and bank loans. The institute would become an important symbol of Musa al-Sadr's leadership; it is still in operation, providing vocational training for about five hundred orphans under the supervision of Musa's strong-willed sister Rabaab.

A physically imposing man of intelligence, widely noted personal charm, and enormous energy—one of his former assistants claims that he frequently worked twenty hours a day—al-Sadr attracted a wide array of supporters, ranging from Shii merchants making their fortunes in West Africa to petit-bourgeois youth. The Shia who had migrated to West Africa, fleeing the poverty of Lebanon to seek their fortunes, proved to be an important source of financial support for Musa al-Sadr. Many of these men had done very well, and they were attracted to a man who promised to bring down an old system that had humiliated them and denied them a political voice.

Imam Musa—as he came to be called by his followers—set out to establish himself as the paramount leader of the Shii community in Lebanon, which was most noteworthy at the time for its poverty and general underdevelopment. He helped to fill a yawning leadership void that had resulted from the growing inability of the *zaims* (traditional political bosses) to meet the mushrooming needs of their clients. From the 1960s on, the Shia had experienced rapid social change and economic disruption, and the old village-based patronage system, which presumed the underdevelopment and apathy of its clients, was proving an anachronism.

Musa al-Sadr could see beyond the villages, the patronage networks, and the clans of the Shia. He was able to stand above a fragmented and often victimized community and see it as a whole. Through his organizational innovations, his speeches, and his personal example, he succeeded in giving many Shia an inclusive communal identity. Furthermore, he reminded his followers that their deprivation was not to be fatalistically accepted, for so long as they could speak out through their religion they could overcome their condition. As he once observed, "Whenever the poor involve themselves in a social revolution it is a confirmation that injustice is not predestined" (Norton 1987:40).

He shrewdly recognized that his power lay in part in his role as a custodian of religious symbols. He used the central myths of Shiism, especially the martyrdom of Imam Husain at Karbala centuries before, to spur his followers.

However, as the record of his political alliances shows, he was above all else a pragmatist. It is both a tribute to his political skill and a commentary on his tactics that well-informed Lebanese have commented that nobody knew where Imam Musa stood.

His followers today often characterize him as a vociferous critic of the Shah of Iran (Mohammad Reza Pahlavi*), but it was only after the October War of 1973, when Iran supported Israel against the Arabs, that his relations with the Shah deteriorated. Starting in the fall of 1973 he became a vehement critic of the Shah, accusing him of suppressing religion in Iran, denouncing him for his pro-Israel stance, and describing him as an "imperialist stooge." However, for more than a decade he had maintained close, even cordial ties with the Pahlavi regime, and during his visits to Tehran in the 1960s and early 1970s he was warmly received by the Shah.

Musa al-Sadr was a strong supporter of Ayatollah Ruhollah Khomeini.* Indeed, the last article he published was an article in *Le Monde* (August 23, 1978), castigating the Shah of Iran and praising Khomeini. However, al-Sadr's vision of Shiism was more moderate and more humanistic than Khomeini's. He was a friend of Ali Shariati (who died in 1973), the writer who propounded a liberal, modernist Shiism and thereby inspired many opponents of the Shah (including the Mujahidin al-Khalq, the organization that has proved to be the staunchest opponent of the Islamic Republic regime). Many observers suspect that al-Sadr would have moderated the course of the revolution in Iran if he had not been consumed by it.

Imam Musa was not averse to hedging his bets. Thus, as his relations with Iran deteriorated after 1973 to the point where his Iranian citizenship was revoked, he improved his relations with Iraq, from which he may have received significant funding in early 1974. According to reliable reports, Musa was friendly with both King Hussein of Jordan and President Anwar al-Sadat* of Egypt, and he traveled regularly throughout the Arab world and Europe. He was hardly a provincial.

Like the Maronite Christians, the Shia are a minority in a predominantly Sunni Muslim Arab world, and for both sects Lebanon is a refuge in which sectarian identity and security can be preserved. Imam Musa's message to the Maronites in the period before the civil war of 1975–1976 was a combination of muted threat and impassioned egalitarianism. In his ecumenical sermons to Christian congregations he won many admirers among his listeners. It is not surprising that many Maronites saw a natural ally in Imam Musa. He was a reformer, not a revolutionary. He sought the betterment of the Shia in a Lebanese context. He often noted, "for us Lebanon is one definitive homeland."

Musa al-Sadr recognized the insecurity of the Maronites, and he acknowledged their need to maintain their monopoly on the presidency. However, he was critical of the Maronites for their arrogant stance toward the Muslims, and particularly the Shia. He argued that since independence the Maronite-dominated government had neglected the south, where as many as 50 percent of the Shia lived, and had made the Shia into a disinherited class in Lebanon.

Musa al-Sadr was anticommunist, one suspects not only on principled grounds but because the various communist organizations were among his prime competitors for Shii recruits. While the two branches of the Bath party (pro-Iraqi and pro-Syrian) were making significant inroads among the Shia of the south and the Beirut suburbs, he appropriated their pan-Arab slogans. Although the movement he founded, Harakat al-Mahrumin (the Movement of the Deprived), was aligned with the Lebanese National Movement (LNM) in the early stages of the Lebanese civil war (1975–1976), he found its Druze leader, Kamal Jumblatt,* irresponsible and exploitative of the Shia. As he once noted, the LNM was willing "to combat the Christians to the last Shii." He imputed to Jumblatt the prolongation of the war: "Without him the war in Lebanon would have been terminated in two months. Because of him, it has been prolonged two years and only God knows how long the encore will last" (Norton 1987: 42).

Thus, it was hardly inconsistent with his political stance that he should have deserted the LNM in May 1976, when Syria intervened in Lebanon on the side of the Maronite militias and against the LNM and its Palestinian allies. He was a friend and confidant of Syrian president Hafez al-Assad,* yet he mistrusted Syrian motives in Lebanon. It was, in Imam Musa's view, only the indigestibility of Lebanon that protected it from being engulfed by Syria. Nonetheless, the Syrians were an essential card in his very serious game with the Palestinian resistance.

He claimed to support the Palestine resistance movement, but his relations with the PLO (Palestine Liberation Organization) were tense and uneasy at best. During the 1973 clashes between the PLO and the Lebanese army, Imam Musa reproached the Sunni Muslims for their chorus of support for the guerrillas. On the one hand he chastised the government for failing to defend the south from Israeli aggression, but on the other he criticized the PLO for shelling Israel from the south and hence provoking Israeli retaliation. He consistently expressed sympathy for Palestinian aspirations, but he was unwilling to countenance actions that exposed Lebanese citizens, and especially Shii citizens of the south, to additional suffering. In Musa al-Sadr's view, Israel was an "absolute evil," yet he was realistic enough to understand the overwhelming dominance of Israeli military power. Thus, his ambition vis-à-vis Israel was not to destroy it, but to see it respect the 1949 armistice line that substituted for a border between Israel and Lebanon.

After the 1970 PLO defeat in Jordan, the bulk of the PLO fighters relocated to south Lebanon, where they proceeded to supplant the legitimate authorities. Imam Musa prophetically warned the PLO that it was not in its interests to establish a state within a state in Lebanon. It was the organization's failure to heed this warning that helped to spawn the alienation of their "natural allies"— the Shia—who actively resisted the Palestinian fighters in their midst only a few years later. For their part, some PLO officials believed that Musa al-Sadr was a creation of the army's Deuxième Bureau (the Second, or intelligence, Bureau).

However, his unremitting opponent was Kamil al-Asad, the powerful Shii political boss from the south, who quite accurately viewed al-Sadr as a serious threat to his political power base and opposed him at almost every move. For Imam Musa and his followers, al-Asad was the epitome of all that was wrong with the zaim system.

In 1967 the Chamber of Deputies (the Lebanese Parliament) passed a law establishing a Supreme Islamic Shii Council (SISC), which would for the first time provide a representative body for the Shia independent of the Sunni Muslims. The council actually came into existence in 1969, with Imam Musa as its chairman for a six-year term—a stunning confirmation of his status as the leading Shii cleric in the country, and certainly one of the most important political figures in the Shii community. The council quickly made itself heard with demands in the military, social, economic, and political realms, including improved measures for the defense of the south, the provision of development funds, construction and improvement of schools and hospitals, and an increase in the number of Shia appointed to senior government positions.

One year after the formation of the SISC, Musa al-Sadr organized a general strike "to dramatize to the government the plight of the population of southern Lebanon vis-à-vis the Israeli military threat." Shortly thereafter, the government created the Council of the South (Majlis al-Janub), which was funded at thirty million Lebanese pounds and was chartered to support the development of the region. Unfortunately, the Majlis al-Janub reputedly became more famous as a locus of corruption than as the origin of worthwhile projects. The creation of the council was a victory for al-Sadr, but it was the formidable Kamil al-Asad who dominated its operation.

By the early 1970s, the existing social and economic problems of the Shia were compounded by a rapidly deteriorating security environment in the south. While the SISC seemed a useful vehicle for the promotion of the community's interests (as mediated by Musa al-Sadr of course), the council was ineffectual in a milieu that was quickly becoming dominated by militias and extralegal parties. Hence, in March 1974, at a well-attended rally in the Biqa Valley city of Baalbak, Imam Musa declared the launching of a popular mass movement, the Harakat al-Mahrumin (Movement of the Deprived). With his movement he vowed to struggle relentlessly until the social grievances of the deprived, the Shia, were satisfactorily addressed by the government.

Just one year later, al-Sadr's efforts were overtaken by the onset of civil war in Lebanon. By July 1975 it became known that a militia adjunct to Harakat al-Mahrumin had been formed. The militia, Afwaj al-Mugawama al-Lubnaniya (the Lebanese Resistance Detachments), better known by the acronym AMAL (which also means "hope"), was initially trained by al-Fatah (the largest organization in the PLO), and it played a minor role in the fighting of 1975 and 1976. Musa al-Sadr's movement was affiliated with the LNM and its PLO allies during the first year of the civil war, but it broke with its erstwhile allies when the Syrians intervened in June 1976 to prevent the defeat of the Maronite-dominated Lebanese Front.

Four months before the Syrian intervention, President Sulaiman Franjiya accepted a Constitutional Document that Imam Musa indicated was a satisfactory basis for implementing political reform. The document—which called for an increase in the proportion of parliamentary seats allocated to the Muslims, as well as some restrictions on the prerogatives of the Maronite president—seemed to offer a basis for restoring peace to Lebanon. Then it was combined with the prospect of bringing the PLO under control through the Syrian intervention, there appeared to be a prospect for a new beginning. Unfortunately, the opportunity to stop the carnage was more apparent than real. While the pace of fighting had decreased by the end of 1976, the violence continued.

The growing influence of Musa al-Sadr prior to the civil war was certainly a bellwether of the increased political importance of the Shia; however, it bears emphasizing that Imam Musa led only a fraction of his politically affiliated coreligionists. It was the multiconfessional parties and militias that attracted the majority of Shii recruits, and many more Shia carried arms under the colors of these organizations than under Amal's. Even in war, the Shia suffered disproportionately; by a large measure they incurred more casualties than any other sect in Lebanon. Perhaps the single most important success achieved by al-Sadr was the reduction of the authority and influence of the traditional Shii elites, but it was the civil war and the associated growth of extralegal organizations that conclusively rendered these personalities increasingly irrelevant in the Lebanese political system.

Whatever he may have been, despite his occasionally vehement histrionics Musa al-Sadr was hardly a man of war. (He seems to have played only a most indirect role in directing the military actions of the Amal militia.) His weapons were words, and as a result his political efforts were short-circuited by the war. He seemed to be eclipsed by the violence that engulfed Lebanon.

Ironically, it was his disappearance in 1978 that helped to retrieve the promise of his earlier efforts. In August 1978, he visited Libya with two companions, the Sheikh Muhammad Shahhadih Yaqub and journalist Abbas Badr al-Din. The party has not been heard from since. While his fate is not known, it is widely suspected that he was killed by the henchmen of the Libyan leader, Colonel Muammar Qaddafi* for reasons that remain obscure. The Libyans did attempt a clumsy cover-up, sending a trio of impersonators armed with doctored passports and the luggage of the ill-fated group to Rome, but good evidence suggests the group never left Libya. It is clear that the disappearance of Musa al-Sadr has been of enormous importance to the Shia of Lebanon. (The anniversary of his disappearance, August 31, is celebrated annually with a national strike.)

Musa al-Sadr has become a hero to his followers, who revere his memory and take inspiration from his words and his suffering. The symbol of a missing imam—reminiscent as it is of the central dogma of Shiism—is hard to assail, and even his blood enemies are now heard to utter words of praise. The movement he founded, now simply called Amal, has since his disappearance become the largest Shii organization in Lebanon and one of the most powerful.

Many of Musa al-Sadr's key followers and associates are now dead: Mustafa Chamran died in 1980 while serving as the chairman of Iran's Supreme Defense Council; Khalil Jaradi and Muhammad Saad, key leaders of the post–1982 resistance to Israel's occupation, were blown up—ironically in Musa's ancestral home village of Marakey—in 1985; Sadeq Ghotbzadeh, aide to Khomeini, was executed in 1982 for plotting to execute the Ayatullah; and Daoud Sulaiman Daoud, devoted aid to Imam Musa and later the dynamic leader of Amal in the South, was killed on September 22, 1988, by an antitank rocket fired at his car (probably by his Shii opponents). Others remain active on the political scene, especially Nabih Berri, who has headed Amal since 1980, and Husain al-Husaini, formerly general secretary of Amal, and since 1984 the speaker of the Lebanese Parliament.

The battle for supremacy that now rages in Lebanon among the Shia is in large measure a conflict over who is the rightful heir to the legacy of Musa al-Sadr. On the one side is *Hizballah* (the Party of God), under the strong influence of Muhammad Husain Fadlallah, which emerged after the Israeli invasion of Lebanon and has been authoritatively associated with the kidnappings of foreigners. On the other side is Amal, still a reform movement, but an angrier, more vengeful one than it was under al-Sadr's leadership. He would probably recognize neither organization, and he would shed tears for both.

BIBLIOGRAPHY

Ajami, Fouad. *The Vanished Imam: Musa al-Sadr and the Shia of Lebanon*. Ithaca: Cornell University Press, 1986.

Bulloch, John. *Death of a Country: The Civil War in Lebanon*. London: Weidenfeld and Nicolson, 1977.

Cole, Juan R. I., and Nikki Keddie (eds.) *Shi'ism and Social Protest*. New Haven: Yale University Press, 1986.

Khalidi, Walid. *Conflict and Violence in Lebanon: Confrontation in the Middle East*. Cambridge, Mass.: Harvard University Center for International Affairs, 1979.

Norton, Augustus Richard. *Amal and the Shia: Struggle for the Soul of Lebanon*. Austin, Tex.: University of Texas Press, 1987.

Pakradouni, Karim. *La Paix manquée*. Beirut: Editions FMA, 1983.

Salibi, Kamal S. *Crossroads to Civil War: Lebanon 1958–1976*. Delmar, N.Y.: Caravan Books, 1976.

Theroux, Peter. *The Strange Disappearance of Imam Moussa Sadr*. London: Weidenfeld and Nicolson, 1987.

U.S. Congress, House. Subcommittee on Europe and the Middle East of the Committee on Foreign Affairs. *Islamic Fundamentalism and Islamic Radicalism*. 99th Cong., 1st Sess. Washington, D.C.: U.S. Gov't. Printing Office, 1985.

Wright, Robin. *Sacred Rage: The Wrath of Militant Islam*. New York: Linden Press, Simon & Schuster, 1985.

AUGUSTUS RICHARD NORTON

NURI SAID (1888–1958), Iraq's leading politician in the last two decades of the monarchy, did more than any other Iraqi figure to shape the institutions of the Iraqi state and to achieve and consolidate its independence. However, he failed to appreciate the need for social and economic reform or the spirit of nationalism that swept the Arab world in the 1950s, and in 1958 he was killed in a bloody coup that swept away the monarchy and the pro-Western policy he had so carefully constructed.

Nuri's early life mirrored many of the forces that would shape the Iraqi state in its early decades. He was born in December 1888 to a modest Baghdad family of mixed Turco-Arab origin. His father held a middle-level position in the Ottoman bureaucracy. After graduation from a government primary school, Nuri chose a military career and attended the military secondary school in Baghdad and then the Ottoman Military College in Istanbul, where, in September 1906, at age eighteen, he received a Turkish commission.

On his return to Iraq, Nuri joined an infantry unit responsible for protecting caravan trade and collecting taxes from unwilling tribesmen, tasks that gave him firsthand knowledge of his country and friendships with tribal leaders that he later put to good political use. In 1910, he returned to Istanbul to attend the Ottoman Staff College, from which he graduated in 1912. That same year he saw action against Bulgaria in the Balkan War. In the meantime he had married, and fathered his only child, a son, Sabah.

Nuri had rather radical ideas in his youth. Like the Young Turks who had seized control of the Ottoman government in 1909, he wanted modernization and reform of the empire. More important for the later history of Iraq, Nuri was an ardent and an early supporter of Arab nationalism. In February 1915, Aziz Ali al-Misri, an Egyptian officer in the Ottoman Army, established *al-Ahd* (the Covenant), a secret society of Arab officers dedicated to achieving autonomy for the Arab areas of the empire. Nuri was a founding member, although such activities were perilous. An order was put out for Nuri's arrest, and in April 1914 he left the Ottoman army and departed for Iraq, hoping to work for the Arab cause.

Nuri attached himself briefly to Talib al-Naqib of Basra, then a leading figure in the Arab movement. When the British occupied Basra in November 1914, Nuri was sent to India as a prisoner of war, where he was kept under a very loose house arrest. In 1916, when the British began recruiting for the Arab revolt, Nuri volunteered and was sent first to Cairo and then to the Hejaz.

Nuri's early attachment to the cause of the Sharif Hussein of Mecca and his leading role in the Arab revolt helped assure his later rise to power in his native country. The revolt cemented Nuri's personal ties to Hussein's son, Faisal. Nuri participated in the campaign to capture Aqaba (December 1916 to July 1917), and was subsequently promoted to general and made Faisal's chief of staff. At the war's end, he accompanied Faisal to the Paris Peace Conference as a military adviser.

Nuri returned to Iraq in 1920 to become the first chief of staff of the Iraqi army in the government appointed by the British. During 1921, he played an active and important role in the campaign to crown Prince Faisal king of Iraq, using his previous contacts with tribal leaders to good advantage. Ultimately, a well-greased British referendum elected Faisal monarch, and his Hashemite supporters were soon awarded high political posts. Nuri was among them.

Nuri played a major role in establishing the Iraqi army and in making it one of the chief pillars of the new Iraqi state. In 1922 he was made acting minister of defense, and from 1923 to 1930 served as minister of defense. He was also temporarily made chief of police in 1922, and for a time helped shape this security force as well. In 1920, the first infantry battalions, some pack batteries, and a cavalry regiment took shape. The basis of the new army lay in some 640 ex-Turkish, pro-Hashemite officers moved up into important positions. These not only provided a core of military experience, but a power base for Feisal and Nuri as well. In 1924, the old Turkish-style military college was replaced with a new Royal Military Academy. Although the director, his assistant, and most instructors were British, Nuri personally saw to it that the curriculum was Arabized. Nuri, like other nationalists of his day, saw the army as the backbone of the new state and a means of instilling patriotism into new recruits. He also felt a native Iraqi army might hasten Iraq's independence from Britain. In 1927 Nuri was part of a group that fought for conscription, a move thwarted by the British government, which did not want to force conscription on a reluctant population.

Nuri's relations with the British in this period were not always smooth. In 1929, the high commissioner took exception to his first appointment as prime minister, fearing that he might mean trouble for Britain. This assessment was to prove mistaken. Nuri's reliance on and ties to Britain were to be demonstrated throughout his career. So, too, were his political skills. Gregarious, loyal to friends, energetic, resourceful, and intelligent. Nuri soon showed that he could outmaneuver competition from other officers as well politicians from wealthy and established families.

It was Nuri's negotiation of the Anglo-Iraq Treaty of 1930 and his ability to secure its passage through Parliament that changed British opinion of him and inaugurated his career as Iraq's dominant politician, although his preeminent status was not fully realized for another decade.

Appointed prime minister in November 1929 after a deadlock in treaty negotiations, Nuri faced severe opposition to a new treaty from nationalists who wanted complete independence and an end to the British tie. He suppressed this opposition with tactics for which he later became famous—muzzling the press, proroguing Parliament, and holding a new and strictly controlled election. The resulting Parliament dutifully ratified the Treaty of 1930, which gave Britain leases on two air bases and a continued strong influence over Iraq's foreign and defense policy until its expiration in 1955. Nuri also led the Iraqi delegation to the League of Nations, which, in 1932, admitted Iraq as a member, thus recognizing its independence, the first Arab state to achieve such status.

Nuri's growing power made King Faisal uneasy. In November 1932, as soon as Iraq was safely in the league, Faisal peremptorily dismissed Nuri as prime minister. Nuri lost even more influence after Faisal's death in 1933. Ghazi, Faisal's son and successor, was a young man of a different generation and political outlook, resentful of the influence of Nuri, his cohorts, and the British.

From 1936 to 1941, Nuri played only a sporadic role in politics. The period was marked by tribal rebellions, military coups, and the emergence of new political forces such as leftist reformers and anti-British nationalists. Nuri had no foothold among these groups, although he still had influence with the British and the army.

In 1936 an army coup led by General Bakr Sidqi overthrew the cabinet in which Nuri was minister of foreign affairs. The coup perpetrators murdered Nuri's brother-in-law, Jafar al-Askari, then minister of defense, thereby creating a personal as well as a political vendetta with Nuri. After a temporary refuge in the British embassy (indicating his close British ties) Nuri left Baghdad for Cairo. It was not until October 1937, after a new government had come to power, that he was able to return to Iraq. For the next few years, Nuri was consumed with two desires—to get back into power and to get revenge on the perpetrators of the coup.

To regain influence, Nuri intrigued behind the scenes with a group of young army officers, who were mainly Arab nationalist in orientation. Nuri was instrumental in hastening the rise of these officers who, in 1941, almost put an end to the Hashemite dynasty and its pro-British policy, an outcome certainly unforeseen by Nuri. A covert military coup they engineered in 1938 finally resulted in Nuri's appointment as prime minister, and he seemed to be in the ascendency once again.

In 1937 King Ghazi was killed in an auto accident and Nuri played a role in the appointment of Abd al-Ilah, Ghazi's cousin, as regent to Ghazi's infant son, Faisal II. A relatively unknown figure, Abd al-Ilah was young (twenty-seven), educated in a British school (Victoria College in Alexandria), and impressionable, leading Nuri and others to believe that he would be both pro-British and malleable. In this they were not mistaken. Nuri then used his good relations with Abd al-Ilah to strengthen his political position, but his good fortune was not to last.

The war and Britain's pressure on Iraq to fulfill its treaty obligations caused a split between Nuri and his supporters in the army. As prime minister, Nuri had been able to break relations with Germany in 1939 at the request of the British with little domestic opposition. When France was defeated in June 1940, however, the officers felt that Nuri's pro-British stand was no longer in Iraq's interest. Anti-British sentiment, always beneath the surface in Iraq, had been exacerbated by British support of the Jews in Palestine. Iraqi feelings were stirred by the Palestinian leader, al-Hajj Amin al-Husseini, *mufti* (chief judge) of Jerusalem, who had taken refuge in Baghdad.

In June 1940, when Nuri wanted to break relations with Italy, the officers refused unless Iraq got some concessions on Palestine; this was an unrealistic demand. The split between the two camps became complete when the pro-British party attempted to transfer the officers out of Baghdad. The officers refused to go and their revolt resulted in Nuri losing influence and any real ability to affect events. As the crisis deepened, the crown prince fled the country along with Nuri and a few of his supporters. A relative of Abd al-Ilah was put in as regent, and a nationalist politician, Rashid Ali al-Gailani, backed by the officers, assumed the prime ministership in a series of events known as the "Rashid Ali coup."

This rift, and the split in the governing forces that it caused, marked a divide in modern Iraqi history which was papered over but never healed. The British, fearing to lose Iraq in the midst of a life and death struggle with the Axis powers, forced the issue by landing troops in Iraq. In May 1941 these troops confronted Iraqi forces in a short war that ended in defeat for the Iraqi army and the demise and flight of the Rashid Ali government. A second British occupation of Iraq then began, and behind the British troops came Abd al-Ilah and those Iraqi politicians able to work with the British. Chief among them was Nuri.

The second British occupation lasted from 1941 to 1945. In this occupation, as in the first, the British preferred to govern indirectly. Embarrassed to use Nuri because he was so closely identified with them, they acquiesced in the appointment as prime minister of a moderate peacemaker, Jamil al-Midfai. He was expected to remove the extreme nationalists from positions of importance and to correct the excesses of the Rashid Ali government. Midfai interned some of the most avid anti-British nationalists and put the key perpetrators of the 1941 coup on trial in absentia, but he did not go far enough to suit the British or the regent. In October 1941, Nuri was brought back from Cairo to become prime minister, a post he held until June 1944. In this period, he cooperated closely with the British in placing nationalists in concentration camps, in trying and executing the four key army officers behind the anti-British movement, and in drastically reducing the size of the army and weeding out its nationalist elements. At the same time, he strengthened his own position in the army and civil service by appointing supporters to key posts. To compensate for the loss of support from Arab nationalist elements, the left was tolerated. It was in this period that communists established roots in schools and labor organizations and among intellectuals.

For the remainder of the war, Nuri managed to keep Iraq quiet and in the British camp, thereby making himself indispensable to the British, the regent, and the conservative establishment. He emerged from the war as Iraq's indisputable strongman, but at a price to himself and the regime. His activities on behalf of the British thoroughly discredited the Hashemite dynasty in the eyes of the populace. The wartime execution of the nationalist officers and the purge of the army created bitterness in the army officer corps. Meanwhile, wartime inflation widened the gap between the rich and the poor, allowing the newly strengthened leftists to champion the lower classes. Nevertheless, Nuri's wartime activities bought time for the regime, unquestionably strengthened the two key institutions of state—the military and the civil service—and provided the basis for a postwar period of development.

In the postwar decade, Nuri was the undisputed leader of Iraq. He formed seven cabinets as prime minister, and joined an eighth as minister of defense. Even when not in office he influenced government policies through his nominees in the cabinet and through his "arranged" majorities in Parliament. Throughout this period he kept Iraq solidly in the Western camp, repressed local communists and leftists, inaugurated Iraq's oilbased development program, and gave Iraq a period of relative political stability. This surface stability, however, was increasingly punctuated by riots, demonstrations, and uprisings, clearly indicating the unpopularity of the regime's domestic and foreign policies with the growing urban lower and middle classes.

One reason for relative domestic stability was an improvement in the situation of the Kurds and Shia. In 1941 Nuri brought into his cabinet the first Shia minister of the interior—Salih Jabr—and groomed him to be prime minister. (In the postwar period there were three Shia and two Kurdish prime ministers.) As government education spread to the shia south and shia graduates were sent abroad for higher education, shia professionals and technocrats joined the middle class in increasing numbers, although they were greatly underrepresented in the higher reaches of power. Shia were also among the many landlords and merchants who became wealthy in this period.

Kurds also advanced, mainly in the army and bureaucracy. In 1945, in the aftermath of a Kurdish rebellion in the north led by the emerging Kurdish leader, Mustapha Barzani, Nuri, with British backing, cracked down on the Kurds. Barzani and his men were pushed out of the north and kept in exile in the postwar period. As a result, the north was quiet, and schools, hospitals, and other projects could be undertaken in Kurdish areas.

Nuri also played a major role in laying the foundations of Iraq's economic development program and in pioneering economic planning. In 1950, Nuri engineered the passage of a law establishing a Development Board, composed of Iraqi and foreign experts, to lay down five-year development plans. Between 1950 and 1958, four such plans were drawn up. Some 70 percent of oil revenues were devoted to long-term development. In 1952, Nuri negotiated a fifty-fifty profit split with IPC (Iraq Petroleum Company) that doubled Iraq's revenues per ton. Between 1951 and 1958, Iraq's oil revenues rose dramatically from 32 to 237 million dollars. Iraq's dependence on oil revenues also rose; by 1958, they accounted for 28 percent of its GNP and 60 percent of its budget.

Oil revenues enabled Iraq to make a sustained effort at long-term development for the first time in centuries. The Development Board's main priority was agriculture, which employed 70 percent of Iraq's workers but produced only 30 percent of its income. The bulk of the board's agricultural allocations went toward large-scale flood control and irrigation schemes. By 1958, irrigation projects completed or nearing completion included the Tharthar Dam, which prevented the flooding of Baghdad; the Habbaniyya scheme, a water-storage facility on the Euphrates; and two dams in Kurdish territory, the Dukan Dam on the Lesser Zab and the Darbandikhan Dam on the Diyala. Iraq's transportation and communications network was expanded. By 1958 the development program had generated an economic boom; begun to mobilize Iraq's resources; and marginally improved health, education, and living standards in urban areas.

These benefits were not accompanied by the necessary changes in social structure. The benefits of agricultural projects went mainly to tribal leaders and urban merchants who had already bought up or gained control of huge tracts of irrigated land. By 1958, less than 2 percent of the landowners held 63 percent of the farmland, while 45 percent owned only 1 percent of the land. Eight landlords owned over 1 million dunums (250,000 hectares). Nuri was not unaware of these social problems, but tended to downplay them. A land-distribution scheme he favored was too small in scope to break the hold of the large landowners over the peasants, or over Parliament, where they held at least a third of the seats. Nuri and the Hashemite dynasty relied on the landed proprietors and the urban wealthy for support, and refused to tamper with their privileges.

The development of Iraq's human resources also lagged behind its needs. Between 1950 and 1958, Iraq's higher educational institutions expanded, but they graduated only about a thousand students a year. Secondary education was concentrated largely in urban areas. Nevertheless, higher education and occupational opportunities did produce a small but growing middle class.

It was from this middle class that Nuri faced increased opposition. Educated elements and the youth were restive because of his ties to Western interests, his lack of social reform, and the absence of democratic processes. To control the political system, Nuri relied on a carrot-and-stick policy. The carrot consisted of buying off the discontent with economic benefits, coopting opposition leaders with seats in Parliament, and strengthening benefits for the army and police. The stick consisted of police actions, martial law, closure of the press and schools, arrests, and, in a few cases, executions of the opposition. In typical Ottoman fashion, Nuri preferred to work behind the scenes with a few "reliable" people; his interest in or concern for public opinion was virtually nonexistent.

Opposition increasingly erupted into street violence. In July 1952, when riots broke out at one of Baghdad's colleges, they quickly spread throughout Iraq's urban centers and the American Information Office in Baghdad was burned down, indicating a new anti-American focus to the opposition. A military government had to be appointed to maintain order.

Nuri's most significant impact on Iraq in the postwar period was in foreign policy. He tied Iraq firmly to a pro-Western alliance system—the Baghdad Pact—which provided a shield against the encroachment of the USSR but seriously isolated Iraq from its Arab neighbors. Under his leadership, Iraq became an important player in Arab, and even international, politics.

Nuri never entirely forsook his early Arab nationalist goals. During the war, in 1942, he wrote a plan for Arab unity, the "Blue Book," which proposed to unite Arab countries beginning with those in the Fertile Crescent. The Jews in Palestine were to receive autonomy. The Blue Book also proposed an Arab League with a permanent council for defense, foreign affairs, and other matters. The Arab League saw fruition in 1945, but the Fertile Crescent scheme never materialized. By the mid–1950s, with the establishment of independent states in the Arab world, including Israel, Nuri became more of an Iraqi nationalist, emphasizing a strong, independent state within the boundaries bequeathed Iraq by the British.

Nuri's main thrust in the postwar period was consolidating the British tie and expanding it to include the United States. The Western alliance, however, became increasingly difficult to foist on an unwilling population, no matter what its international benefits. The first indication of this came in 1948 when, under the aegis of the regent and Salih Jabr, the regime attempted to renegotiate the Anglo-Iraq Treaty of 1930. The new treaty would have been an improvement on the old one, but it would not have ended the British tie. The result was a major popular uprising, the Wathbah, which was repressed by the police with many deaths. The abortive Portsmouth Treaty had to be cancelled.

The 1930 treaty with Britain was due to expire in 1955, and Nuri searched for a way to remove the onus of the British connection but at the same time preserve the Western security umbrella. One possibility was to join an emerging alliance of "northern-tier" states (Turkey, Iran and Pakistan) in a collective defense arrangement then taking shape under the guidance of U.S. Secretary of State John Foster Dulles. Nuri was favorably disposed toward the idea, but wanted to bring in other Arab countries, specially Egypt, as well as Britain, the cornerstone of Iraq's external defense. However, Gamal Abdul Nasser, who had just succeeded in removing British troops from the Suez Canal, wanted no part of such a treaty and refused. Nevertheless, in February 1955, Nuri took the first step in the formation of such an alliance by signing an agreement with Turkey. In September of that year, Iran joined, and in November, Pakistan followed, completing the "Baghdad Pact." Britain adhered to the pact, dissolving the Anglo-Iraq Treaty and turning its two air bases over to Iraq. The United States did not join the pact, but did attend meetings as an observer.

The Baghdad Pact had profound repercussions for Nuri and the regime he symbolized. On the positive side, it strengthened Iraq's external and internal defenses, helped build up its military infrastructure, and paid dividends in peace with the Kurds and the shia through good relations with Turkey and Iran. However, its disadvantages proved overwhelming. The pact marked the beginning of the end of Nuri and the "old regime," as the Hashemite monarchy came to be called.

To get the treaty passed, Nuri dismissed a recently, and relatively freely, elected parliament and substituted one of his own making. In the summer of 1954, with Parliament in abeyance, he issued a series of decrees that virtually ended all open political activity. They allowed the deportation and denationalization of communists and others, prohibited meetings that might disturb public order, and broke off diplomatic relations with the Soviet Union. From 1954 through 1958, while Nuri governed through a controlled parliament, the opposition was driven underground and into the officer corps.

The pact also isolated Iraq from the rest of the Arab world. Nuri had underestimated the rise of new forces in the Arab world—forces that were anti-Western and proreform. These were symbolized by Nasser who, from the moment it was signed, mounted a media attack on the Baghdad Pact, on Nuri, and on the regime that had signed it. These attacks further eroded Nuri's domestic support.

Opposition intensified in 1956, when Britain, France, and Israel attacked Egypt in the wake of Nasser's nationalization of the Suez Canal. Nuri faced uprisings in Baghdad and elsewhere, and only weathered the storm by applying martial law. In February 1958, Egypt and Syria, both hostile to Iraq, announced the formation of the United Arab Republic. Although the step was taken mainly to avoid further communist penetration of Syria, it created fears in Iraq and Jordan that their regimes were in danger. Iraq and Jordan hastily put together their own Arab Federation. Nuri's last post was as its prime minister, and one of his last political acts was an attempt to get Kuwait to join the federation, a move opposed both by Britain, then Kuwait's protector, and Kuwait itself.

While Nuri was involved in foreign affairs, his domestic opposition gathered strength. By 1957 the moderately nationalist *Istiqlal* (Independence) Party, and the left-of-center NDP (National Democratic Party) had turned to more radical elements in the political spectrum—the pan-Arab *Bath* (Renaissance) Party and the communists—to form a United National Front. Far more serious was disaffection in the army, where junior officers had formed a Free Officers group modelled on that of Egypt. In 1956 a plot to overthrow the regime was discovered, but the suspected officers were merely transferred. Nuri, who had received new warnings of trouble in 1958, ignored them, evidently thinking that generous benefits to the military would keep the officers loyal. In May 1958, civil war broke out in Lebanon, and fearing that it might spread to Jordan, King Hussein* of Jordan asked Iraq for troops. In the early hours of the morning of July 14, 1958, the Iraqi army units, which had been ordered to march to Jordan, marched instead on Baghdad. They occupied the Radio Station, the Ministry of Defense, and the Royal Palace, killing the regent and the young King Feisal II in a bloody and violent coup. Nuri escaped from his house on the Tigris by boat and made his way to the home of a friend. However, the following day he was caught on a public street attempting to escape disguised in a woman's cloak and was killed.

With the fall of Nuri, the old regime ended, and with it ended many of the policies he had espoused for forty years. Treaty ties to the West were broken;

Iraq turned increasingly to the Soviet Bloc for arms, and an era of domestic conservatism came to an end. However, the independent state itself, together with its main pillars, the army and the bureaucracy, remained, perhaps the greatest monument to Nuri's enduring legacy of statecraft.

BIBLIOGRAPHY

Batatu, Hanna. *The Old Social Classes and the Revolutionary Movements of Iraq.* Princeton: Princeton University Press, 1978.

Birdwood, Lord. *Nuri as-Said.* London: Cassel, 1959.

Gallman, Waldemar. *Iraq under General Nuri.* Baltimore: Johns Hopkins University Press, 1964.

Kanna, Khalil. *Al-Iraq, Amsuhu wa Ghadahu* (Iraq, Its Yesterday and Tomorrow). Beirut: Dar al-Rihani, 1966.

Khadduri, Majid. *Independent Iraq, 1932 to 1958.* London: Oxford University Press, 1960.

Marr, Phebe. *The Modern History of Iraq.* Boulder, Colo.: Westview Press, 1985.

Simon, Reeva. *Iraq between the Two World Wars.* New York: Columbia University Press, 1986.

al-Suwaidi, Tawfiq. *Mudhakirati* (My Memoirs). Beirut: Dar al-Katib al-Arabi, 1969.

Tarbush, Mohammad. *The Role of the Military in Politics, a Case Study of Iraq to 1941.* London: Kegan Paul, 1982.

LOUAY BAHRY AND PHEBE MARR

SAID BIN TAYMUR (1910–1972) ruled from 1932 to 1970 as the thirteenth ruler in the Al Bu Said dynasty. In the early part of his reign as sultan of Muscat and Oman, Said engineered a modest revival of the state's fortunes. In the 1950s, he presided over the reunification of the country, with British assistance. In his later years, however, Said's reign was characterized by his efforts to keep Oman isolated and his refusal to permit the sort of development that was occurring in neighboring oil states. Finally, unable to deal effectively with a major rebellion, Said was overthrown by his son Qabus bin Said* in 1970.

The first Al Bu Said ruler of Oman was an elected *imam*, the secular and religious leader of the Ibadi sect of Islam. His descendants, however, dropped the title when they moved their seat from inner Oman to Muscat on the coast, which has been the capital ever since, and eventually became known as *sultans*. Since the great Said bin Sultan (ruled 1807–1856), the sultans have been drawn from his descendants or the Al Said branch of the family. While the shift to the coast facilitated the creation of a maritime empire in the early nineteenth century, Al Bu Said legitimacy among the tribes of the interior diminished. Gradually, the domain of the sultans was reduced to Muscat and the coast while periodic attempts were made to revive the traditional imamate in the tribal interior.

The Al Bu Said sultanate had come close to extinction by the early twentieth century, and increasingly weaker sultans forced the British to take a greater role in the nominally independent sultanate's affairs. Said bin Taymur's father, Taymur bin Faysal (ruled 1913–1932) was never comfortable as sultan and had indicated to the British his desire to abdicate on numerous occasions. Leaving state administration largely to a British adviser, Taymur traveled widely throughout Asia, where he met and married several women. Taymur's requests for abdication, however, were not met until his son reached twenty-one.

Said bin Taymur was born in Muscat on August 13, 1910, to Sultan Taymur and Bibi Fatima bint Ali bin Salim. Of the five sons of Taymur bin Faysal, only Said's mother was from the Al Said or was even Arab, and therefore he was always regarded the heir apparent. Like his father, he was sent abroad for education, first in Baghdad and then at Mayo College in Ajmere, India (the so-called "Chiefs' College"). While this Indian connection was promoted by the British, it was not illogical as Oman traditionally has looked outward more overseas to the Indian Ocean littoral than to neighboring Arabia. His experience in India perhaps found form in Said's later "maharaja" approach to governing, as opposed to the more collegial approach of other rulers in the Gulf with their emphasis on consultation and consensus.

Upon his return to Muscat at the age of eighteen, Said effectively was made regent in the absence of his father and was given substantial authority for the state's administration. His reign then effectively dates from 1929 and falls into three main periods. The first (1929–1945) centered on consolidation of his control over the state. Said moved first to regain supremacy over his family by facing down his semiindependent uncles who governed the major towns of the coastal plain. Next, he took over active administration of the state from his British adviser and worked to have individual advisers removed from Muscat and the positions abolished. In 1932, following a formal letter of abdication from Taymur bin Faysal (who continued to live and travel in Asia until his death in 1965), Said formally was declared sultan.

Throughout the next decade, he worked assiduously to reduce British influence over his small state. Because Muscat's indebtedness served as the tool of British control, Said gradually put the state on a sound financial footing by ruthlessly cutting budgetary expenditures, paying off debts owed to the (British) government of India, and utilizing several small British subsidies wisely. By the end of World War II, he had accomplished the near-impossible task of putting the state in the black, and had eliminated Britain's direct involvement in state administration. Henceforth, he insisted on symbolic acknowledgment of his legally independent status by declining to submit annual budgets to the British and addressing the local British representative as consul (later consul general) instead of political agent, as was the case elsewhere in the Gulf.

The second period of his rule revolved around the reunification of Oman (1945–1959). While he was bound to respect the 1920 Agreement of al-Sib, which guaranteed autonomy for the interior tribes and imamate, this did not prevent him from working in the 1940s to secure the agreement of tribal leaders to recognize his sovereignty after the death of the long-serving Imam Muhammad al-Khalili. Sultan Said's hope for a peaceful reassertion of Al Bu Said control over the interior fell victim in the following decade to the advancing tide of

Arab nationalism, as promoted by Egypt, and to a recrudescence of Saudi expansionism, sparked by expectations of oil in eastern Arabia.

In 1952, a Saudi military contingent occupied part of al-Buraymi oasis, a collection of nine villages administered by the sultan and the ruler of neighboring Abu Dhabi. This provided a window for Saudi Arabia and its improbable ally of revolutionary Egypt through which to intrigue in inner Oman. They found willing partners in two of the principal Omani tribal leaders and two brothers in the service of the imam, all of whom sought an independent state in inner Oman. Upon the death of Imam Muhammad, they secured the election of Ghalib bin Ali al-Hinai, one of his brothers, as his successor.

Expectations of oil were held also by the British-Dutch company, PDO; or Petroleum Development (Oman). PDO formed a small regiment to escort an oil exploration party into the interior, which set off in late 1954. A few months later, the Saudis were driven from al-Buraymi by the British-officered Trucial Oman Scouts, and the regiment accompanying the oil party subsequently occupied Nizwa, the traditional capital of inner Oman. Imam Ghalib abdicated, one of the tribal leaders capitulated, and the others fled to Saudi Arabia and later established "Imamate of Oman" offices in Egypt and Damascus. Sultan Said cemented the unification of his country with an epic overland journey from the southern province of Dhufar to Nizwa and al-Buraymi.

However, in 1957 several of the leaders and their followers stole back into the country and joined forces with those who had remained to restore the rebel flag over Nizwa. Several months later, a combined sultanate and Trucial Oman Scouts force recaptured the interior with the help of British air cover. The rebel leaders fled to the heights of al-Jabal al-Akhdar mountain and from there carried out sporadic land-mining and assassination attempts until the sultanate, with the assistance of the British Special Air Service, secured al-Jabal al-Akhdar in January 1959. The leaders once again managed to escape to Saudi Arabia but thereafter had to be satisfied with a propaganda war against the sultanate until Oman was admitted to the Arab league and the United Nations in 1971.

Said bin Taymur's reunification of Oman did not solve all his problems. Instead, this success was followed by a third period in which the political situation significantly deteriorated (1959–1970). The country remained impoverished and woefully undeveloped, a problem aggravated by the migration of thousands of Omanis who left to work in neighboring oil-rich states. Said refused to institute any development projects without having the total funds required by such commitments in hand at the inception. This attitude guaranteed the failure of British-initiated development efforts during the late 1950s, except in the expansion of the military, which Said saw as the key to maintaining his authority over the interior.

In addition, Said had long practiced the tendency of his father to spend much of his time isolated at the palace in Salala, the capital of the southern province of Dhufar. Said considered Dhufar to be his personal estate and not part of the state. He married in succession several Dhufari women, who bore him two daughters and a son. From 1958, he resided permanently in Dhufar and never returned to Muscat. Nevertheless, he continued to rule the country in a strong authoritarian manner and imposed a myriad of petty restrictions on his subjects, especially the Dhufaris.

Like the northern Omanis, many Dhufaris had escaped the country to find work elsewhere in the Gulf, and their experiences there prompted some to carry out acts of sabotage and other violent crimes in Dhufar during the early 1960s. By 1965, these efforts had coalesced in the formation of the Dhufar Liberation Front (DLF); and a nearly successful attempt was made on Said's life in the following year. In 1968, Marxist elements gained control of the DLF and renamed it the Popular Front for the Liberation of Oman and the Arabian Gulf (PFLOAG, later just PFLO). With help from South Yemen, China, and the Soviet Union, the rebels were able to overrun the Dhufari mountains and threaten settlements on the coastal plain.

The combination of resented stagnation in the north and escalating rebellion in the south prompted Said's son Qabus to join other plotters in Muscat to overthrow the old sultan. Following a brief gun battle in Said's palace in Salala in July 1970, a wounded Said bin Taymur was flown first to Bahrain for medical treatment and then to London, where he resided in the Dorchester Hotel until his death in October 1972. He was buried near the old mosque in nearby Woking.

The impact of Said bin Taymur on his state was complex. On the positive side, he could be regarded a precursor of modern Omani nationalism, as he removed the British from actively governing Oman and secured the state's financial independence. The costs of these successes were high, however, the weakness of the Al Said family and the strength of Said's character encouraged a type of one-man rule that continued into the reign of his son Qabus. His parsimony, useful in erasing the state's indebtedness in the early part of his reign, appeared more like unwarranted miserliness after the state began exporting oil in 1967. His attempts to isolate Oman from the changes occurring elsewhere in the Gulf led to his subjects' resentment and even to rebellion. In a larger sense, it can be said that Said was responsible for the first step in the transformation of the modern Sultanate of Oman. By eliminating the possibility of a rival imamate and reestablishing strong physical control over the entire country, he laid the groundwork for the subsequent step of establishing a social welfare state after 1970.

BIBLIOGRAPHY

Anthony, John Duke, with J. E. Peterson and Donald Abelson. *Historical and Cultural Dictionary of the Sultanate of Oman and the Emirates of Eastern Arabia.* Metuchen, N.J.: Scarecrow Press, 1976.

Landen, Robert Geran. *Oman Since 1856: Disruptive Modernization in a Traditional Arab Society.* Princeton: Princeton University Press, 1967.

Morris, James. *Sultan in Oman: Venture into the Middle East.* New York: Pantheon, 1957.

Peterson, J. E. *Oman in the Twentieth Century: Political Foundations of an Emerging State*. London: Croom Helm; New York: Barnes and Noble, 1978.

————. "Legitimacy and Political Change in Yemen and Oman." *Orbis* 27, no. 4 (Winter 1984): 971–998.

Pridham, B. R. "Oman: Change or Continuity?" In Ian Richard Netton, (ed.). *Arabia and the Gulf: From Traditional Society to Modern States*. London: Croom Helm, Barnes & Noble, 1986, pp. 132–155.

Skeet, Ian. *Muscat and Oman: The End of an Era*. London: Faber and Faber, 1974. Repr. 1985.

Townsend, John. *Oman: The Making of a Modern State*. London: Croom Helm; New York: St. Martin's Press, 1977.

J. E. PETERSON

ALI ABDULLAH SALIH (1942–   ) became leader of the Yemen Arab Republic (YAR) after the assassination of Ahmad Hussein al-Ghashmi on June 24, 1978. Salih, then the military governor of Taiz in the southern part of Yemen, defeated other contenders for leadership, and on July 17 the People's Constituent Assembly elected him president and commander in chief of the armed forces. Since then, President Salih has worked to improve relations with South Yemen while assuring Saudi Arabia that there will be no alliance with the Soviet Union by pledging to maintain a policy of non-alignment. He has sought to improve economic and social conditions for the Yemenis by taking advantage of the country's newly developed oil resources.

Salih's perceptions and policies were shaped by several elements in his life and career. Born in 1942, Salih comes from the village Bayt al-Ahmar, of the Sanhan tribe which is part of the Hashid confederacy. He belongs to the dominant Zaydi denomination and got his Quranic primary education in his village school. Salih was a conscientious tribal member, who understood and even favored the dominance of tribes in Yemeni public life. Unlike other army officers and some of Yemen's civilian and urban-based politicians, who despised tribal elements and sought to remove them from politics, Salih has continuously aspired to integrate them into Yemen's political community.

Salih also grew as a military man and, in his youth, served as a tribal irregular in the forces of Imam Ahmad, the ruler of Yemen. He joined the armed forces in 1958, and went to a noncommissioned officers' school in 1960. The revolution of 1962 ended the Imam's regime and precipitated a civil war between republican, prerevolutionary forces, aligned with Egyptian contingents, and tribal groups who were supporters of the old order. Then a sergeant, Salih joined the revolutionary forces. Salih became an officer and, in 1964, attended the armored school. He became a supporter of a modernizing state that would bring improvements in health, education, and economic well-being and would generate cohesion in society. This drive to bring Yemen to the twentieth century guided his policies in later years.

Salih's political perceptions were shaped during the Presidency of Ali al-Hamdi (1974–1977). Following years of internal warfare fostered by foreign intervention, Hamdi seemed to find a way of relaxing Yemen's internal vicissitudes and balancing Yemen's opposing conservative and radical factions. His strategy was to reconcile opposing groups rather than to defeat one of them. To achieve this aim it was also necessary to halt the interference of neighboring states in Yemeni politics. Wedged between the conservative Kingdom of Saudi Arabia in the north and the Marxist Peoples Democratic Republic of Yemen (PDRY) in the South, Yemen's unstable internal political situation provided fertile ground for these states' intervention in Yemen, and each sought to establish influence for itself and to neutralize the other party. The Saudis sought to turn the Hashid tribal groups into a conservative antileftist force in Yemen, and did so through bestowing financial doles on these tribes. With Saudi help, opposition elements from the PDRY based themselves in Yemen and attempted to subvert the regime in Aden. In April 1977, tribal elements engaged in a rebellion, which was suppressed by Hamdi's regime. The PDRY in turn cultivated relations with urban leftist elements in Yemen in order to counter the opposition to the PDRY that was based in Yemen and to revolutionize the regime in Sana. Such attempts led to frontier clashes in the summer of 1971, and to subsequent efforts to establish unity between the two Yemens. The National Democratic Front (NDF) was founded in the mid–1970s to subvert the Yemen regime. Each initiative waged by either Saudi Arabia or the PDRY, or by their proxies within Yemen, triggered a nervous and often violent response of the other party. Hamdi tried to improve relations with both states, thereby seeking to reduce their motivation to subvert the country. Hamdi was suspected by both the leftists and the conservatives within Yemen (and by their external patrons) of being subservient to the other party, which finally brought about his demise. During Hamdi's rule, Salih commanded a variety of armored units and the al-Mandab district. Moreover, he followed Hamdi's balancing strategy as a guideline for internal and foreign affairs. Salih then received his military appointment at Taiz from Hamdi's successor, Ghashmi.

Salih's paramount mission during the first four years of his reign was to terminate the prolonged civil war with its foreign intervention. Salih thereby hoped to assure the survival of his own regime, which had been burdened by turbulence from its inception, and to lay the foundation for a sound regime in the future.

The most dangerous challenge emanated from the NDF. Spurred by the rising, leftist-oriented South Yemeni leader Abd al-Fattah Ismail,* a group of leftist officers in Yemen, which operated in exile in the PDRY, attempted to overthrow Salih's regime on October 15, 1978. The plot was thwarted and its perpetrators were tried and executed. However, in February 1979, NDF subversive activity reemerged in the southern parts of Yemen. As Yemeni forces sought to curb this opposition, PDRY forces came to the NDF's aid and invaded Yemen. The Yemen army performed poorly and it was mediation by the Arab League, notably Iraq and the Gulf States, which led to the withdrawal of the PDRY forces and a cease-fire in March 1979.

Until then, Salih only reacted to activities of the NDF, and he remained in power as a consequence of foreign mediation. However, he soon became more active, and he embarked on several initiatives. These included continuous negotiations with NDF leaders aimed at reincorporating the NDF into the Yemeni public and even into its government. Salih undoubtedly wished to achieve this aim with a show of strength that would allow him to handle the NDF in favorable conditions. The intermittent negotiations that ensued were sometimes interrupted by clashes in the southern parts of Yemen. According to NDF sources, the parties reached an agreement in 1980 which the government failed to uphold.

Salih's attempts to achieve reconciliation and supremacy were more evident in other initiatives. In late 1978, Salih announced elections for the Confederation of the Yemeni Development Association. In March 1979, the government was reshuffled, bringing in both tribal leaders and professionals who could rally the support of urban civilian intellectuals and socialists. Salih attempted to develop representative bodies. In May 1980 he announced the foundation of the National Dialogue Committee, a body composed of leading figures, whose aim was to explore ways of generating a consensus among different societal factions. They drafted a document, the National Pact, which thereon became the cornerstone for internal cooperation and reconciliation in Yemen. Moreover, under the committee's auspices, a questionnaire was passed out among different groups in different parts of the country, and followed by conferences in various regions, whereby the population was rallied in support of Salih's plans.

As this process was being completed in late 1981, Salih also appointed new people, mainly his confidants, to key positions in the army and the government. Abd al-Karim al-Iryani's assumption of the role of prime minister in October 1980 signified an improvement in the internal stability of the Yemen government. Attempts were made to provide an infrastructure for economic development. Yemen started drawing funds from the Arab Monetary fund and the World Bank to facilitate the Second Five-Year Plan, in 1982. A combination of new appointments, the building of a broad societal concensus, and the suppression of the NDF were the main policy trends during this period.

Salih also sought to achieve internal stability by improving relations with neighboring states. He took advantage of the joint Yemen-PDRY committees, which had been established after the 1972 crisis and reconvened in March 1979. While the official aim of the negotiations was unity, the parties used this framework to settle disputes outstanding between the two Yemens. Yemen was particularly anxious to improve relations with the PDRY, in part to persuade Aden's leaders to reverse their support of the NDF, and meetings between the parties were parallel to Yemen's negotiations with the NDF. The coup of April 21, 1980, in the PDRY, which toppled Abd al-Fattah Ismail and brought to power the more pragmatic Ali Nasser Mohammed,* enabled Salih to intensify contacts with the PDRY. Yemen's forces engaged in small-scale clashes with the NDF during this period to facilitate Sana's supremacy.

Yemen's relations with Saudi Arabia were supposed to balance and supplement Sana's relations with Aden, but until 1981 they did not fulfil that aim. While Riyadh was anxious to see Yemen surmount the leftist challenge that the PDRY-supported NDF posed to Sana, it facilitated its interests through tactics that offended Salih. Saudi Arabia formed an "Islamic Front" which posed a right-wing check on concessions Salih might make to the left. The arrest of Yemen's Foreign Minister Abdullah al-Asnaj in March 1981 on suspicion of spying for an "unnamed Arab State" (presumably Saudi Arabia) indicated that Riyadh's reach in Yemen might have gone considerably further. Moreover, though Riyadh had paid for a huge arms deal that Yemen negotiated with the United States after the clashes between Yemen and the PDRY in 1979, it actually conditioned the delivery of these arms on Sana distancing itself from contacts with the Soviet Union, including the reversal of a contemplated arms purchase. The Saudis also demanded that Yemen halt unity plans with the PDRY. American arms arrived in Sana only gradually.

Salih presumably sensed by then that the Yemen's relations with its neighbors did not produce the desired internal stability, and both Saudi or PDRY initiatives could entangle Sana's internal and regional conflicts. Salih's initiatives from summer 1981 attest to a more resolute and resourceful course of action. In summits he held with Ali Nasser Mohammed in June and September 1981, Salih and his counterpart each agreed to refrain from supporting subversion directed against the other. Salih fostered this agreement on a visit he paid to Moscow in October 1981, during which he obtained the Soviet Union's support for overall regional relaxation, a policy that Moscow then influenced the PDRY to accept. As this aim was also supported by the pro-Western states in the region, a broad regional consensus for the improvement of regional interstate relations emerged. In a further meeting between Salih and Ali Nasser, hosted in and mediated by Kuwait on November 27, 1981, the two presidents not only reiterated their earlier agreement but also agreed on a series of steps leading to cooperation and unity, notably the establishment of a Supreme Yemeni Council composed of the two presidents, a forum that would convene every six months and supervise the course toward unity.

Salih's endeavors bore fruit only in mid–1982, but not before the NDF once again challenged the regime. Encouraged mainly by a new hard-line leader in Aden and aided by Libya's Muammar Qaddafi,* NDF units engaged in subverting the southern parts of Yemen. Salih initiated a counterattack which, by late April 1982, managed to attenuate the NDF's forces. In a meeting between Salih and Ali Nasser which convened in Taiz on May 5, 1982, Salih agreed to the South Yemeni demand to declare an amnesty for NDF members and even to reincor-porate those who so wished in Yemen's administration and its political life. He apparently did so after his forces dealt a severe military blow to the NDF, and as it became evident that those remaining could be neutralized by administrative means. In return, Ali Nasser undertook to enforce Aden's commitment to cease aiding the NDF.

The subsequent Israeli operation against the PLO in Lebanon in June 1982 enabled Salih to participate in a joint mission with Ali Nasser, who then visited Riyadh and Damascus in a show of Arab solidarity. He sent volunteers to aid the PLO (Palestine Liberation Organization) in Lebanon, among which were NDF members. Yemen's regional stature and internal stability were thereby reaffirmed.

In the next years Salih embarked on more elaborate strategies aimed at strengthening his rule, and developing Yemen's economy and regional position. In foreign affairs, Salih sought international and regional nonalignment. Located between two states that constituted opposite poles in both regional and international terms, Sana had to exercise, in Salih's view, a policy that would avoid irking the PDRY and Saudi Arabia into retaliation against Yemen, or into manipulating any of Yemen's political groups against the government. Moreover, by exercising such a policy, Salih also sought to obtain for Yemen diversified and wide-ranging assistance from both Western and Eastern Bloc states.

In 1985 Salih supported nonalignment with this statement: "We believe that the pursuance of an independent policy based on the principles of positive neutrality and non-alignment has given our country and people the guarantee to enjoy a distinctive standing through which they have avoided all forms of subservience" (Middle East Contemporary Survey 1987:708).

This foreign policy was exercised in several spheres. Salih was particularly careful to develop close relations with the PDRY. He adopted the notion of unity as a future goal and a focal point for Sana's relations with Aden, but he set this goal as a long-term one, almost an ideal, that was not practical in the immediate range. Salih stressed that unity should develop on solid foundations, after practical stages of cooperation between the parties had been enacted. This was a sober approach, basing unity on gradual progress and the achievement of well-built fundamentals. In practice, this approach permitted Salih to adhere to unity as a prestigious long-term goal, to use it as a framework for the development of solid cooperation with the PDRY, and to resolve frontier disputes that threatened Yemeni stability. Moreover, as unity was not set for the immediate future, Salih viewed it as a goal that should not deter the Saudis and the tribal groups in Yemen who feared to be compromised under unity with the Marxist regime in the PDRY.

Salih met Ali Nasser under the auspices of the Yemen Council in 1983 and 1984. Ministerial and professional committees of the two parties concluded agreements that allowed citizens of one country free passage into the territory of the other; steps were taken to unify the educational system and currency of the two Yemens. A constitution for the United Yemeni state was drafted that determined that Salih would be the president, Sana its capital, and Islam its religion, all of which marked concessions on Aden's side. It was to be ratified by the two states' supreme institutions.

The bloody war in South Yemen in January 1986 frustrated Salih's policies. The weakening of Ali Nasser's party during the fighting stirred Salih to intervene on his behalf. However, Salih apparently had second thoughts (presumably after a Soviet warning) which made him wait and witness Ali Nasser's downfall. Salih then permitted him to settle in exile in the southeastern part of Yemen. Tens of thousands of South Yemeni refugees then fled to Yemen, escaping the new PDRY regime. Since that time Salih attempted in vain to mediate between Ali Nasser in exile and the new leaders in Aden. Aden's fear of an infiltration of Ali Nasser's forces burdened the relations of the two states. Moreover, death sentences that an Adenese court passed on Ali Nasser and some thirty-four of his followers in absentia in December 1987 further soured this relationship. However, renewed cooperation emerged during 1988, as the fear of clashes between the Yemens over Ali Nasser's fate and over the undemarcated frontiers in the Marib region where oil was found led Salih into more serious negotiations over unity with South Yemen. In May 1988, a program of mutual exploitation of the oil-rich region and unity was agreed upon between the two presidents to become effective in 1989, but the real prospects remained unclear.

Salih also sought to stabilize Yemen's relations with Saudi Arabia. Once Sana surmounted the NDF's subversion and regional relaxation supported by the Soviet Union was introduced, Riyadh's anxiety that Yemen would become an extension of Aden's aggressive Marxist base was allayed. Saudi support for tribal elements to check Salih's regime declined in 1983–1984. Moreover, under the auspices of a joint Saudi-Yemeni Coordinating Council, Saudi financial doles were given annually to Sana to boost its budget. Salih was firm in exercising control over the smuggling of goods from Saudi territory into Yemen, and Yemeni troops occasionally even engaged in shooting and pursuit of smugglers, engaging Saudi forces, but these were small-scale skirmishes that did not destroy the calm relations between the two states.

Another form of regional balancing exercised by Salih was a policy of pursuing agreed-upon and undisputable inter-Arab causes and avoiding taking any controversial position that might expose Sana as a one-sided participant in Arab politics. Hence, Yemen was a supporter of Iraq in its war with Iran, a policy justified in the name of Arab solidarity. Close contacts, manifested in mutual visits of high-ranking officials in both states and telephone calls between Salih and Iraq's president, Saddam Hussein,* often occurred. Salih took one step further by sending volunteers to fight alongside Iraqi's forces.

Salih supported the PLO after its expulsion form Lebanon in 1982–1983. He opened Yemen to PLO fighters expelled from Lebanon, providing them with training facilities, and he supported the reunification of the PLO under Yasser Arafat's* leadership. Together with the leaders of the PDRY and Algeria, Salih mediated between the PLO factions. However, Salih did not push PLO reunification to the extent of alienating Syria, the supporter of anti-Arafat factions within the PLO. Similarly, Salih favored improvement of relations between the Arab states and Egypt which had been severed after Egypt signed the peace treaty with Israel in March 1979. However, to avoid controversy Salih insisted that only a collective decision at an Arab League Summit should decide the fate of relations with Egypt.

Salih extended the policy of nonalignment to Sana's relations with the great powers. Yemen used U.S.-made weapons but did not expand or substantially improve relations with Washington. However, Sana signed agreements that made it possible to acquire technical assistance from different Western states, mostly in Western Europe. On the other hand, in October 1984, Salih renewed a twenty-year Treaty of Friendship and Co-operation with the Soviet Union. originally signed in March 1964, and Moscow remained the power that extended the majority of economic, technical, and military assistance to Yemen.

Under the umbrella of regional relaxation, Salih embarked on policies that would stabilize and even improve the political and economic situation in Yemen. These included a government reshuffling on November 12, 1983, which placed the Yemen government firmly under Salih's control. Reports in the summer of 1985 indicated that the government had succeeded in infiltrating the NDF and forced it to resort to nonsubversive means. In view of the improved relations with the PDRY, Aden did not counteract Yemen's policies. There were other reports that indicated an increase in popular support for the Islamic Front. However, a decline in the activity of this conservative group was also evident. In March 1985 a "Constituent Assembly" of religious divines (*ulema*) was founded by the government as a means aimed at exerting government control over the ulema, thereby blocking the growing tendency of the until-then unheeded Islamic-conservative power. Salih and his government have foregone governments' ambitions to defeat tribalism and establish a uniform, urban society in Yemen. Salih developed a pluralist outlook, which focused on the legitimate role of various groups in Yemeni society and politics, and on the nobility and uniqueness of tribal descent. Moreover, Salih encouraged an active dialogue among these groups that would encourage nationwide reconciliation and broad support for the government.

The main organ that epitomized these ambitions was the General Peoples Congress. Convened in October 1982, the Congress was composed of one thousand delegates from different sectors and regions of Yemen. Salih was elected its secretary general. It was aimed at exercising what Salih called the "democratic process" in Yemen, based on the National Pact. The Congress has acted as a mechanism to improve interfactional relations and facilitate mass political participation. Elections to the General Peoples Congress Standing Committee were held in July 1985 and to its provincial committees in summer 1987. Salih was thereby undoubtedly able to spread the government's word nationwide, to rally wide support, and to encourage a national dialogue, all of which stabilized the Yemeni regime.

Salih's reign is also marked by economic development, which was made possible by the relative political calm. In addition to a balance-of-payment deficit with which Salih had to deal, in December 1982 an earthquake hit the central mountainous region in the Yemen, leaving four hundred thousand people homeless and forty-five hundred dead. Salvage and reconstruction expenses, which were estimated at circa two billion dollars were mainly afforded by Saudi Arabia and the Gulf States.

Oil was discovered in the summer of 1984 in the Marib-Jawf area, but already by 1987 it was stated that the expected income would rise to 740 million dollars per year. Salih can be credited for the contacts with the American companies, which facilitated the beginning of the oil industry in the Yemen. The oil income is intended to facilitate the development of agriculture and basic industries and to boost the infrastructure of the Yemen's economy.

The development of an entrepreneurial group in Yemen, investments in the local economy and the attraction of both Saudi Arabia and the PDRY to Yemeni oil pose both benefits and dangers to Salih's regime. The growing numbers of PDRY refugees in the Yemen (approximately four hundred thousand), whose quantities kept increasing since the 1986 civil war in the PDRY, have further burdened the delicate balance in Yemen society. Ali Abdullah Salih will have to cope with growing difficulties in the future, but his initiatives to stabilize and reconcile Yemeni societal factions have provided a solid basis for potentially troublesome times.

BIBLIOGRAPHY

Abir, Mordechai. *Oil, Power and Politics: Conflict in Arabia, the Red Sea and the Gulf.* London: Frank Cass, 1974.
Bidwell, Robin. *The Two Yemens.* London: Longmans, 1982.
Burrowes, Robert. *The Yemen Arab Republic.* Boulder, Colo.: Westview, 1987.
Halliday, Fred. *Arabia without Sultans.* N.Y.: Penguin, 1974.
Goldberg, J., and J. Kostiner. Annual chapter on Yemen Arab Republic. In D. Dishon, H. Shaked, and I. Rabinovich, (eds.) *Middle East Contemporary Survey.* New York: Holms and Meir, 1976–1985; Boulder, Colo.: Westview, 1986, 1987.
Ingrams, Harold. *The Yemen: Imams, Rules, and Revolutions.* London: Murray, 1963.
Page, Stephen. *The Soviet Union and the Yemens: Influence in Asymmetrical Relationships.* N.Y.: Praeger, 1958.
Peterson, John E. *Conflict in the Yemens and Superpower Involvement.* Washington, D.C.: Georgetown University, Center for Contemporary Arab Studies, 1981.
———.*Yemen: The Search for a Modern State.* Baltimore: Johns Hopkins, 1982.
Pridham, B. R. (ed.). *Contemporary Yemen: Politics and Historical Background.* N.Y.: St. Martins, 1984.
———.*Economy, Society and Culture in Contemporary Yemen.* London: Croom Helm, 1985.
Stookey, Robert W. *Yemen: The Politics of the Yemen Arab Republic.* Boulder, Colo.: Westview, 1978.
Wenner, Manfred W. *Modern Yemen: 1918–1966.* Baltimore: Johns Hopkins, 1968.

JOSEPH KOSTINER

YITZHAK SHAMIR (1915–   ) became prime minister of Israel and leader of the Likud party, succeeding Menachem Begin,* in October 1983. During his political career he held a number of senior positions including foreign minister, speaker of the Knesset (parliament), and chairman of the Herut Party's Executive

Committee. In the period preceding the establishment of the State of Israel, he played an active but controversial role as a leader in the Jewish underground, where he developed a reputation as an uncompromising leader with strongly held views. Unlike Begin, Shamir entered politics relatively late in life and rose rapidly to positions of power in the party and the government. Of all Israel's prime ministers he was probably the least well-known before taking office, despite a decade of public service in positions of responsibility.

Yitzhak Shamir (formerly Yzernitzky) was born in Rozhinay in eastern Poland in 1915. He was educated at a Hebrew secondary school in Bialystok, where he became a disciple of Vladimir (Ze'ev) Jabotinsky, the father of Revisionist Zionism, and joined the Revisionist youth movement, Betar. Shamir studied law at Warsaw University until 1935, when he emigrated to Palestine and changed his name from Yzernitzky to Shamir. He completed his studies at Hebrew University in Jerusalem.

Revisionist Zionism represented a more militant approach than mainstream Labor Zionism, and had fewer followers among those Eastern European Jews who emigrated to Palestine. It was less compromising with regard to the geographic boundaries of the proposed Jewish state, which Jabotinsky believed encompassed all of British-mandated Palestine on both sides of the Jordan River. The Revisionists established their own organizations, including the Irgun, which was formed in 1931 as an alternative to the Labor-dominated defense force, the Haganah. The Irgun and the Haganah differed both in policy and tactics, chiefly in the use of violent measures against British troops and Arabs in Palestine. Shamir joined the Irgun in 1937 and rose through the ranks of the organization into leadership positions. Menachem Begin became the commander of the Irgun in 1943 and remained its leader until its dissolution in 1948.

In 1940 the Irgun suspended attacks against the British Mandatory authorities in Palestine and offered its cooperation in the war effort against Germany. This caused a split within the organization and led to the creation of a smaller and more militant group, which Shamir joined. This faction, LEHI (Lohamei Herut Yisrael—Israel Freedom Fighters) was known as the "Stern Gang." It was named after Abraham Stern (Yair), the group's first leader, and viewed the British as the main obstacle to the establishment of a Jewish state in Palestine.

After Stern was killed by the British police in 1942, Shamir helped to reorganize LEHI, establishing a high command known as LEHI Central, which included Shamir, Nathan Yellin-Mor, and Dr. Israel Scheib (Eldad). Shamir directed LEHI's operations, which became increasingly violent. A terror campaign was conducted against the British, which included the assassination of Lord Moyne, Britain's senior Middle East official stationed in Cairo, in 1944. Two gang members were captured, tried, convicted, and executed for the crime. The Stern Gang was also suspected in the assassination of Swedish Count Folke Bernadotte, who had sought to mediate an end to Israel's War of Independence (1948–1949) on behalf of the United Nations. These charges have not been substantiated, however, and Shamir refuses comment on the matter.

Shamir was arrested twice by the British authorities, in 1941 and 1946, but managed to escape both times. The arrest in 1946 was related to the bombing of the King David Hotel, which had been carried out by the Irgun. Shamir was sent to a detention camp in Eritrea, but he escaped and traveled through Ethiopia to Djibouti, ultimately arriving in France where he was given political asylum. He remained in France until he returned to the newly established State of Israel in May 1948.

As Israel declared its independence, armies of the Arab states entered Palestine with the declared intent of preventing the establishment of the Jewish state, thus assuring that all Palestine would remain in Arab hands. Prime Minister David Ben-Gurion* attempted to consolidate the various Jewish-Zionist military organizations operating in Palestine into one national army. This required the Irgun and LEHI to concede their operational independence and accept a subordinate position under Ben-Gurion, who also served as defense minister. Despite initial opposition and some clashes this was ultimately achieved.

Shamir found it difficult to enter Israel's new political system, which was dominated by former Haganah members and others who had been associated with the Labor Zionist movement. Shamir sought election to the Knesset in 1949 with a list of candidates comprised of former LEHI members, but this effort failed. Shamir did not pursue elective office again until he joined the Herut (Freedom) party of Menachem Begin in 1970.

During the period from 1948 to 1955, Shamir remained in private life, where he was active in a number of commercial ventures including directing an association of cinema owners. These were not particularly successful. Isser Harel, then head of the Mossad, (''institute,'' Israel's central intelligence agency) recruited Shamir into the organization in 1955 where his operational experience from the Mandate period could be put to use. Shamir spent a decade with the Mossad and rose to a senior position. He was stationed in Paris for a part of that time, where he was involved in Operation Damocles which was designed to coerce German scientists into discontinuing their assistance to Egyptian President Gamal Abdul Nasser* in his efforts to develop atomic-weapons production capability.

Shamir left the Mossad in 1965 and returned to private life, where he pursued commercial interests with only moderate success. He remained active in public life primarily through his efforts at increasing Soviet Jewish immigration to Israel. In 1970, Menachem Begin offered him a leadership position in Herut, which Shamir had recently joined; he was elected to the Executive Committee and became the director of the Immigration Department. Shamir successfully ran for election to the Knesset for the first time on the Herut list in 1973, and became a member of the State Comptroller Committee and the influential Defense and Foreign Affairs Committee. He directed the party's Organization Department, and in 1975 he was elected chairman of Herut's Executive Committee, a post to which he was unanimously reelected two years later.

The 1977 Knesset election was a watershed in Israeli politics. Likud, into which Herut had merged, secured the largest number of votes, and Menachem Begin became Israel's first non-Labor prime minister, thus ending Labor's dominance of Israeli politics which had begun during the Yishuv (prestate) period. Begin formed the government and took control of Israel's bureaucracy as well as of the formulation and implementation of domestic and foreign policy. Shamir was elected speaker of the Knesset in June 1977, and continued to be a loyal supporter of Begin.

Loyalty characterized Shamir's service to Begin both within the party and in the Begin-led governments in which he served. The most significant issue to separate the two was Begin's decision to negotiate and sign the Camp David Accords (1978) and the Egypt-Israel Peace Treaty (1979). Shamir opposed the treaty, as did other Likud leaders including Moshe Arens and Ariel Sharon, because he believed Israel was sacrificing too much in return for what he viewed as uncertain guarantees of peace. He saw the withdrawal from the Sinai Peninsula and the relinquishing of the security buffer it provided and the sophisticated air bases located there, as well as the destruction of Jewish settlements, as too high a price for Israel to pay. Shamir abstained on the final Knesset vote when the treaty was approved.

Begin appointed Shamir as his foreign minister in March 1980, five months after Moshe Dayan* resigned from that position. Shamir's view of the Camp David process changed during his tenure as foreign minister, where he was responsible for implementing the agreements reached. He became an advocate of the Camp David approach for future negotiations between Israel and the Arab states, and stated, "It must be clear to all that the Camp David Accords are the only document agreed on by all and, therefore the only way to continue the [peace] process" (Reich 1984:26). Shamir was also active in efforts to reestablish diplomatic relations with several African states that had been severed at the time of the Yom Kippur War of 1973. Contacts were initiated with these states and in several instances relations were restored. He also supported legislation declaring united Jerusalem the eternal capital of Israel (July 1980), as well as the bombing of the Iraqi nuclear reactor in June 1981 and the "annexation" of the Golan Heights in December 1981. He saw these actions as contributing to Israel's security.

The 1981 Knesset election was not conclusive in identifying a popular preference for Likud or Labor. The electorate divided its votes between the two blocs, but awarded neither a majority of votes or seats in the Knesset, and coalition politics continued to characterize the system. Begin received the mandate to form the new government, and he succeeded in establishing a Likud-led coalition that subsequently received the endorsement of the Knesset. Shamir continued to serve as foreign minister.

Begin's second government (1981–1983) was marked by severe economic difficulties including triple-digit inflation, and by the continuation of the Arab-Israeli peace process. The government's tenure was overshadowed by the sixth

Arab-Israeli war—the June 1982 Israeli military action against the Palestine Liberation Organization (PLO) in Lebanon, known as Operation Peace for Galilee.

A tragic episode of Israel's involvement in Lebanon was the massacre of Palestinians by Christian Phalangist forces at the Sabra and Shatila refugee camps in West Beirut in September 1982. A Commission of Inquiry chaired by Supreme Court Chief Justice Yitzhak Kahan, inter alia criticized Shamir because he failed to pass on to appropriate individuals information he had received from Communications Minister Mordechai Zippori suggesting that massacres were taking place in the camps. Although others were more severely chastized and punished, the commission found that Shamir erred in not passing on the information, and found it difficult to justify "such disdain for information that came from a member of the Cabinet" (Brinkley 1988:74).

Menachem Begin resigned from office in September 1983, apparently believing that he could no longer carry out his responsibilities in an effective manner. The death of his wife, Aliza, and the continuing casualties suffered by Israel's forces in Lebanon apparently were significant factors. His resignation brought to an end a major era in Israeli history. Efforts by many of his colleagues, supporters, and followers to convince him to reconsider his decision were to no avail. Shamir was the compromise choice to follow Begin, and he formed the new government.

Shamir's personality and style were dramatically different from those of Begin, despite strong accord on ideology and policy. Shamir apparently had been affected by his many years in the underground prior to Israel's independence and in the Mossad afterward. Unlike Begin's dominating personality, Shamir's is more soft-spoken. Many of the same programs were followed but in a more quiet, unostentatious, and less confrontational manner. He has tended to avoid publicity and the media, and is relatively uncommunicative about his past activities. He is seen as methodical and hardworking, with a pleasant exterior masking a tough inner personality. He was perceived, especially in Washington, D.C., as more diplomatic and less pugnacious than Begin. Some described him as a low-key, colorless, noncharismatic but determined figure.

Shamir's initial efforts were directed toward reconstituting the government around the personalities and policies of the outgoing one. He pledged to continue along the course Begin had charted, and said that his government would be bound by the basic principles and the coalition agreement of the previous government as submitted to the Knesset in 1981. On October 10, 1983, the Knesset endorsed the government and its programs, and Yitzhak Shamir became the prime minister of Israel, but many viewed him as merely an interim leader who would last only until the next Knesset election in 1984. Some observers pointed to Shamir's decision to continue serving as foreign minister as well as prime minister during this period as evidence that he anticipated the return of Menachem Begin to the leadership of the party and the government.

Shamir focused on both domestic- and foreign-policy issues. His economic policies were directed toward reducing government subsidies on essential commodities, decreasing private and public consumption, and lowering the standard of living. The overriding foreign-policy issue was Israel's continued presence in Lebanon, which Shamir felt was necessary for maintaining the security of northern Israel. He called for implementation of the Israel-Lebanon Agreement of May 1983 and the withdrawal of all foreign forces from Lebanon, and named Syria as the primary obstacle to peace in the region.

Despite the absence of Menachem Begin in the 1984 Knesset election, the Likud, led by Shamir, and other rightist parties maintained their electoral support and their strength in the Knesset. Nevertheless, the results of the elections were inconclusive, and after a period of intense, lengthy, and complex negotiations, neither Shamir nor Labor Party leader Shimon Peres* succeeded in their efforts to establish a coalition government. This division in the Israeli body politic led, in September 1984, to the formation of a government of national unity, the basis of which was a series of compromises and concessions. According to the terms of the agreement, Shamir and Peres each were to serve for twenty-five months as prime minister while the other held the position of vice prime minister and foreign minister. Peres was prime minister during the first period, and rotated positions with Shamir as agreed in October 1986.

The National Unity Government (NUG) was successful in dealing with issues where a broad consensus of opinion existed, such as the withdrawal of Israel's forces from Lebanon and the problems facing the economy. However, the government and the country remained divided on key issues such as the modalities for the peace process. While Peres accepted the concept of an international conference, Shamir was steadfast in his rejection of that approach, preferring direct negotiations between Israel and the Arab states. This stalemate was compounded by a lack of dynamic and imaginative leadership from either Shamir or Peres. They differed from their predecessors (particularly Ben-Gurion and Begin) in their inability to produce new initiatives and directions for Israeli policy, especially for the peace process.

The 1988 Knesset election campaign focused almost exclusively on foreign-policy issues, particularly the modalities for continuation of the peace process. Shamir again received his party's nomination for the leadership of Likud and of the next government, as did Peres for Labor. They presented the electorate with sharply different visions of Israel's future and of the most desirable path to achieve peace and security.

As in 1984, the 1988 election did not demonstrate a clear preference for either Likud or Labor among the electorate. Both lost Knesset seats to smaller and more ideologically oriented parties on the extreme right and left of the political spectrum, and fifteen parties gained representation in the Knesset. Likud won forty seats, one more than Labor and, by tradition, Shamir received the mandate from President Chaim Herzog to form a coalition government. Shamir expressed initial confidence that he could form a coalition, but this required the support of the religious parties. During the coalition negotiations it became clear that the substantial and controversial demands of the religious parties threatened the harmony of the body politic. This was particularly true with changes demanded by the religious parties restricting the interpretation of who is a Jew under the Law of Return of 1950, which grants citizenship and special privileges to any Jew upon immigration to Israel. This alarmed not only secular Israelis but also numerous American Jews who were firmly opposed to changes in the definition of Jewish identity.

After weeks of intensive negotiations, Shamir entered into a new coalition agreement with Labor. The religious parties lost much of their bargaining strength as a consequence of this arrangement. The agreement placed Labor in an equal position with Likud in the government; however, Shamir would remain the prime minister for the full tenure. The distribution of cabinet portfolios among the two blocs was equal, with Shimon Peres becoming finance minister, Moshe Arens becoming foreign minister, and Yitzhak Rabin* continuing as defense minister. The policy guidelines adopted were virtually identical to the 1984 coalition agreement, which required mutual consent for controversial issues such as territorial compromise and the modalities for continuation of the peace process.

Shamir's success as prime minister has depended to a significant degree on the advice and assistance of his closest aides. His working style, developed during his years outside political life—in the Mossad and in business—seems to have commended to him the value of good staff and teamwork as well as the importance of expertise. Unlike Begin's individualism, Shamir tends to rely on others. Also, unlike many of Israel's senior political figures, Shamir came to office without the usual coterie of advisers and protégés that have accompanied many of his predecessors. He built a team of aides after securing public office.

Shamir's views on foreign policy are complex. He abstained from the Knesset vote on the Camp David Accords, in part because they required Israel to dismantle the settlements in Sinai. He sees Israel's 1967 frontiers as indefensible. Shamir supports the peace treaty with Egypt (although he disagreed with some of its clauses), and believes that Israel must work within its framework. He saw a security risk in giving up Sinai, but believed that it was necessary for peace, which he sees as essential for Israel. He preferred a faster and smoother normalization process with Egypt but recognized that there were obstacles. Shamir has suggested that a stand softer than that adopted by Likud on many of the Arab-Israeli conflict issues would probably help the autonomy talks go more smoothly, but also suggested that this would be "at the expense of our vital interests." He supported the bombing of the Iraqi nuclear reactor in June 1981, the "annexation" of the Golan Heights in December 1981, and the war in Lebanon. In retrospect, he sees actions such as these as contributing to Israel's security.

Shamir has been a consistent advocate of maintaining an Israeli presence on the West Bank, and supports the continued construction of Jewish settlements there. He is unwilling to relinquish any part of the Golan Heights and the Gaza

Strip, and suggests that previous land-for-peace agreements such as the Camp David Accords and the consequent Egypt-Israel Peace Treaty should not necessarily be seen as guidelines for future settlements. He stated his position on the matter: "Do not forget that in Camp David we have paid a tremendous price for the peace. We have taken great risks . . . and we have already reached the limits of concessions we are able to make" (Reich 1984:27). Nevertheless, Shamir appears to want some form of working arrangement with the Palestinians, but adamantly refuses to negotiate with the PLO.

The Palestinian uprising (the *intifada*), which began in December 1987 in the West Bank and Gaza Strip, placed the rejuvenation of the peace process at the forefront of political debate in Israel. It focused attention on the question of the disposition of the territories and their inhabitants. Shamir worked closely with Defense Minister Yitzhak Rabin to quell the disturbances and restore order to the territories through the use of force in an "iron fist" policy employing the Israel Defense Forces (IDF). The intifada loomed large over Shamir's tenure as prime minister, and although there was widespread (but not universal) public support within Israel for the measures employed, they generated unease at home and had a negative effect on Israel's international image.

Relations between the United States and Israel continued to improve during Shamir's tenure. Strategic cooperation was enhanced and institutionalized by the Memoranda of Understanding of December 1987 and April 1988, which formalized cooperation on a range of military, political, economic, and intelligence matters. Shamir has been a consistent advocate of close relations with the United States, and said that "relations of trust, friendship, and close cooperation between ourselves and the United States are vital for us and for the stability of the whole Middle East . . . and the government of Israel will do all it can to foster and deepen our ties with the United States" (ibid.). He noted that the differences in political positions appearing at times between the two states were a "natural and understandable phenomenon," and did not cloud the atmosphere of friendship and the strong alliance that characterized the relationship.

After reassuming power in 1988, Shamir once again became the subject of speculation concerning his future as leader of the party and the government. Shamir has been challenged for the leadership of Likud since Begin's resignation, but has retained his position at the head of the party. His rivals have included David Levy, who has a strong base of support among the considerable Oriental constituency of Herut, and General Ariel Sharon, the former defense minister. Moshe Arens, who has been Shamir's chief ally, has credentials as defense minister, foreign minister, and ambassador to the United States. Some argue that Shamir has retained his leadership of the party because of the lack of a single obvious successor. Certainly infighting among various factions has helped Shamir and made him the continued compromise choice.

Shamir's performance as prime minister and the direction Israel pursues as a result will serve as his political legacy. He is confronted by difficult circumstances and decisions that will bear heavily on Israel's future. Shamir has described the next four years from 1988 to 1992 (the tenure of his government) as "my last cadence . . . At the end of this next term I will be 77, maybe that's enough" (Brinkley 1988:77).

Shamir has expressed a desire to spend more time with his wife, Shulamit, his two children, and his five grandchildren on his retirement from public office. When he retires he will leave behind a lifelong commitment to the State of Israel and the Jewish people. He has dedicated over fifty years to advancing his vision of Zionism, often in controversial positions. Whether his legacy is that of a great statesman will largely be determined by his final term in office and his accomplishments at that time. He will need to have domestic- and foreign-policy successes to build an image as an effective and appropriate successor to Menachem Begin and the earlier prime ministers of Israel.

BIBLIOGRAPHY

Works by Shamir:

"Israel's Role in a Changing Middle East." *Foreign Affairs* 60 (Spring 1982): 789–801.
"Israel at 40." *Foreign Affairs* 66 (America and the World 1987–1988): 574–590.

Other Works:

Arian, Asher. *Politics in Israel: The Second Generation*. Chatham, N.J.: Chatham House, 1985.
Arian, Asher, and Michael Shamir (eds.) *The Elections in Israel—1984*. New Brunswick, N.J.: Transaction Books, 1986.
Brinkley, Joel. "Israel's Shamir." *New York Times Magazine*, August 21, 1988.
Peleg, Ilan. *Begin's Foreign Policy, 1977–1983: Israel's Move to the Right*. New York: Greenwood Press, 1987.
Reich, Bernard. "The Shamir Government: Policy and Prospects." *Middle East Insight* 3 (January/February 1948): 25–31.
———. *Israel: Land of Tradition and Conflict*. Boulder, Colo.: Westview Press; London and Sydney: Croom Helm, 1985.
Reich, Bernard, and Gershon R. Kieval (eds.). *Israel Faces the Future*. New York: Praeger, 1986.
———. *Israel National Security Policy: Political Actors and Perspectives*. New York: Greenwood Press, 1988.
Sachar, Howard M. *A History of Israel: From the Rise of Zionism to Our Time*. New York: Alfred A. Knopf, 1979.

BERNARD REICH AND JOSEPH HELMAN

W

CHAIM WEIZMANN (1874–1952) was the first president of the State of Israel. He devoted his entire life to help bring the Jewish state into existence. He did this not as a leader of the Jewish community in Palestine, but as the official and sometime unofficial head of the World Zionist Organization (WZO). A consummate diplomat, his strength was the moral fervor he brought to his mission.

Weizmann was born in Motol, a small hamlet some twenty-five miles from Pinsk, on November 27, 1874, the third of Ozer and Rachel-Leah Weizmann's fifteen children. Many of Motol's persecuted Jews sought escape through emigration to America, while others sought salvation through the centuries-old dream of a return to Palestine.

The Weizmann family were ardent Zionists and belonged to the *Hovevei Zion*, a proto-Zionist group founded in 1884 to support modern Jewish settlements in the Holy Land. The yearning for Zion and for the recreation of a modern Jewish homeland there, became the lodestar of Weizmann's life. As a student in Germany, where he earned his doctorate in chemistry, Weizmann became a leader of the Russisch-Juedischer Wissenschaftlicher Verien, an association of Russian Jewish intellectuals, many of whom would later become leaders in the Zionist movement. After Berlin, Weizmann claimed, "no fundamental change took place; my political outlook, my Zionist ideology, my scientific bent, my life's purposes, had crystallized" (Rose 1986:44).

Although elected a delegate, Weizmann did not attend the First Zionist Congress in 1897, but he attended the second congress and would be a major figure at many others in his life. While he admired and even respected Theodor Herzl, the founder of modern political Zionism, he also considered him naive as far as Jewish aspirations were concerned. Weizmann helped found and became a leader of the Democratic Faction, which opposed Herzl's political program with a demand for practical work, emphasizing the need for new Jewish settlements in Palestine. (Ironically, years later Weizmann himself would be attacked as relying too much on political negotiations and ignoring the practical needs of the *Yishuv*, the Jewish community in Palestine.) He and Herzl did agree on a plan for a great Jewish university in Palestine, a dream that Weizmann labored tirelessly to bring to reality.

In 1904, following Herzl's death and the split in the Zionist movement over the British offer of land in east Africa, Weizmann moved with his bride Vera Khatzman to England, where he began his career as a scientist at the University of Manchester. It took him a number of years to establish himself, but Weizmann's success in his chemical research had two important benefits. His patents on dyestuffs provided him with an ample and independent income, and it introduced him to men who played important roles in Britain's political, cultural, and intellectual affairs. Although he had vowed to give up Zionist politics and its frustrations when he moved to England, he did not do so. At the Eighth Zionist Congress in 1907, he delivered an important speech calling for continued practical work in building up Jewish settlements as well as continued diplomatic activity to win international support for a Jewish homeland. "If we achieve a synthesis of the two schools of Zionism," he said, "we may get past the dead points" (Rose 1986:103). Ultimately, this "synthetic Zionism" became the dominant theme of the movement, and remained the pattern for Weizmann's entire career.

When war broke out in 1914, the international leadership of the Zionist movement collapsed. As a result, great opportunities opened up for Weizmann, who by this time had become the de facto leader of the nascent English Zionist movement. His war work in chemicals gave him access to political figures whom he lobbied on behalf of his scheme. American Zionists under the leadership of Justice Louis D. Brandeis helped get President Woodrow Wilson to agree to the idea, but the major credit for securing the Balfour Declaration belongs to Chaim Weizmann. He overcame opposition from the anti-zionist British Jewish elite, and won over important figures in the government and the press. On November 2, 1917, Foreign Minister Arthur Balfour informed Lord Rothschild that "His Majesty's Government view with favour the establishment in Palestine of a national home for the Jewish people, and will use their best endeavours to facilitate the achievement of this object."

The Balfour Declaration constituted the greatest diplomatic achievement of Weizmann's career. It was the political charter that Herzl had dreamed about, and it set the Zionist movement irreversibly on the road to transforming a handful of settlements into a Jewish state. In one stroke, it also made Weizmann the undisputed leader of international Zionism, even though he held no formal office. When the British government wanted to send a commission to Palestine to investigate the status of Jewish settlements there and to draw up a plan for postwar development, it turned to Weizmann, and in doing so treated him as if he were the president-in-exile of the Jewish state to be.

Although the "charter" fulfilled few of the grandiose expectations it generated, it did appear to be the key to the realization of the Zionist dream, and it made Great Britain the sponsor of that dream. From November 1917 until his death, Weizmann persisted in viewing England as the only partner the Zionists could have in their work, despite one British betrayal after another. His success as a chemist, his acceptance by the great, the comfort he felt with English society, and, finally, the Balfour Declaration, made Weizmann an anglophile. Access to His Majesty's Government gave Weizmann enormous influence; it also created the blind spot that was his greatest liability.

Following World War I and a bitter struggle with the Americans over the course Zionism should take, Weizmann emerged in the 1920s as the leader both in name and in fact of the World Zionist Organization. Royalties from his chemical patents gave him the financial independence to devote the rest of his life to Zionism, although he often returned to the laboratory, especially when he despaired over Jewish affairs. He eventually built a home in Palestine near Rehovot, and shuttled back and forth between the United States, Great Britain, Europe, and Palestine until the outbreak of World War II.

Although Weizmann's name became synonymous with Zionism and the creation of a Jewish homeland, paradoxically he enjoyed only limited influence in Palestine itself. There David Ben-Gurion* emerged as the leader of the labor Zionist movement, which would be the dominant force in prestate political affairs as well as during the first three decades of the State of Israel. As a result, Weizmann had relatively little impact on the internal development of the Jewish state's political, economic, and social instrumentalities. The only exception was the Hebrew University in Jerusalem, whose cornerstone Weizmann laid on his trip to Palestine in 1918, and later on the Sieff Institute for Science, which ultimately became part of the Weizmann Institute in Rehovot.

Weizmann's contribution to the creation of Israel came in other areas. As head of the Zionist movement, he had the responsibility for providing financial support to the Yishuv and its institutions. He became, as he jokingly referred to himself, the "great *schnorrer*" (beggar) of Jewish life, constantly importuning Jewish communities around the world to support the Zionist enterprise. He even managed to involve non-Zionist Jews through the creation of the Jewish Agency in 1929, a partnership between the World Zionist Organization and non-Zionists who opposed a Jewish state but believed in the religious and cultural regeneration of the Holy Land. The depression and then the war prevented the agency from developing along the lines he had planned.

Most important, Weizmann served from 1917 to 1949 as Zionism's leading diplomat. When he went to Palestine in 1918 as head of the Zionist Commission, he traveled to Aqaba to meet with the Amir Feisal, the acknowledged leader of Arab nationalism. In a letter to Weizmann dated January 3, 1919, Feisal promised to recognize Zionist claims in Palestine if the Allies supported Arab national aspirations in Iraq and Syria. When the Western powers, for their own reasons, failed to support Arab plans, Feisal considered his pledge to Weizmann to be void. This appears to have been the only major effort by Weizmann, whose focus was always on Jewish nationalism, to reach out for some cooperation between Arabs and Jews in the Middle East, although many times he showed sensitivity to the Arab problem.

In 1919 Weizmann headed the Zionist delegation to the Paris Peace Conference, where he pleaded for international recognition of the Balfour Declaration. In 1921, the Allies awarded the mandate for Palestine to Great Britain. Throughout the world, Jewish communities rejoiced, and believed that restoration of a Jewish commonwealth in Palestine would now proceed with the encouragement and protection of His Majesty's Government.

However, the very moment of triumph masked the fact that Britain had already begun to reconsider the Balfour pledge. With each outbreak of riots in Palestine, the British government attempted to appease the Arabs, and always at the expense of Jewish interests. First, the British separated Palestine, with that part west of the Jordan reserved specifically for the Arabs. Throughout the 1920s, a perceptible shift took place in British policy on the assumption that British interests in the Middle East could better be served by placating the Arabs than by championing the Jews. Weizmann protested continuously against this policy, but to no avail.

Following the 1929 Arab riots in Palestine against the Jews, the colonial secretary, Lord Passfield (Sidney Webb), issued a White Paper essentially abrogating all British obligations to the Jews, especially the major premise of the Mandate that a Jewish homeland be created in Palestine. As Weizmann noted, the Passfield White Paper was intended "to make our work in Palestine impossible" (1949:333).

The issuance of the Passfield White Paper touched off a storm of protest. Weizmann, no longer able to apologize for the British, resigned from the Jewish Agency, which had been designated the official liaison between the Jewish people and the British government. Within the British Parliament both Liberals and Conservatives attacked Passfield vehemently, and even his own Labour Party wanted to disown the document. Finally the Labour Government beat a tactical retreat, and Prime Minister Ramsey MacDonald wrote to Weizmann disavowing any intention to undermine the Jewish settlement. His Majesty's Government, MacDonald assured Weizmann, would carry out the intention of the Mandate.

The MacDonald letter was Weizmann's last major political success for many years, and it bought seven years of breathing space for the Zionist movement. Weizmann himself found little peace during these years. He had put all his eggs in the British basket, and now he had to pay the price. On the right, the Revisionist Zionists led by Vladimir Jabotinsky attacked him and demanded that the British restore the land taken away to create Transjordan. On the left, a militant social Zionist contingent of Palestinians led by David Ben-Gurion scolded him for failing to protect the interests of the Yishuv. Justice Brandeis's group, now once again in control of American Zionism, also joined in the attack. At the 1931 Zionist Congress, the delegates showed their dissatisfaction by refusing to reelect him as president, but they elected Weizmann's closest colleague, Nahum Sokolow, to head the Executive Committee. Although personally absent from the leadership for the next four years, the Zionist policy Weizmann had shaped changed hardly at all: reliance on Britain while building up the Yishuv, "house by house, dunam by dunam" (1949:339).

The rise of Nazism in the 1930s emphasized the need for a Jewish homeland; British leaders, however, saw the necessity of wooing Arab leaders in order to protect imperial interests in the Middle East. In Palestine, the Yishuv enjoyed economic prosperity and easily absorbed the tens of thousands of Jews who immigrated annually. However, Arab resentment increased, and the familiar pattern played itself out again—Arab rioting, a Royal commission, and further British withdrawal from the Balfour promise.

The Peel Commission appointed in May 1937 to investigate the Jewish-Arab unrest, recommended the partition of Palestine into Jewish and Arab states as a possible solution to the problem, the first time an official British body had ever recommended a Jewish state. Weizmann's testimony before the Peel Commission is credited by some with leading the members to recommend a state, and at the 1937 Zionist Congress, Weizmann urged the delegates to accept the principle of partition while seeking to improve the territorial provisions.

Weizmann, along with Ben-Gurion and many of the Palestinian Jewish leaders, accepted the partition proposal not with rejoicing, but with a fatalistic necessity. As Nazi persecution of Jews increased, it became all too clear that no country other than Palestine would take in Jewish refugees, and Palestine could not control immigration so long as it remained a British colony. An independent Jewish state, they reasoned, even a truncated one, would at least be a haven to which the victims of Hitler could flee.

However, the Arabs rejected the proposal out of hand. At the St. James's Conference in February 1939, Weizmann led the Jewish delegation in what would be Great Britain's last effort to arrange a negotiated agreement between Jew and Arab. The conference provided the pretext for the British to issue a White Paper that imposed severe restrictions on Jewish land purchases and placed a cap on Jewish immigration, after which there could be no further immigration without Arab approval.

The outbreak of war a few months later temporarily made moot the impact of the White Paper. Weizmann immediately offered his services to the British government, both out of patriotism and out of the hope that his success during World War I could be repeated. Circumstances had changed, however, and although he could still gain audience with government leaders, he could not influence them at all. His requests for a Jewish military unit, his offer to do scientific work, and his pleas to allow stateless refugees to land in Palestine all were rebuffed. He, and other Jewish leaders, had no idea of the extent of the Holocaust, and all anticipated there would be two to three million Jewish refugees seeking access to Palestine after the hostilities ended. Nonetheless he continued to work toward the goal of securing a satisfactory political settlement after the war, and if his efforts in Great Britain went unrewarded, he would go to the United States, which he and other Jewish leaders assumed would be the dominant force in the postwar settlement.

While Weizmann sought to replicate his past triumph, command of Zionist affairs shifted to David Ben-Gurion,* who vowed to fight the White Paper as if there were no Hitler, and Hitler as if there were no White Paper. The Nazis had taught the Zionist leadership a lesson—Jews had to control their own destiny, and not be dependent on the good will of others. Britain had been hailed as the savior of the Jews in 1917; appeasement condemned millions of Jews to death a quarter-century later. Weizmann could continue to seek a political solution; the Yishuv prepared to do battle for its independence.

During the war a weary Weizmann, devastated by the death of his son in battle, commuted between England and the United States seeking audience with British and American leaders, who assured him that they supported Zionism, but did nothing concrete to demonstrate that support. Nonetheless, for all his frustration with the British, Weizmann continued to believe that only a political solution with England's blessing would bring the Jewish state into being. Within the Zionist movement he may still have been president of the WZO and revered by Jews all over the world, but Ben-Gurion in Palestine and the equally militant Abba Hillel Silver in the United States reflected the new mood of Zionism—action and not words would establish the Jewish state.

Once the war ended and the world realized the devastation wrought by the Holocaust, Weizmann hoped that conscience would lead the Western democracies to implement the Zionist plan at once. However, Winston Churchill, for all his promises of support during the war, now told Weizmann that nothing could be done until the Allies were seated at the peace table. By then Franklin Roosevelt was dead, and a few months after that Churchill had been voted out of office. The new Labour Government, which had castigated the Conservatives for failing to keep British promises to the Zionists, now adopted exactly the same posture of placating the Arabs. Weizmann, his health severely undermined by glaucoma, continued his efforts to seek a political solution to keep the Yishuv and Britain tied together, but to no avail. In the years immediately following the war, Weizmann knew little but pain, rejection, and defeat.

At the first postwar Zionist Congress in Basle, Switzerland, in 1946, Weizmann defended his policies in one of the greatest speeches of his life, and tried to warn the movement away from an open confrontation with Great Britain. In part, this derived from his view of what a Jewish state ought to be, one devoted to peace and a shining symbol of Jewish values. Weizmann himself was heartsick from British betrayal, and had few illusions left by this time over British intentions. Nonetheless, he believed the Yishuv was too weak to fight either the Arab states that surrounded Palestine of the British army that ruled it. The delegates, however, had had enough of English perfidy, and on a vote of confidence, rejected both Weizmann and his anglocentric policies.

One might have thought that Weizmann's career had ended, but he still had a part to play in the birth of Israel. When a frustrated British government turned the Palestine problem over to the United Nations, everyone assumed that it would be Weizmann who would present the Jewish case to the UN Special Commission on Palestine. In the fall of 1947 he addressed the United Nations General Assembly to plead for the partition of Palestine and the establishment of a Jewish State. Regarding the latest Arab proposal that the Yishuv should accept minority status within an Arab state, he declared simply that those of us who immigrated to Palestine did not intend to become citizens of an Arab state.

That fall and winter the aging and sick old man showed he was still the master of diplomacy. Weizmann secured an interview with U.S. President Harry Truman, who promised to aid in the creation of a Jewish state. Weizmann twice appealed to Truman for help, both times successfully. When the U.S. State Department seemed willing to cut out the Negev from the proposed Jewish state, Truman overrode them and ordered the American delegate to support the plan that included the Negev, and on the day Israel declared its independence, the United States immediately extended recognition to the new Jewish state, thus fulfilling a promise Truman had made to Weizmann.

The armed conflict that had erupted in Palestine even before independence had sickened Weizmann, and he declared, "This is not the way!" (Laqueur 1972:575). However, as the Mandate neared its end, Weizmann too came to realize that while the Yishuv prayed for peace, it would have to fight for its life.

With the declaration of Israel's independence and the establishment of a provisional government, Weizmann's status changed overnight. From being the unofficial special pleader for Zionism, he became president of Israel, and was accorded all the honors due to a foreign head of state. On an official visit to Washington, D.C., he stayed at Blair House, rode in a parade down Pennsylvania Avenue, and called at the White House. There he and Truman discussed the problems of the new state, and Weizmann secured the president's promise of loans and other aid.

In February 1949, the first elected Israeli *Knesset* (Parliament) selected Weizmann as the first president of Israel, a post he held until his death. However, although he had lived to see the promised land, he had little satisfaction in the honors that now came to him. Ben-Gurion had structured the government along British lines, so that the prime minister held all the power, while the president, like the British king, had little more than a ceremonial role. One can understand Ben-Gurion's desire to keep political power in his own hands, but there is no excuse for the spitefulness he displayed in keeping Weizmann's name off the list of signers of the Declaration of Independence. An aged, sick Weizmann had little interest in ceremony, and called himself the "prisoner of Rehovot" (Rose 1986:457). His health continued to fail, and he died on November 9, 1952, mourned by Jews all over the world.

BIBLIOGRAPHY

Works by Weizmann:

The Letters and Papers of Chaim Weizman. Series A: Letters. 23 vols. *Series B: Papers.*
    2 vols. Oxford: Oxford University Press; Jerusalem: Israel Universities Press,
    1968–1984.
Trial and Error. New York: Harper & Brothers, 1949.

Other Works:

Bethel, Nicholas. *The Palestine Triangle*. New York: G. P. Putnam's, 1979.
Halpern, Ben. *A Clash of Heroes*. New York: Oxford University Press, 1987.
Laqueur, Walter. *A History of Zionism*. New York: Holt, Rinehart & Winston, 1972.
Litvinoff, Barnet. *Weizmann: Last of the Patriarchs*. New York: G. P. Putnam's, 1976.
Reinharz, Jehuda. *Chaim Weizmann: The Making of a Zionist Leader*. New York: Oxford
        University Press, 1985.
Rose, Norman. *Chaim Weizmann*. New York: Viking, 1986.
Stein, Leonard. *The Balfour Declaration*. New York: Simon and Schuster, 1961.
Weizmann, Vera. *The Impossible Takes Longer*. New York: Harper & Row, 1967.

MELVIN I. UROFSKY

Y

YAHYA (1869–1948). King Yahya Muhammad Hameed ad-Deen was the founder and first ruler of modern North Yemen. He fought the Ottoman Turks for nearly two decades to achieve the independence of contemporary North Yemen in 1919. He clashed with the British and the Saudis in his attempt, in the 1920s and 1930s, to reunite all the territories of Biblical Yemen under his religious leadership and to sustain the independence of those territories already under his rule. He was the longest ruler of a Middle Eastern state in modern times (1904–1948) which led to political stability and governmental continuity in Yemen. Yet, his rigid form of government, his harsh treatment of his subjects, his closing of Yemen to outside influences, and his lack of enthusiasm for internal socioeconomic development were factors in the popular revolt against his rule and his death in 1948.

He was born in Sanaa City, the capital of North Yemen, in June 1869. Yahya grew up in Sanaa at the house of his father, Muhammad, a famous Zaydi religious scholar and later a Zaydi imam of Yemen (1890–1904). He received both his primary and secondary education in Islamic law and Arabic classical literature from his father—who during the late 1870s and early 1880s was Sanaa's first *mufti* (Islamic law interpreter)—and several other prominent Zaydi scholars. In sum, he was raised within an Islamic scholarly environment and under religious circumstances.

As for his career, Imam Yahya was raised politically and militarily by his father within a very troubled and truculent tribal society and under warring circumstances during the Yemeni resistance to the Turkish and British occupation of Yemen. By the late 1880s, his father was already distinguished not only as a famous religious scholar but also as a prominent political figure challenging the Turkish authority and presence in Yemen. He was already known for his good and successful offices in mediating tribal disputes and reconciling conflicts among the many warring Yemeni tribes. After the death of the previous imam in 1890, Yahya's father became the favorite candidate of both the *ulama* (the religious scholars) and the tribal leaders to assume the Zaydi imamate in Yemen and lead the struggle of independence against the Turks in North Yemen and the British in South Yemen. In 1890 he was proclaimed Yemen's new Zaydi imam in the city of Saadah, and soon assumed the religious title of *al-Mansur Billah* (the Victorious by God). From Saadah, al-Mansur and his son Yahya called for and initiated a general revolt throughout the stronghold mountains of North Yemen against the Turks that resulted by the end of 1891 in the siege of Sanaa itself. Though the siege lasted for about a year, the Turkish troops were able to break it and drive al-Mansur's tribal army away; however, he continued his national struggle for Yemen's independence from Turkey until his death in 1904. Soon after his death, his son Yahya succeeded him to the Zaydi imamate and assumed the religious title of *al-Mutawakkil Ala Allah* (the One Who Relies on God). Moreover, he often used to be called *Mawlana Amir al-Muaminin* (His Highness, or literally, Our Lord the Commander of the Faithful). His domain came to be known also as the Yemeni Mutawakkilite Kingdom, after his al-Mutawakkil title, especially after achieving the full independence of North Yemen from Turkey in 1919 in the wake of the latter's defeat in World War I. Similarly, each of Yahya's eighteen sons assumed the title of *Sayf al-Islam* (Sword of Islam), except for Ahmmad who, as the oldest son, was distinguished by the title *Wali al-Aahd* (the Crown Prince). These princes, especially Ahmmad, were their father's right hand in governing and administering the major provinces of the kingdom as well as his main commanders later during his external wars with the Turks, the British, the Idrisis, and the Saudis. However, most surprisingly, most of these "Swords of Islam," including Ahmmad, were Yahya's iron fist in his internal reign of terror against his subjects. Ahmmad, by the way, was the only son to assume the Zaydi imamate in North Yemen, which he did between 1948 and 1962, following his father's death.

Much of the time al-Mansur insisted that his son Yahya accompany him in order to train him for his future career. By the age of twenty, Yahya was already helping his father in solving legal disputes, visiting tribal sheikhs and heads of major clans to call for their support, collecting money for his father's cause, and recruiting troops and drawing up plans for attacking the Turkish centers throughout the central mountains of Yemen. Nevertheless, the death of Yahya's father had a deep influence on his career and his life. Al-Mansur left Yahya a troubling political career and a divided tribal society and domain. Furthermore, he left Yahya alone facing the powerful foreign penetration of Yemen, including the Turkish occupation of most of North Yemen, the British colonization of South Yemen and Dhofar in present Oman, and the Idrisi and later the Saudi occupation of Wadi Najran, Asir, and Jizan in northern Tihamah and southern Hejaz (the northern territories of Biblical Yemen)—to all of which Imam Yahya had laid geographical, historical, and political claim. In doing so Imam Yahya hoped to reunite the whole historical and natural territories of *al-Yemen al-Kubra* (the Great Yemen) under his religious and political leadership.

Imam Yahya's claim for greater Yemen is important, and is one of five major factors deriving from his childhood, his educational and political training, and his political career and leadership. Those five factors can be regarded as the most significant historical, social, and political instruments in formulating his personality as a political leader, determining the major course of political events during his unstable era, affecting his overall political contributions to his country, and, finally, influencing both his positive and his negative achievements.

The first factor is the influence of Yahya's childhood, youth, and adult experiences in life, including his early education and his political socialization and training during his father's era. The second factor is the perception in modern Yemen of al-Yaman al-Kubra, or Great Yemen, and Yahya's strong desire to reunite all the regions of historical, ancient, and biblical Yemen in one political entity under his own Zaydi rule. Imam Yahya's vision of greater Yemen did not grow out of mere political ambitions. Before the eighteenth century, ancient, historical, and biblical Yemen had for about four thousand years included geographically, demographically, socially, and politically the lower and southern half of what is known in modern history as the Arabian Peninsula, including the two present-day Yemens, the current Sultanate of Oman, and the northern Tihamah regions that are now under Saudi control. Likewise, historically and politically Yemen was the home of one of the greatest ancient agricultural and commercial civilizations of the world. The Greeks and the Romans called Yemen *Arabia Felix* (happy or prosperous Arabia), referring thus to its wealthy agricultural, commercial, and industrial society. As a matter of fact, the word "Yemen" is derived from the Arabic word *yumn*, which means prosperity. Similarly, the Holy Torah and the Quran describe the land of Saba (Sheba) in Yemen, and narrate the story of the historical visit of its queen—who is called Bilqees by Yemeni, Arab, and Muslim historians, to King Solomon in Jerusalem. The Quran, furthermore, devotes a *surah* (chapter) called Saba describing Sheba's highly sophisticated and unique irrigating and agricultural systems, and refers to the construction and collapse of its huge dam in Marib city, the historical capital of Sheba and a modern agricultural center in the eastern part of the present North Yemen. Last, the Yemenis are proud above all of the description of their sincere belief in Islam and their general wisdom and breadth of vision by the great Muslim Prophet Muhammad in his famous saying, "The faith is a Yemeni and the wisdom is a Yemenite." Finally, from the dynasties of the five major kingdoms that ruled Yemen for more than two thousand years before the advent of Islam, the rulers of the Himyarite dynasty were politically distinguished by their ability to exercise sovereignty and tight political control over the entire ancient Yemeni territories in the southern portion of the Arabian Peninsula after the fifth century B.C. The Himyarite king Karb Ali Water, the first unifier of ancient Yemen, became, therefore, one of Imam Yahya's political heroes.

The religious and political legacy of the Zayid imamate can be identified as the third factor that affected Imam Yahya's political career. The Arabic word *Imamate* refers here to the religious and political leadership of the Muslim community. It was developed within Shiism, the smaller of the two great branches of Islam, as a political term opposite or equal to the Sunni traditional term *Caliphate*, or the succession to the Islamic leadership after the death in 632 of the Prophet Muhammad. The latter has been maintained within Sunnism (Orthodoxy), the largest mainstream of Islam. Zaydism, on the other hand, is one of the major divisions of Shiism. It is a term that derived its name from that of its founder Zayd ibn Ali, a great-grandson of the fourth and last orthodox Muslim Caliph, Ali ibn Abi Talib. The latter was also the cousin and son-in-law of the Prophet Muhammad and the husband of his daughter Fatimah. Ali and Fatimah's great-grandson Zayd rebelled militarily against the Umayyad caliph, but he was killed in A.D. 740 by the caliph's soldiers. His Zaydi doctrine focused on the conditions that he required for any leader to assume the imamate of the Muslim nation, including the qualifications of being just, pious, and a descendant of Ali and Fatimah.

Zaydism in Yemen was introduced by Imam Yahya al-Hadi, a descendant of Ali and Fatimah who came to Yemen from Persia in 893. Later, he declared himself Yemen's first Zaydi imam (897–911). His era was characterized by his violent behavior toward his Yemeni subjects in clear violation of the Zaydi principles of justice and compassion. Al-Hadi's violent methods of rule were employed eleven centuries later by Imam Yahya and his son and successor Ahmmad. By contrast, Imam Qasim and his sons Imam Muhammad and Imam Ismail, who ruled Yemen between 1598 and 1676, were said to have been just, pious, and very capable political leaders. They were best known for their successful guerrilla campaigns, which terminated the first Ottoman invasion of Yemen during the sixteenth century and resulted in the reunification of the whole southern part of the Arabian Peninsula under the rule of one central political government for the first time since the Himyarite rule. This was an achievement that Imam Yahya was so proud of three centuries later that in 1904 he chose as his religious title al-Mutawakkil and named his Mutawakkilite kingdom after that of al-Mutawakkil Ismail. In sum, it was the Himyarite and the Zaydi reunifications of all the territories of ancient Yemen under the rule of one central government that influenced the political thinking of Imam Yahya and inspired his powerful desire to embark on the same attempt to try to reunite under his own personal Zaydi rule all the lands that he considered the property of his Zaydi ancestors.

A fourth factor is the geopolitical and socioeconomic division of Yemeni society into large numbers of truculent and quasi-independent tribes and communities. It is within the North Yemeni domain, which remained under Imam Yahya's control after 1934, that more socioeconomic divisions can be found. Socially, North Yemen can be divided into two major classes: Zaydi tribal communities residing mostly in the central and northern mountains as well as the eastern desert plain, and a *Shafii* (Sunni orthodox) peasantry and clan families that are spread today throughout the southern mountains and the western coastal plain along the southeastern shore of the Red Sea. The first class, with its large number of big and small quasi-independent tribes, has always given political leaders in Yemen, and especially Imam Yahya, a difficult time to control. Most of these independent tribes will not submit easily to any central authority or control. Though it seemed more passive than the tribes, the peasantry had its own independent social tendencies and similarly gave Imam Yahya a troubling time to control and subdue. The popular uprising of the Zaraniq Shafii tribes in the coastal plain against Imam Yahya during the late 1920s is evidence of the difficulties that Imam Yahya's rule encountered even from the pacific segments in his domain. Finally, in terms of the economic and demographic division of North Yemen's populace, there are two mixed categories within both tribal and rural classes. First, there is the wealthy group, mostly *Sayyids* (descendants of the house of the Prophet), *Qadis* (religious judges), *sheikhs* (tribal leaders), merchants, large landowners, and others. Second, there are the less fortunate individuals who compose the majority of the Yemeni population and include mostly the ordinary tribal members, farmers, fishermen, and workers. The misfortune of this larger group springs further from the fact that it was its income that Imam Yahya and his sons, *ummal* (local administrators), soldiers, and tax system sought.

The last factor is the long history of foreign penetration and occupation of most of historical Yemen that resulted after 1934 in the Saudi occupation of the northern segments of ancient Yemen and in the later separation of North Yemen, South Yemen, and Oman into three independent political entities. This particular factor and the two previous ones had a great impact on Imam Yahya's political thinking, behavior, and methods of governing. The violent history of the Zaydi imamate in Yemen, especially during the reign of its founder al-Hadi; the reluctance of most Yemeni tribes and communities to sacrifice their political and social independence in favor of any central authority; and the frequent foreign intrusion on and invasion of Yemen all contributed to Imam Yahya's violent treatment of his people. Although his father left him highly decentralized and troubled tribal communities, especially in the central mountainous region of North Yemen, he did not teach him the violent and suppressive political and social methods that Imam Yahya conducted for more than four decades against his subjects. This included the hostage system that Yahya developed after 1904, in which he demanded from every tribal sheikh and every clan head throughout his domain either a son, a brother, or a close relative and deposited most of them in his jails as political *rahinahs* (hostages) to forcibly guarantee the loyalty of their relatives to his rule. His heavy-handed and oppressive methods also included the mass execution of even minor opponents and sometimes ordinary and friendly reformers who advised him and called his attention to the necessity of having normal Yemeni foreign relations with the Arab and Islamic states and with the rest of the world in order to benefit the very poor and less-developed Yemeni society from the technological exchange with the more advanced and developed nations. Among Yahya's subjects who were unjustifiably slaughtered were many popular Muslim scholars and intellectuals such as Ahmmad al-Mutaa, Abdulwahab al-Wareeth, and Ahmmad al-Azab.

Yahya's entire life (1869–1948) can be divided chronologically into five major periods, including the four periods that constituted his entire political reign

(1904–1948). The first period (1869–1903) included his birth, growth, education, and early political training and socialization, as well as his participation in the early battles for the independence of Yemen during his father's era. The second period (1904–1911) began with Imam Yahya's accession to the Zaydi imamate, followed by both his initiation of a long inward violent domestic crackdown to silence his opponents and subdue his subjects, and his immediate vigorous outward resumption of the Yemeni resistance to the Turkish occupation. Imam Yahya's methods in dealing with his society not only during this period but also during his whole era have already been described. As for his external war against the Turks, soon after assuming the Zaydi imamate in 1904, King Yahya immediately led a very large-scale attack against the Turks, laying siege to Sanaa itself and entering it victoriously in April 1905. This was a task that his own father could not accomplish during his 1891 siege. Furthermore, Imam Yahya's tribal army was said to have slain the Turkish occupiers in the thousands and turned Yemeni mountains into their graveyard, but after 1905, the Turks regrouped their forces and fought back to recapture Sanaa after the arrival of large and better equipped troops sent by the Ottoman Sublime Porte. Imam Yahya had to retreat into the northern mountain stronghold of Hajjah, located to the north of Sanaa. From there he resumed a very large-scale guerrilla warfare against the Turks until in 1911 he forced them to conclude with him the Daan peace agreement, named after the village in which it was signed. In that treaty, the Turks finally acknowledged, at the least, Imam Yahya's religious leadership over the northern highland of central Yemen.

The third phase was from 1912 to 1919. Here Yahya's high-handed methods of suppressing and subduing the members of his Zaydi domain continued as in the previous stage, but in terms of Imam Yahya's external wars, he stuck to the Daan treaty and remained at peace with the Turks until they handed over to him in 1919 what is now North Yemen, the only Yemeni territory that remained under their control in the wake of their defeat in World War I. The independence of the Yemeni Mutawakkilite Kingdom at least from Turkey was thus completed. This accomplishment by itself has been considered by many as Imam Yahya's greatest political achievement for his society, namely, the foundation, struggle for, and leadership, for the first time, of twentieth-century modern North Yemen. However, between 1919 and 1925, that independence was already in danger. In fact, although this third period (1912–1919) saw a calm in Yahya's relations with the Turks, it also saw, on the other hand, the launching of his resistance to both the British occupation of the southern part of Yemen and the Idrisi presence and encroachment on the northern territories of Yemen. During this period, Imam Yahya continued to attack most of the British colonies, or the so-called Nine Protectorates, in South Yemen. The British responded during World War I by attacking and seizing Hudaydah (North Yemen's first port and third largest city) and relinquishing it in 1919 to their new Idrisi allies, thus threatening Imam Yahya's entire domain. Meanwhile, Imam Yahya was already attacking the Idrisis, members of a Moroccan family that came to Yemen and took control of the northern Yemeni territories of Asir, Jizan, and Najran after the conclusion of Imam Yahya's 1911 peace treaty with Turkey.

In the fourth period (1920–1934), Imam Yahya's internal battles to subdue his citizens and control his domain and his external war of independence for the liberation of the southern portion of Yemen from British control continued vigorously. At the same time, his external war of independence continued against the Idrisi control of Hudayah and the northern segments of Yemen until the mid–1920s. In 1925, Imam Yahya drove the Idrisis out of Hudaydah and the central Tihamah coastal region. During 1926 he continued to follow and attack the now-weakening Idrisis in all the northern frontiers. The major cities of Asir, Jizan, and Najran began to fall under the control of Yahya's forces throughout 1926, forcing the Idrisis to request an immediate agreement that would give the imam the status of the religious leader of these three northern territories and guarantee the Idrisis' own status as the administrators of these regions for the imam. However, the victorious imam refused that opportunity to at least guarantee the maintenance of important territorial segments of historical Yemen instead of losing them later to the Saudis. Imam Yahya was said to have arrived at the conclusion that the Idrisis were nothing but recent intruders on Yemeni historical lands who, along with the British, ought to be driven out of Yemen permanently. The Idrisis turned in 1926 into King Abdal-Aziz ibn Saud,* the founder in 1932 of present-day Saudi Arabia, seeking his protection against Imam Yahya. However, in 1932 the Idrisis broke their 1926 protection accord with ibn Saud and went back to Imam Yahya, seeking help and protection against ibn Saud himself, who had begun by the late 1920s to liquidate their authority and express his real desire to annex those Yemeni territories into his own Saudi domain.

The last period of Yahya's life began in 1934 and ended with his death in 1948. In this period Imam Yahya's rule and Yemen's modern history entered a very critical point as Yahya's powerful drive for al-Yaman al-Kubra came to a sudden and sad end and greater Yemen became geographically smaller and politically more divided than ever. This period began in early 1934 with the humiliating defeat of Imam Yahya in Jizan and central Tihamah by the Saudis, who surprised him by invading and occupying the port and the city of Hudaydah itself. Here the Saudis seemed to imitate the clever British move during World War I when they invaded and occupied Yahya's most vital port, thus threatening his entire domain. The Saudis were said to have further laid at that time a false territorial claim to all the Yemeni coastal region of Tihamah on the shore of the Red Sea, including the famous second Yemeni city port of Mocha and the famous religious city of Zabid, inexplicably arguing that those areas were part of Hejaz, which was then under the control of ibn Saud. Finally, in 1934 ibn Saud demanded that in order to return Hudaydah to Imam Yahya, the latter should not only relinquish his geographical, historical, political, and territorial claims to the Yemeni territories of Asir, Jizan, and Najran, but also hand over the Idrisis to the Saudi leader. Out of fear about Hudaydah Yahya did submit to ibn Saud's wishes, and Asir, Jizan, Najran, and the Idrisis vanished, as a result, from the

Yemeni official political arena after 1934. Still, Yahya could have done better. He could have simply reorganized the powerful Zaydi tribes of the mountains as he and his ancestors used to do against the Turkish and British intruders and have left the rest up to those strong tribes to use their guerrilla warfare skills and experiences to confront the bedouin and coastal capabilities of the Saudis and turn the Yemeni lands that they captured into another graveyard.

Meanwhile, this period also saw under similar circumstances the end of Imam Yahya's active military campaign and political drive to recapture the southern Yemeni regions from the British. Also at the end of 1934, the defeated Yahya concluded another unfortunate treaty recognizing British political control over the southern territories of Yemen. South Yemen and Oman would not, as a consequence, be reunited with North Yemen and the other lost northern territories of historical Yemen. South Yemen, in particular, would after 1967 fall into the hands of radical pro-Soviet regimes. Finally and most significantly, the end of Yahya's external adventure and quest for greater Yemen did not halt his risky political doings within his own domain. His high-handed methods of suppressing his subjects and his draining of their financial resources and possessions through an elaborate and harsh tax system that was managed by a large number of his greedy so-called *ummal* (local administrators) intensified more than ever during this stage of his reign. One reason was perhaps to compensate for the psychological and financial losses of his shocking military and political defeats during the mid–1930s.

Hence, as a result of the humiliating defeats and territorial losses of 1934, and because of Yahya's continuous internal reign of terror, a natural response emerged throughout the Yemeni strata questioning the political legitimacy of the Hameed ad-Deen family and its reasons for improperly ruling Yemen and savagely isolating and enslaving its society as Imam Yahya and his sons, especially Ahmmad, had been doing. Indeed, a more direct response to all these grievances was the immediate birth after 1934 of a small, talented, intellectual, religious, tribal, political, and social underground opposition to Yahya's rule. Mujtamaa an-Nidhal (Society of Struggle) was founded first by a small group of ulama and intellectuals, including Ahmmad al-Mutaa, who came to be recognized later as the father of the Yemeni resistance to the Hameed ad-Deen family's rule in Yemen. After 1935, the opposition to Imam Yahya grew gradually and surfaced internally, especially in the three major North Yemeni cities of Sanaa, Taiz, and Hudaydah. It was also spread externally outside North Yemen, particularly in Aden and Cairo, which by the mid–1940s had become vital centers of Yemeni intellectuals who escaped Yahya and his sons' persecution. By 1944 a second political organization was formed in Aden and was led by Yemen's greatest modern political poet, Qadi Muhammad az-Zubayri. It was called Harakat al-Ahrar al-Yamaniyyin (the movement of the Free Yemenis). In 1946 it was joined by Yahya's moderate son Ibrahim, who escaped from his father's stronghold to Aden and sided with the growing opposition to Yahya's rule. He was thus renamed by his fellows in Aden Sayf al-Haqq (Sword of Truth). Finally, the civil and military branch of the opposition to Imam Yahya in Sanaa was able to assassinate him on February 17, 1948.

Imam Yahya's life, from 1904 through 1948, as well as the period of his entire political imamate and reign, was marked by several general characteristics. The first one was his rigidity and inflexibility. Imam Yahya was a rigid, obstinate, and narrow-minded political leader. His personal rigidity also applied to his methods of rule, government, and political decision making. Such a trait alone was dangerous due to the fact that his imamate and era lasted for four and a half decades. Indeed, his can be considered the longest rule in Middle Eastern society. Not even Iran's former shah Mohammad Reza Pahlavi* broke Yahya's long record. The second feature was his incredible hesitation, especially in making initiatives or quick and clever political decisions. His hesitation caused Yemen to lose its northern regions to ibn Saud who, in comparison, sagely accepted the Idrisis' offer which Yahya had earlier mistakenly rejected. The third trait was the tight centrality of decision making or initiation, whether political or social, to the degree that any of Yahya's citizens was said to need an explicit written permission from his highness the imam in order to travel from one city to another, even for visiting a relative or doing minor business. A small merchant was reported to spend months waiting in Hudaydah for the imam's written approval to allow him to go back to his family in Sanaa. Also used to waiting were foreigners, journalists, reporters, or even visiting teachers, including those from other Arab and Muslim countries.

Fourth, the intolerable isolation of North Yemen by Imam Yahya from the rest of the world was the worst feature of all. Notwithstanding, between 1926 and 1945 Imam Yahya signed friendship agreements with several Arab, Muslim, and European countries; however, most of them were for short periods (no more than ten years) and provided for only minor cultural, commercial, medical assistance, and for military training purposes. Even Yahya's entry into the so-called Treaty of the Arab Brotherhood Alliance in 1937 along with Saudi Arabia and Iraq, and his joining of the Arab League in 1945 and the United Nations in 1947, never changed his rigid and isolationist position toward his underdeveloped society. Indeed, by the time of his death in 1948, Yemen was reported to be under such severe isolation that only five elementary schools, three high schools, three small health centers in Sanaa, Taiz, and Hudaydah, one pharmacy, very few cars, one official newspaper, and one radio station existed throughout the whole of North Yemen. Moreover, the three small health centers were said not to be decent hospitals by modern standards. The pharmacy, the newspaper, the radio, and the few cars were, moreover, among the private properties of his highness Yahya. Last, there was no television in North Yemen and there was only one small, old private airplane for his majesty's special travel abroad. As for the rest of his subjects, one of Yahya's sons once told an Egyptian teacher in Sanaa that it would be against religion for citizens to fly on the air while his highness or his sons were on land. Finally, so much misery, poverty, and hunger existed throughout Yemen that al-Fadheel al-Wartlani, a famous Islamic scholar and one of the prominent leaders of Algeria's resistance to the savage French colonial rule, came from Cairo in late 1947 to call Imam Yahya's attention to the severe situation in Yemen and to recommend a general reform program to change the situation. Yahya responded irresponsibly to Wartlanis' suggestions, arguing that an owner of a dog should always starve his dog in order for the dog to closely follow him. Wartlani then warned him that a very hungry dog may attack and even bite his owner's body. Still, the careless dictator did not listen. Though wisdom is a Yemenite, as the great Prophet Muhammad said, had King Yahya been a true Yemeni and listened to the conventional wisdom that Wartlani gave him, he and his family could have survived the Yemeni anger that took his life in the 1948 coup, expelled his family, and terminated his entire dynasty after the 1962 social republican revolution of North Yemen against his grandson Imam Muhammad al-Badr.

Finally, so exploitative was Yahya and his family of the Islamic religion and the Zaydi doctrine that for more than four decades they took advantage of the Yemeni love for Islam and respect for the descendants of the virtuous house of its great Prophet Muhammad for their own benefit and political and financial gains. So simple and so innocent were the Yemeni people, by contrast, that their sons and loved ones could spend up to more than three decades as political hostages in the jails of the Hameed ad-Deen family, as in the case of Sheikh Ali N. al-Qardai, who spent about thirty years in Yahya's jail as a political hostage on behalf of his father. When Ali tried to open his eyes outside the prison upon his release, he swore that from then on he would live only to kill Imam Yahya for wasting his life behind bars. Ali fulfilled his promise. During the quiet afternoon of February 17, 1948, Ali lead a fifteen-man group that interrupted Yahya's return from a short trip outside Sanaa and deposited a flood of bullets into his old, partially paralyzed body.

Yahya's assassination was commissioned by the civil and military branch of the political opposition in Sanaa in collaboration with the Aden branch. Abdullah al-Wazeer, head of the civilian opposition, was elected the new imam, while Jamal Jameel, a former member of the 1940 Iraqi training mission in Yemen and later the head of the military opposition to Imam Yahya, became head of the army. However, Yahya's oldest son Ahmmad escaped into the northern mountains and a month later hired a huge tribal army to attack Sanaa with the political and large financial support of ibn Saud and other Arab monarchs and leaders who felt threatened by revolutions and political change in neighboring Arab societies. Sanaa was severely plundered and Wazeer was executed a few weeks later while Jameel was jailed until he was murdered in 1949 with the approval of Nuri al-Said* of Iraq. Ahmmad became Yemen's new imam, ruling it savagely with an iron fist from his new capital, Taiz. Although he escaped two major coups in 1955 and 1961, he died on September 19, 1962, from serious wounds that he suffered during the 1961 assassination attempt on his life. His son and successor Muhammad was ousted a week later by North Yemen's republican political and social revolution of September 26, 1962.

In conclusion, although Imam Yahya's two greatest reputations, first as the founder and first governor of modern twentieth-century North Yemen and second as the enforcer of peace and stability among the members of his divided and truculent tribal society, may be regarded as his greatest domestic positive political achievements for his country, most of his other political and nearly all his socioeconomic contributions to the development and prosperity of that society were negative. In addition, a third positive political contribution may be Yahya's regional participation during 1944 and 1945 with the leaders of Egypt, Iraq, Jordan, Lebanon, Saudi Arabia, and Syria in establishing the Arab League in early 1945. However, even his two internal positive achievements, which are sometimes thus classified by some Western writers, are often refuted by many Yemeni, Arab, and Islamic writers and scholars. The latter argue that the fact that it was Imam Yahya himself who suddenly surrendered the northern segments of natural Yemen to ibn Saud and let the British split the southern portions after 1934 and hand them over later to the pro-Soviet communists in 1967 renders that first positive achievement of his less significant. As for Yahya's alleged enforcement of peace and stability in North Yemen, it is argued that this was not done without a sea of blood and without what can be measured and considered by human standards as savage and high-handed methods and tactics. Moreover, most large and small Yemeni tribes were said to remain mostly as truculent as ever even during Yahya's whole era. Furthermore, it is significant that most of the fifteen men who executed the murder of Imam Yahya in the 1948 coup were young sons of tribal sheikhs who had spent most of their lives behind Yahya's bars as political hostages to ensure their fathers' loyalty to his highness the imam. Thus, the refutation of Yahya's two greatest positive achievements for the North Yemeni society provides a sixth and final feature that marked his dark forty-four-year era. This feature can simply be described as the internal and external instability of his domain: internal instability due to his nearly four decades and a half of inward battles of domination, and external instability because of his three-decade war (1904–1934) of unfulfilled independence.

BIBLIOGRAPHY

Bidwell, Robin. *The Two Yemens*. Boulder, Colo.: Westview Press, 1983.

Jacob, Harold F. *Kings of Arabia*. London: Mills and Boon, 1923.

Nyrop, Richard F. (ed.) *The Yemens: Country Studies*. Washington, D.C.: U.S. Government Printing Office, 1986.

al-Rihani, Amin. *Muluk al-Arab* (Kings of the Arabs). Beirut: Dar ar-Rihani for Publication, 1960.

as-Saidi, Ahmmad Qayid. *Harakat al-Muaradhah al-Yamaniyah fi Aahd al-Imam Yahya bin Muhammad Hameed ad-Deen, 1904–1948* (The Yemeni Opposition Movement during Imam Yahya Muhammad Hameed ad-Deen's Reign, 1904–1948). Beirut: Dar al-Adab, 1983.

Salim, Sayyid Mustafa. *Takwin al-Yaman al-Hadith: Al-Yaman Wal Imam Yahya, 1940–1948* (The Foundation of Modern Yemen: Yemen and Imam Yahya, 1904–1948). Cairo: Ayn Shams University, 1971.

ash-Shakaah, Mustafa. "Mughamarat Missry Fi Majahil al-Yaman" (The Adventures of an Egyptian in the Mysteries of Yemen). In *Thalath Wathaiq Arabiyah Aan Thawrat 1948* (Three Arab Documents about the 1948 Revolution). The Yemeni Center for Research and Studies. Beirut: Dar al-Awdah, 1985).

Stooky, Robert. YEMEN, THE POLITICS OF THE YEMEN ARAB REPUBLIC. Boulder, Colo.: Westview Press, 1978.

al-Wasai, Abdulwasi. *Tareekh al-Yaman al-Kubra al-Musamma Furjat al-Humum Wal Hazan Fi Hawadith Wa Tareekh al-Yaman* (History of Great Yemen Which Is Called the Solver of Problems and Sadness in The Events and History of Yemen). Cairo: al-Maktabah as-Salafiyah, 1927.

Wenner, Manfred. *Modern Yemen: 1918–1966*. Baltimore, Md.: Johns Hopkins Press, 1967.

AOWS IBN SABA

Z

ZAYED BIN SULTAN AL NUHAYYAN (1918?–   ). The career of Sheikh
Zayed bin Sultan Al Nuhayyan as a political leader is one of the longest and
most distinguished in the Arab world. For more than forty years he has exercised
political authority at several levels, beginning with a twenty-year governorship
of al-Ain province. Since 1966 he has been ruler of Abu Dhabi and since 1971
he has served as the first and only president of the United Arab Emirates, after
playing the leading role in bringing about the federation's creation. Over the
past decade he has assumed the role of an elder Arab statesman, playing a key
part in composing regional disputes and promoting the cause of the moderates
in the Arab world. In all these roles it seems certain that his imprint will be
lasting and important.

The date of Zayed's birth is uncertain; most probably he was born toward the
end of World War I. His early education was traditional, providing exposure to
the Koran and some secular Arab literature. What prepared him to exercise
political authority was his keen observation of the tribal society in which he
grew up, in the course of which he would almost certainly have developed an
acute awareness of his own family's position, how its preeminence had been
maintained, and what was required to continue it.

The Al Nuhayyan have ruled Abu Dhabi for more than two centuries in their
capacity as leaders of the Al Bu Falah clan, preeminent within the Bani Yas
tribal confederation which has dominated the amirate's traditional bedouin society. If there is a single example of rulership that the young Zayed would have
regarded as a model it would undoubtedly have been the reign of his own
grandfather, Zayed the Great, who ruled from the mid-nineteenth century to the
early twentieth century, extending the sway of the Bani Yas and making himself
the dominant figure in the lower Gulf.

Though born in Abu Dhabi town on the coast, Zayed grew up in the interior
of Abu Dhabi where he effectively absorbed the lessons and developed the
qualities necessary to exercise authority in a tribal society. The display of physical
courage and endurance remained essential in a ruler, as did the practice of

magnanimity and generosity toward bedouin subjects. Equally, a capacity for mastering the arts of *shura* (endless consultation over issues in dispute) and *tawassut* (mediation between disputing parties) was a prerequisite. It must have been in his early, formative years that Zayed cultivated that quality of character so evident in his later career, which is defined in Arabic by the word *hilm* (denoting forbearance, patience, and discernment). The great English travel writer Wilfred Thesiger was a witness to the young Zayed's capacity as a leader in 1948, not long after he had assumed the duties of governor of al-Ain. In *Arabian Sands*, Thesiger wrote: "Zayed was a powerfully built man of about thirty with a brown beard. He had a strong, intelligent face, with steady, observant eyes, and his manner was quiet but masterful . . . He had a great reputation among the Bedu" (p. 250).

Until 1966 Zayed's energies and abilities were engaged in governing the villages and adjacent territory claimed by Abu Dhabi in the al-Ain (Buraimi) oasis area. Al-Ain, secured for Abu Dhabi by Zayed the Great, was significant strategically, economically, and emotionally to the Al Nuhayyan. It was the key to the amirate's hinterland, provided the bulk of its agricultural production, and had become the favored home of the ruling family, where Zayed himself had grown up. As successor to an ineffective governor, taking power at a critical juncture, Zayed moved quickly to reestablish the loyalty of the tribes from the interior to Abu Dhabi. This was crucial for the subsequent fate of both Abu Dhabi itself and for the United Arab Emirates (UAE), the federation it was later to lead. In the face of competing territorial claims from Oman and, especially, from Saudi Arabia, Zayed's popular and effective authority over the tribes consolidated Abu Dhabi's hold on al-Ain, thereby maintaining Abu Dhabi's territorial integrity and its continued preeminence among the Trucial States.

Almost as important were the economic and social accomplishments of Zayed's governorship, which foreshadowed policies that would later mark his stewardship as ruler of Abu Dhabi and as president of the UAE. Earlier neglect had caused deterioration of the irrigation system on whose successful maintenance and functioning the prosperity of al-Ain depended. Key to the system were underground channels, which brought water run off to the fields from the mountains some miles away. These required constant, labor-intensive care, which only strong political authority could ensure. Zayed restored damaged and neglected channels, constructed a major new water course, and provided equipment such as water pumps to those farmers who demonstrated a willingness to cultivate new areas. In the pre oil era of extremely scarce resources, this was economically significant.

At the same time, Zayed's policies as governor reflected an animus essentially bedouin in character, which was against wealth, whether that of landowners or merchants, and a strong concern that social justice be coupled with economic development. He confronted prosperous farmers who had cornered most of the water distribution rights, thus denying adequate irrigation for many small landholders, and who refused Zayed's request to provide the latter with free water. Zayed prevailed by providing free water from the Al Nuhayyan's holdings and denying the wealthy landholders access to the newly constructed water channel. Also during his governorship of al-Ain, Zayed took the lead in establishing an elementary school for boys, a harbinger of his keen interest in promoting education as amiral and national leader. In 1966 Zayed moved to a much larger political stage as ruler of Abu Dhabi, prepared by a lengthy apprenticeship and already enjoying a wide reputation for able leadership. His twenty-two years as amir have been marked by a number of important contributions to Abu Dhabi's political life, all of them likely to have enduring consequences.

In a state where rule is hereditary, the first task of the ruler is to consolidate and strengthen the political position of the family. Zayed's accession as ruler came as a result of the deposition of his elder brother Shakhbut, not unusual in Arab patriarchal systems of government where there is no precise order of succession and a leader perceived to lack the ability to govern effectively is often replaced by another, abler family member. Lacking the qualities of flexibility and self-confidence that Zayed had already exhibited, Shakhbut seems to have feared the uncertainties of rapid economic development, preferring to preserve the social-economic status quo, even as large oil revenues began to accumulate. Zayed and other members of the family were persuaded that if Shakhbut remained amir of Abu Dhabi, the state would face a worsening crisis that could jeopardize the continued control of the Al Nuhayyan. Thus, to preserve the position of the family, Zayed was prepared to act with the protecting British government (which was anxious not to allow exploitation of the amirate's oil to lag) against his brother.

Once installed as amir, Zayed displayed the deft mastery of genealogical politics that is key to the successful governance of a patriarchal state. Apart from Zayed and his sons, the most important members of the family are the more numerous Bani Khalifah, grandsons of one of the brothers of Zayed's father. The claim to rule of these nephews of Zayed is alive and may one day be exercised. In the meantime, however, Zayed has shared with them the perquisites of power and wealth in a way that has appeared to satisfy them. Immediately after becoming the ruler of Abu Dhabi, Zayed included several of the Bani Khalifah in key positions in the amiral government and was careful to provide generous stipends as well. He enlisted their support for the idea of a federation before independence, and today several of the Bani Khalifah have key positions in the UAE government, including Sheikh Mubarak bin Muhammad, minister of the interior, and Sheikh Suroor bin Muhammad, a key adviser to Zayed.

Although the political system of Abu Dhabi is scarcely an open one in the Western sense, the ruler must practice the politics of inclusion with respect to certain key groups of commoners in order to ensure his base of support. Zayed has done this skillfully, showing appropriate solicitude for the *ulema*, the religious scholars who oversee the application of Islamic law or Sharia, as well as for the still important tribal elements of society. It has also meant including in the government representatives of leading commoner families, particularly young university graduates from such families as the al-Suwaydi, (Ahmad al-Suwaydi was appointed chairman of the amiri court in 1967) and the al-Otaiba (Mana Saeed al-Otaiba was appointed Abu Dhabi petroleum minister at about the same time). This helped to secure support from the younger, increasingly educated generation. One of the hallmarks of Zayed's rule from the outset has been a strong commitment to rapid development and a broadly inclusive sharing of Abu Dhabi's wealth throughout the population. Also reflecting his commitment to promoting social progress was a dramatic expansion of the education system. The growth of political radicalism in nearby Aden and the violent birth of the Marxist state of South Yemen that followed had the effect of reinforcing his conviction that there was a link between an improved life for the people and their continued support for a moderate, conservative, hereditary government.

Another significant aspect of Zayed's leadership of Abu Dhabi is what might be called the politics of stewardship—a closely personal involvement in preserving and improving the condition of the amirate, physically and otherwise, for the future. This has encompassed an enlightened environmentalism, for example, protecting endangered species of wildlife, reintroducing indigenous forms that had become extinct, and undertaking a major effort at afforestation. Whether the last-mentioned program will eventually alter the climate sufficiently to be self-sustaining remains an open question; what is certain is that the greening of Abu Dhabi has greatly enhanced the quality of life of its citizens. Zayed has also devoted considerable effort to reinforcing his people's awareness of their past in the midst of dizzying change. Just two years after he became Abu Dhabi's ruler, Zayed established the Center for Documentation and Research which, under the direction of an able scholar, Dr. Muhammad Morsy Abdullah, has made a major effort to gather archival material that will be used to illuminate the historical past of Abu Dhabi and the lower Gulf region. At the popular level, folklore and traditional forms of recreation, such as camel and horse racing and falconry, have been promoted. The last-mentioned sport is Zayed's own special passion. He likes nothing better than to relax in the desert with his falcons and retainers, pursuing the hunt. Indeed, under his patronage, in December 1976, an international conference on falconry was held in Abu Dhabi, and he is himself the author of *Falconry as a Sport: Our Arab Heritage*. Zayed also has a deep affection for the poetry indigenous to the UAE, Nabati poetry, and has provided material support to encourage continuation of this art form, which he has also practiced himself.

A key element in solidifying his political control of Abu Dhabi has been Zayed's moderate, Islamic conservatism. His own pious, if unostentatious, adherence to Islam, together with generous support to Islamic centers and promotion of religious education, has affirmed his commitment to religious values, which comprise the most crucial component in the legitimation of rule in Abu Dhabi and its traditional Gulf Arab neighbors. At the same time, Zayed's characteristic flexibility has been apparent in the practical application of Islamic principles.

On frequent occasions he has exercised his prerogative as ruler to set aside what he deemed to be excessively harsh judgments rendered by the Sharia courts.

Finally, a major political accomplishment that greatly boosted his stock in Abu Dhabi and beyond was Zayed's quiet but forceful self-projection as a nationalist. As governor of al-Ain and ruler of Abu Dhabi he stood up to the Saudi challenge in the Buraimi crisis of the mid–1950s and afterwards, thereby defending the state against possible truncation through loss of most of its hinterland. As independence approached at the end of the 1960s, his vigorous role as leader in the effort to respond to the challenge of independence from Great Britain by promoting a federation in the lower Gulf provided a further enlargement of his stature.

It is undoubtedly Zayed's role in bringing into existence the federation of the United Arab Emirates and ensuring its survival that will be remembered as his most obvious political legacy. At the birth of the UAE on December 2, 1971, most informed outside observers gave the experiment little chance to succeed, both because of the rivalries among its six (later seven) members, and because of external threats on virtually all sides. That the federation has survived and appears likely to endure is overwhelmingly due to the actions of Zayed as president, which largely mirror policies he had successfully pursued as governor of al-Ain and as ruler of Abu Dhabi.

Zayed as UAE president had the obvious advantage of being hereditary ruler of the state with 40 percent of the federation's population, close to 90 percent of its territory, and the great bulk of its wealth. Nonetheless, an artful and energetic exploitation of these assets was necessary to launch and sustain the UAE. At the outset it was Zayed's politics of magnanimity and generosity which were most evident. To secure the cooperation in the federal venture of his principal rival, Sheikh Rashid bin Said Al Maktum, the ruler of Dubai, he made far-reaching concessions. Despite their states' disparity in size and resources, Zayed essentially yielded parity to Rashid in agreeing to share with his state Abu Dhabi's right of veto within the UAE's principal governing body, the Supreme Council, and to accept the principle that any measure must have the support of each of the two states to be adopted by the federal government. Even before independence, Zayed had committed himself to sharing Abu Dhabi's incipient oil wealth with the other Trucial States that were to form the UAE. In 1968 he supplied 90 percent of the funds for the Trucial States Fund and, as president of the UAE, he has provided the vast bulk of financing for all federal projects.

At the time of the federation's launching, the recently born People's Democratic Republic of Yemen (PDRY or South Yemen) had shown how lack of social and economic development could help promote political radicalism. The PDRY's subsequent support of a rebellion in western Oman, which was aimed at eventually toppling the Arabian Peninsula's conservative governments, gave further power to fears already aroused. This added urgency to Zayed's commitment to rapid development of the UAE's physical and human infrastructure, symbolized by the establishment and rapid expansion of a national university, now headed by Zayed's own nephew. Despite continued social conservatism and an indefinite dependence on imported human technical and managerial skills, important progress has been made in opening up both private- and public-sector opportunities to educated men and, at least in a modest way, educated women.

Also in an extension of earlier policy at the amirate level, Zayed has given solicitous attention to pursuing balance and inclusion in the composition of the federal government. Rashid was UAE vice president and later prime minister. Rashid's son Muhammad has been defense minister, and members of other ruling families have been carefully placed in key ministries. Similarly, capable non-Abu Dhabi commoners have been given significant responsibilities. Said al-Ragabani, the minister of agriculture from Fujeirah, is an example.

On the federal as at the amiral level, Zayed has established strong credentials as a nationalist. He continued to resist, for example, the efforts of the Saudis to force territorial claims that after 1971, became a UAE as well as an Abu Dhabi challenge. He has equally proved himself an Arab nationalist, further consolidating his position as a national leader. During the 1973 October War, Zayed was the first Arab ruler to pledge financial contributions to Cairo and Damascus, and was the first to announce an embargo on oil to the United States. He has verbally and materially supported the Palestinian cause, making a sizable personal donation to the West Bank and Gaza Palestinians in the early phase of their *intifada* or uprising against Israeli occupation in 1987–1988.

The most difficult challenge Zayed has faced as president of the UAE is to manage interamirate relations in such a way as to promote federal interests. At the outset, federal authority was successfully asserted. Zayed and Rashid combined to reject what were seen as excessive political demands by the amirate of Ras al-Khaimah to join the federation and again acted in concert to use federal power in thwarting an attempted coup in the amirate of Sharjah, in which the ruler was killed by a cousin. The latter event, which resulted in the federal government rather than the ruling family itself installing a new amir, confirmed the legitimacy and efficacy of that government in its infancy.

Once the formative stage was passed, however, traditional rivalries—especially that between Abu Dhabi and Dubai—reasserted themselves and have since undermined efforts to extend the reach of federal power. Zayed has pressed for rapid progress toward a strong, centralized federal government, while Rashid has insisted on a slower pace and retention of greater autonomy by each amirate. Periodic crises, including one in 1976 when Zayed threatened to quit the presidency, have brought some concessions to those seeking a stronger central government. However, with basic matters such as security and oil policy left largely in the hands of individual amirates, Zayed's goal of a more closely knit federation is not in sight. With the UAE now sufficiently well established to be secure against dissolution, Zayed has largely turned his attention to the wider stage of the Arab world.

With the preindependence establishment of the Abu Dhabi Fund for Arab Economic Development, Zayed had already involved himself significantly in inter-Arab affairs, using the state's wealth to promote stability and moderation. His greatest concern has focused on proximate threats in the Persian Gulf–Arabian Peninsula area and, in this context, Zayed carried out one of his most significant inter-Arab initiatives—mediation between Oman and the PDRY. Together with Kuwait he had, from the late 1970s, sought to use much needed economic assistance to soften the Aden regime's radicalism and improve its relations with its neighbors. This bore significant fruit in 1983 when aid and patient diplomacy brought about a rapprochement between South Yemen and Oman, ending the former's support of efforts to overthrow the Omani government and leading to mutual diplomatic recognition.

Zayed was also one of several heads of state who made significant efforts to mediate the Iran-Iraq war. That he, like other mediators, had little apparent impact on the course of events should not obscure the fact that in being able to credibly undertake such a mission he gave evidence of the stature he had achieved in Gulf and Arab circles. Moreover, his ability to play such a role indicated how deftly Zayed had contrived to steer his course between Iraq and Iran, thereby helping to safeguard the UAE's security and preserve its political and economic ties with each Gulf power into the postwar period.

When Zayed went to Tehran in February 1988 to attempt to mediate it was as the spokesman of the Gulf Cooperation Council (GCC), selected by the heads of state of its members (Saudi Arabia, Kuwait, Bahrain, Qatar, and Oman in addition to the UAE). Establishment of the GCC was first proclaimed at a meeting in Abu Dhabi in May 1981, and Zayed and the UAE have since played a key role in the organization as Zayed's selection as Iran-Iraq mediator would suggest. However, the UAE's own divisions—with Dubai and Sharjah economically motivated to preserve close ties to Iran during the conflict—have prevented Zayed from assuming as large a part in the GCC context as might otherwise have been the case.

In the wider realm of OPEC (the Organization of Petroleum Exporting Countries) Zayed has pressed for a policy giving the UAE the position of a major player. With Saudi Arabia and Kuwait, the UAE has formed an effective bloc threatening massive price-reducing production increases if other OPEC members do not observe their quotas. The UAE has been especially aggressive in expanding its sales of oil in an effort to warn both Iran and Iraq against expansion of their production quotas. Whatever the outcome of this bold policy, the UAE under Zayed will be a central factor in determining the fate of OPEC at a critical juncture in its existence.

In the sphere of the wider Arab world and beyond, Zayed has become a respected elder statesman, actively engaged in a range of issues and concerns. In the first six months of 1988 he made visits to five countries, received four heads of state, and met with sixteen other high-ranking officials from the United States, Western Europe, the Soviet Union, and India, as well as from the Arab

world. Zayed was the first to restore diplomatic ties with Egypt after the November 1987 Arab League Summit, he has vigorously pressed the case for
Palestinian rights, and, in the wake of the Lebanese constitutional crisis of 1988,
he has tried to promote a general Arab effort to bring that country's divided
leadership together.

Undoubtedly the high point of Zayed's international career was reached at the
November 1987 Arab League Summit in Amman. The summit was a high water
mark for the moderates, in large part because the GCC states, having determined
to use their oil as a weapon against Iran, asserted their influence with decisive
results. Zayed was a prominent spokesman for the moderate agenda in the days
leading up to the summit, arguing for an end to the Iran-Iraq war as being in
the best interests of both combatants and pressing the case for Egypt's reinte-
gration in the Arab League. At the summit Zayed was a dominant figure, rallying
and reinforcing the moderate forces in the Arab world at a critical juncture. This
appears to be the role he seeks for the remaining active years of his political
career, and could well be his most important political legacy. Toward the end
of a long and remarkable career of leadership at various levels, the same qualities
that led to his early success as the governor of a handful of villages and small
tribes—flexibility, magnanimity, pragmatism, and moderation—sustain his efforts in the international arena.

BIBLIOGRAPHY

Work by Zayed:

Falconry As a Sport. Our Arab Heritage. Abu Dhabi: n.p., 1976.

Other Works:

Abdullah, Muhammad Morsy. *The United Arab Emirates: A Modern History.* London:
    Croom Helm, New York: Barnes and Noble, 1978.
Anthony, John Duke. *Arab States of the Lower Gulf: People, Politics, Petroleum.* Wash-
    ington, D.C.: The Middle East Institute, 1975.
Daniels, John. *Abu Dhabi: A Portrait.* London: Longman Group, 1974.
Heard-Bey, Frauke. *From Trucial States to United Arab Emirates: A Society in Transition.*
    London and New York: Longman Group, 1982.
Kelly, J. B. *Arabia, the Gulf and the West: A Critical View of the Arabs and Their Oil
    Policy.* New York: Basic Books, 1980.
Khalifa, Mohammed Ali. *The United Arab Emirates: Unity in Fragmentation.* Boulder,
    Colo.: Westview Press, 1979.
Peck, Malcolm C. *The United Arab Emirates: A Venture in Unity.* London and Boulder,
    Colo.: Westview/Croom Helm, 1986.
Tammam, Hamdi. *Zayed bin Sultan Al Nahayyan: The Leader and the March.* Abu
    Dhabi/Tokyo: Dai Nippon Printing Co., 1981.
Zahlan, Rosemarie Said. *The Origins of the United Arab Emirates: A Political and Social
    History of the Trucial States.* London: MacMillan Press, 1978.

MALCOLM C. PECK

LISTING OF SUBJECTS
BY COUNTRY

Fahd bin Abd al-Aziz Al Saud

Faisal bin Abd al-Aziz Al Saud

SOUTH YEMEN

Salim Rubay Ali

Ali Nasser Mohammed

Abd al-Fattah Ismail

SUDAN

Sadiq al-Mahdi

Jafar Mohammed Nimeiri

SYRIA

Michel Aflaq

Hafez al-Assad

Salah al-Din Bitar

Shukri al-Quwatli

TUNISIA

Zine el-Abidine Ben Ali

Habib Bourguiba

TURKEY

Suleyman Demirel

Bulent Ecevit

Ismet Inonu

Adnan Menderes

Turgut Ozal

UNITED ARAB EMIRATES (UAE)

Rashid bin Said Al Maktum

Zayed bin Sultan Al Nuhayyan

YEMEN

Ali Abdullah Salih

Yahya

CHRONOLOGY

1869	June: Birth of Imam Yahya of Yemen.
1874	November: Birth of Chaim Weizmann.
1879	June: Birth of Mustafa al-Nahhas.
1882	Birth of King Abdullah ibn Hussein of Jordan
	June: Birth of Mohammed Mossadegh of Iran.
1884	September: Birth of Ismet Inonu of Turkey.
1886	October: Birth of David Ben-Gurion.
1888	Birth of Nuri Said of Iraq.
1889	Birth of Idris I of Libya.
1891	Birth of Shukri al-Quwatli of Syria.
1895	Birth of Levi Eshkol.
	Birth of Abdallah al-Salim al-Sabah.
1897	First Zionist Congress meets in Basel, Switzerland.
1898	Birth of Golda Meir.
1899	Birth of Adnan Menderes of Turkey.
	October: Birth of Ferhat Abbas of Algeria.
1900	April: Birth of Camille Chamoun.
1902	September: Birth of Ruhollah Khomeini.
1903	Birth of Habib Bourguiba.
	Birth of Fuad Chehab.
1904	Death of Imam al-Mansur, Yahya elected as successor.
1905	November: Birth of Pierre Gemayel.
1906	Granting of Iranian constitution.
	April: Birth of King Faisal bin Abd al-Aziz Al Saud of Saudi Arabia.
1908	Hussein ibn Ali is appointed sharif of Mecca.

1909   Birth of Mohammed V of Morocco.
1910   Birth of Michel Aflaq.
        Birth of Allal al-Fasi of Morocco.
        Birth of Said bin Taymur of Oman.
1912   Birth of Salah al-Din Bitar.
1913   August: Birth of Menachem Begin.
1914   December: Birth of Abdul Karim Qassem of Iraq.
1915   Birth of Yitzhak Shamir.
        May: Birth of Moshe Dayan.
1916   June: Arab Revolt declared.
1917   November: Balfour Declaration.
        Birth of Kamal Jumblatt.
1918   January: Birth of Gamal Abdul Nasser.
        December: Birth of Anwar al-Sadat.
1919   Birth of Mohammed Reza Pahlavi.
        May: Kemal Ataturk organizes rebellion in Anatolia.
1920   February: Birth of Farouk I, King of Egypt.
        July: French troops occupy Damascus.
1921   Birth of Rashid Karami.
        Birth of Turgut Ozal.
        Birth of Fahd bin Abd al-Aziz Al Saud of Saudi Arabia.
1922   March: Birth of Yitzhak Rabin.
1923   Nuri Said becomes minister of defense of Iraq.
        August: Birth of Shimon Peres.
1924   Birth of Suleyman Demirel of Turkey.
1925   Inonu becomes prime minister of Turkey.
        Great Syrian Revolt begins.
        May: Birth of Bulent Ecevit.
1926   Birth of Jabir al-Ahmad of Kuwait.
        King Abd al-Aziz ibn Saud conquers Hijaz.
        Birth of George Habash.
1927   Birth of Houari Boumediene of Algeria.
        Mohammed V becomes Sultan of Morocco.
1928   Birth of Musa al-Sadr.
        March: Birth of Hosni Mubarak.
1929   April: Birth of Chadli Bendjedid of Algeria.
        July: Birth of King Hassan II of Morocco.
        December: Birth of Yasser Arafat.

1930   October: Birth of Hafez al-Assad of Syria.

Faisal becomes first minister of foreign affairs of Saudi Arabia.

Constitution is promulgated in Syria.

Birth of Jafar Mohammed Nimeiri of Sudan.

1932   Faisal appointed president of Saudi Arabian Council of Deputies.

Birth of Khalifa ibn Hamad Al Thani of Qatar.

Said bin Taymur formally declared sultan of Oman and Muscat.

1933   June: Birth of Sheikh Isa bin Sulman al-Khalifa of Bahrain.

1935   Birth of Hussein ibn Talal of Jordan.

1936   April: Farouk inaugurates reign in Egypt.

November: Pierre Gemayel creates the Phalange.

Shukri al-Quwatli becomes minister of defense and minister of finance of Syria.

Birth of Zine el Abidine Ben Ali of Tunisia.

Birth of Sadiq al-Mahdi of Sudan.

1937   Birth of Sabri Khalil al-Banna (Abu Nidal).

Yitzhak Shamir joins Irgun.

April: Birth of Saddam Hussein of Iraq.

October: Allal al-Fasi is arrested in Morocco and begins nine-year exile.

1938   Death of Kemal Ataturk.

Ismet Inonu becomes president of Turkey.

1940   Birth of Qabus bin Said of Oman.

1941   June: Free French and British oust Vichy French from Lebanon and Syria.

Allies occupy Iran until 1945; the Soviet Union remains until 1946.

August: Mohammed Reza Pahlavi becomes shah of Iran upon forced abdication of his father, Reza Khan.

1942   Yitzhak Shamir helps to reorganize the ''Stern Gang.''

Birth of Ali Abdallah Salih of Yemen Arab Republic (YAR).

Spring: Birth of Muammar Qaddafi of Libya.

1943   Shukri al-Quwatli becomes first president of independent Syria.

Ferhat Abbas delivers the ''Manifesto of the Algerian People'' to French and American officials.

December: Istiqlal (Independence) Party formed in Morocco.

1944   February: Menachem Begin, commander of Irgun Zvai Leumi, proclaims revolt against British.

1945   March: Arab League created.

June: Faisal bin Abd al-Aziz Al Saud signs United Nations Charter, making Saudi Arabia a founding member.

August: Fuad Chehab named commander of Lebanese Army.

November: Anglo-American Committee of Inquiry established.

1946   January: Iranian appeal to United Nations Security Council to seek Soviet troop withdrawal.

May: Report of the Anglo-American Committee of Inquiry.

May: Soviet troops withdraw from Iran.

Independent Kingdom of Trans-Jordan created; Abdullah ibn Hussein becomes king.

1947   Yemen joins the United Nations.

March: Truman Doctrine.

April: Founding congress of Baath Party.

May: United Nations Special Committee on Palestine (UNSCOP) created.

November: United Nations Partition Plan for Palestine.

1948   February: Assassination of Imam Yahya of Yemen.

May: Termination of British Mandate over Palestine.

Israel proclaims its independence.

David Ben-Gurion becomes first Prime Minister of Israel.

Beginning of first Arab-Israeli war.

Allal al-Fasi elected general secretary of the Committee for the Liberation of the Arab Maghrib.

1949   Spring: Armistice agreements between Israel and Jordan, Egypt, Syria, and Lebanon.

August: Birth of Walid Jumblatt.

December: Syrian coup d'état. Government of Shukri al-Quwatli replaced by military regime.

Kamal Jumblatt founds Progressive Socialist Party.

1950   May: Democratic Party replaces People's Republican Party in Turkish elections. Adnan Menderes becomes prime minister and Celal Bayar becomes president.

Abdallah al-Salim al-Sabah becomes amir of Kuwait.

September: Turkey joins NATO (North Atlantic Treaty Organization).

1951   March: Iranian oil industry nationalized.

April: Mohammad Mossadegh becomes prime minister of Iran.

July: King Abdullah of Jordan is assassinated.

December: Libya becomes independent.

1952   Arafat is among the organizers of Palestinian Students' Union in Cairo.

July: Revolution in Egypt led by Gamal Abdul Nasser and RCC (Revolutionary Command Council). Farouk forced to abdicate.

August: Hussein ibn Talal becomes King of Jordan.

September: Camille Chamoun becomes President of Lebanon.

October: Shimon Peres becomes acting director general of the Defense Ministry.

November: Death of Chaim Weizmann.

1953   David Ben-Gurion resigns as prime minister and moves to Sde Boker in the Negev.

USSR renounces claims to Kars and Ardahan regions of Turkish Armenia.

March: Libya joins the Arab League.

July: King Idris of Libya signs Treaty of Friendship and Alliance with Great Britain.

August: Shah Mohammad Reza Pahlavi returns to power in Iran. Mohammad Mossadegh placed under arrest.

France exiles Moroccan royal family.

November: Moshe Sharett becomes prime minister of Israel, replacing David Ben-Gurion.

Mohammad Mossadegh placed on trial and sentenced to three years in jail and exile.

King Abdal-Aziz ibn Saud of Saudi Arabia dies. Saud bin Abdal-Aziz becomes king.

1954   September: Libya signs Treaty of Friendship with the United States.

November: Algerian War of Independence begins.

Moshe Dayan appointed chief of staff of IDF (Israel Defense Forces).

Gamal Abdul Nasser becomes prime minister and president of Egypt.

1955   Yitzhak Shamir recruited into the Mossad.

April: Gamal Abdul Nasser attends Bandung Conference.

June: Franco-Tunisian accord signed.

September: Announcement of Czechoslovakia-Egypt arms deal. Beginning of major Soviet arms supply to Egypt and the Arab world.

November: David Ben-Gurion again becomes prime minister of Israel.

Baghdad Pact signed.

Shukri al-Quwatli becomes president of Syria.

Sultan Said bin Taymur consolidates power and unites Oman.

Mohammed V returns to Morocco from exile.

1956   January: Sudan declares its independence.

March: Independence officially declared in Morocco.

July: Gamal Abdul Nasser nationalizes the Suez Canal.

October: Israel invades Sinai.

November: Anglo-French force invades Suez Canal zone.

December: Anglo-French withdrawal from Suez completed, replaced by UNEF troops.

Salah al-Din Bitar becomes foreign minister of Syria.

Golda Meir appointed foreign minister of Israel.

1957   January: Eisenhower Doctrine announced.

        March: Israeli troops complete withdrawal from Sinai and Gaza Strip.

1958   January: Sheikh Isa bin Sulman al-Khalifah of Bahrain designated as heir apparent.

        February: United Arab Republic of Egypt and Syria created.

        Spring: Insurrection against President Camille Chamoun of Lebanon.

        July: Revolution in Iraq. Abdul Karim Qassem comes to power. Death of Nuri al-Said.

        U.S. marines land in Lebanon.

        September: Formation of Provisional Government of the Algerian Republic (GPRA); Ferhat Abbas becomes president.

        September: Fuad Chehab inaugurated president of Lebanon.

        November: General Ibrahim Abboud seizes power in Sudan.

        Rashid Karami named prime minister of Lebanon.

        Salah al-Din Bitar and Michel Aflaq dissolve Syrian Baath party.

        Salah al-Din Bitar named union minister of state of UAR (United Arab Republic).

        Zine el Abidine Ben Ali appointed director of military security of Tunisia.

1959   Salah al-Din Bitar becomes union minister of culture and guidance of UAR (United Arab Republic).

        March: Iraq officially withdraws from Baghdad Pact.

        Britain, Greece, and Turkey sign agreement concerning Cyprus.

1960   May: Coup in Turkey led by General Cemal Gursel overthrows government of Celal Bayar and Adnand Menderes.

        December: David Ben-Gurion resigns as prime minister of Israel.

1961   January: Mohammad V hosts meeting that leads to the formation of the Organization of African Unity.

        February: Death of Mohammed V of Morocco.

        March: Hassan II becomes King of Morocco upon the death of his father Mohammed V.

        June: Kuwait declares independence from British control.

        September: Syria withdraws from the United Arab Republic.

        October: Second Turkish Republic established under President Cemal Gursel.

        November: Sheikh Sulman bin Hamad of Bahrain dies.

        December; Sheikh Isa bin Sulman al-Khalifah accedes to the throne of Bahrain.

        December: Attempted coup by the Parti Popularie Syrien against Fuad Chehab.

1962   Ismet Inonu survives coup attempt in Turkey.

        March: Evian Accords establish procedures for transition to Algerian independence.

        July: Algeria becomes independent.

September: Mohammed al-Badr becomes imam of Yemen.

Yemen civil war begins.

October: King Saud of Saudi Arabia resigns as prime minister in favor of Faisal bin Abd al-Aziz Al Saud.

Kuwait becomes independent.

1963   Musa al-Sadr granted Lebanese citizenship.

February: Coup in Iraq ousts Abdul Karim Qassem.

March: Baathist coup in Syria.

June: Levi Eshkol becomes prime minister of Israel.

August: Ferhat Abbas resigns as president of the National Constituent Assembly and then is expelled from the FLN (National Liberation Front) by Ahmed Ben Bella.

November: Iraqi President Abd al-Salam Arif removes Baath Party from power.

1964   March: YAR (Yemen Arab Republic) and Soviet Union sign a Treaty of Friendship and Cooperation.

May: PLO established under Ahmed Shuqayri.

October: Suleyman Demirel becomes prime minister of Turkey.

Revolution in Sudan ends military rule.

November: Faisal bin Abd al-Aziz Al Saud officially replaces Saud as king of Saudi Arabia.

1965   January: Fatah's first attack against Israel.

February: Ismet Inonu resigns as prime minister of Turkey. Suleyman Demirel replaces him.

March: Death of King Farouk.

April: Michel Aflaq steps aside as secretary general of the Baath Party.

June: Movari Boumediene ousts Ahmed Ben Bella in bloodless coup.

July: David Ben-Gurion, Moshe Dayan, and Shimon Peres form splinter political party, Rafi.

August: Death of Mustafa al-Nahhas.

Dhofar Liberation Front wages guerrilla war against Oman.

Death of Sheikh Abdallah al-Salem of Kuwait.

Sheikh Sabah becomes amir of Kuwait.

1966   January: Golda Meir resigns as Israel's foreign minister; succeeded by Abba Eban.

February: General Salah Jaddid leads military coup in Syria. Michel Aflaq goes into exile.

March: General Cevdet Sunay becomes president of Turkey.

July: Sadiq al-Mahdi becomes prime minister of Sudan.

1967   March: Death of Mohammed Mossadegh.

May: Egyptian forces replace UNEF (United Nations Emergency Force) forces in Sinai.

Gamal Abdul Nasser announces blockade of Straits of Tiran. Jordan joins Defense Pact of Egypt and Syria.

June: Moshe Dayan becomes defense minister of Israel.

Third Arab-Israeli (Six Day) war.

August: Egypt ends involvement in Yemen.

August-September: Arab Summit meeting at Khartoum.

November: United Nations Security Council Resolution 242 dealing with the Arab-Israeli conflict is adopted.

December: Ahmed Shuqayri resigns as head of PLO (Palestine Liberation Organization).

December: South Yemen becomes independent.

Death of Shukri al-Quwatli.

1968   Michel Aflaq accepts post of secretary general in Baghdad-based Baath Party.

July: Coup in Iraq. President Abd al-Salam Arif ousted. Ahmed Hasan al-Baker becomes president.

October: Hafez al-Assad becomes leader of Syria following a coup.

December: Israel raids Beirut International Airport in retaliation for Palestinian aircraft hijackings.

1969   Musa al-Sadr becomes chairman of the Supreme Islamic Shia Council of Lebanon.

Faisal bin Abd al-Aziz Al Saud convenes first Pan-Islamic Summit Conference in Rabat.

February: Yasser Arafat becomes head of the PLO (Palestine Liberation Organization).

Hafez al-Assad takes over direct control of the Syrian government.

Death of Saud, former king of Saudi Arabia.

Death of Levi Eshkol.

March: Golda Meir becomes prime minister of Israel.

Spring: War of Attrition begins along the Suez Canal and continues until cease-fire of August 1970.

May: Jafar Mohammed Nimeiri seizes power in the Sudan.

July: Saddam Hussein becomes president and chairman of RCC (Revolutionary Command Council) in Iraq.

September: Revolution in Libya. Muammar Qaddafi takes power.

1970   July: Qabus bin Said overthrows his father in a palace coup in Oman. Said bin Taymut flees to Bahrain and London.

September: Black September. Civil war in Jordan between armed forces and the PLO (Palestine Liberation Organization).

September: Gamal Abdul Nasser dies. Anwar al-Sadat becomes president of Egypt.

December: South Yemen officially becomes the People's Democratic Republic of Yemen (PDRY).

1971 February: Hovari Boumediene nationalizes Algerian oil industry.

March: Hafez al-Assad endorsed as president of Syria following a referendum.

May: Soviet-Egyptian Treaty of Friendship signed.

Anwar al-Sadat becomes uncontested leader of Egypt.

July: Unsuccessful coup against King Hassan II of Morocco.

August: Sheikh Isa bin Sulman al-Khalifah declares Bahrain an independent state and applies to both the United Nations and the Arab League for membership.

August: Ali Nasser Mohammad becomes prime minister of South Yemen.

September: Qatar declared an independent nation.

December: Creation of the United Arab Emirates.

Oman enters the Arab League and the United Nations.

Abortive communist coup in Sudan.

1972 Ismet Inonu resigns from leadership of Turkey's Republican party.

February: Sheikh Khalifa becomes ruler of Qatar.

March: Addis Ababa Accord ends Sudanese Civil War.

April: Soviet-Iraqi Treaty of Friendship signed.

May: U.S. President Richard Nixon and Secretary of State Henry Kissinger visit Tehran, Iran.

August: King Hassan II of Morocco survives coup attempt.

October: Border war between the two Yemens.

Kamal Jumblatt receives Lenin Medal from the USSR for championing world peace.

October: Sultan Said bin Taymur of Oman dies in exile in London.

1973 Yitzhak Shamir elected to Israeli Knesset.

Death of Ismet Inonu.

Algeria assumes leadership of nonaligned movement.

April: Death of Fuad Chehab.

October: Egyptian and Syria troops attack Israeli positions in the Sinai Peninsula and Golan Heights. The Yom Kippur (Ramadan) War begins. United Nations Security Council adopts Resolution 338 calling for a cease-fire. Israel and Egypt begin negotiations at Kilometer 101 on the Suez-Cairo road.

December: Geneva Conference convenes to discuss Arab-Israeli conflict.

December: Death of David Ben-Gurion.

1974   Habib Bourguiba agrees to merge Tunisia with Libya.

Habib Bourguiba elected president-for-life.

King Hussein ibn Talal suspends Jordanian parliament.

Bulent Ecevit becomes prime minister of Turkey.

January: Israel and Egypt sign disengagement agreement after U.S. Secretary of State Henry Kissinger's shuttle diplomacy achieves accord.

March: Musa al-Sadr launches his Movement of the Deprived in Lebanon.

April: Golda Meir resigns as prime minister of Israel.

May: Kissinger shuttle diplomacy achieves disengagement agreement between Israel and Syria.

Death of Allal al-Fasi of Morocco.

June: Shimon Peres named minister of defense of Israel.

July: Turkey invades Cyprus.

October: Arab summit meeting at Rabat, Morocco, recognizes PLO (Palestine Liberation Organization) as sole legitimate representative of the Palestinian people.

1975   Suez Canal reopens.

Defense treaty between Libya and Algeria.

United States Congress suspends arms sales to the Republic of Turkey over its invasion of Cyprus.

March: King Faisal bin Abd al-Aziz Al Saud of Saudi Arabia is assassinated.

Khalid becomes King of Saudi Arabia.

March: Saddam Hussein of Iraq signs Algiers Agreement with Shah Mohammed Reza Pahlavi of Iran.

April: Khalid becomes King of Saudi Arabia. Civil war in Lebanon "officially" begins. Hosni Mubarak appointed vice president of Egypt.

July: Musa al-Sadr of Lebanon forms Amal militia.

September: Signing of Egypt-Israel Agreement (Sinai II).

November: Morocco lays claim to the Western Sahara.

December: Sultan Qabus bin Said defeats rebels in Dhofar region of Oman.

1976   June: Algerian Charter approved.

July: Sadiq al-Mahdi sponsors unsuccessful coup in Sudan.

Syrian intervention in Lebanese civil war.

Sheikh Sabah suspends Kuwaiti National Assembly.

1977   Bulent Ecevit becomes prime minister of Turkey.

March: Assassination of Lebanese Druze leader Kamal Jumblatt. His son Walid succeeds him.

May: Israeli Knesset elections; Menachem Begin emerges as Israel's prime minister.

June: Yitzhak Shamir elected speaker of the Israeli Knesset.

November: Somalia expels Soviet Union from its Berbera facilities and abrogates Treaty of Friendship and Cooperation.

Egyptian President Anwar al-Sadat flies to Israel.

December: Sheikh Sabah dies and Jabar al-Ahmad becomes Amir of Kuwait.

Zine el Abidine Ben Ali appointed director general of national security of Tunisia.

Moshe Dyan becomes foreign minister of Israel.

1978   Musa al-Sadr of Lebanon disappears while visiting Libya.

Death of Golda Meir.

Death of Algerian Presiden Hovari Boumediene.

Bulent Ecevit becomes prime minister of Turkey.

Reelection of Hafez al-Assad as president of Syria.

March: Large-scale Israeli military operation in southern Lebanon.

June: Ali Abdullah Salih succeeds the assassinated Ahmad Husayn al-Ghashmi of the Yemen Arab Republic (YAR). Salim Rubay Ali of South Yemen killed in mysterious bomb explosion.

Ali Nasser Mohammad briefly takes over presidency of South Yemen.

September: Camp David Accords signed by Anwar al-Sadat of Egypt, Menachem Begin of Egypt and U.S. President Jimmy Carter.

October: Unsuccessful coup attempt against Ali Abdallah Salih of the YAR.

1979   January: Shah Mohammed Reza Pahlavi leaves Iran. Ayatollah Ruhollah Khomeini returns to Iran.

February: Chadli Bendjedid becomes president of Algeria.

PDRY (South Yemen) invades Yemen Arab Republic.

March: Egypt-Israel Peace Treaty signed in Washington, D.C.

April: Islamic Republic established in Iran.

July: Saddam Hussein becomes president of Iraq.

October: Moshe Dayan resigns as Israeli foreign minister.

November: United States embassy in Teheran, Iran, is seized and hostages are taken.

December: Soviet Union invades Afghanistan.

1980   January: Libya openly backs a raid on Tunisian town of Gafsa by Tunisian rebels.

March: Yitzhak Shamir appointed foreign minister of Israel.

April: Abd al-Fattah Ismail forced to resign from Yemeni government. Lives in exile in Moscow.

July: Salah al-Din Bitar assassinated.

August: Mohammed Reza Pahlavi dies in Cairo.

September: General Kenan Evren leads military coup in Turkey. End of the

Second Turkish Republic. Iraq declares Algiers Agreement null and void as response to Iranian provocations.

Iraq invades Iran and starts Iran-Iraq War.

October: Soviet-Syrian Treaty of Friendship and Cooperation signed.

1981   Jabar al-Ahmad reconvenes Kuwait's National Assembly.

January: United States hostages released by Iran.

June: Menachem Begin leads Likud to victory in Israeli elections. Ariel Sharon appointed minister of defense.

June: Israel destroys Iraqi nuclear reactor near Baghdad.

June: Ayatollah Ruhollah Khomeini dismisses Iranian president Bani-Sadr.

August: Fahd Peace Plan presented for resolution of Arab-Israeli conflict.

October: Anwar al-Sadat assassinated. Hosni Mubarak becomes President of Egypt.

October: Death of Moshe Dayan.

December: Israel annexes the Golan Heights, which it had captured from Syria.

1982   February: Massacre at Hama; Syrian Army puts down revolt of the Muslim Brotherhood.

April: Israel completes withdrawal from the Sinai Peninsula.

June: Israel invades Lebanon.

King Khalid of Saudi Arabia dies. Replaced by Crown Prince Fahd bin Abd al-Aziz al Saud. Abdullah becomes Crown Prince.

August: Bashir Gemayel is elected president of Lebanon.

September: Bashir Gemayel is assassinated. Amin Gemayel is elected president of Lebanon.

1983   May: Turgut Ozal forms Motherland Party (MP), and becomes prime minister of Turkey in landslide election victory.

September: Menachem Begin resigns as prime minister of Israel.

September: Israel begins first phase of withdrawal from Lebanon.

September: Jafar Mohammed Nimeiri enacts a sweeping Islamic code.

October: Yitzhak Shamir confirmed as Israeli Prime Minister.

November: Turgut Ozal becomes prime minister of Turkey.

Zayed bin Sultan Al-Nuhayyan of the UAR (United Arab Republic) helps bring about a rapprochement between South Yemen and Oman.

1984   January: Chadli Bendjedid reelected president of Algeria.

March: Ali Abdallah Salih renews YAR (Yemen Arab Republic)–Soviet Treaty of Friendship and Cooperation.

August: King Hassan II of Morocco and Muammar Qaddafi form Arab-African Union.

September: Shimon Peres begins term as Israeli prime minister while Shamir remains foreign minister.

1985   Amir Jabir al-Ahmad of Kuwait's motorcade attacked. Jabir survives.

Jabir al-Ahmad suspends National Assembly of Kuwait.

Hafez al-Assad reelected president of Syria.

January/February: Abd al-Fattah Ismail returns to South Yemen from exile in Moscow.

February: Yasser Arafat and King Hussein sign agreement for joint diplomatic coordination.

February: Ali Nasser Mohammad resigns as prime minister of South Yemen.

April: Coup in Sudan topples Jafar Mohammed Nimeiri.

October: Zine el Abidine Ben Ali named minister of national security of Tunisia.

Tunisia and Libya sever diplomatic relations.

December: Death of Ferhat Abbas.

1986   January: Ali Nasser Mohammad assassinates rivals during a Politburo session in Yemen and is exiled to North Yemen.

February: Egyptian security police riot for economic reasons.

April: United States bombs Libyan cities of Tripoli and Benghazi.

April: Zine el Abidine Ben Ali becomes minister of the interior of Tunisia.

May: Sadiq al-Mahdi becomes prime minister of Sudan.

June: Zine el Abidine Ben Ali appointed under secretary general of the Destourian Socialist Party (PSD) of Tunisia.

July: Israeli Prime Minister Shimon Peres visits King Hassan II in Morocco.

October: Yitzhak Shamir becomes Israeli prime minister while Shimon Peres assumes position of foreign minister.

1987   April: Yasser Arafat abrogates agreement with King Hussein ibn Talal of Jordan.

May: Ruhollah Khomeini abolishes Islamic Republican Party in Iran.

August: Death of Camille Chamoun.

September: Bulent Ecevit of Turkey becomes Democratic Socialist Party chairman following referendum lifting ban on political activity. Suleyman Demirel elected to head True Path party.

October: Hosni Mubarak reelected president of Egypt.

October: Zine el Abidine Ben Ali appointed Tunisian prime minister and secretary general of the PSD (Destourian Socialist Party).

November: Habib Bourguiba, president of Tunisia, deposed by Zine el Abidine Ben Ali.

December: Uprising (*intifada*) on the West Bank and Gaza Strip.

December: Ali Nasser Mohammed and associates condemned to death in absentia in South Yemen.

1988   Turgut Ozal of Turkey meets with Greek Prime Minister Andreas Papandreou.

         February: Zayed bin Sultan Al Nuhayyan of the United Arab Emirates goes to Teheran as spokesman of the Gulf Cooperation Council (GCC) in an attempt to mediate Iran-Iraq War.

         July: Iran and Iraq accept UN Security Council Resolution 598 leading to a cease-fire.

         November: Palestinian National Council declares independence of Palestine.

         December: Yitzhak Shamir forms coalition government after November Israeli elections.

         King Hassan II agrees to talk with the Polisario to determine the future of the Western Sahara.

1989   Death of Khomeini.

ROBERT OWEN KRIKORIAN

BIBLIOGRAPHICAL NOTE

The reader who wishes to pursue the subjects of the profiles in this volume further is referred to the brief bibliography at the end of each entry in which the author has listed the most valuable English-language works on the personality profiled. The reader may also wish to consult the bibliographies of other figures from that country for further information.

To supplement the individual bibliographies there are listed below a number of works that focus more broadly on the political elite of the Middle East and North Africa and the roles these personalities have played in the politics of the region.

Be'eri, Eliezer. *Army Officers in Arab Politics and Society*. New York: Praeger, 1970.

Bill, James A. and Carl Leiden. *Politics in the Middle East*. 2d ed. Boston and Toronto: Little, Brown and Company, 1984. See especially the chapters "The Genes of Politics: Groups, Classes, and Families", "The Politics of Patrimonial Leadership"; and "The Politics of Leaders and Change."

Dekmejian, R. Hrair. *Patterns of Political Leadership: Lebanon, Israel, Egypt*. Albany, N.Y.: State University of New York Press, 1975.

Frey, Frederick W. *The Turkish Political Elite*. Cambridge, Mass.: M.I.T. Press, 1965.

Halpern, Manfred. *The Politics of Social Change in the Middle East and North Africa*. Princeton, N.J.: Princeton University Press, 1963.

Khadduri, Majid. *Arab Contemporaries: The Role of Personalities in Politics*. Baltimore and London: Johns Hopkins University Press, 1973.

Lenczowski, George (ed.). *Political Elites in the Middle East*. Washington, D.C.: American Enterprise Institute for Public Policy Research, 1975. Includes sections on "Some Reflections on the Study of Elites," "The Patterns of Elite Politics in Iran," "Patterns of Elite Politics in Turkey," "Patterns of Association in the Egyptian Political Elite," "The Political Elite in Iraq," "Aspects of the Political Elite in Syria," "The Political Elite and National Leadership in Israel," and "Political Elite of Lebanon."

Long, David E., and Bernard Reich (eds.). *The Government and Politics of the Middle East and North Africa*. 2d ed., rev. and updated. Boulder, Colo., and London: Westview Press, 1986.

Seligman, Lester G. *Leadership in a New Nation: Political Development in Israel*. New York: Aldine-Atherton, 1964.

Tachau, Frank (ed.). *Political Elites and Political Development in the Middle East*. New
    York: Schenkman, Halsted Press Division, John Wiley and Sons, 1975. Includes
    sections on "Political Elites and Political Development in the Middle East,"
    "Elites and Modernization in Turkey," "Egypt: Neo-Patrimonial Elite," "Syria:
    Downfall of a Traditional Elite," "Saudi Arabia: Survival of Traditional Elites,"
    "The Political Elite of Iran: A Second Stratum?" "Israel: The Persistent Elite,"
    and "Algeria: A Post-Revolutionary Elite."
Waterbury, John. *The Commander of the Faithful: The Moroccan Political Elite—A Study
    in Segmented Politics*. New York: Columbia University Press, 1970.
Zartman, I. William (ed.). *Political Elites in Arab North Africa*. New York: Longman,
    1982.
Zonis, Marvin. *The Political Elite of Iran*. Princeton, N.J.: Princeton University Press,
    1971.

INDEX

CONTRIBUTORS

AOWS IBN SABA is a Middle Eastern Ph.D. candidate at George Washington University.

LOUAY BAHRY was Associate Professor of Political Science at the University of Baghdad and at King Abdul Aziz University in Jidda, Saudi Arabia. He has written several books on modern Middle Eastern history and politics, including *The Baghdad Railway* (Baghdad, 1967).

BAHMAN BAKTIARI is Assistant Professor of International Relations in the Department of Political Science at the University of Maine. His publications have focused on various aspects of Iran's politics and foreign policy.

AMAZIA BARAM has been a Fellow of the School for Advanced Studies, Hebrew University, Jerusalem, and the Woodrow Wilson Center, Washington, D.C., and a senior associate member at St. Antony's College in Oxford. Dr. Baram teaches in the Department of Middle Eastern History at Haifa University and is the author of a number of works on modern Iraq.

SALLY ANN BAYNARD is a Visiting Assistant Professor of Political Science at George Washington University. Dr. Baynard has written and lectured on the Sudan and other aspects of Middle East politics.

PETER K. BECHTOLD is Chairman for Near East and North African Area Studies at the Foreign Service Institute. He has conducted field research in Sudan on ten separate occasions covering a period of twenty-two years. In addition to publishing numerous articles about the Sudan, he is the author of *Politics in Sudan* (Praeger, 1976).

MARVER H. BERNSTEIN was a member of the faculty of Politics at Princeton University from 1947 to 1972, where he served as Chairman of the Politics

Department and as Dean of the Woodrow Wilson School of Public and International Affairs. From 1972 to 1983 he was President of Brandeis University. He is University Professor of Philosophy and Politics at Georgetown University. His book *The Politics of Israel* (1957) analyzed the first decade of statehood. He has also published articles and chapters in books dealing with Israeli politics.

JEROME B. BOOKIN-WEINER is Professor of History and Director of International Programs at Bentley College in Waltham, Massachusetts. Dr. Bookin-Weiner has taught in Morocco at both the Ecole Nationale Forestière d'Ingenieurs and the Université Mohammed V. He is the author of many articles on Morocco.

LOUIS J. CANTORI is Professor of Political Science at the University of Maryland, Baltimore County, and Adjunct Professor at the Center for Contemporary Arab Studies at Georgetown University. His most recent major publications are *Local Politics and Development in the Middle East* (1984) and *Comparative Politics in the Post-Behavioral Era* (1988).

HELENA COBBAN was a Beirut-based correspondent for *The Christian Science Monitor* from 1976 through 1981. She is the author of *The Palestinian Liberation Organization: People, Power and Politics* (1984) and *The Making of Modern Lebanon* (1985).

JILL CRYSTAL is Assistant Professor in Political Science at the University of Michigan. Dr. Crystal is the author of *Oil and the State: The Politics of Change in Kuwait and Qatar*. Her research included a year's fieldwork in Kuwait and the Gulf.

MARIUS DEEB has written extensively on the politics and contemporary history of the Middle East. Dr. Deeb's publications include *Party Politics in Egypt: The Wafd and Its Rivals 1919–1939* (1979); *The Lebanese Civil War* (1980); *Libya Since the Revolution: Aspects of Social and Political Development* (coauthored with Mary-Jane Deeb, 1982).

MARY-JANE DEEB is Professorial Lecturer in the School of Public Affairs at the American University in Washington, D.C. She is the author of *Libya's Foreign Policy in North Africa*, and coauthor with Marius Deeb of *Libya Since the Revolution: Aspects of Social and Political Development*.

JOHN F. DEVLIN has specialized in the modern history of the Fertile Crescent. He is the author of *The Ba'th Party: A History from Its Origins to 1986* (1976) and *Syria: Modern State in an Ancient Land* (1983), as well as shorter articles.

STEVEN R. DORR is Director of Conferences and Programs at the Defense Intelligence College in Washington, D.C. He was Director of Programs at the

Middle East Institute and Book Review Editor for *The Middle East Journal*. He is a specialist in Gulf affairs with particular research interests in Qatar. His publications include *A Scholars' Guide to Washington, D.C., for Middle Eastern Studies*.

ELLIS GOLDBERG is Assistant Professor of Political Science at the University of Washington in Seattle. Dr. Goldberg is the author of *Tinker, Tailor, and Textile Worker: Class and Politics in Egypt* (1986), as well as various articles on contemporary Egyptian and Arab politics.

ARTHUR GOLDSCHMIDT, JR., is Professor of Middle East History at the Pennsylvania State University. Dr. Goldschmidt is the author of *A Concise History of the Middle East*, 3d edition (1988) and *Modern Egypt: The Formation of a Nation State* (1988), as well as articles on the Egyptian nationalist movement.

MAX L. GROSS is Professor of Middle East Studies at the Defense Intelligence College in Washington, D.C. He is a specialist in the modern history of Syria and Lebanon, about which he has written numerous articles.

PETER GUBSER, President of American Near East Refugee Aid (ANERA), has written two books on Jordan: *Politics and Change in Al-Karak, Jordan—A Study of a Small Arab Town and Its District* and *Jordan: Crossroads of Middle Eastern Events*; and numerous articles on Syrian, Lebanese, and Jordanian subjects.

WILLIAM MARK HABEEB is an international consultant in Washington, D.C., and a Research Fellow at the Middle East Institute. Dr. Habeeb is the author of *Power and Tactics in International Negotiation* (1988) and coauthor of *State and Society in the Modern Maghrib* (1989).

GEORGE S. HARRIS is Director of the Office of Analysis for Near East and South Asia, Bureau of Intelligence and Research, U.S. Department of State. Dr. Harris is the author of *Turkey: Coping with Crisis and Troubled Alliance: Turkish-American Problems in Historical Perspective, 1945–1971*.

GABRIELLA HEICHAL teaches at Ben-Gurion University of the Negev in Israel and previously taught at Tel Aviv University and at the Hebrew University of Jerusalem. She has been a fellow of Hebrew University of Jerusalem. She has been a fellow of Hebrew University's Leonard Davis Institute for International Relations and is a member of its Center for Security Studies.

JOSEPH HELMAN is a Ph.D. candidate and Graduate Teaching Fellow in the Department of Political Science at George Washington University in Washington, D.C. He is coauthor of a number of articles on Israeli politics and foreign policy.

PHILIP S. KHOURY is Associate Dean of the School of Humanities and Social Science at the Massachusetts Institute of Technology, where he teaches Middle Eastern History. He is the author of *Urban Notables and Arab Nationalism* (1983) and *Syria and the French Mandate* (1987). He is also coeditor of *Tribes and State Formation in the Middle East*.

GERSHON R. KIEVAL is an Adjunct Professor in the Department of Political Science at George Washington University, Washington, D.C. He is the author of *Party Politics in Israel and the Occupied Territories* (Greenwood, 1983), and coauthor and coeditor of *Israeli National Security Policy* (Greenwood, 1988) and *Israel Faces the Future* (Praeger, 1986).

JOSEPH KOSTINER is a lecturer in the Department of Middle Eastern and African History and research fellow at the Dayan Center, Tel Aviv University. He is the author of *The Struggle for South Yemen* (1984), has published articles on the contemporary history of the Arabian Peninsula, and is a contributor to *Middle East Contemporary Survey*.

ROBERT OWEN KRIKORIAN holds an M.A. degree in Political Science from George Washington University where he specialized in Middle East politics.

RAYED KRIMLY is a Ph.D. candidate at George Washington University in Washington, D.C., and a member of the political science faculty at King Saud University in Riyadh, Saudi Arabia.

ELLEN LAIPSON is a Specialist in Middle East and North African Affairs at the Congressional Research Service of the Library of Congress. She has written numerous reports on U.S. policy in the Maghreb.

FRED H. LAWSON teaches international relations and Middle East politics in the Department of Government at Mills College. He is the author of *Bahrain: The Modernization of Autocracy* (1988) and "Labor Politics, Economic Change and the Modernization of Autocracy in Bahrain," in P. Chelkowski and R. Pranger, eds., *Ideology and Power in the Middle East* (1988).

DAVID E. LONG is a Diplomat in Residence at Georgetown University. He has served for the United States Department of State in posts in the Sudan, Morocco, Saudi Arabia, and Jordan, and as a member of the U.S. Policy Planning Staff and the Office of Counter Terrorism. Dr. Long's publications include *The Persian Gulf, Saudi Arabia, The Hajj Today*, and *The United States and Saudi Arabia*.

PHEBE MARR is Senior Fellow at the Institute for National Strategic Studies of the National Defense University, Washington, D.C. She has taught Middle

Eastern history at the University of Tennessee and California State University, Stanislaus, and has authored numerous articles on Iraqi history, as well as *The Modern History of Iraq* (1985).

MOSHE MA'OZ is a Professor of Islamic and Middle East Studies at the Hebrew University of Jerusalem. This article is based on his book, *Asad: The Sphinx of Damascus, A Political Biography* (1988), a shorter version of which appeared in *Orbis*, summer 1987.

AARON DAVID MILLER is a member of the Policy Planning Staff of the Department of State. Previously he served in the U.S. State Department's Office of the Historian and in the U.S. Bureau of Intelligence and Research. Dr. Miller has written three books and various articles on the Middle East.

JAMES ANDREW MILLER is Associate Professor of Geography at Clemson University and is the author of *Imlil: A Moroccan Mountain Community in Change* (1984) and coauthor of *A Question of Place: World Regional Geography* (1989). Dr. Miller has been a Fulbright researcher in Morocco.

AUGUSTUS RICHARD NORTON is Associate Professor of Comparative Politics at the United States Military Academy, West Point, New York, and the author of a number of works on Lebanon.

STEPHEN PAGE is an Associate Professor, Department of Political Studies, Queen's University, Kingston, Ontario, Canada. He is the author of *The Soviet Union and the Yemens: Influence in Asymmetrical Relationships*, and articles on Soviet activities in Southwest Asia.

MALCOLM C. PECK is a program officer at the Visitor Program Service of Meridian House International. Previously he was director of programs at the Middle East Institute and served as Arabian Peninsula affairs analyst at the U.S. Department of State. He is the author of *The United Arab Emirates: A Venture in Unity* and has contributed a number of chapters to books and written numerous articles on Middle Eastern issues, concentrating on the countries of the Arabian Peninsula.

ILAN PELEG is Professor and Head, Department of Government and Law, Lafayette College in Easton, Pennsylvania. Dr. Peleg is the author of *Begin's Foreign Policy, 1977–1983: Israel's Move to the Right* (Greenwood Press, 1987) and a coeditor of *The Emergence of a Binational Israel: The Second Republic in the Making* (1989).

J. E. PETERSON is an author and consultant. His publications include *Oman in the Twentieth Century* (1978), *Yemen: The Search for a Modern State* (1982),

The Politics of Middle Eastern Oil (editor, 1983), *Defending Arabia* (1986), *The Arab Gulf States: Steps toward Political Participation* (1988), and *Crosscurrents in the Gulf* (coeditor, 1988).

R. K. RAMAZANI is Harry F. Byrd Professor of Government and Foreign Affairs at the University of Virginia. He is the author of ten books and numerous articles and book chapters on Iran's foreign policy and other aspects of the politics and international relations of the Middle East. Among his most recent books are *Revolutionary Iran: Challenge and Response in the Middle East* and *The Gulf Cooperation Council: Record and Analysis.*

NAZI RICHANI holds an M.A. degree from the American University of Beirut and worked as a researcher for the Institute of Arab Development. His articles have been published in a number of Middle East newspapers such as *al-Safir* and *al-Fajr*. He is a Ph.D. candidate in Political Science at George Washington University.

JOHN RUEDY is Associate Professor of History at Georgetown University, where he specializes in the history of the Maghreb. He also chairs the Advanced Area Studies Seminar on Northern Africa at the Foreign Service Institute of the Department of State. He is the author of *Land Policy in Colonial Algeria* and articles on modern Maghrebi history.

EMILE SAHLIYEH is Associate Professor of International Relations and Middle East Politics at the University of North Texas. Between 1978 and 1984 he taught at Birzeit University in the West Bank. He also served as a fellow at the Woodrow Wilson International Center for Scholars and at the Brookings Institution. In addition to numerous chapters and articles, he is the author of *The PLO after the Lebanon War* (1986) and *In Search of Leadership* (1988).

SABRI SAYARI is a consultant at the RAND Corporation. Formerly a Professor of Political Science at Bogazici University in Istanbul, Dr. Sayari has held visiting teaching and research appointments at a number of European and American academic institutions. He has published extensively on Turkish politics and foreign policy.

ARYEH SHMUELEVITZ is Associate Professor of Middle Eastern History in the Department of Middle Eastern and African History of Tel-Aviv University and at the Dayan Center for Middle Eastern and African Studies. He was one of the founders of the Shiloah (now Dayan) Center in 1959 and of the *Middle East Record*. His publications include books and articles on contemporary Middle Eastern and Ottoman history, and chapters on contemporary political and social developments in Turkey, Iran, and the Persian Gulf in the *Middle East Record* and *Middle East Contemporary Survey.*

SANFORD R. SILVERBURG is Professor of Political Science and Chairman of the Department of Political Science at Catawba College, Salisbury, North Carolina. His research interests and publications have focused on Middle Eastern politics and international law.

JENAB TUTUNJI was born in Amman, Jordan, and lived in Beirut for twelve years. He was managing editor of the *Jordan Times* for 1976–1980, and assistant editor of the *Journal of Palestine Studies* from April 1975 to February 1976. He is completing a Ph.D. dissertation on the Lebanese civil war at George Washington University.

MELVIN I. UROFSKY is professor of history at Virginia Commonwealth University in Richmond. He has written extensively on relations between Israel and American Jewry, and is the author of a history of American Zionism, as well as biographies of Louis D. Brandeis and Stephen S. Wise.

L. B. WARE is Professor of Middle East studies and Chief of the Political-Military Affairs Division, Center for Aerospace Doctrine, Research, and Education of Air University at the Maxwell Air Force Base, Montgomery, Alabama.

MARY C. WILSON teaches history at the University of Massachusetts at Amherst. She received her doctorate at Oxford University and is currently at work on a comparative history of the Arab states under mandate. Her book, *King Abdullah, Britain and the Making of Jordan* was published in 1987.

MARVIN ZONIS is a Professor in the Department of Behavioral Sciences at the University of Chicago. His writings include *The Political Elite of Iran* (1971) and *Khomeini, the Islamic Republic of Iran, and the Arab World* (1987), as well as numerous other monographs and articles. Professor Zonis has served as President of the American Institute of Iranian Studies, Chairman of the Committee on the Middle East of the Social Science Research Council and the American Council of Learned Societies, and the Director of the University of Chicago's Center for Middle Eastern Studies.